AF262604

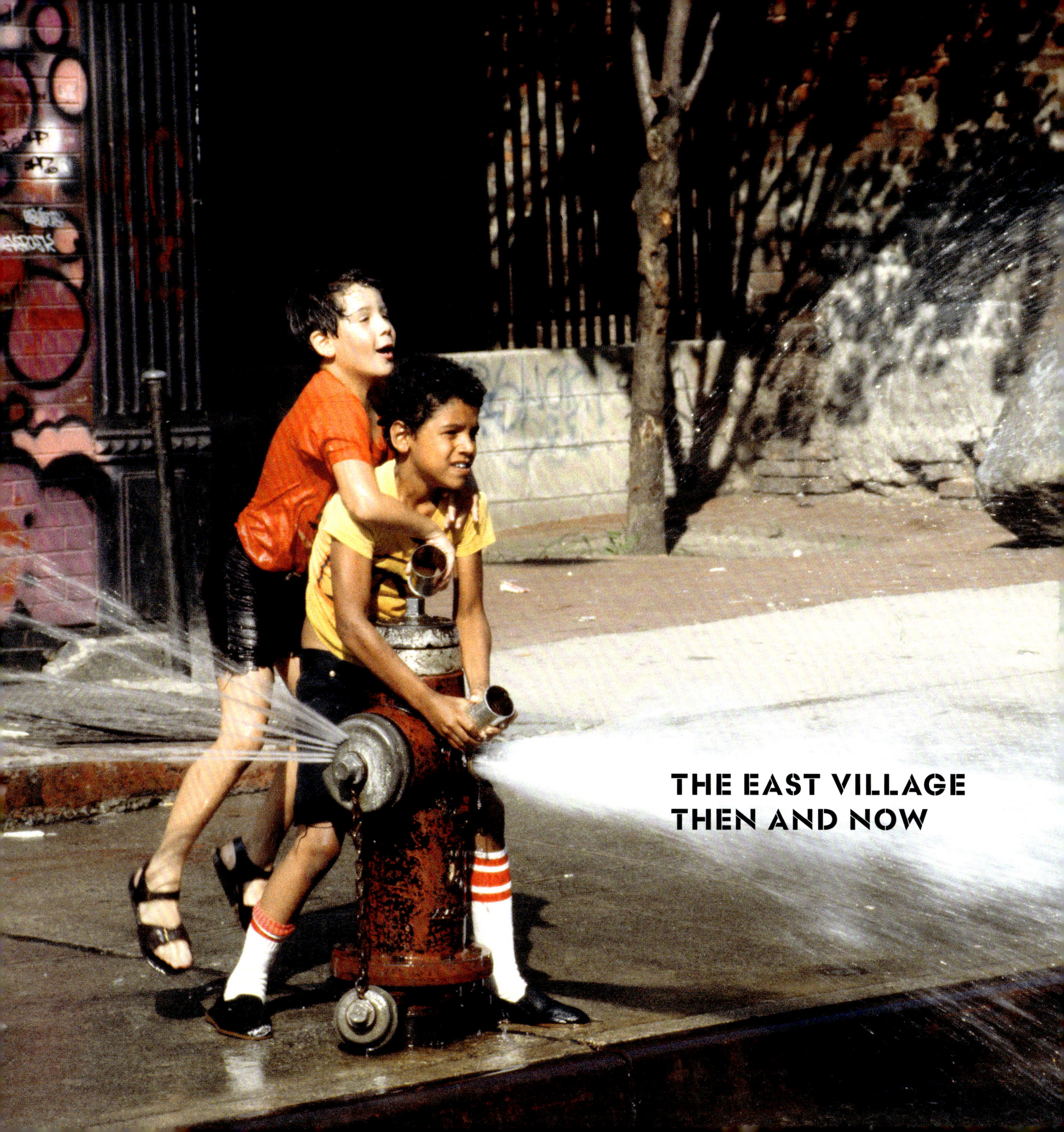
THE EAST VILLAGE
THEN AND NOW

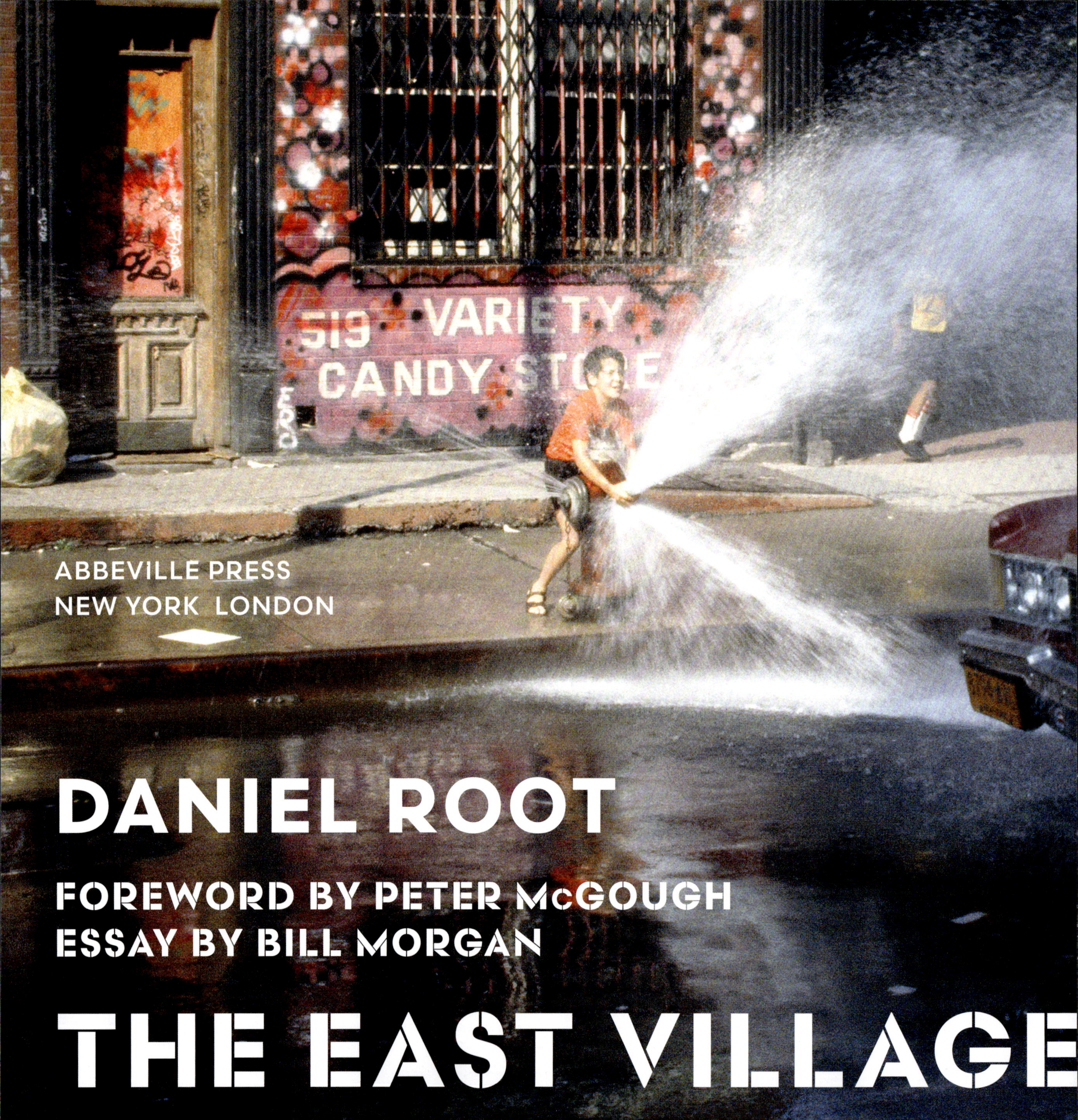
513 VARIETY CANDY STORE
ABBEVILLE PRESS
NEW YORK LONDON
DANIEL ROOT
FOREWORD BY PETER McGOUGH
ESSAY BY BILL MORGAN
THE EAST VILLAGE

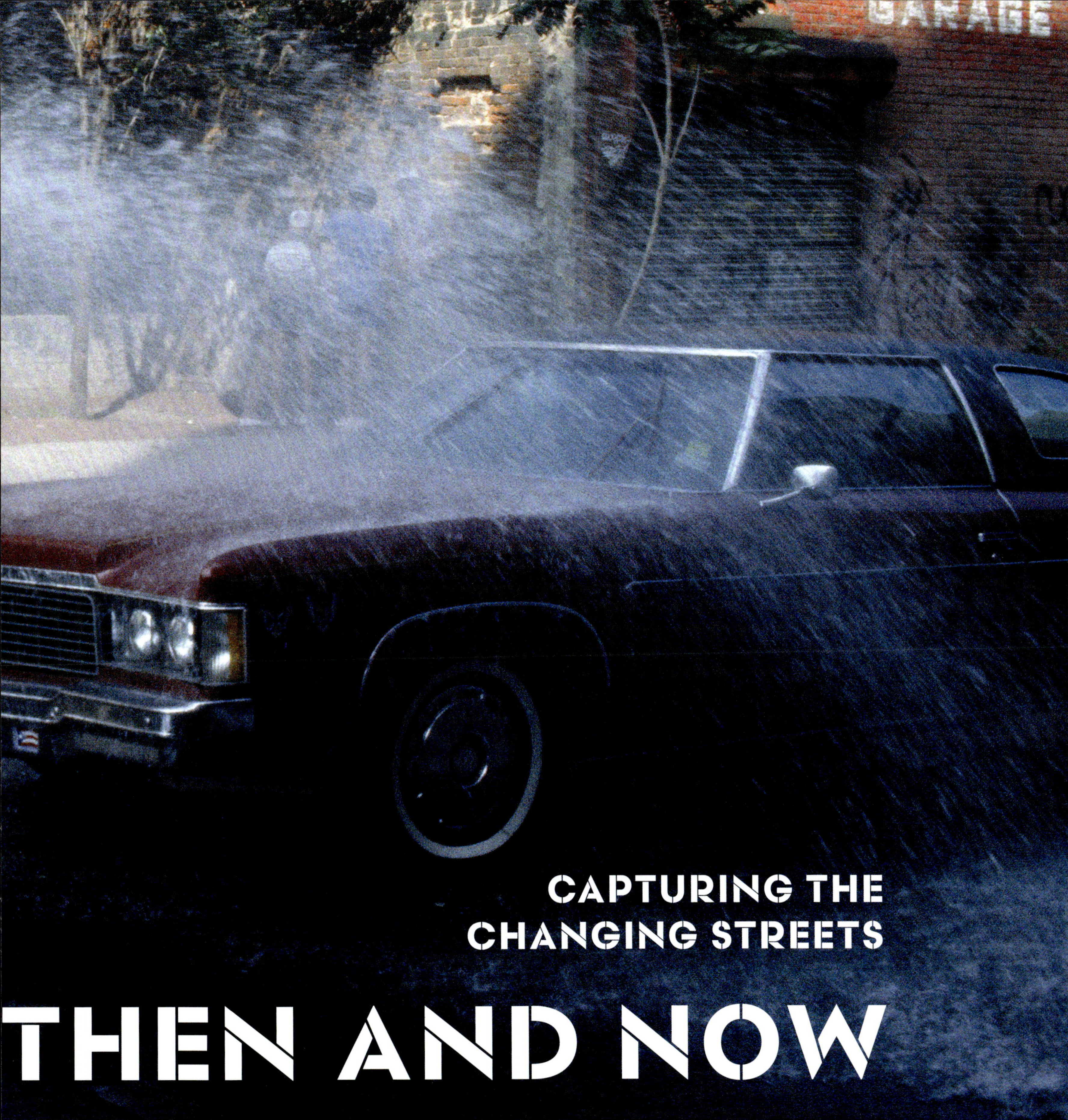
CAPTURING THE
CHANGING STREETS
THEN AND NOW

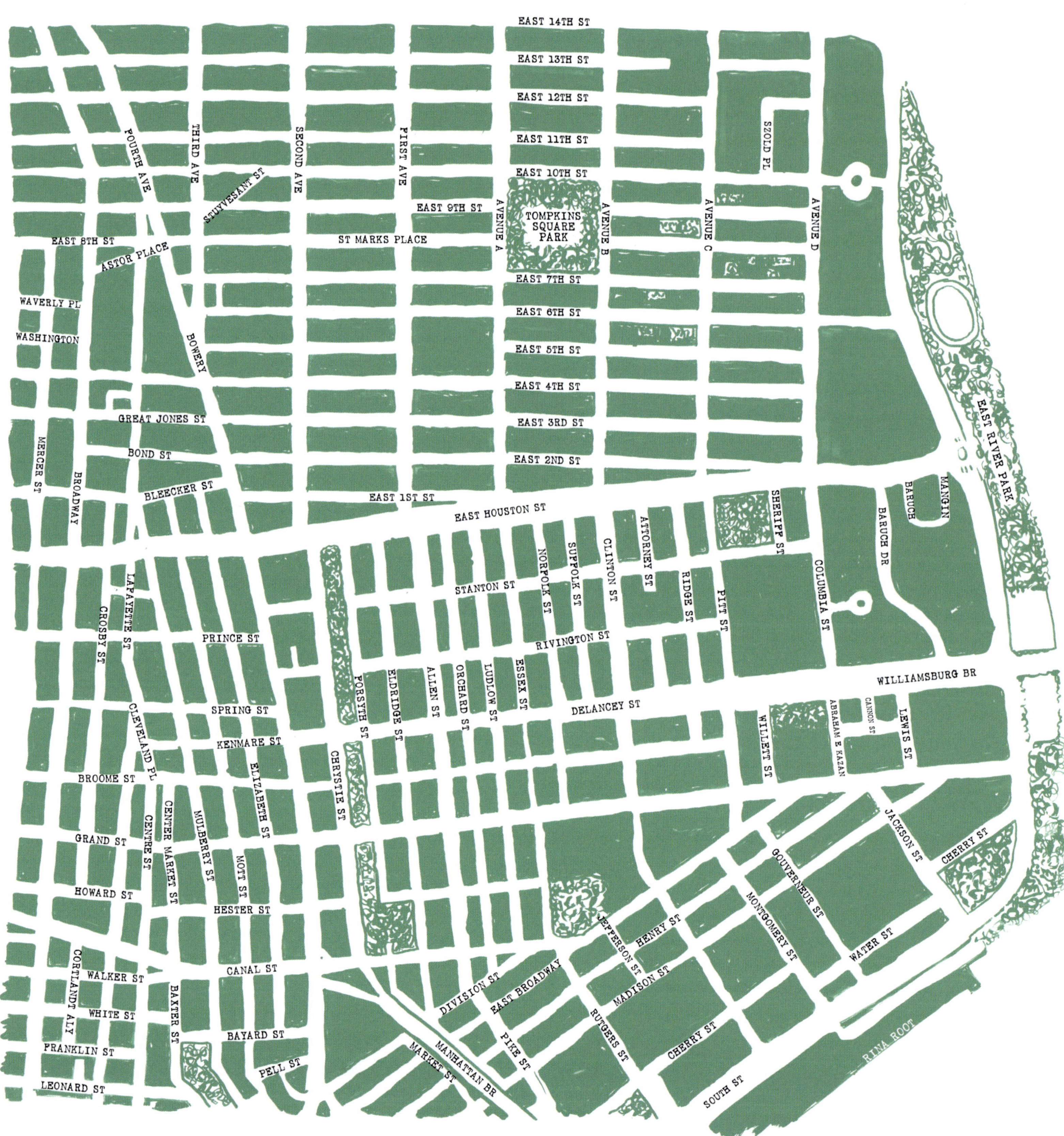

EAST 14TH ST
EAST 13TH ST
EAST 12TH ST
EAST 11TH ST
EAST 10TH ST
EAST 9TH ST
EAST 8TH ST
ST MARKS PLACE
TOMPKINS SQUARE PARK
EAST 7TH ST
EAST 6TH ST
EAST 5TH ST
EAST 4TH ST
EAST 3RD ST
EAST 2ND ST
EAST 1ST ST
EAST HOUSTON ST
FOURTH AVE
THIRD AVE
STUYVESANT ST
SECOND AVE
FIRST AVE
AVENUE A
AVENUE B
AVENUE C
AVENUE D
SZOLD PL
ASTOR PLACE
WAVERLY PL
WASHINGTON
MERCER ST
BROADWAY
BOWERY
GREAT JONES ST
BOND ST
BLEECKER ST
LAFAYETTE ST
CROSBY ST
PRINCE ST
SPRING ST
KENMARE ST
CLEVELAND PL
BROOME ST
GRAND ST
CENTRE ST
CENTER MARKET ST
MULBERRY ST
ELIZABETH ST
MOTT ST
CHRYSTIE ST
FORSYTH ST
ELDRIDGE ST
ALLEN ST
ORCHARD ST
LUDLOW ST
ESSEX ST
NORFOLK ST
SUFFOLK ST
CLINTON ST
ATTORNEY ST
RIDGE ST
PITT ST
SHERIFF ST
COLUMBIA ST
BARUCH
BARUCH DR
MANGIN
EAST RIVER PARK
STANTON ST
RIVINGTON ST
DELANCEY ST
WILLIAMSBURG BR
WILLETT ST
ABRAHAM E KAZAN
CANNON ST
LEWIS ST
HOWARD ST
HESTER ST
CANAL ST
WALKER ST
CORTLANDT ALY
WHITE ST
FRANKLIN ST
LEONARD ST
BAXTER ST
BAYARD ST
PELL ST
MANHATTAN BR
MARKET ST
DIVISION ST
EAST BROADWAY
PIKE ST
RUTGERS ST
JEFFERSON ST
HENRY ST
MADISON ST
CHERRY ST
SOUTH ST
GOUVERNEUR ST
MONTGOMERY ST
WATER ST
JACKSON ST
CHERRY ST
RINA ROOT

CONTENTS

FOREWORD 7
Peter McGough

INTRODUCTION 11
Daniel Root

**THE EAST VILLAGE
THEN AND NOW** 14

**FROM PETER STUYVESANT'S
FARM TO CBGB** 221
Bill Morgan

INDEX OF ADDRESSES 230

INDEX OF NAMES 232

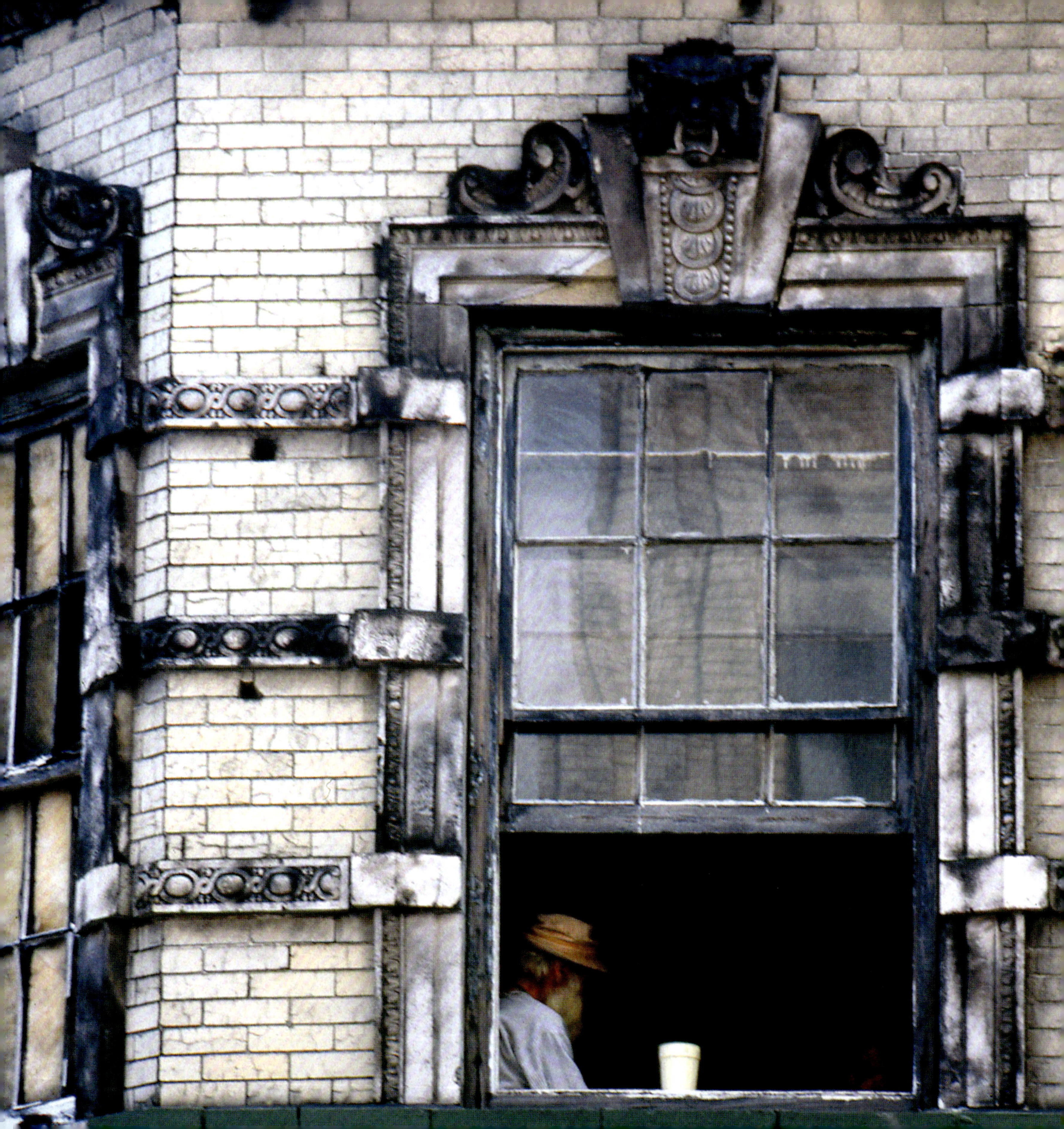

FOREWORD
PETER MCGOUGH

Like the lingering scent of perfume or the aroma of a home-cooked meal, Daniel Root's photographs of the Lower East Side transport me back to the gritty streets I called home in the 1980s. It was a neighborhood in decline, inhabited by European Jews, Hispanics, Poles, and African Americans who hadn't yet fled for more prosperous surroundings. Some aging hippies from the sixties such as Mr. Purple still roamed the streets, his long gray beards and tie-dye shirts a faded echo of another era. On East 3rd Street and Avenue B, the streets teemed with drug buyers and sellers, shouting out the names of heroin brands like "Black Parrot, Black Parrot!" as if oblivious to the thumping music from passing cars. Amid this chaos, an old woman in a housedress and slippers stood by a shopping cart with a small fire inside, cooking and selling skewered meats to passersby.

I would weave through blocks of burned-out brick buildings on my way to my apartment on Avenue C. Friends were terrified to visit me, and taxis often refused to venture into the area. The neighborhood is known as Alphabet City, and each avenue came with its own ominous warning: Avenue A was "A-OK," relatively safe; Avenue B was "Beware"; Avenue C was "See you later," implying you might not make it back; and Avenue D was simply "Do not enter."

I stuck to the south side of Tompkins Square Park on East 7th Street, where I felt a semblance of safety. On the block between Avenues B and C, dealers stood day and night on the stoops of an abandoned building, organizing lines of eager customers. Money would go up in a bucket to the roof, and drugs would come back down to trembling hands. The crowd was a bizarre cross-section of society: businessmen in suits clutching briefcases, punk rockers in ripped stockings, and everyone in between. If I recognized anyone in line, I knew better than to mention it later. Even in the dead of winter, an ice cream truck played its monotonous jingle through the night, a cover for heroin sales from its window.

One night, leaving the Palladium club on 14th Street, I made the mistake of walking tipsily down East 8th Street. I was robbed at gunpoint by three men. The experience is seared into my memory, alongside the faded painted sign on the top of the Palladium building before renovation advertising vaudeville shows for 25 cents—ghosts of a bygone era.

Artists flocked to the neighborhood for its cheap rents. My first apartment, on Avenue A and Houston Street, was $300 a month for four rooms, and even then, I thought it was expensive. Katz's Deli was across the street, where a sandwich now costs $27. We lived in crumbling buildings that horrified middle-class friends—apartments with bathtubs in the kitchen and peeling nineteenth-century moldings, hastily painted over by disinterested landlords. The rents were so low that many of us—artists, writers, musicians—survived without steady jobs. Landlords didn't ask for bank statements, relying instead on word-of-mouth recommendations. Today, those same buildings have been gutted of their history, transformed into sterile white boxes for wealthier tenants.

Life on the Lower East Side felt precariously balanced between danger and possibility. Days often began with an air of quiet desperation—the faint smell of burned wires from tenements that caught fire overnight or the murmur of neighbors discussing the latest eviction. Yet, by nightfall, the streets came alive with the thrum of energy and creativity. Makeshift galleries sprouted up in abandoned storefronts seemingly overnight, hosting spontaneous art shows that blurred the lines between the avant-garde and the absurd. An unflinching homage to the crumbling neighborhood to compete with the more established monied galleries in SoHo.

There were moments of wild camaraderie amid the chaos. At Club 57, a church-turned-nightclub on St. Mark's Place, the creative set gathered to celebrate, collaborate, and forget their woes. Keith Haring's graffiti works adorned the walls. Over at the Mudd Club on White Street, punk bands like the Bush Tetras thrashed out beats that reverberated through the smoky air. I recall one evening when Andy Warhol wandered into the Mudd Club, his silver hair gleaming under the dim lights, and struck up a conversation with a young painter who had just sold his first piece for $50. The room buzzed with possibility, as if anything could happen—and sometimes it did.

Tompkins Square Park was filled with makeshift cardboard or plastic homes. Though dangerous, it was also a space for unexpected moments of community. On summer evenings, musicians would set up impromptu jam sessions, and drag queens in towering wigs performed beneath the stars in a graffitied bandshell. Wigstock, the annual drag festival, began here, with Lady Bunny presiding over a kaleidoscope of joy and irreverence. It was a defiant celebration in the face of adversity, as the specter of AIDS loomed large over the neighborhood. The disease ravaged the community, taking friends, lovers, and collaborators in its merciless grip. Memorials became as common as gallery openings, each loss a devastating blow to the fragile ecosystem of creativity.

The physical decay of the Lower East Side was matched by a sense of moral decay that permeated daily life. Then the Christodora House on Avenue B, once a towering symbol of neglect, began its transformation into luxury condos. Its renovation marked the creeping tide of gentrification. I still remember the graffiti someone scrawled on the sidewalk outside: "JUMP"—a bitter admonishment to the new, wealthier residents who would soon displace the neighborhood's longtime inhabitants.

Despite the hardships, there was something undeniably magical about living in the midst of such raw authenticity. The Pyramid Club on Avenue A became a second home for many of us. Its drag shows, hosted by soon-to-be icons like RuPaul, were riotous celebrations of identity and self-expression. The crowd was a glorious mix of outcasts: queer kids from the suburbs, downtown poets, and the occasional Wall Street escapee. The walls dripped with sweat and glitter, as if the very building were alive with the spirit of rebellion.

The streets themselves were an ever-changing canvas. Graffiti artists like Jean-Michel Basquiat and Futura 2000 left their marks on crumbling walls, their bold lines and cryptic symbols a reflection of the chaos and creativity that defined the era. Even the simplest tags carried a weight of defiance, a claim to space in a city that seemed determined to erase its underbelly. As the 1980s gave way to the 1990s, the character of the Lower East Side began to shift. The rents crept higher, the galleries closed their doors, and the artists scattered to Brooklyn or beyond. Katz's Deli remained, but its neon sign felt like a relic of a bygone era, a lone survivor in a neighborhood that had been almost entirely transformed. Walking down the streets today, it's hard to reconcile the sleek glass condos and upscale boutiques with the rough-edged community I once knew.

Daniel Root's photographs capture the spirit of that lost time—the peeling paint, the tangle of fire escapes, the faces of those who dared to carve out lives in the margins. They remind us that the Lower East Side was more than just a place; it was a state of mind, a crucible of creativity forged in the fires of adversity. For those of us who lived it, the memories remain vivid, as indelible as the graffiti that once adorned its walls. And for those who didn't, Root's images offer a glimpse into a world that, though gone, will never be forgotten.

But the story of the Lower East Side isn't just one of loss. It's also a testament to resilience. Among the artists and eccentrics, there was a sense of collective survival—a deep understanding that this shared chaos, as rough as it was, also fueled creation.

Artists made work from the garbage of the neighborhood, from discarded wood, canvases or flattened old metal trash can lids.

The punk ethos that defined the East Village was not just a style; it was a way of living. You didn't wait for permission to create; you simply did it. Basement theaters put on experimental plays for audiences of ten. Walls became canvases overnight, and poetry readings were held in the back rooms of dingy bars. One night, I saw a performance by a musician who used only a guitar and a loop pedal. His sound was haunting, echoing off the cracked walls as if the building itself were part of the performance. It wasn't polished, but it was real—and that was enough. Even the struggle to survive became a form of art.

INTRODUCTION
DANIEL ROOT

Forty years ago a friend of a friend asked me to photograph the "changing East Village and Lower East Side" for a book she would write, covering an area roughly from Third Avenue and the Bowery to the East River, and from 14th Street to Delancey Street. The photographs happened, but the writing did not. Those photos were filed away until about ten years ago, when I realized I had a collection that documented a moment in an ever-changing area. I printed the photos, framed them, then hung them on the street near the place they were originally taken. A neighbor suggested putting the project on social media, which I did, and quickly the project was "trending." It started getting attention locally, then nationally, and ultimately had an international following. It turns out the East Village of the 1980s, and the East Village in general, represented more to people than I realized. A false start with another publisher put the images back on the shelf. Now they are back in the daylight.

In the 1980s, East Village was home to many immigrants—Ukrainians, Puerto Ricans, Italians, Dominicans, Poles, among others—established artists, younger artists, drugs (lots of drugs). Also, there was an exploding gallery scene, huge empty lots, gentrification, reclaiming, rebuilding—and very much a sense of community. The neighborhood was home to a population diverse in backgrounds, economics, and opinions—but nevertheless functioning as a community.

Older restaurants, bars, and shops originally serving the immigrant communities were next to newer restaurants, bars, and shops serving the incoming artists and younger people. One could eat cheap, sometimes excellent food, sometimes merely filling food, but it didn't cost a day's wages to eat dinner. The city would cinder-block an abandoned building shut, and the drug dealers would just as quickly bash out the cinder blocks so they could deal from the empty buildings. The cinder blocks that remained were often painted with graffti, or with a more traditional mural. Makeshift playgrounds or fledgling community gardens took shape in rubble-filled lots as kids and families made do with what was immediately available.

St. Mark's Place continued to draw the young and the tourists, and Madonna was shooting *Desperately Seeking Susan* all around the neighborhood. Community gardens were starting to better organize and formalize their existence with, at times, a contentious City Hall. Quirky Adam Purple's beautiful "Garden of Eden," between Eldridge and Forsyth, was bulldozed as the real estate pressures started to heat up. There were many efforts to preserve the remaining East Village and the Lower East Side in general as those pressures grew, but the neighborhood's location, popularity, and history were too much of a draw, and gentrification tumbled forward. Even the NYPD found a new interest in what was going on "over there."

I have lived in the neighborhood for over forty years and certainly witnessed many changes. The overriding constant of the neighborhood is change. That and the close second of ruing the change.

Despite the huge changes in the last forty years—some for the better and some for the worse—many people who live here still want the same things . . . safe housing, community, diversity, open space (community gardens!), the arts, and a place to hang.

The neighborhood is still unique despite the constant cries that "it's no different than [insert any place here]!" and it's still worth knowing. There is still a strong sense of community if you're willing to extend yourself, just like you had to extend yourself in the '80s and before.

THE VELOCITY OF MONEY
ALLEN GINSBERG

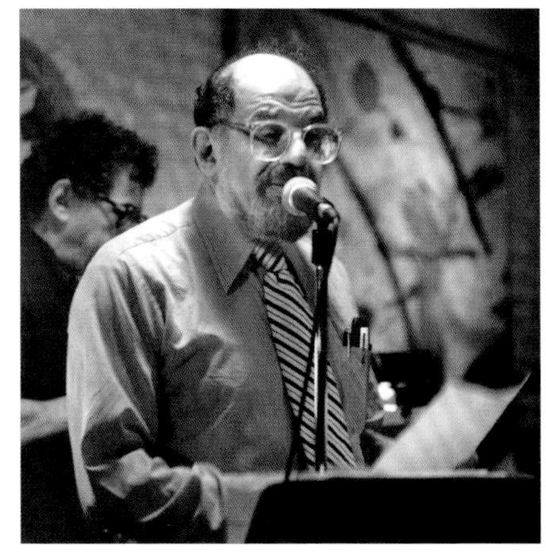

For Lee Berton

I'm delighted by the velocity of money as it whistles
    through windows of Lower East Side
Delighted skyscrapers rise grungy apartments fall on
    84th Street's pavement
Delighted this year inflation drives me out on the
    street
with double digit interest rates in Capitalist worlds
I always was a communist, now we'll win
as usury makes walls thinner, books thicker &
    dumber
Usury makes my poetry more valuable
Manuscripts worth their weight in useless gold—
The velocity's what counts as the National Debt gets
    trillions higher
Everybody running after the rising dollar
Crowds of joggers down Broadway past City Hall on
    the way to the Fed
Nobody reads Dostoyevsky books anymore so they'll
    have to give passing ear
to my fragmented ravings in between President's
    speeches
Nothing's happening but the collapse of the
    Economy
so I can go back to sleep till the landlord wins his
    eviction suit in court

February 18, 1986, 10:00 A.M.

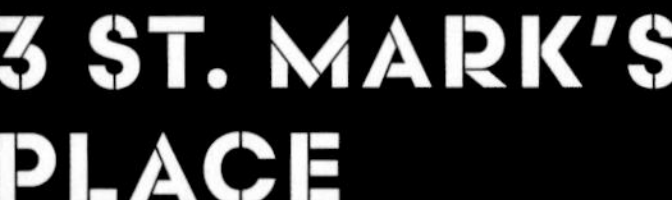

3 ST. MARK'S PLACE

Greetings from the East Village! Gringo with a warm East Village welcome. The mural was painted around 1984 to promote Story of a Junkie, a movie starring John "Gringo" Spacely, an actual local junkie. The mural stayed up for about twenty years.

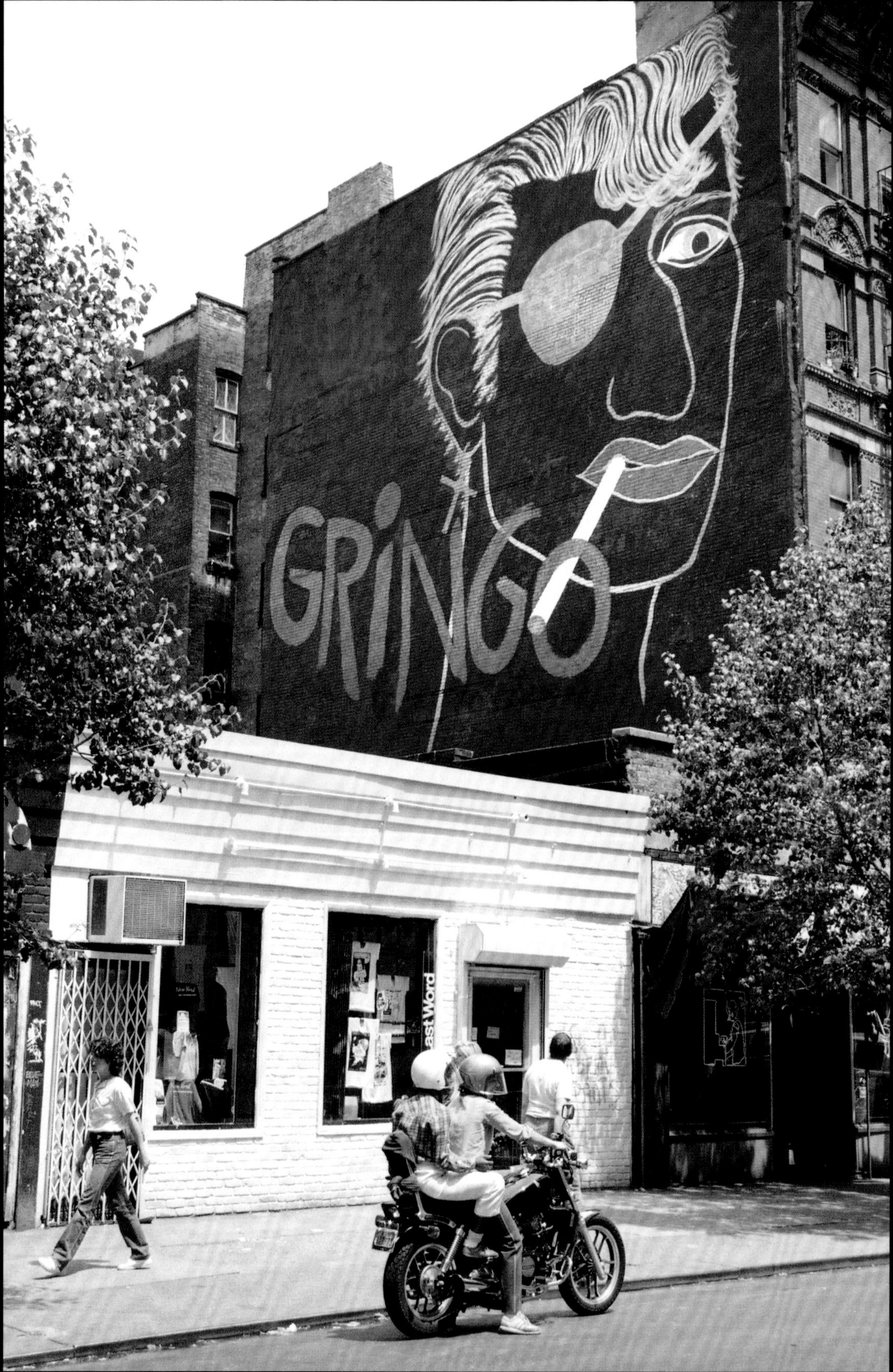

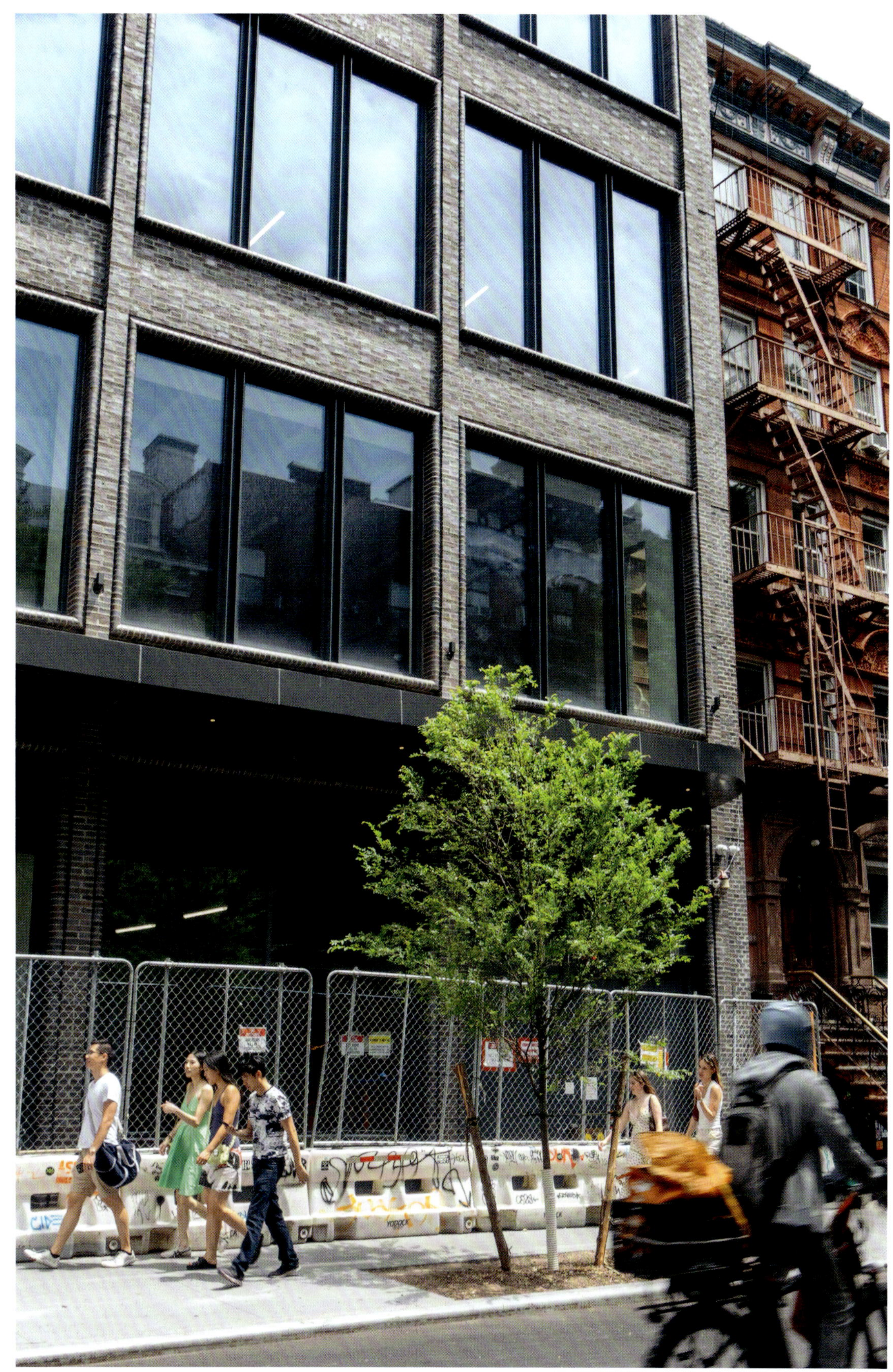

Gringo is long gone; the wall no
longer sees the light of day.

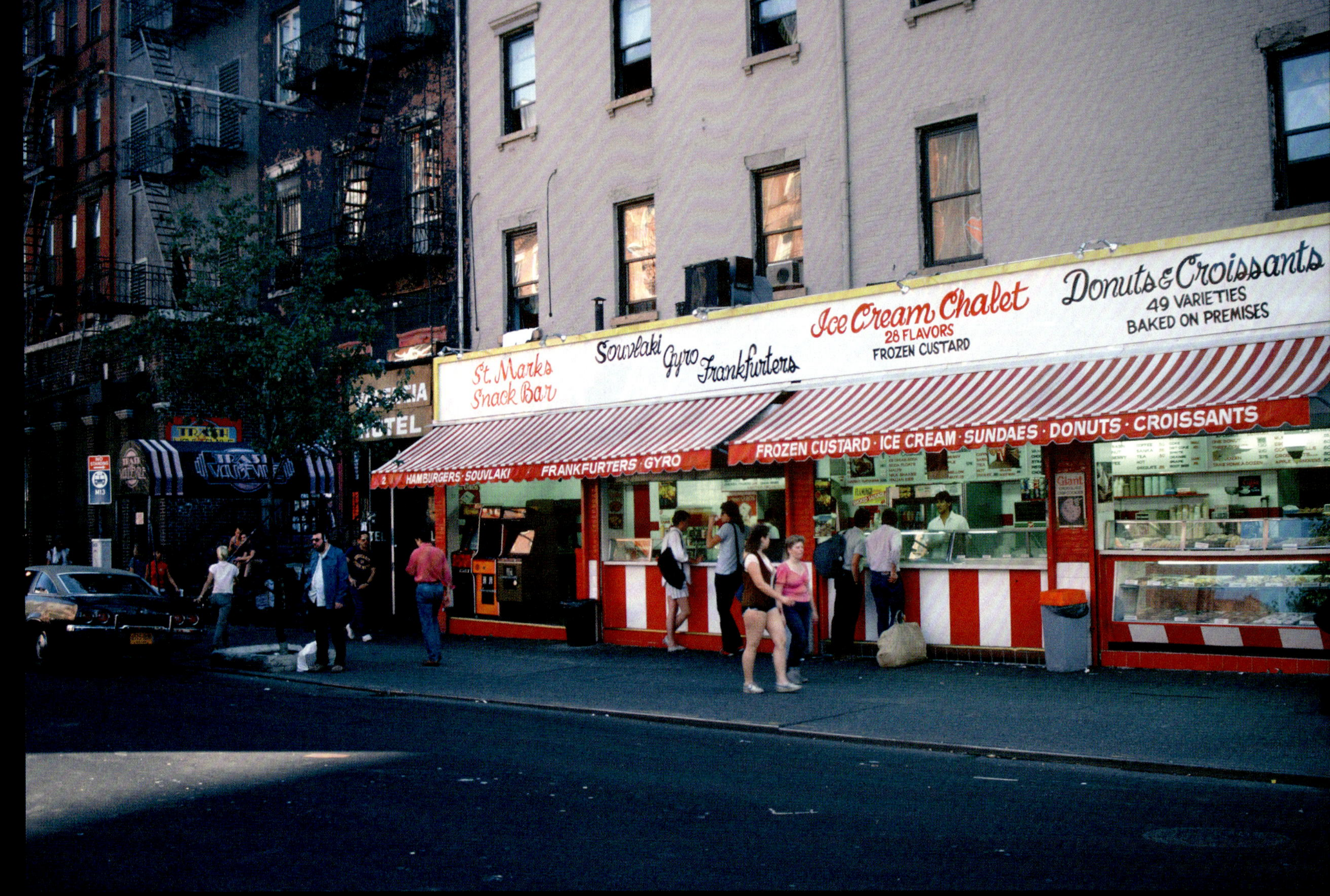

2 AND 4 ST. MARK'S PLACE

The iffy Valencia Hotel and some treats on the way there. The original location of Trash and Vaudeville (1975–2015) next door.

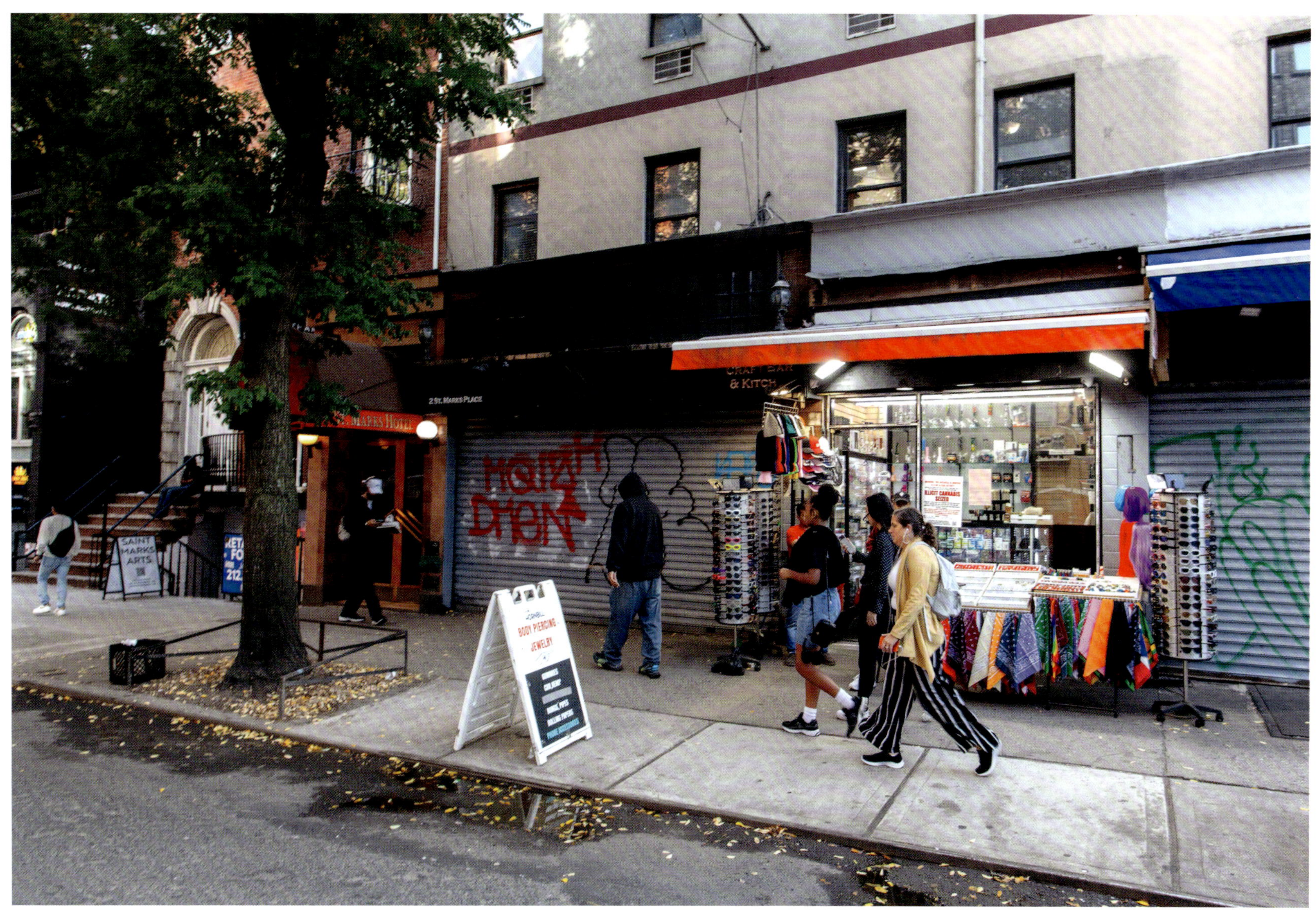

Tourist / junk / plastic doodads shop ("Illicit
Cannabis Seized" sign in window), St. Mark's Hotel.
Next door, 4 St. Mark's, the former home not only
of Trash and Vaudeville but Elizabeth Hamilton,
Alexander Hamilton's widow.

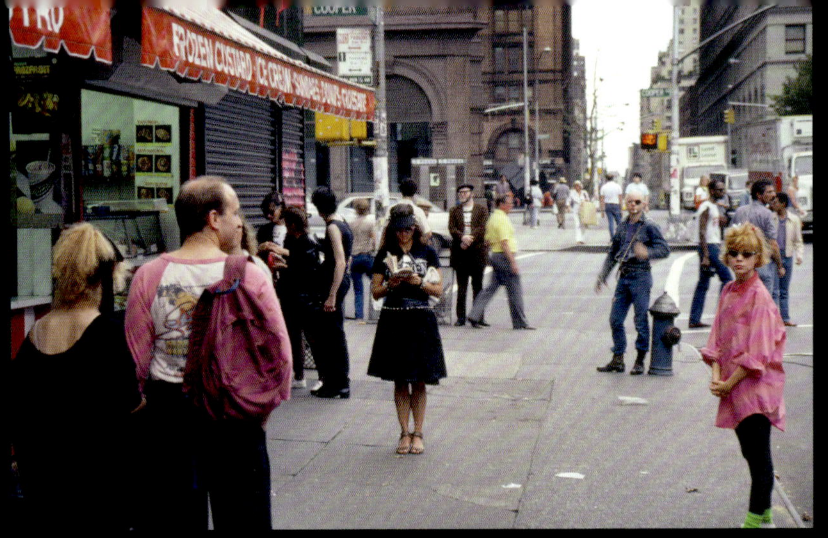
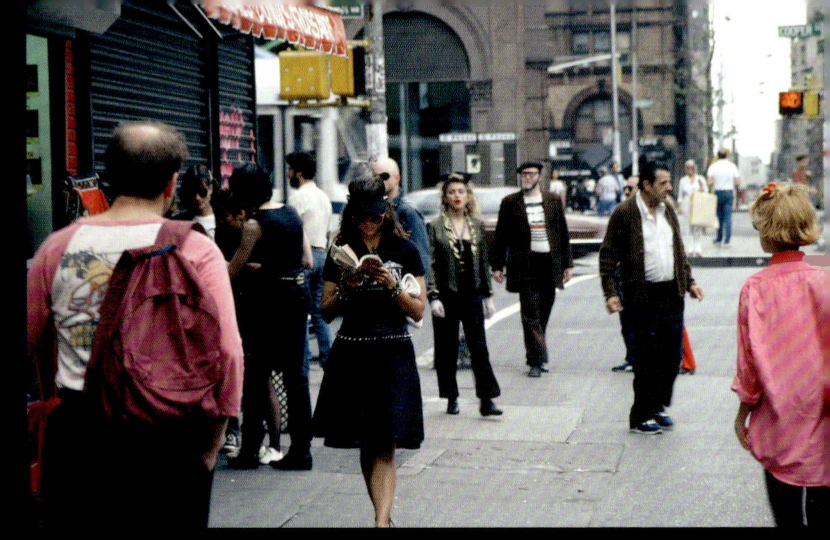

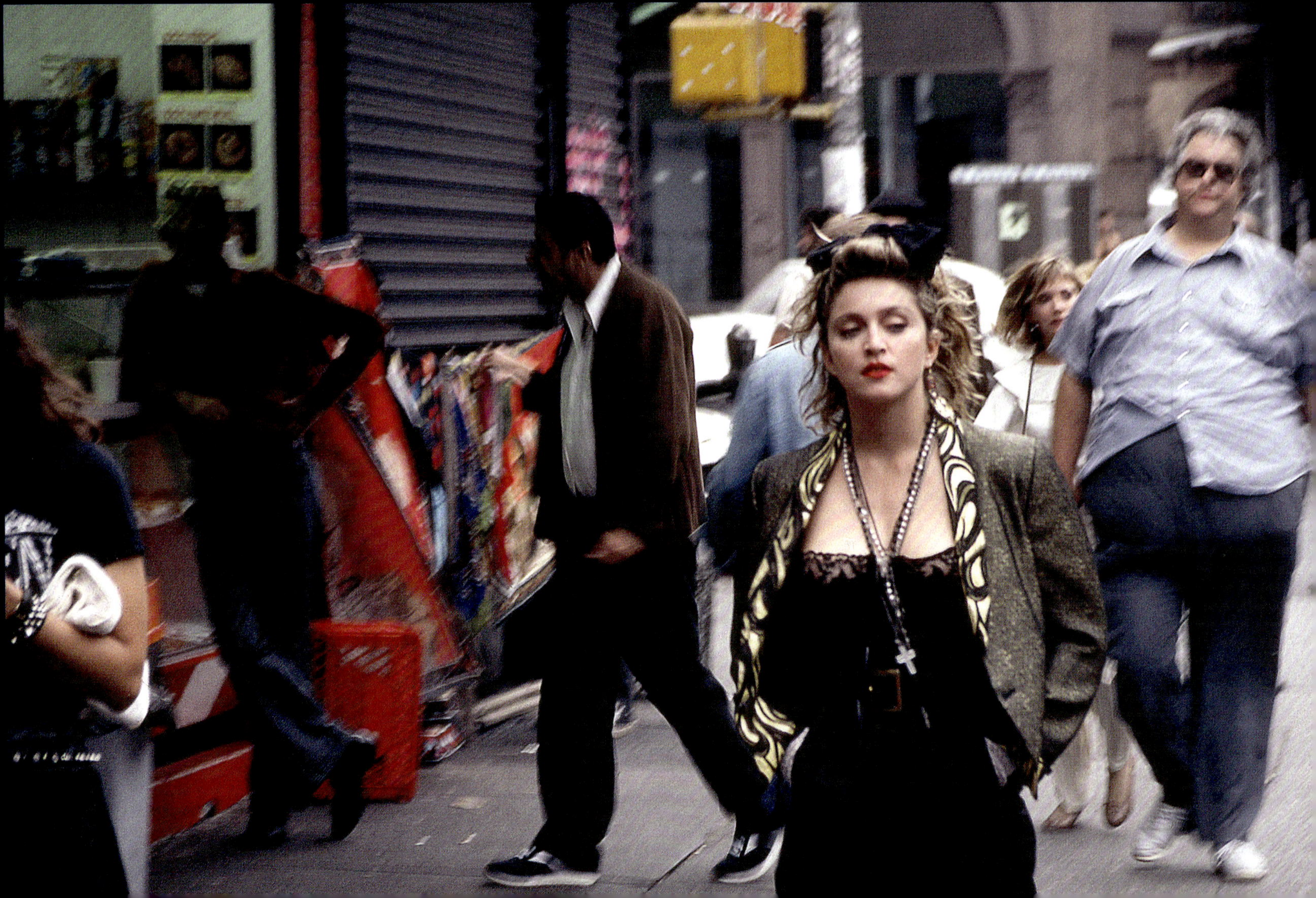

2 SAINT MARK'S PLACE

THEN Madonna strolling in a scene from the movie
Desperately Seeking Susan with Cooper Union in the
background. A lot of the movie was shot around the
East Village and on St. Mark's in particular. Also, various
scenes from the shoot. While taking pictures for a book
about the "changing East Village" that never happened,
I was told I should get to St. Mark's to photograph
Madonna. I barely knew who she was, but I went. A long
story, but these photos ended up getting me many jobs (a
profession!) photographing music and celebrity types.

NOW An after-school walk home.

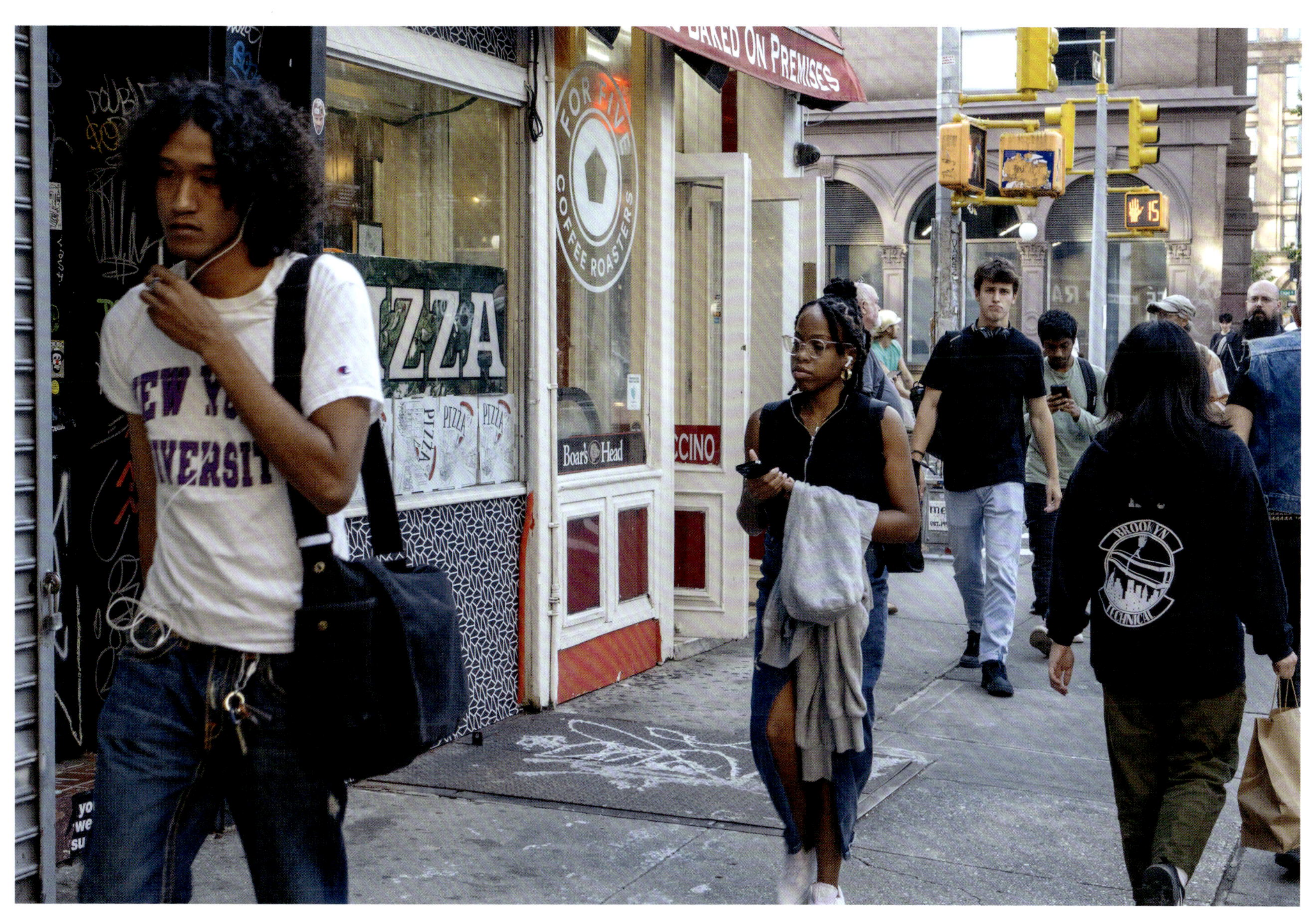

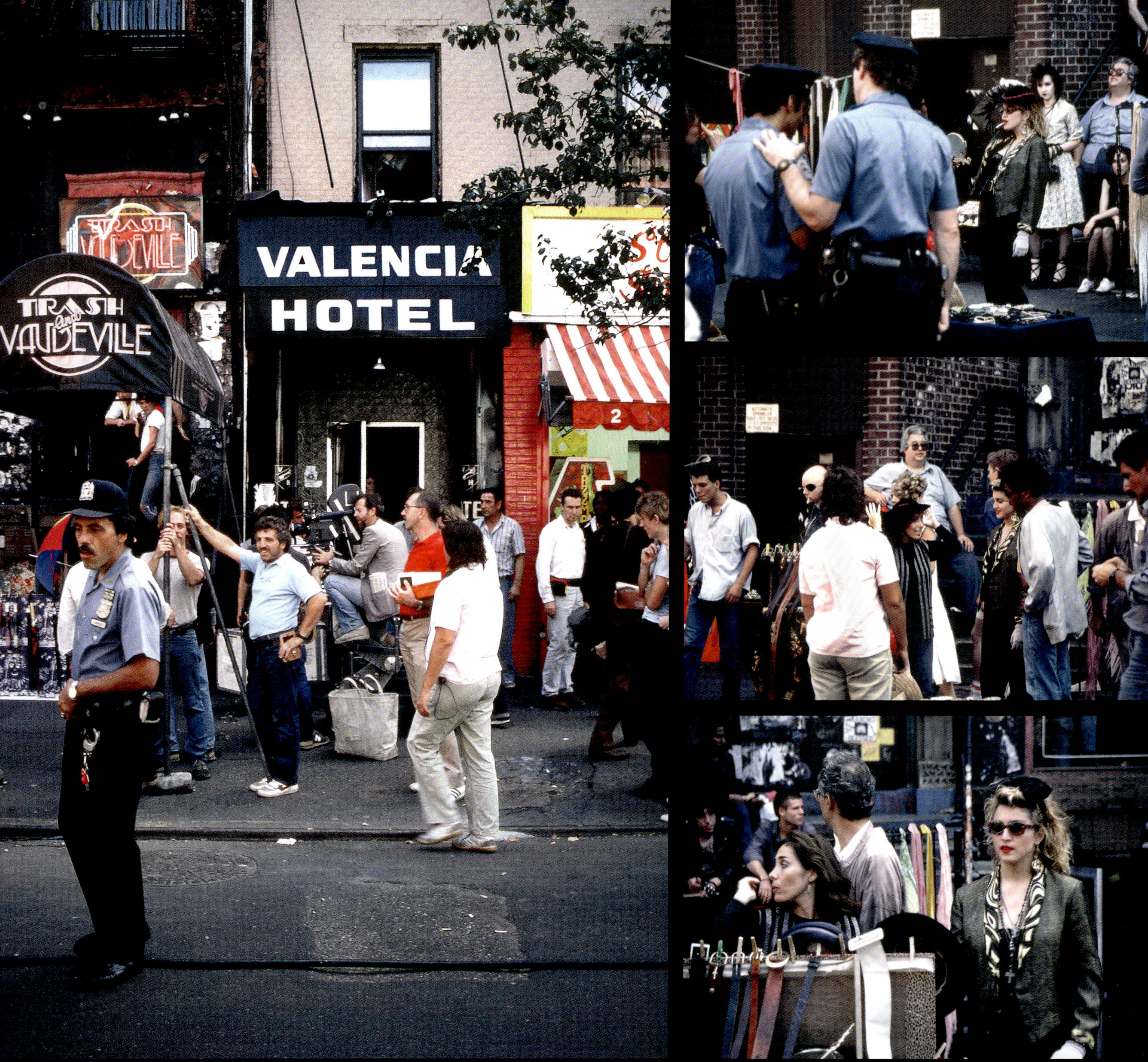
TRASH AND VAUDEVILLE
TRASH AND VAUDEVILLE
VALENCIA HOTEL
2

4 ST. MARK'S PLACE

THEN Trash and Vaudeville and the Valencia Hotel during the filming of *Desperately Seeking Susan*. The cops and crew . . . some working, some watching.

NOW An afternoon stroll, St. Mark's Hotel, and "This Space for Lease."

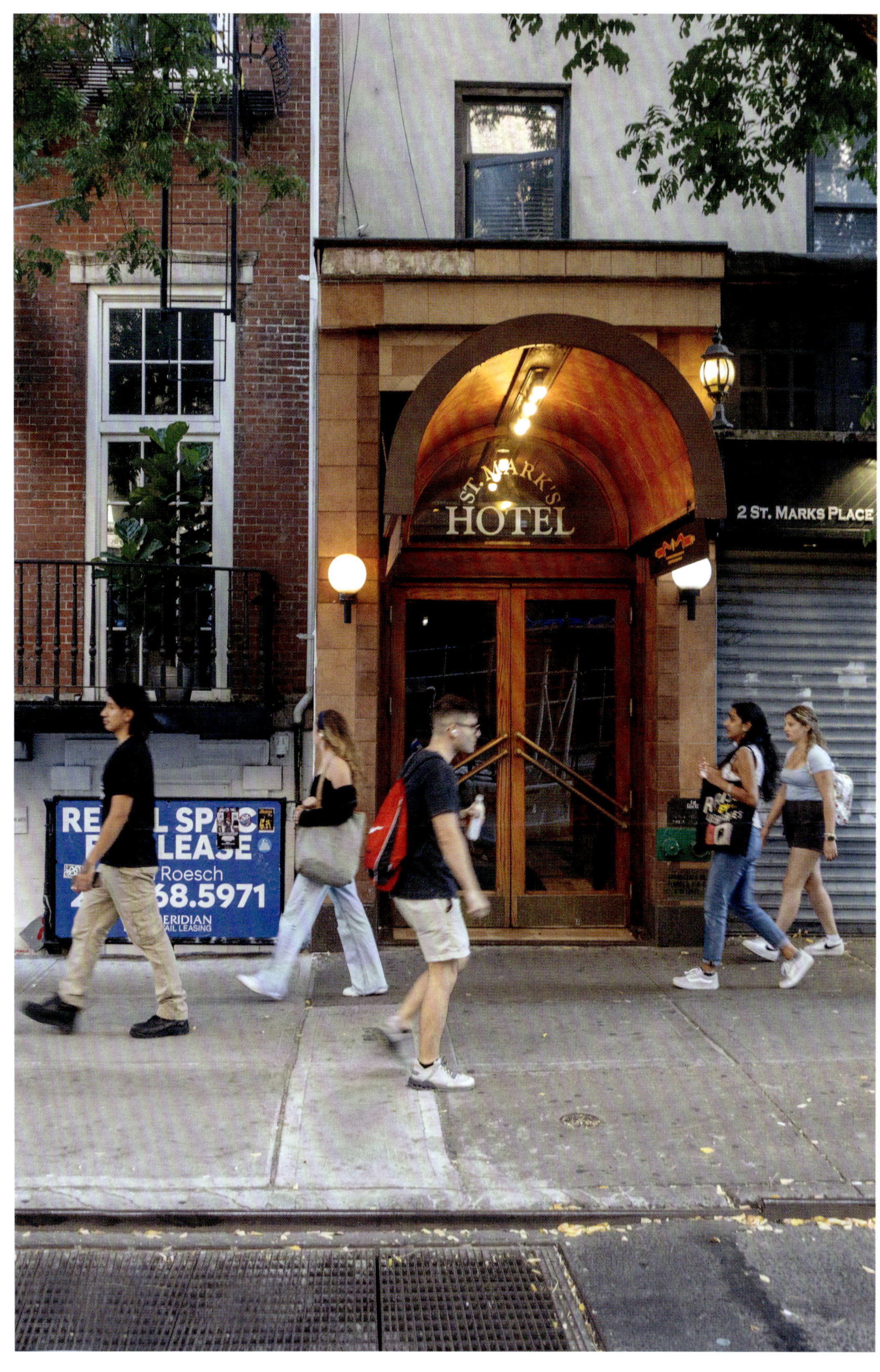

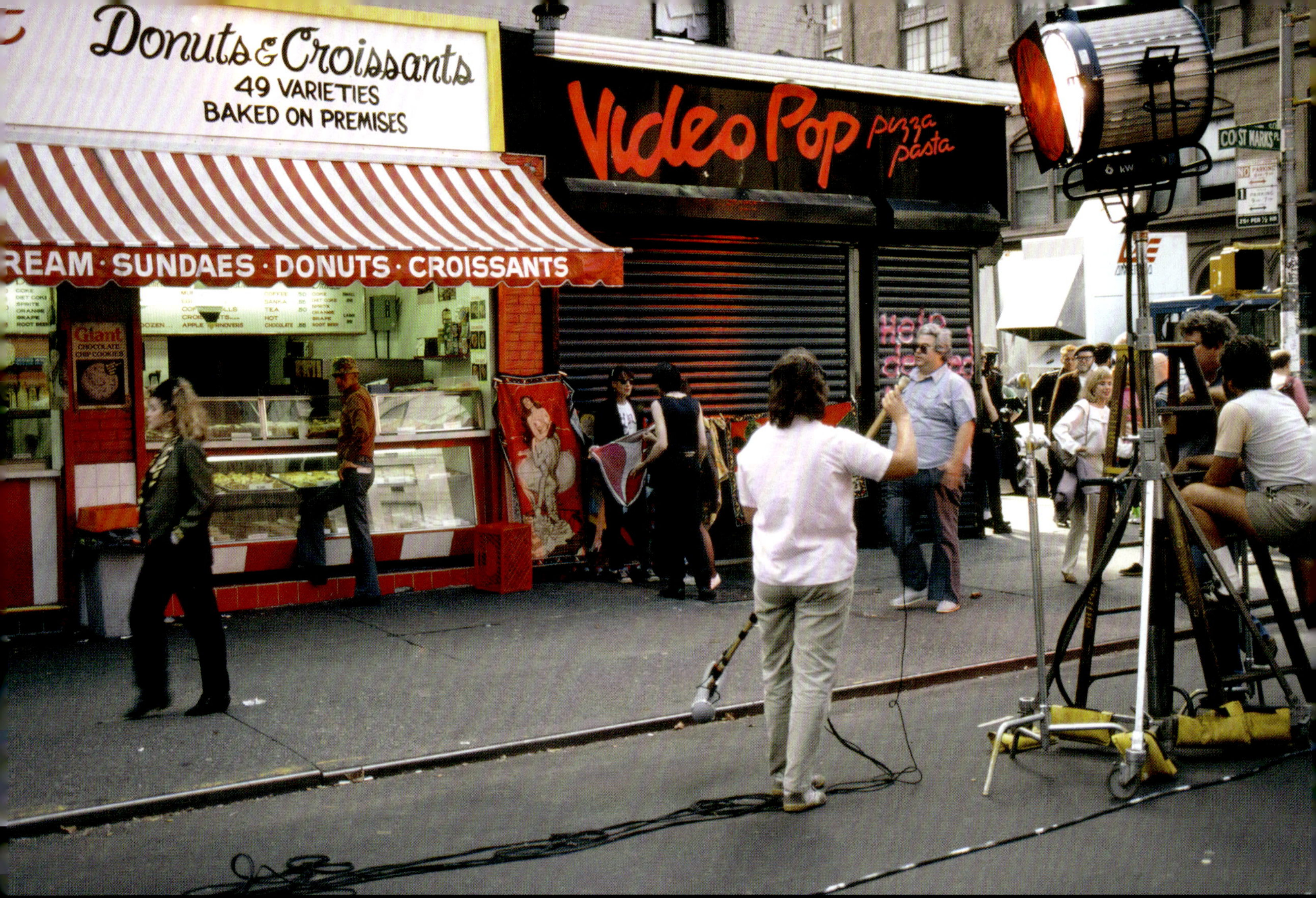

Donuts & Croissants
49 VARIETIES
BAKED ON PREMISES
CREAM · SUNDAES · DONUTS · CROISSANTS
Giant
CHOCOLATE
CHIP COOKIES
Video Pop pizza pasta
6 kW
CO ST MARKS PL

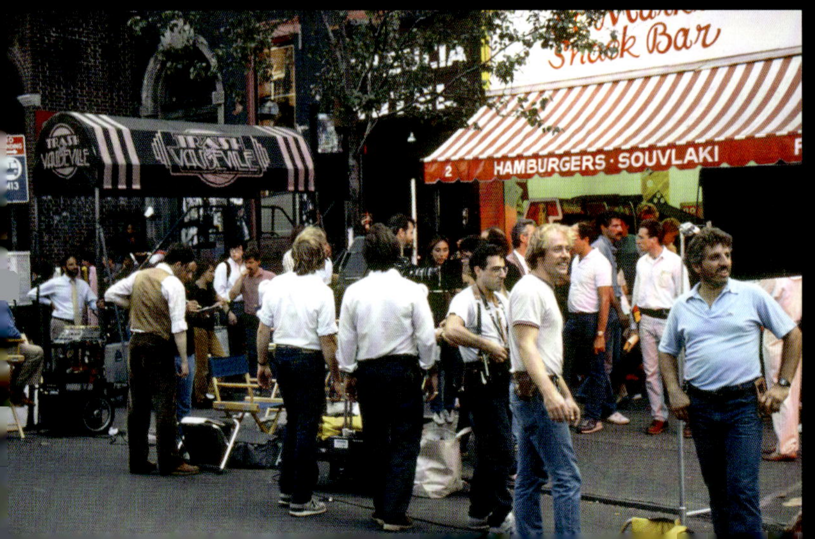
Shack Bar
TRASH
VAUDEVILLE
HAMBURGERS · SOUVLAKI

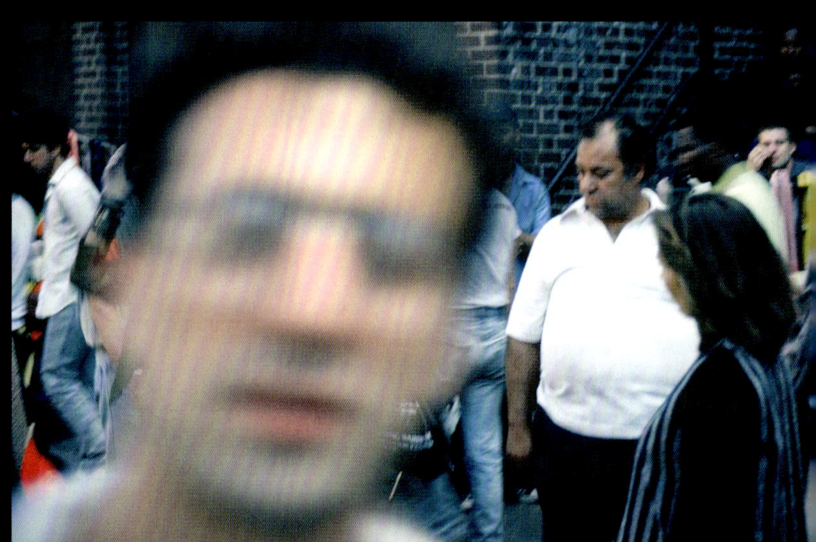

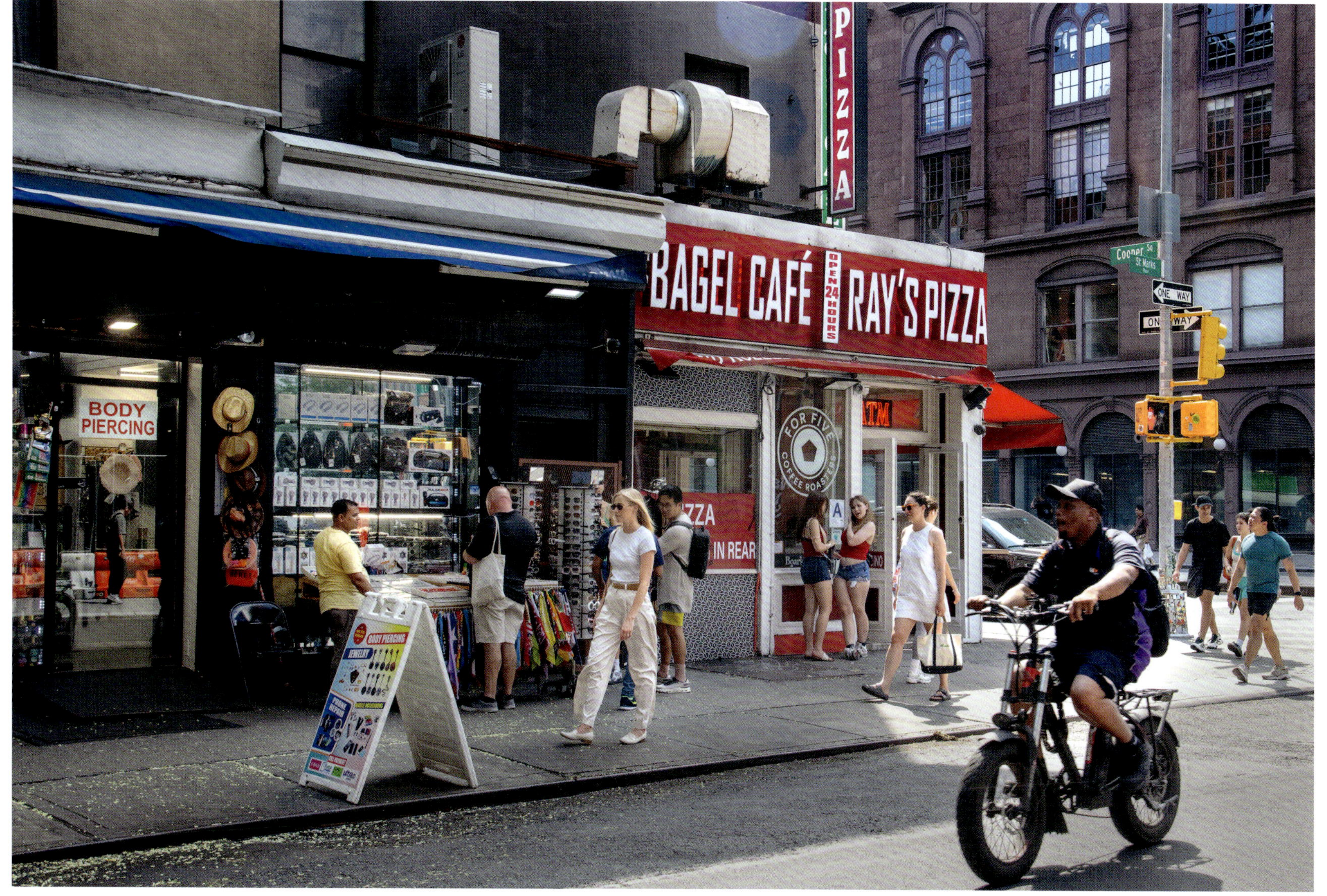

2 SAINT MARK'S PLACE

THEN Madonna eyeing the donuts. The extras and
the crew eyeing Madonna. The production's "still
photographer" had enough of me and got in my face. I
guess he didn't want alternate takes in the Madonna stock
photography business.

NOW Donuts gone, pizza still available, people still walking
(no celebrities at the moment), me and my camera in the
street dodging traffic.

27 SAINT MARK'S PLACE

THEN At the time, one of the many hair salons on the block.

NOW "For rent," but despite the attempts to clean it up, continually tagged and pasted, making for nice photo shoot backgrounds.

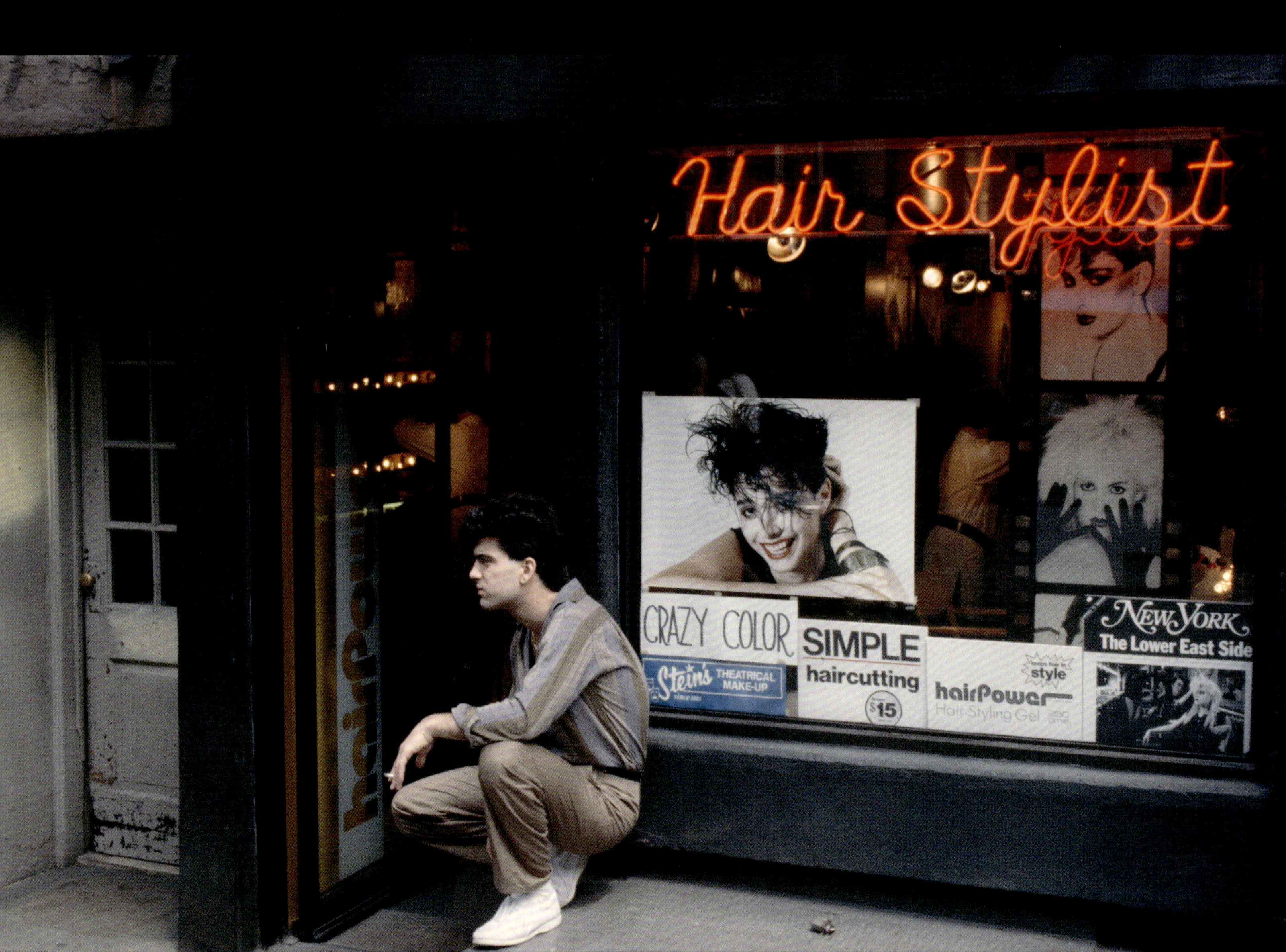

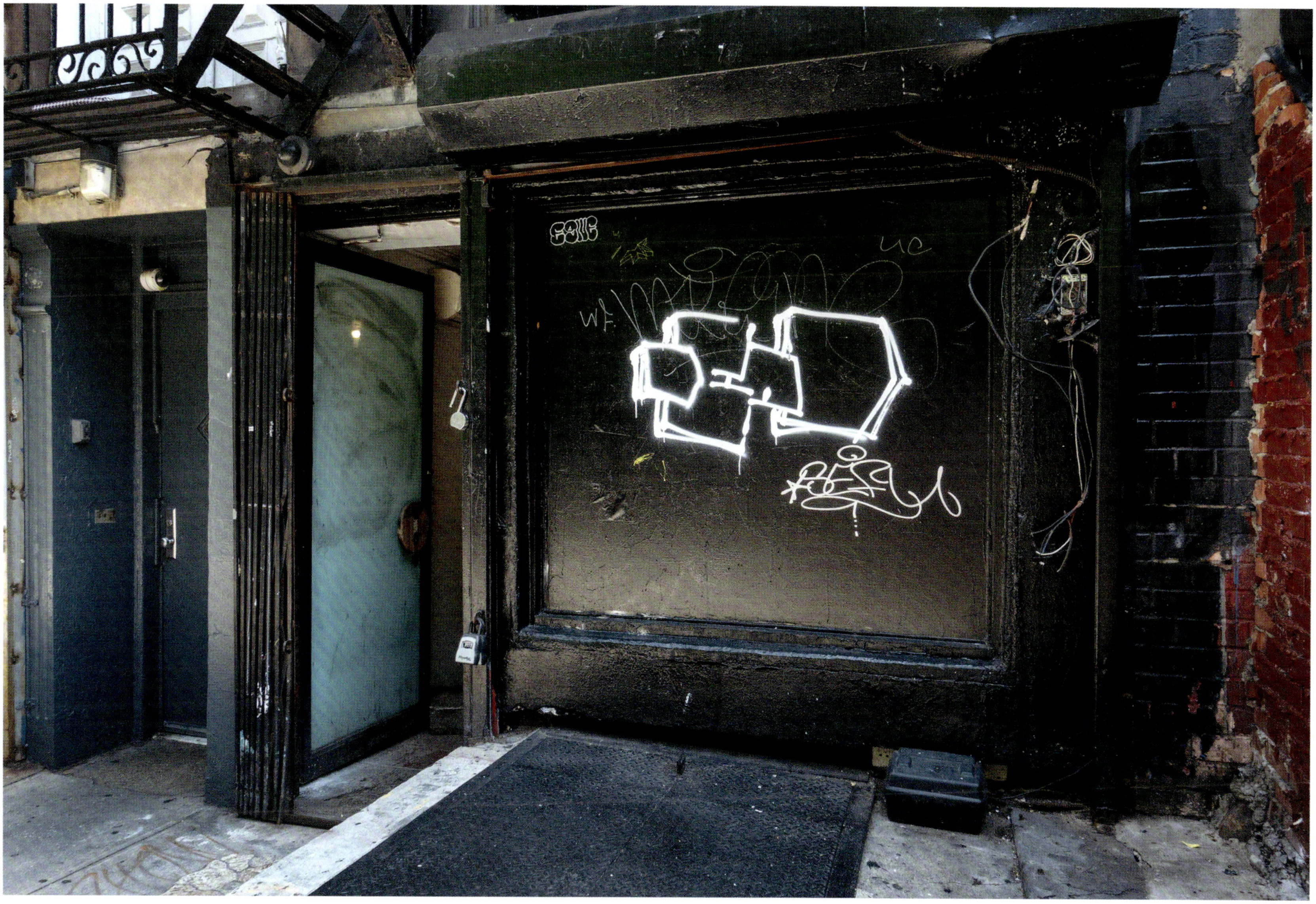

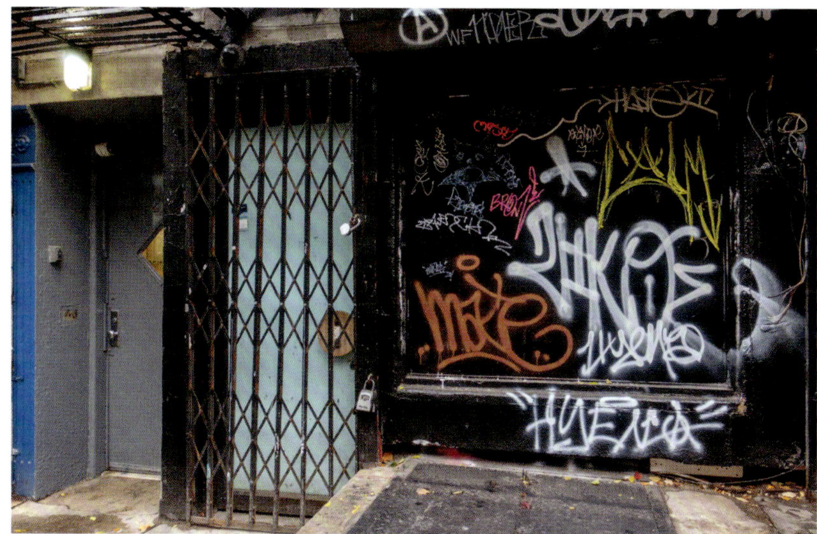
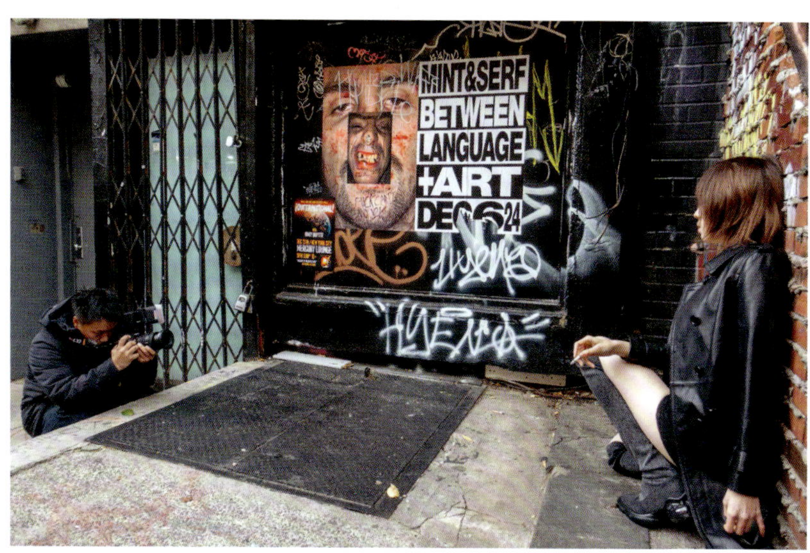

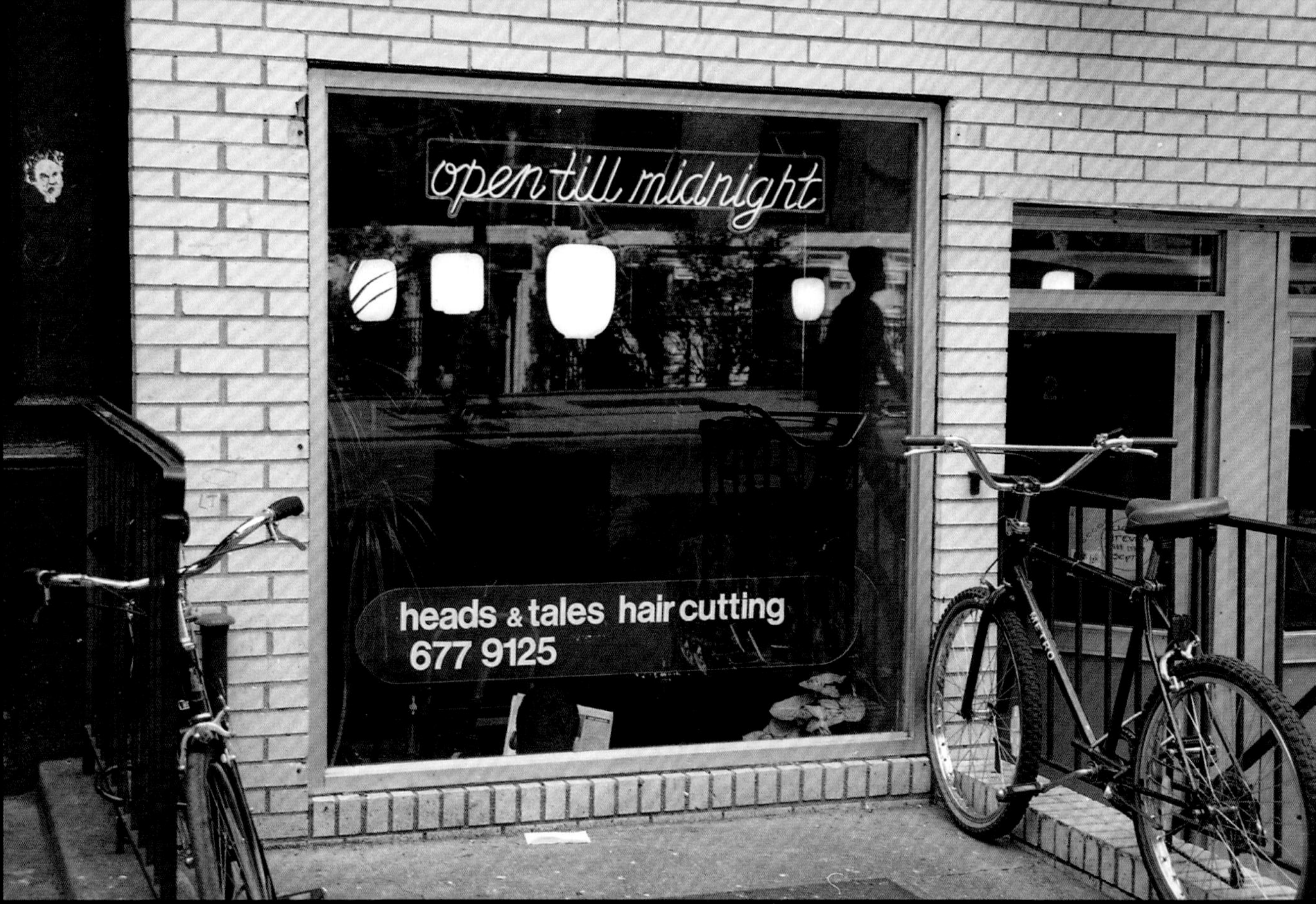

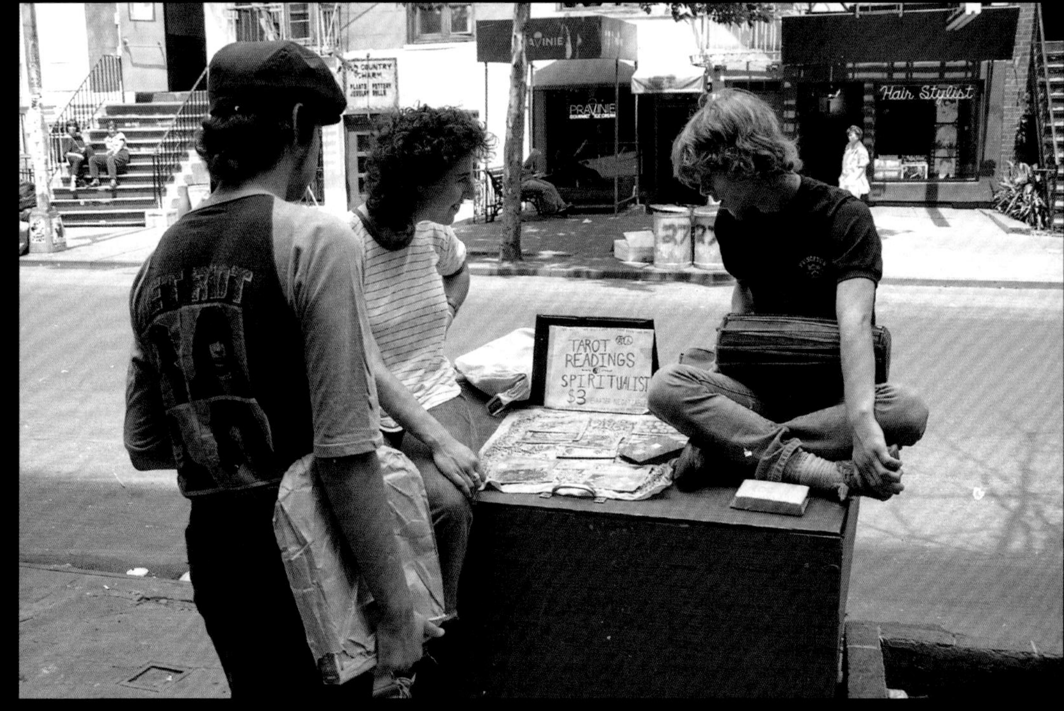

22 ST. MARK'S PLACE

Yet another hairstylist. Sidewalk tarot card readings with the old Electric Circus nightclub and the Dom across the street. In 1966 Andy Warhol and Paul Morrissey transformed an old German and Polish music hall into the Electric Circus. The Velvet Underground were the house band there.

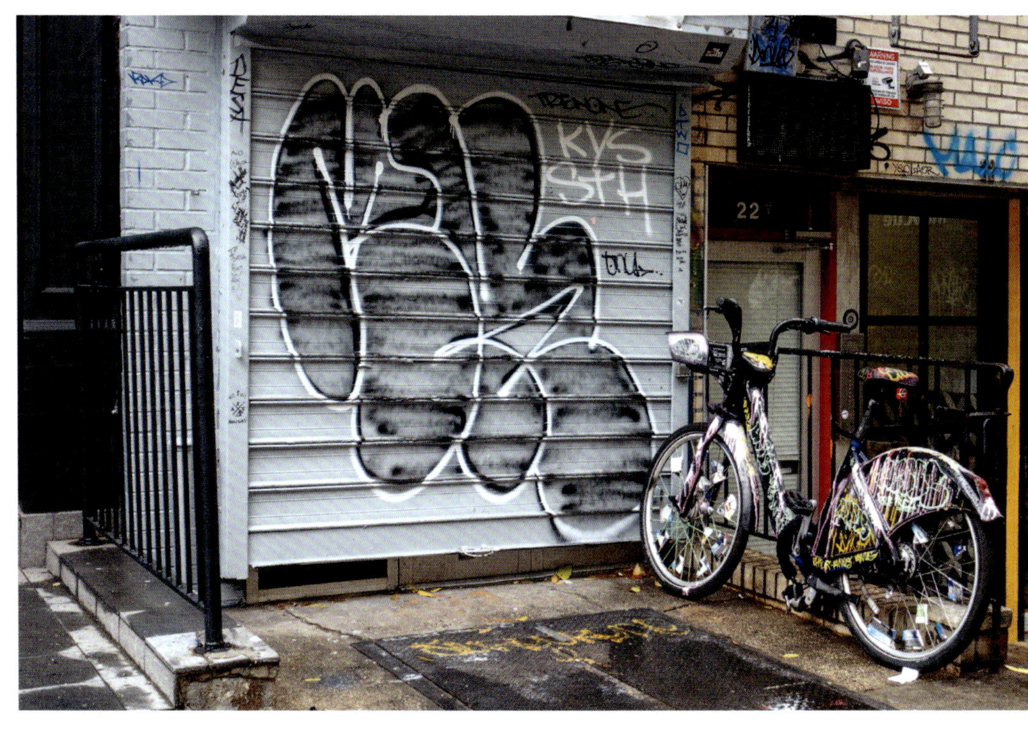

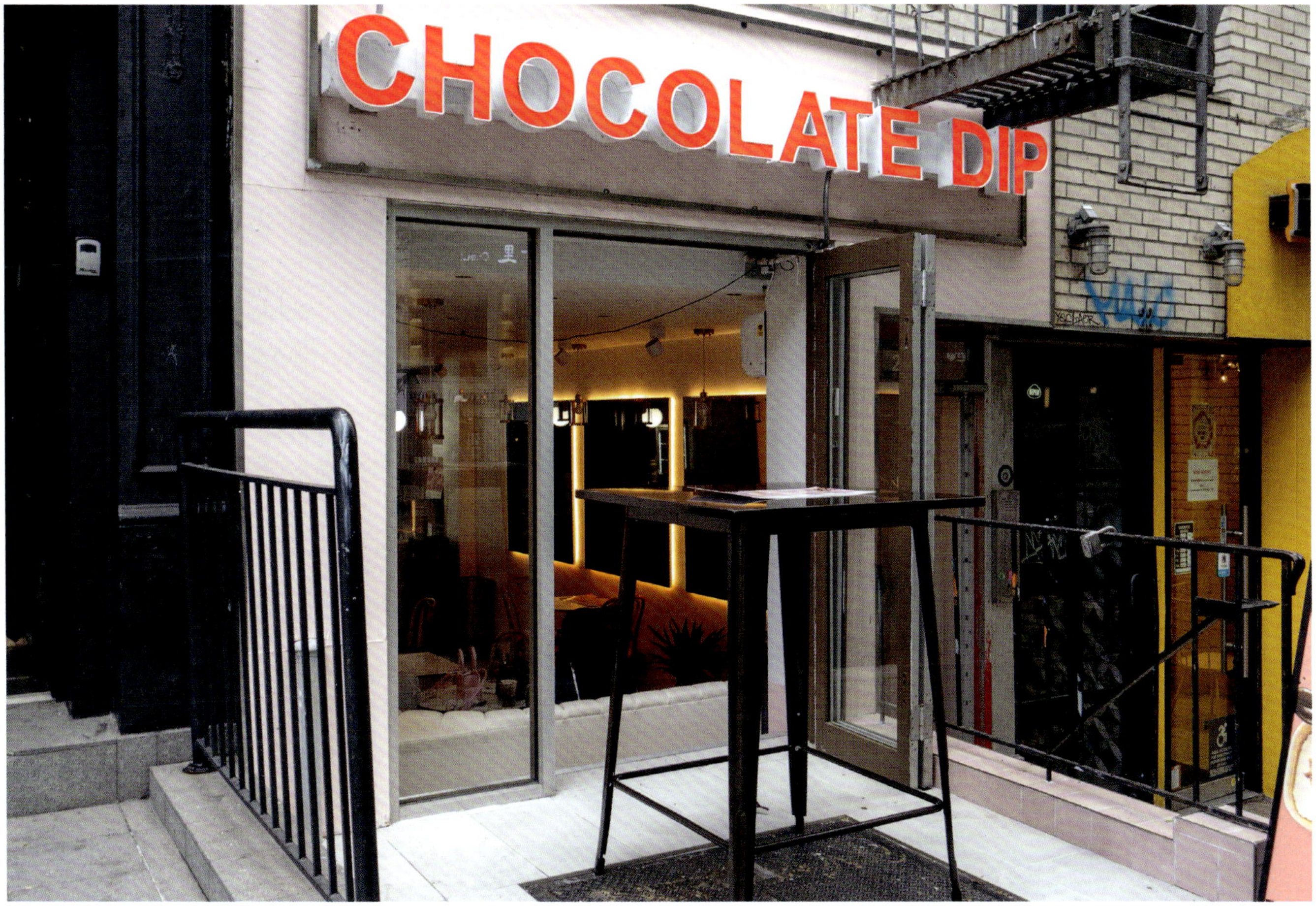

Chocolate Dip
giving it a go.

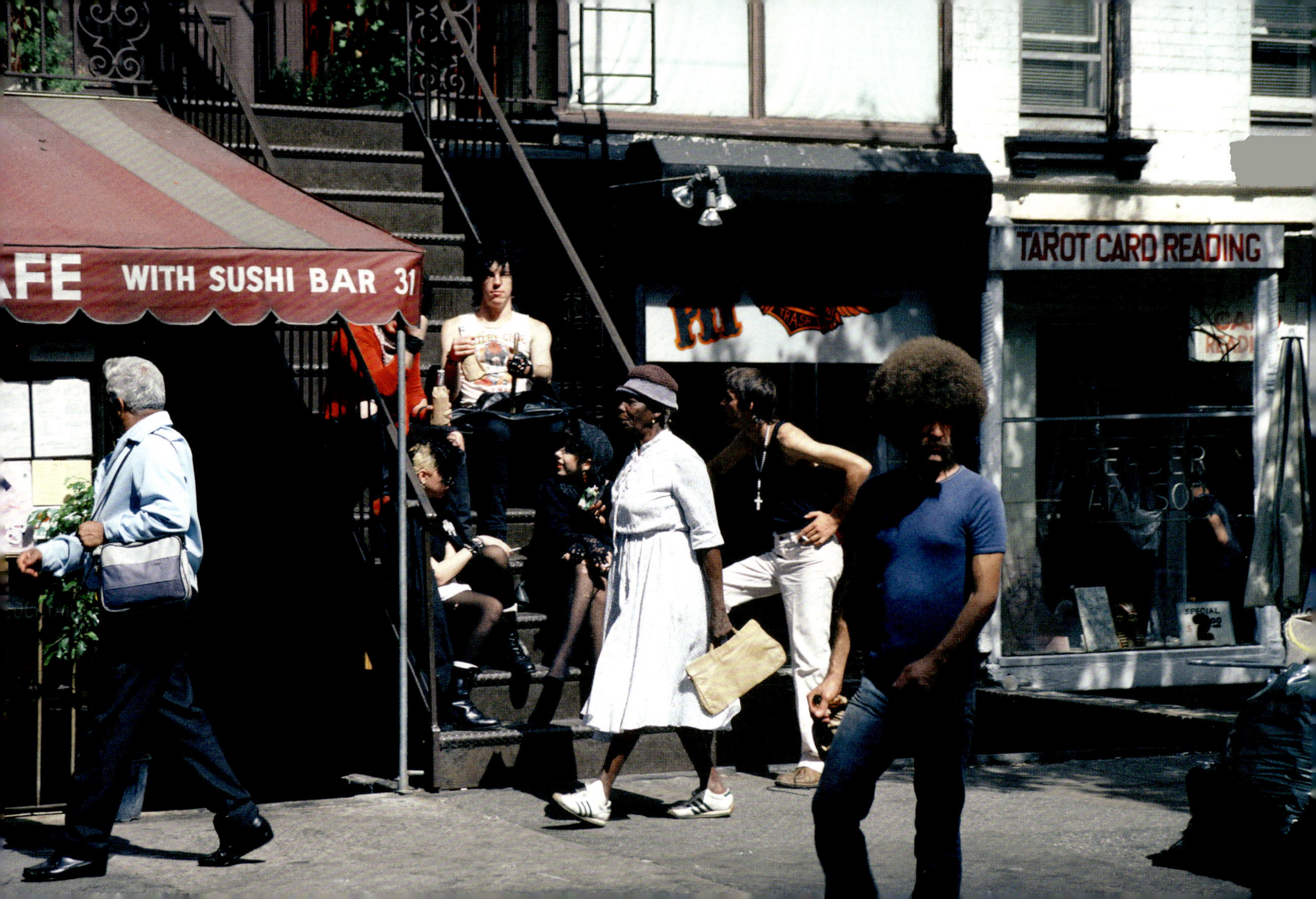

AFE WITH SUSHI BAR 31
TAROT CARD READING

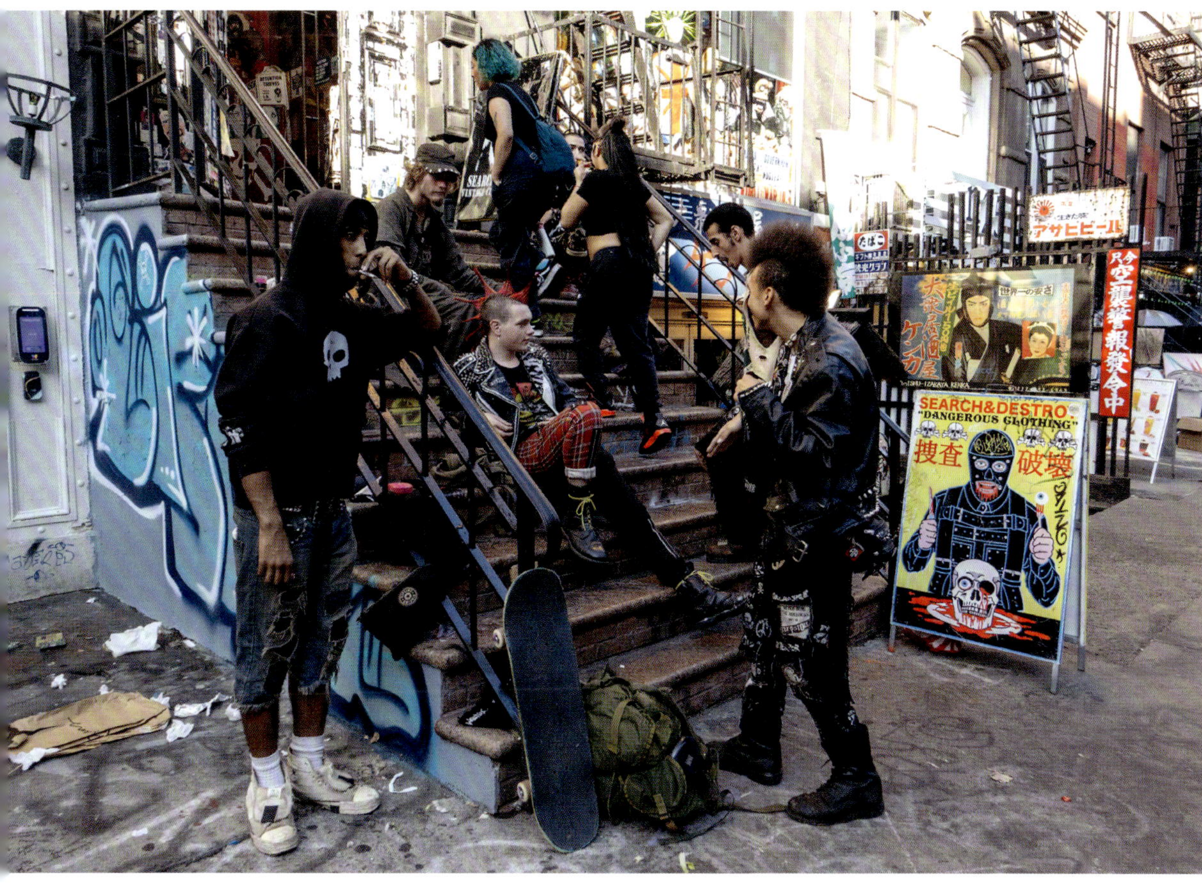
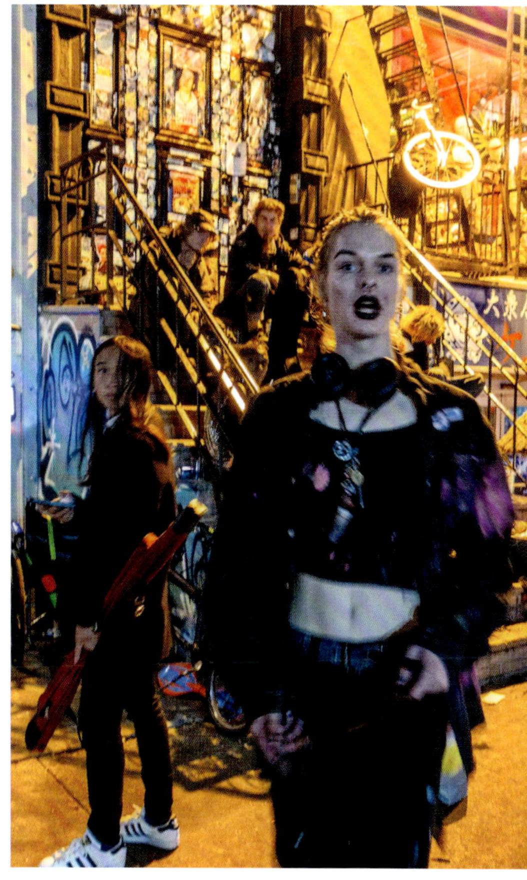

25 ST. MARK'S PLACE

A couple of doors down, forty years apart . . .
Punks on the steps, spike mohawk. (Search
& Destroy.)

Being disagreeable
in the evening.

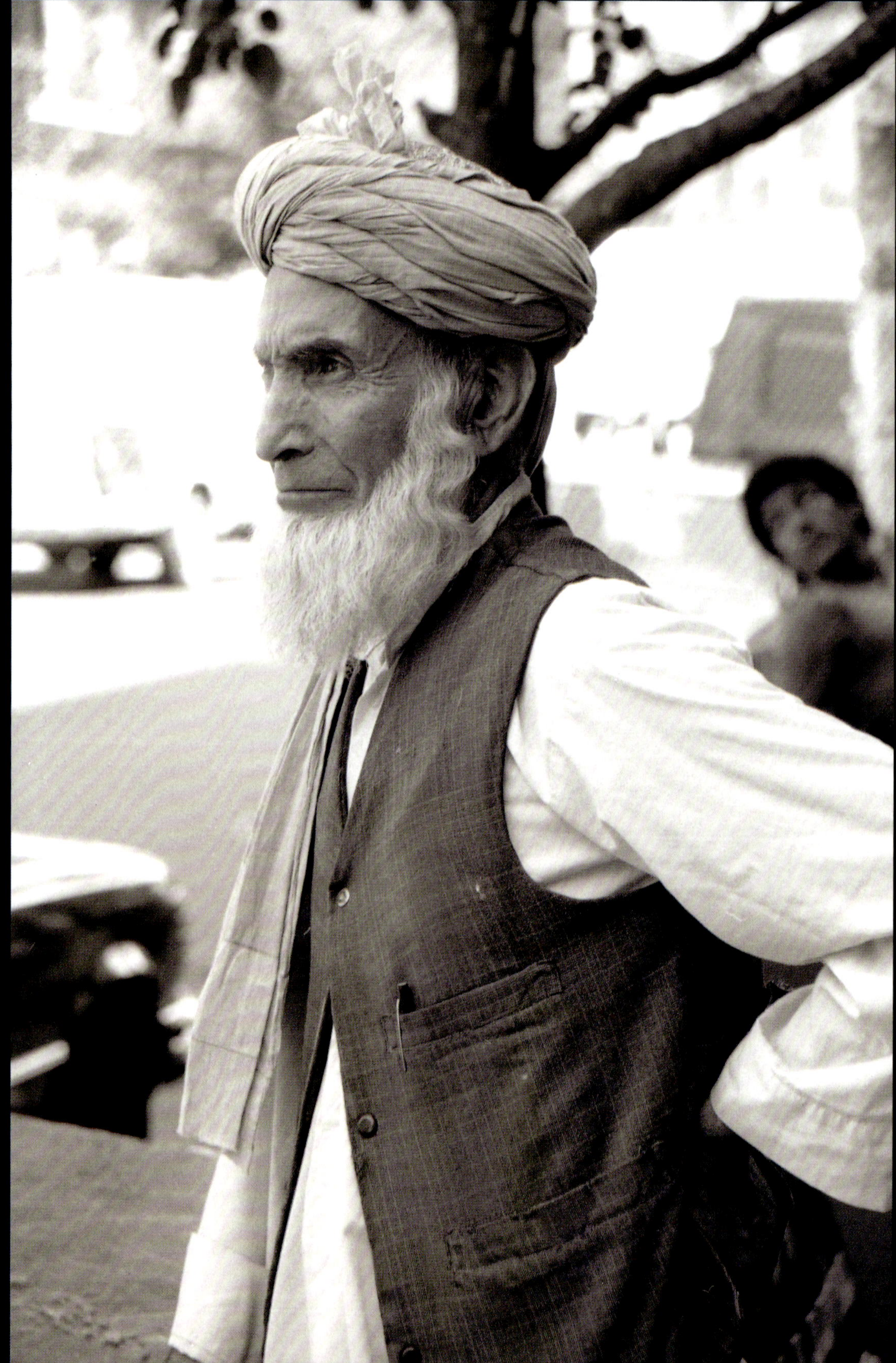

34 ST. MARK'S PLACE

Grandfather and grandson outside Cafe Kabul / Khyber Pass, a longtime Afghan restaurant.

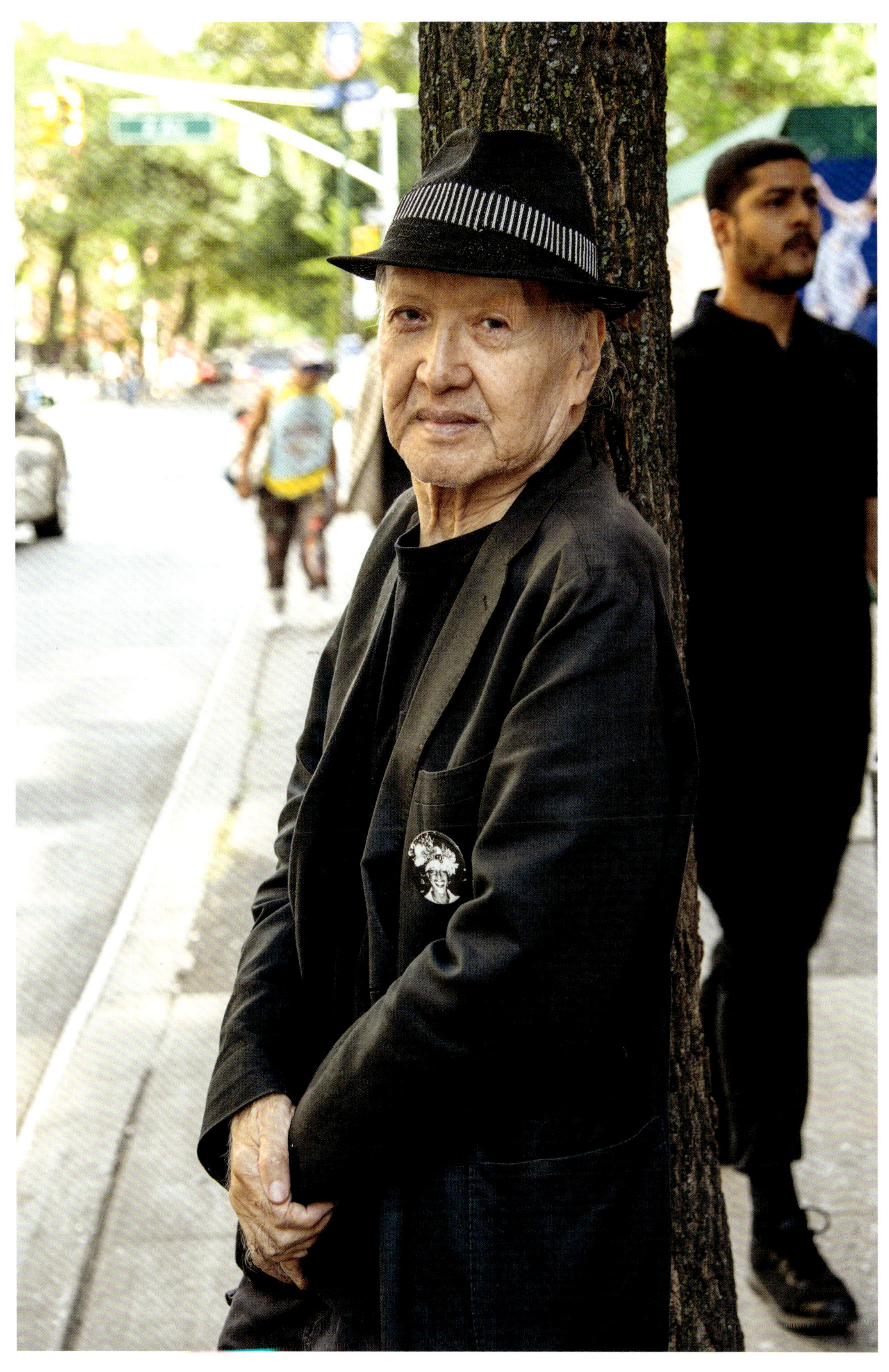

Same tree, now with Agosto Machado. Saw Agosto nearby and asked if he would stand for a portrait. Agosto is a lovely person, as well as (per his gallerist Gordon Robichaux) "a singular figure . . . a Chinese-Spanish-Filipino-American performance artist, activist, archivist, muse, caretaker, and friend to countless celebrated and underground visual and performing artists." MoMA calls him "a crucial figure in the history of Downtown New York." But mainly he is a lovely person.

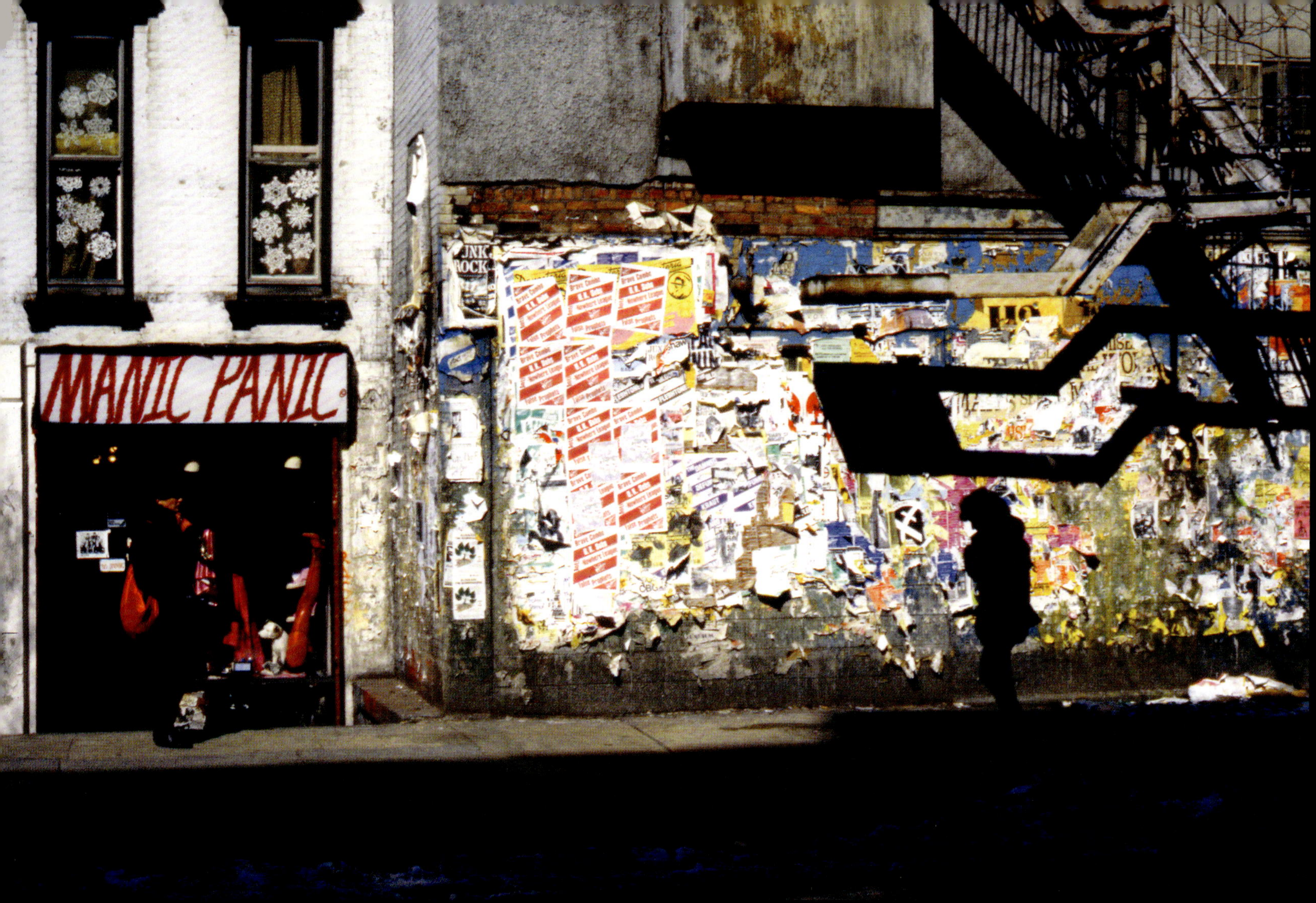

33 ST. MARK'S PLACE

The original location of Manic Panic, owned by
sisters Tish and Snooky, aka the "high priestesses
of punk." Manic Panic opened in 1977 and was the
go-to place for all your punk fashion needs. Tish and
Snooky are still at it but just not here. Next door was
a wheat paste / community info wall.

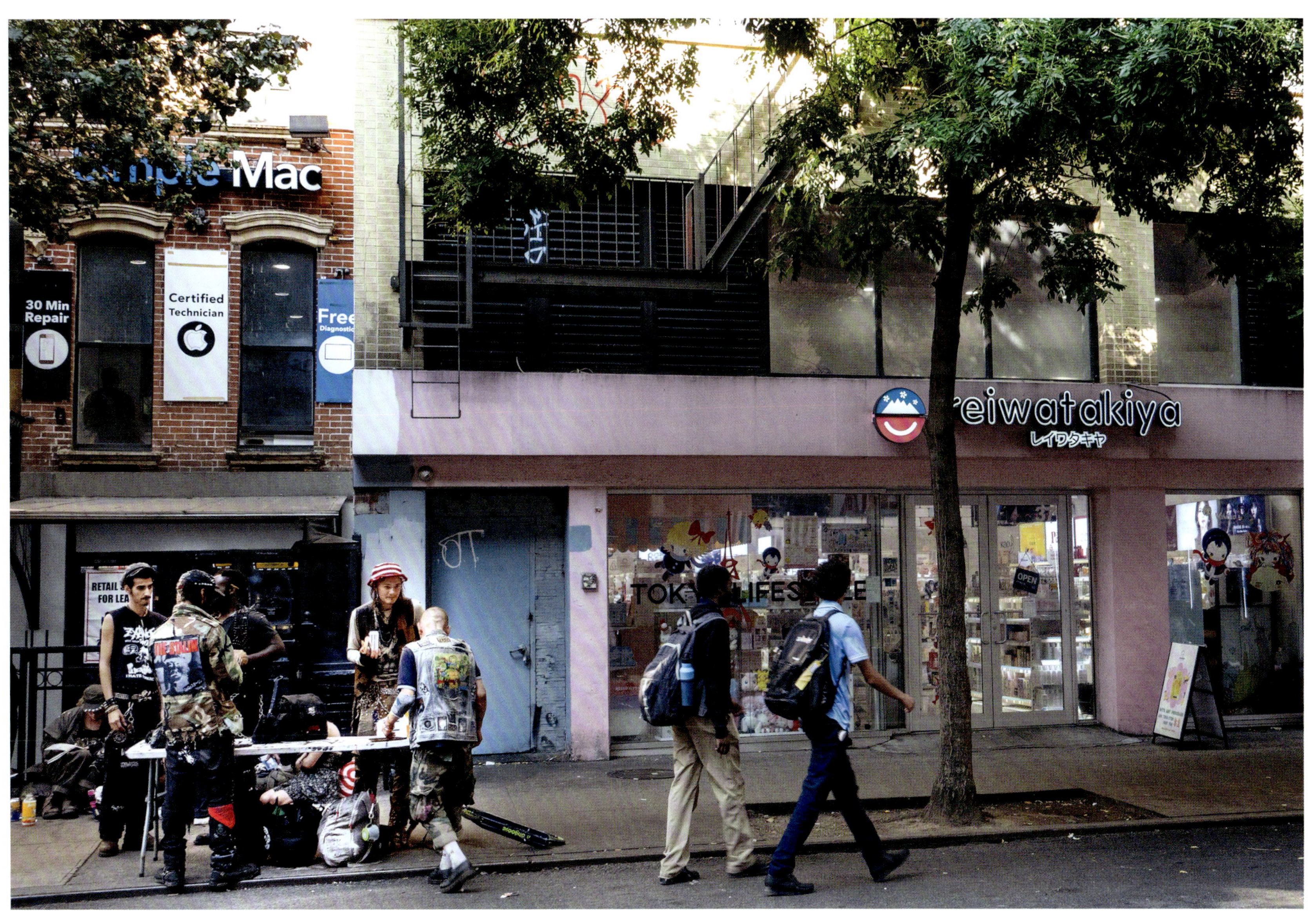

A very different look, almost unrecognizable.

Not quite its 1940s self but as close as you can expect. Borscht, blintzes, and (matzo) balls.

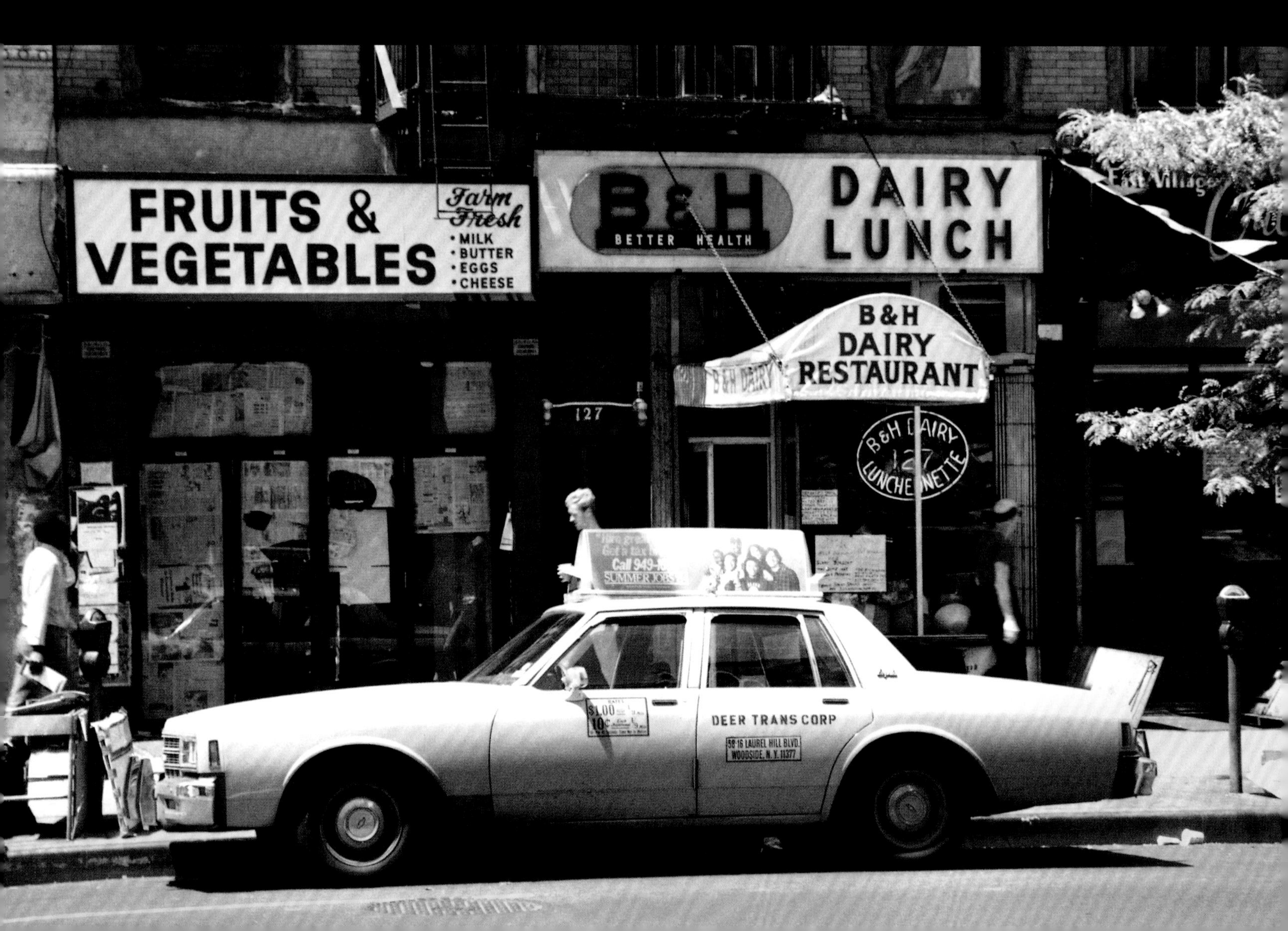

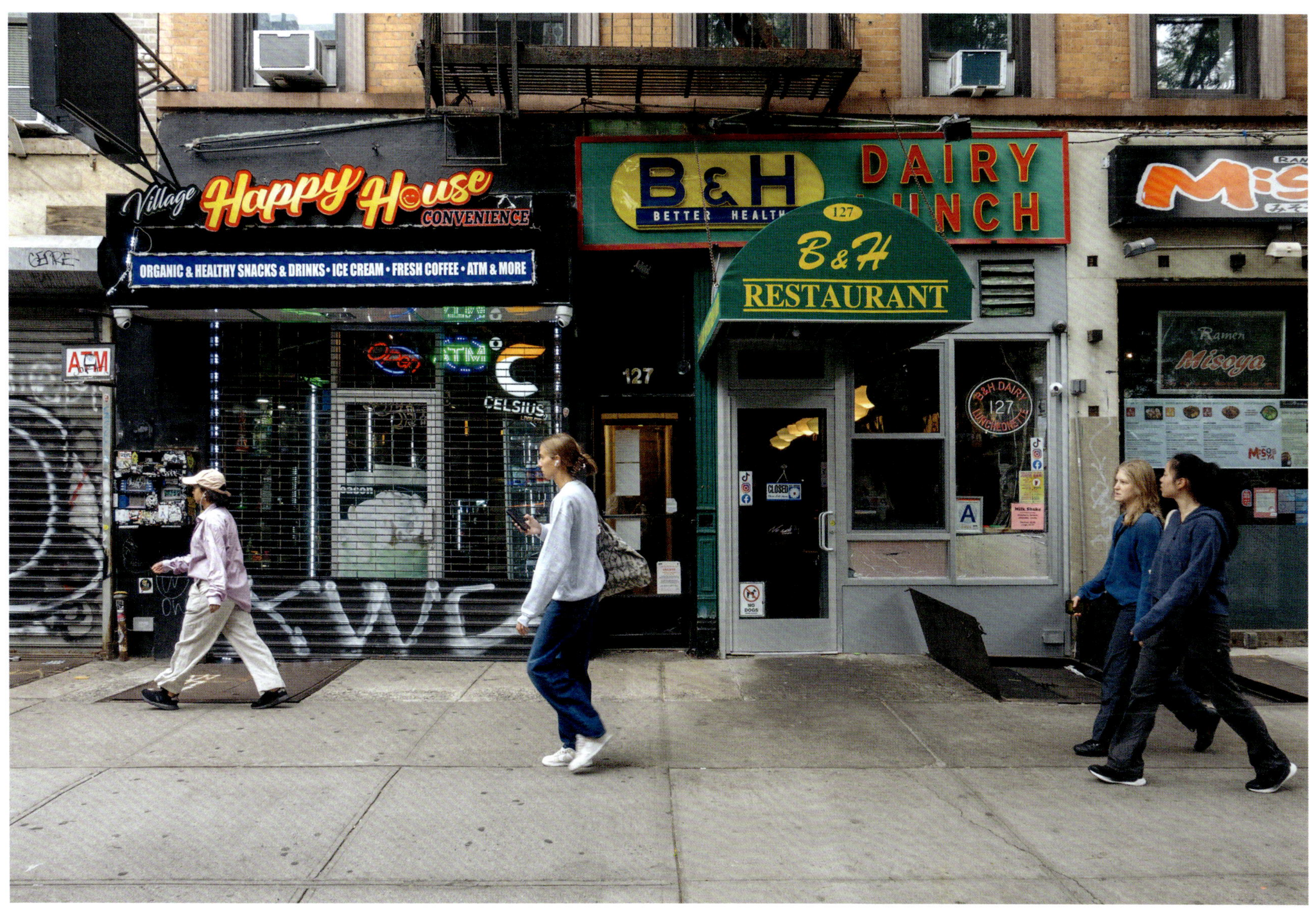

New sign, new neighbors, still "Better Health."

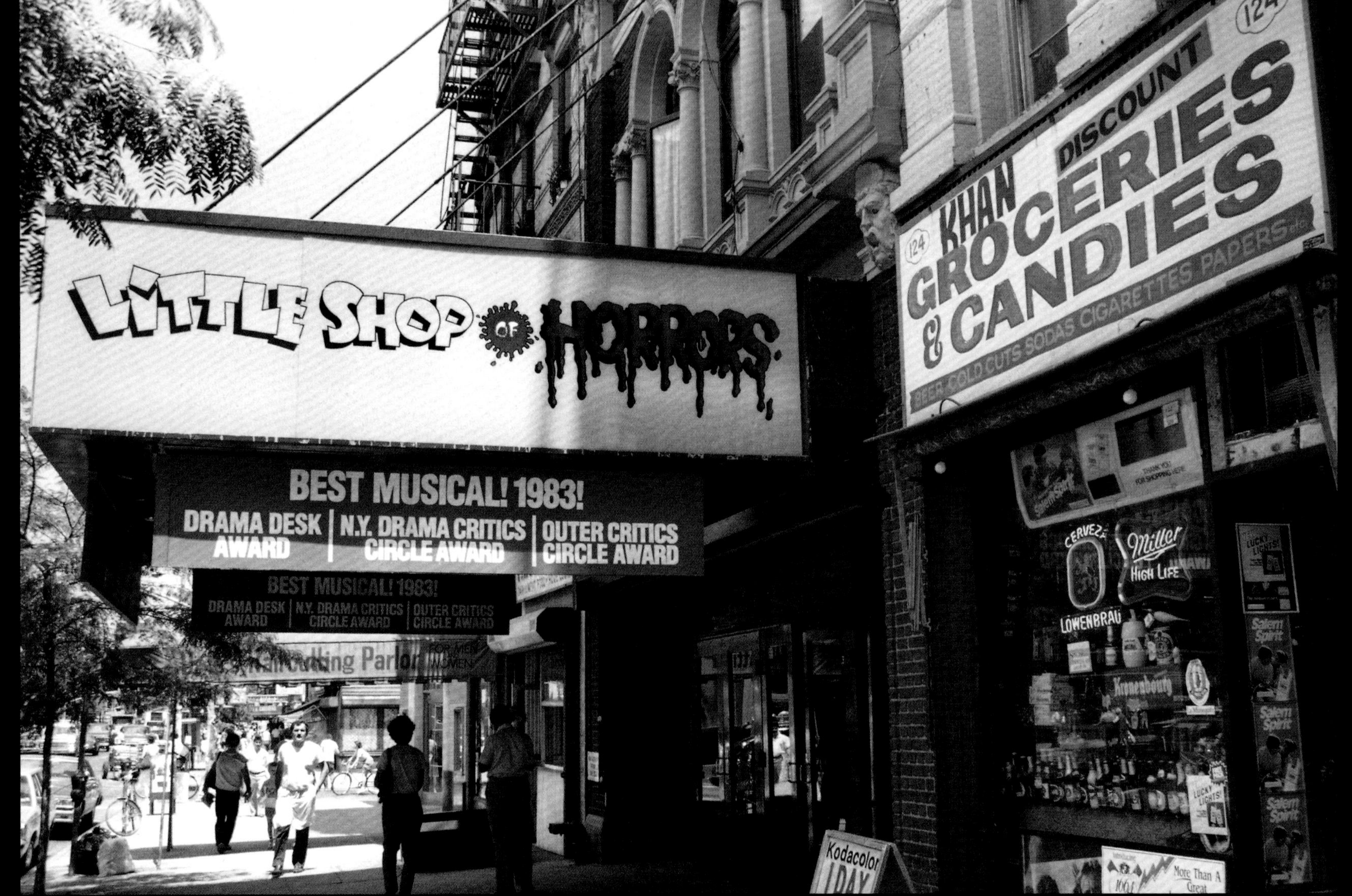

126 SECOND AVENUE

Once part of the Yiddish Theatre District, the Orpheum Theatre transitioned to Off-Broadway in the 1950s. From 1993 to 2023, it was home to *Stomp*.

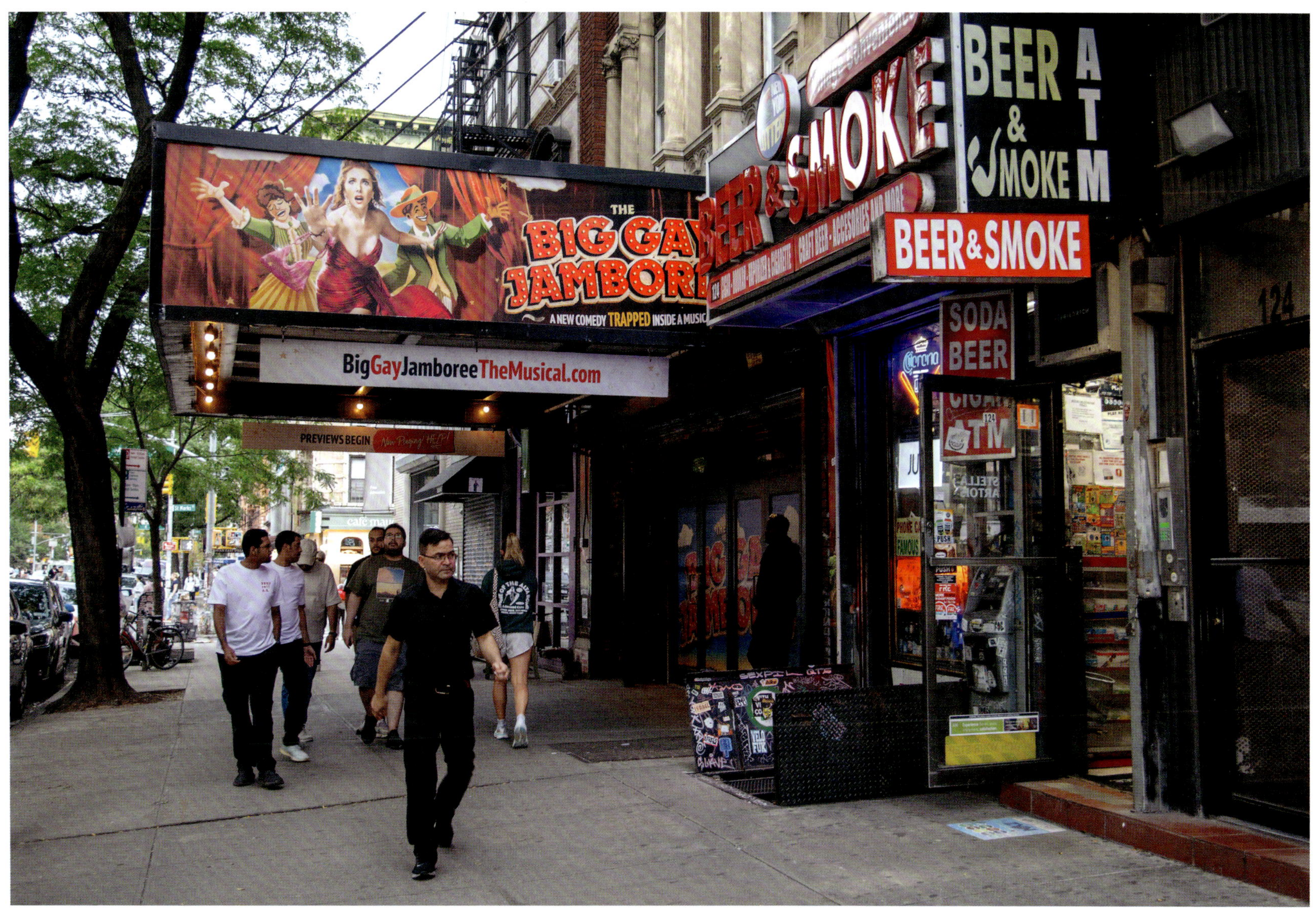

Back to limited-run shows.

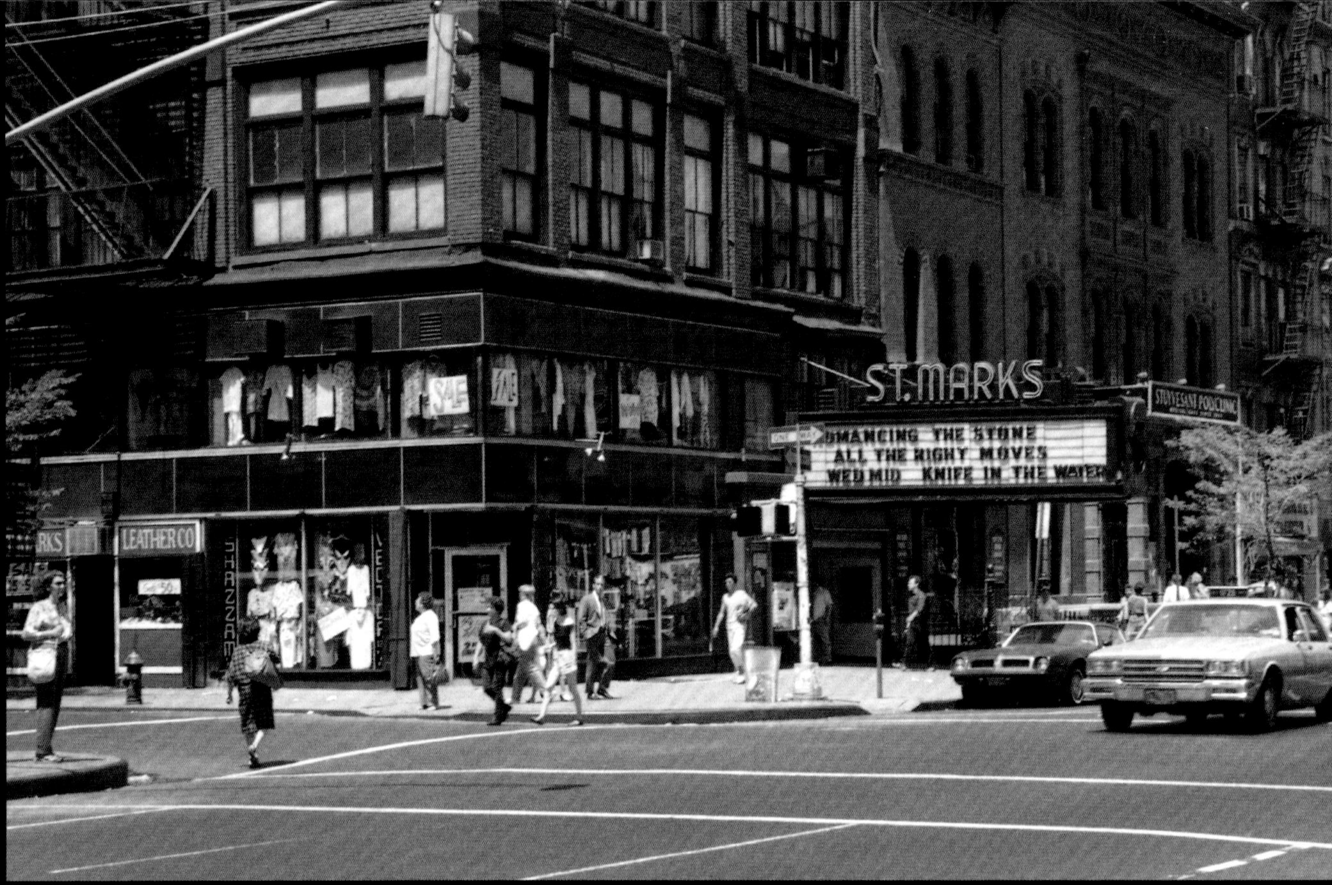

133 SECOND AVENUE

Late nights at St. Marks Cinema and then
over to Kiev for a bowl of borscht.

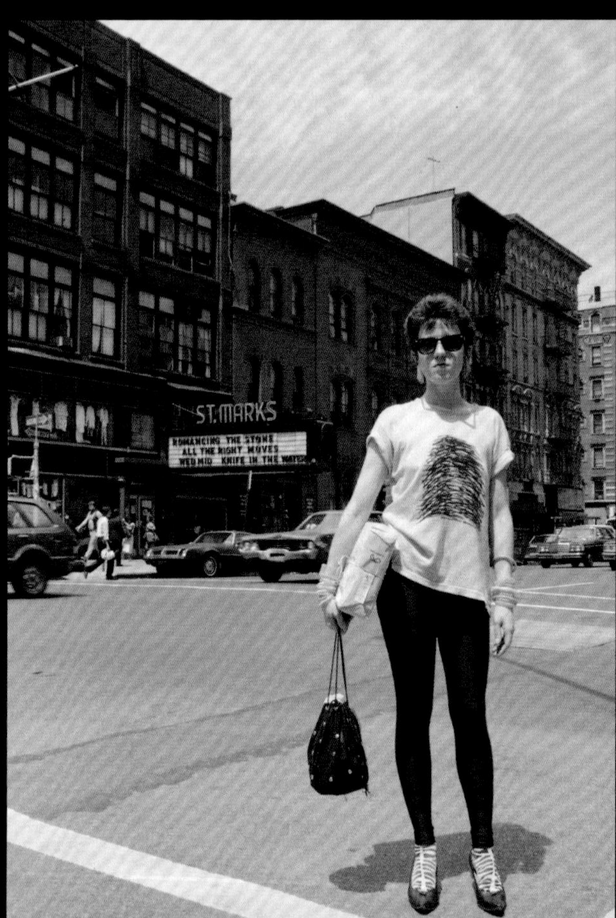

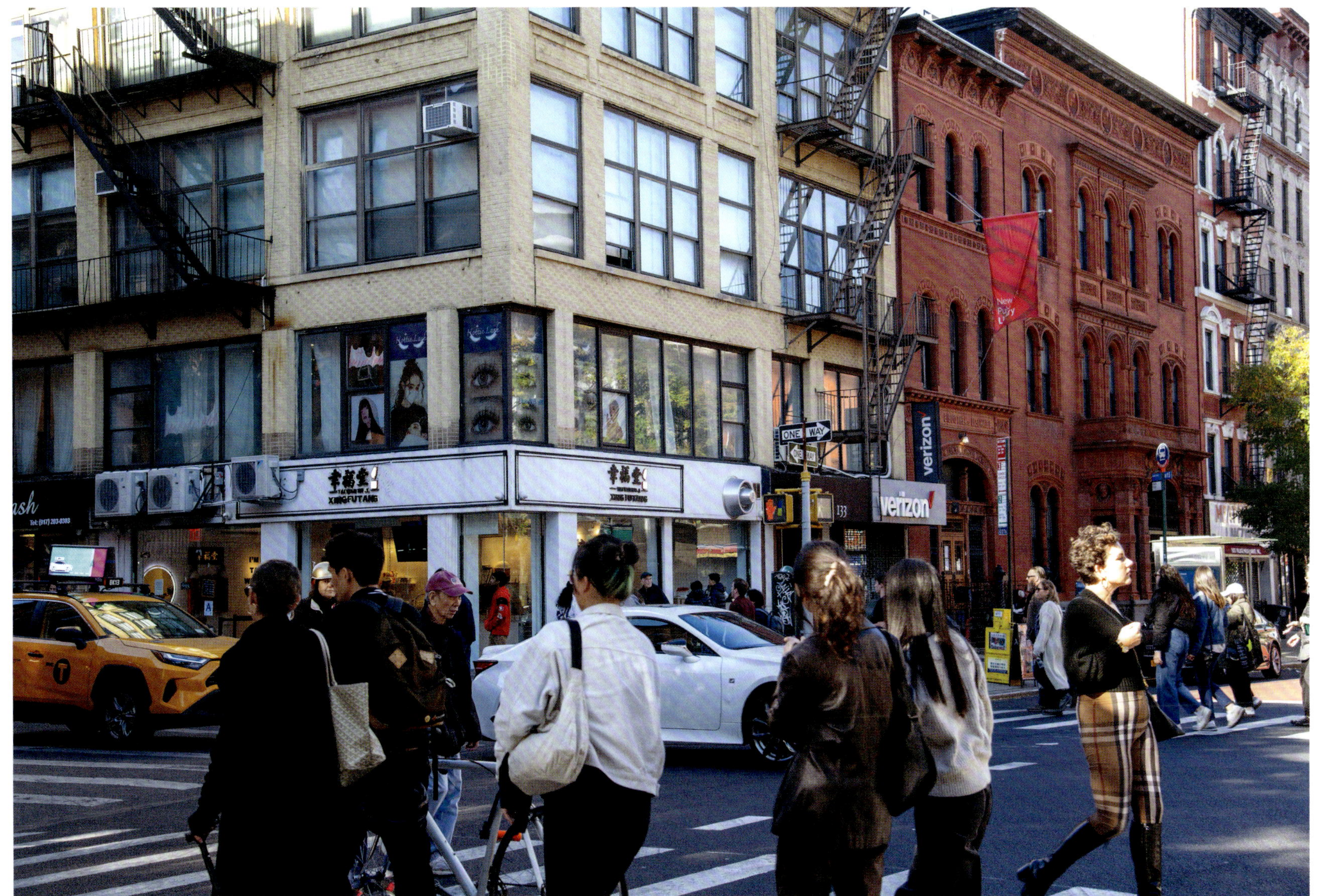

Xing Futang, Verizon, and the Ottendorfer Library, which was the city's first free library (and is now a branch of the New York Public Library).

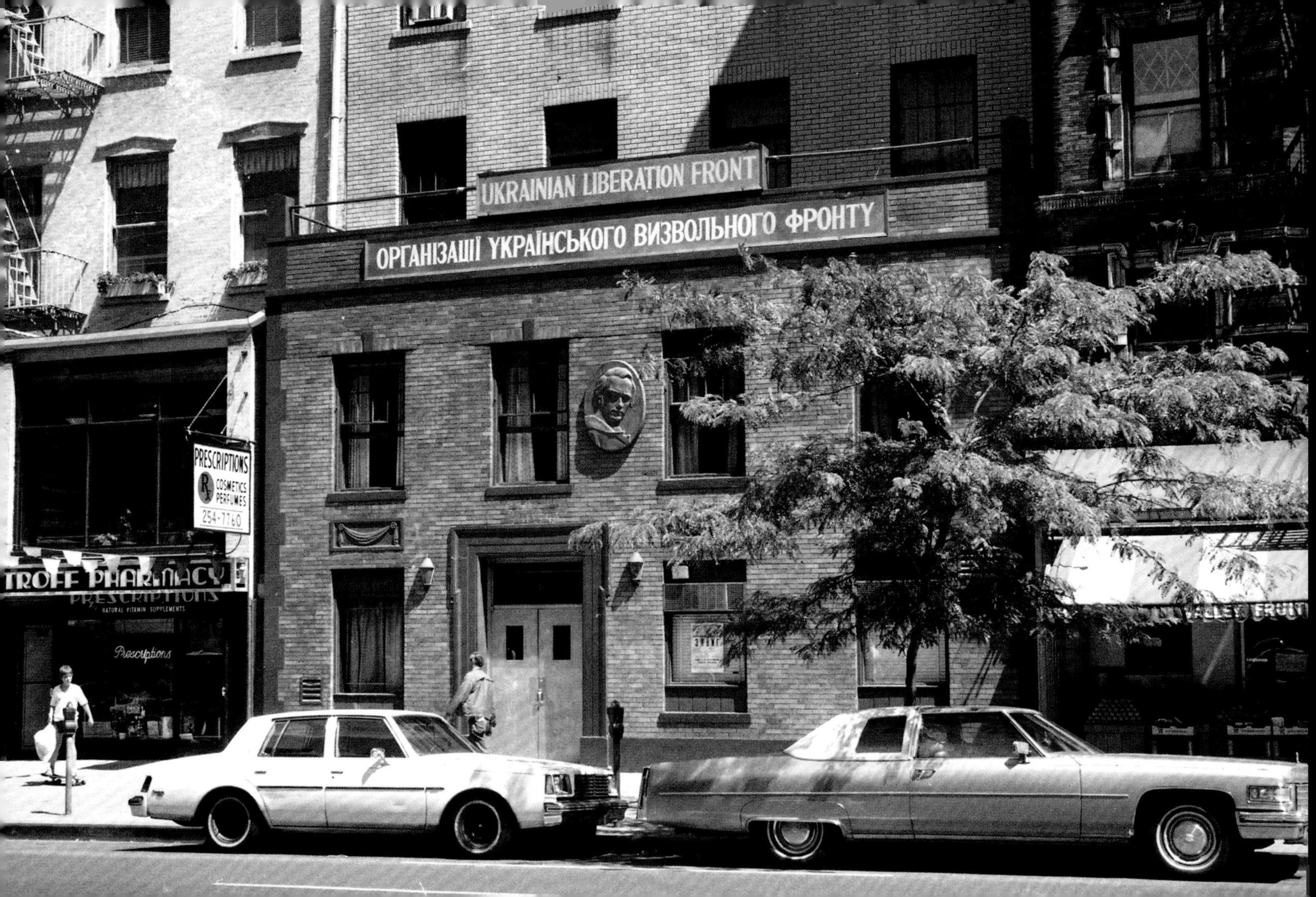

UKRAINIAN LIBERATION FRONT
ОРГАНІЗАЦІЇ УКРАЇНСЬКОГО ВИЗВОЛЬНОГО ФРОНТУ
PRESCRIPTIONS
R
COSMETICS
PERFUMES
254-7760
TROFF PHARMACY
PRESCRIPTIONS
NATURAL VITAMIN SUPPLEMENTS
Prescriptions
VALLEY FRUIT

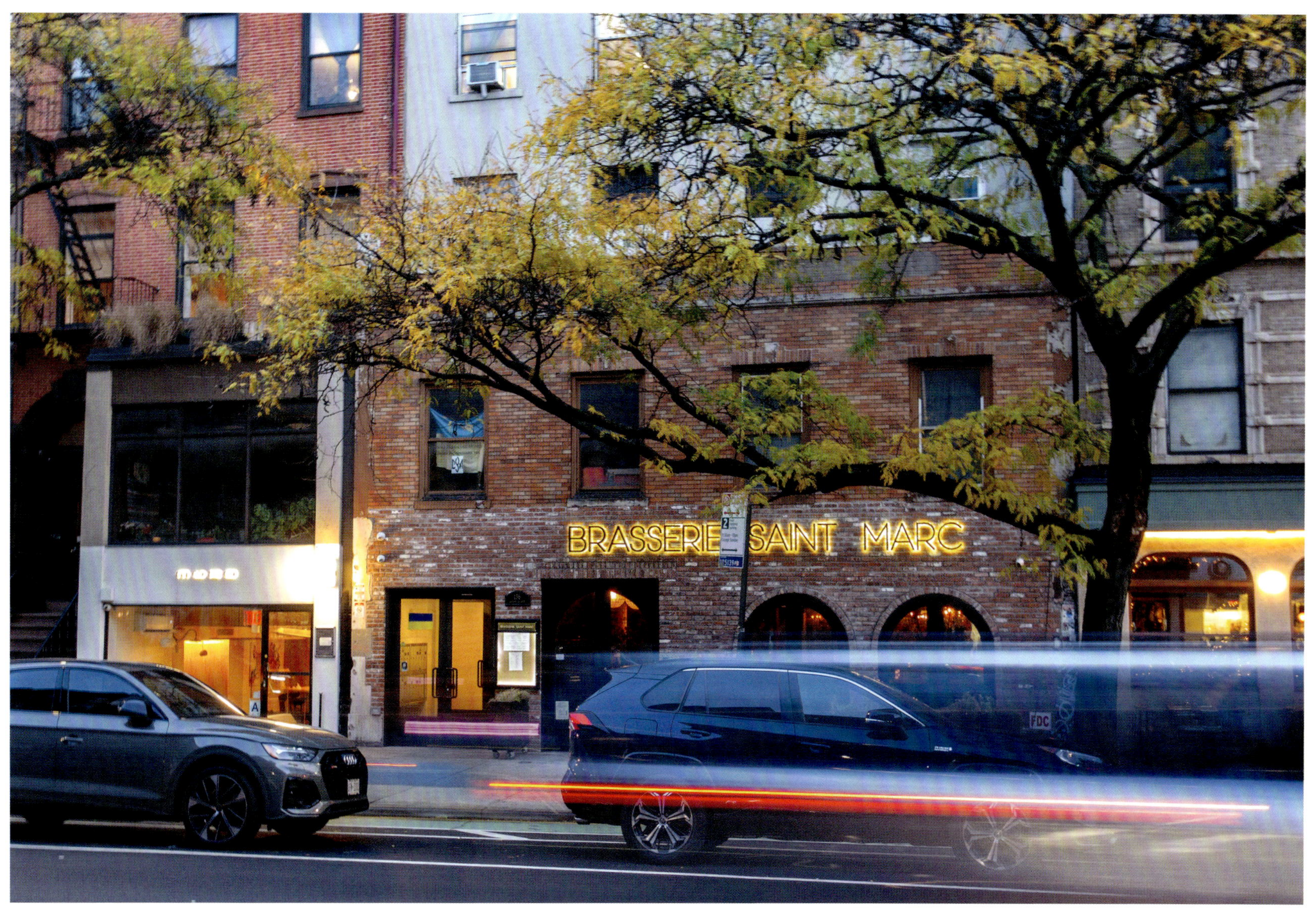

Brasserie Saint Marc, renamed "SAINT"
before this book went to press.

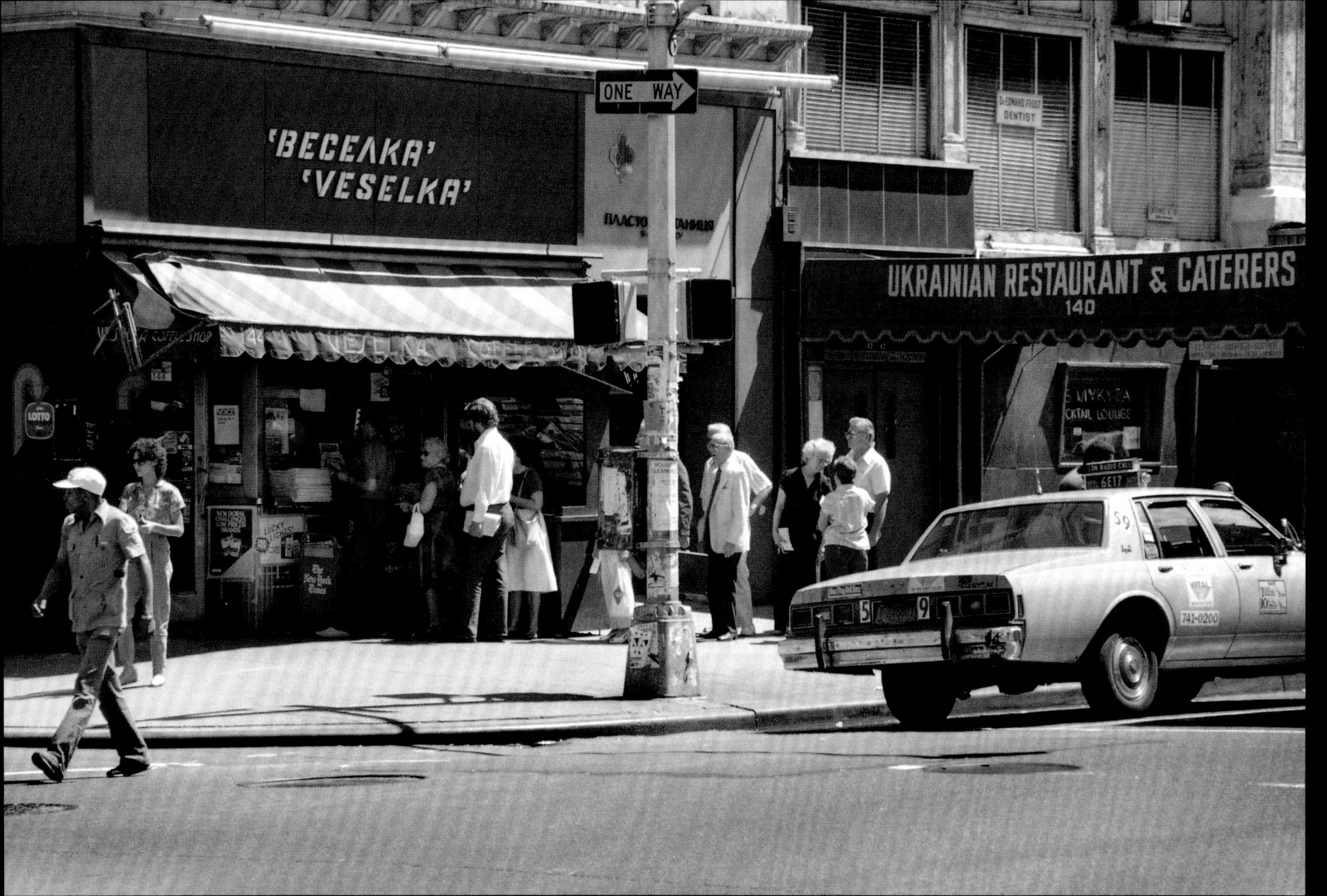

144 SECOND AVENUE

Veselka, since 1954. On the right, Ukrainian
Restaurant and Caterers (aka Ukrainian East Village
Restaurant), located in the Ukrainian National Home.
The immediate neighborhood has gone from German
(Kleindeutschland / Little Germany), to Jewish, to
Ukrainian. Veselka, along with a couple of others,
holding the Ukrainian torch. There were lines in the
early eighties, but they were mainly for lottery tickets.

Still has the lines, but now they're for the food. Especially weekends. They used to be open twenty-four hours, and I would take our daughter there at 5 a.m. After her mother fed her, Hannah and I would sit in a booth (front room, before they expanded), me having coffee, us looking out on the wintry street, while Rina got a little sleep. An extremely happy time of my life.

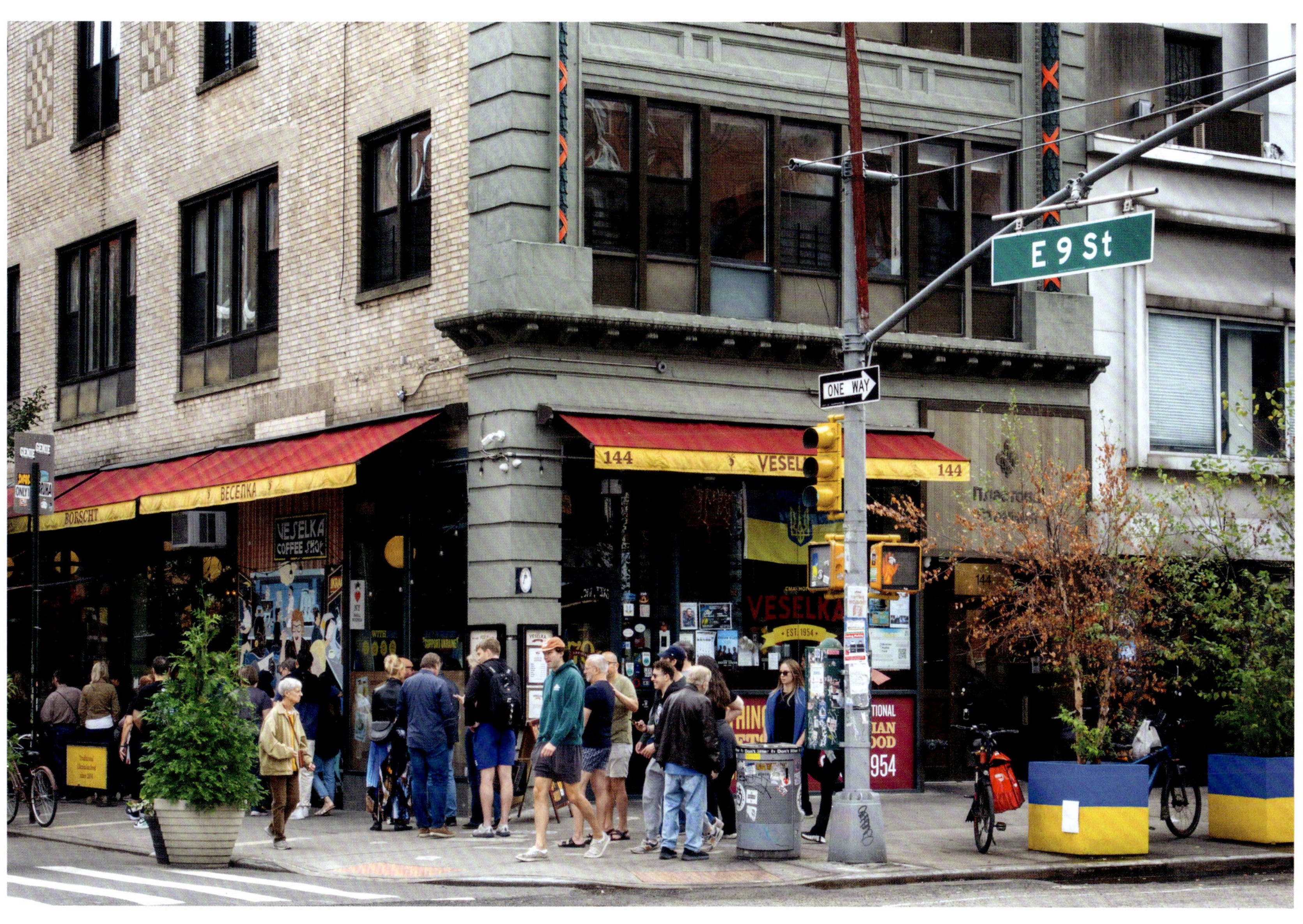

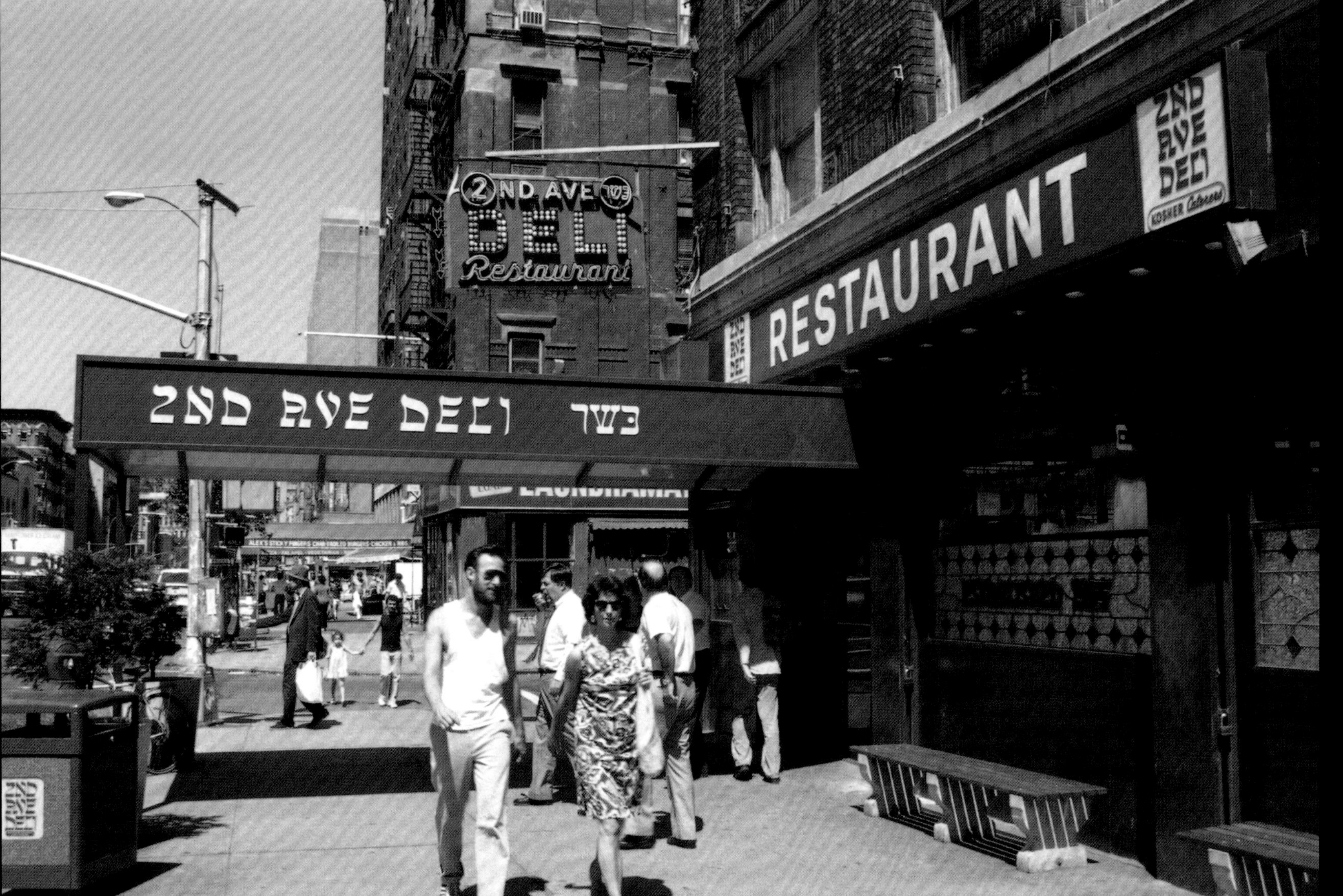

156 SECOND AVENUE

The 2nd Ave Deli opened in 1954 (the same year as Veselka one block south) in the old Yiddish Theatre District. The Yiddish Walk of Fame stars, honoring the old Yiddish performers, were installed shortly after this photograph was taken in 1984.

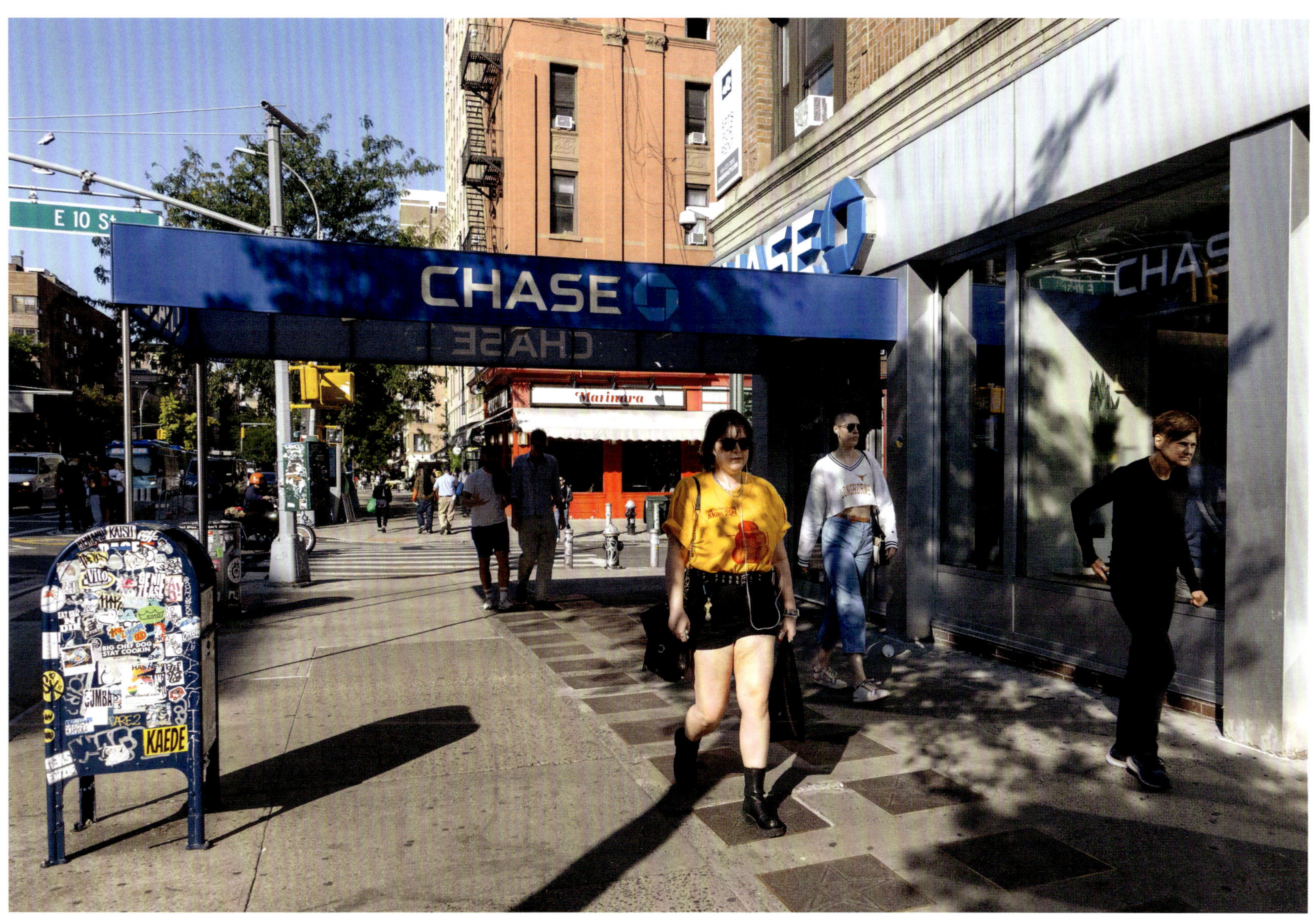

The deli has moved, but the Yiddish Walk of
Fame remains.

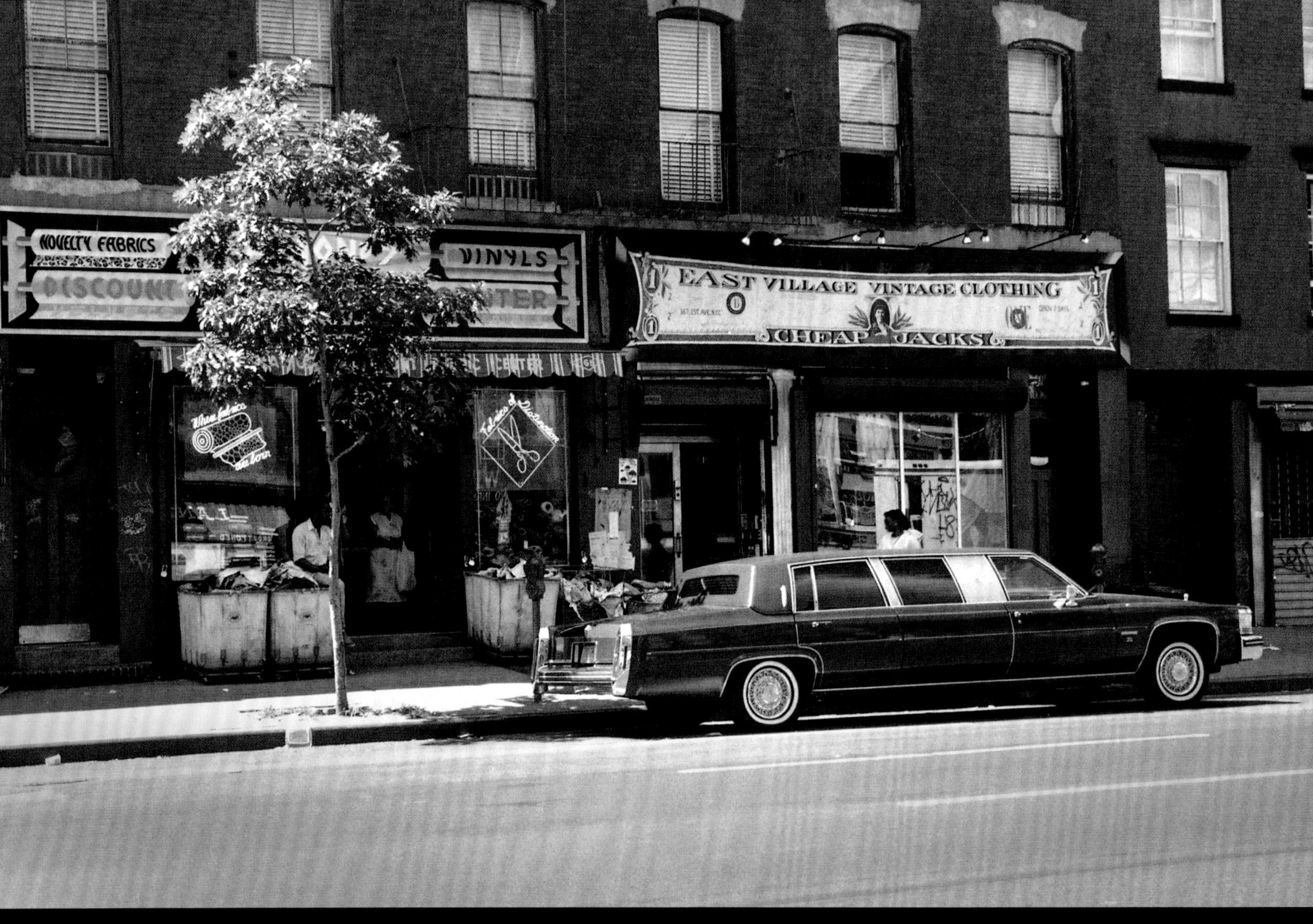

165 AND 167 FIRST AVENUE

Wealthy trendsetters buying vintage.

The remains of Commodities, a relatively early
neighborhood organic grocery, and a minivan. Plus a
touch of color provided by the MTA (a passing bus).

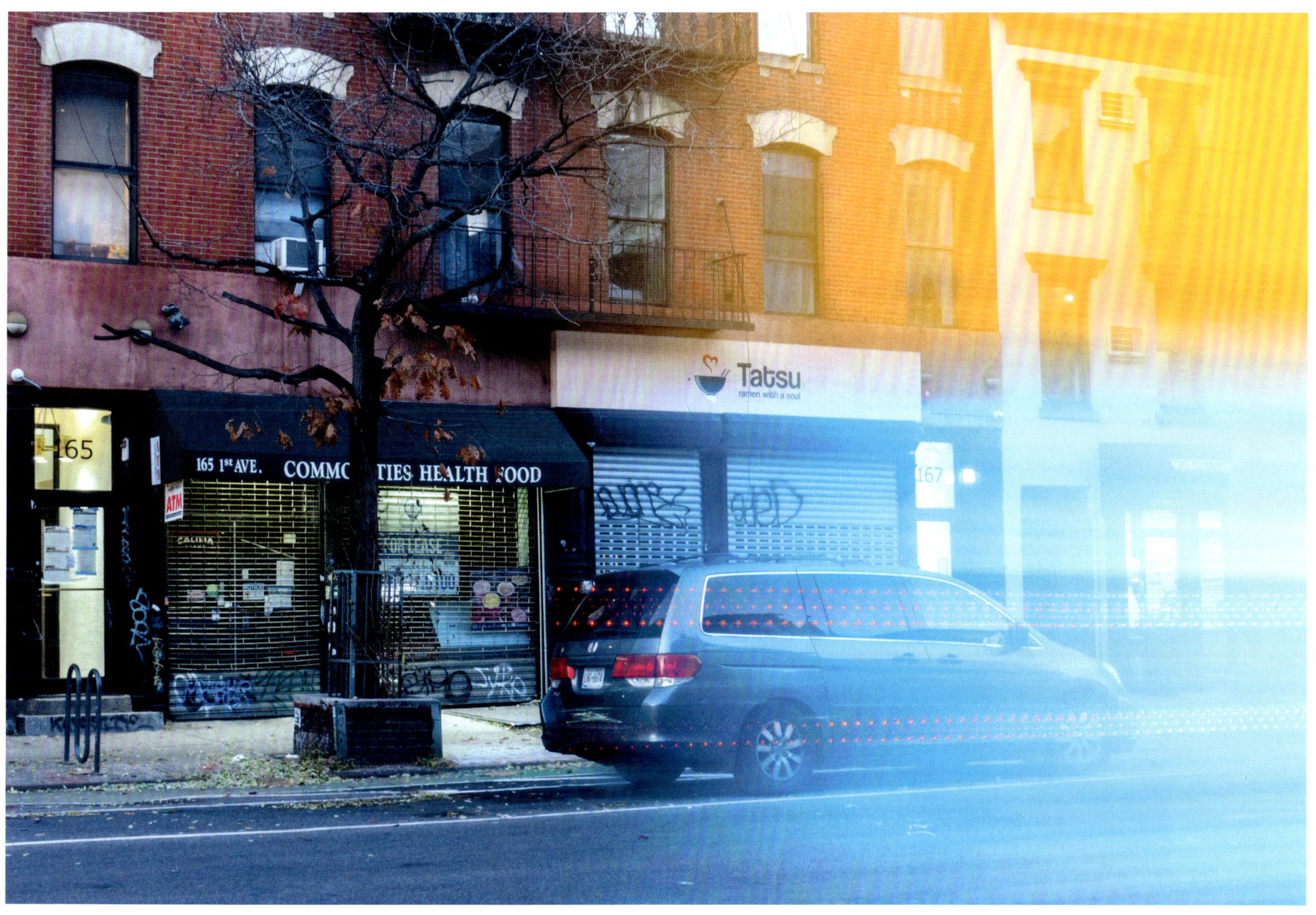

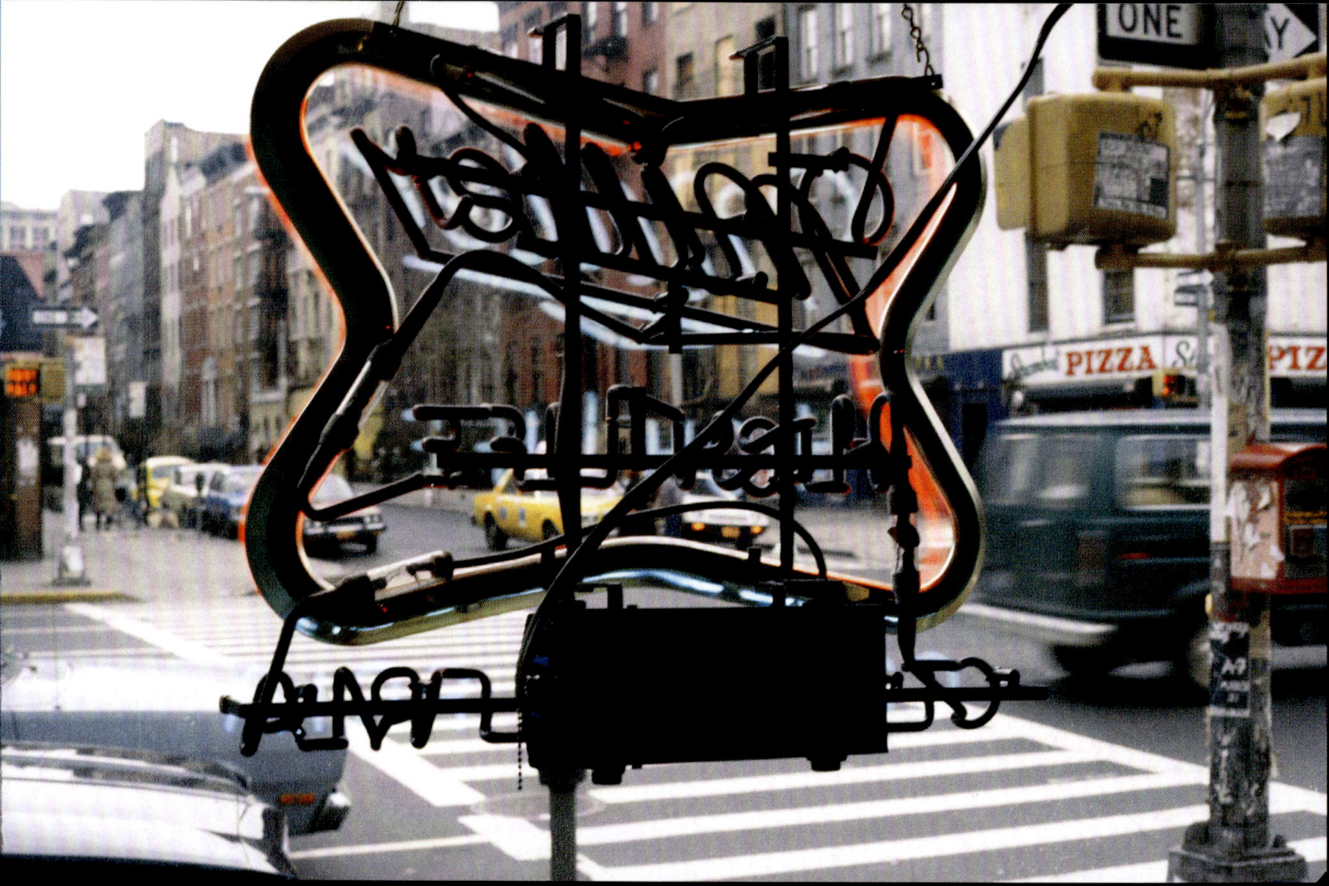

132 FIRST AVENUE

The Miller sign in St. Mark's Bar and Grill, looking toward Stromboli Pizza kitty-corner across First Avenue. Also, the interior and a couple of patrons. The Rolling Stones did the "Waiting on a Friend" video here. Exterior shots in the video include a building a couple of doors east that was on the cover of Led Zeppelin's *Physical Graffiti*.

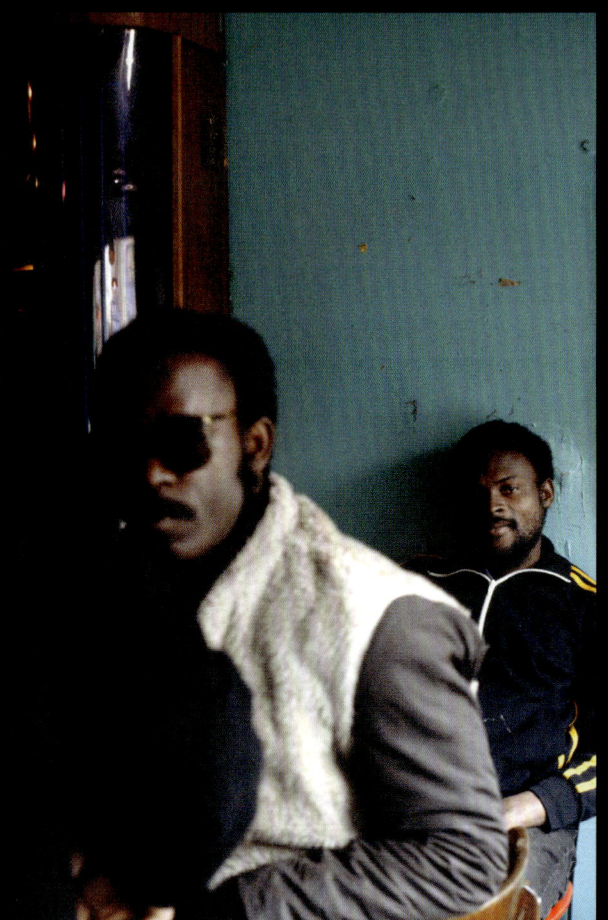

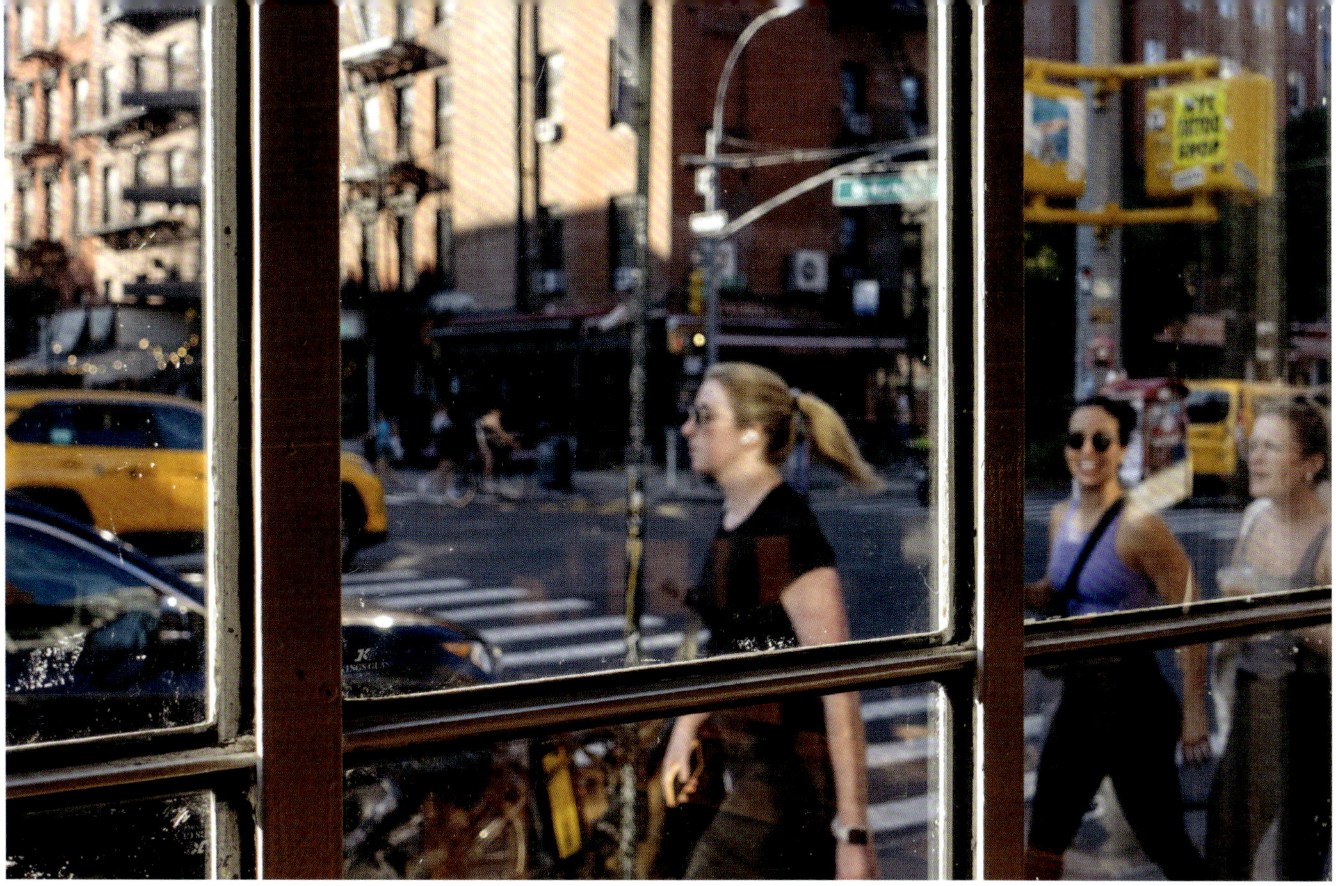

The same view, now from the Lion Bar and Grill, still looking toward Stromboli. People still take photographs of the *Physical Graffiti* buildings and re-create the "Waiting on a Friend" scene.

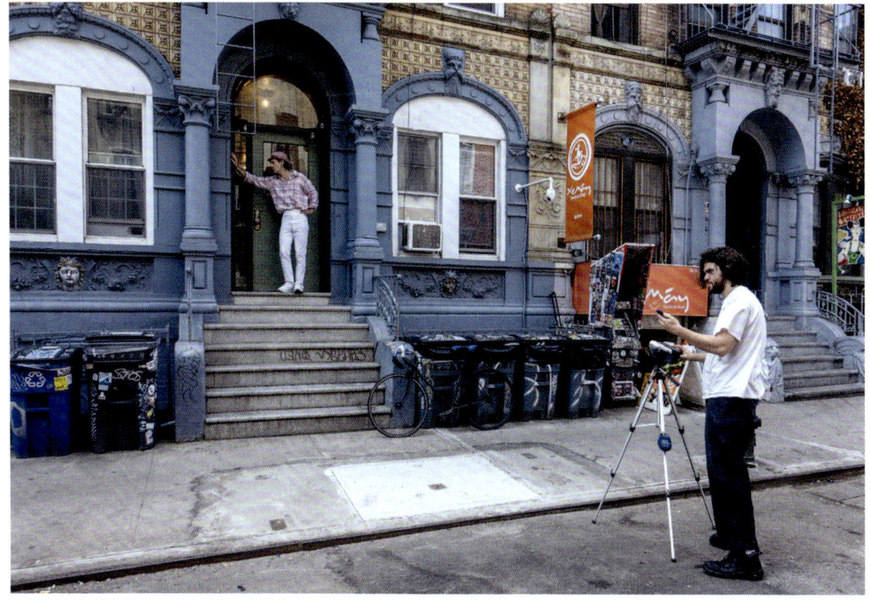

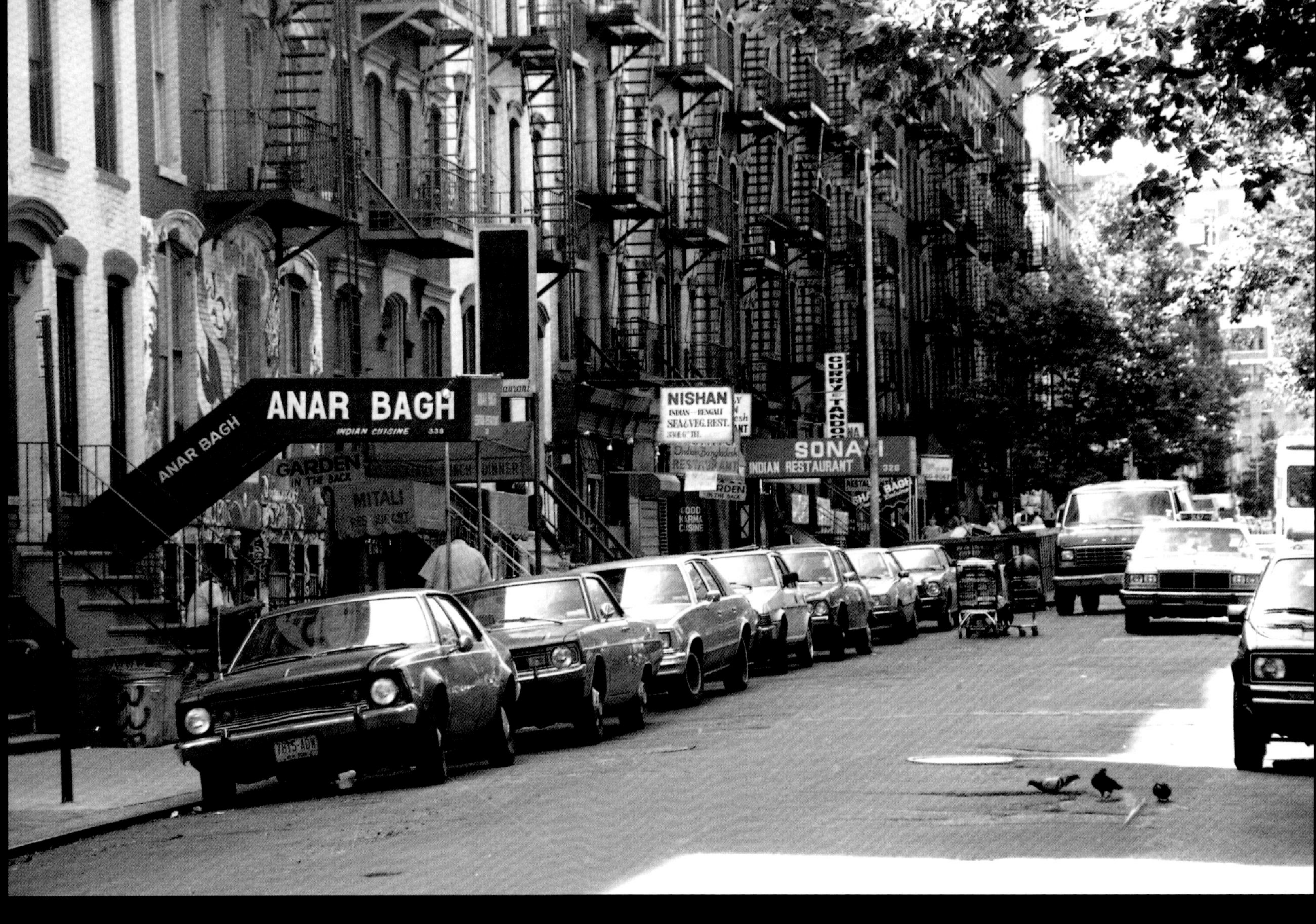

EAST 6TH STREET BETWEEN
FIRST AND SECOND AVENUE

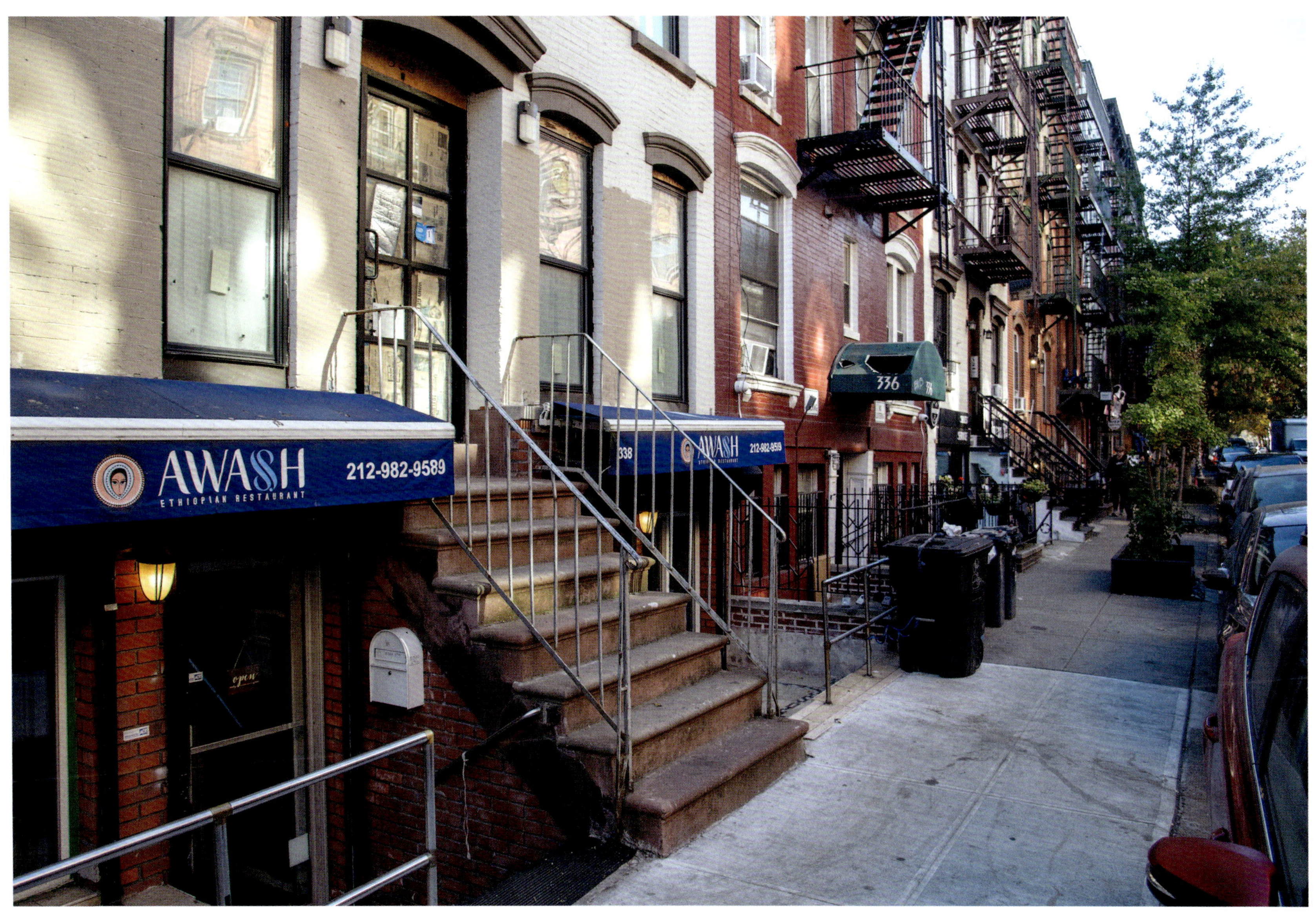

Still a bunch of restaurants but now a variety
in terms of ethnicity, price, and diet.

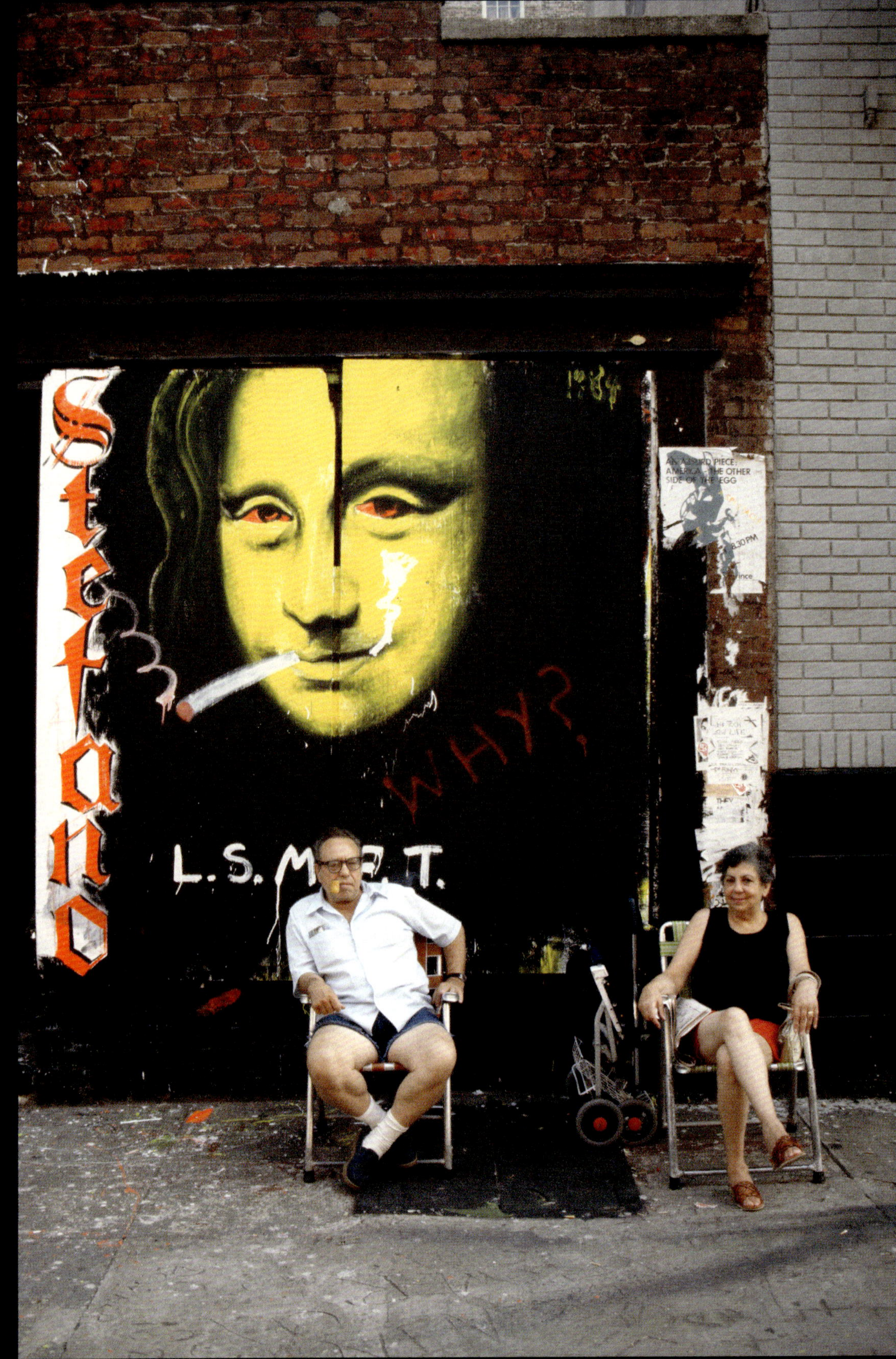

254 EAST 10TH STREET

Smoking Mona Lisa, "Stefano," a neighborhood couple (Jerome Golding, landlord) out for an afternoon smoke in front of Fun Gallery. Fun was one of the first East Village galleries, which would grow to 176 in number over the next decade, according to *Artforum*. Fun Gallery showed Fab 5 Freddy, Keith Haring, Jean-Michel Basquiat, and Kenny Scharf, among many others.

The ritual of a move and
getting rid of books.

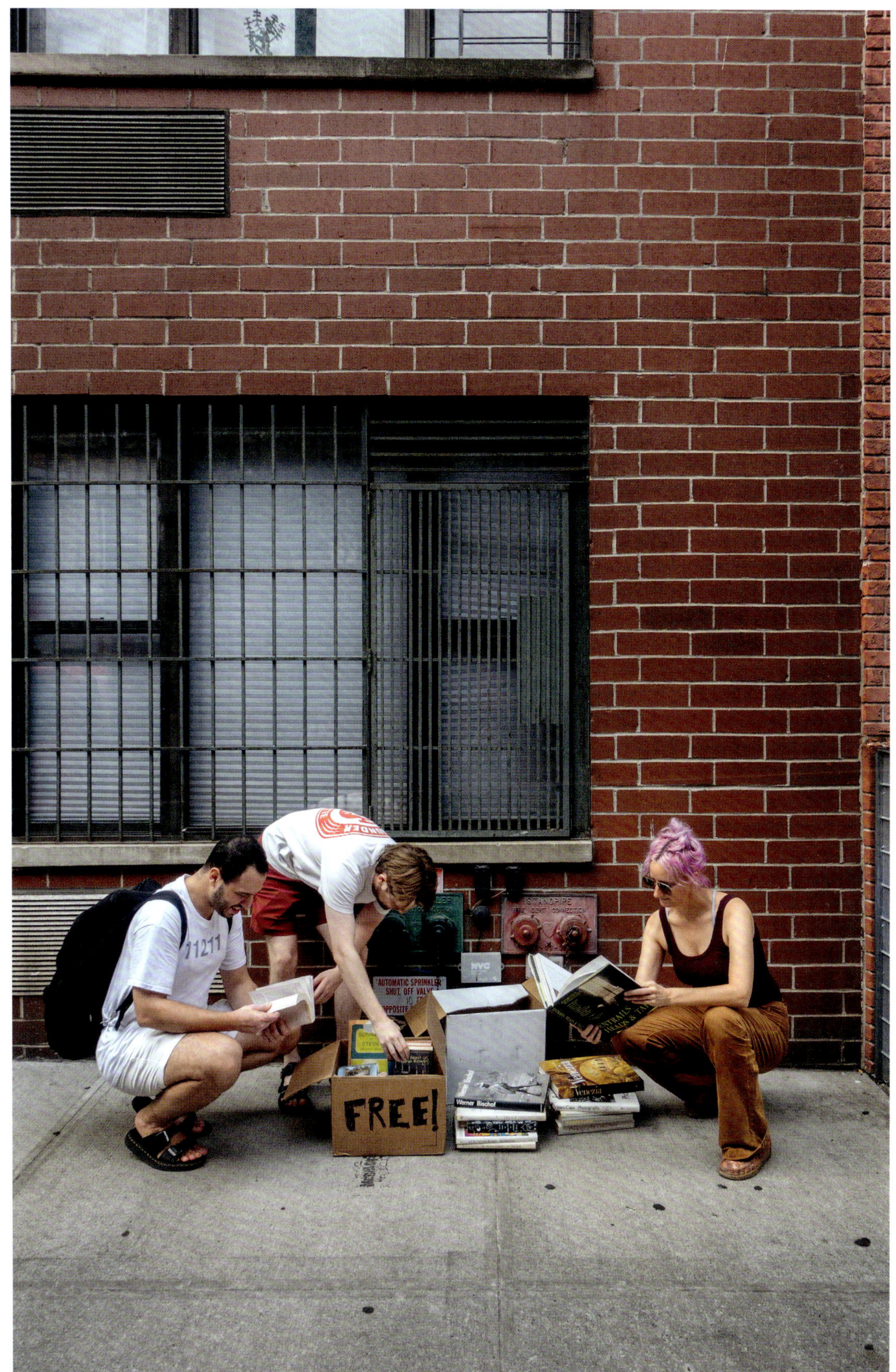

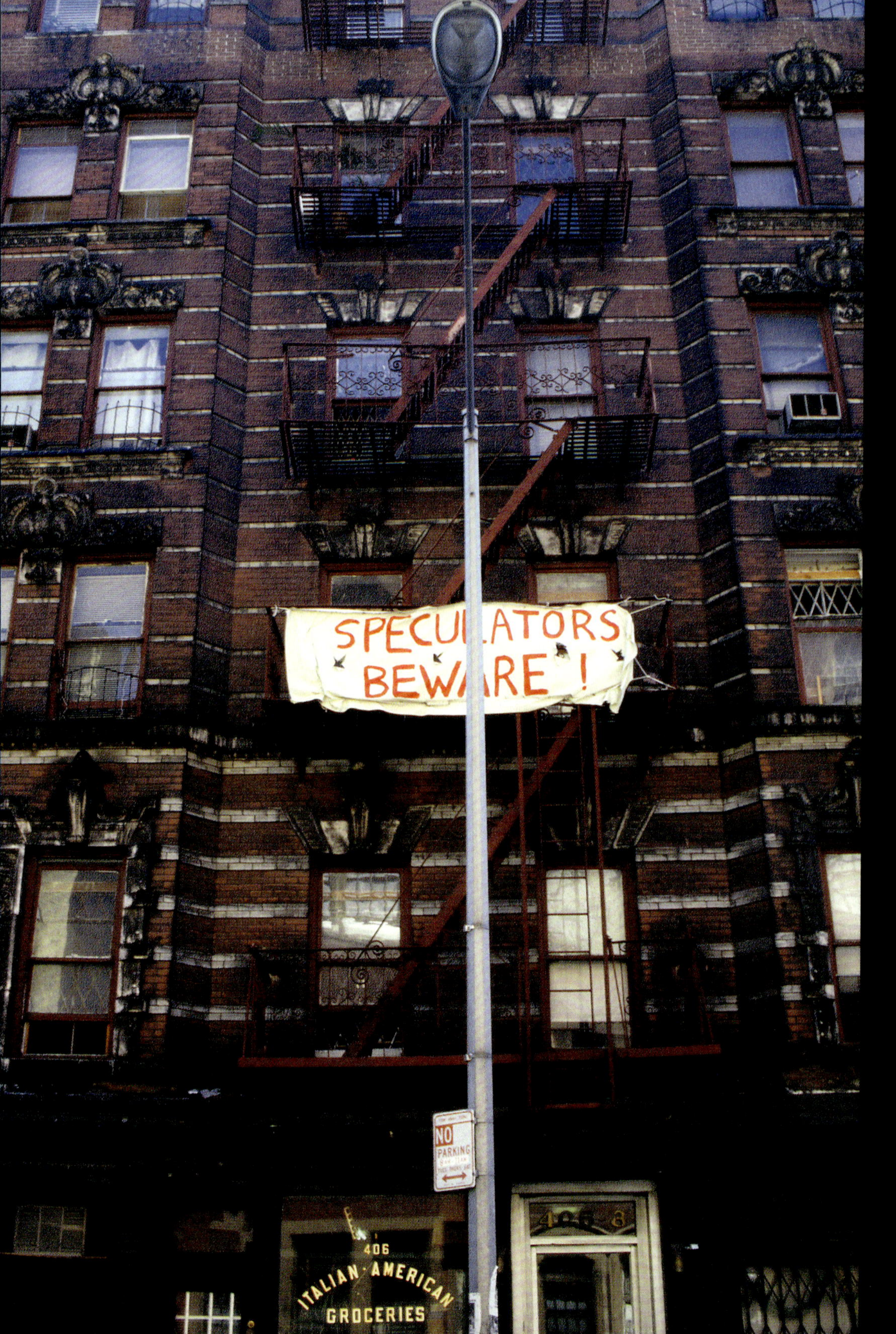

406 EAST 9TH STREET

As the neighborhood changed, the money poured in. Speculators were indeed everywhere and ready to pounce.

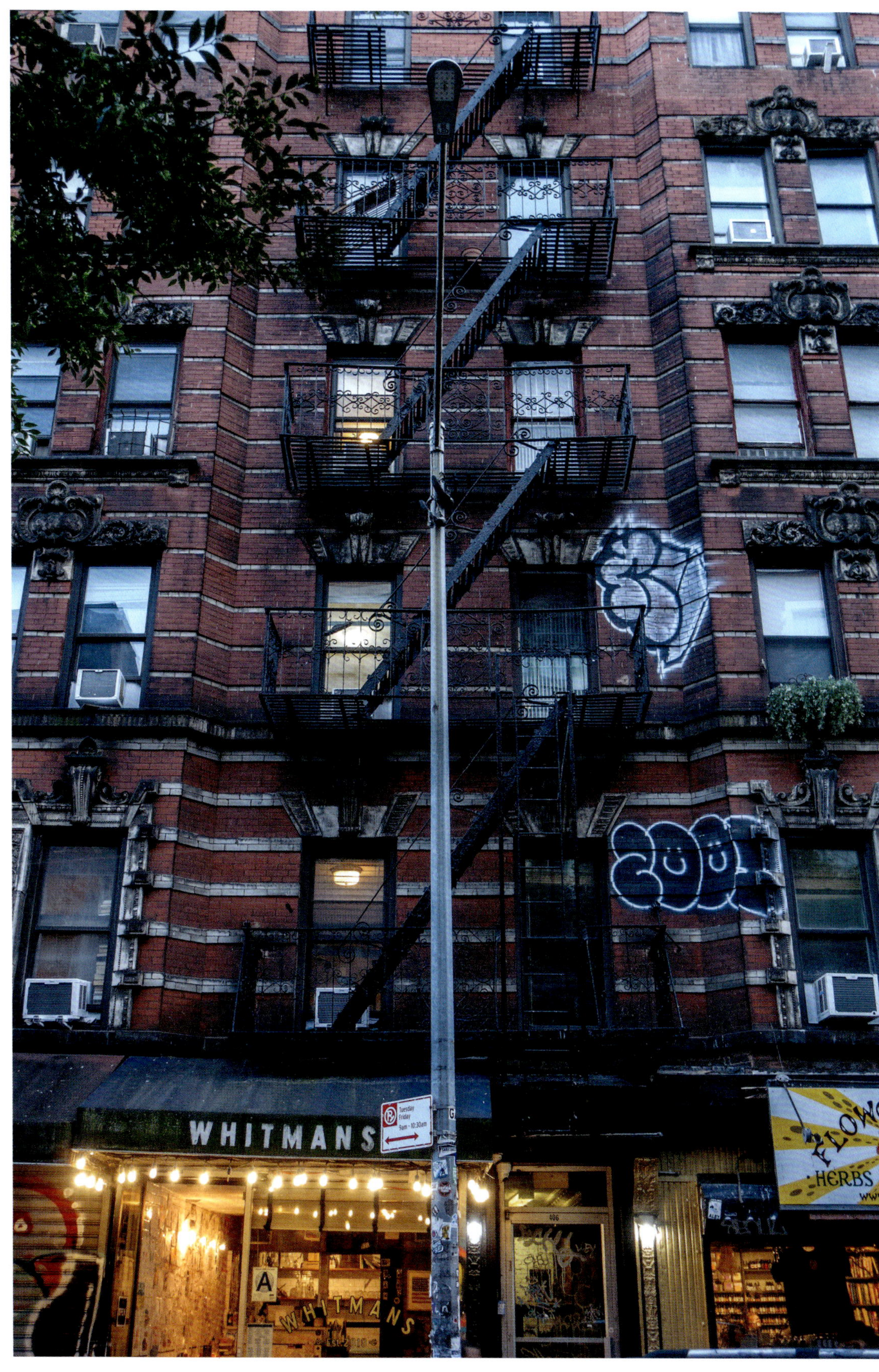

The sign came down
(and Whitman's is in).

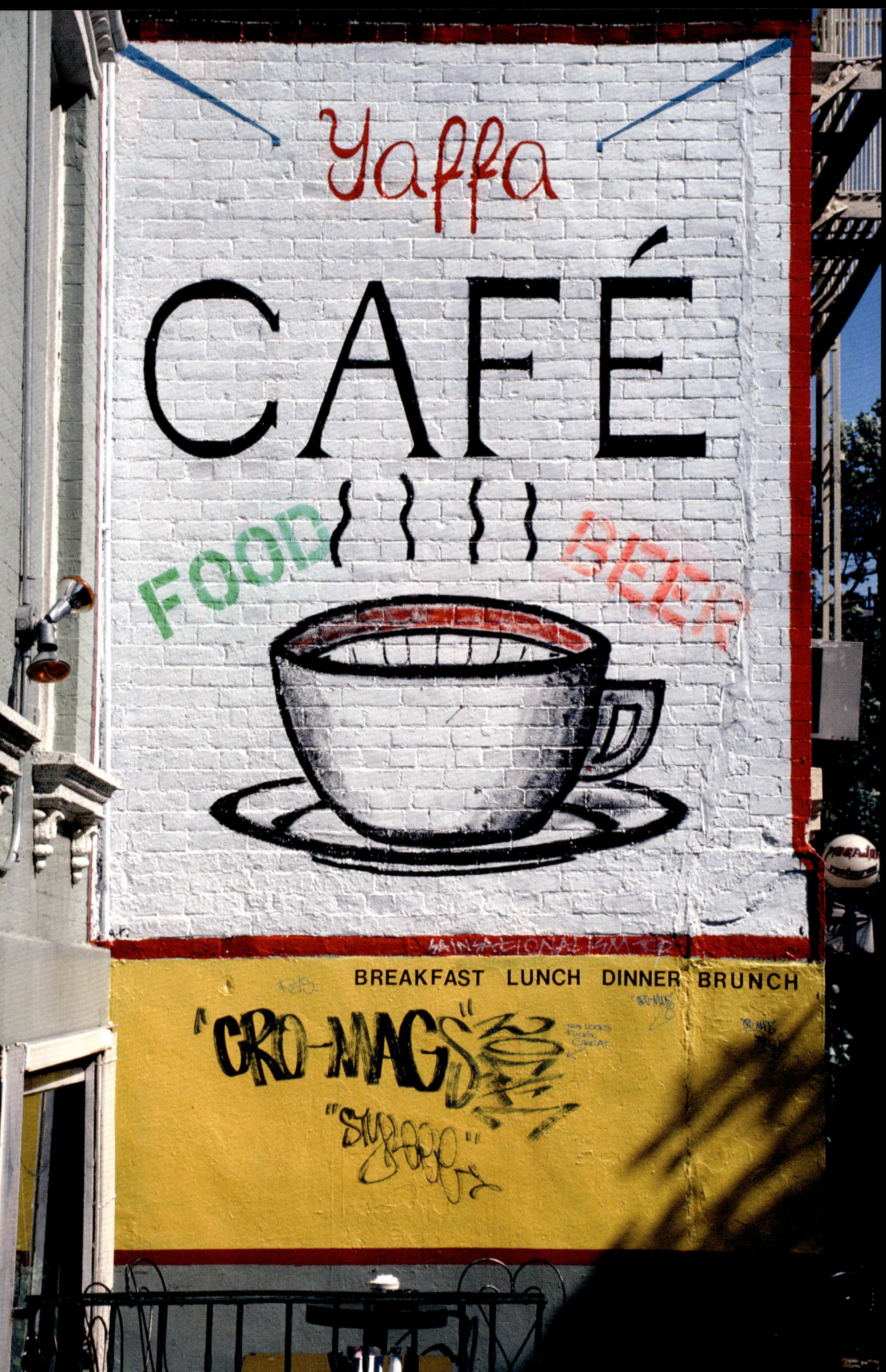

97 ST. MARK'S PLACE

Yaffa Café offered cheap eats, with the mural being a bit of a landmark. The mural meant you were going to the right place, you were going in the right direction, you were almost home.

And the new mural. A nice
successor and a nice new
mural.

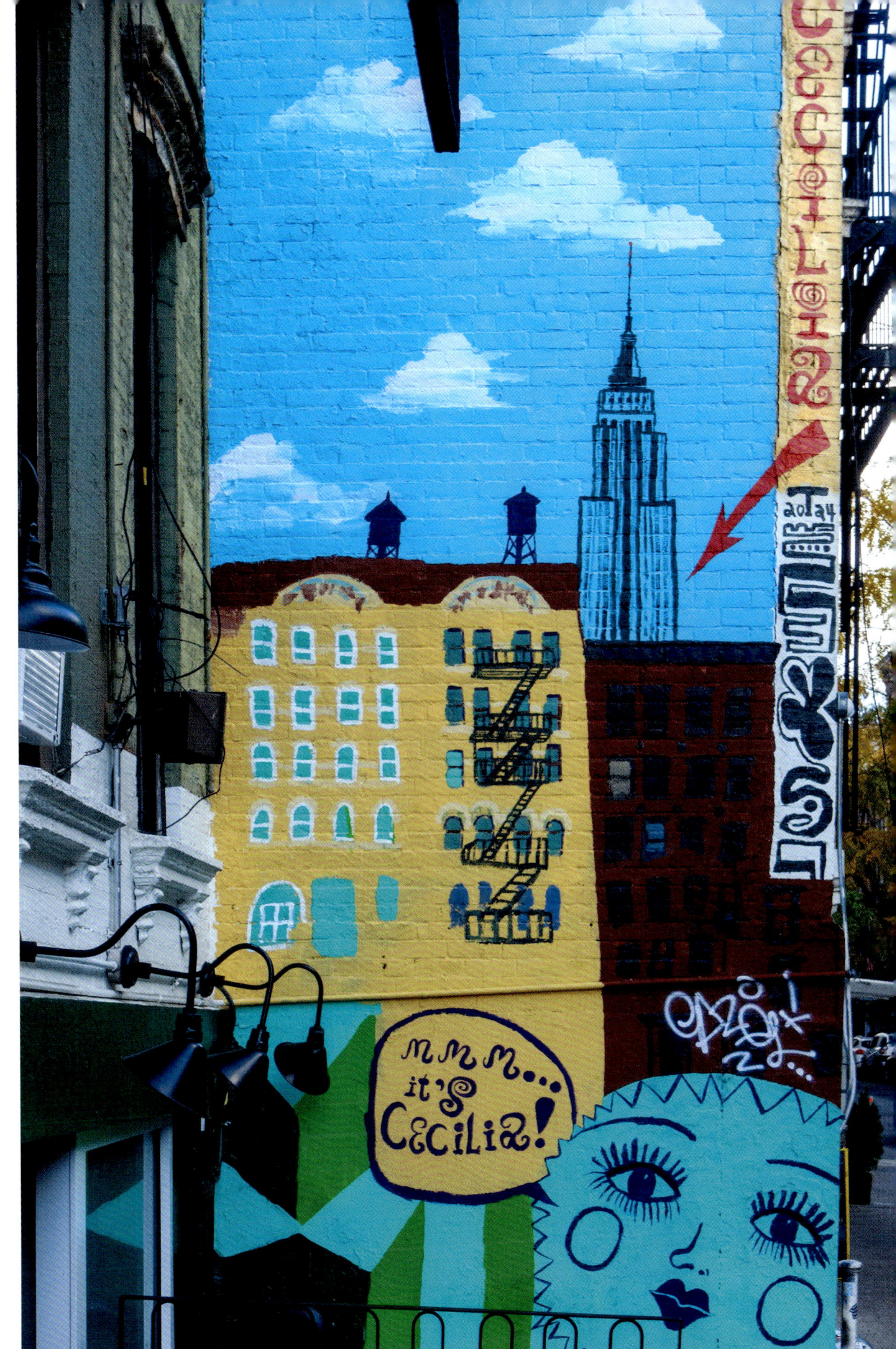

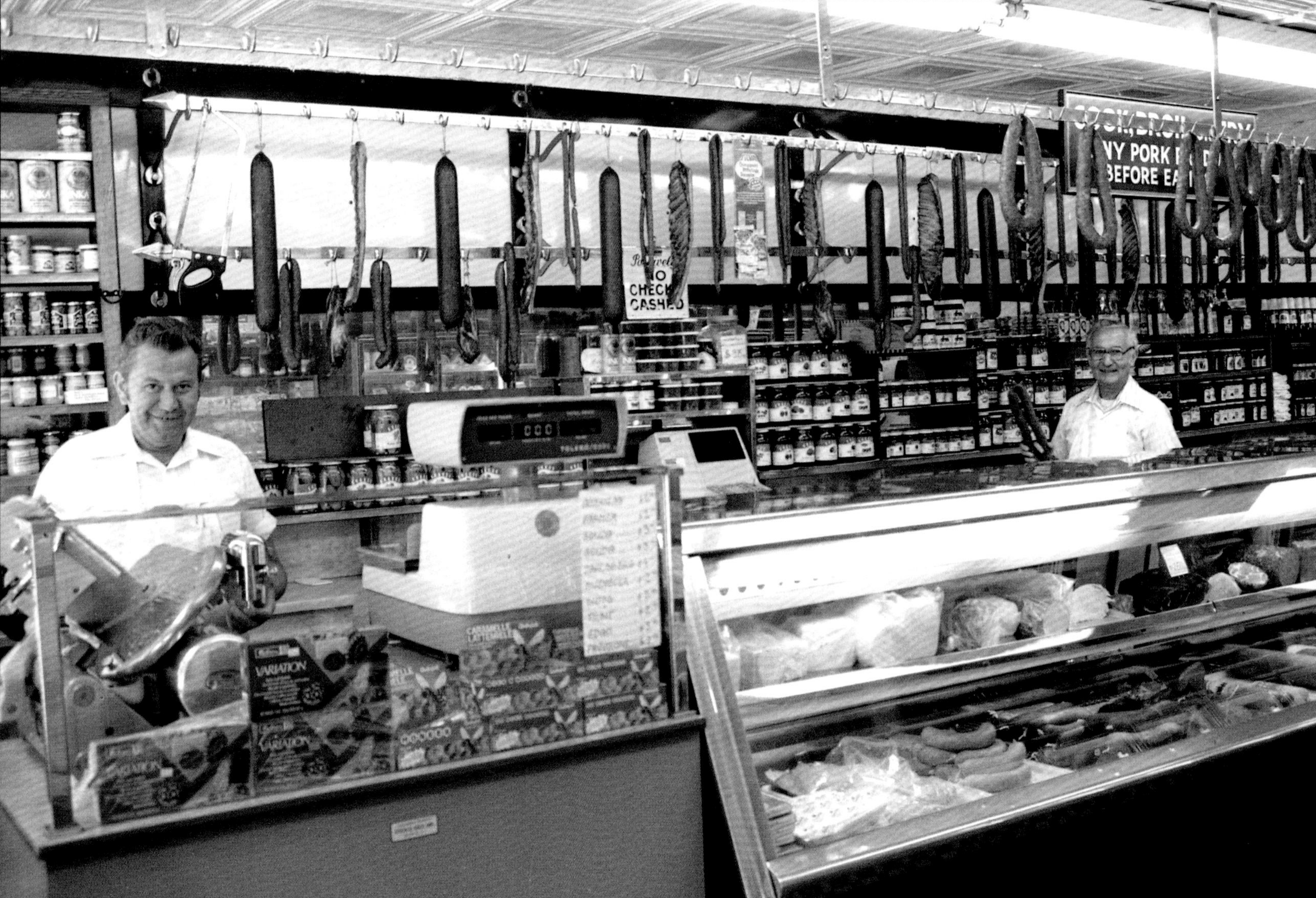

124 FIRST AVENUE

Kurowycky Meat Products: excellent butcher, smoker
in the back of the store, and great hot dogs.

"Of course they're good! I feed them to my own
children!!"
　—Jerry (Jaroslaw) Kurowycky

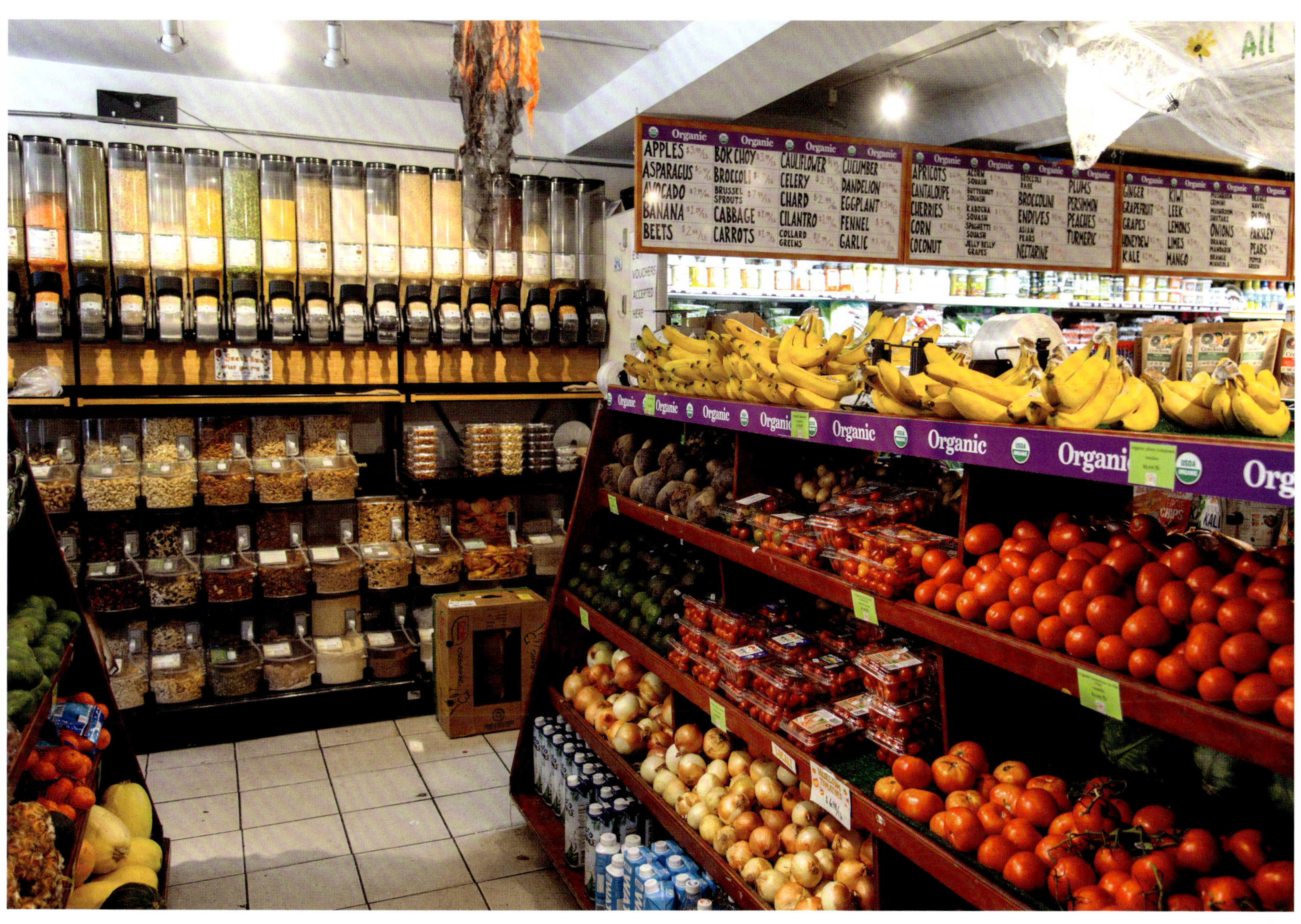

East Village Organic: in line with the
times and a colorful rejoinder.

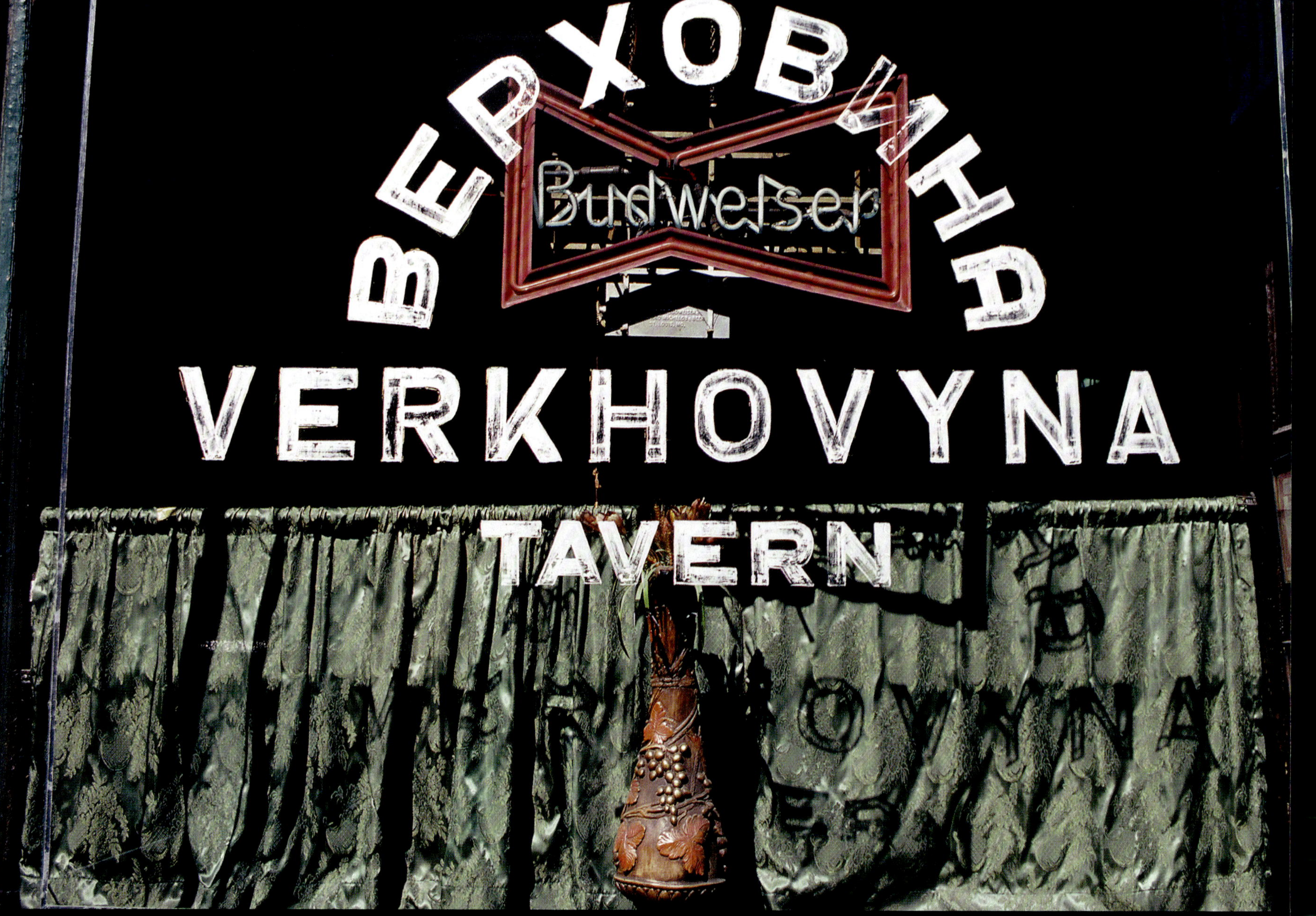

81 EAST 7TH STREET

Verhovyna / George's Bar / Bar 81. One of
several Eastern European bars. Like Bar 82 /
The Blue and Gold next door.

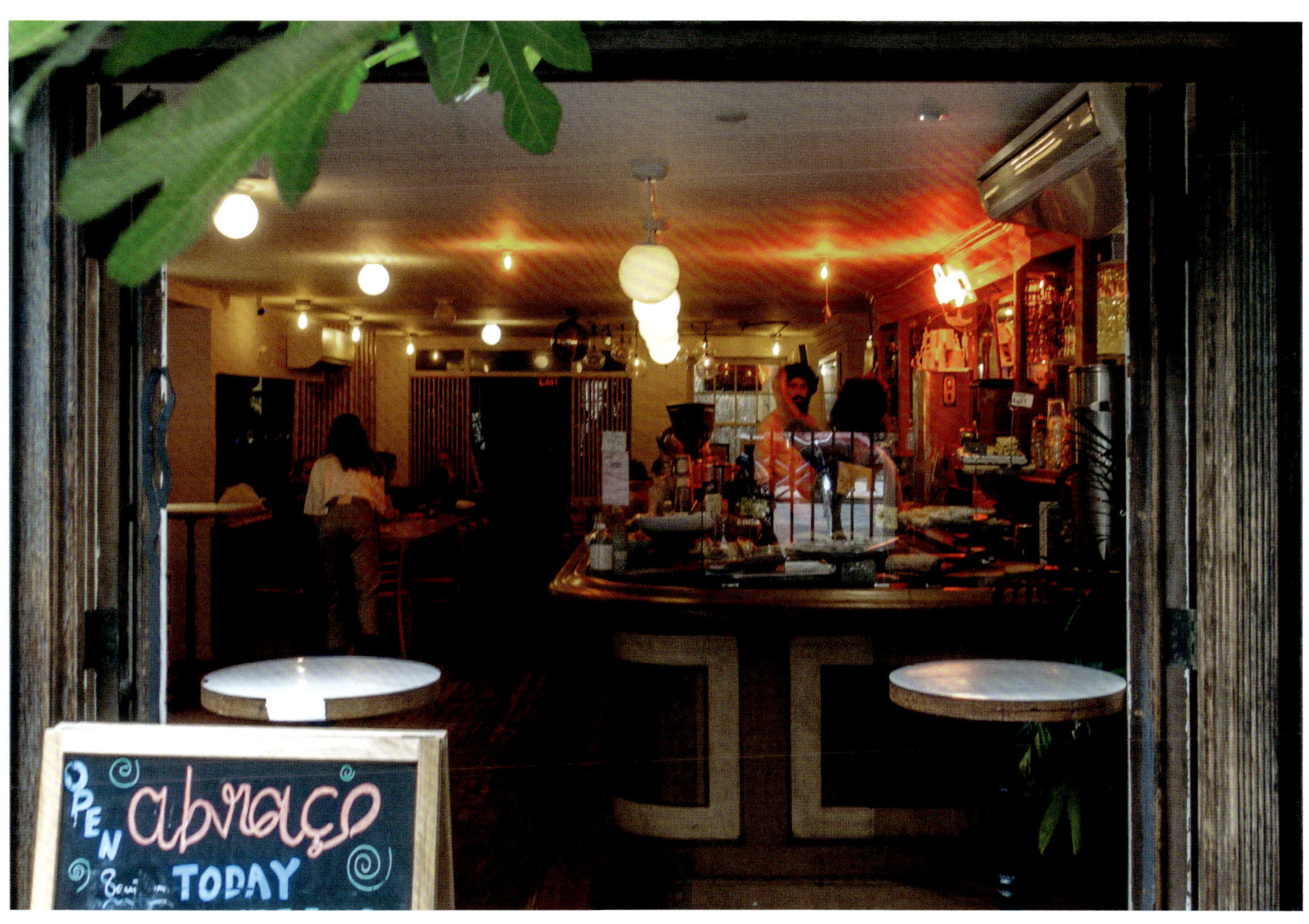

Abraço. A neighborhood coffee spot, with a
little fresh air.

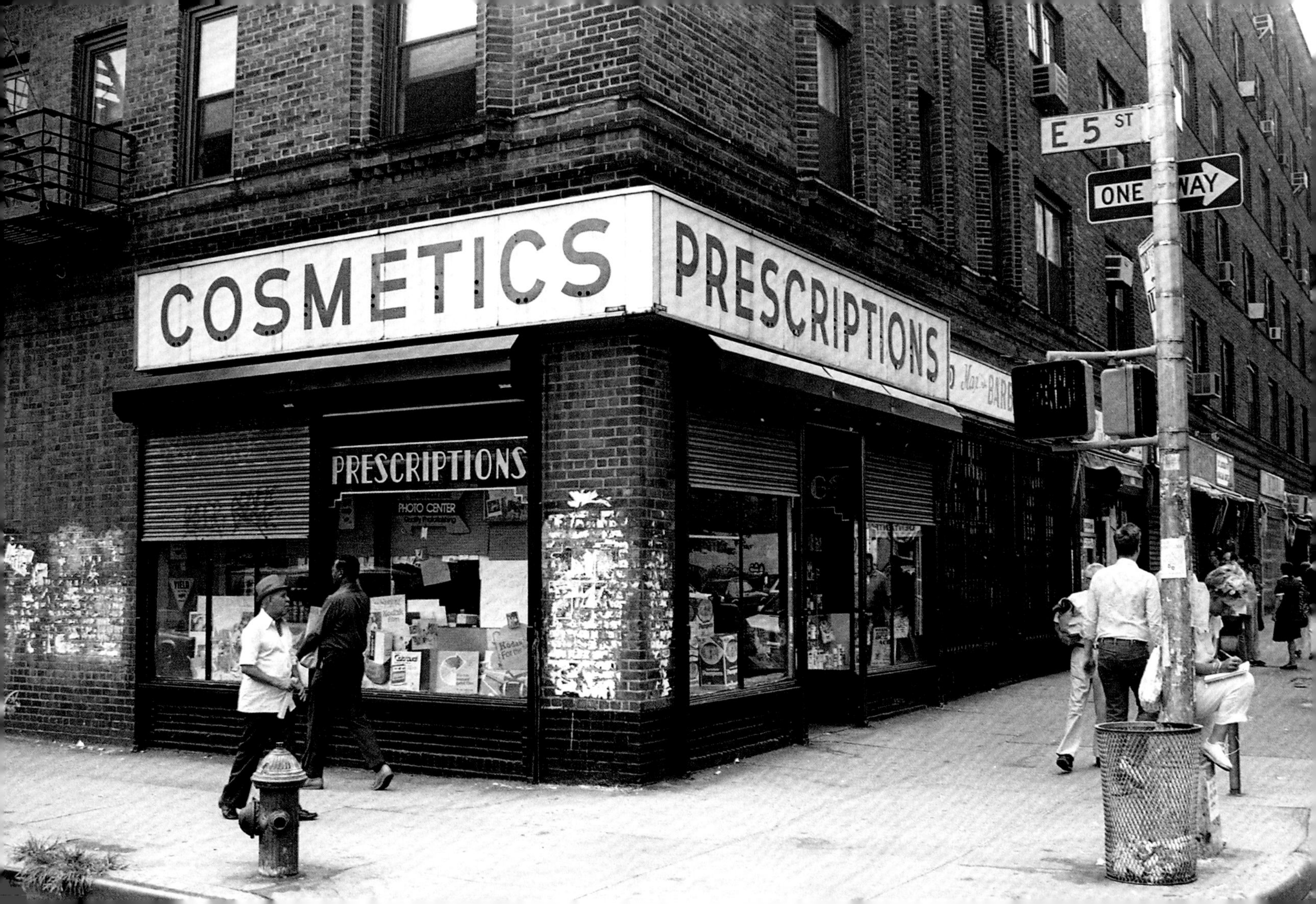

COSMETICS
PRESCRIPTIONS
E 5 ST
ONE WAY
PRESCRIPTIONS
PHOTO CENTER
YIELD

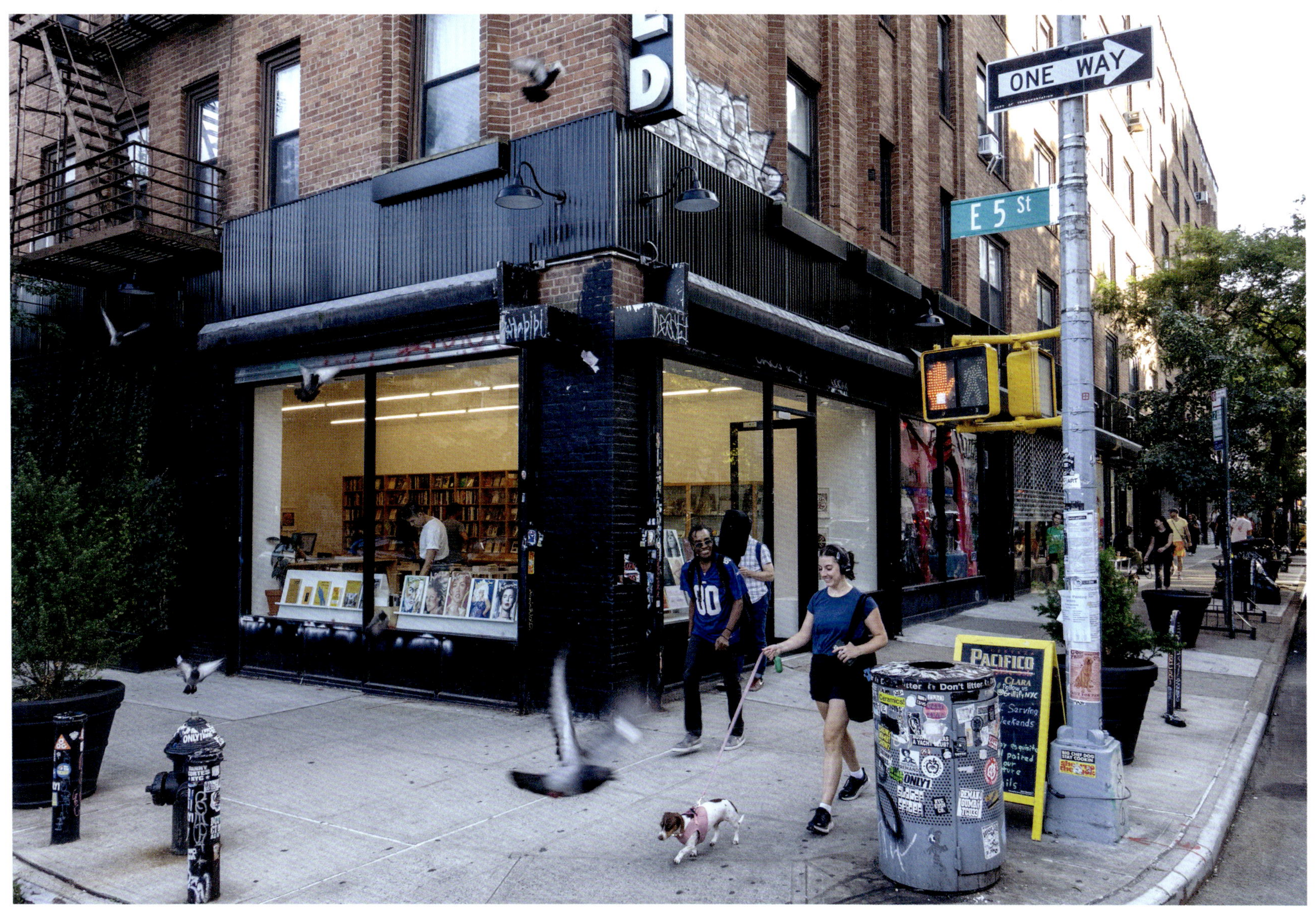

Mast Books, a bookstore with a
great selection of art books.

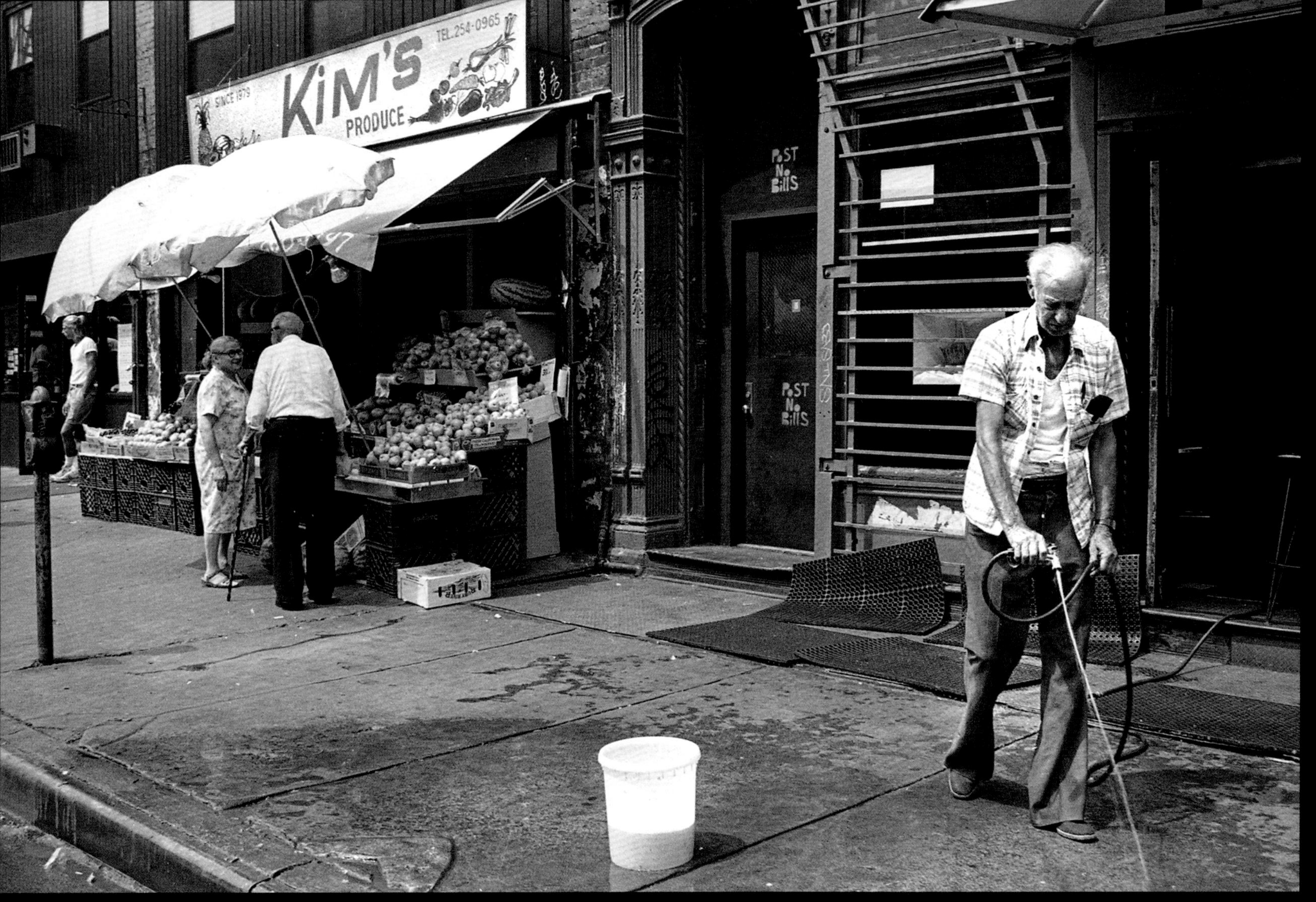

101 AVENUE A

The Pyramid Club, getting a morning hosedown, and Kim's Produce in the background. The Pyramid Club had something for everyone. Gay, Drag, No Wave, Punk, Nirvana, Madonna, Debbie Harry, Red Hot Chili Peppers, Lady Bunny, RuPaul. Plays, performances, comedy; experimental, eclectic, at times outlandish. Kim's Produce changed to Kim's Dry Cleaners when the much larger Syp's Produce moved into the old movie theater / Pioneer grocery store across the street. Kim's Dry Cleaners had a little shelf next to the counter, and they started putting videotapes on the shelf for rent. The videotape rental business did very well, so Kim's Dry Cleaners became Kim's Video and moved down the block to a larger store. Kim's Video eventually had several locations around the neighborhood, including Mondo Kim's, which occupied three floors in the old St. Marks Baths. Kim's huge video and DVD collection eventually moved to Sicily and then came back to the Alamo Drafthouse Cinema.

Club 101 took over Baker Falls, which
took over the Pyramid space. Kim's Dry
Cleaners turned into Best Cleaners on A.

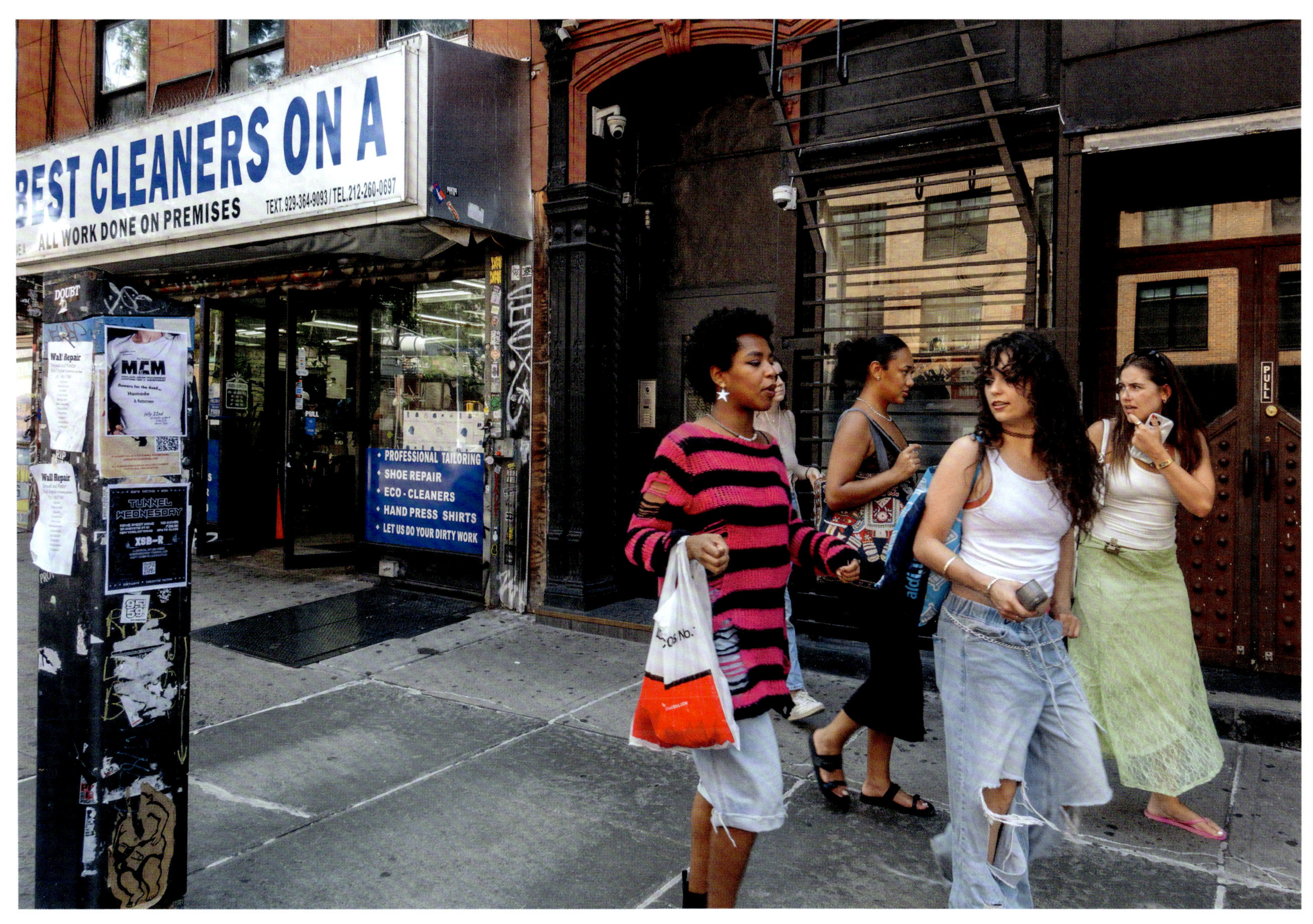

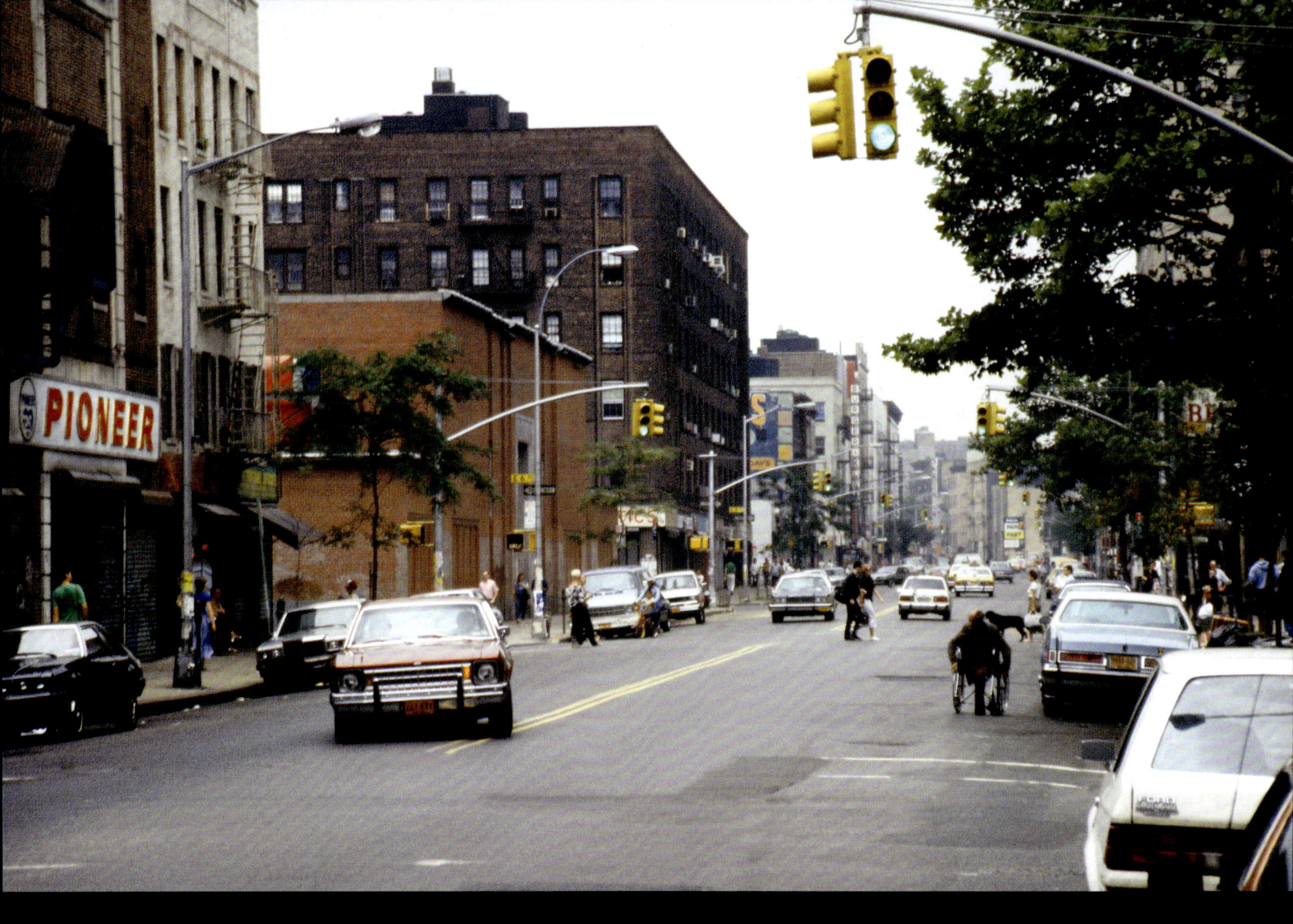

AVENUE A LOOKING SOUTH
BETWEEN 7TH AND 6TH STREET

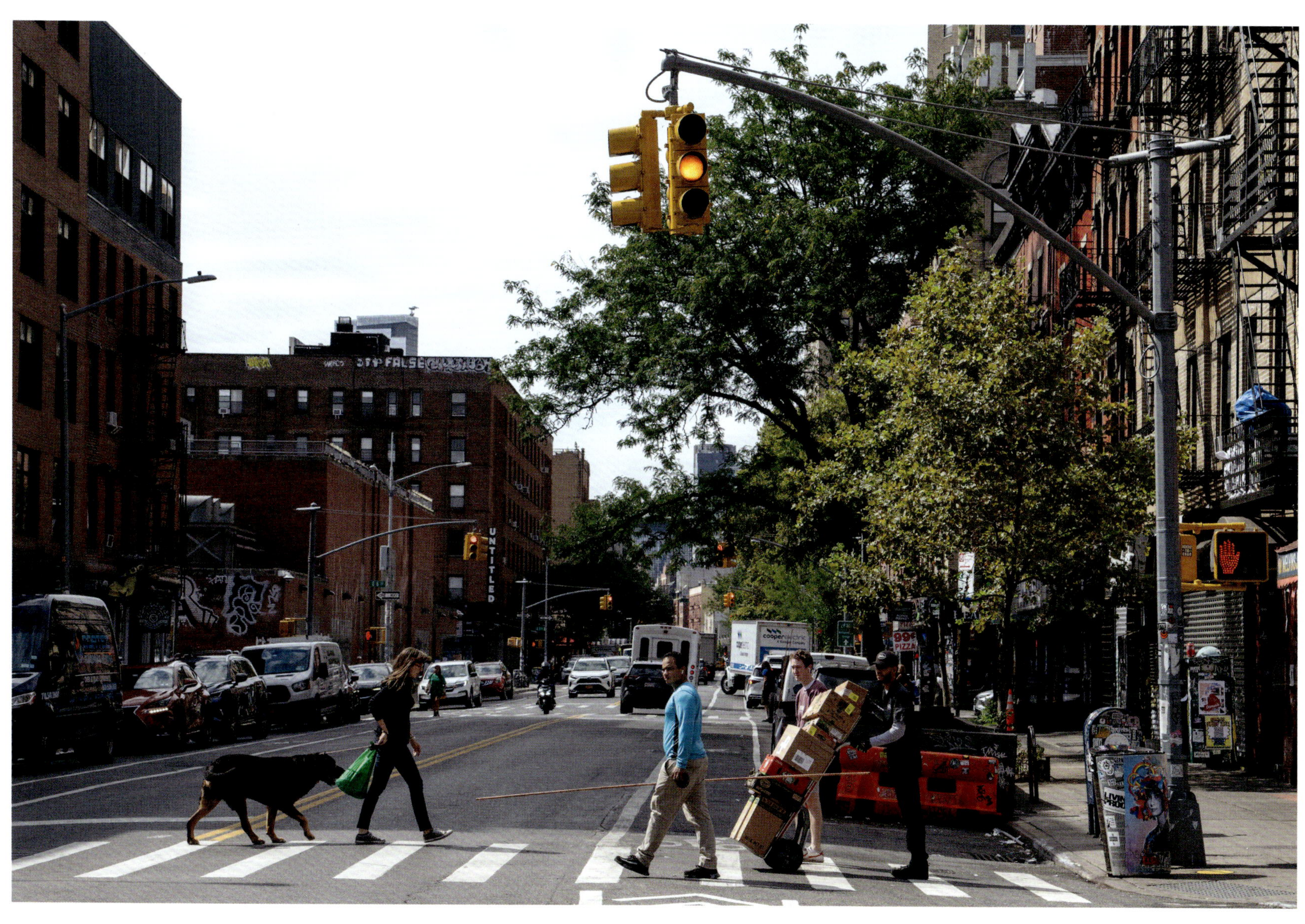

The movie theater / Pioneer / Syp's Produce replaced by a
new building. Con Edison still here.

109 AVENUE A

Avenue A and East 7th Street, a crossroads of sorts. The restaurant 7A on the right.

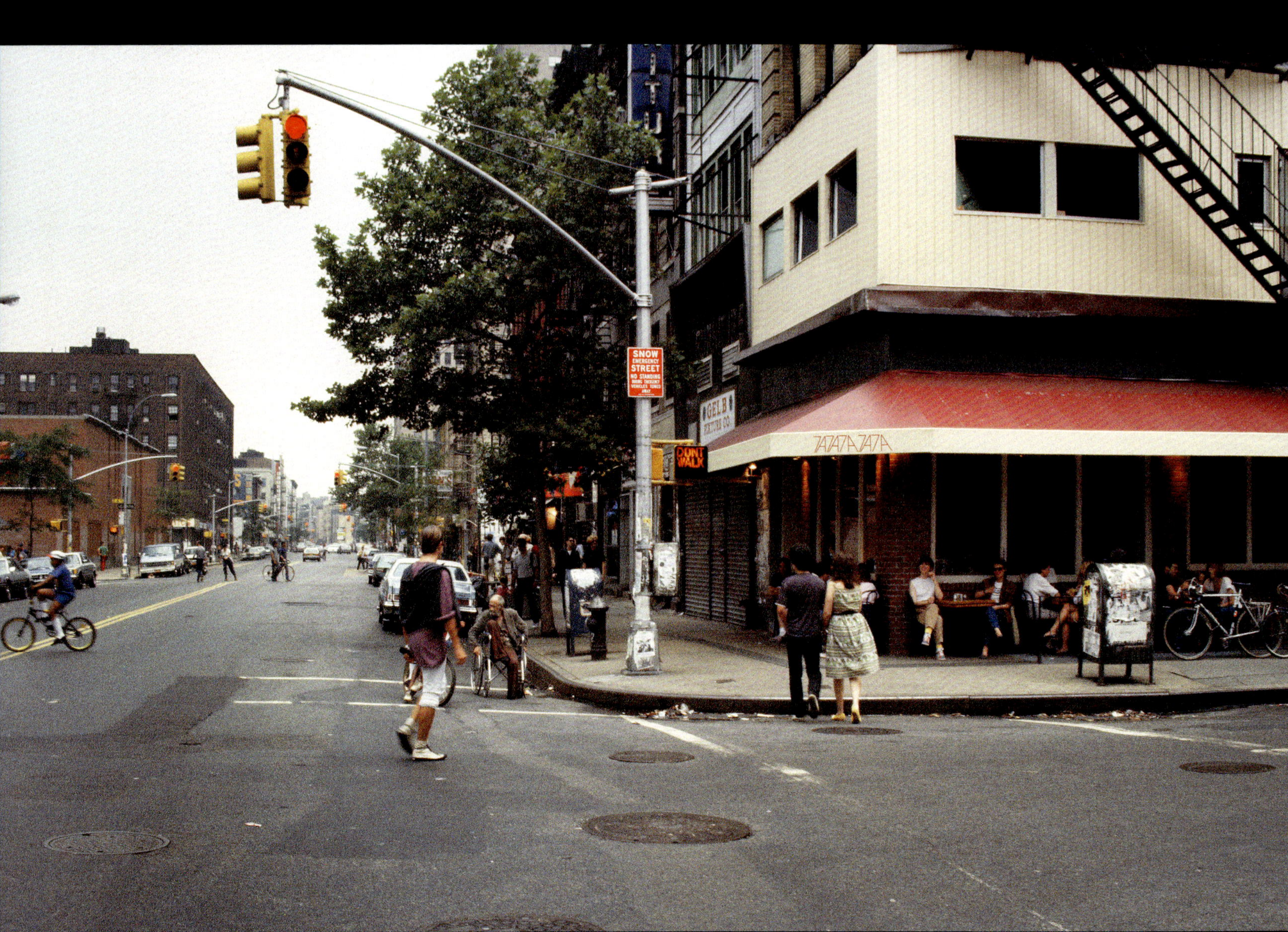

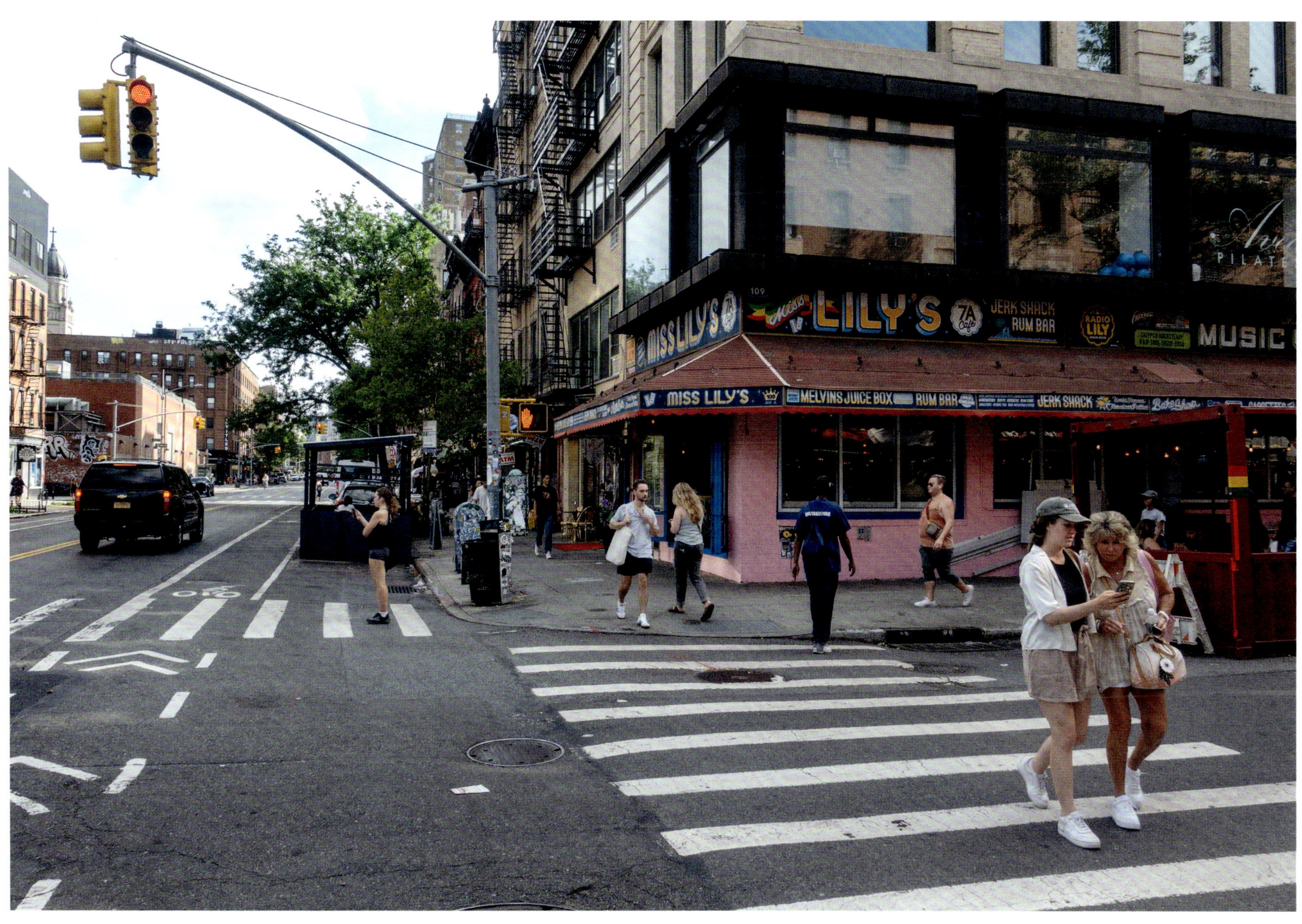

Still a crossroads of sorts. Now
it's Miss Lily's 7A on the right.

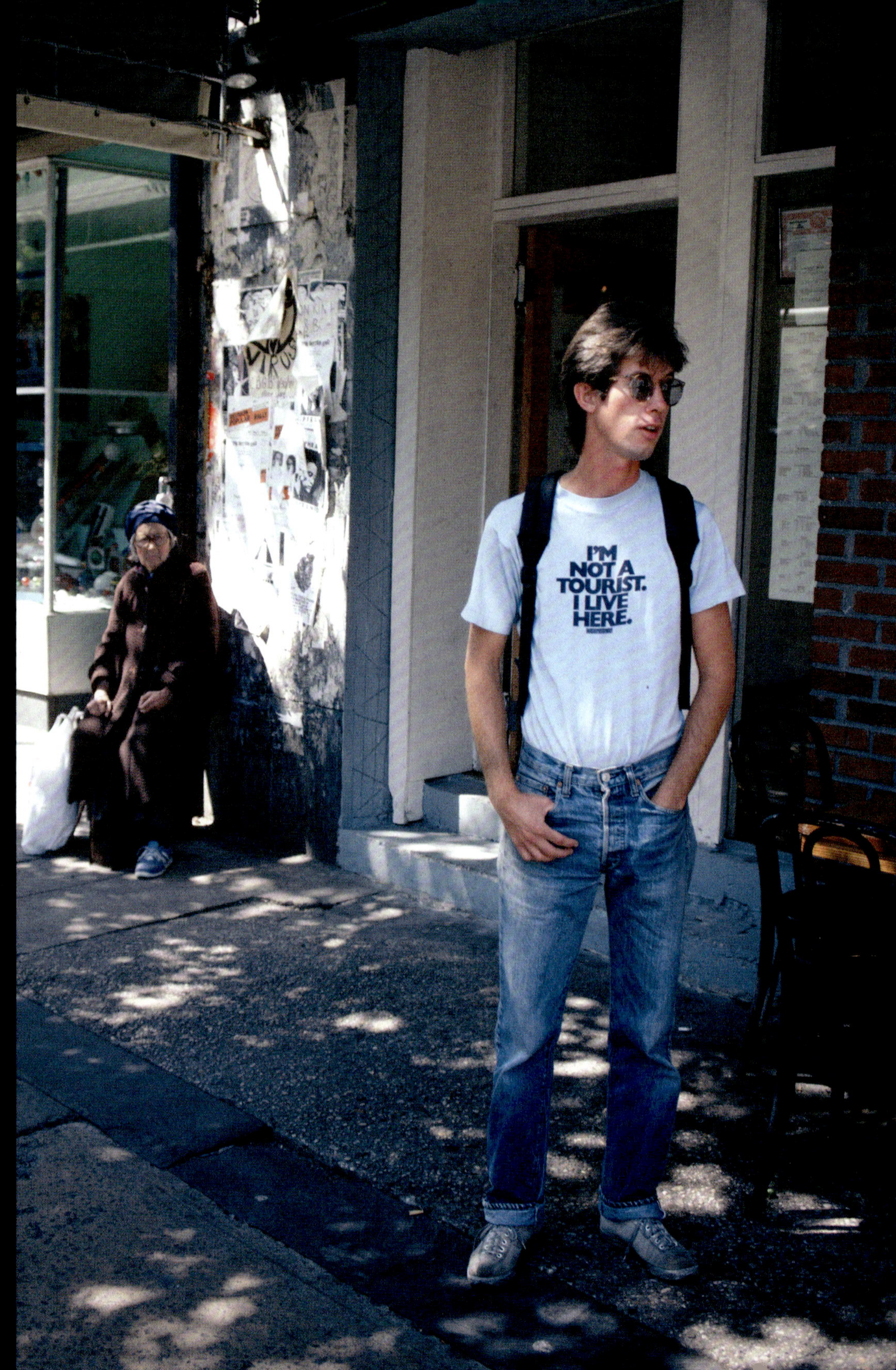

109 AVENUE A

In front of 7A. Things were
changing quickly, with people
of all stripes trying to stake their
claim.

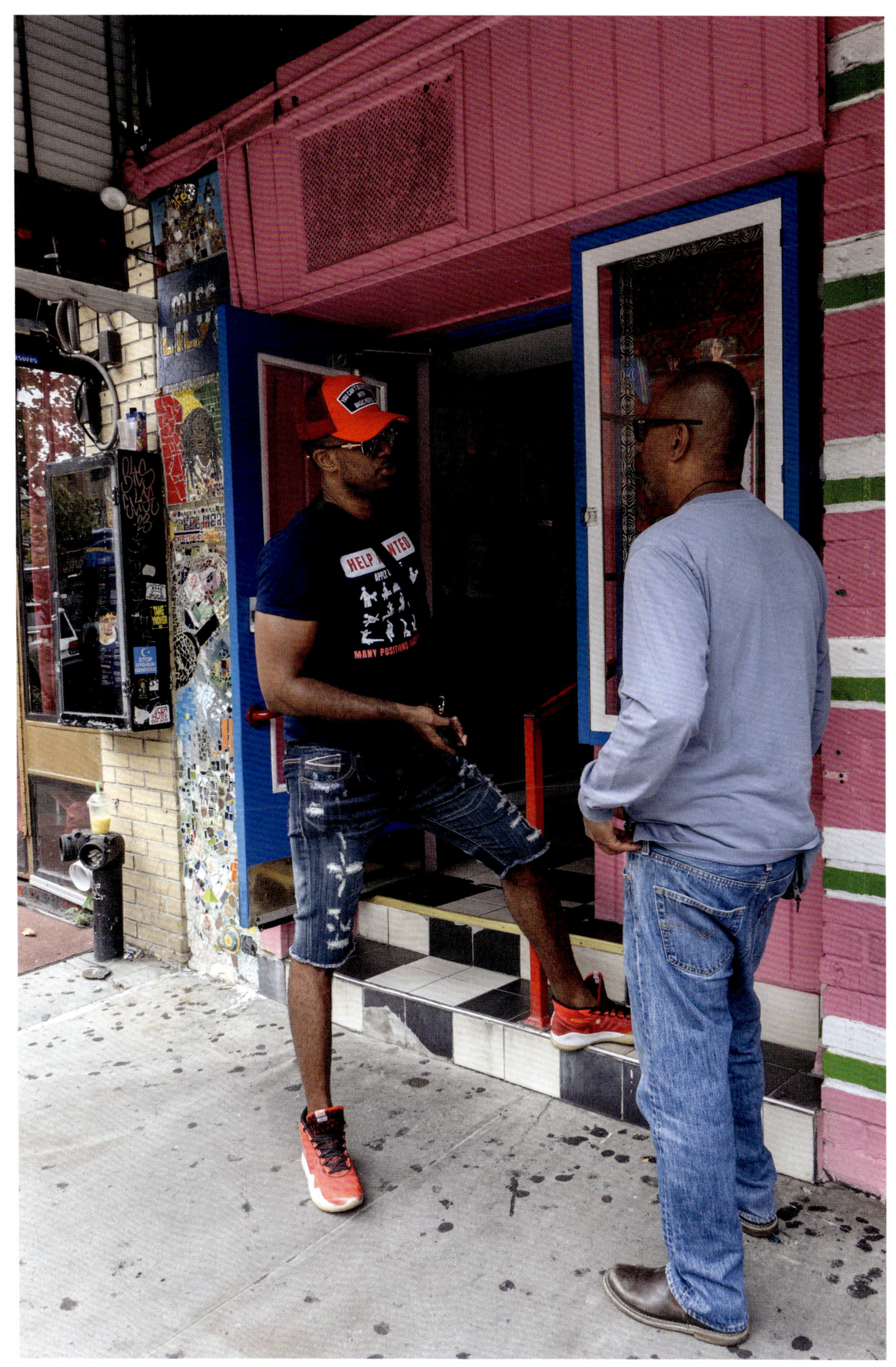

Hanging, talking, but now at
Miss Lily's 7A.

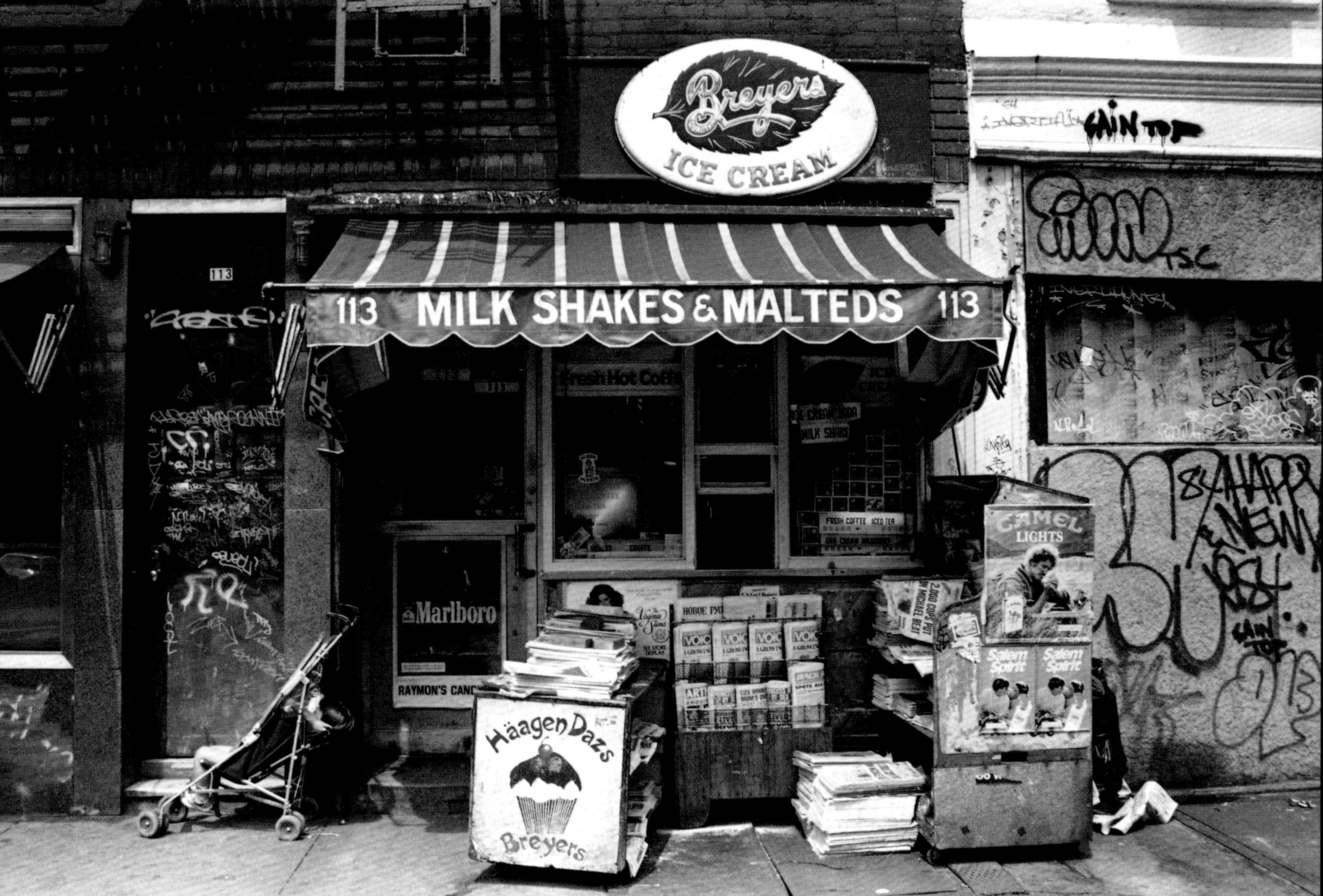

113 AVENUE A

Ray's Candy Store, since 1974. Open
twenty-four hours. Newspapers and
magazines with the egg cream.

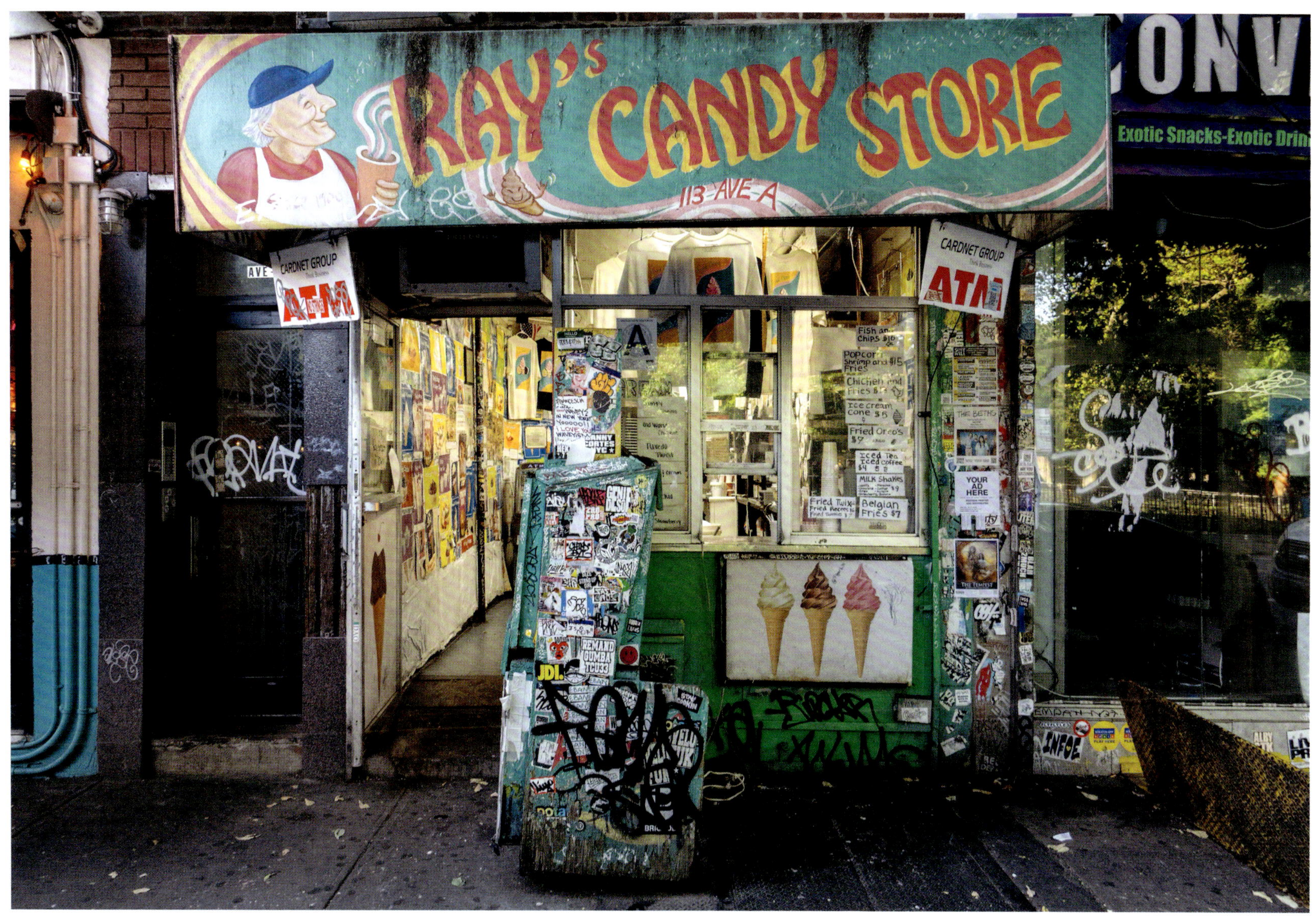

Ninety-one-year-old Ray Alvarez still takes the overnight
shift, with all that "overnight" implies (drunk, high, etc.).
Now Ray's is more sweets and munchies.

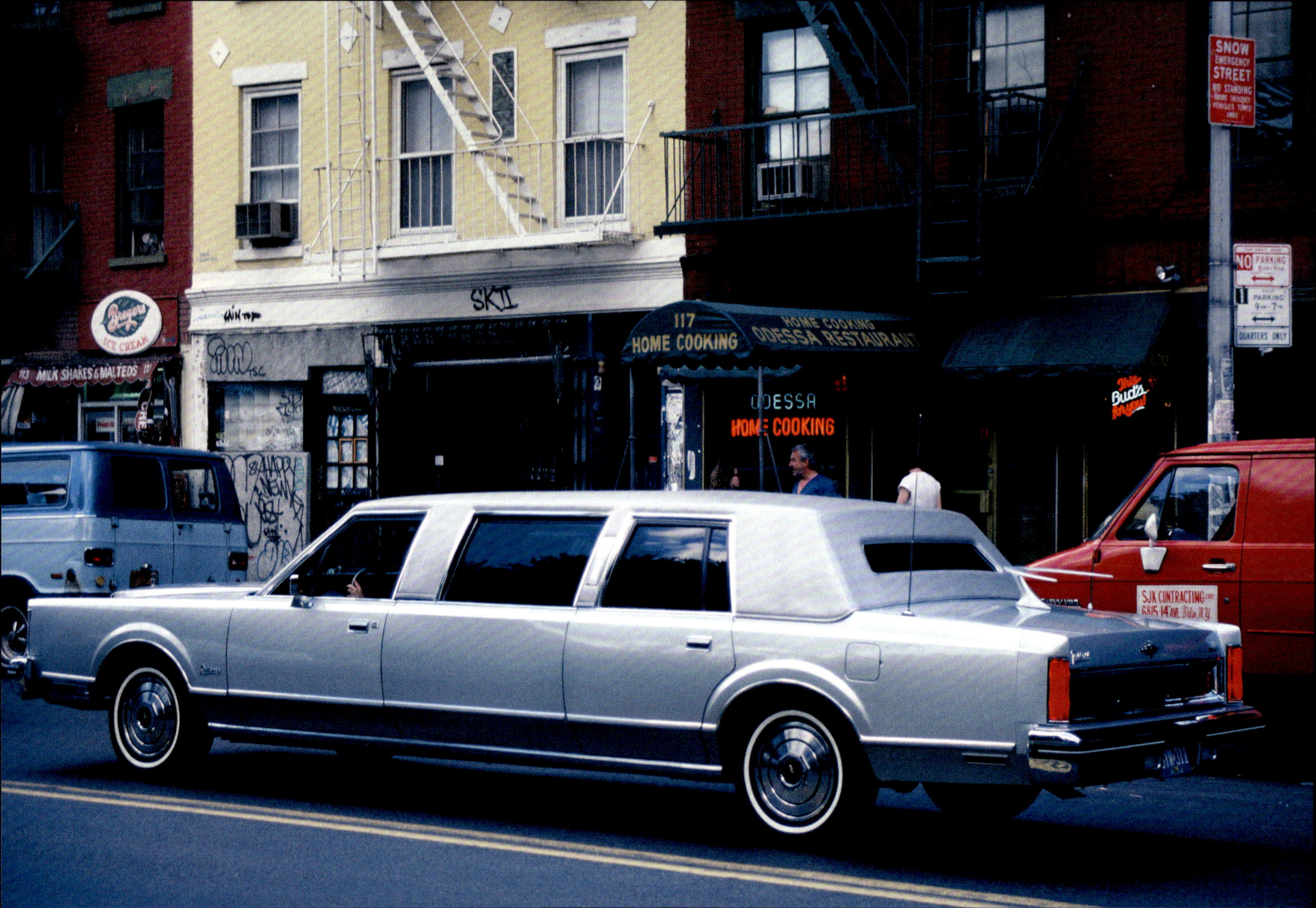

SNOW
EMERGENCY
STREET
NO STANDING
QUARTERS ONLY
NO PARKING
PARKING
Brewers
ICE CREAM
MILK SHAKES & MALTEDS
SK II
117
HOME COOKING
HOME COOKING
ODESSA RESTAURANT
ODESSA
HOME COOKING
This Bud's
SJK CONTRACTING

Now it's St. Dymphna's bar,
and now it's a Bentley.

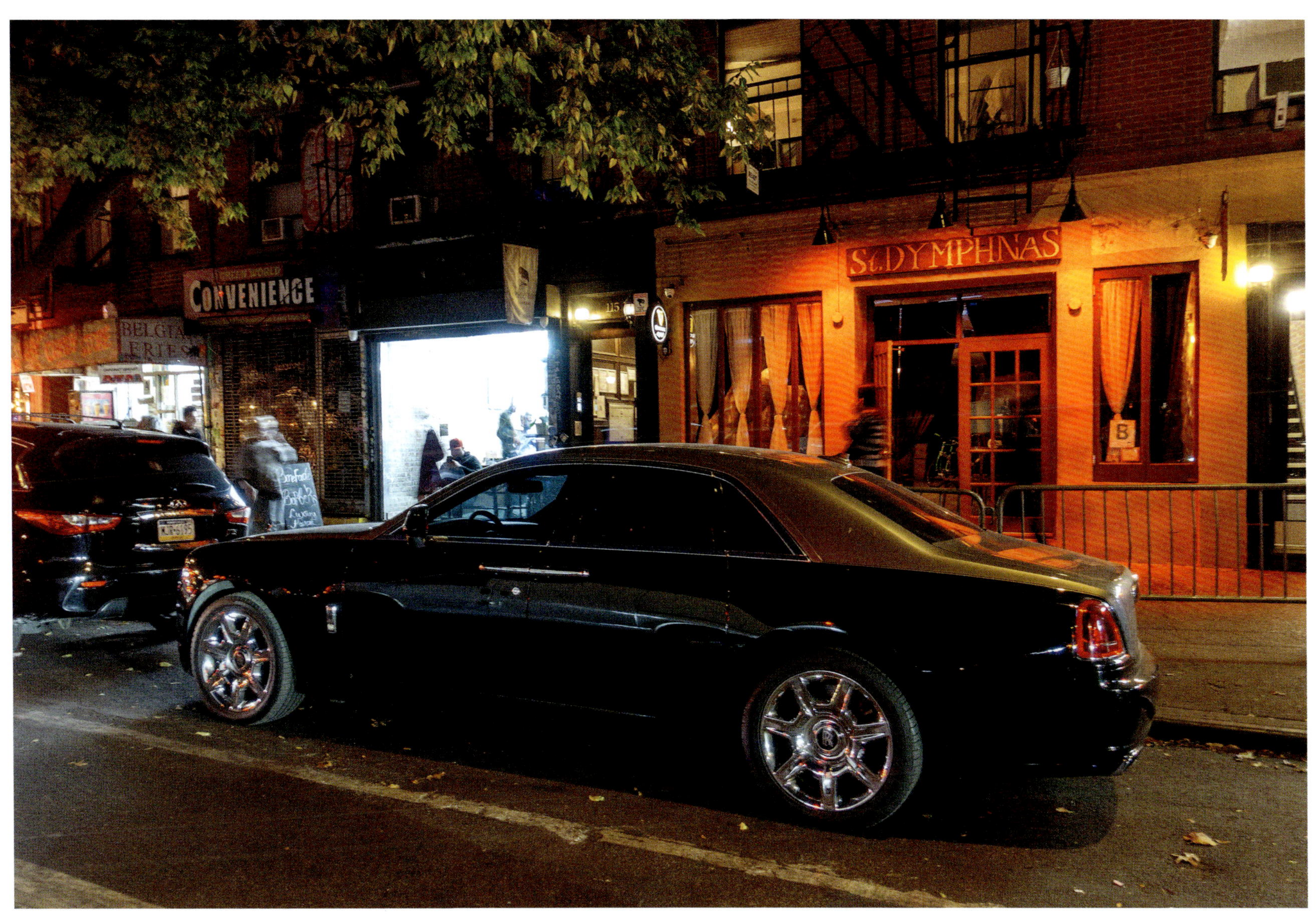

126 ST. MARK'S PLACE

Penny's General Store (Natural Healing Products) before they moved around the corner to East 7th Street.

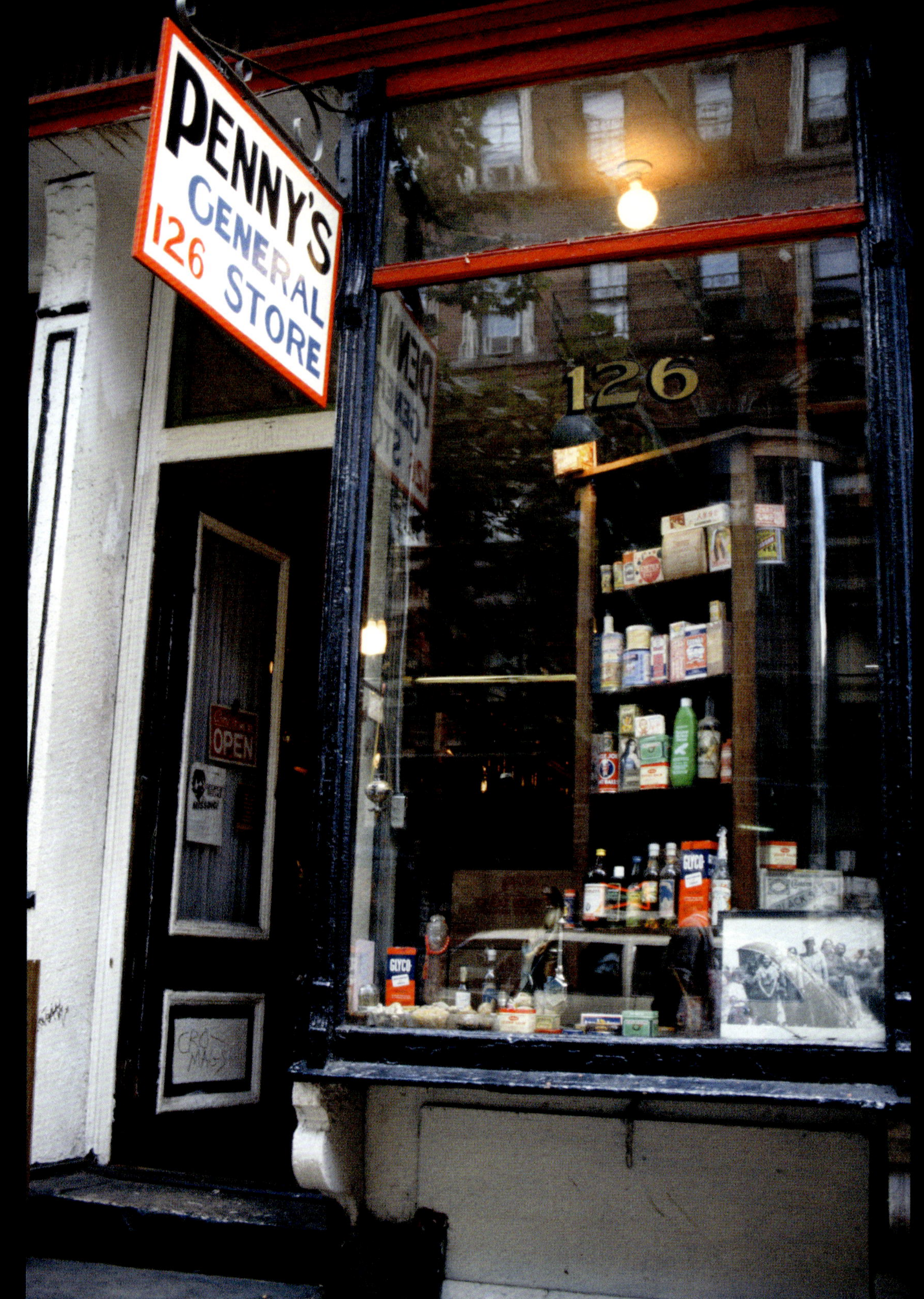

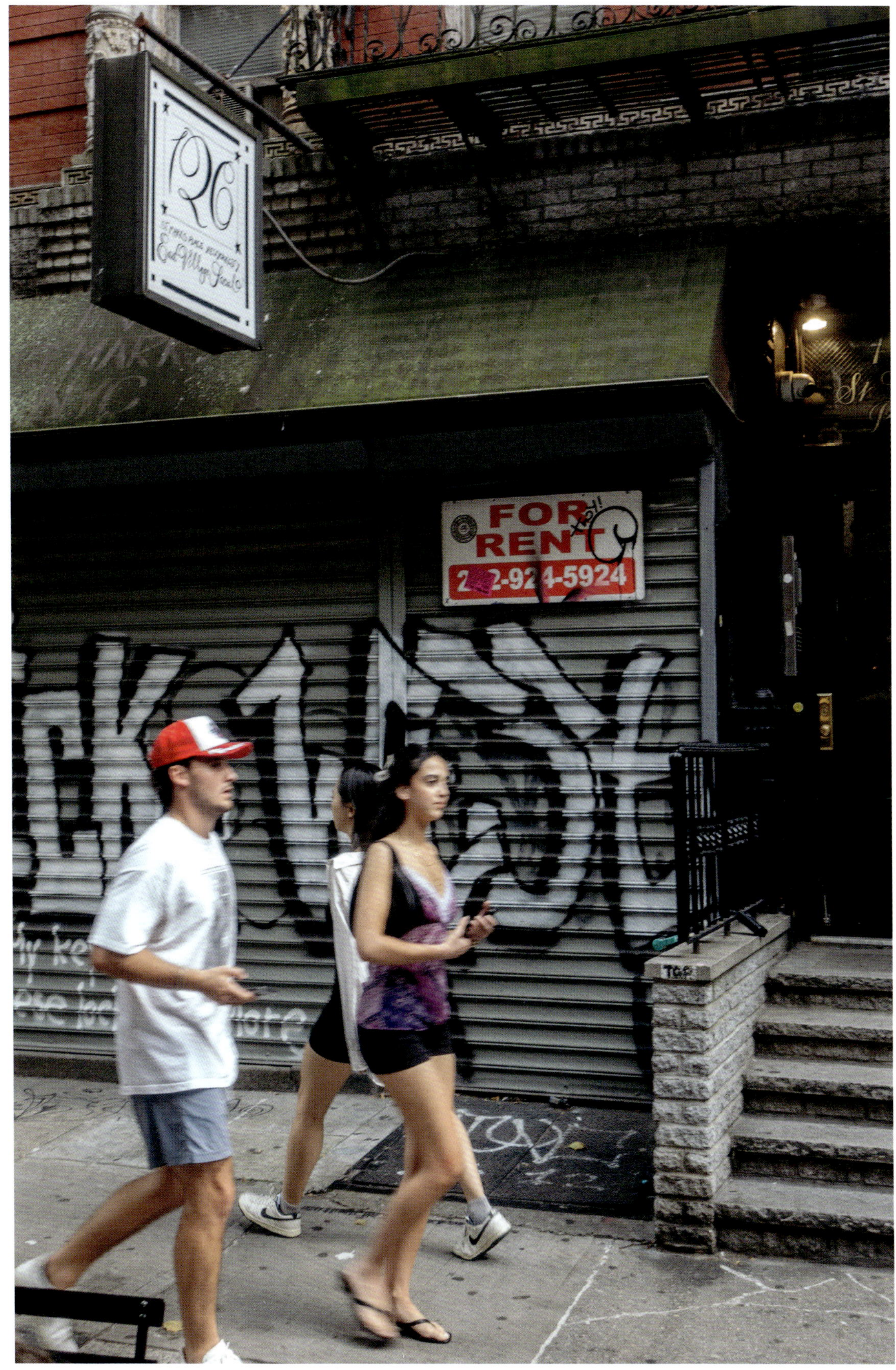

The shuttered East Village Social aka EVS. The bars on St. Mark's Place between Avenue A and First Avenue didn't really follow the Covid protocols during the first summer of the pandemic. Videos of the street prompted then-Governor Cuomo's threat "Don't make me come down there!"

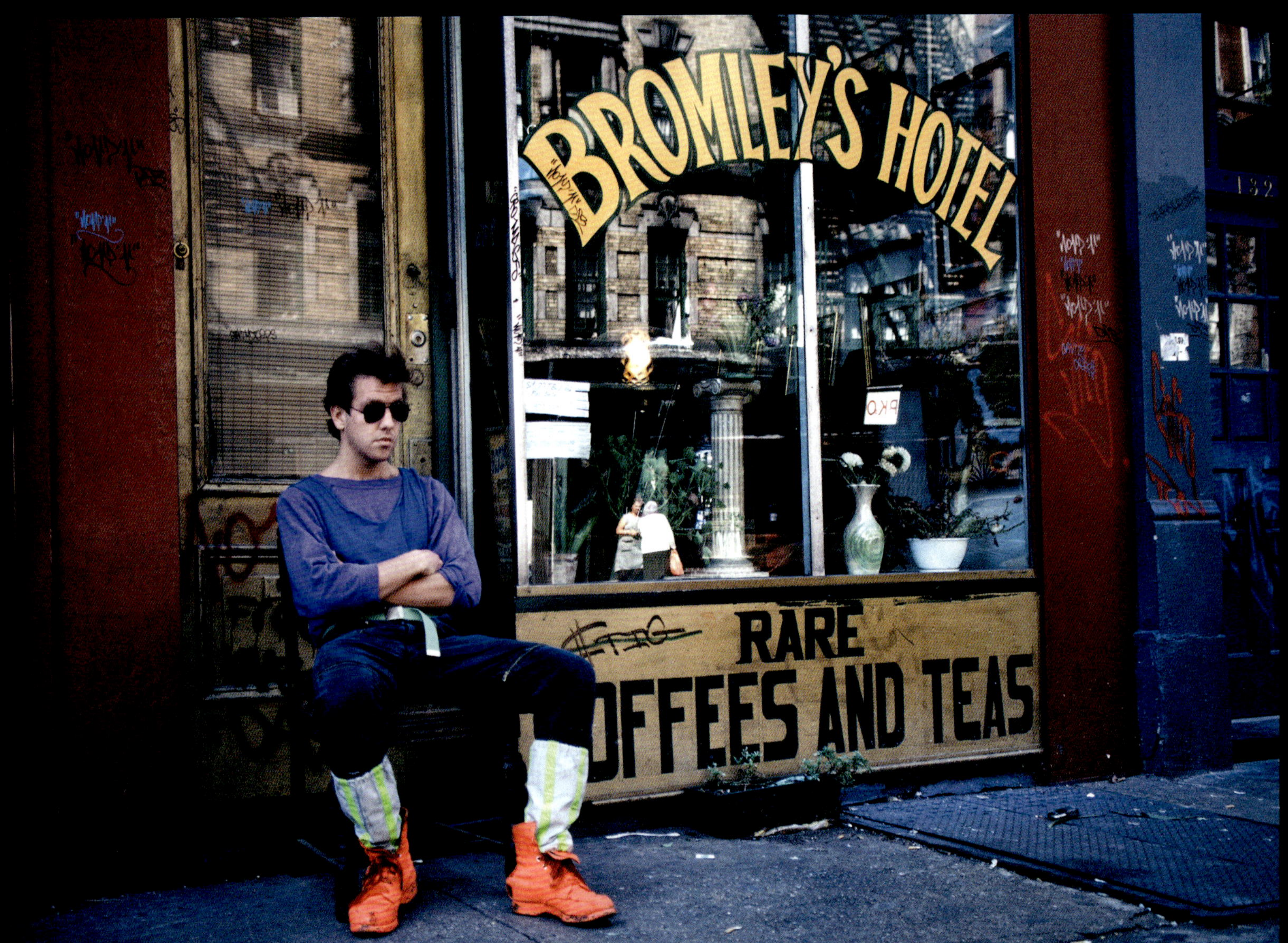
BROMLEY'S HOTEL
RARE
OFFEES AND TEAS

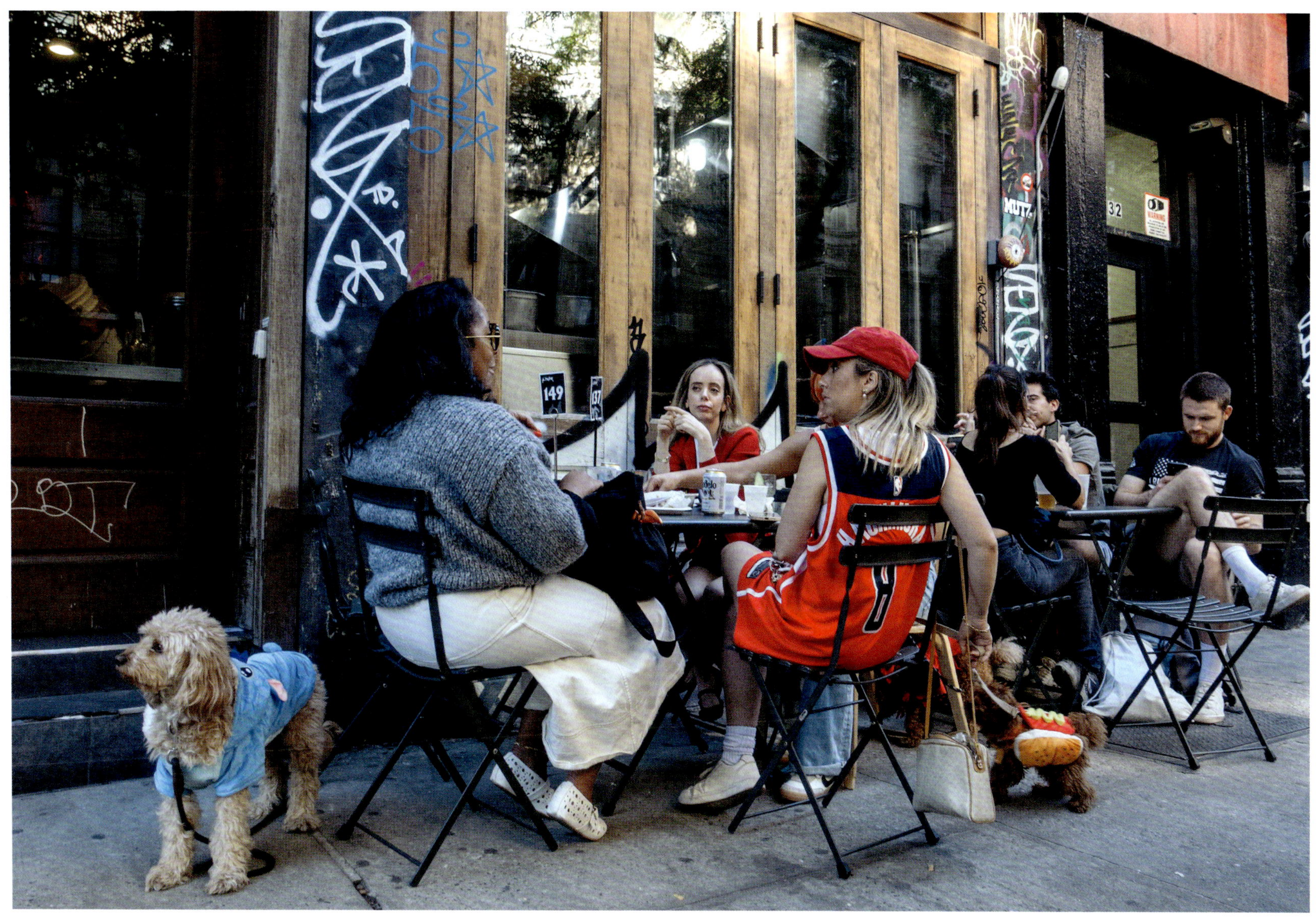

Outdoor seating at Empellón Al Pastor, a
"contemporary Mexican hot spot."

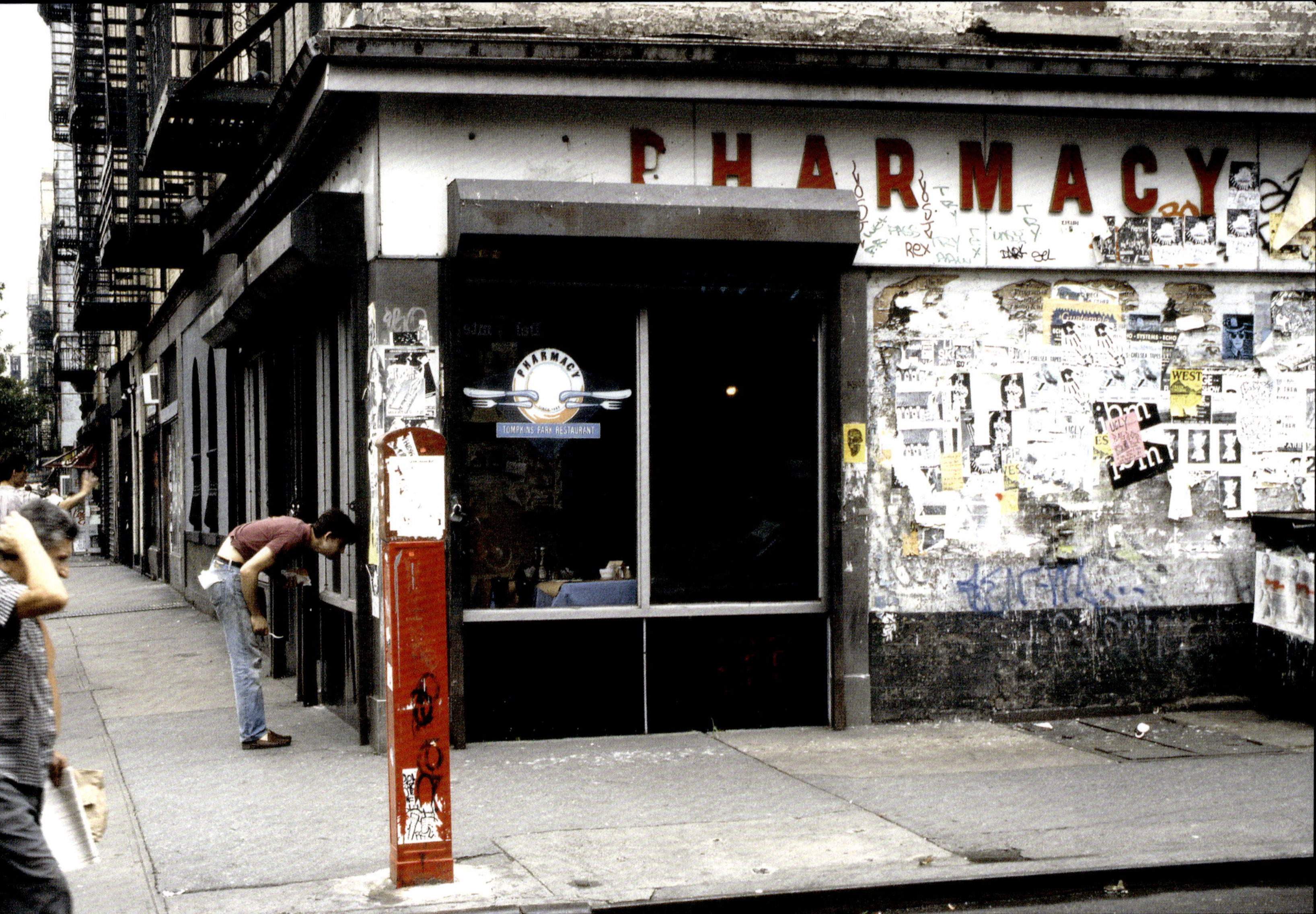

141 AVENUE A

The Pharmacy: a restaurant that went
with the sign, and the name, from the old
business. The kind of restaurant you could
bring relatives to show them you didn't
live in a "shithole" (their word, not mine).

Doc Holliday's, a divey roadhouse-type bar
that's been here for around thirty years.

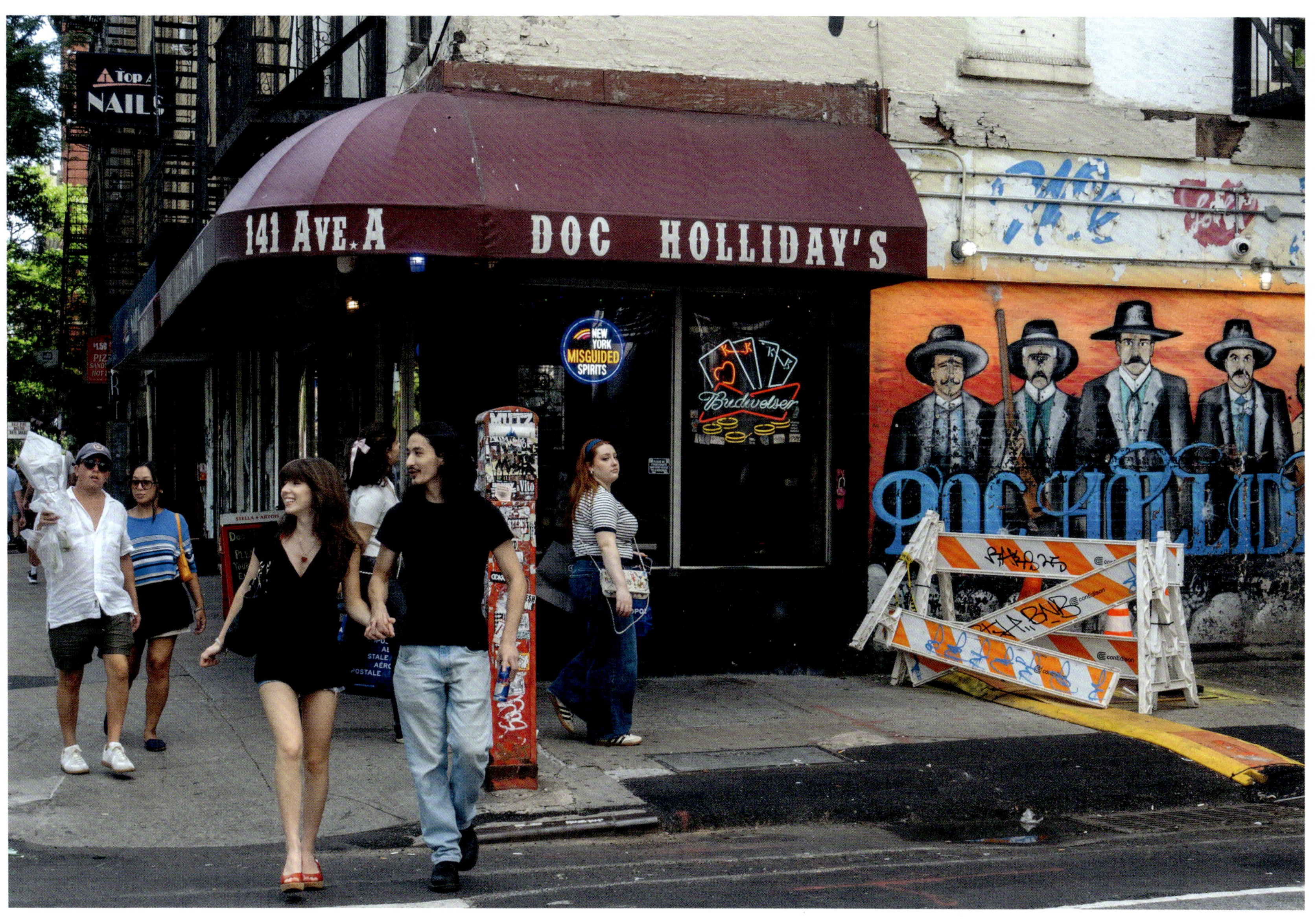

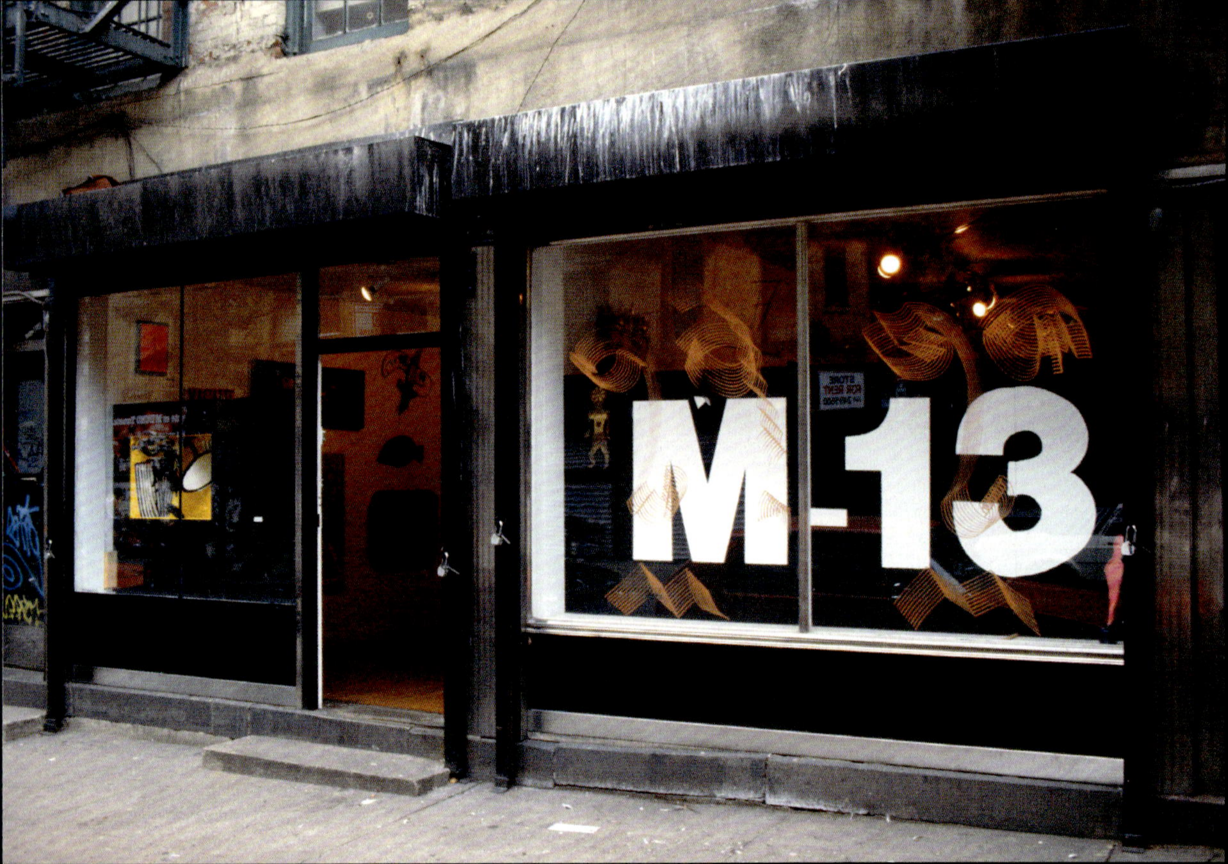

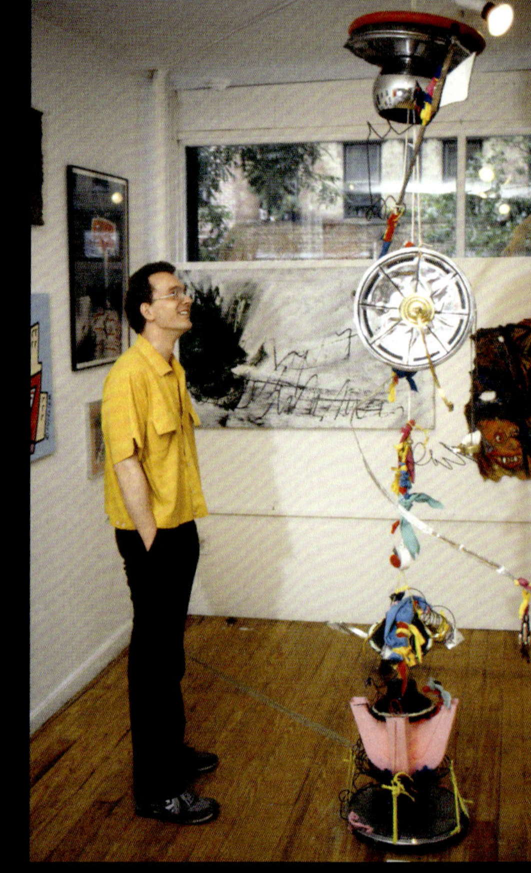

440 EAST 9TH STREET

The M-13 Gallery moved to SoHo and changed
its name to the Howard Scott Gallery. Moved to
Chelsea and is now closed.

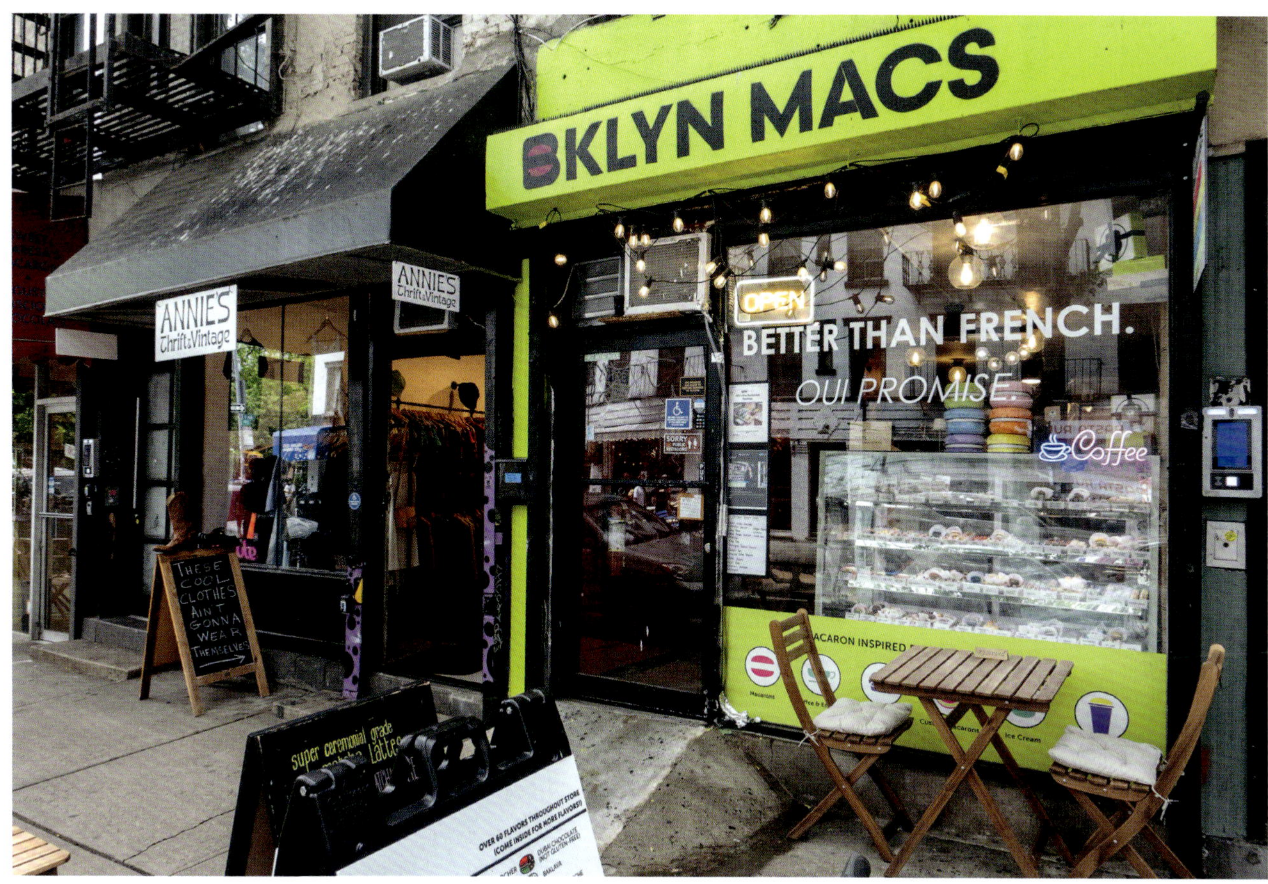

Bklyn Macs, and thrift shop upcycling.

174 AVENUE A

THEN Kids playing in the remains of Paradise Alley and the rear building of the neighboring tenement. Paradise Alley was once a row of tenements that attracted painters and writers including Beat poet Alene Lee. Alene attracted Jack Kerouac, who included Paradise Alley in his book *The Subterraneans* but moved it to San Francisco. In the sixties it was renovated with a fountain and gas lamps, trying to emulate Patchin Place off West 10th Street and Sixth Avenue. That all ended with a fire in the early eighties.

NOW Alliance Apartments for the Elderly. The replacement. The second photo is the rear building of the neighboring tenement (the same one in the eighties photo) seen through the backyard of Alliance.

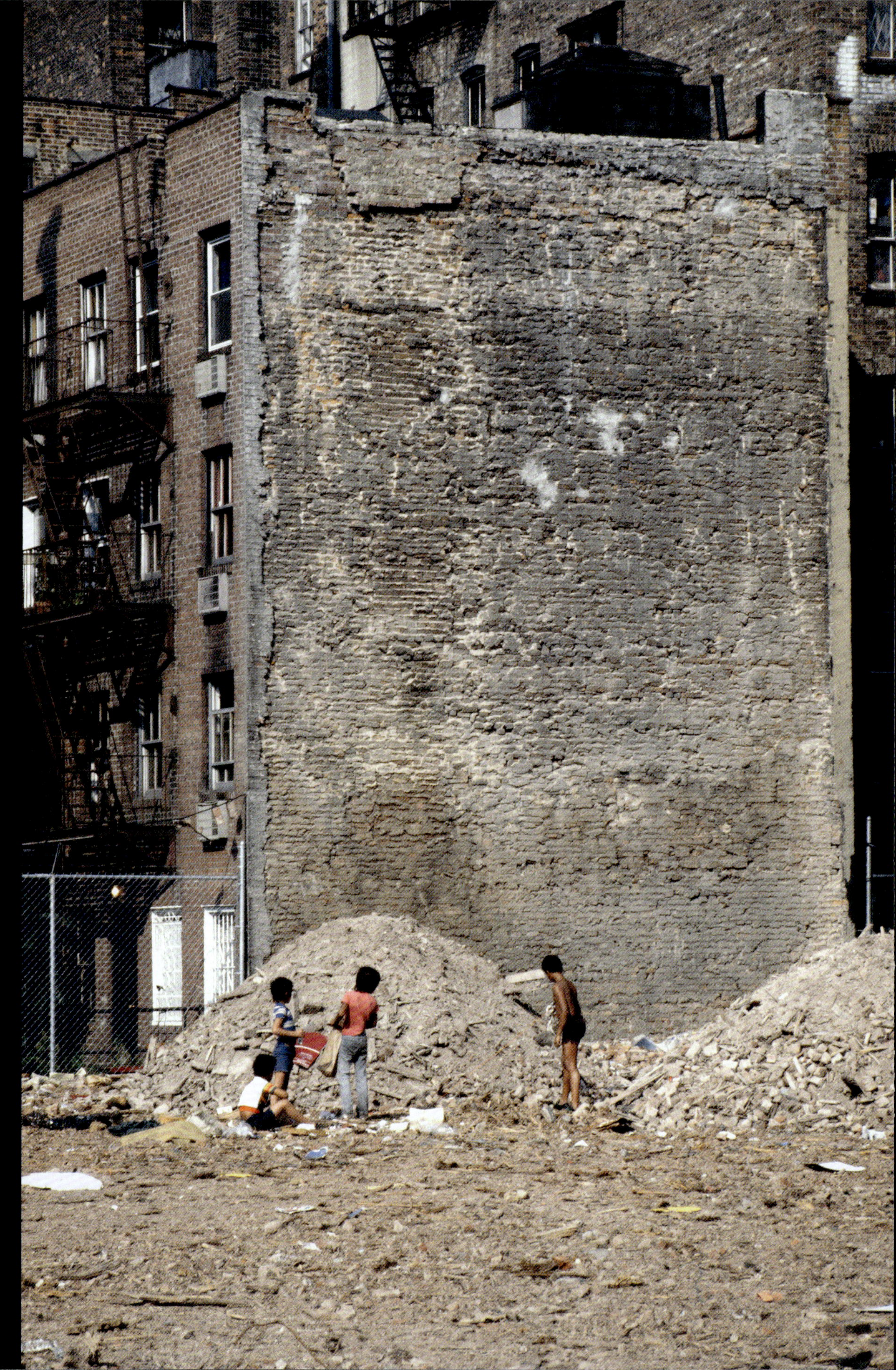

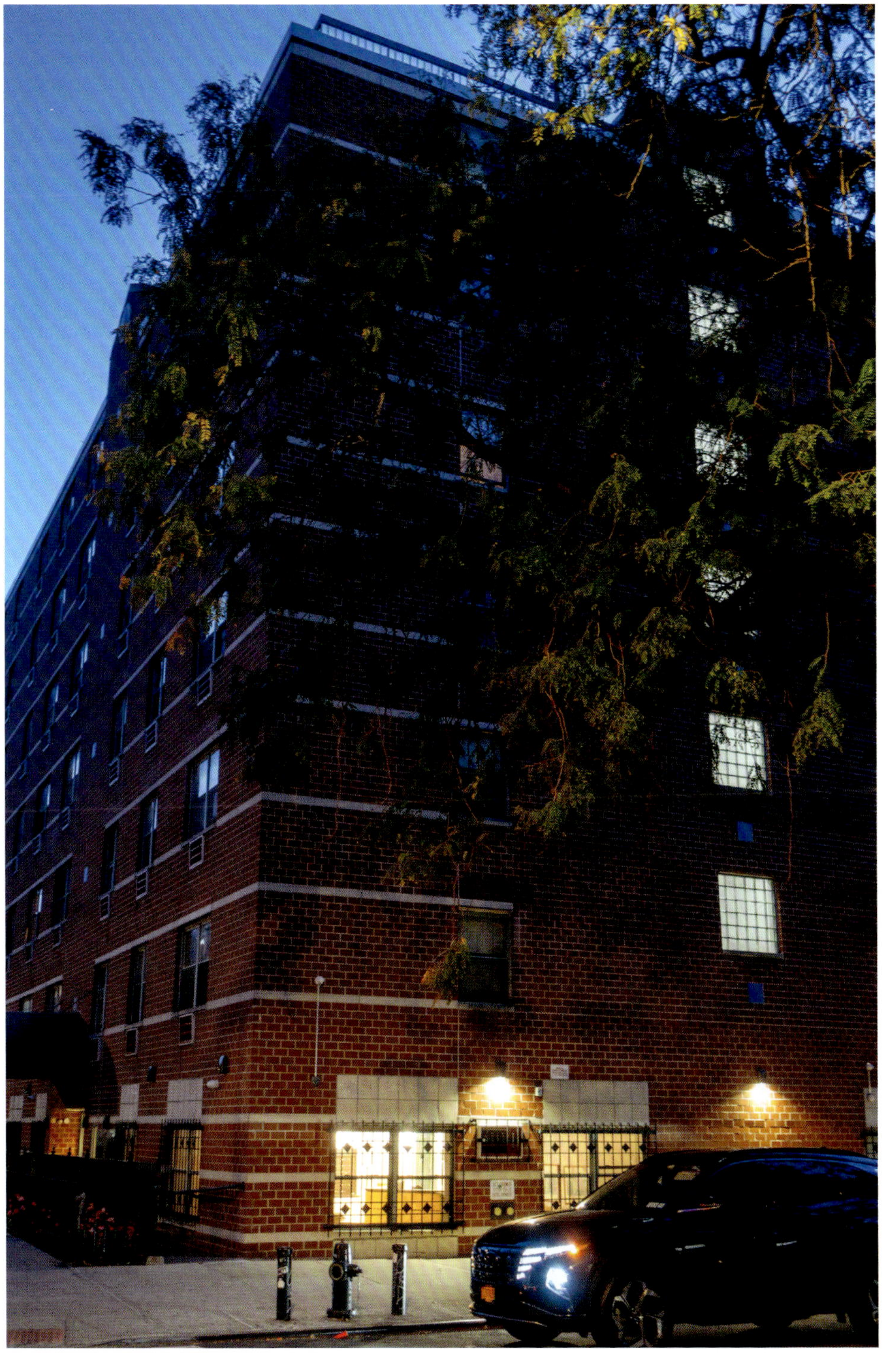

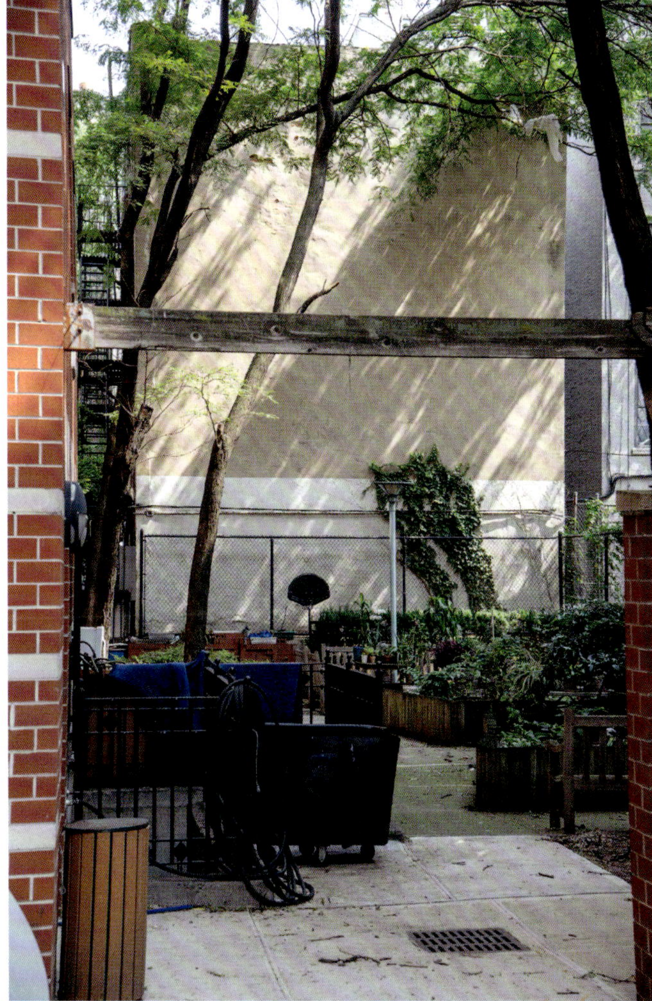

TOMPKINS SQUARE PARK

Samuel Cox giving a warm welcome to Tompkins Square Park and all the visitors. Tomkins Square—it's got something for everyone, including what you don't want and what you don't need. But it's here and it's everyone's. The trees are particularly beautiful and welcome.

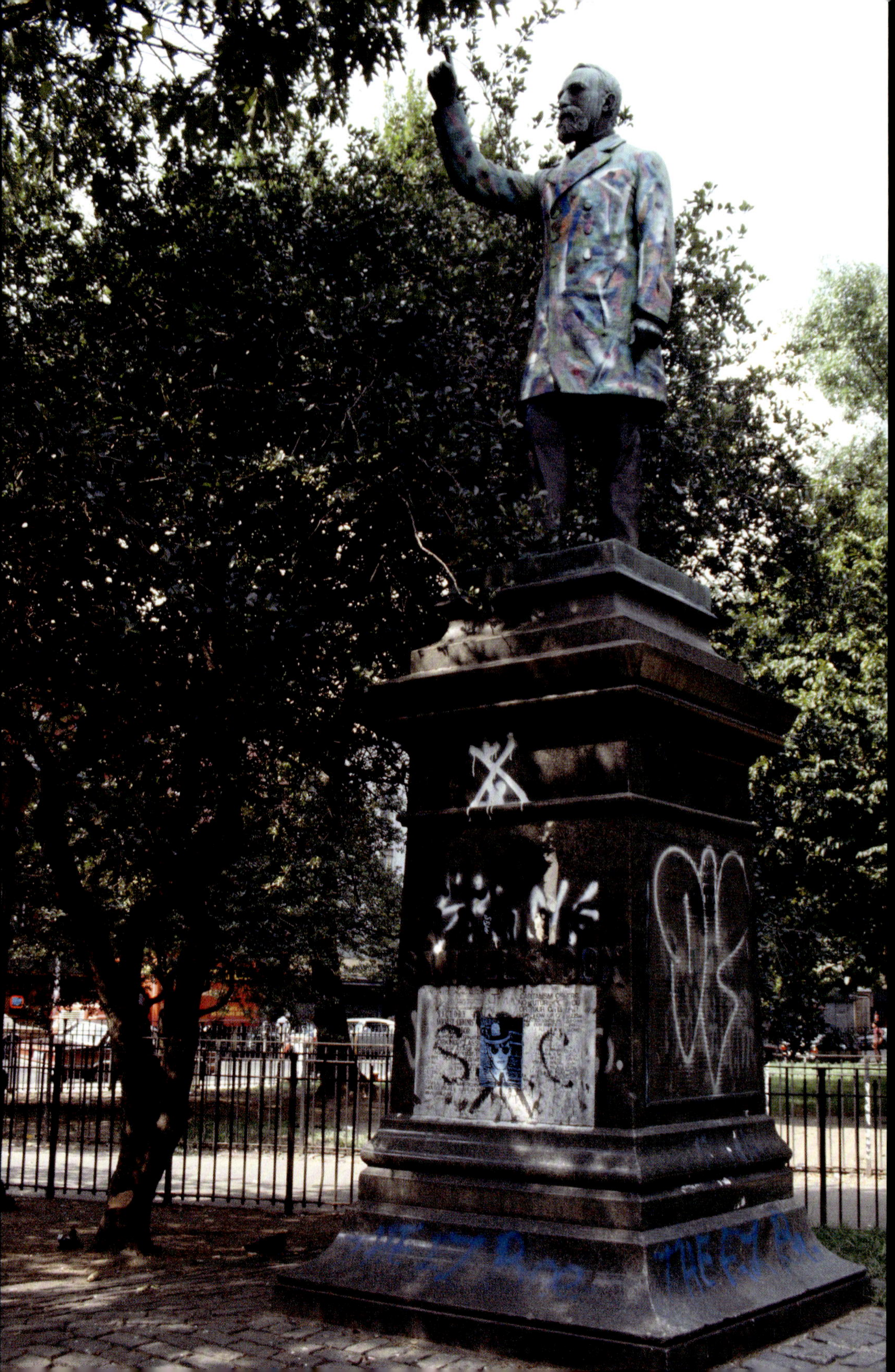

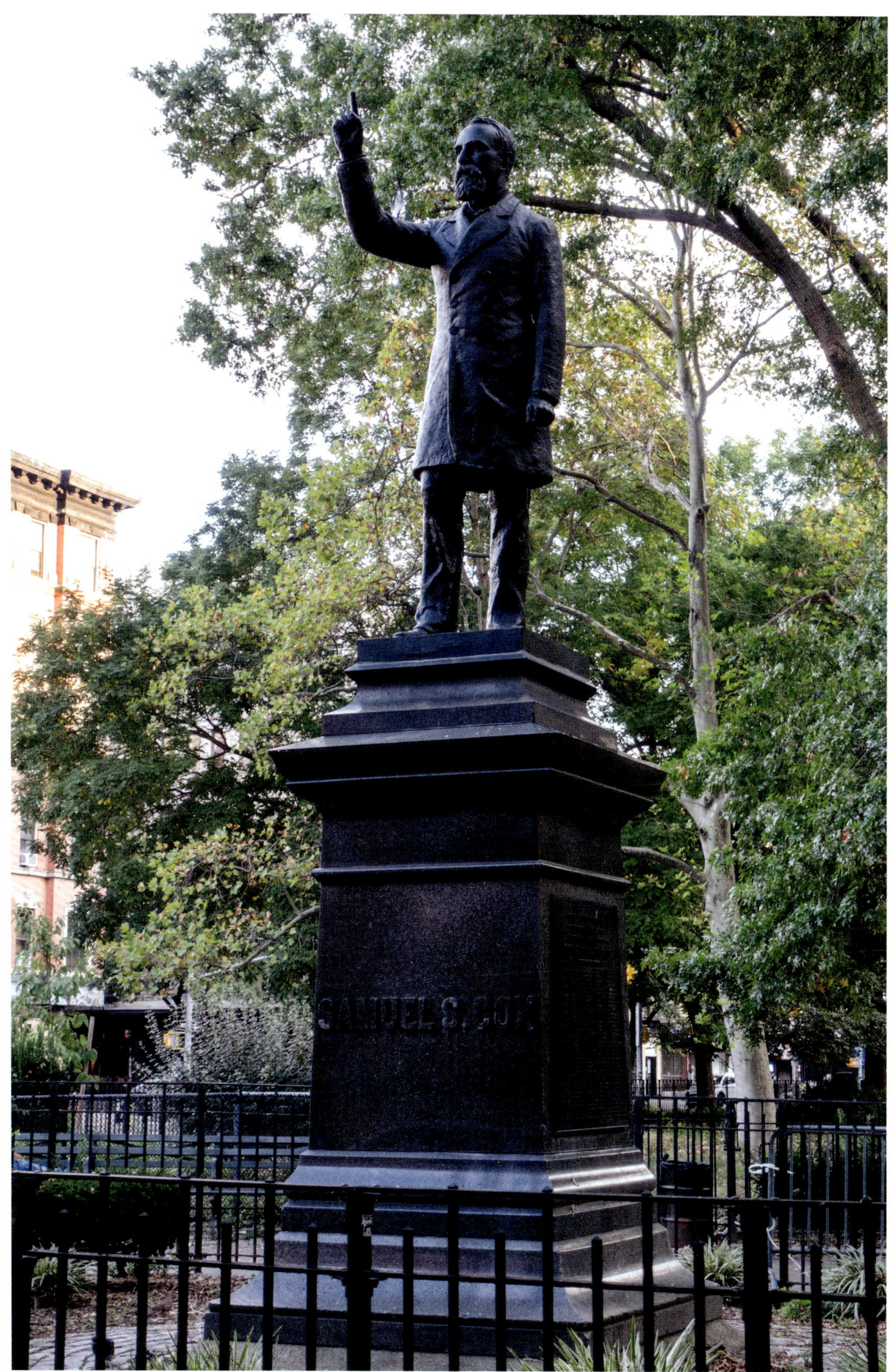

Still here and looking younger.
Still with the warm welcome.

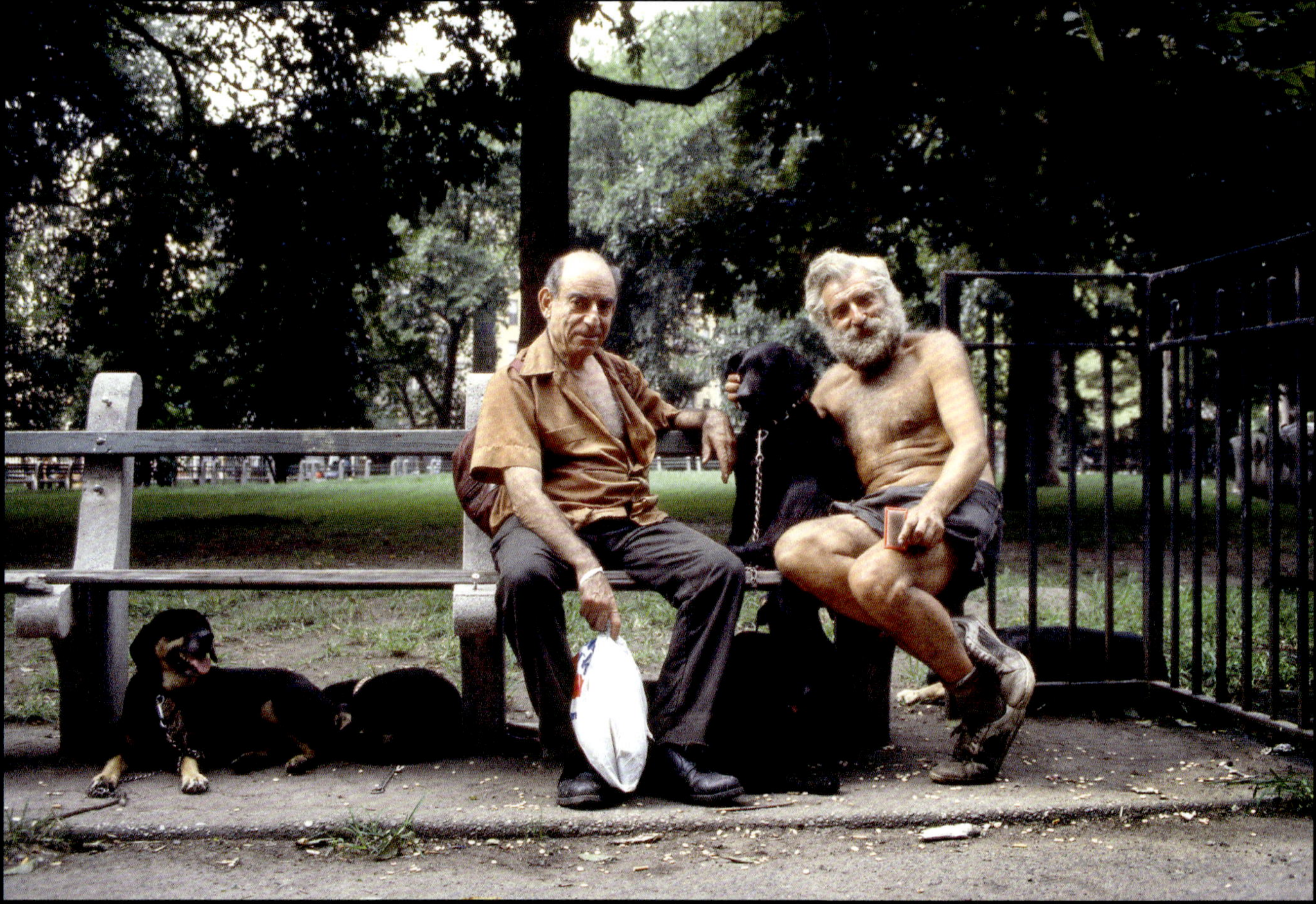

TOMPKINS SQUARE PARK

A guy who lived on the street, in the park, in abandoned buildings, with his ever-reproducing dogs.

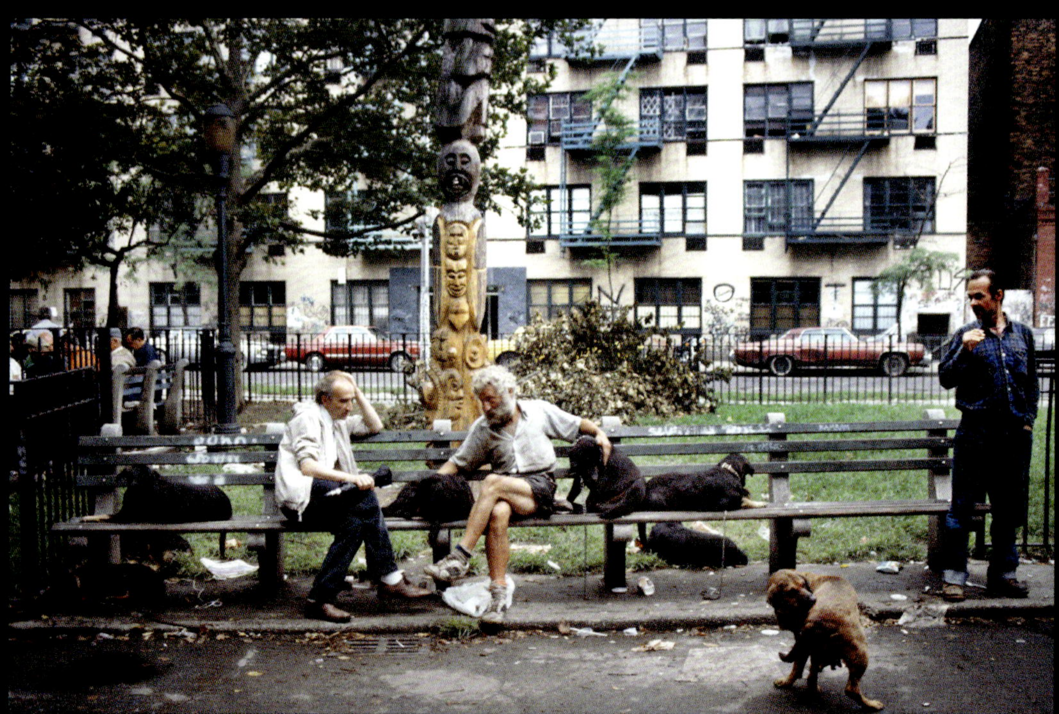

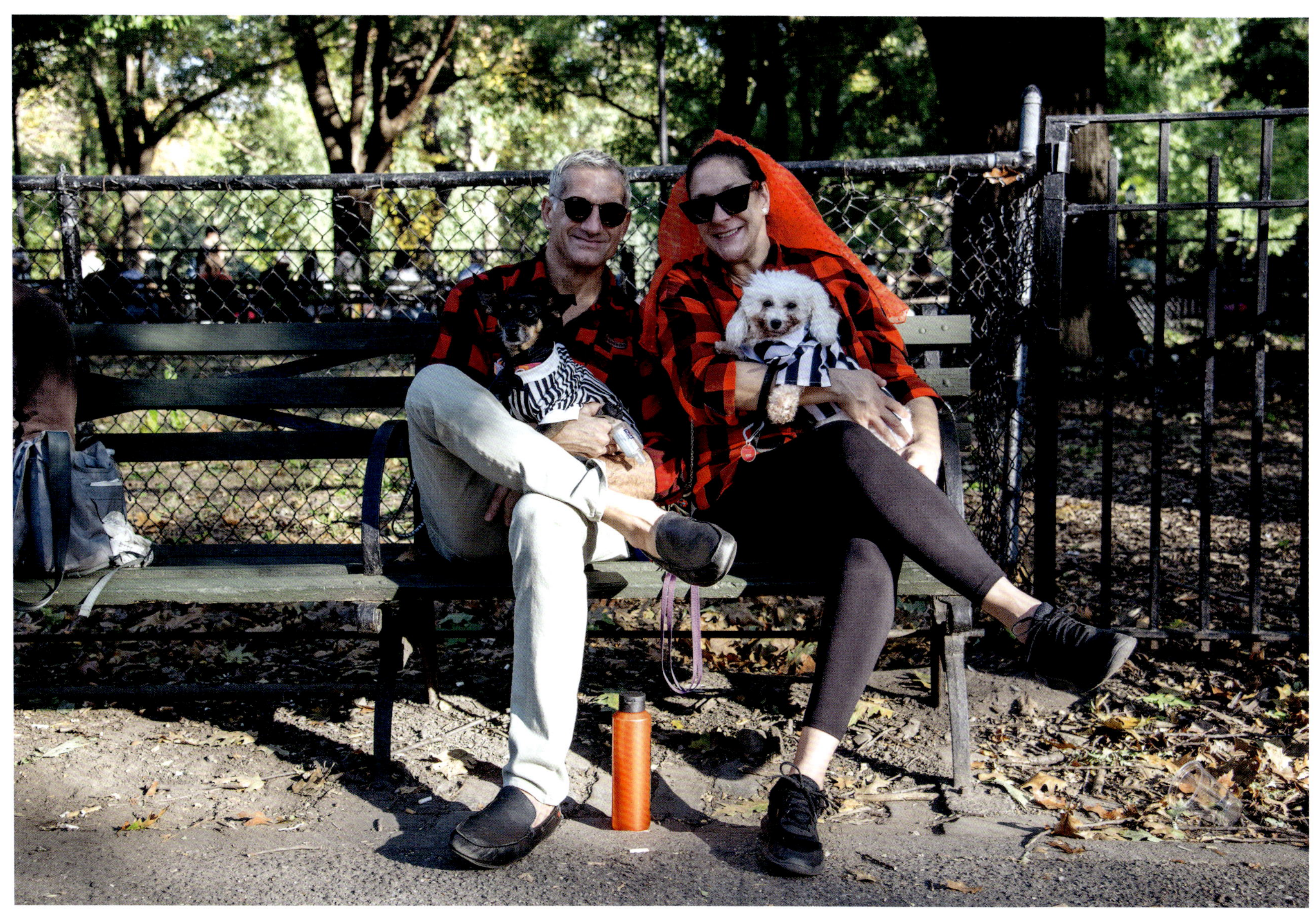

Taking a break from the festivities of the annual
Tompkins Square Halloween Dog Parade.

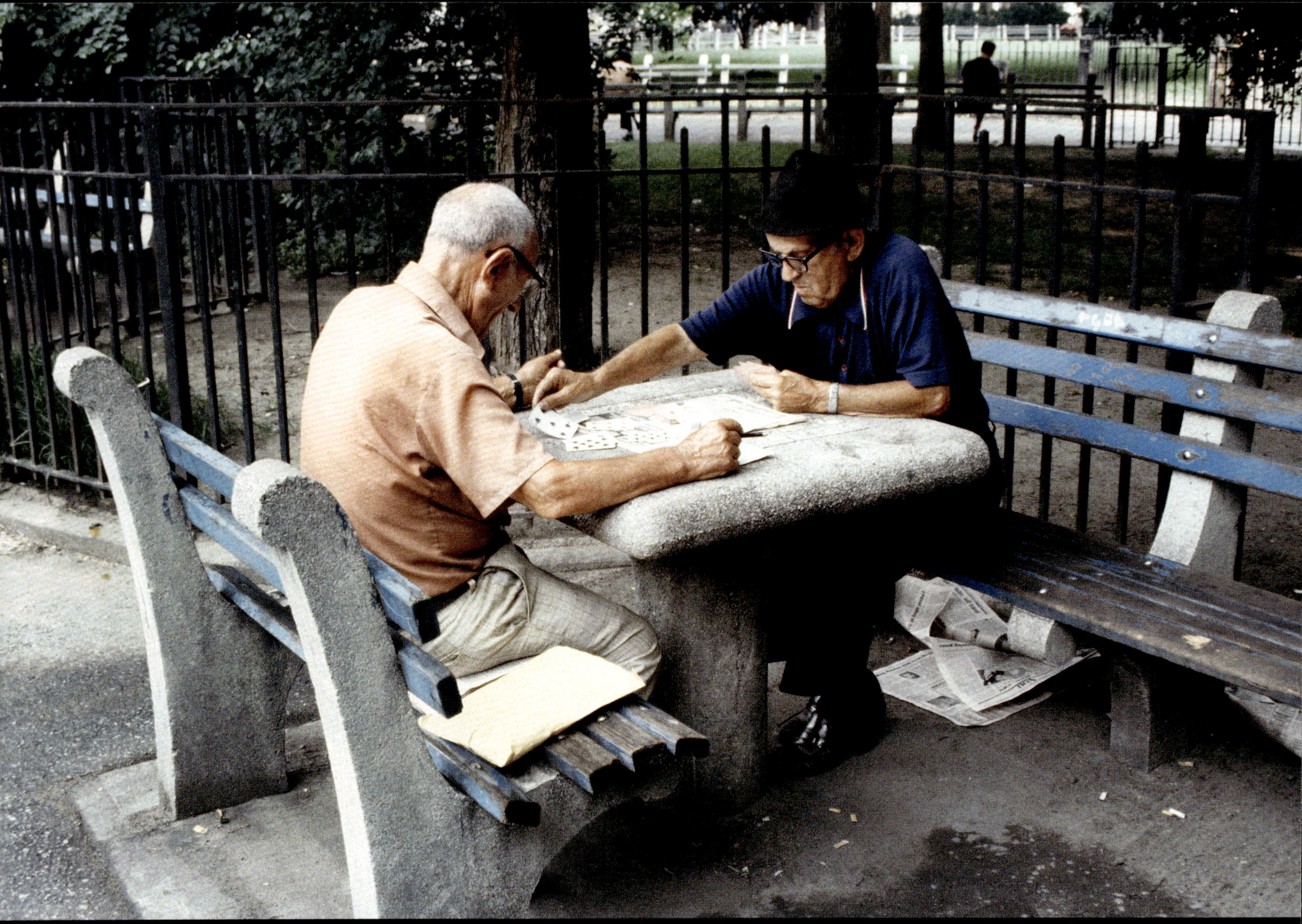

TOMPKINS SQUARE PARK

An afternoon game in retirement.

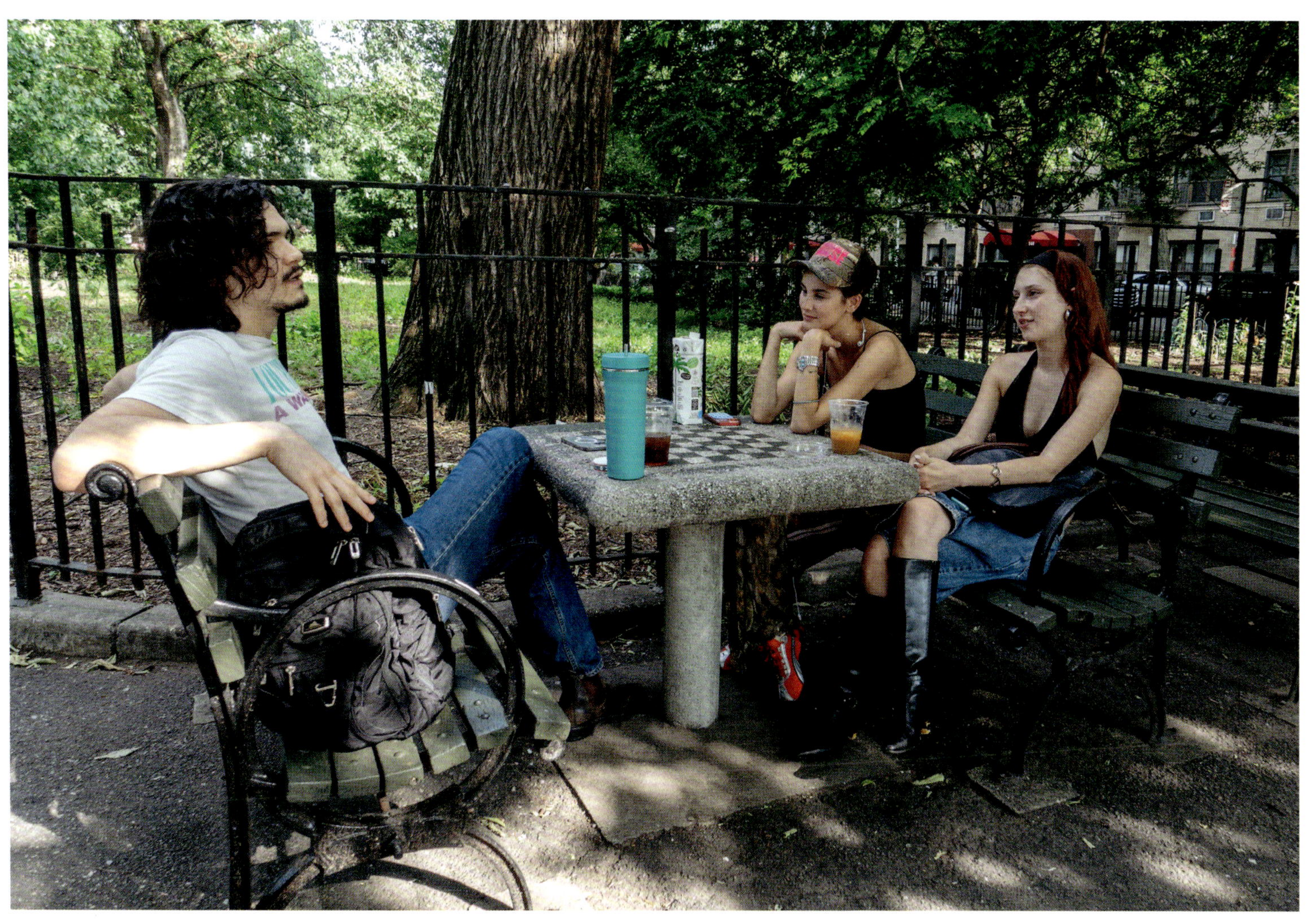

Still a gathering spot.

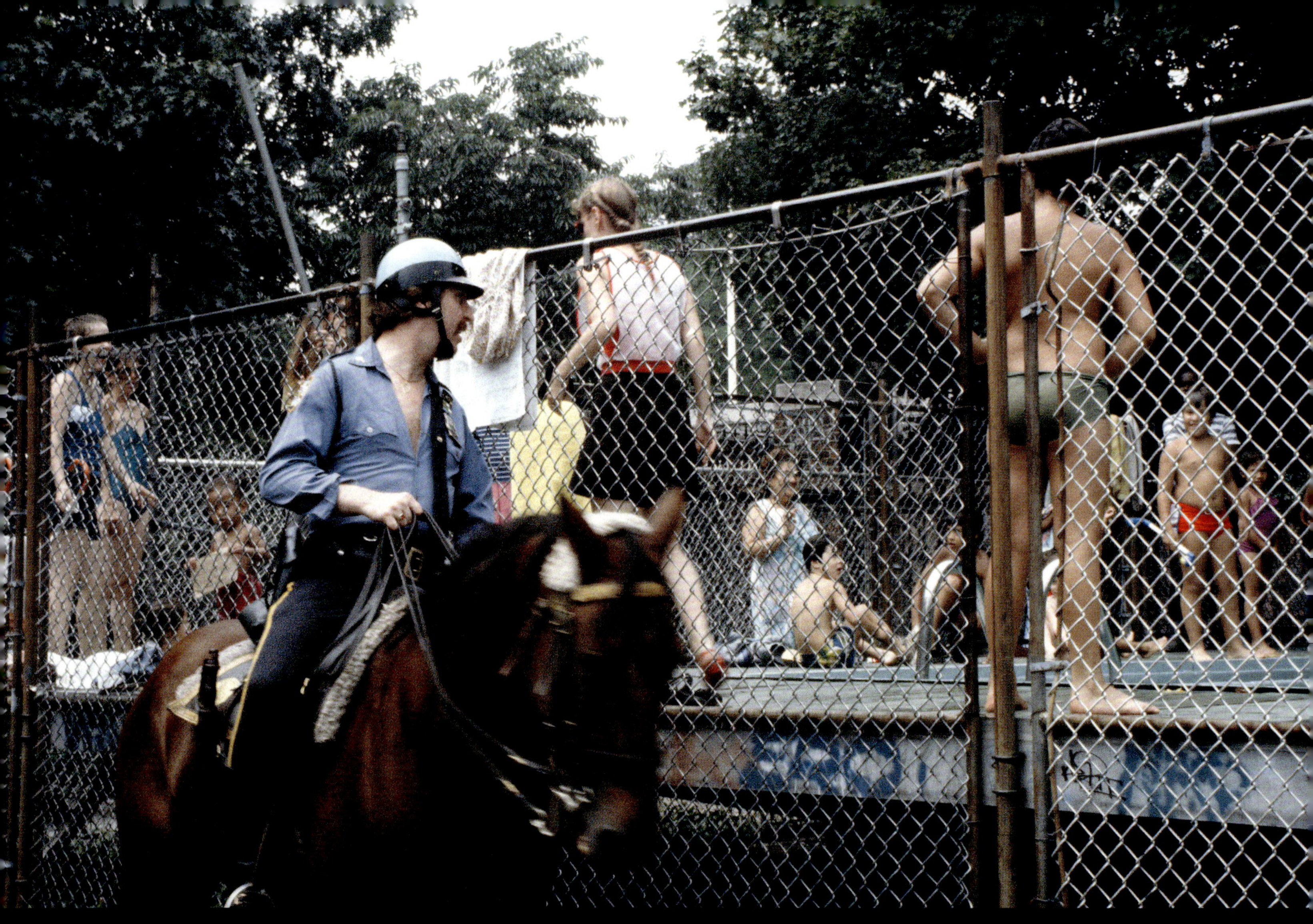

TOMPKINS SQUARE PARK

Kids swimming, cop in "casual dress mode"
checking in, and summer camps taking a break

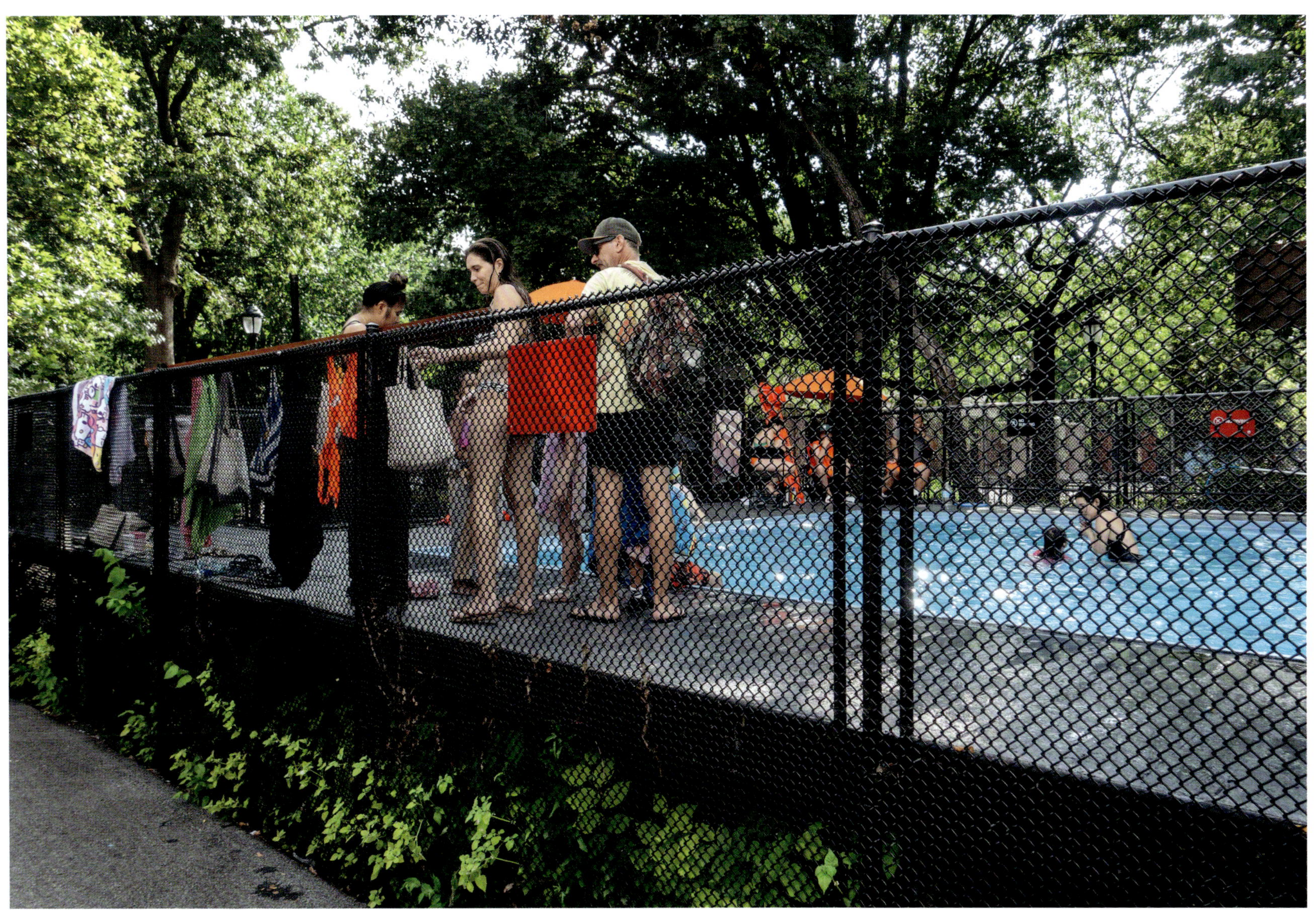

After being closed for years, the
pool finally has water again.

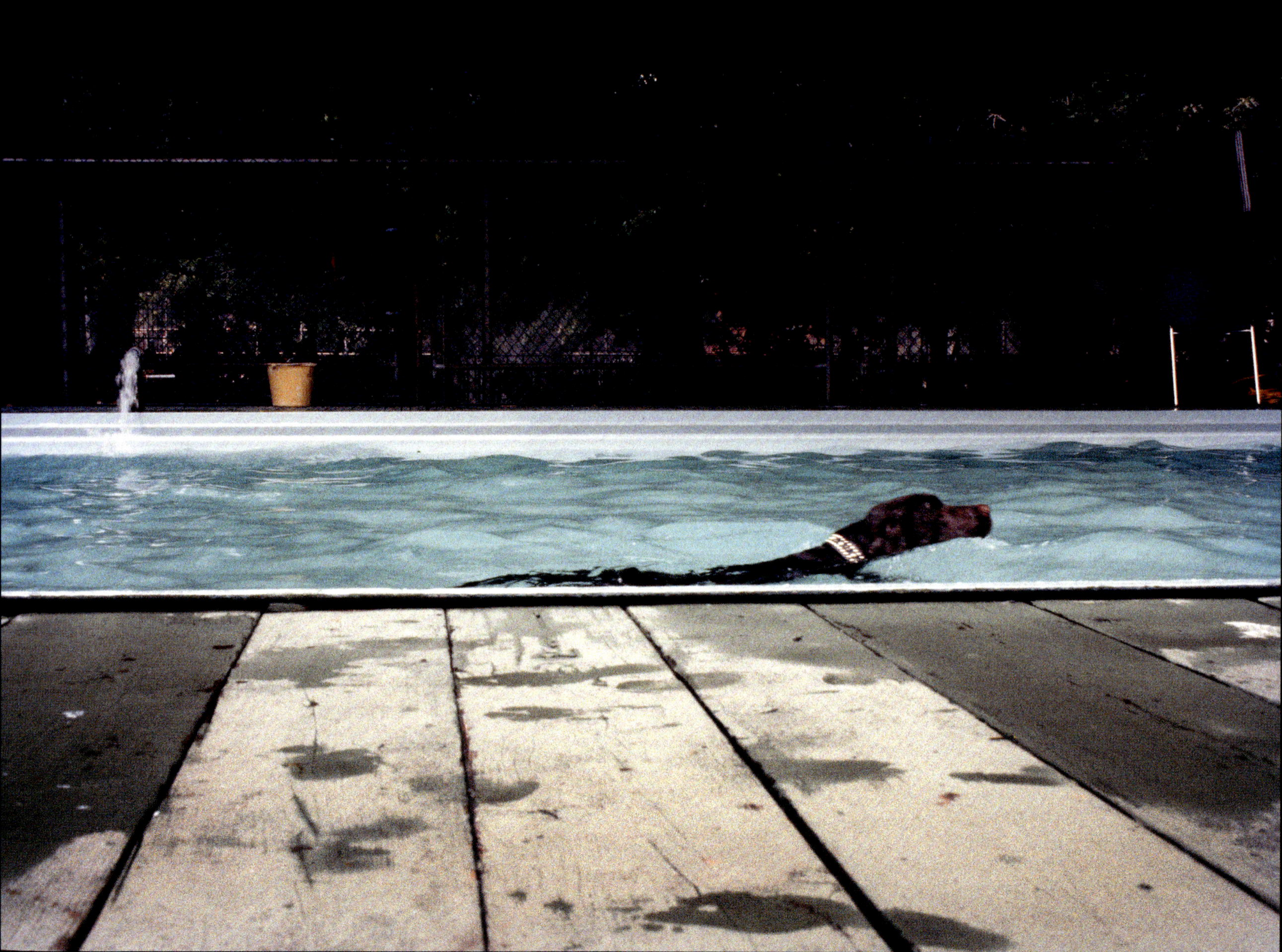

TOMPKINS SQUARE PARK
The dog days of summer and a cool swim.

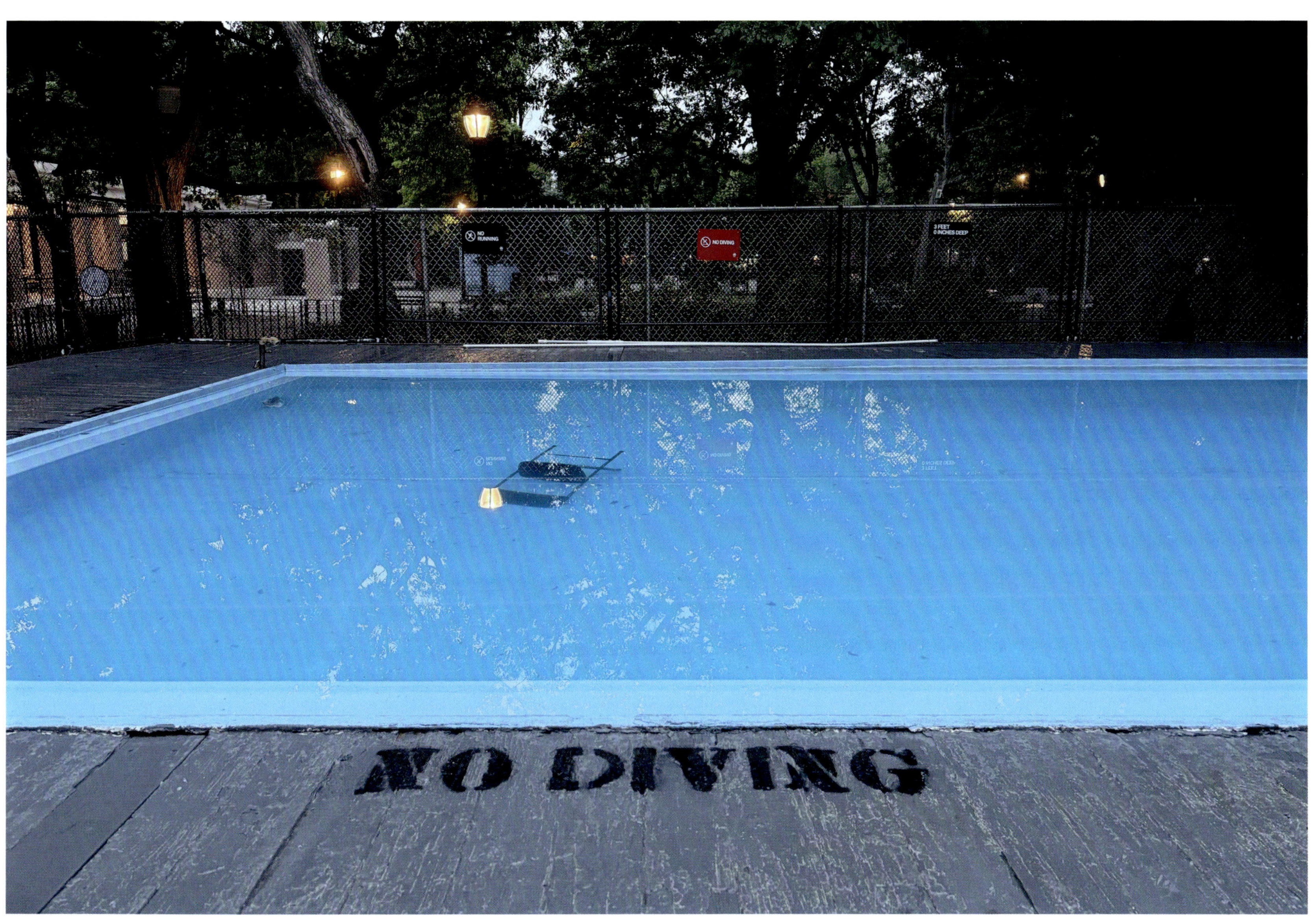

No Diving.

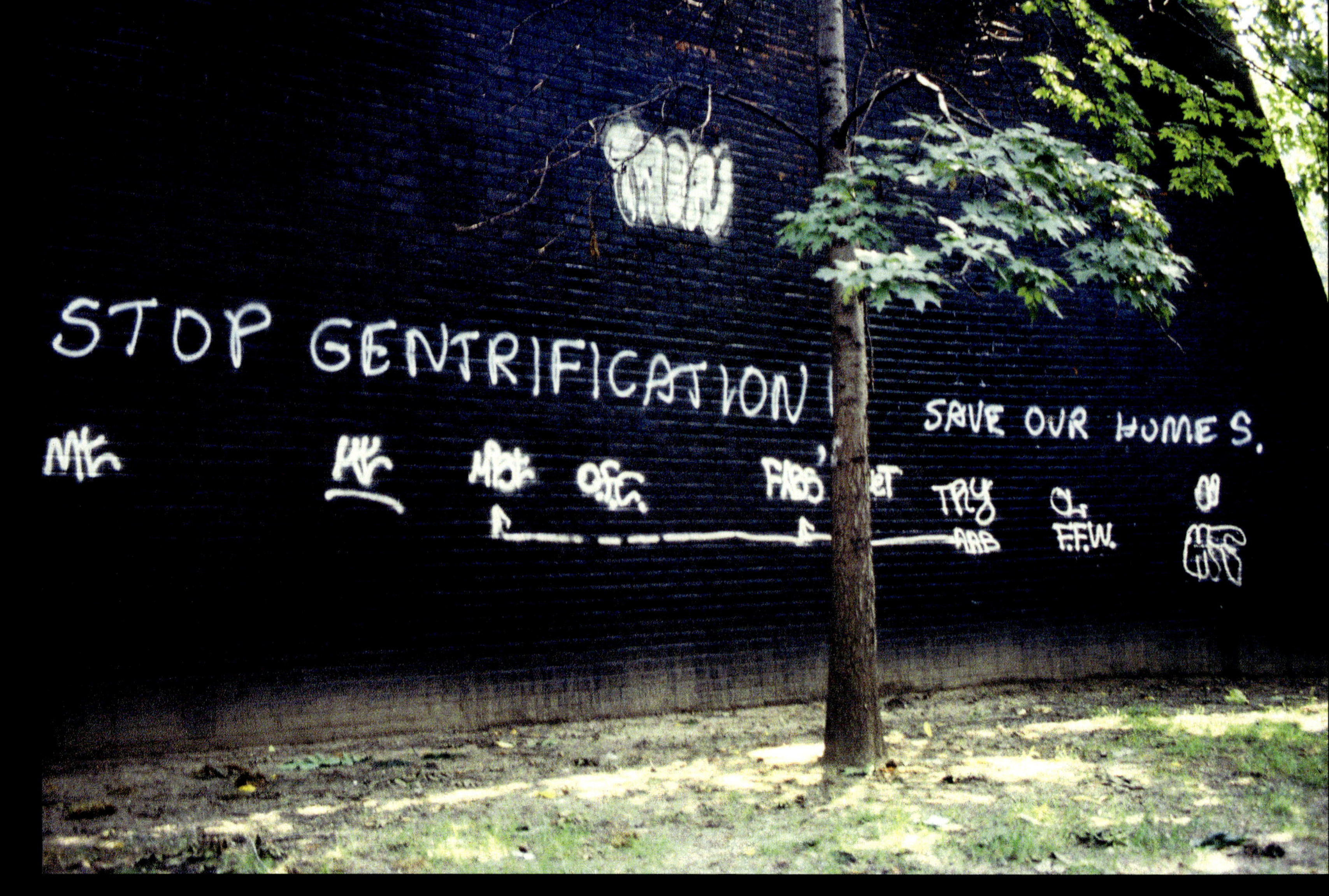

TOMPKINS SQUARE PARK

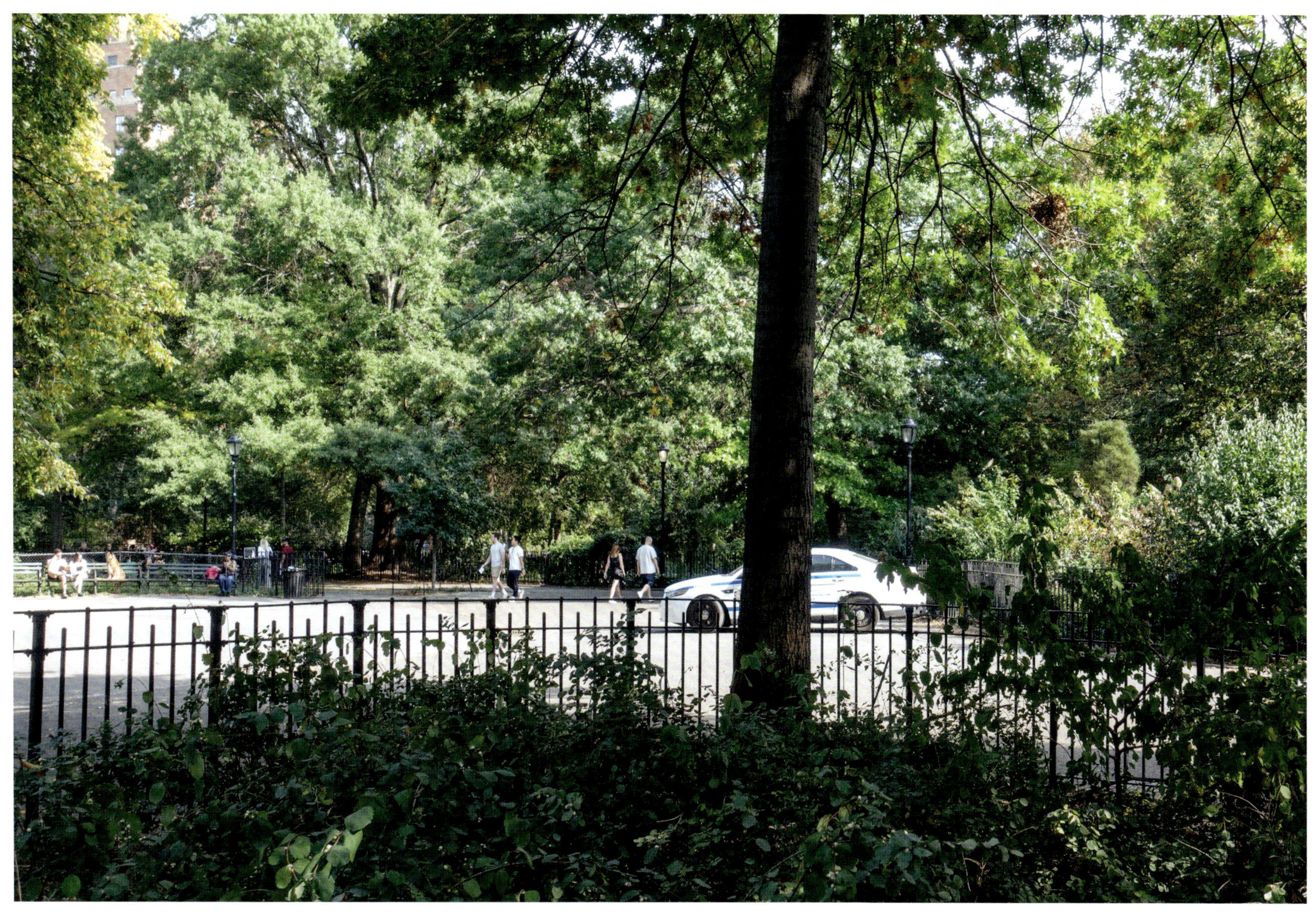

The bandshell is gone. At least
there's a similar tree.

More local opinions being made known on the bandshell.

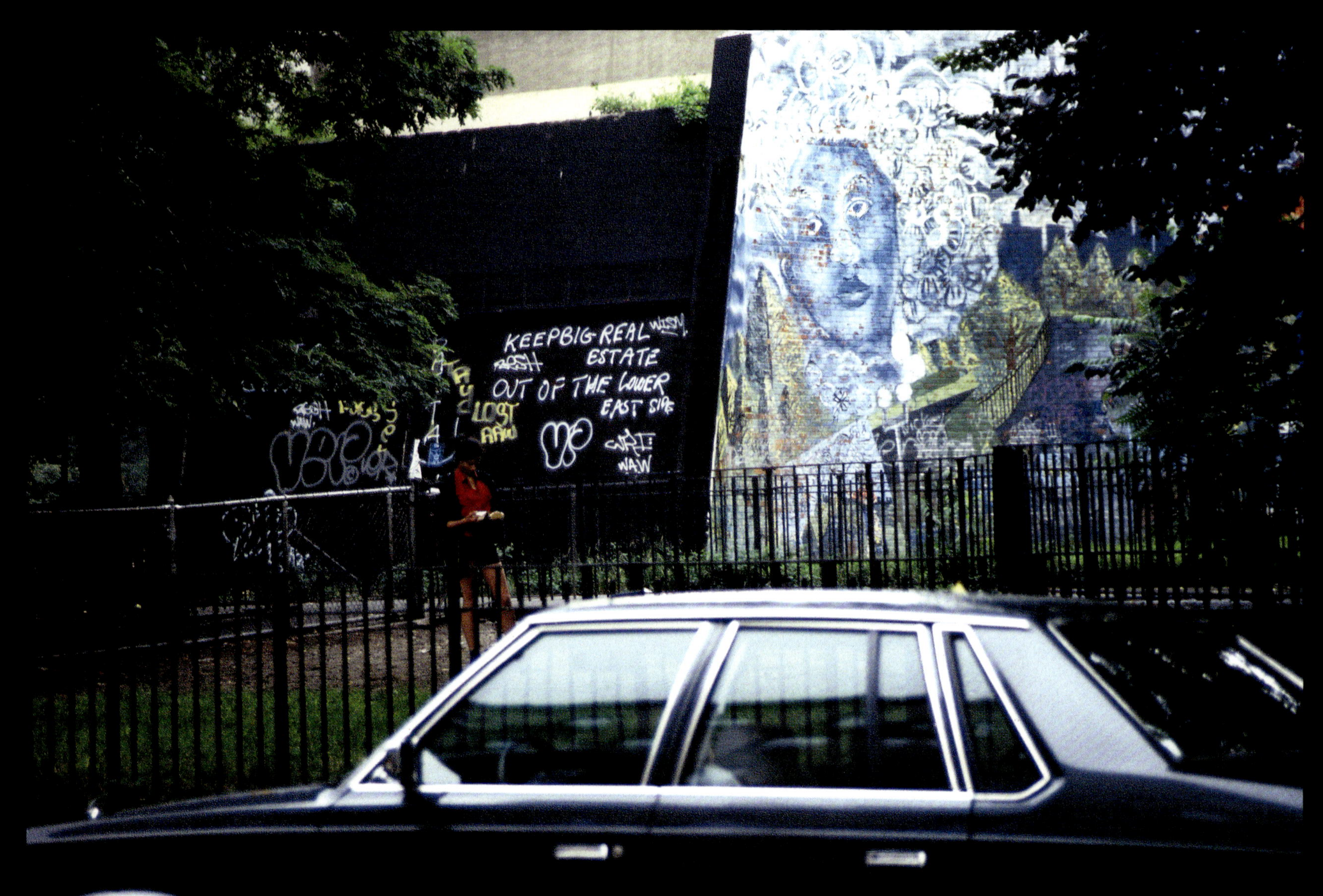

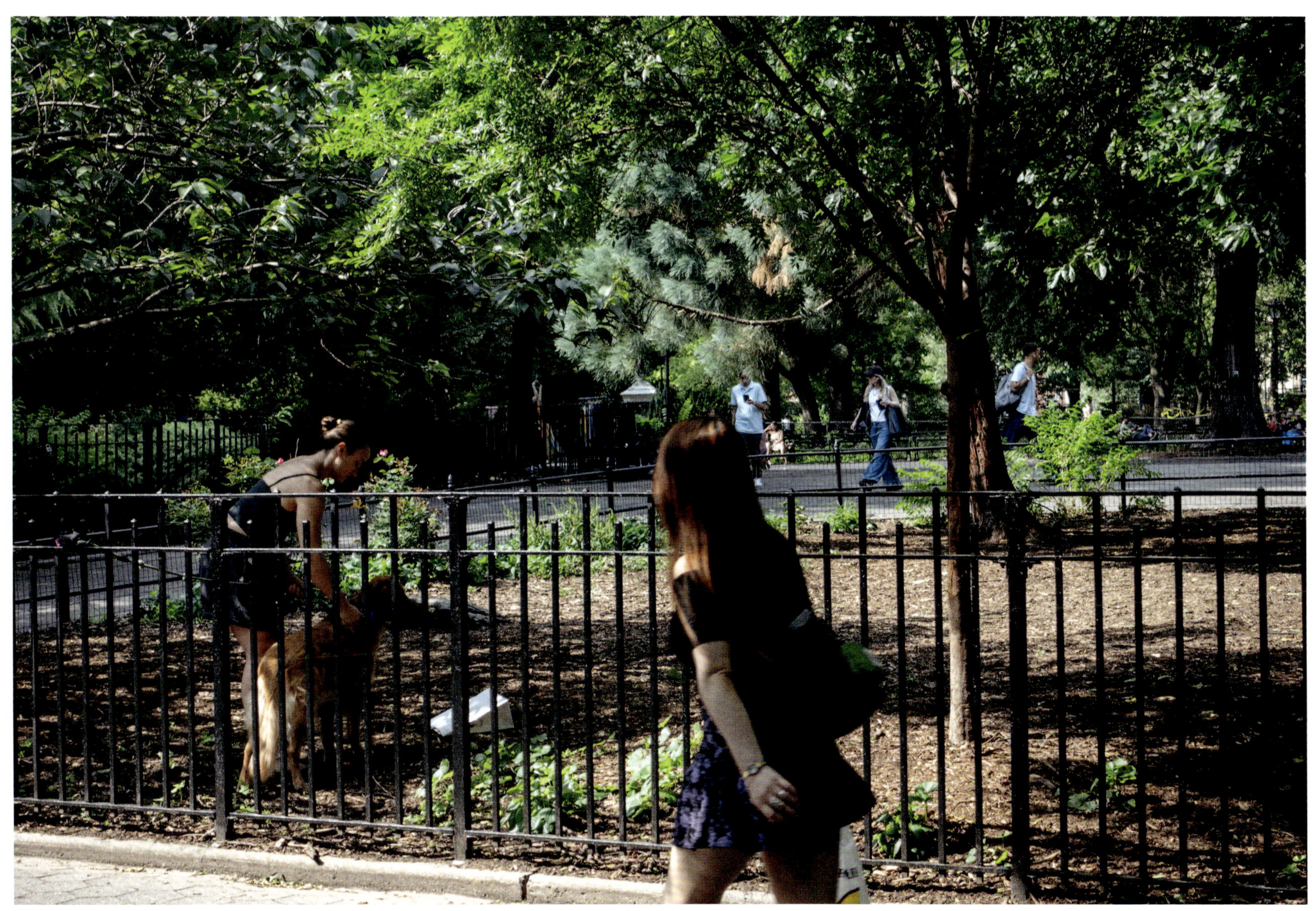

The ghost of the bandshell, from 7th Street.

TOMPKINS SQUARE PARK

THEN Lots of people taking a break.

NOW More people taking a break.

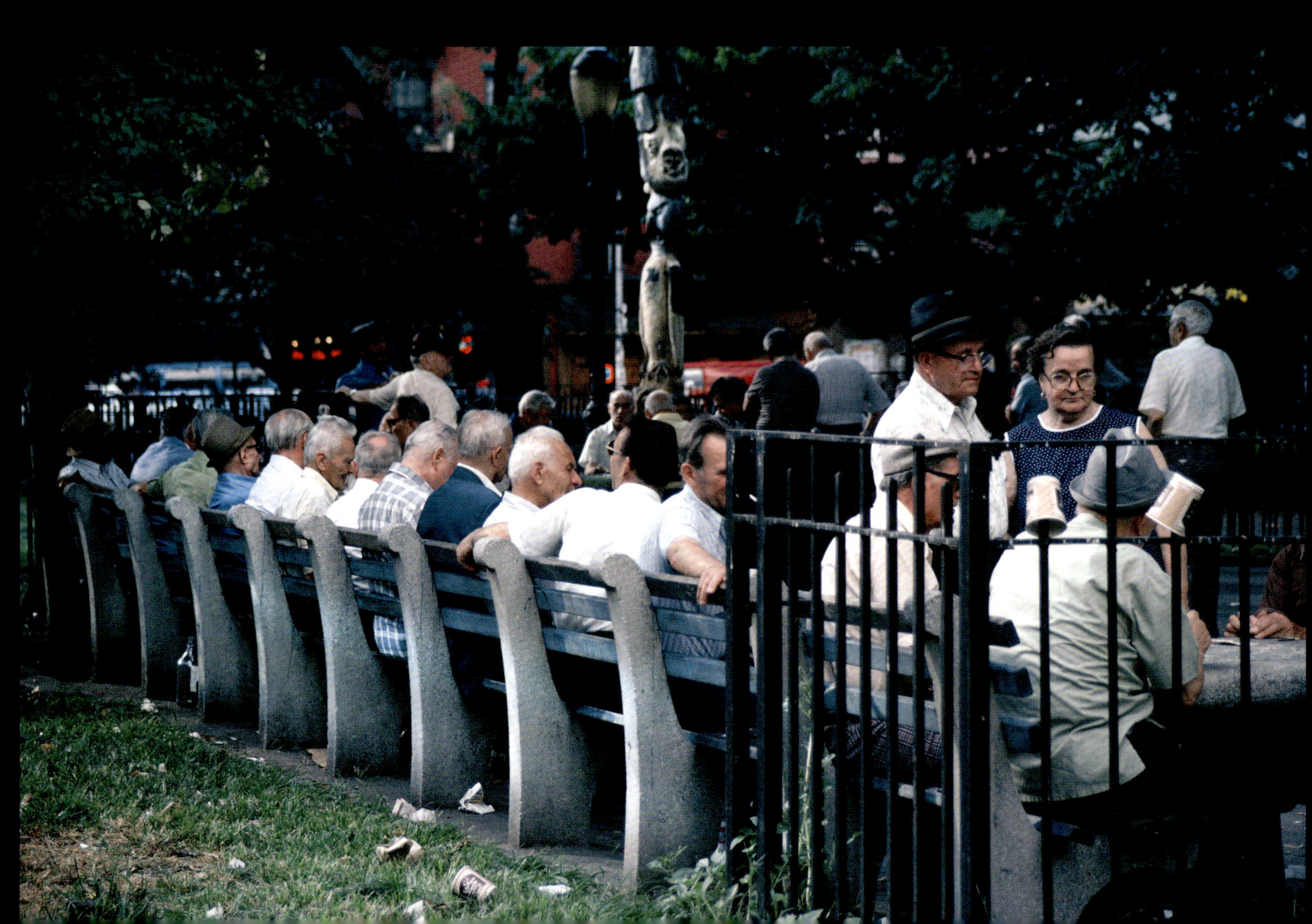

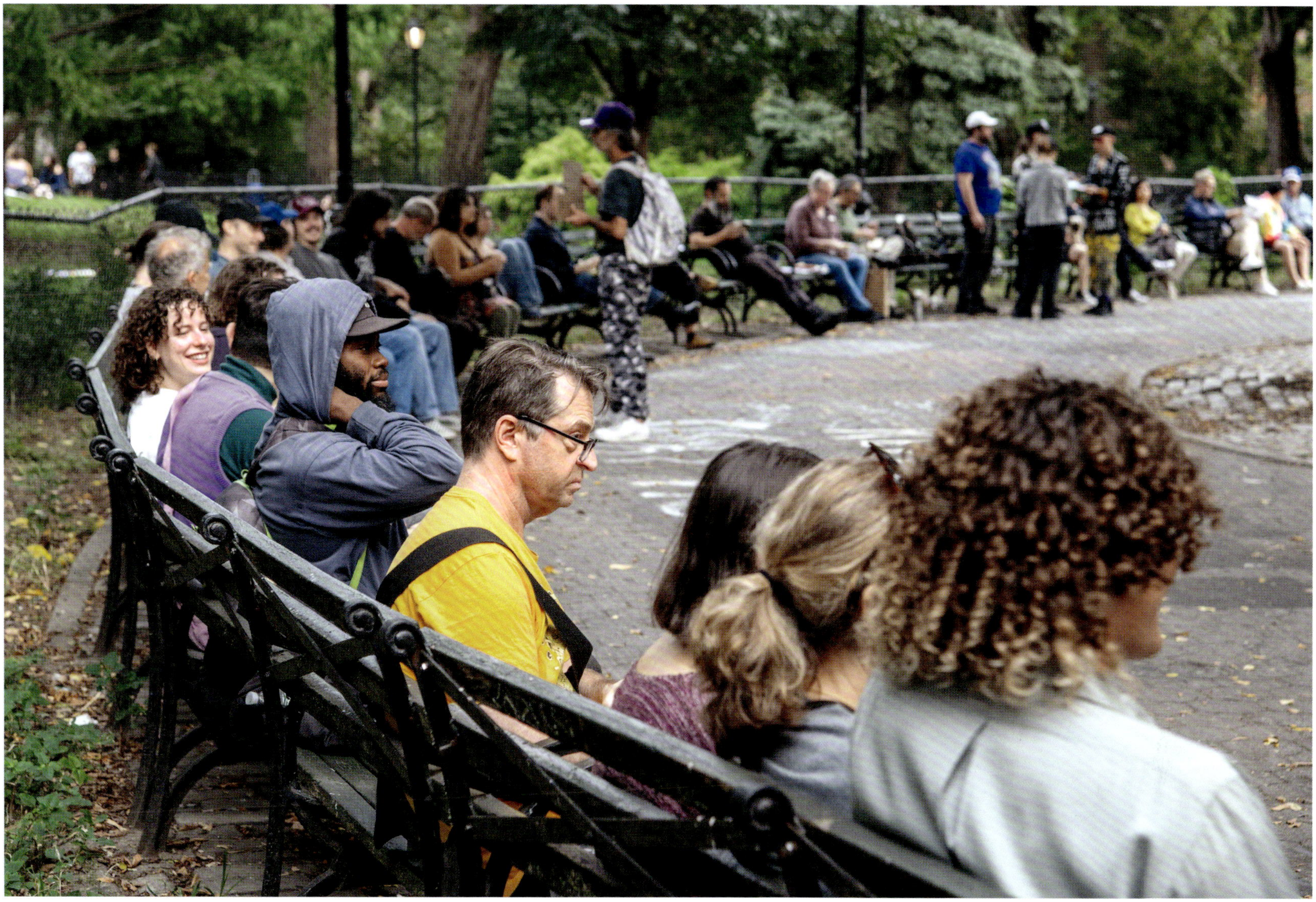

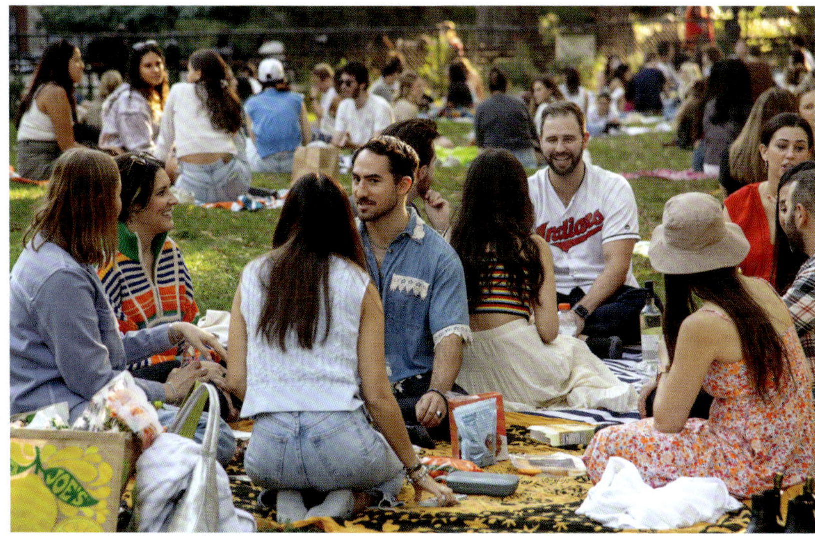

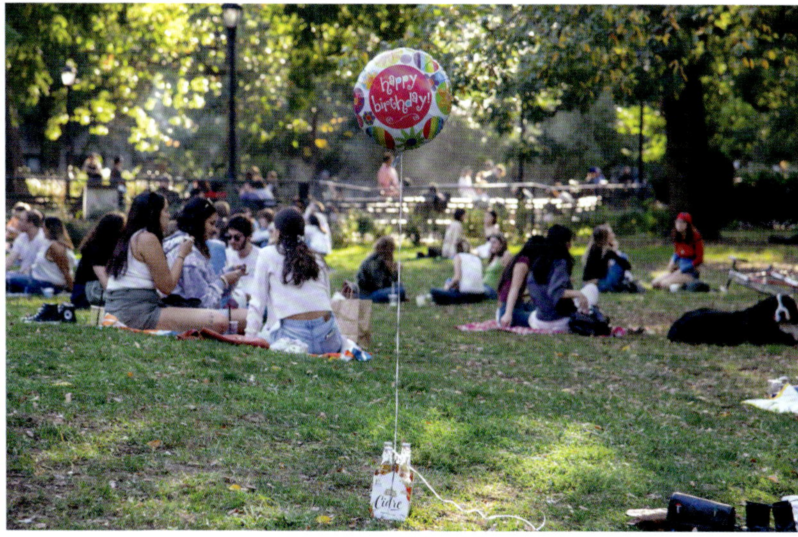

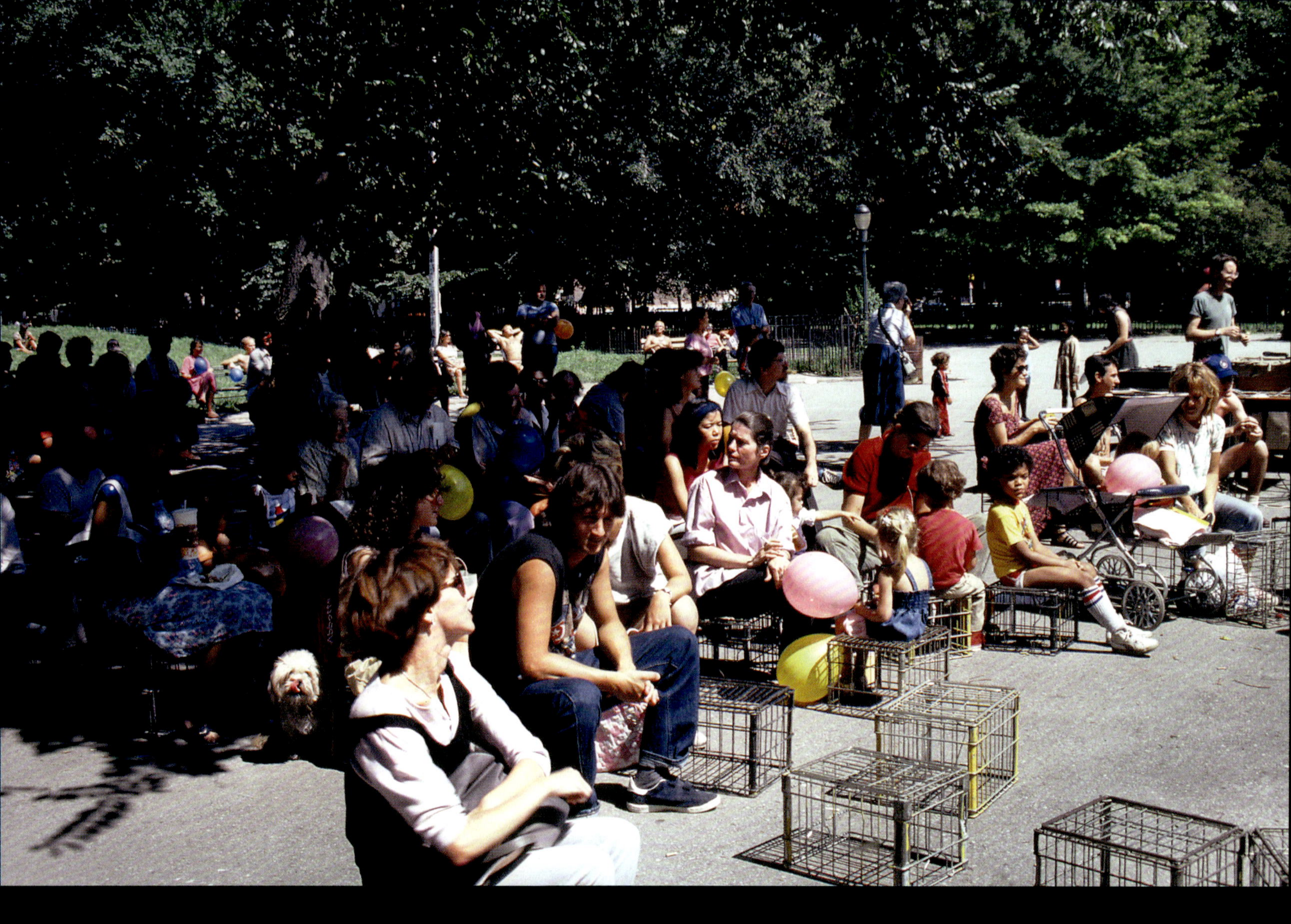

TOMPKINS SQUARE PARK

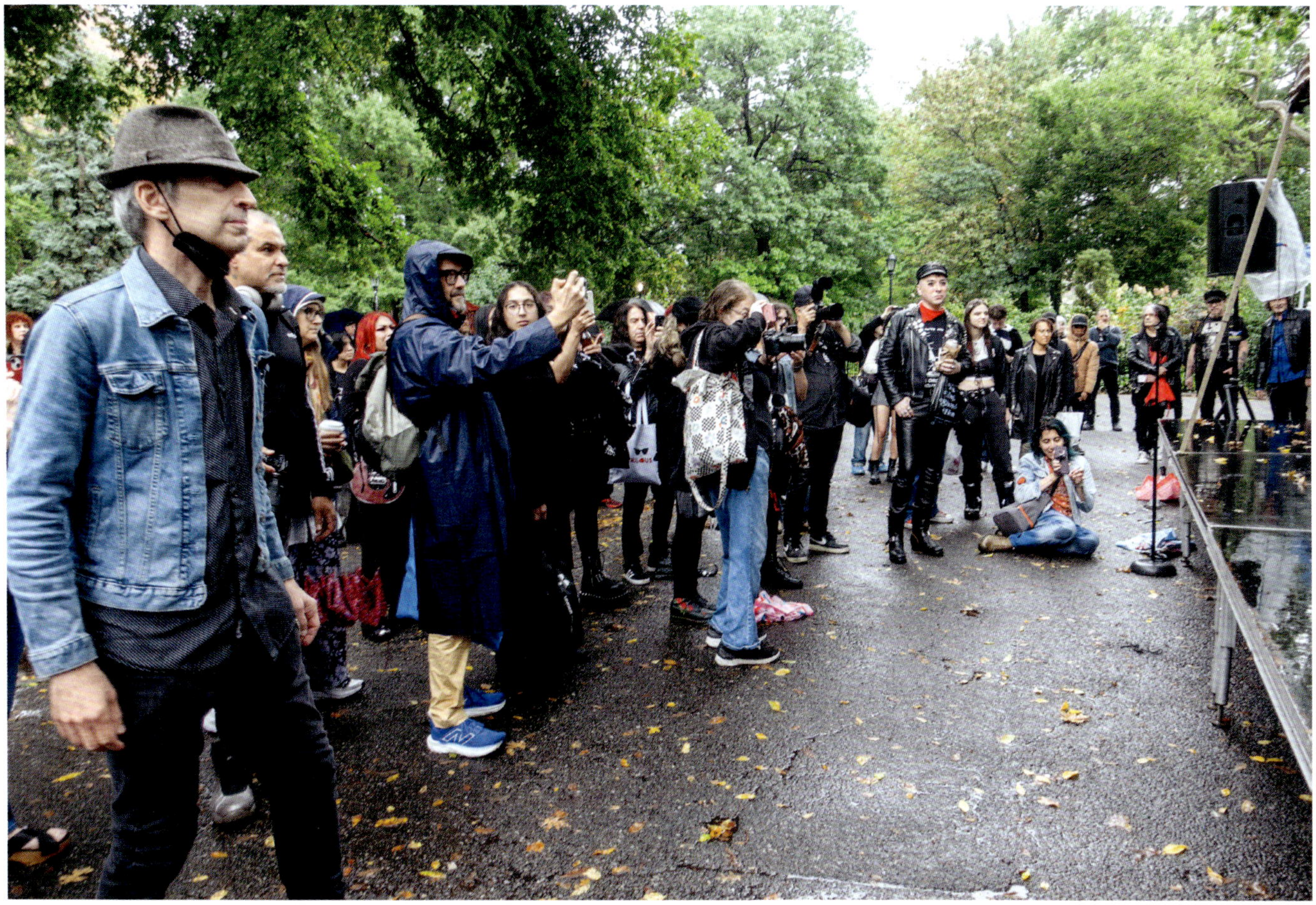

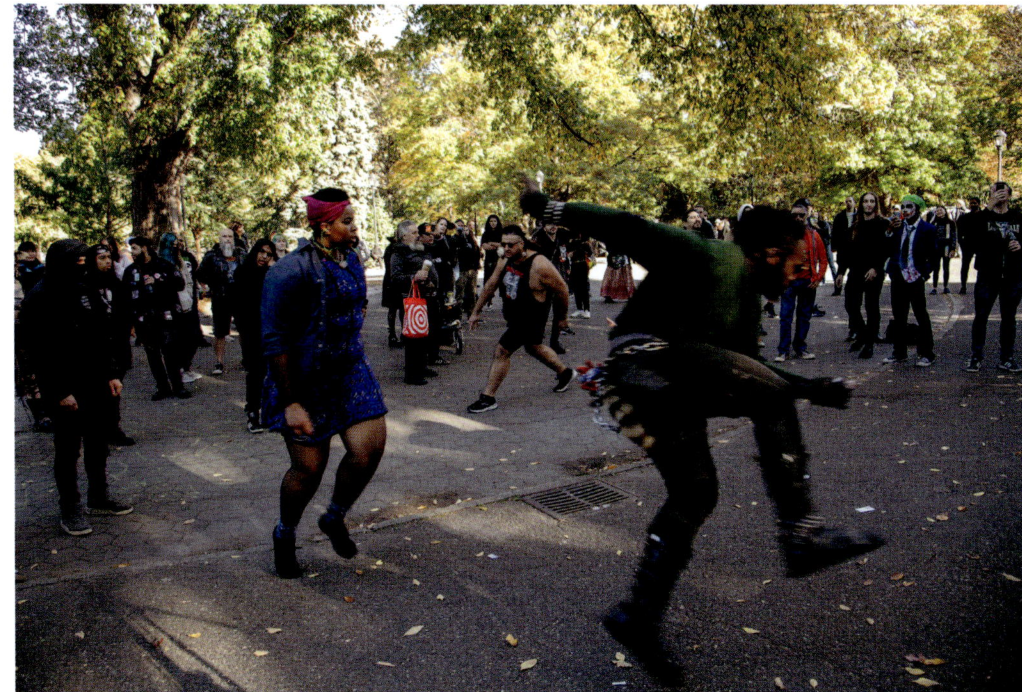

Enjoying the show.

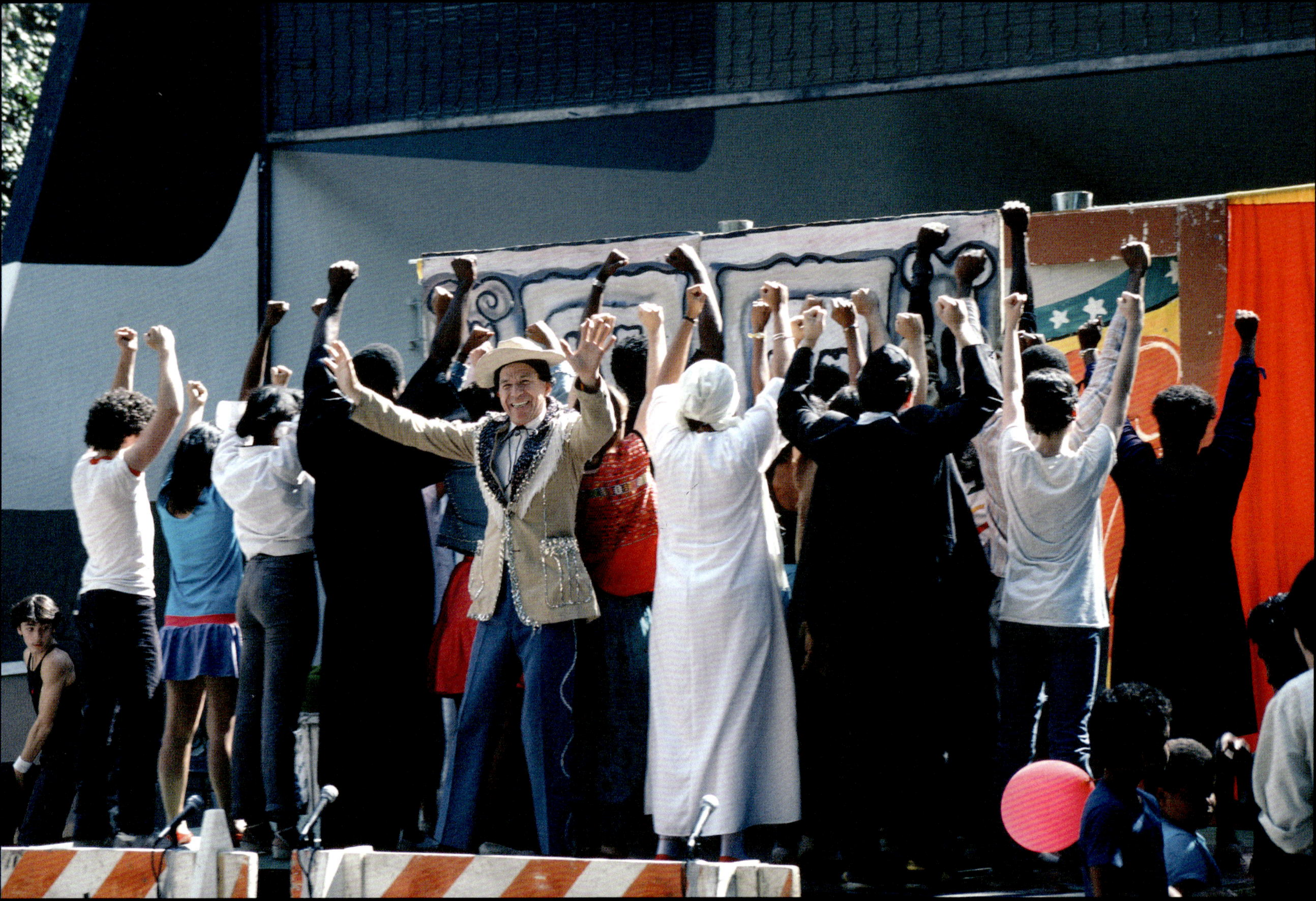

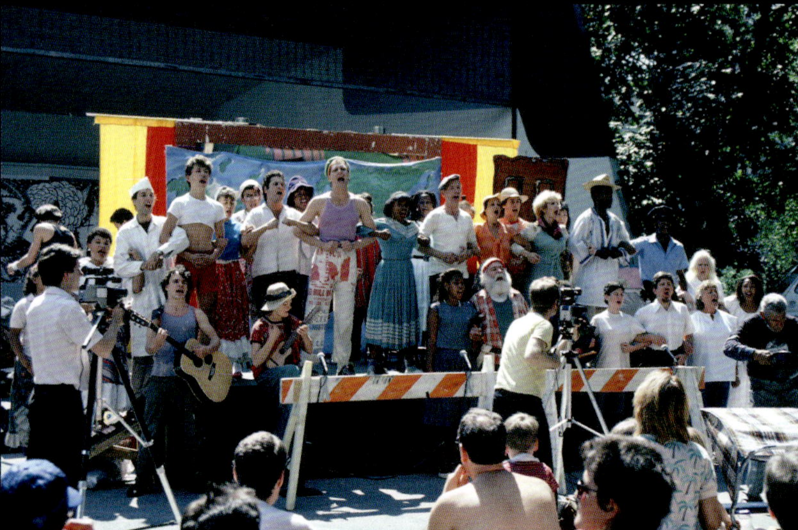

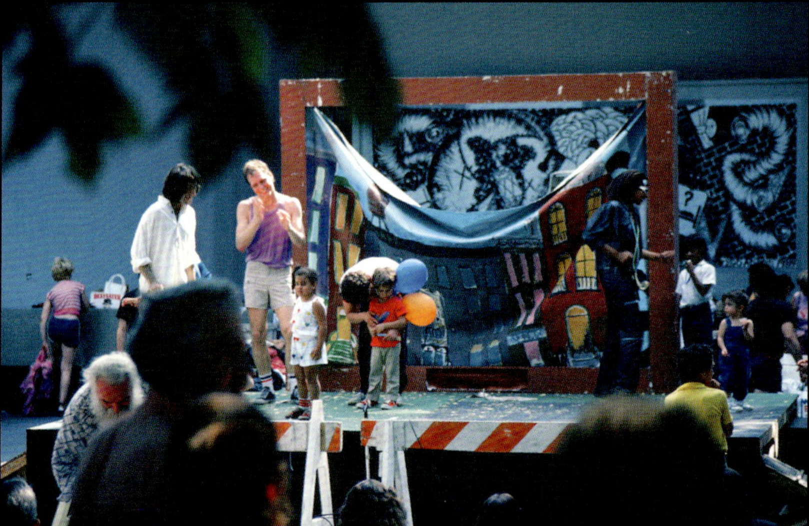

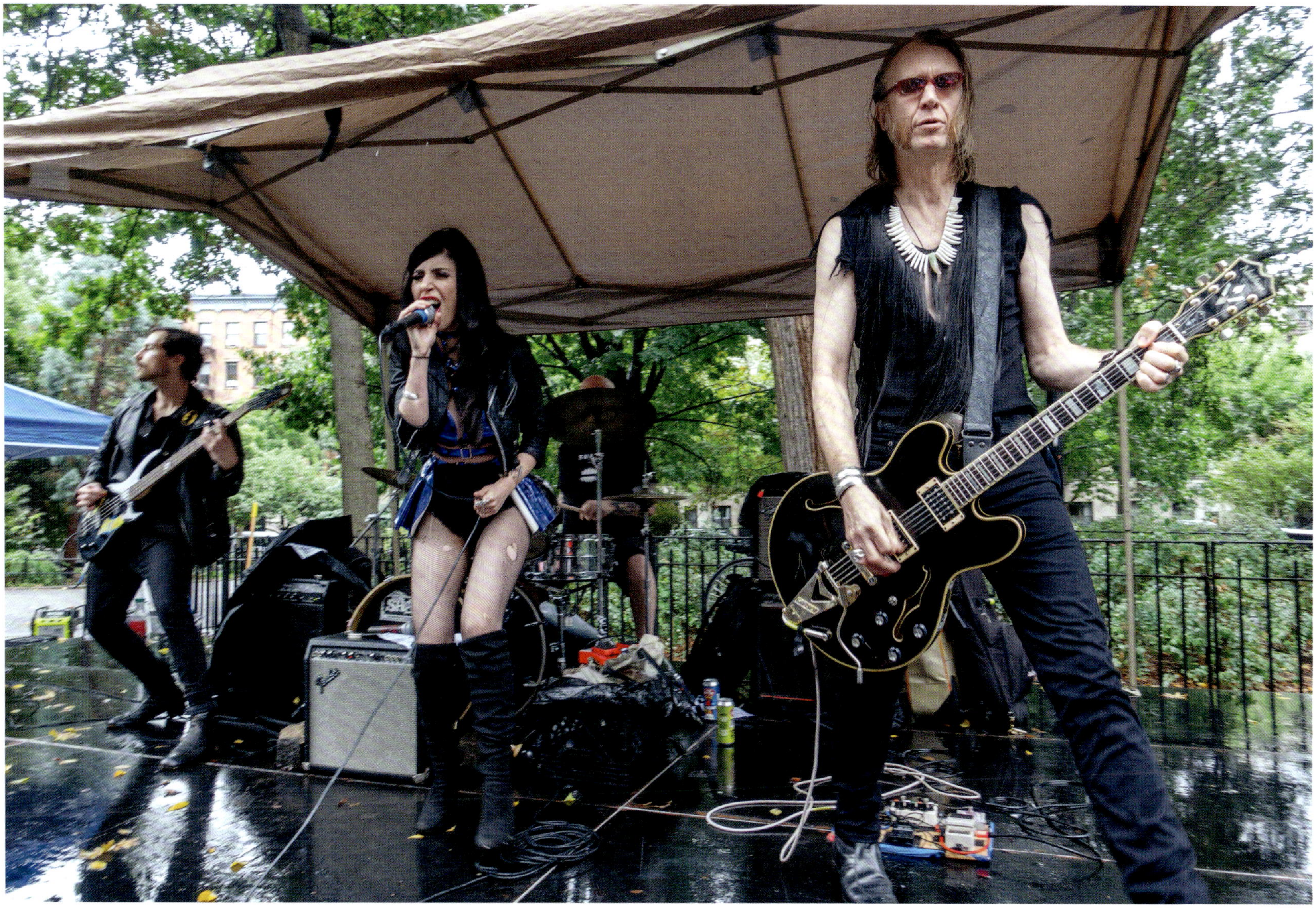

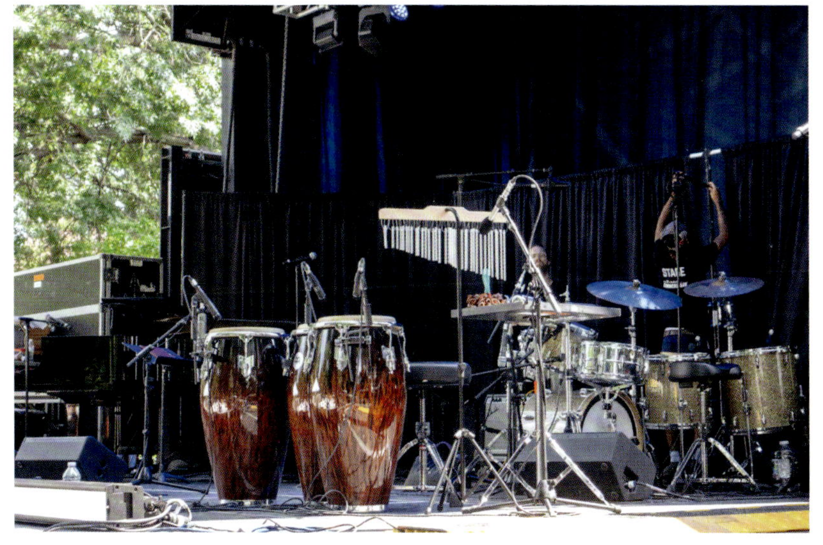

TOMPKINS SQUARE PARK

THEN A performance from the bandshell before it was torn down. That bandshell was the first place the Grateful Dead played in New York City, in 1967.

NOW Making do with temporary bandshells. The big events, like the Charlie Parker Jazz Festival, get the big mobile bandshell. Others, not so much. (Charlie Parker lived on Avenue B between 9th and 10th Street.)

YUPS FROM THE CHRISTODORA VIEW UNSIGHTLY MESS—POVERTY IS OKAY BUT NOT SO CLOSE TO THEIR CO-OP.

THIS IS NOT QUAINT!

NEW MERCHANT

YOUNG PUERTO RICANS HANG OUT (SATURDAY NIGHT AT THE BEACH.)

POOL FOR WASHING UP—DO-GOODERS EVEN SWIM IN IT

EAST 10TH STREET

STONED WORSHIPPERS AT DRUID TEMPLE (REST ROOMS)

SPRINKLERS

NICE SLEEP AREA—WITH CANDLES, MUSIC, DRINKING, DRUGS...

DISGUSTING!

BASEBALL DIAMOND—NEUTRAL, AND GOOD GAMES

CITY OFFICIAL

MOVE 'EM OUT!

DEVELOPER

POLISH, UKRAINIAN VODKA DRINKERS

HARE KRISHNA FOOD WAGON

FOR CRACK, CUSTOMERS GO TO NEARBY STORES →

HIPPIE ACTIVISTS

'60s BURNOUT

LATINO AND BLACK CHESS PLAYERS AND MUSICIANS KNOW IT'S ALL ABOUT REAL ESTATE

GOOD SLEEPING BEATS THE SHELTER

NEIGHBORS FOR FIFTY YEARS

CRIMINAL ON LAM

DOG WALKERS POOPERS HEAVEN

MARAUDING GANG LOOKING FOR UNWARY

LSD DEALER

CHARITY MONUMENT—ALCOHOLICS AND HARE KRISHNAS →

ACTIVIST POET

POLITICAL AGITATOR

RASTAFARIANS SELLING POT, PLAYING MUSIC...

PLAYGROUND—NEUTRAL

CITY CUTS DOWN TREES BECAUSE OF ELM DISEASE (REALLY FOR BETTER SURVEILLANCE)

AVENUE A

AVENUE B

KINDHEARTED PARKS WORKER—WHO LOVES FLOWERS BUT IS AFRAID TO MAKE IT TOO NICE BECAUSE DEVELOPERS WILL MOVE IN FASTER

BAPTISTS' FOOD WAGON

SHADY, COOL, QUIET SIDE OF PARK

CLOSE THE PARK AND RE-DESIGN IT!

ALCOHOLICS

PARKS DEPT OFFICIAL

SEX, DRUGS, DIRT!

TOP JAZZ MUSICIANS

BANDSHELL—NEUTRAL, FOR HARD DRUG USE →

AWFUL URINE SMELL

DELI OWNER

CAMP GROUNDS

EAST 7TH STREET

UKRAINIAN POLISH CHECKER PLAYERS—(DON'T MESS WITH 'EM, MAY BE EX-FREEDOM FIGHTERS)

SKINHEADS—VIOLENT, RIGHT WING PATRIOTS

NONE OF MY BUSINESS!

PUNKS—LEFT WING COMMIES

'BURB BRATS IN FOR THRILLS

7TH DAY ADVENTISTS' FOOD WAGON

©1988 stan mack

TOMPKINS SQUARE PARK

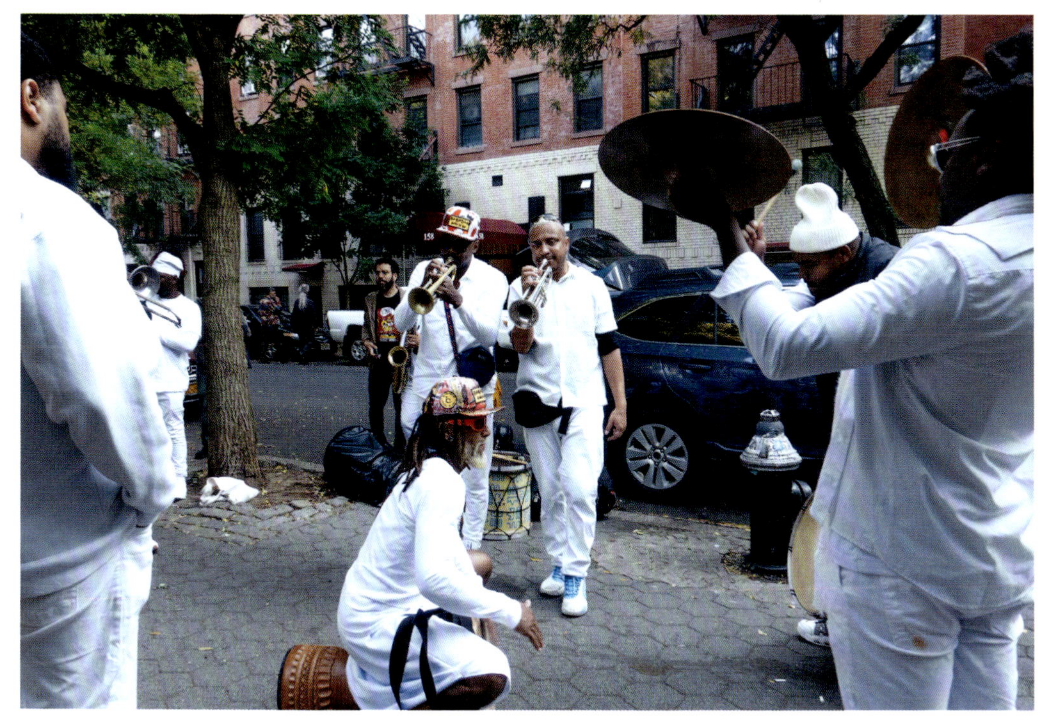

THEN Cartoonist Stan Mack's map of Tompkins Square Park from 1988, the year of the famous riot and three years before the park was closed for restoration.

NOW BaBaDan Banda de Rua (Street Band), from Brazil, picking up the Tompkins Square feel.

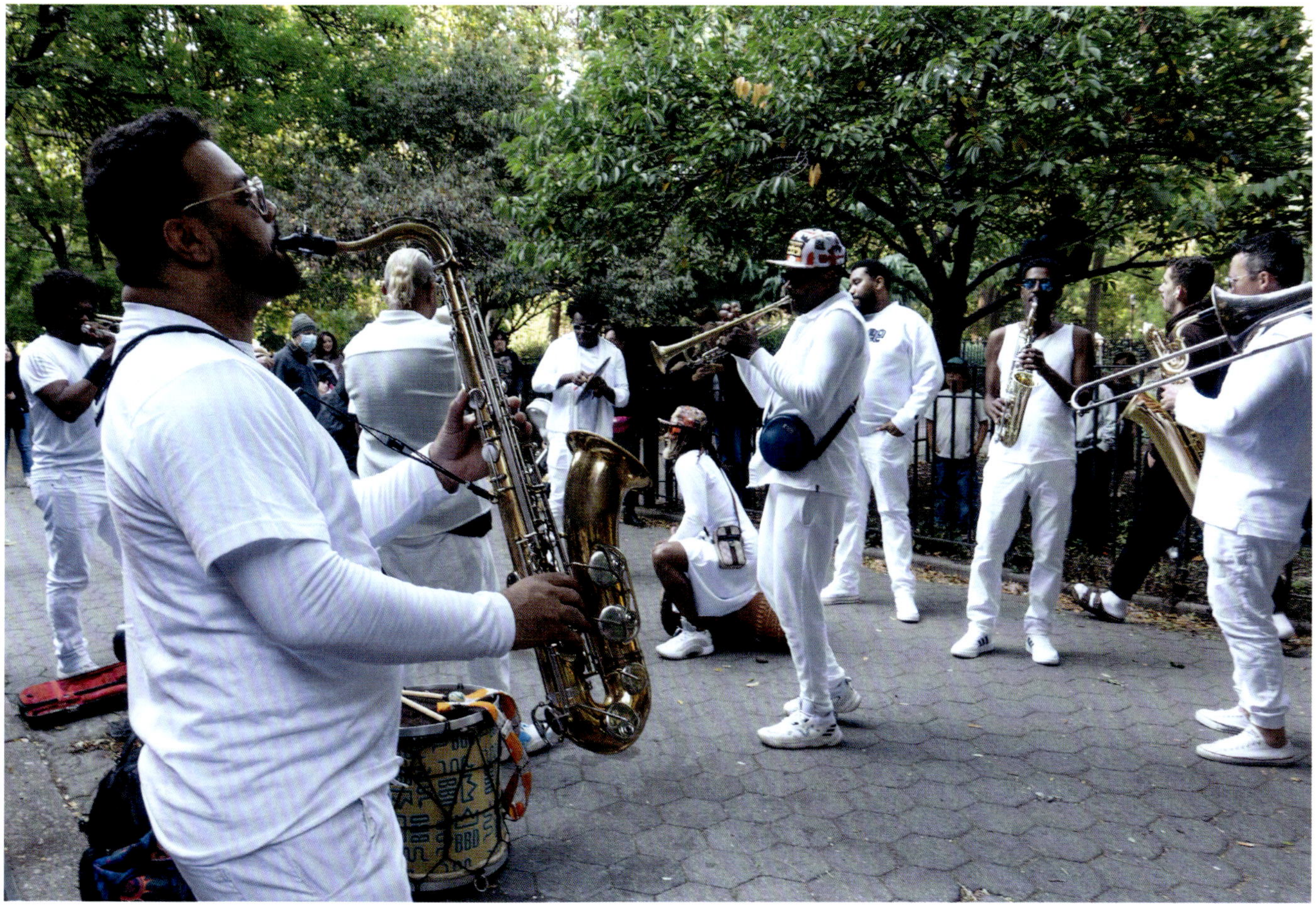

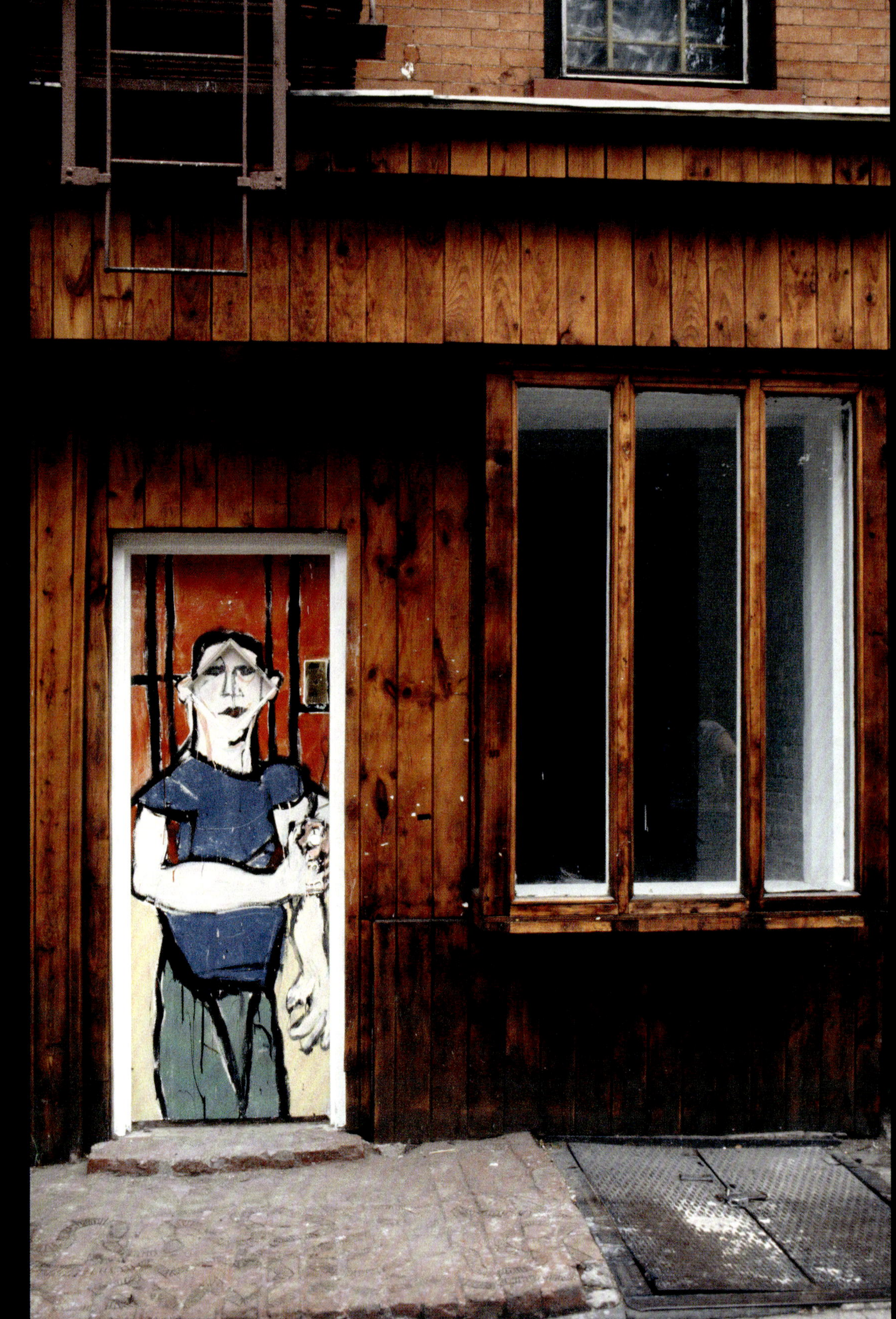

9 EAST 10TH
REET

door to Crowbar.

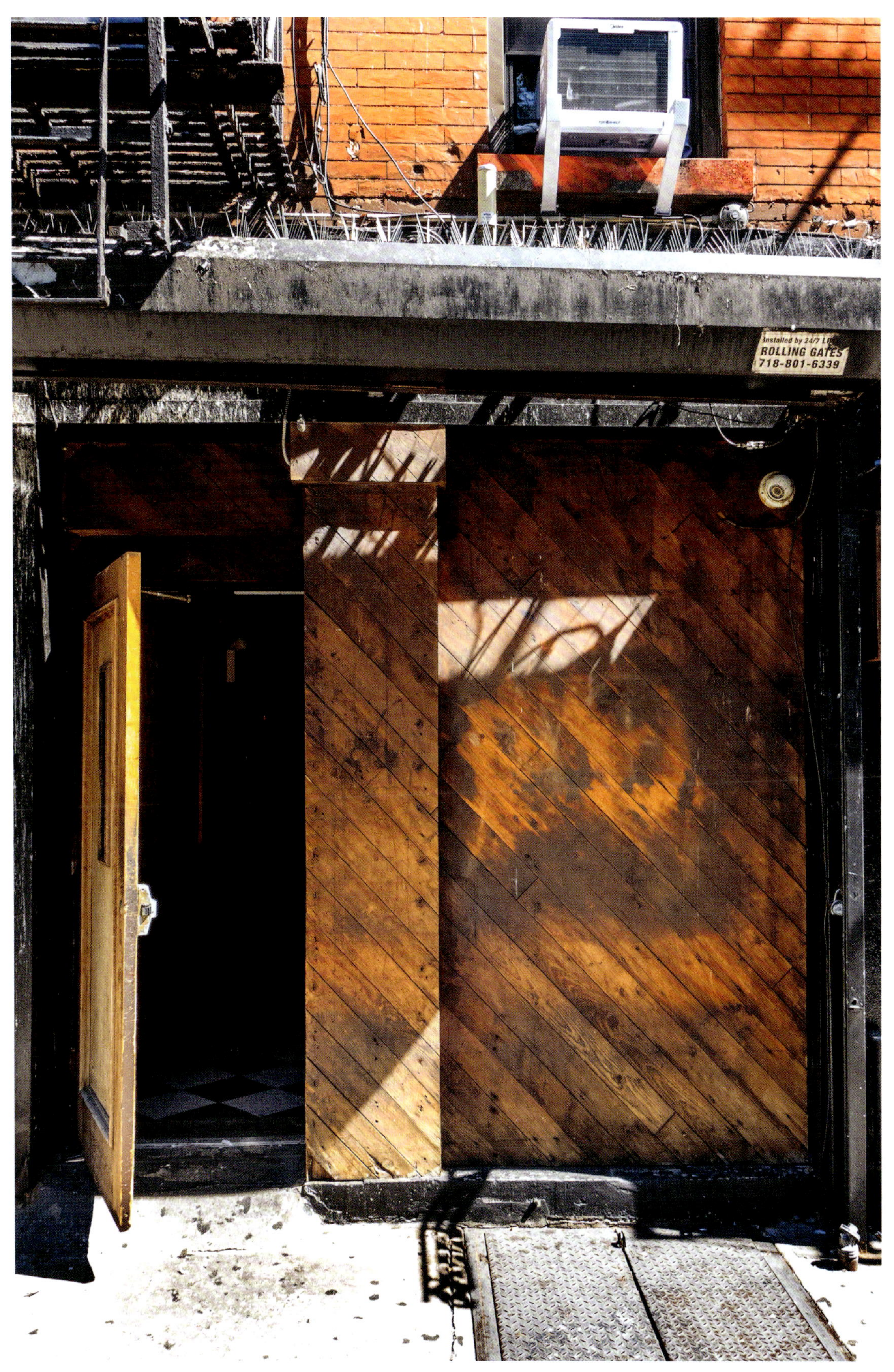

Now it's Blind Barber, entered next
door, through the barbershop.

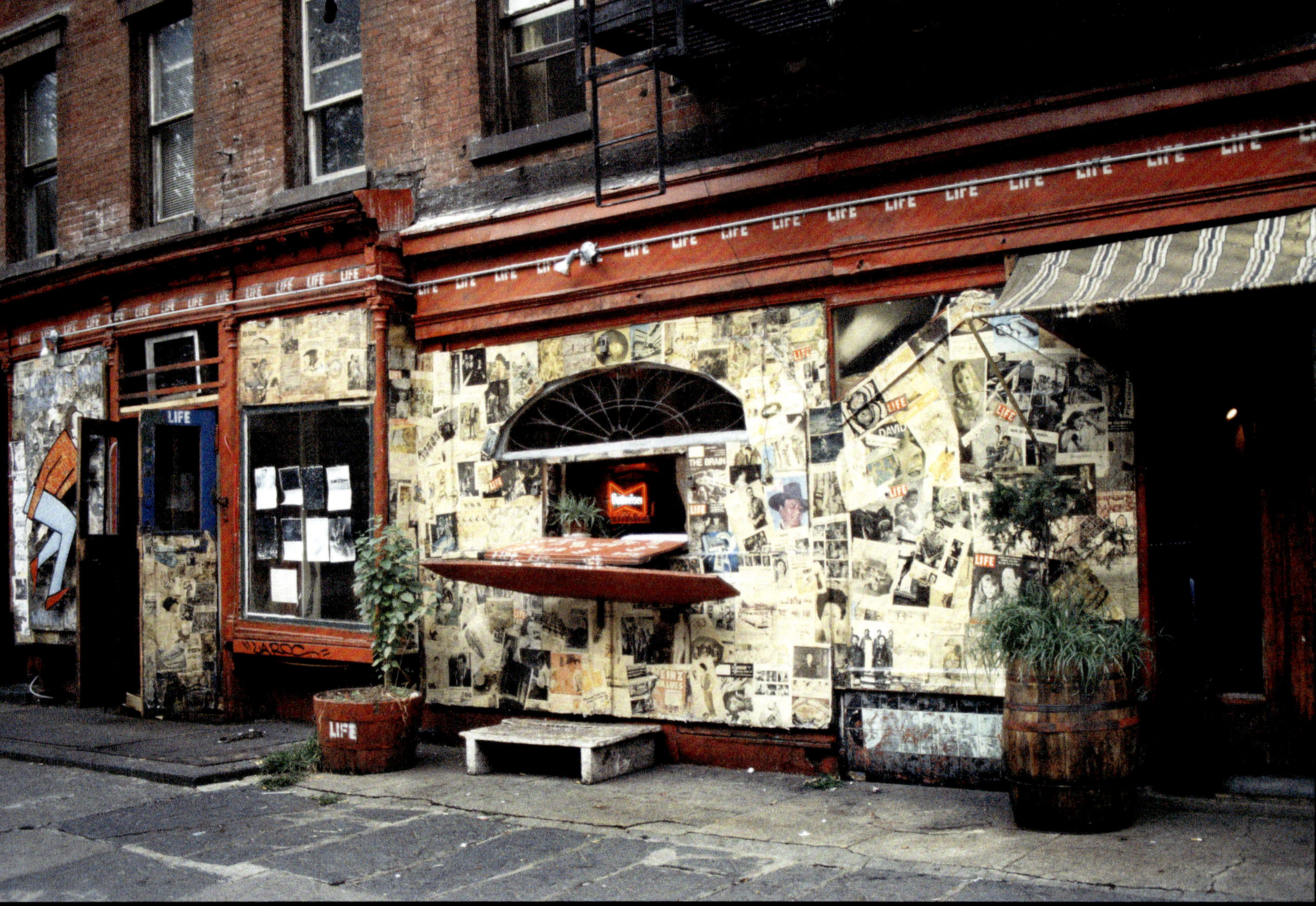

343 EAST 10TH STREET

The original facade of Life Café, with shellacked *Life* magazine pages. Matching bar and tables inside.

Maiden Lane. Beer and food. Tinned fish.

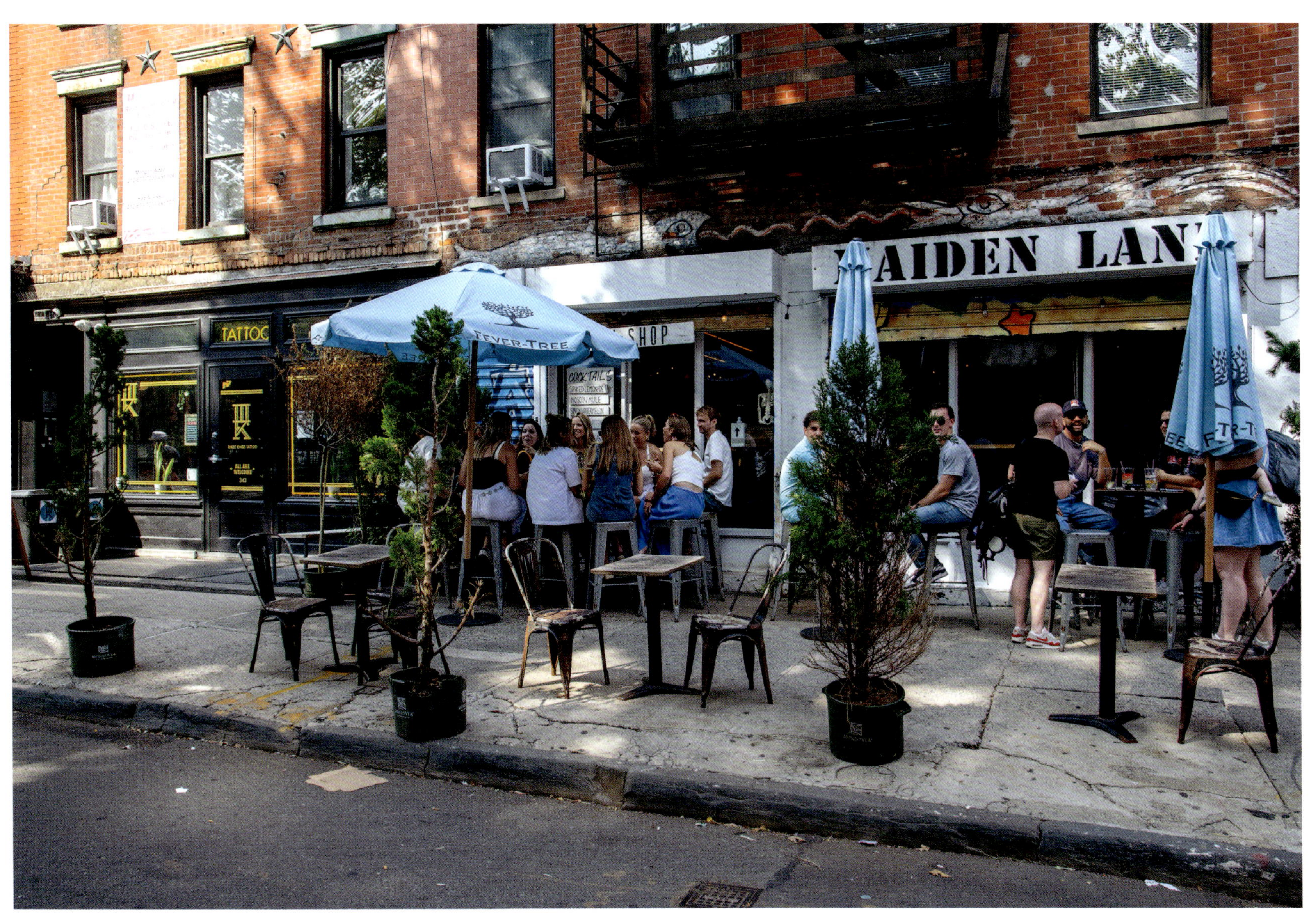

A side door. The unique look of Life Café.

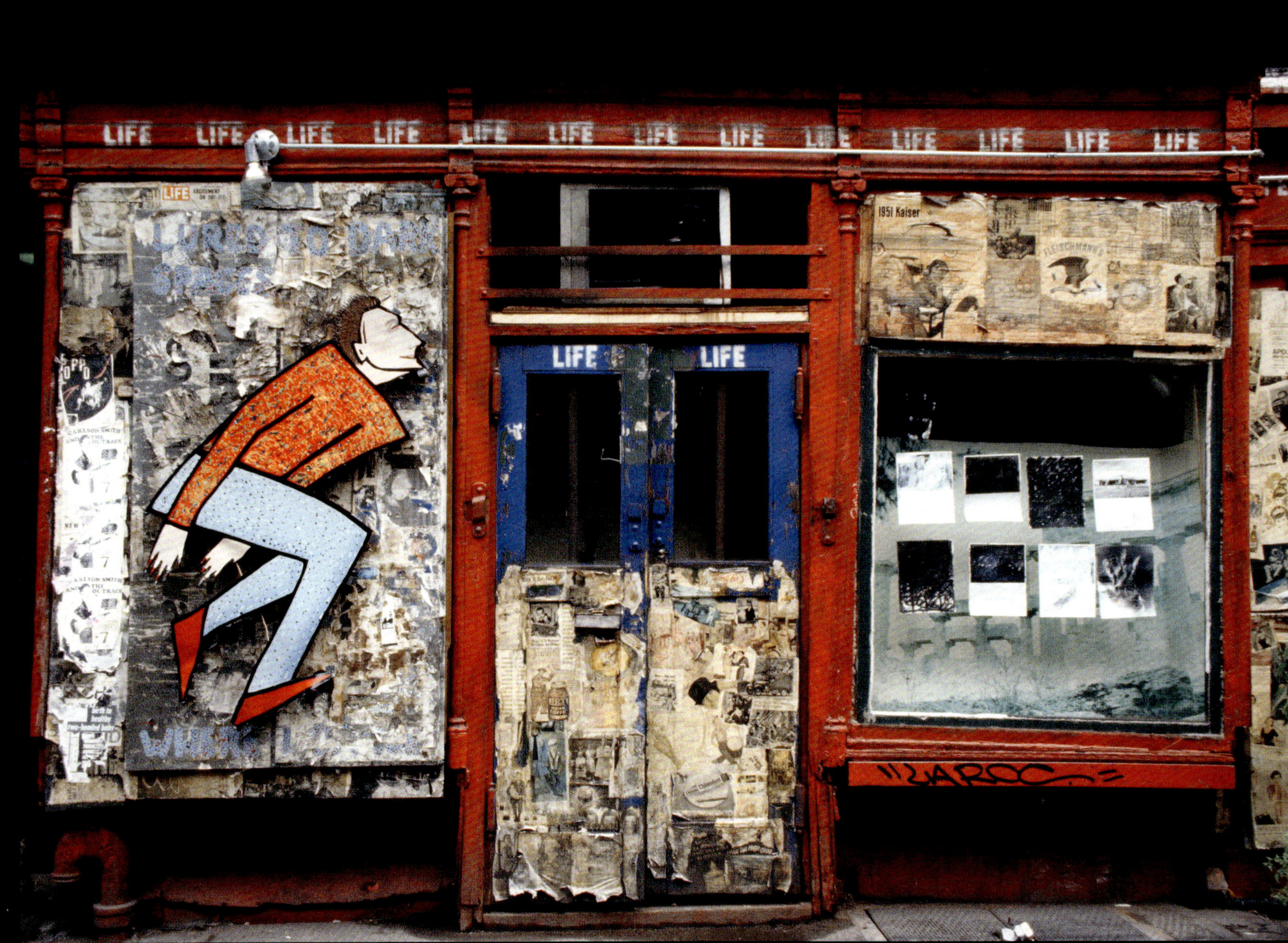

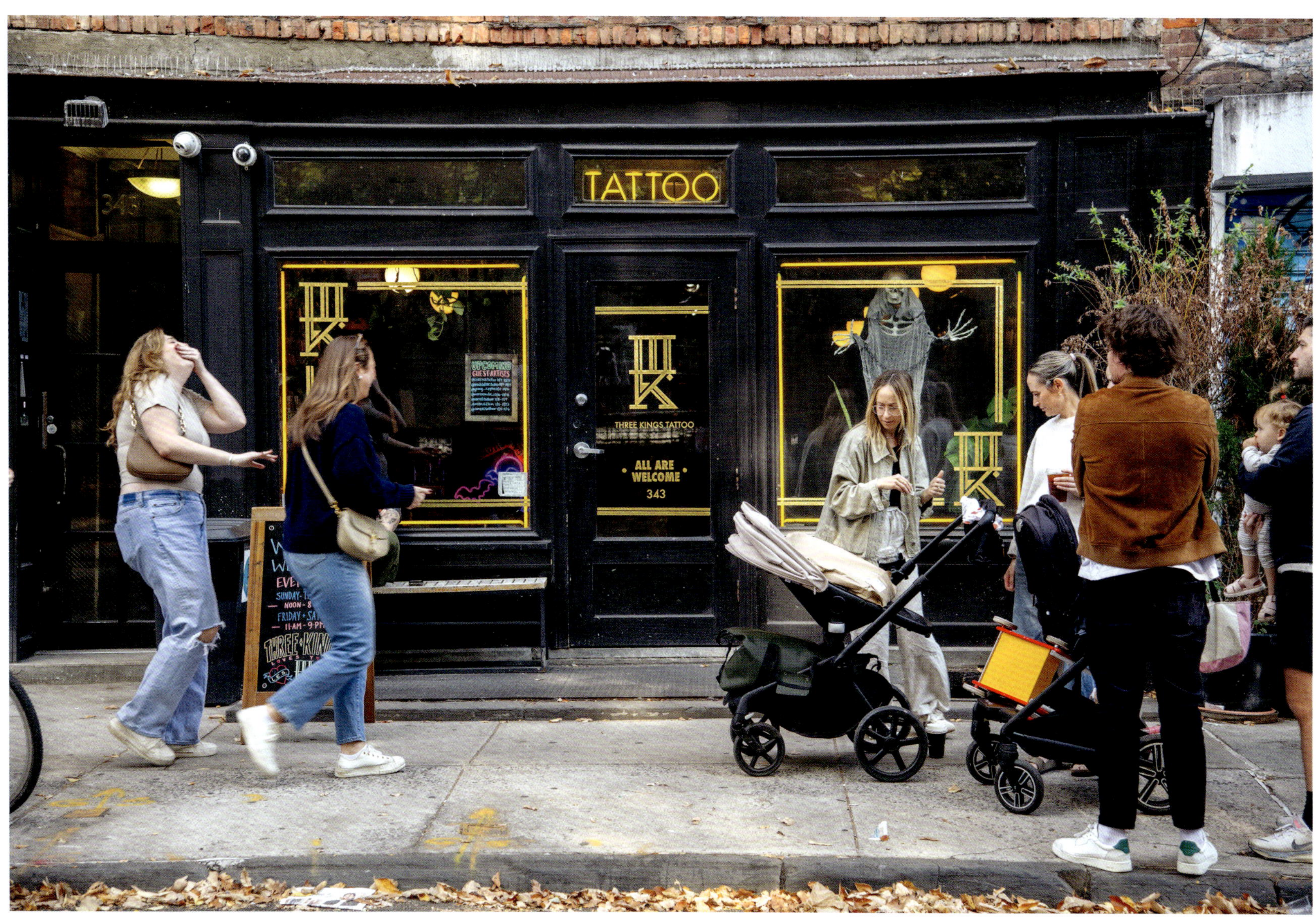

Sunday afternoon strollers.

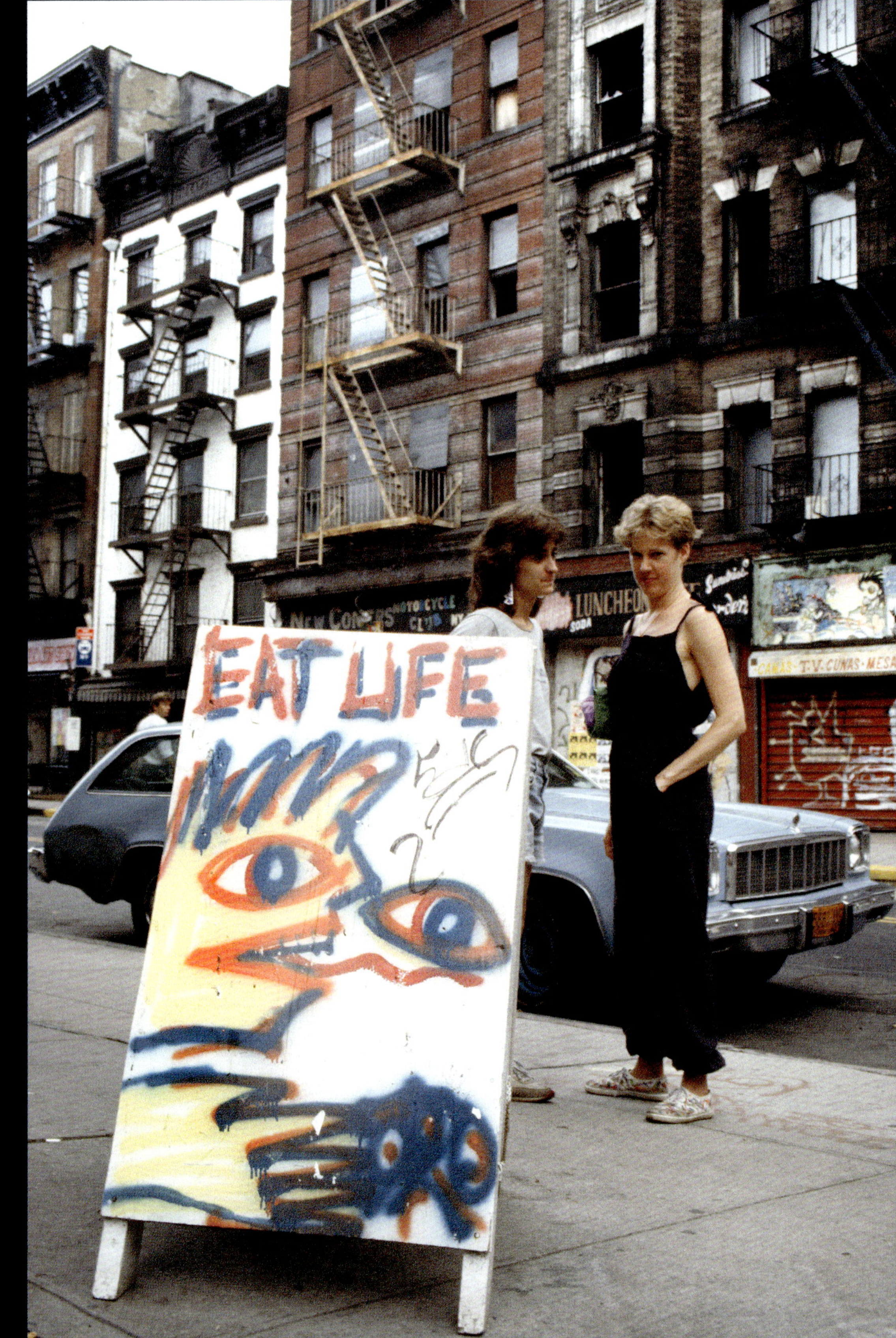

Life," with a side-eye.

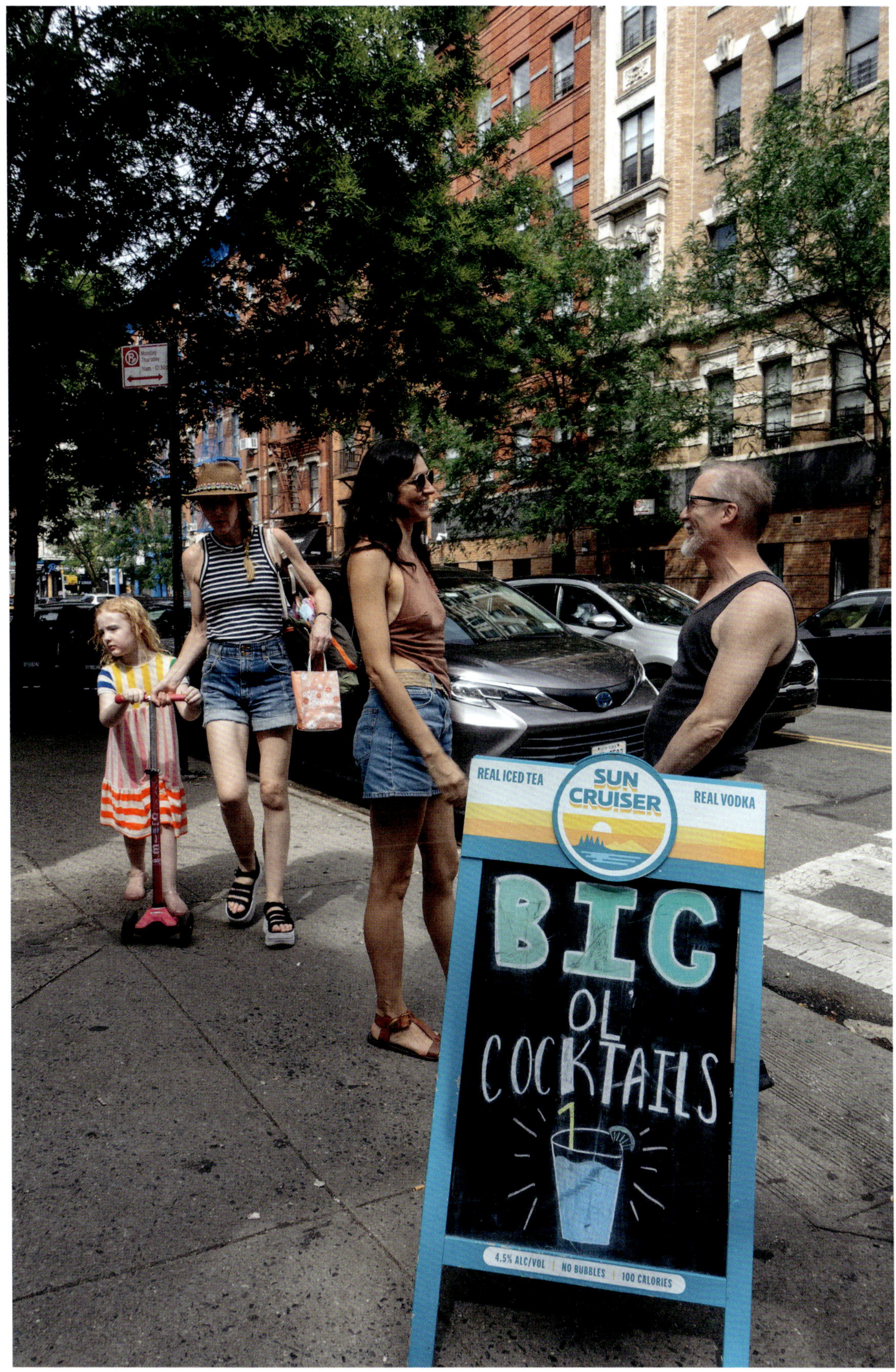

The sandwich boards still seem to work. "Big Ol' Cocktails."

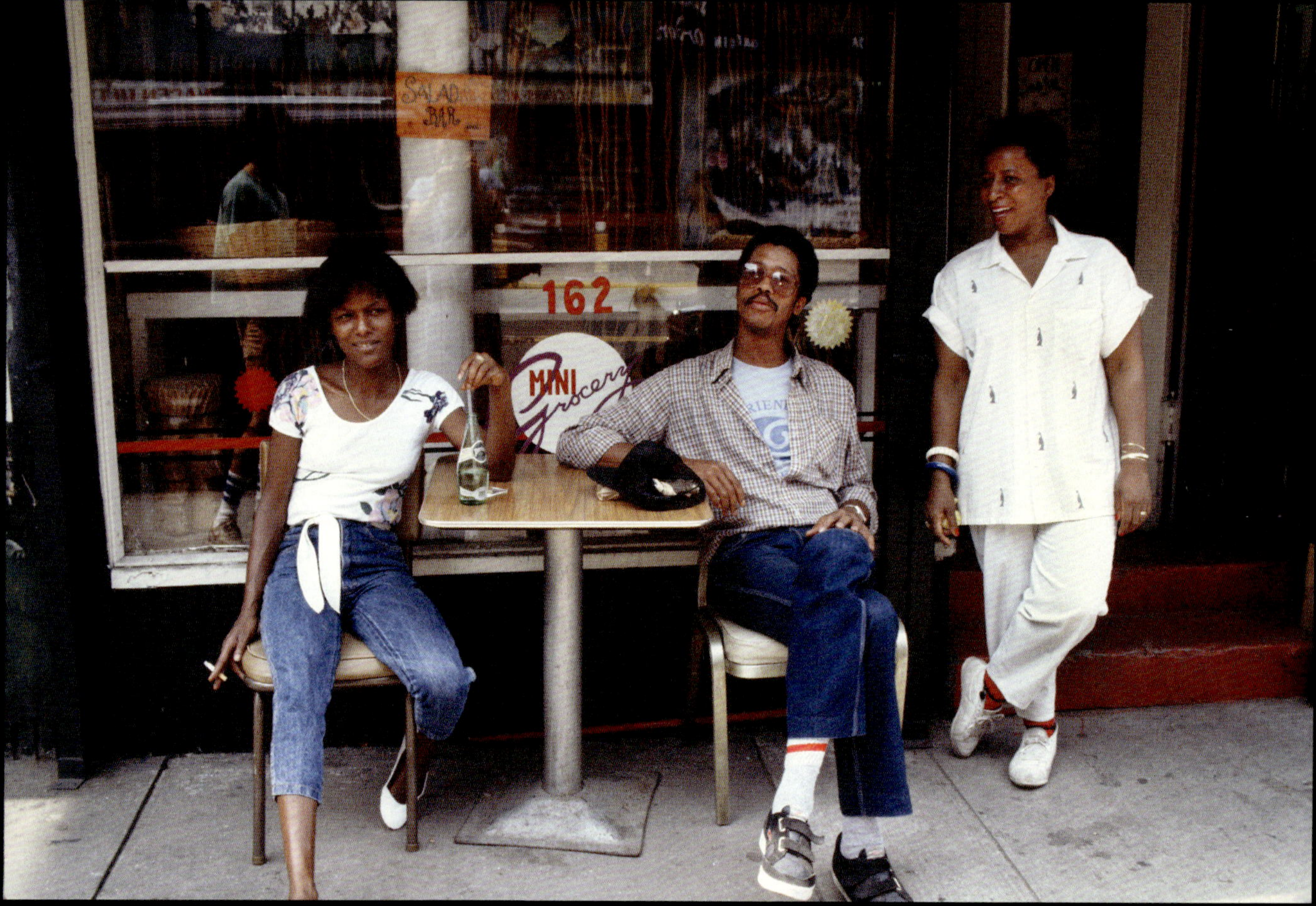

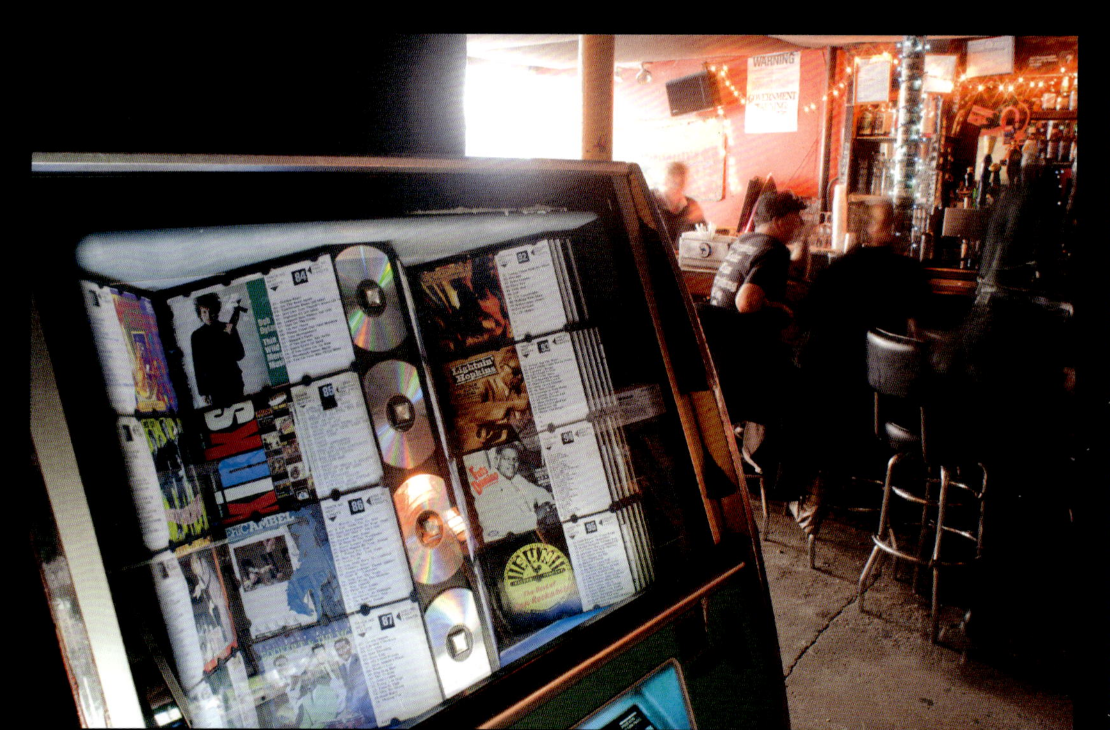

162 AVENUE B

A Jamaican bakery/restaurant that later became the Lakeside Lounge. A fine bar indeed, with a fine jukebox (seen here at the closing in 2012).

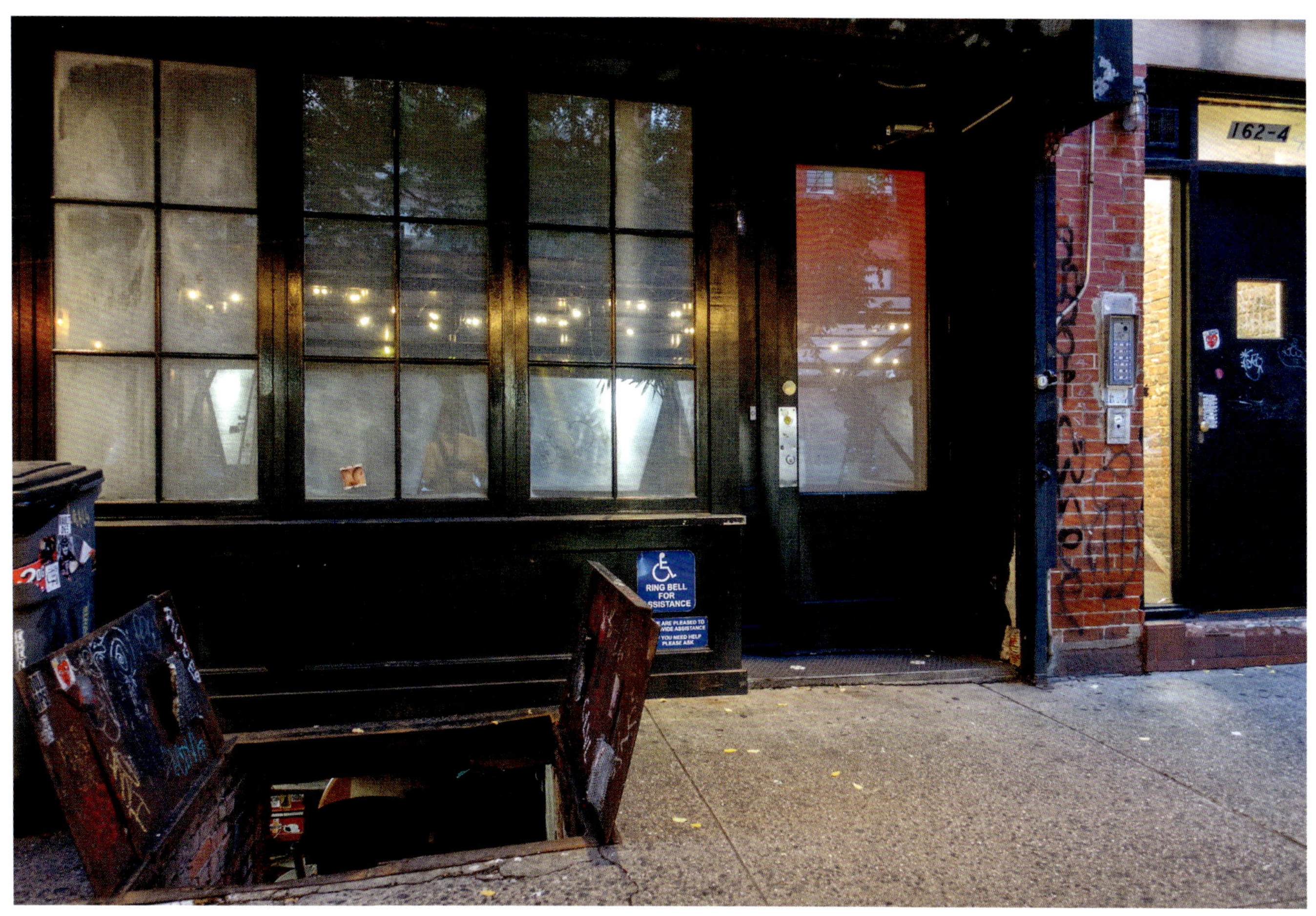

Side door of Dream Baby, the successor
to Lakeside Lounge, and a glimpse into
the basement.

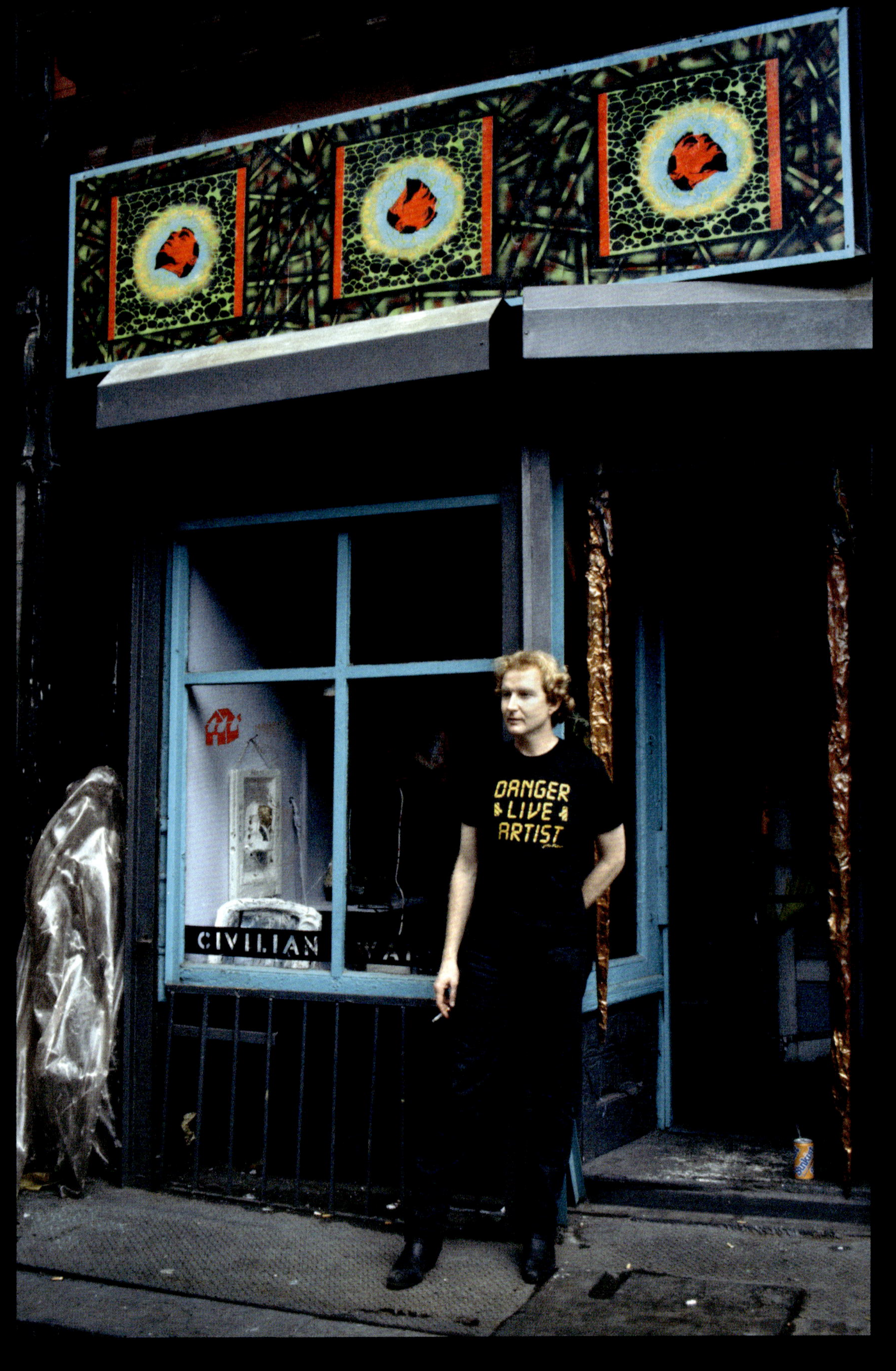

526 EAST 11TH STREET

Civilian Warfare Gallery. Alan Barrows, a cofounder with Dean Savard, taking in the street. David Wojnarowicz and Greer Lankton among others got early support from Civilian Warfare.

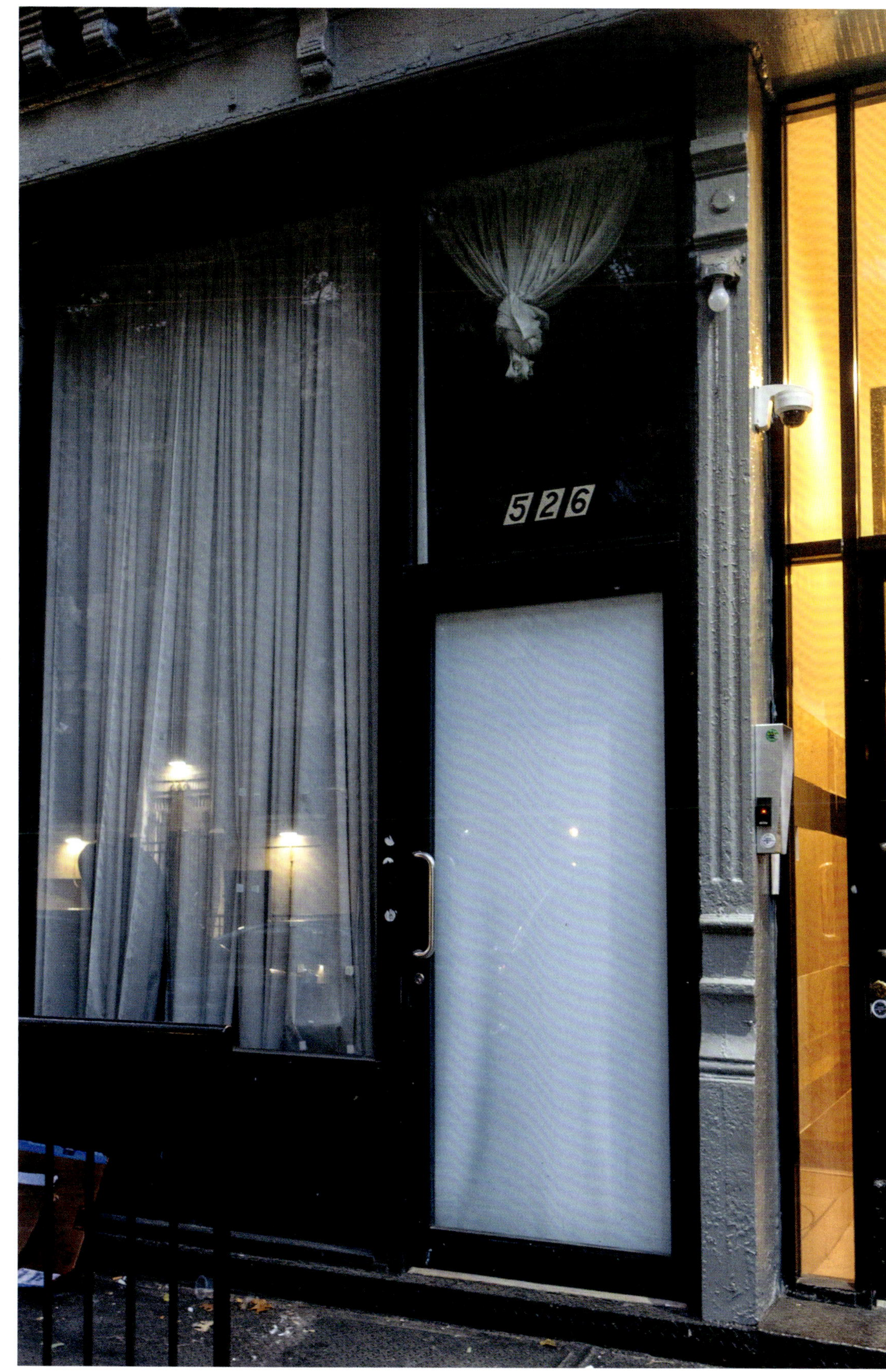

Not a lot to say.

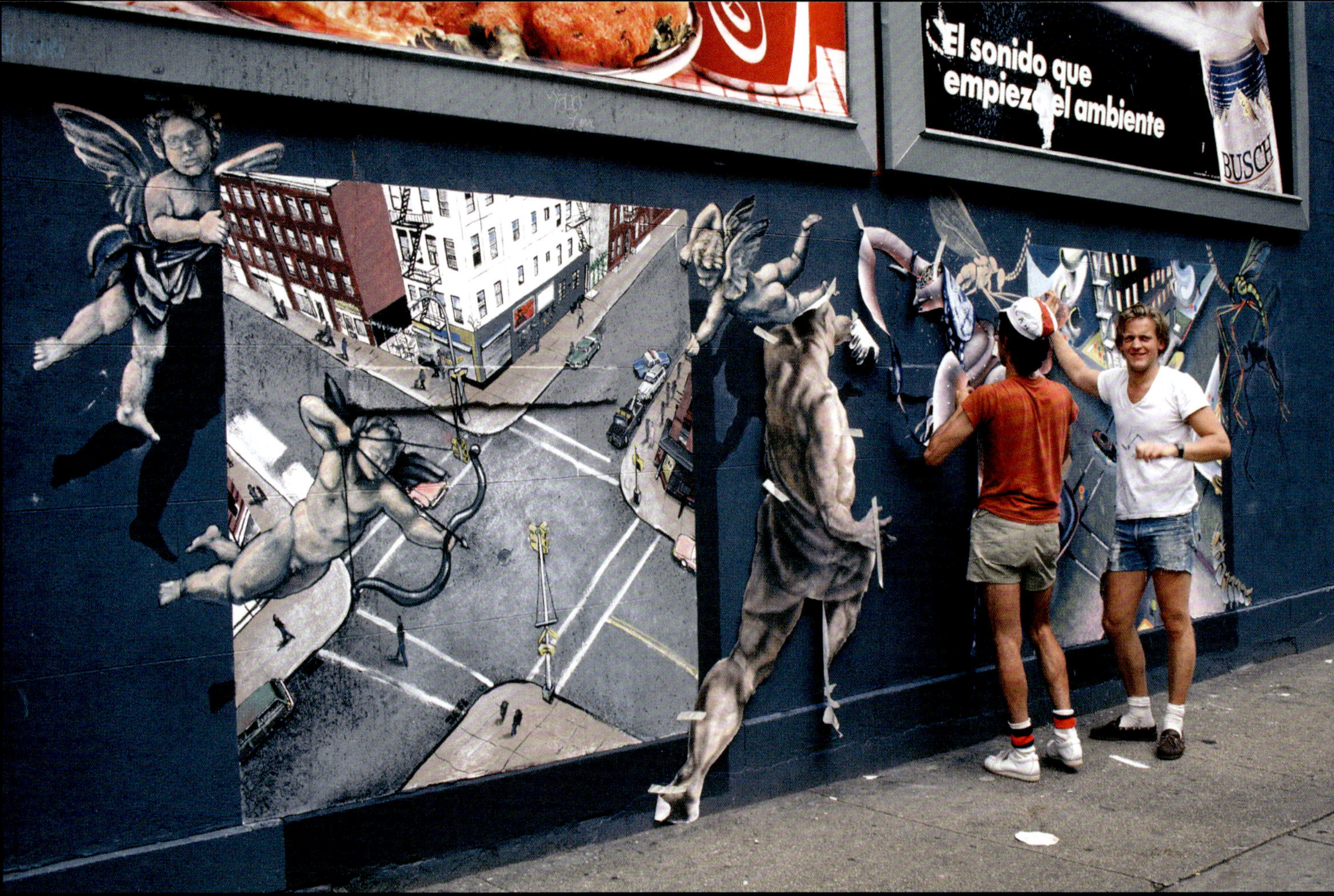

AVENUE B

[...]er elaborate
[...] going up.

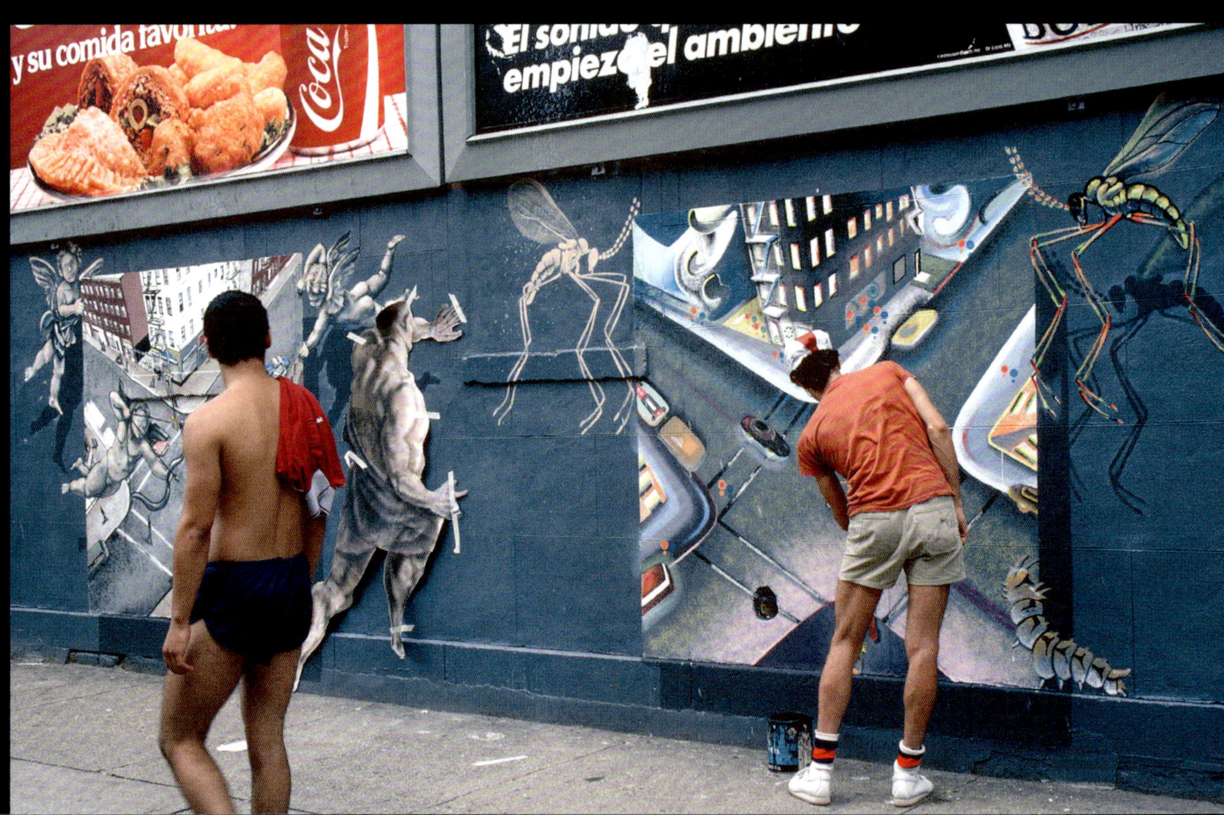

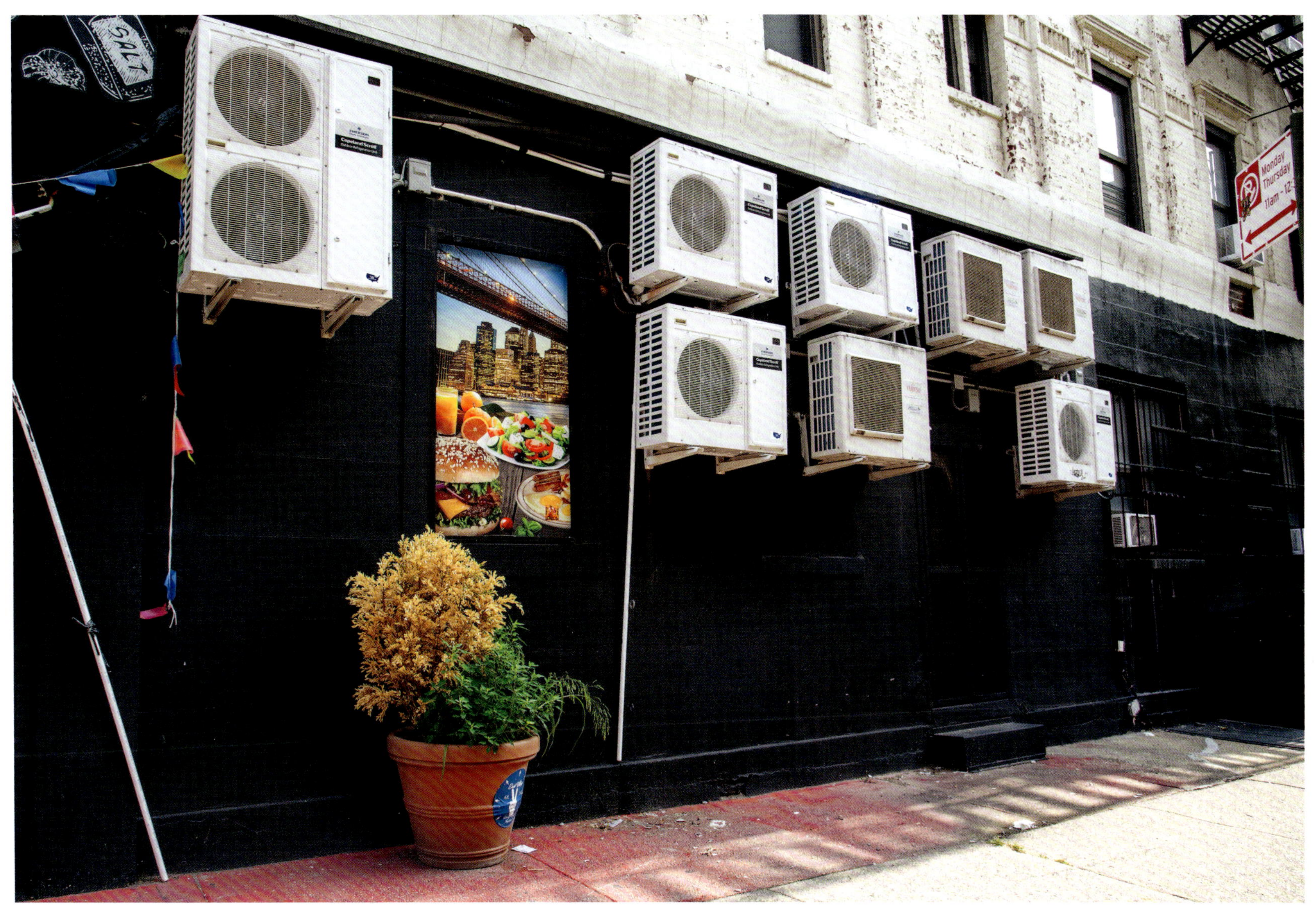

Paradise Deli, mini splits. Sign of
the times, new street decor.

PS 361 from the roof of 633 East 11th Street.

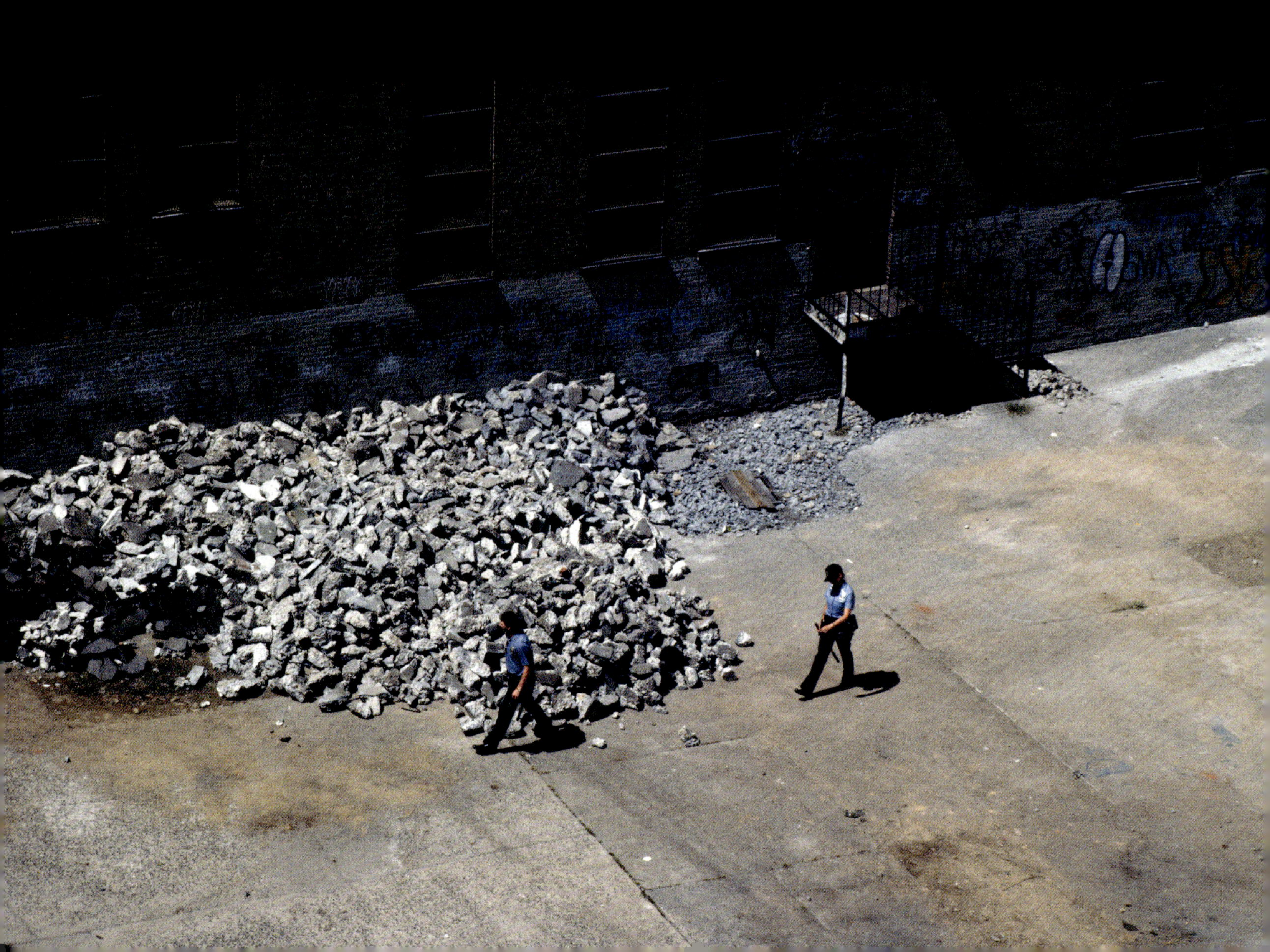

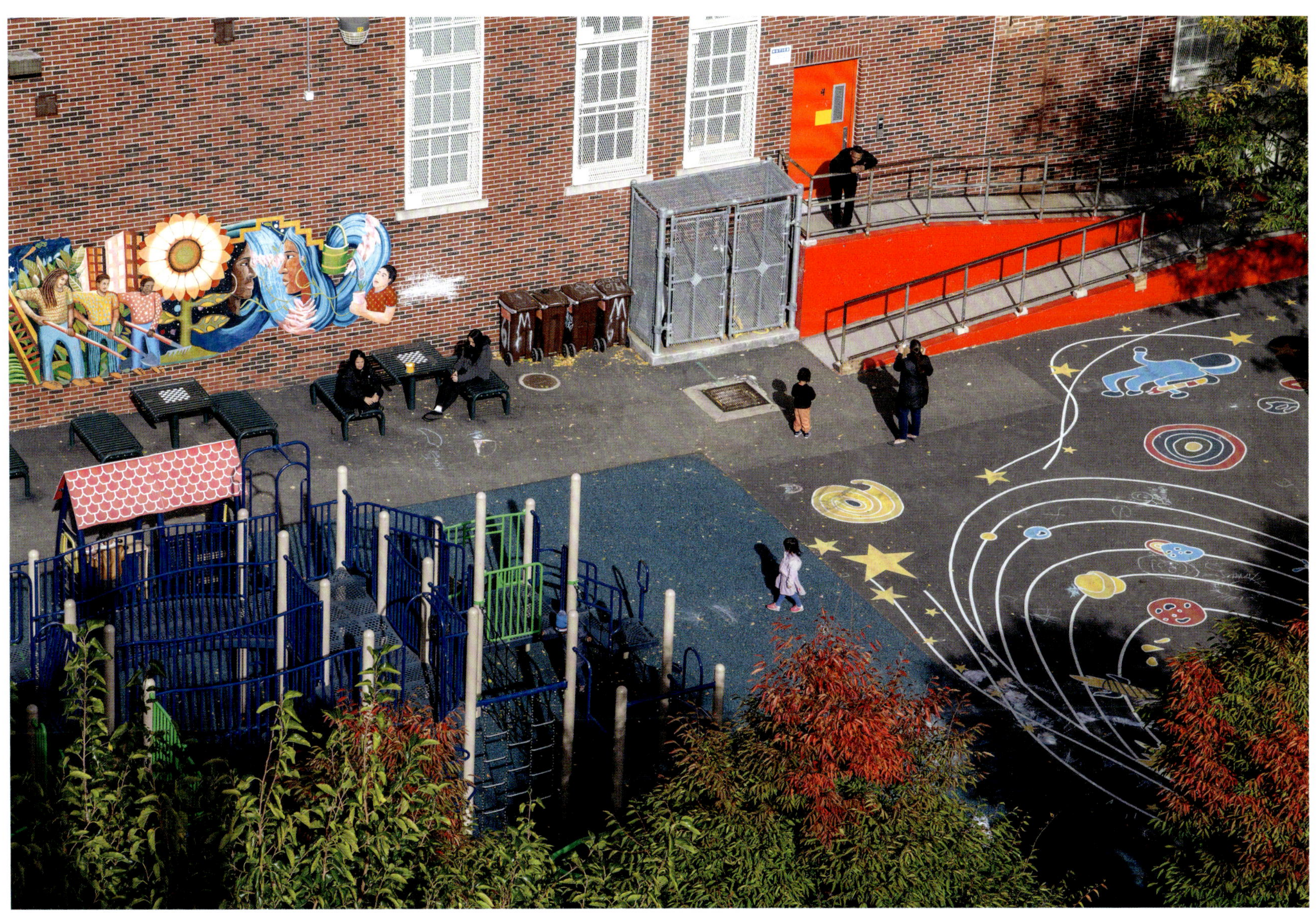

Ditto.

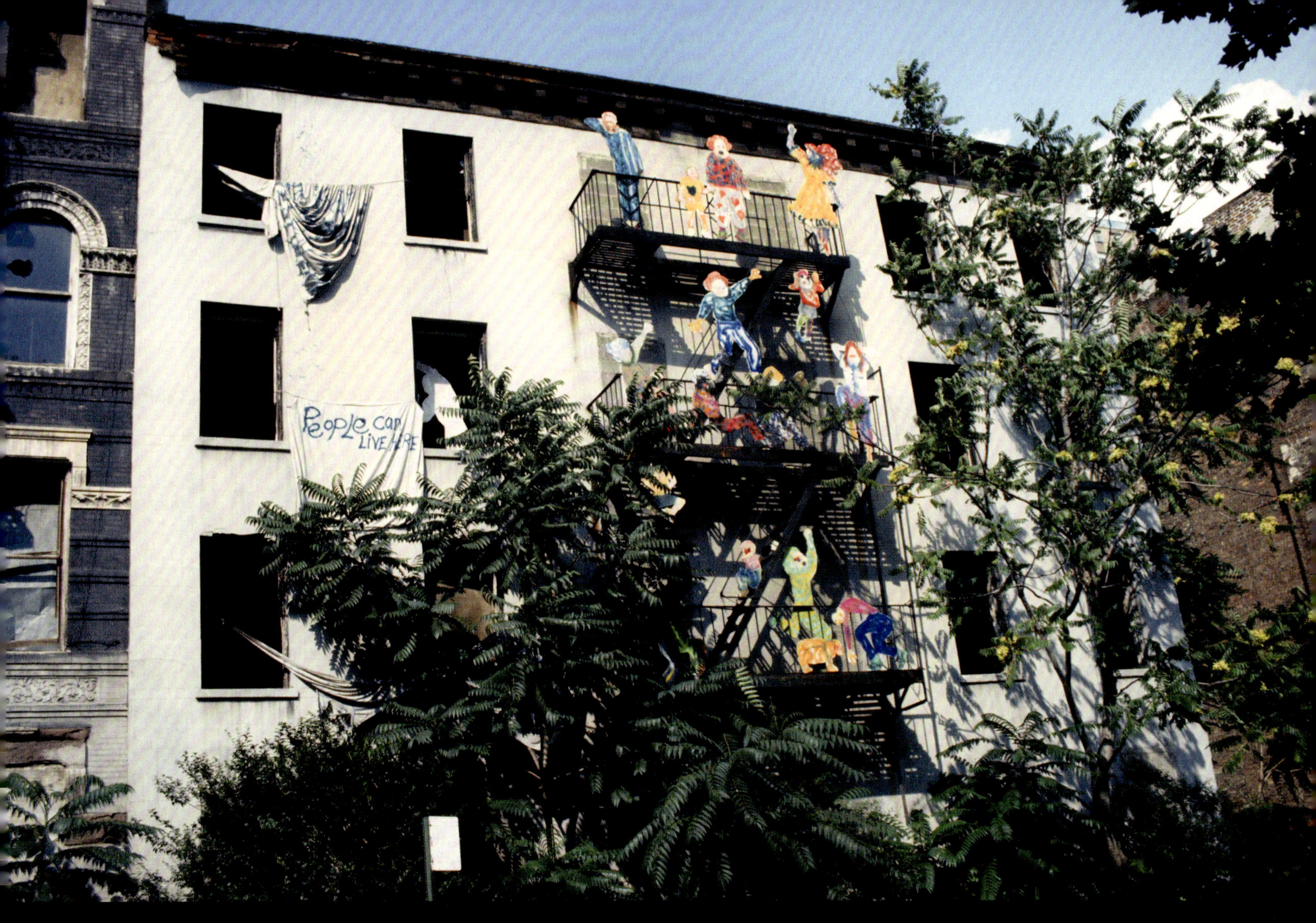

641 EAST 11TH STREET

"People can live here" and cutouts

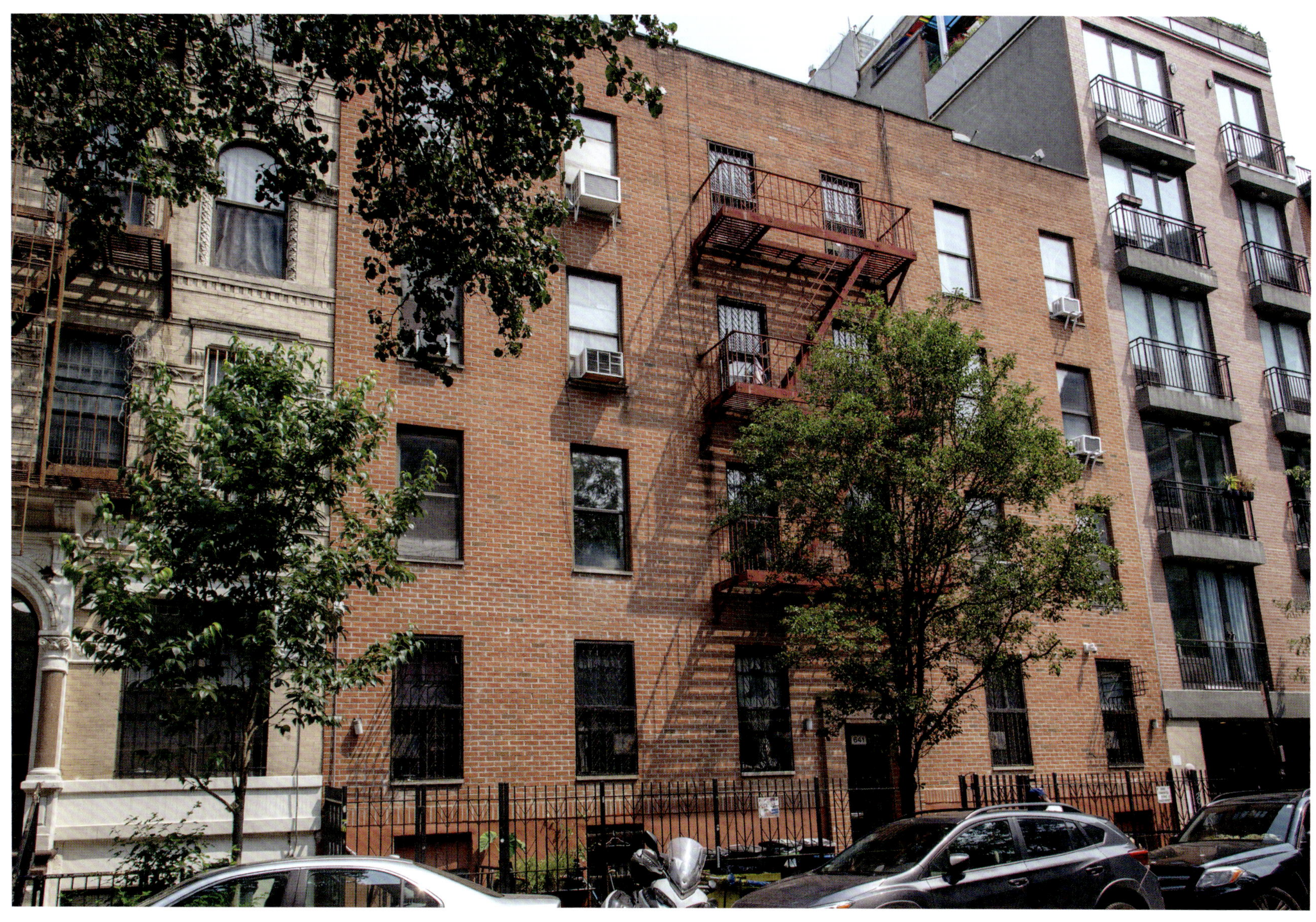

Now people do.

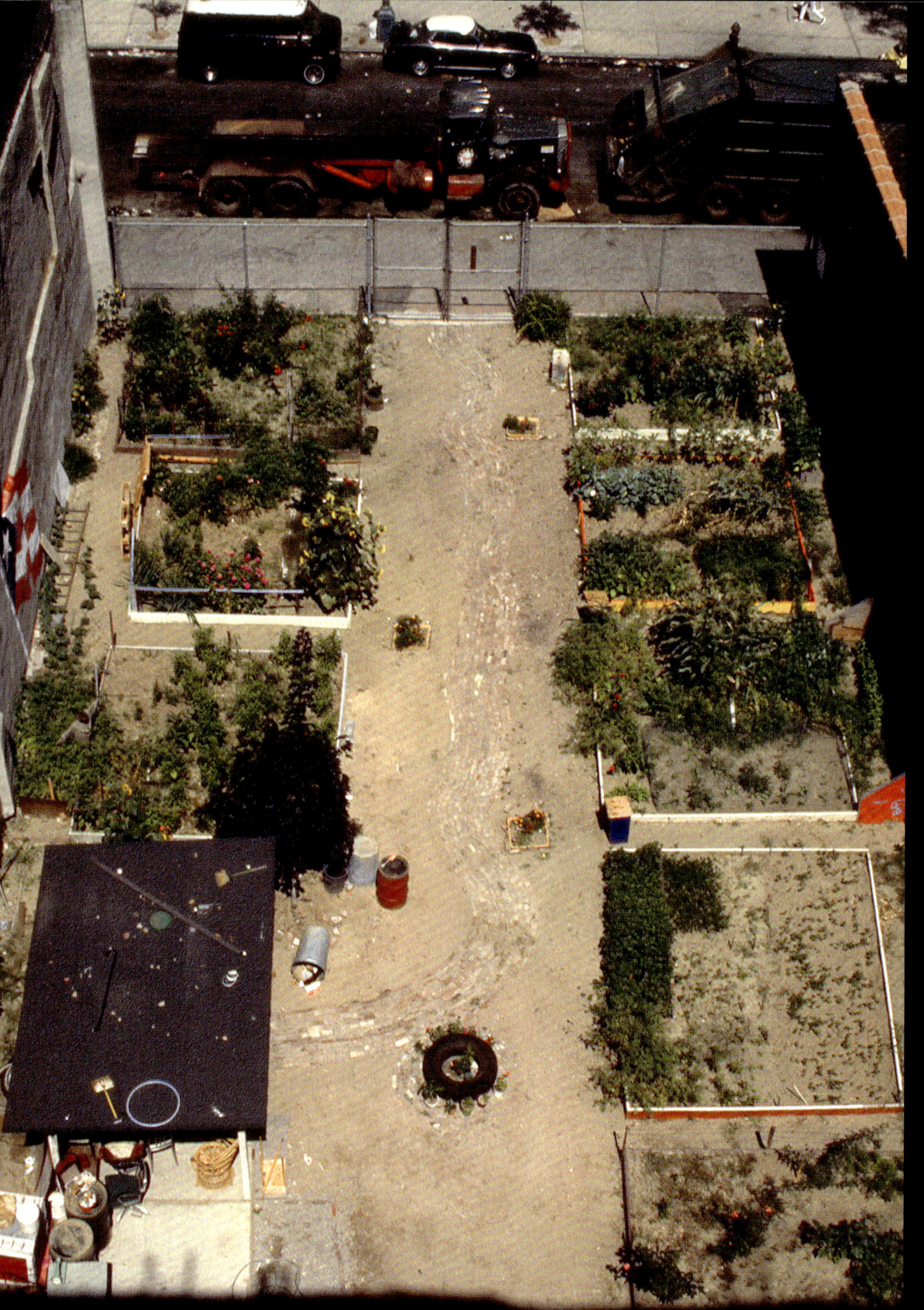

644 EAST 12TH STREET

A community garden getting a start.

Campos Community Garden
in full bloom.

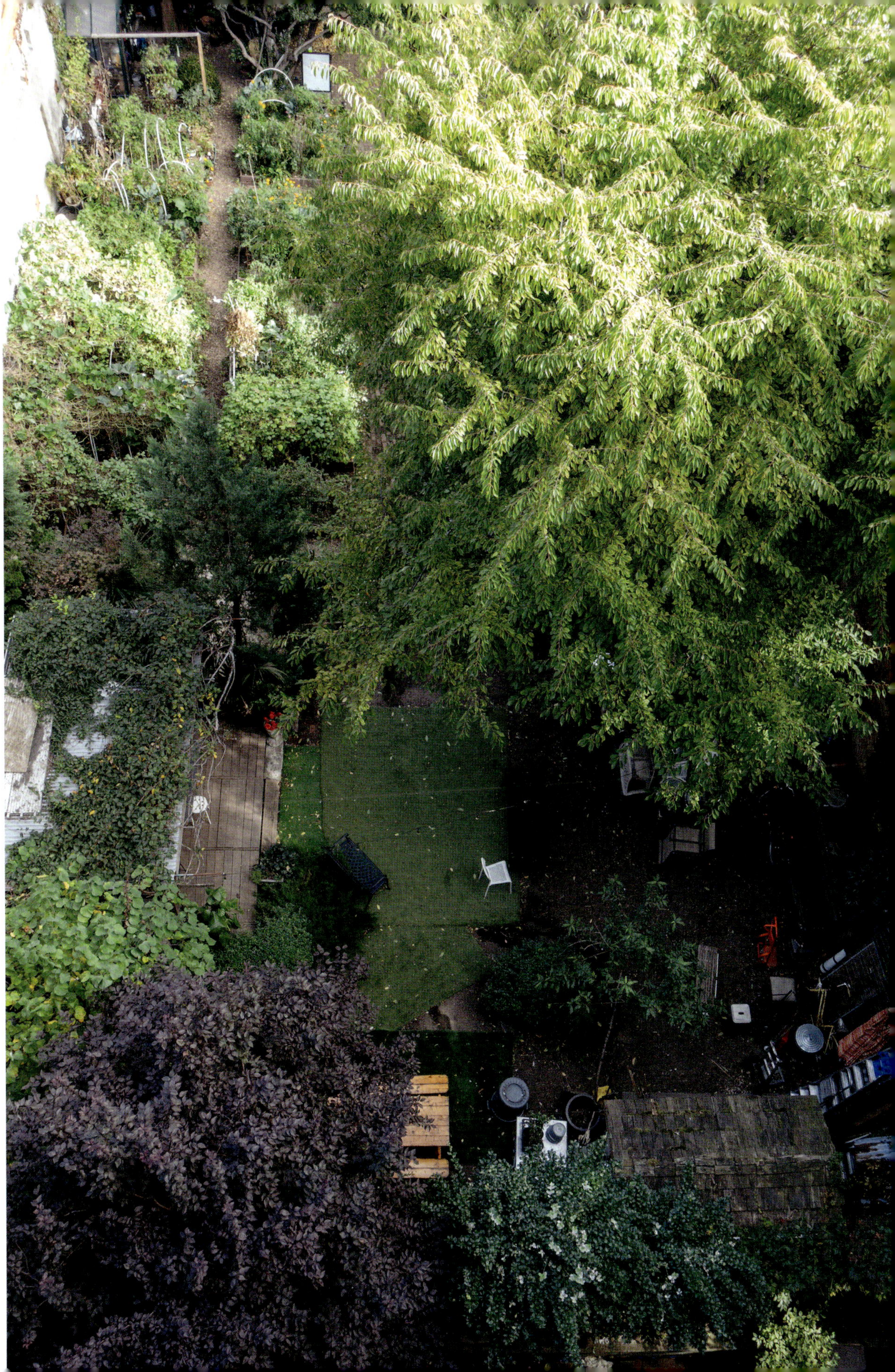

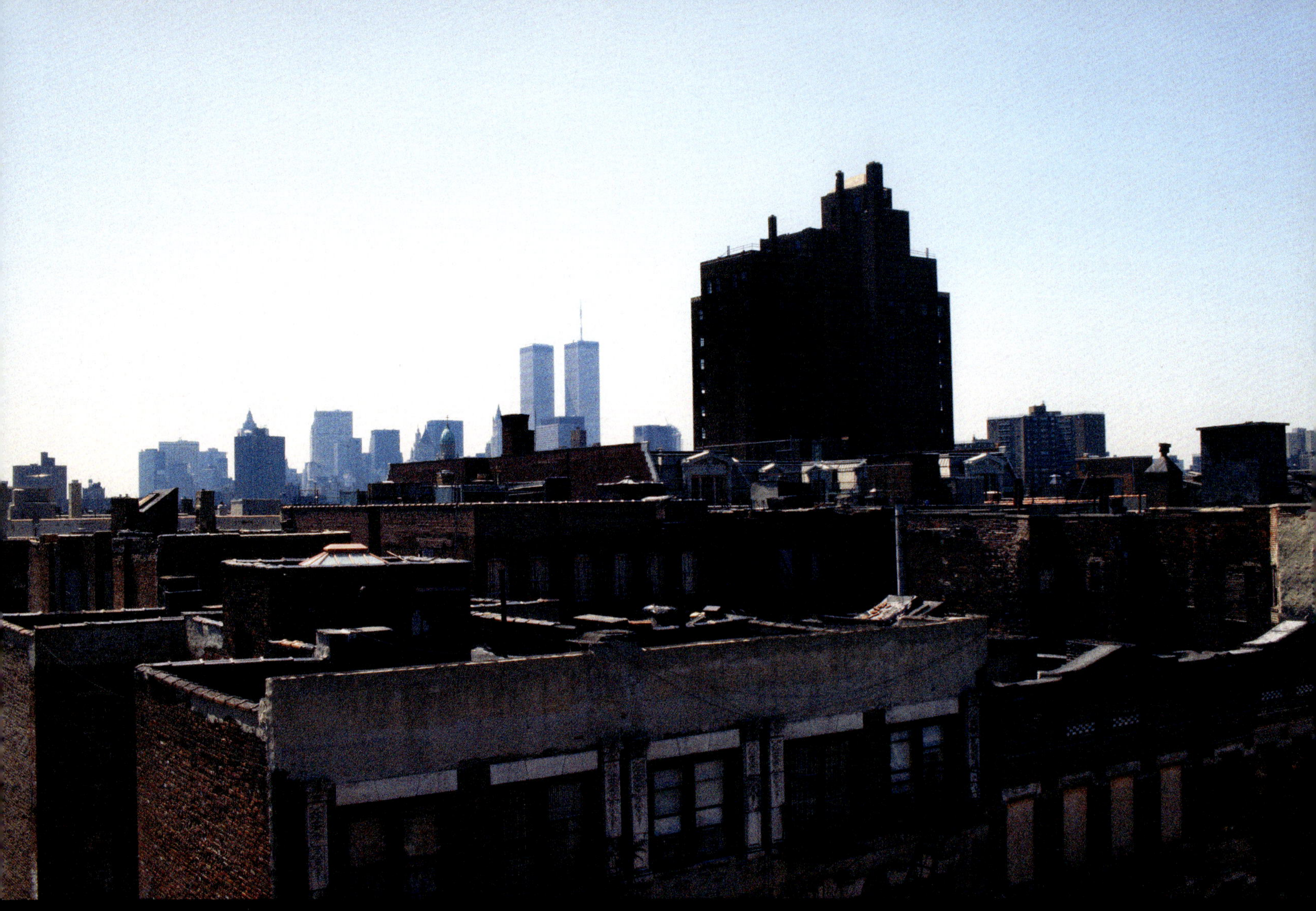

633 EAST 11TH STREET

From the roof looking downtown.
Christodora House and WTC skyline.

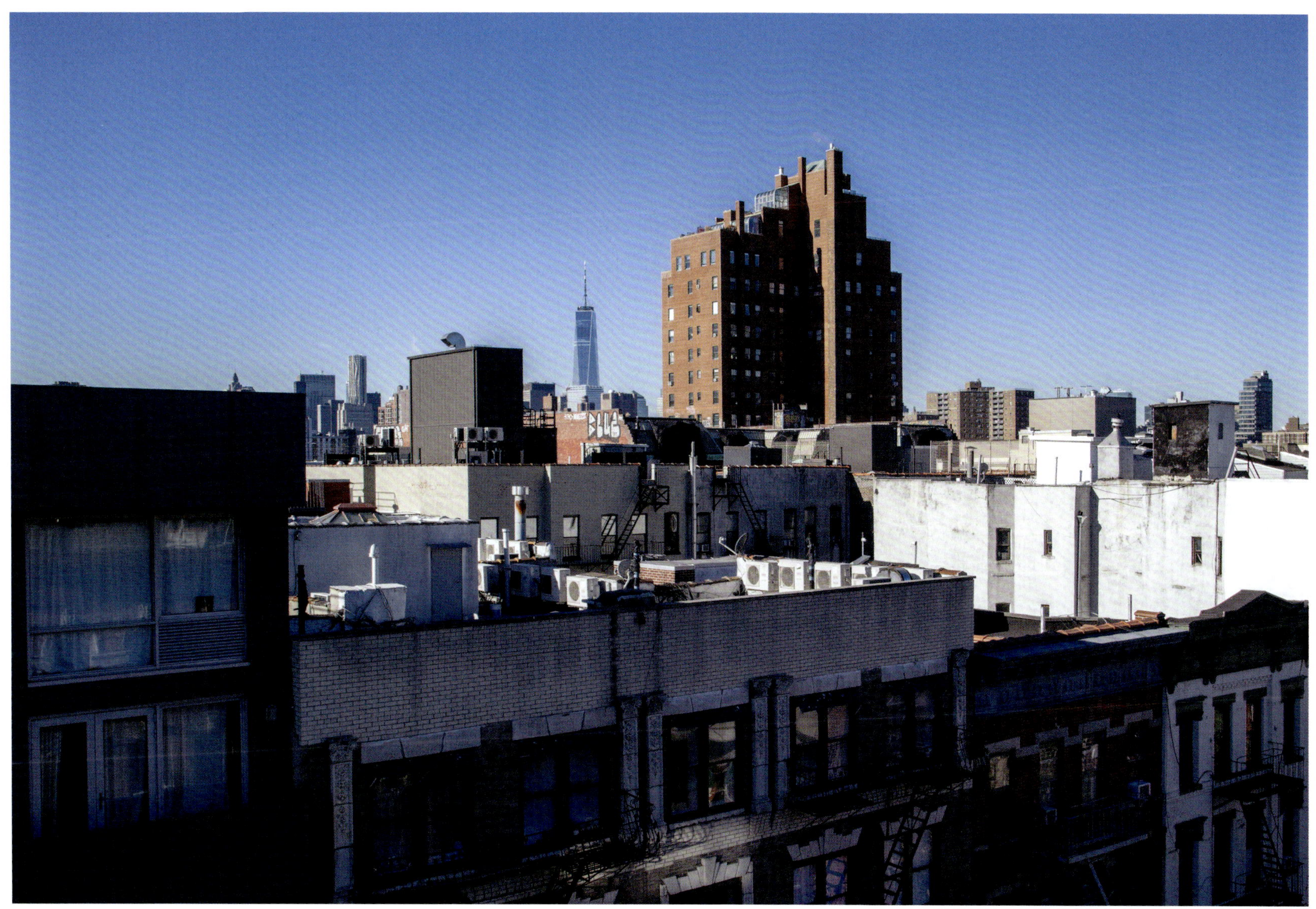

From the roof looking downtown.
Christodora House and One WTC skyline.

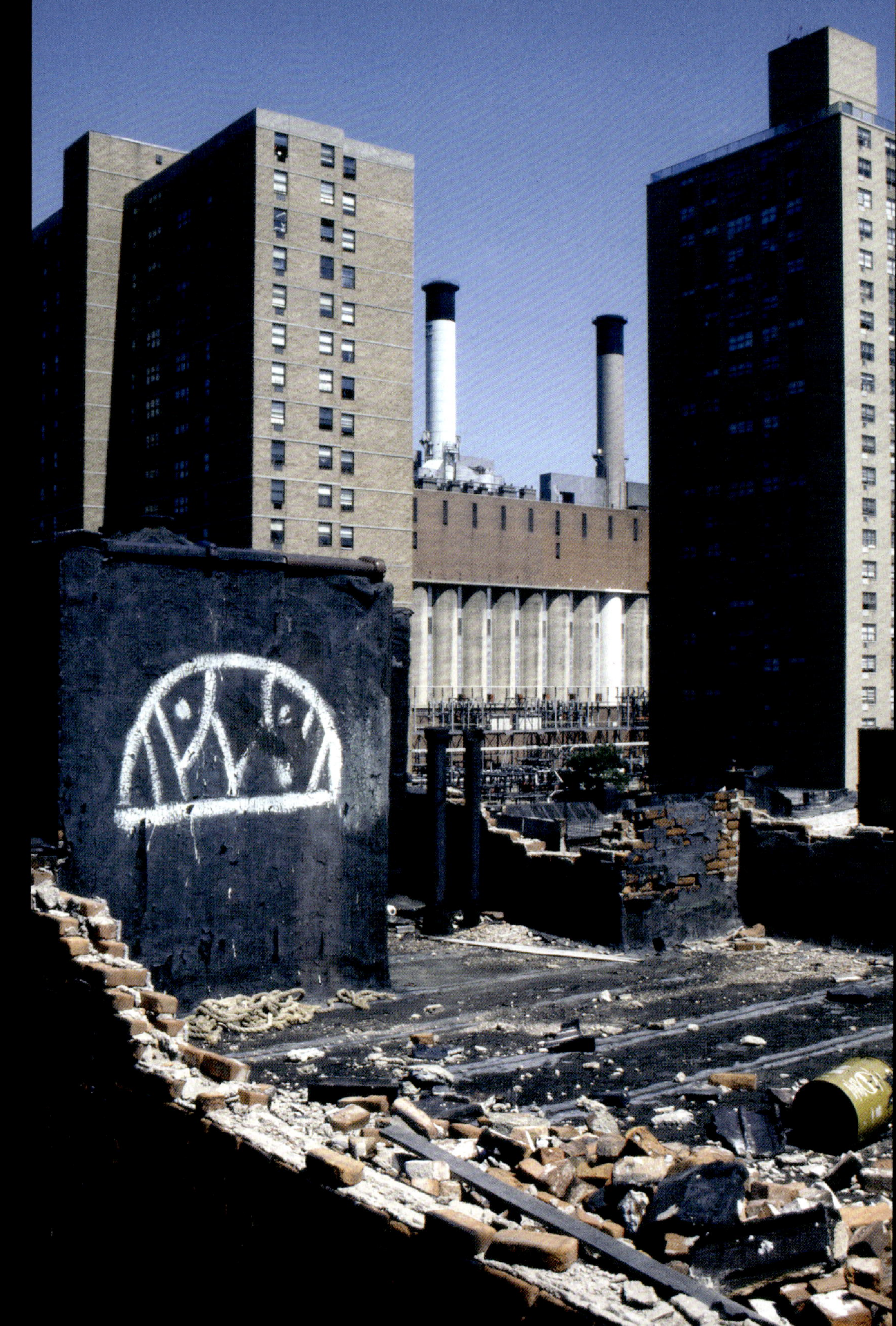

633 AND 635 EAST 11TH STREET

Over the roof of 635 East 11th Street when it was abandoned. Shooting toward the Con Edison plant.

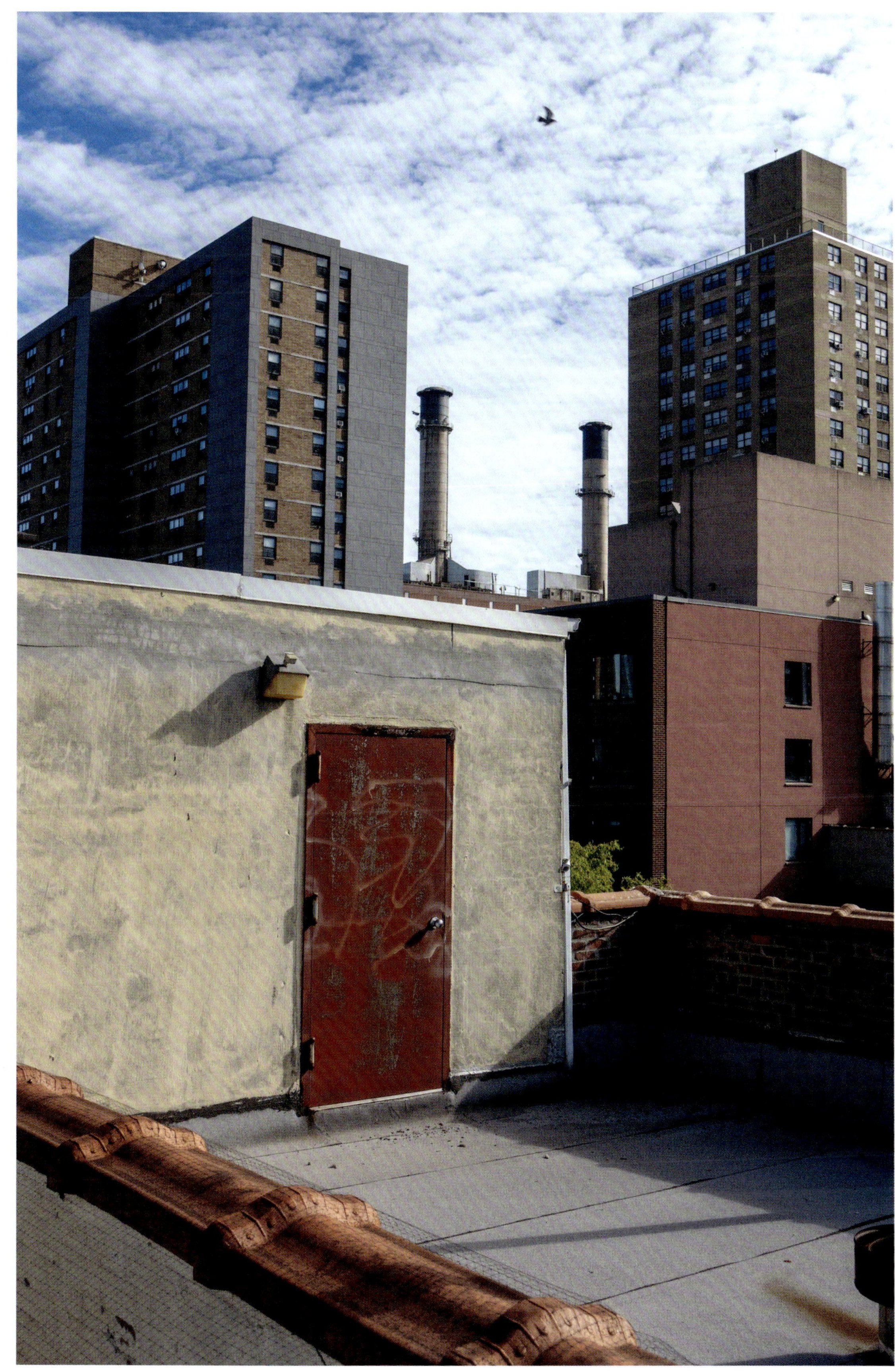

Over the roof of 635 East 11th Street now that it's occupied.

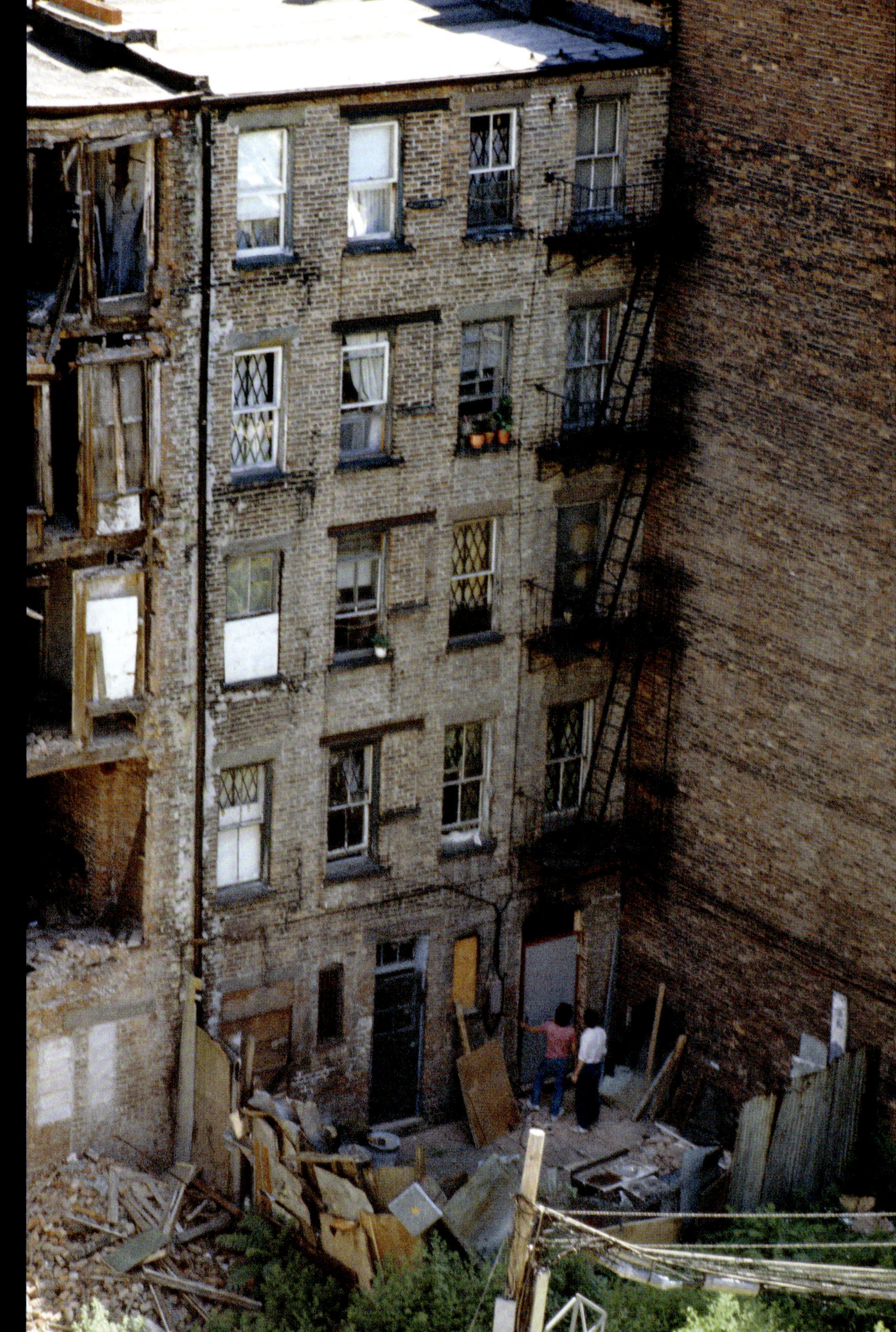

635 EAST 11TH STREET

Looking at 175 Loisaida Ave from the roof, with some activity going on. Next to a building about to come down.

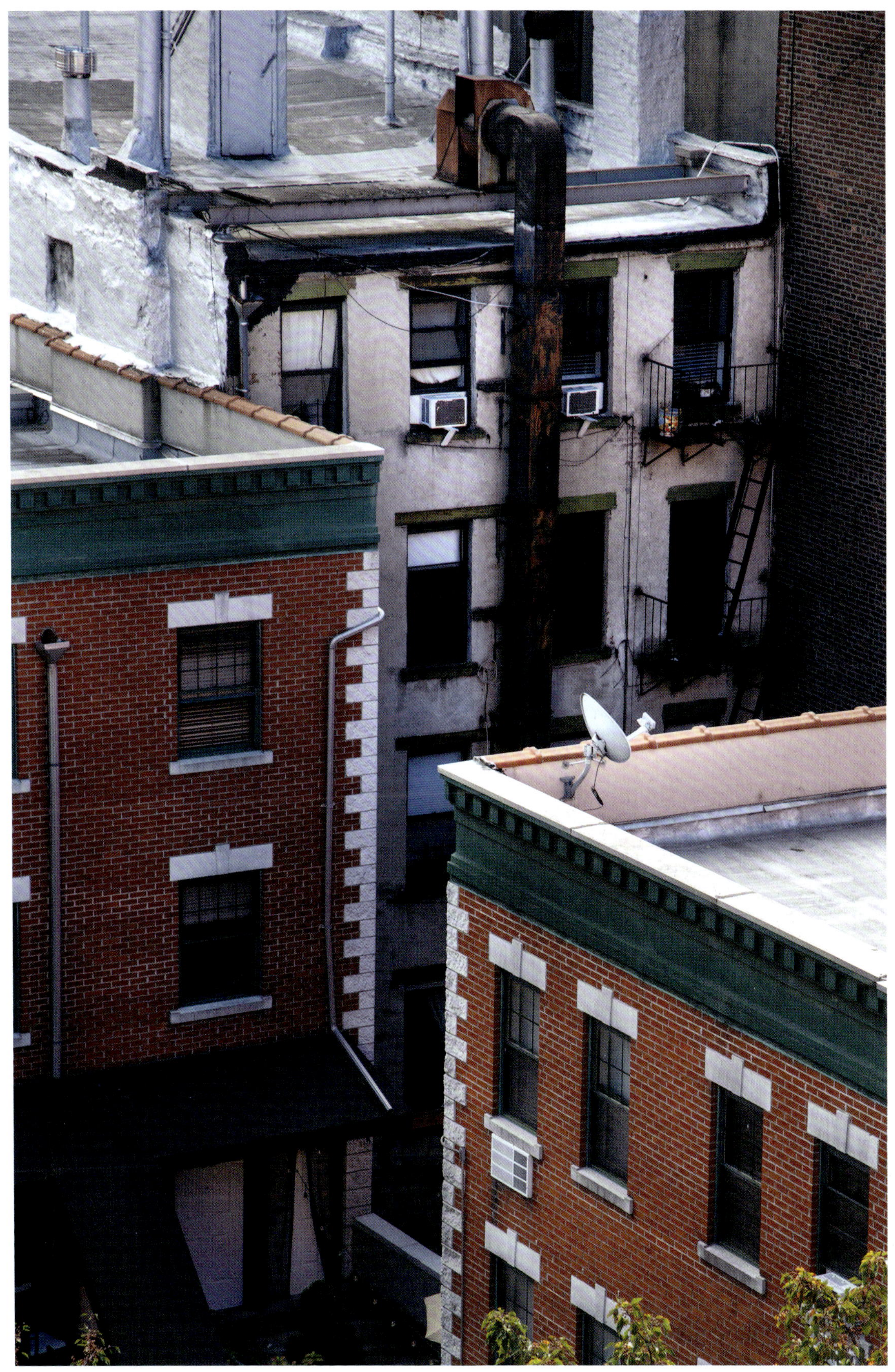

All spiffed up, and
new neighbors.

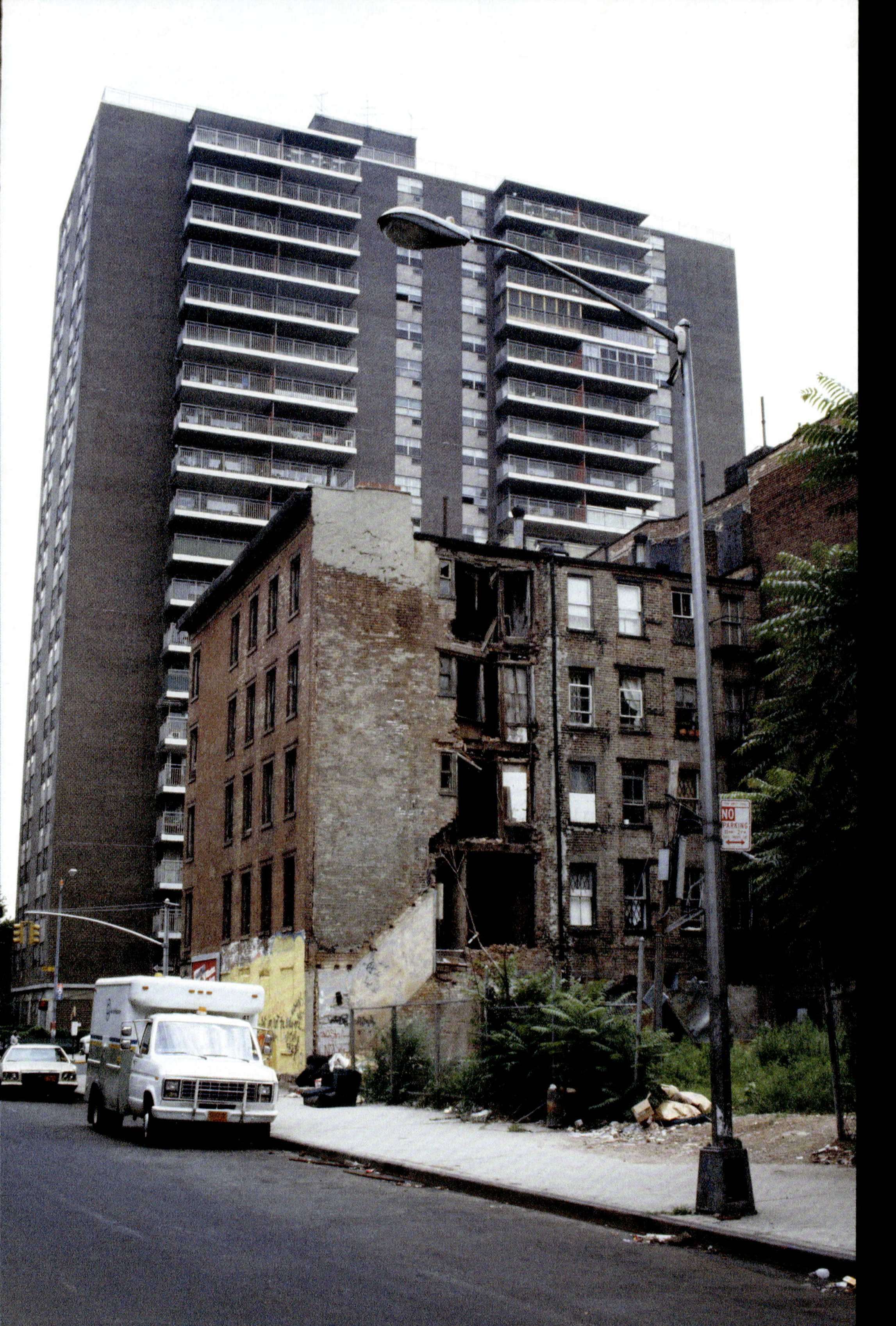

640 EAST 11TH STREET

Looking toward Avenue C and the Village East Towers from East 11th Street

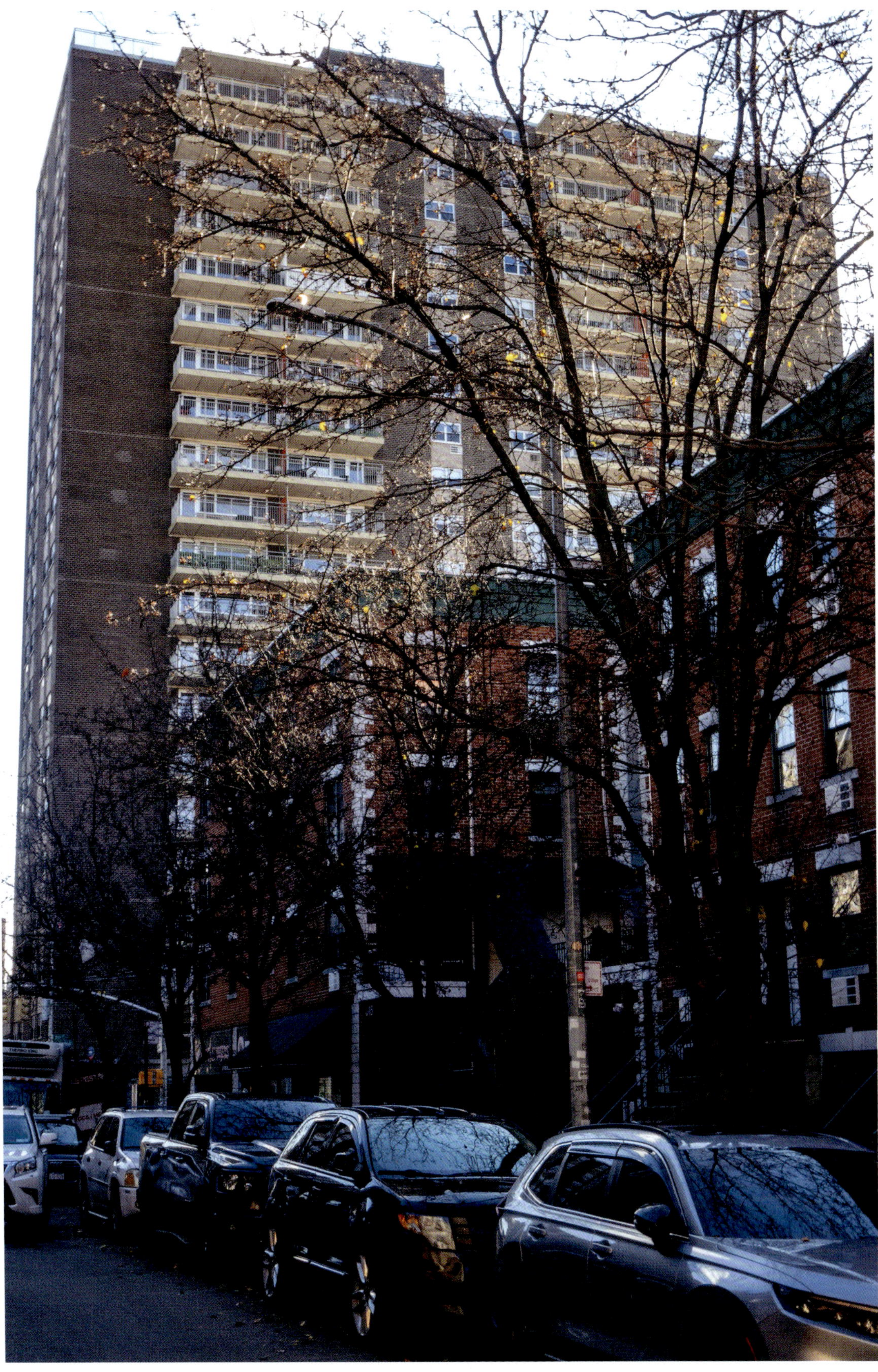

Now with housing on 11th Street.

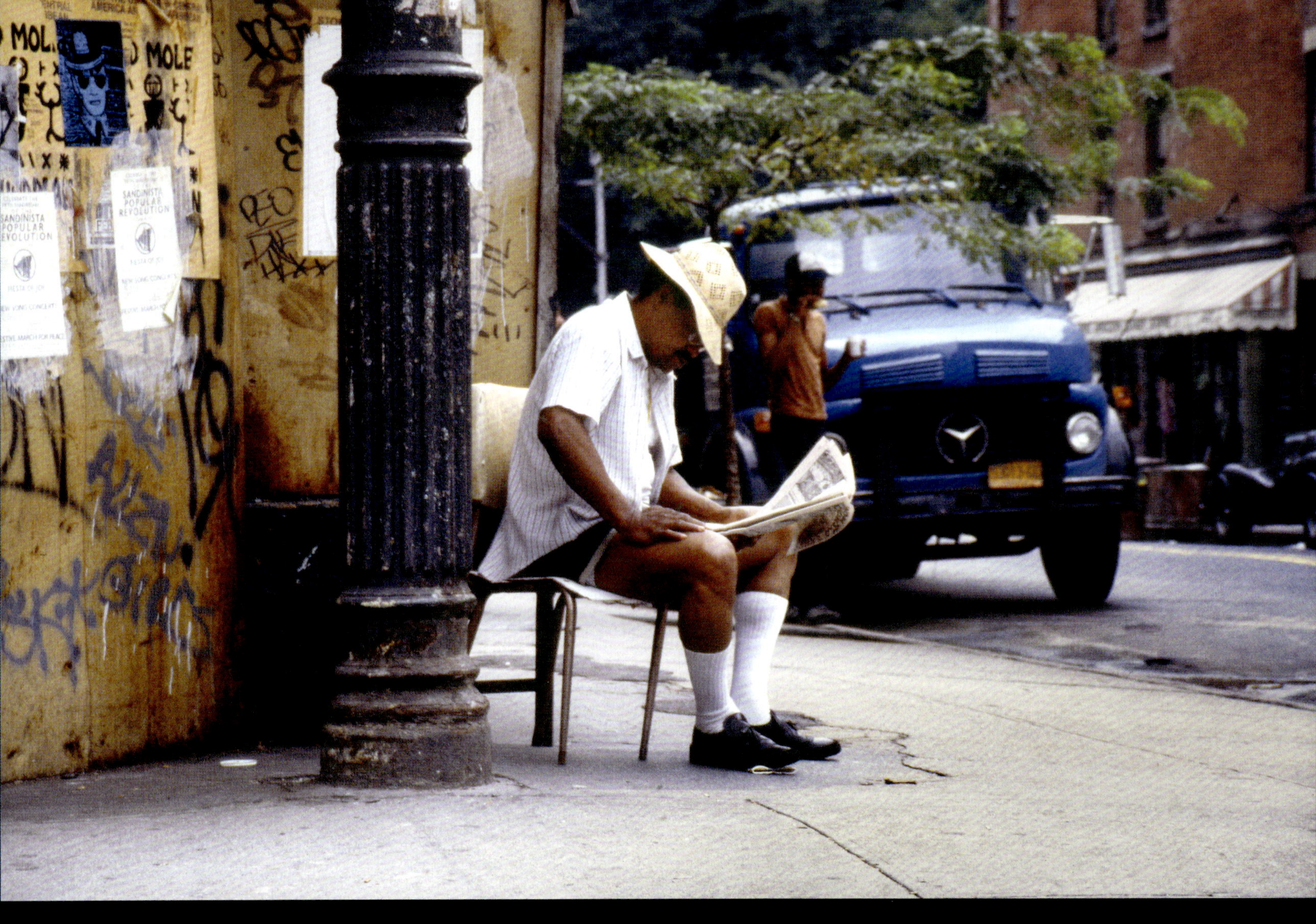

**AVENUE B AND
EAST 11TH STREET**

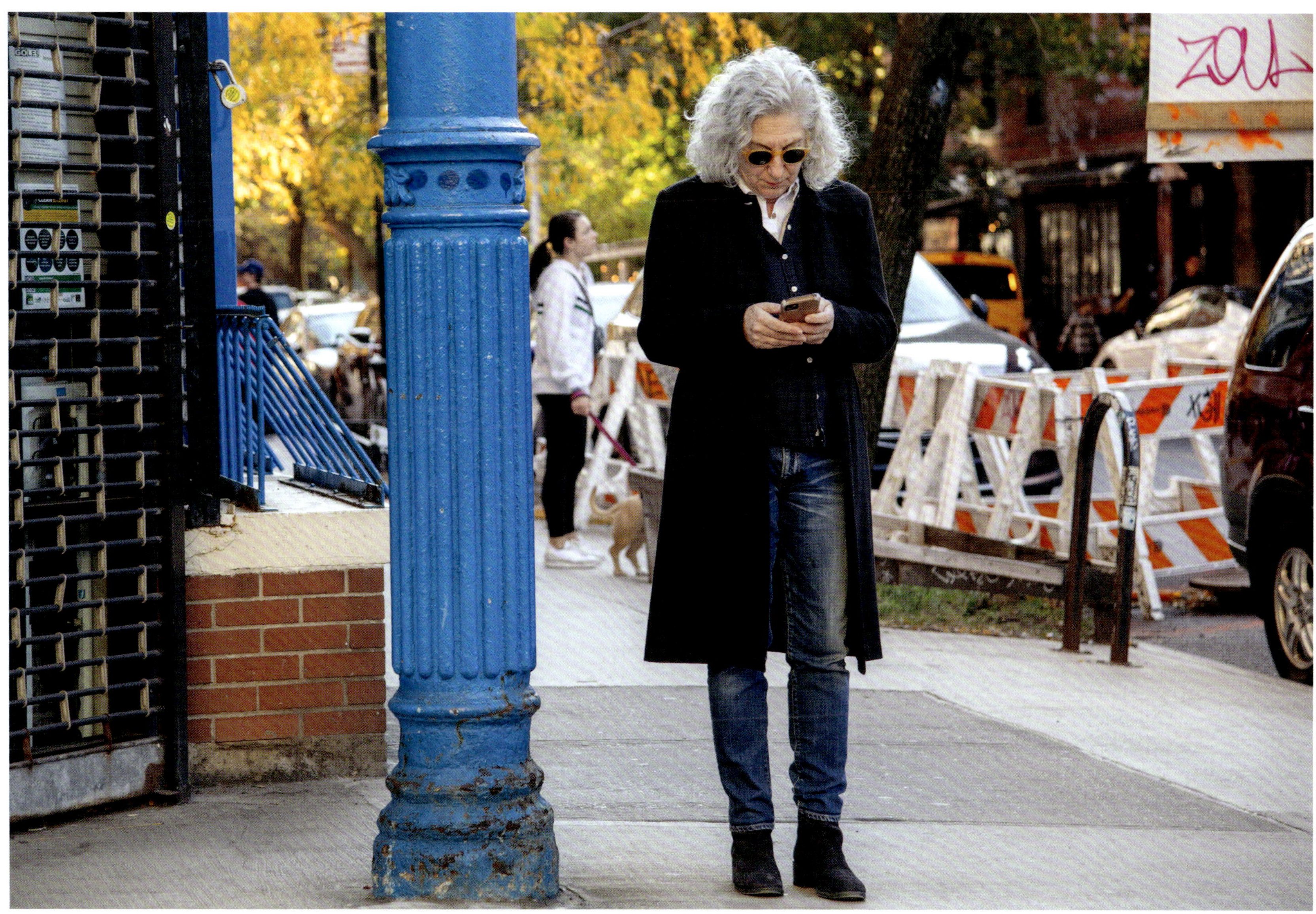

Reading on the corner, the phone kind.

Looking north toward 12th Street. NewComers Motorcycle Club at the corner of 12th Street, a dominoes club on the left.

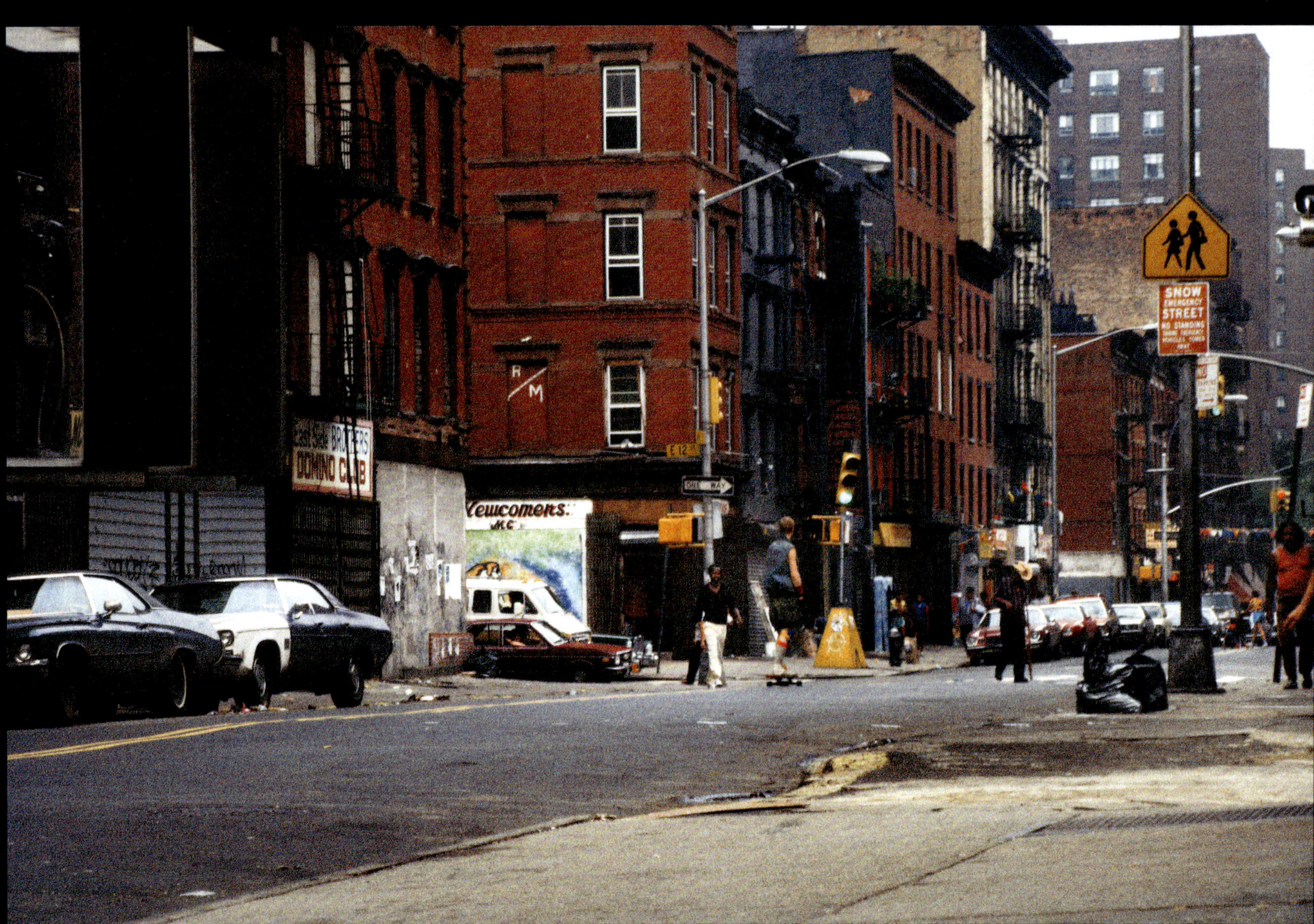

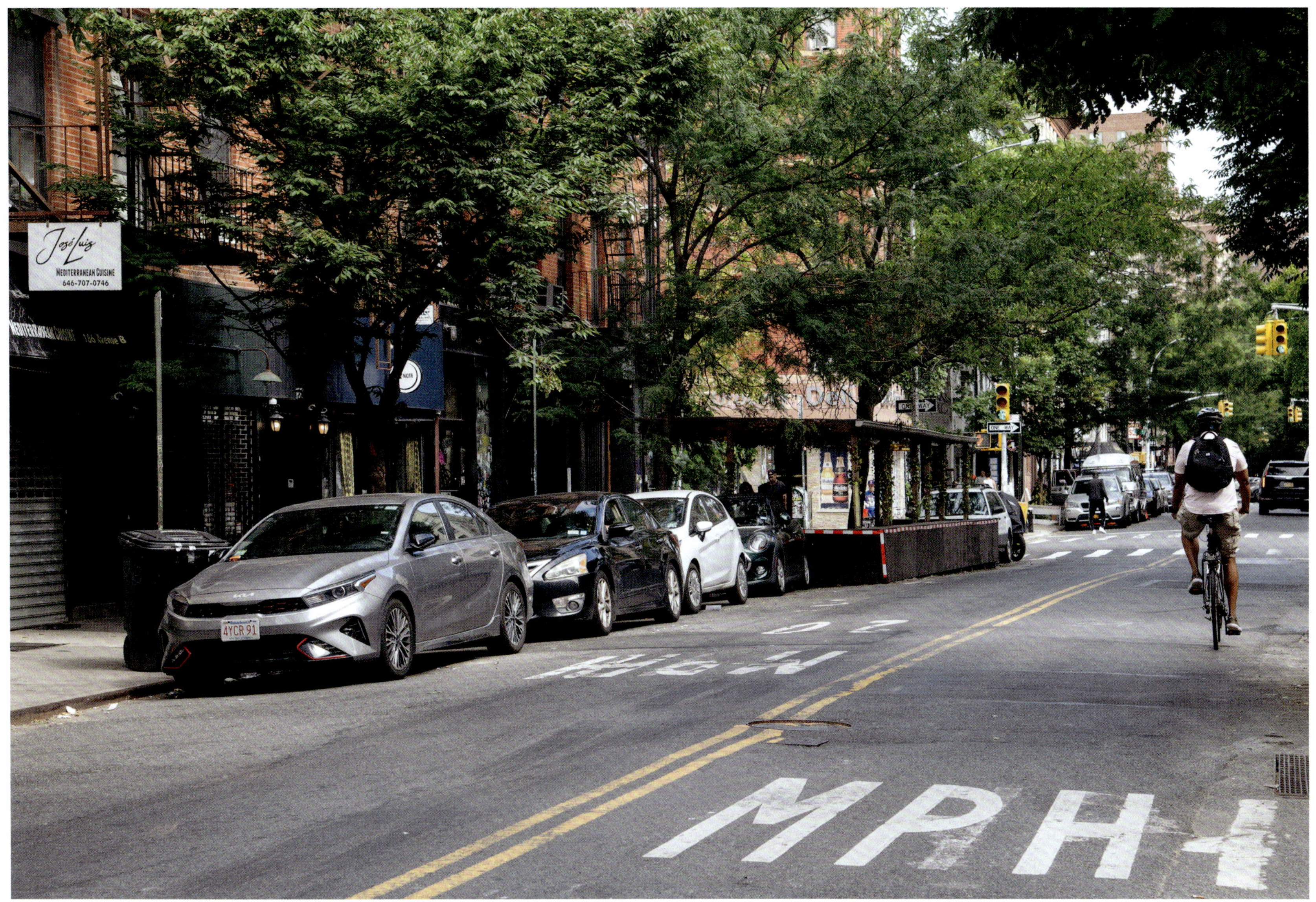

A deli in place of the NewComers, and Ama
Raw Bar in place of the dominoes club.

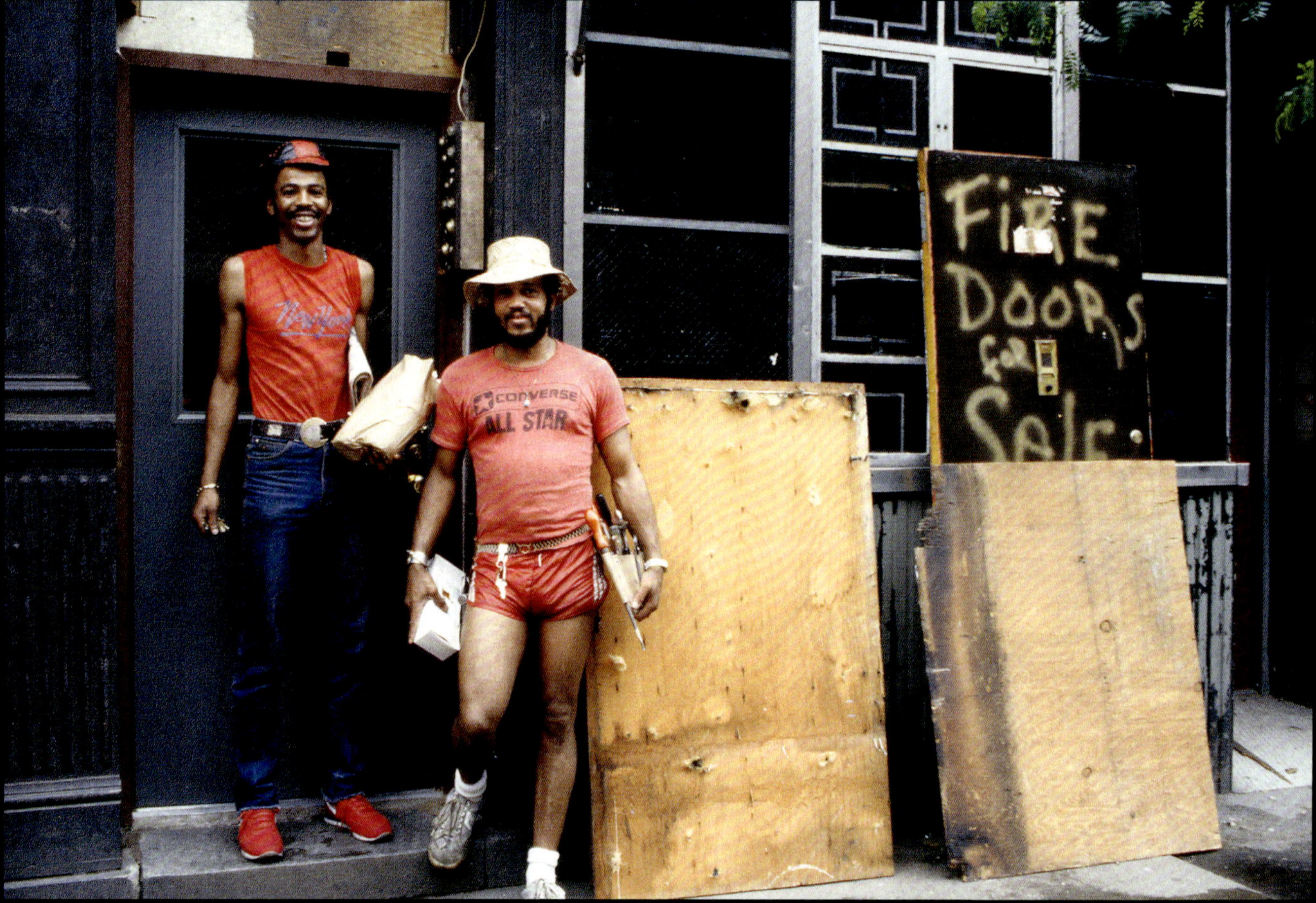

167 AVENUE B

Home repair with a couple of forties.
Family and friends, street art.

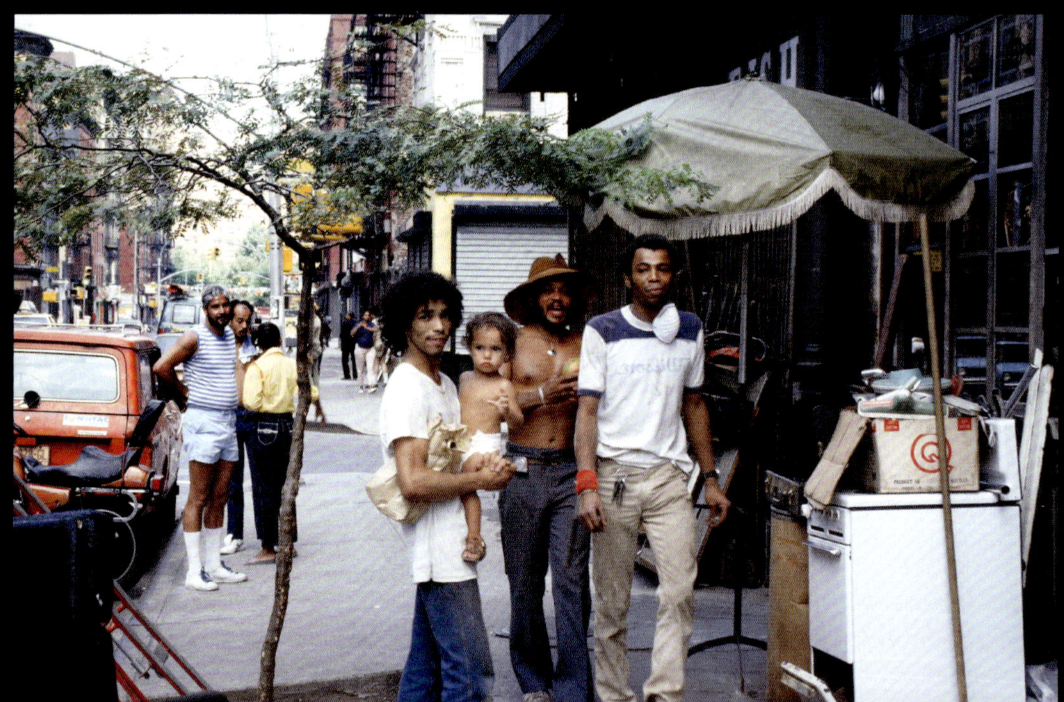

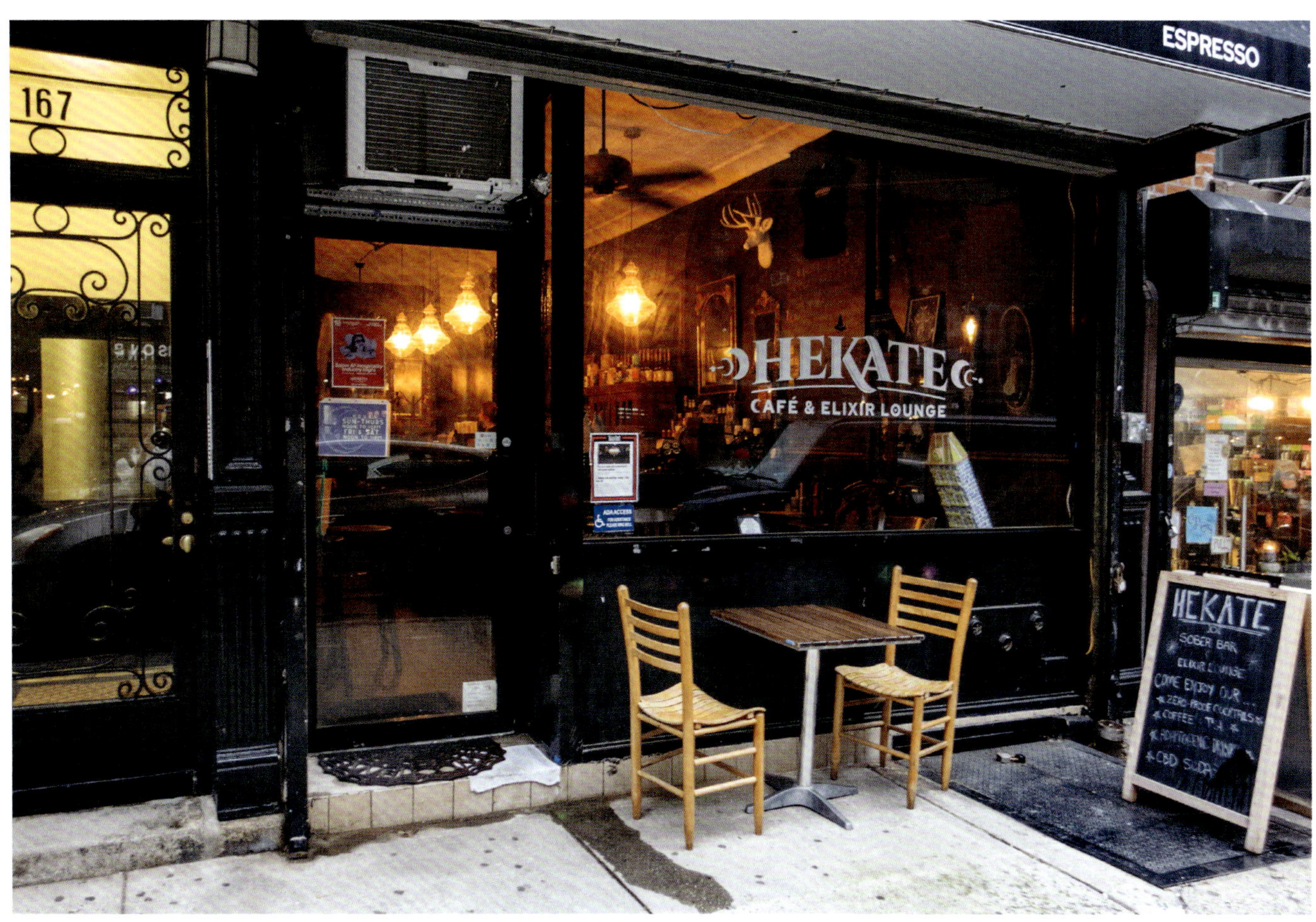

Hekate Café and Elixir
Lounge (sober bar).

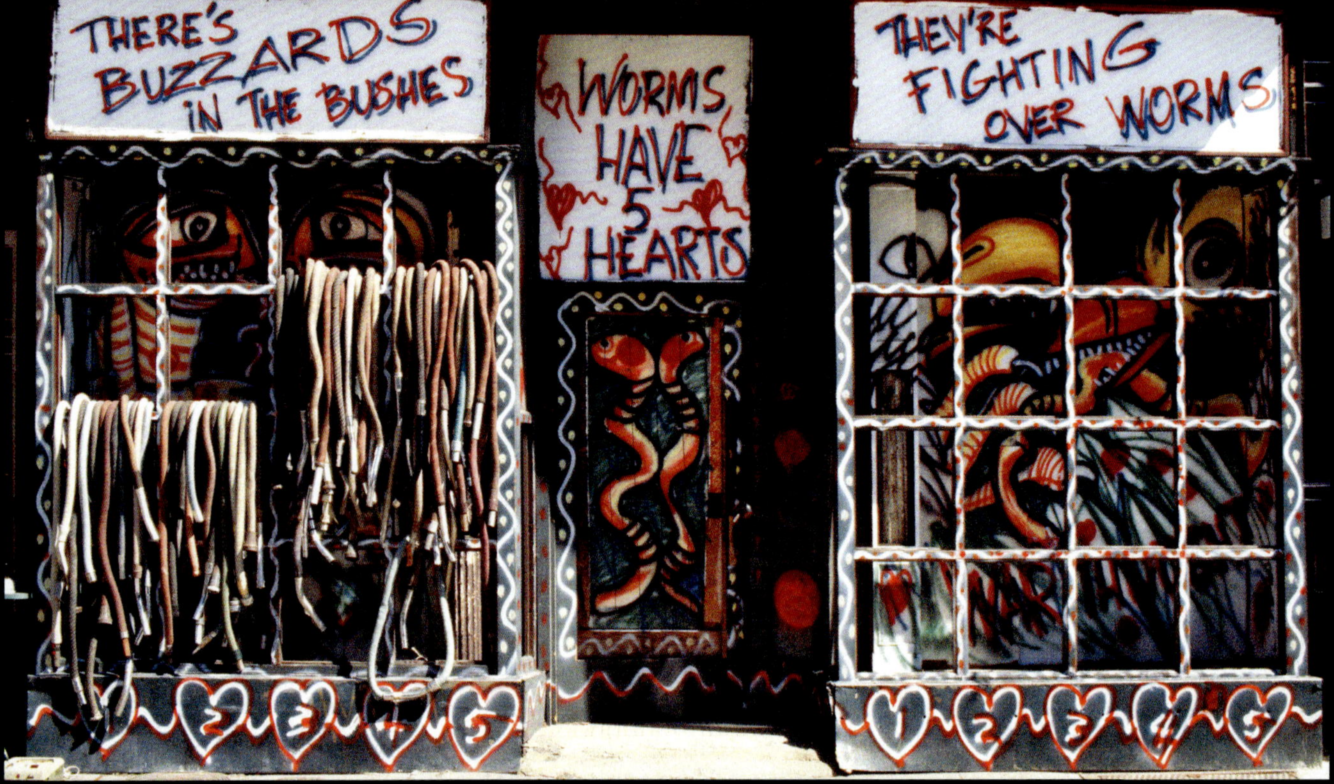

171 AVENUE B

Vacuum hoses and messaging.

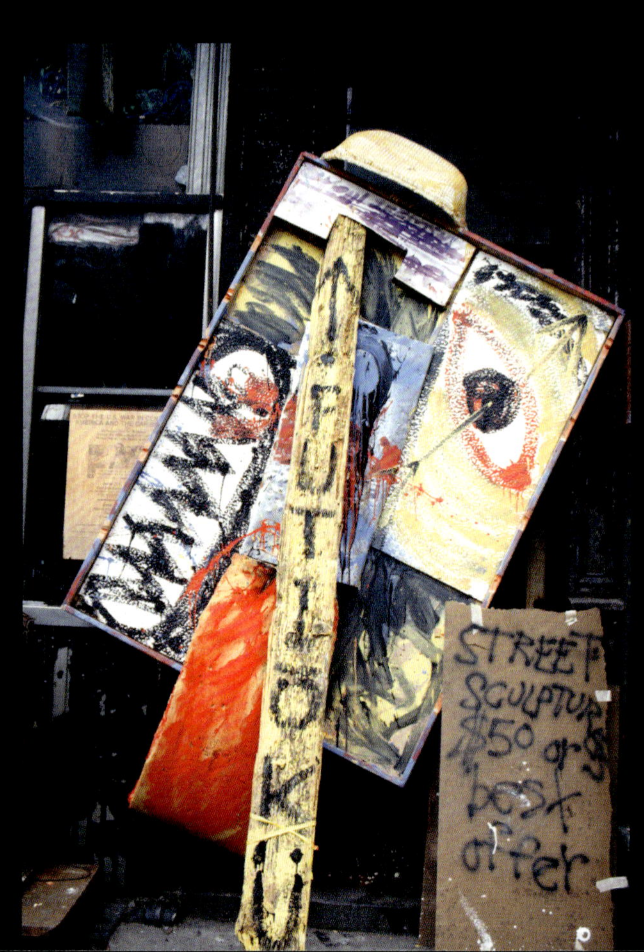

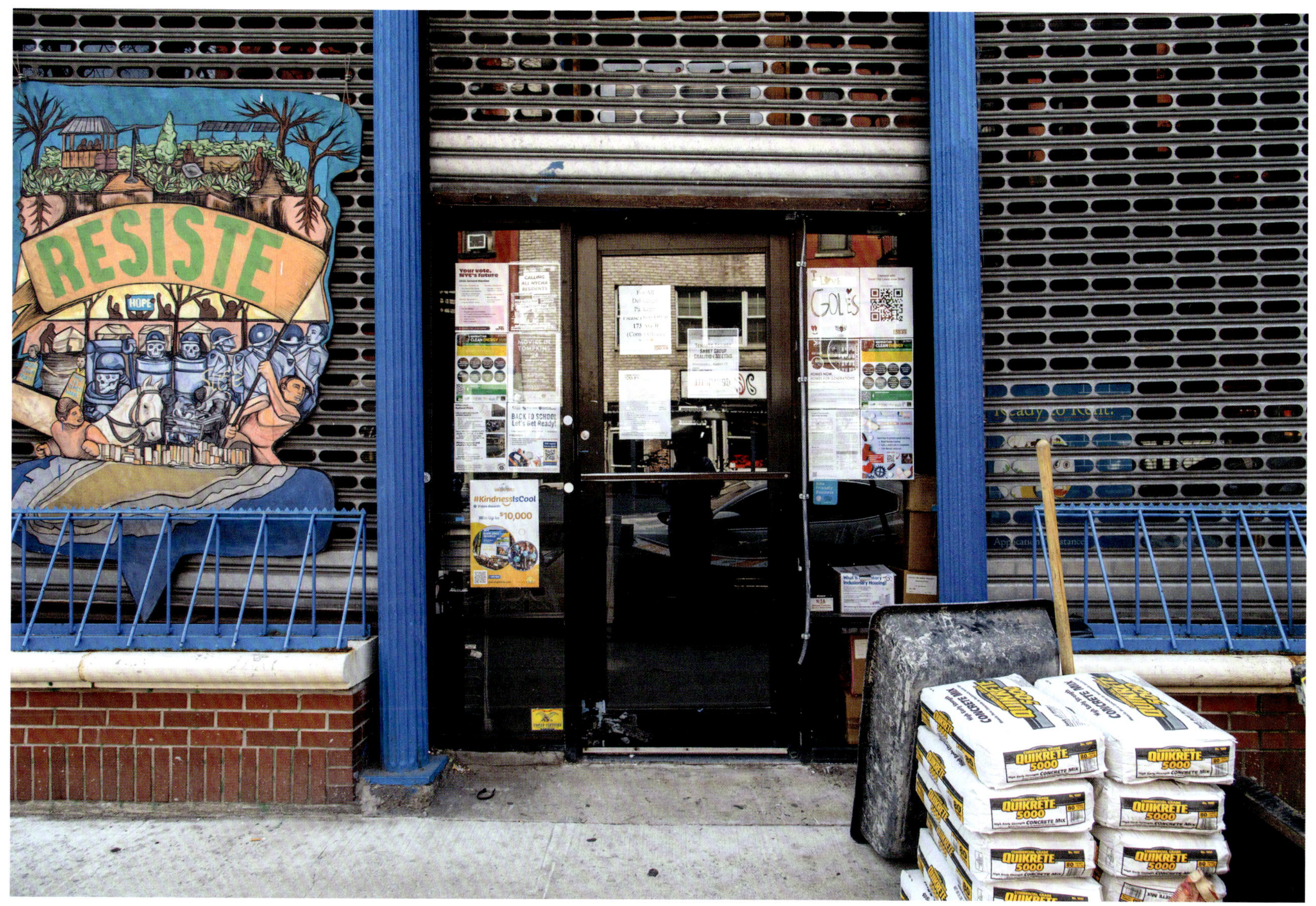

Good Old Lower East Side (GOLES), a
neighborhood housing advocate since 1977.

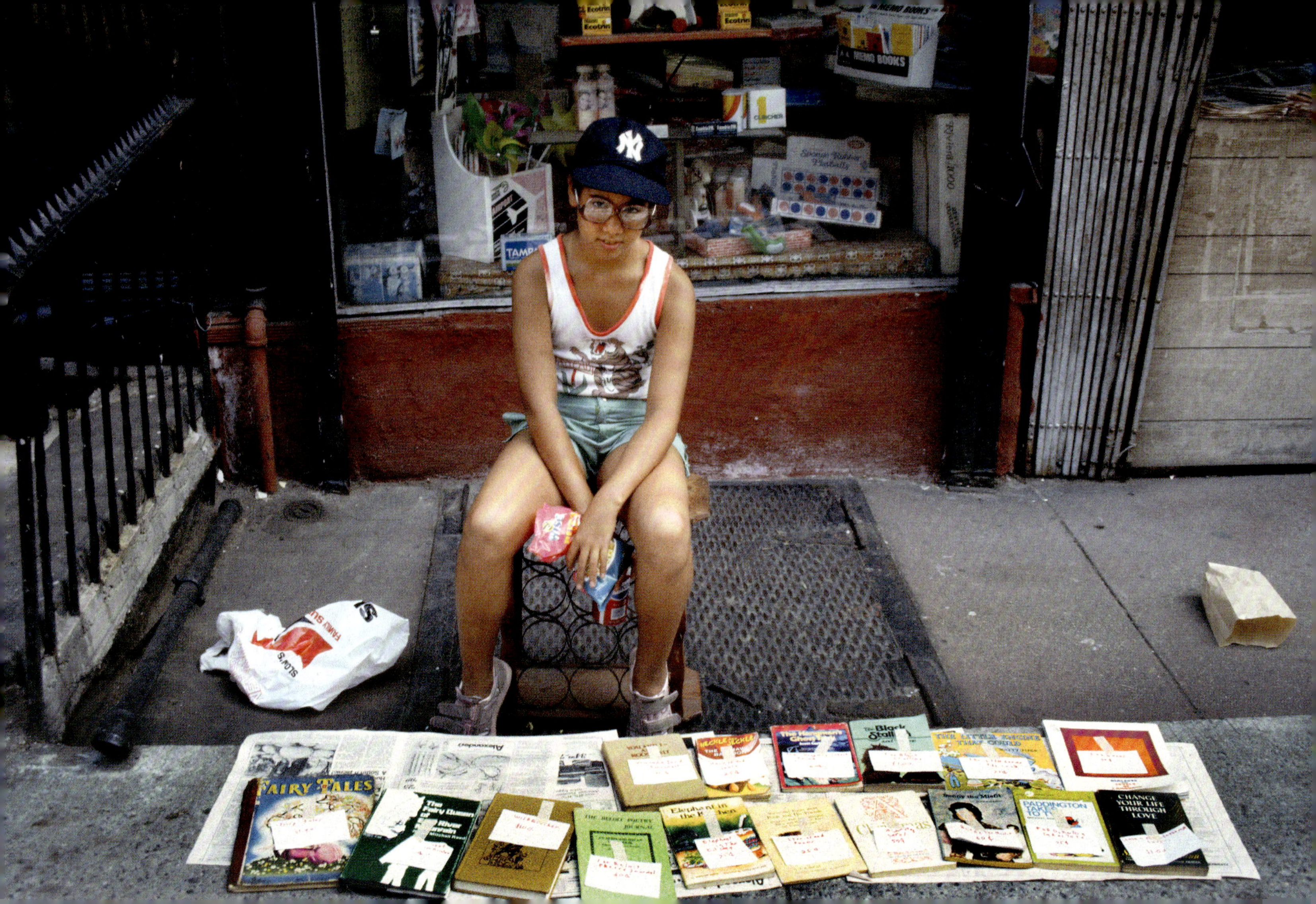

Afternoon Metaphysical Supply seller.

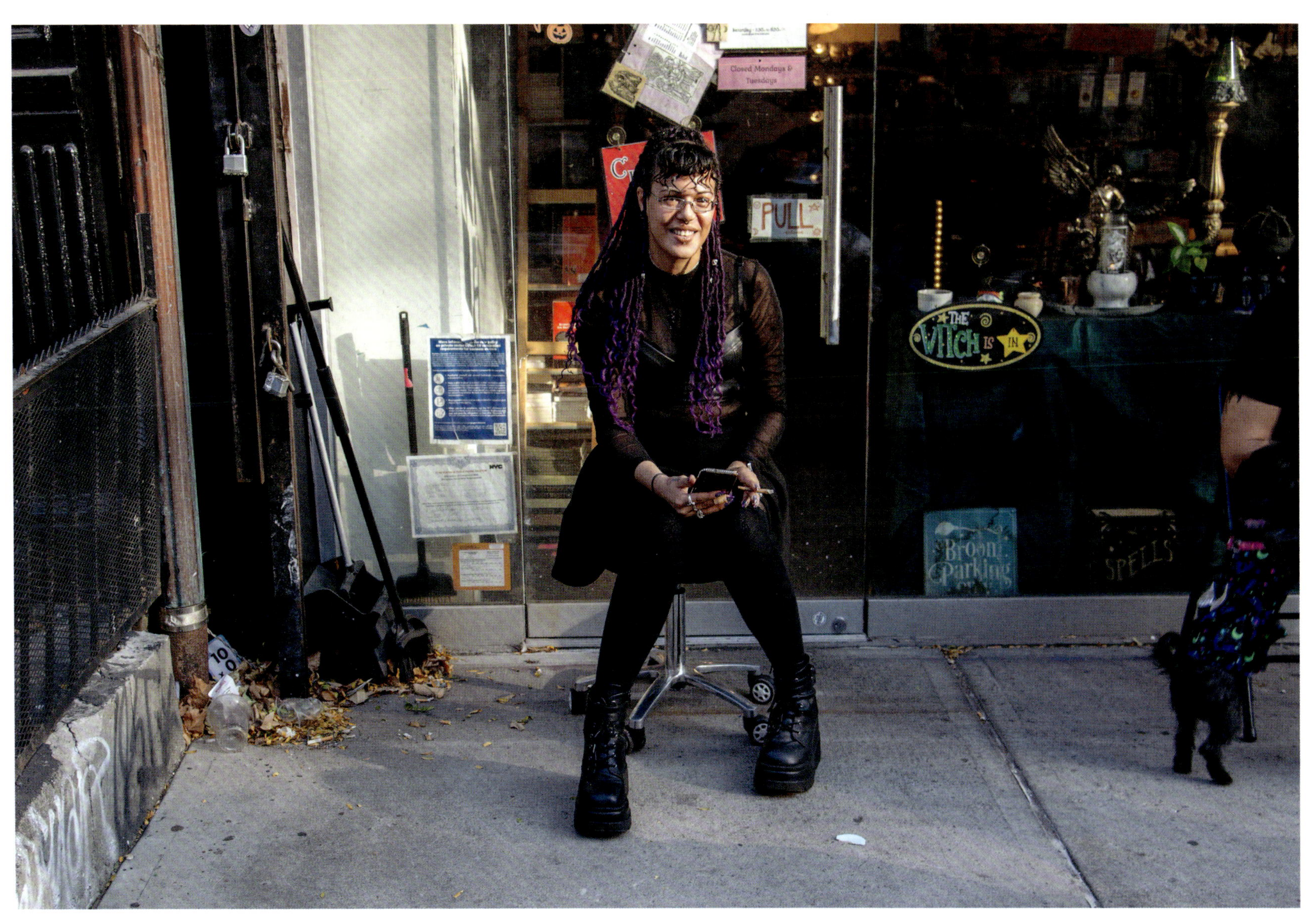

AVENUE B AND EAST 10TH STREET

Burned-out building /
drug dealer hang / squat.

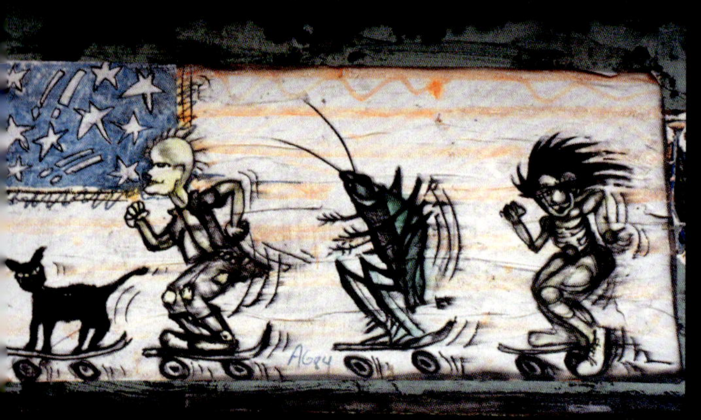

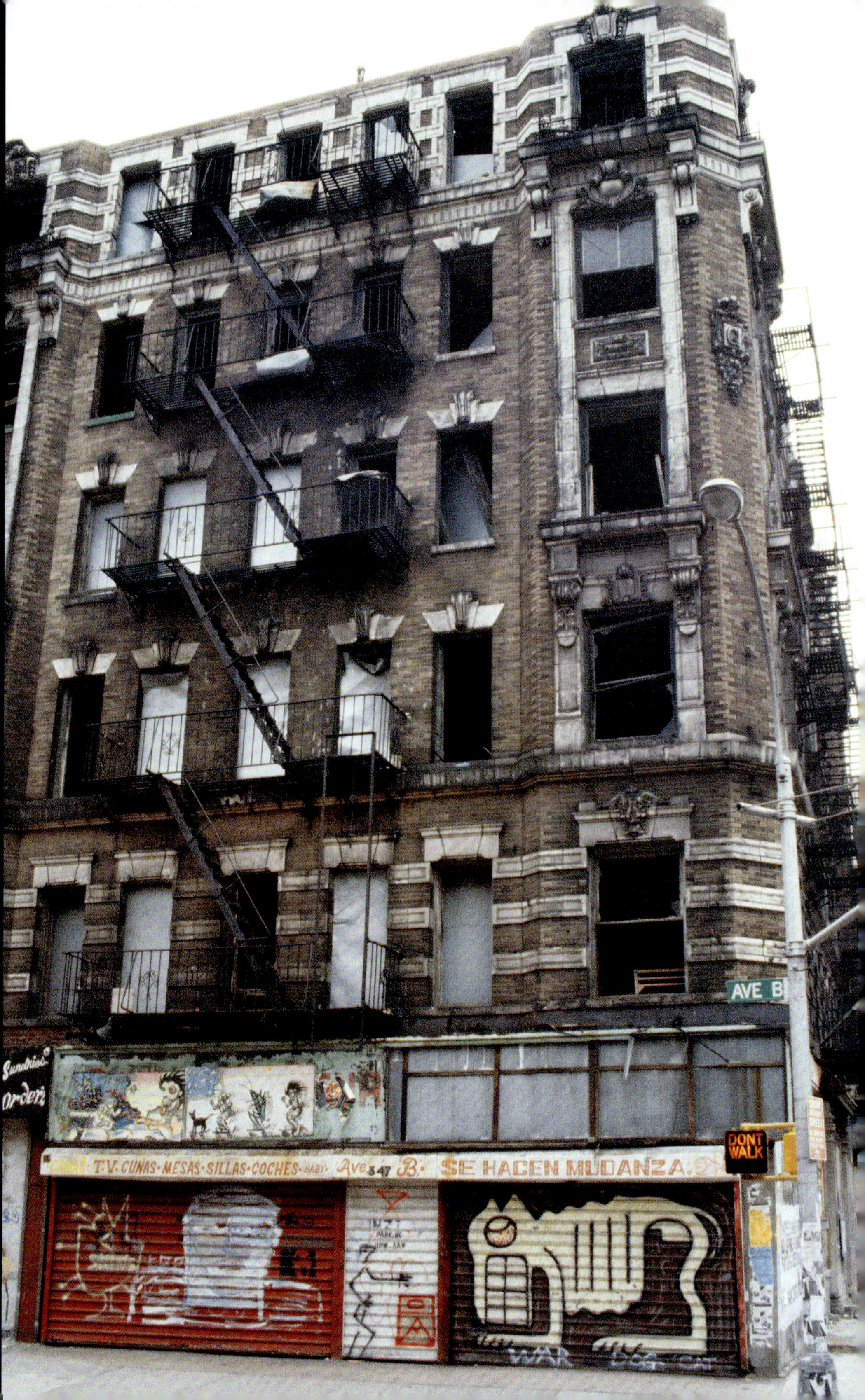

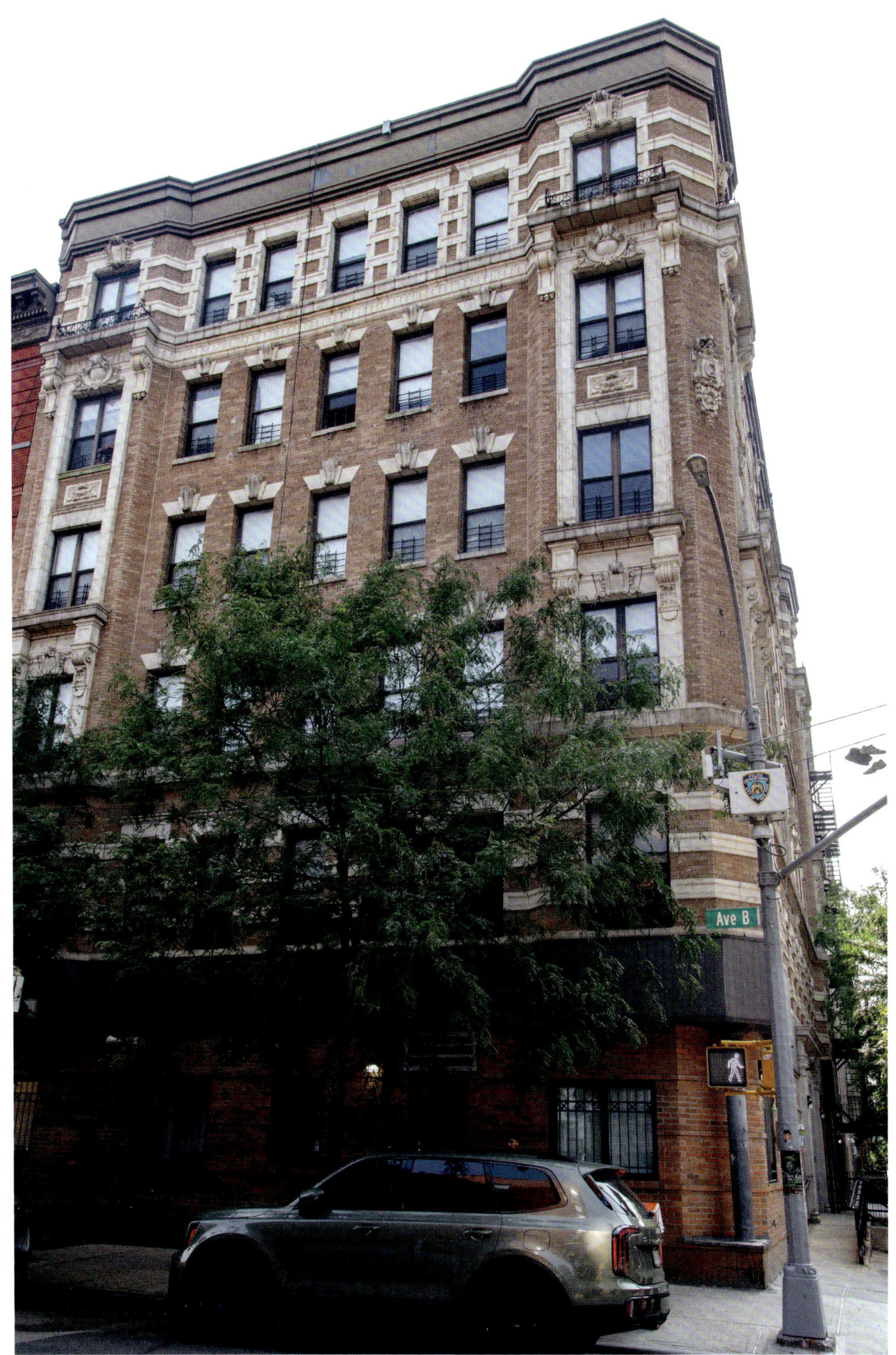

Avenue B and East 10th Street
cleaned up.

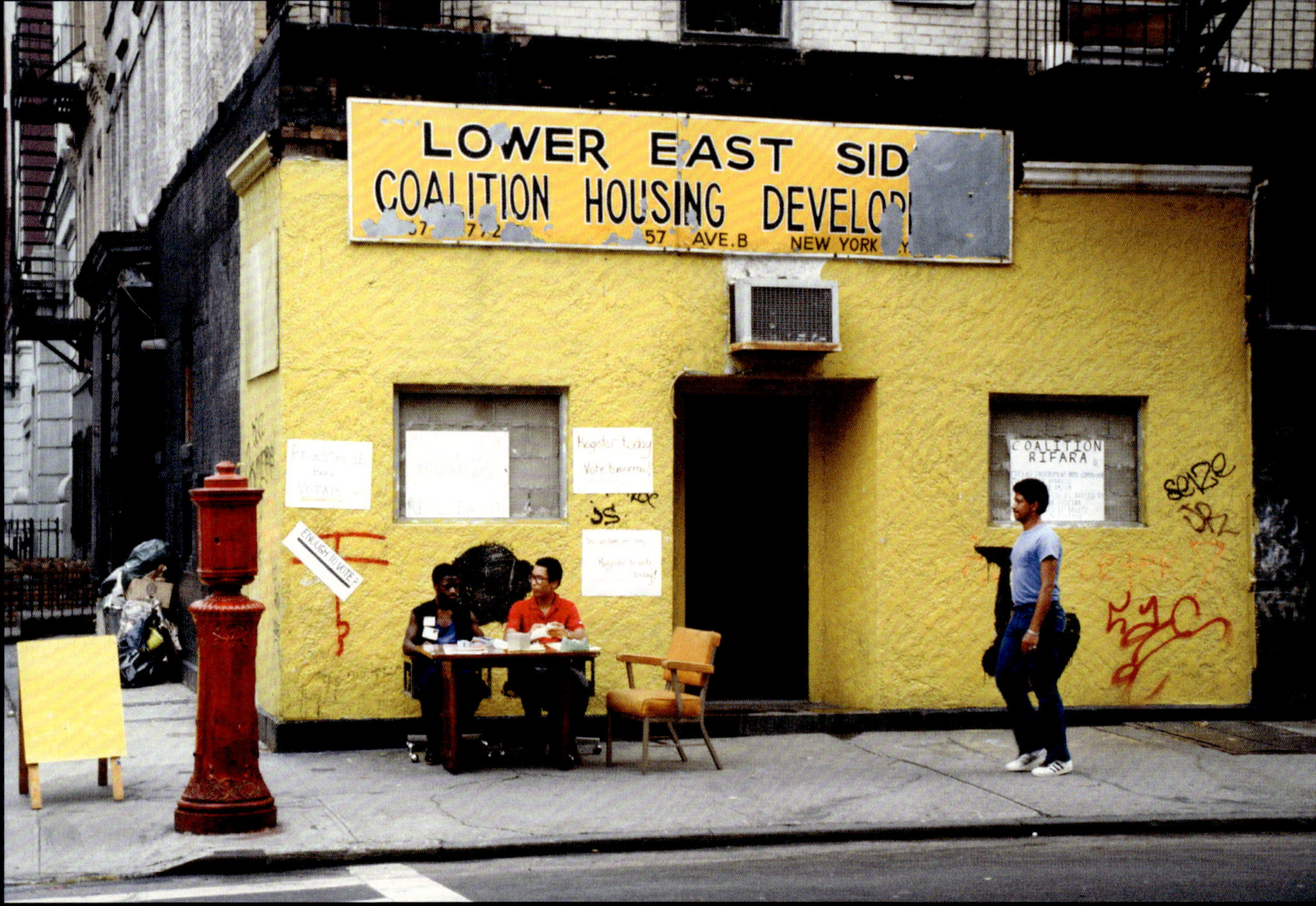

157 AVENUE B

Lower East Side Coalition Housing
Development, voter registration drive.

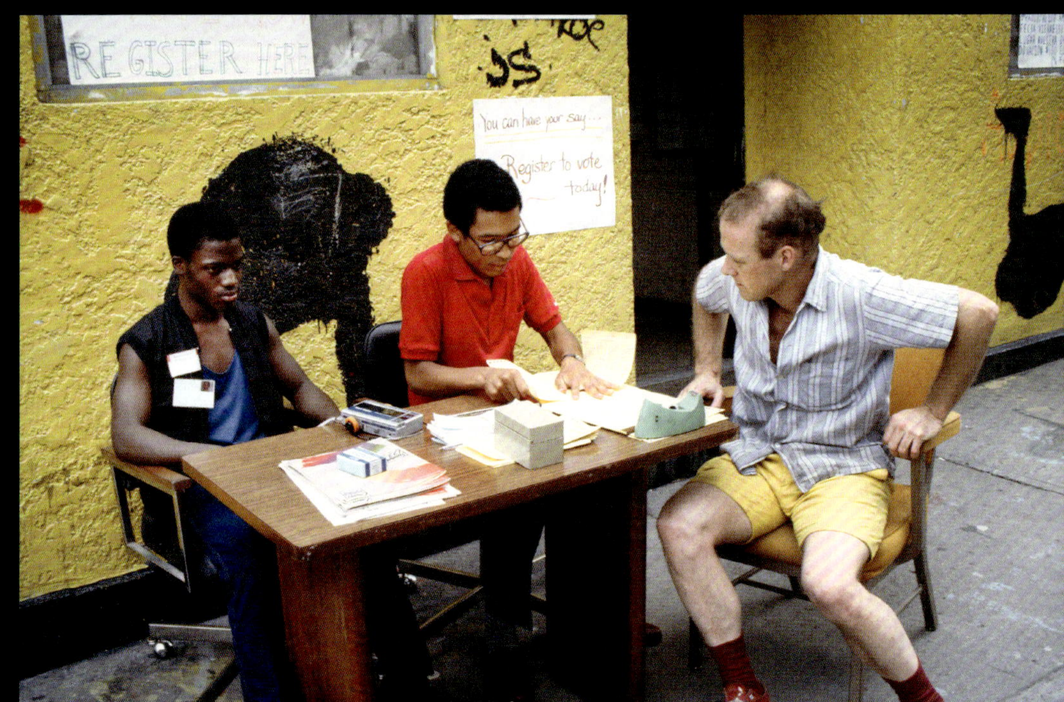

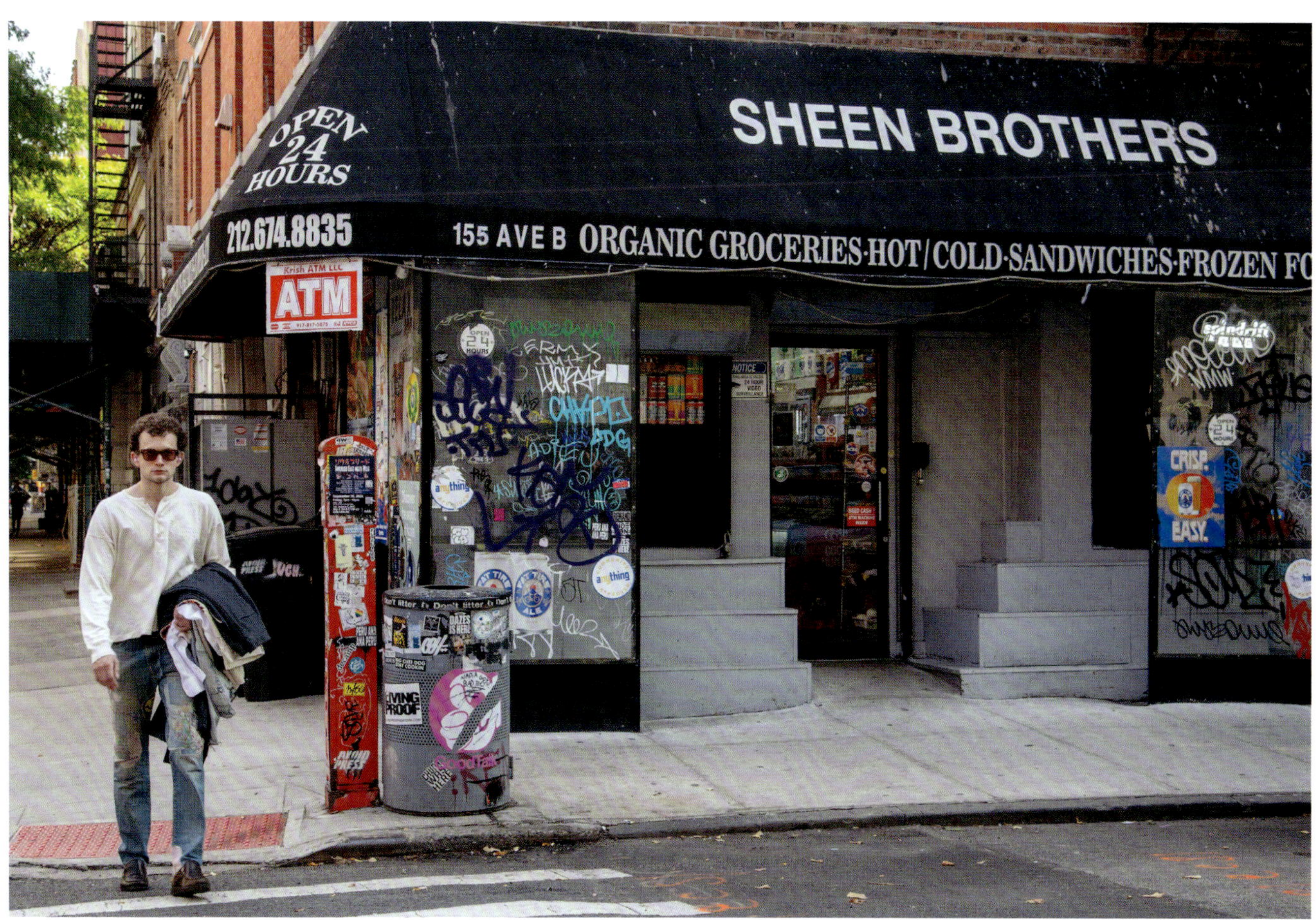

Convenience store.

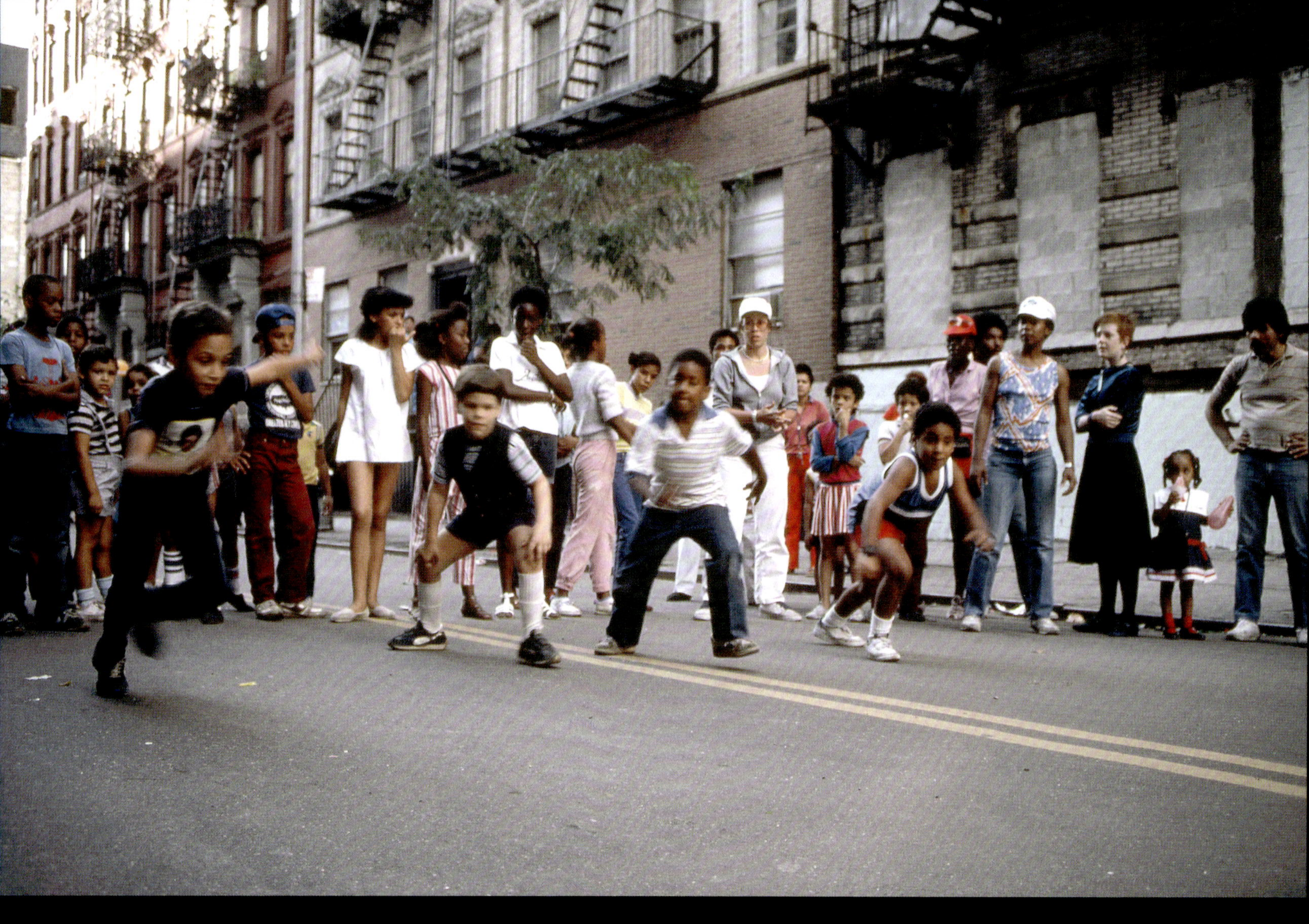

367 EAST 10TH STREET

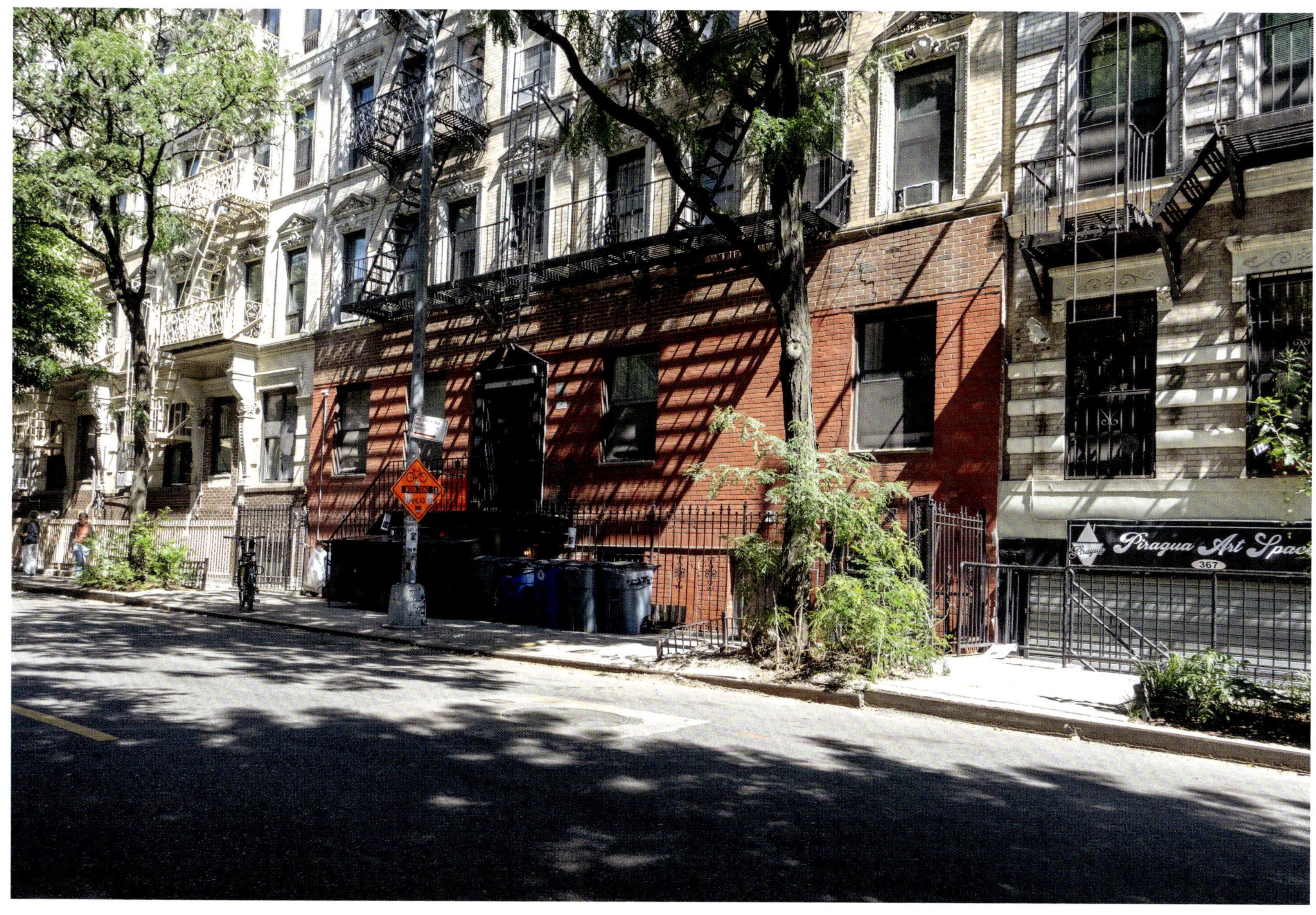

Piragua Art Space in the basement level.

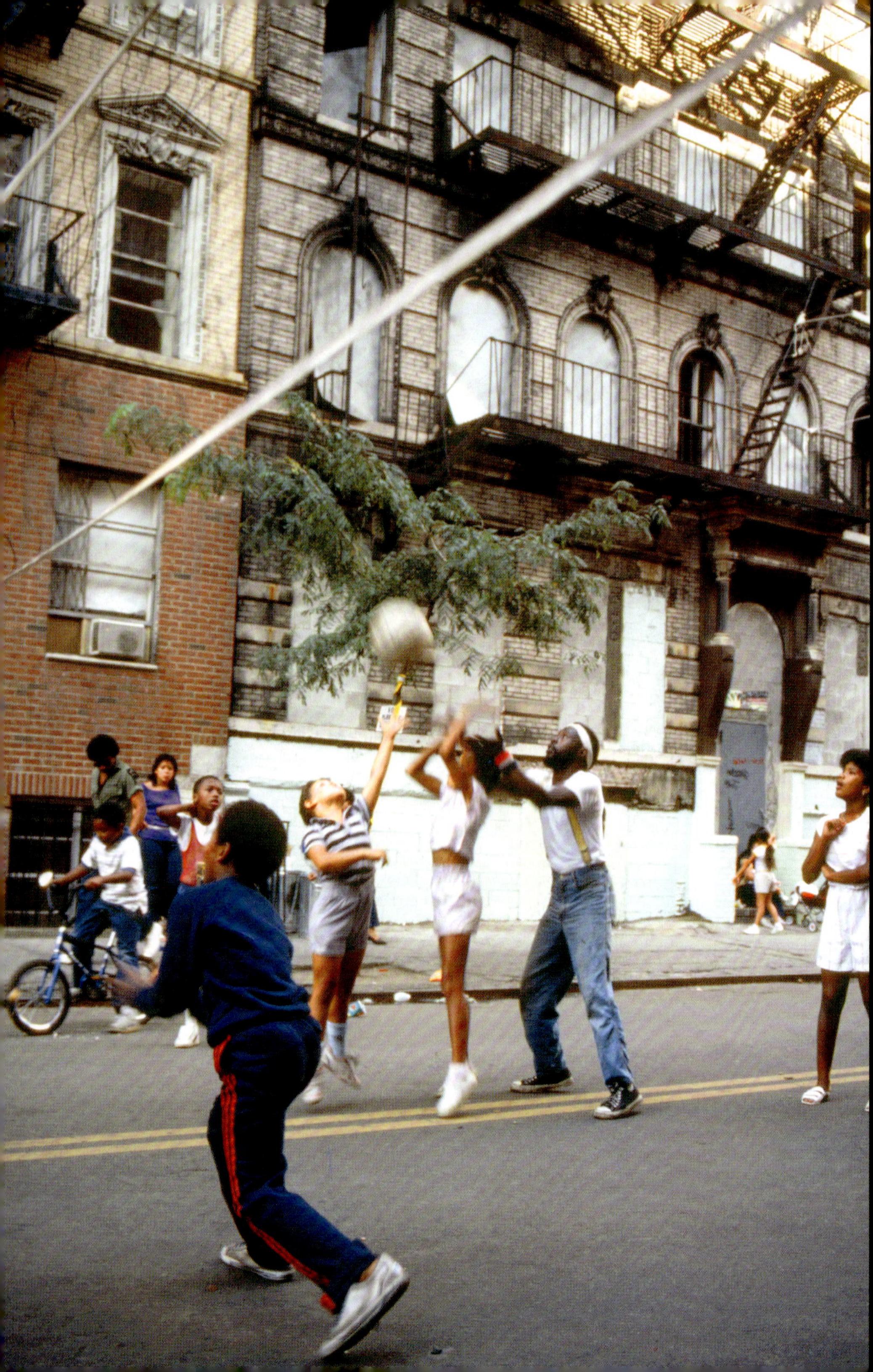

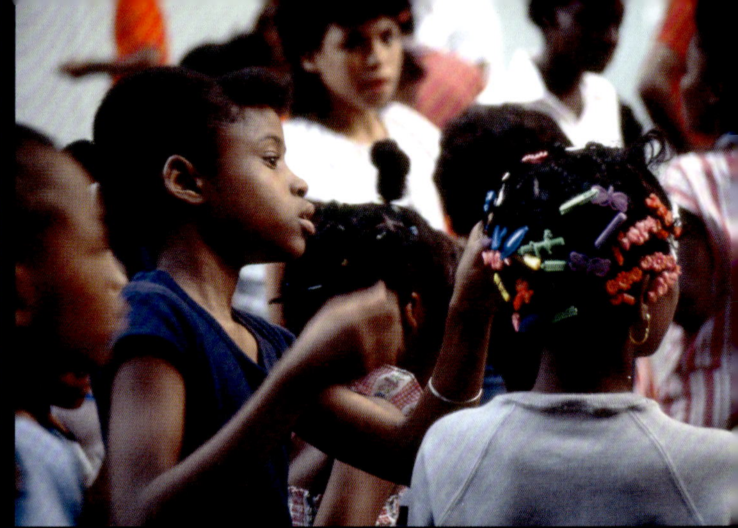
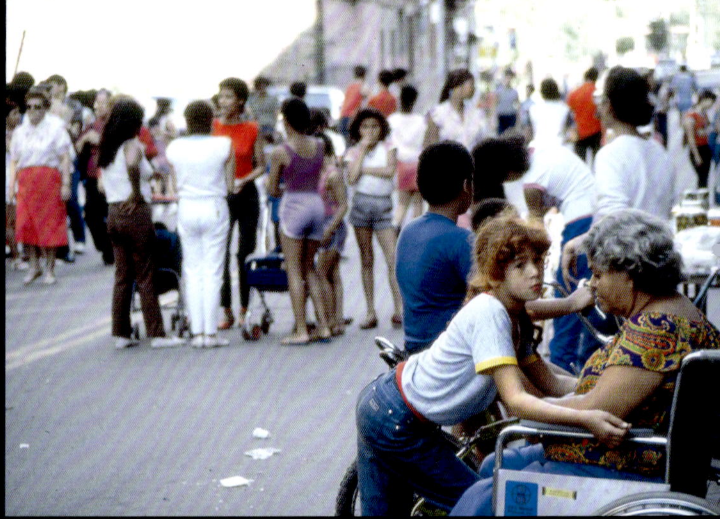
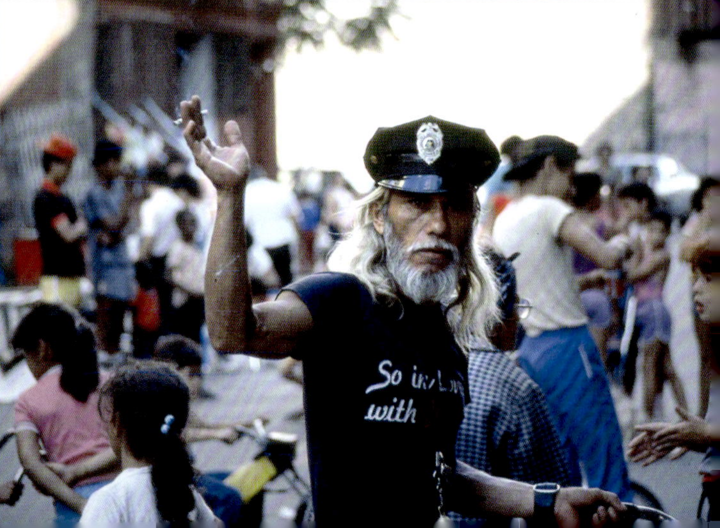

367 EAST 10TH STREET

THEN Block party.

NOW The trees have grown.

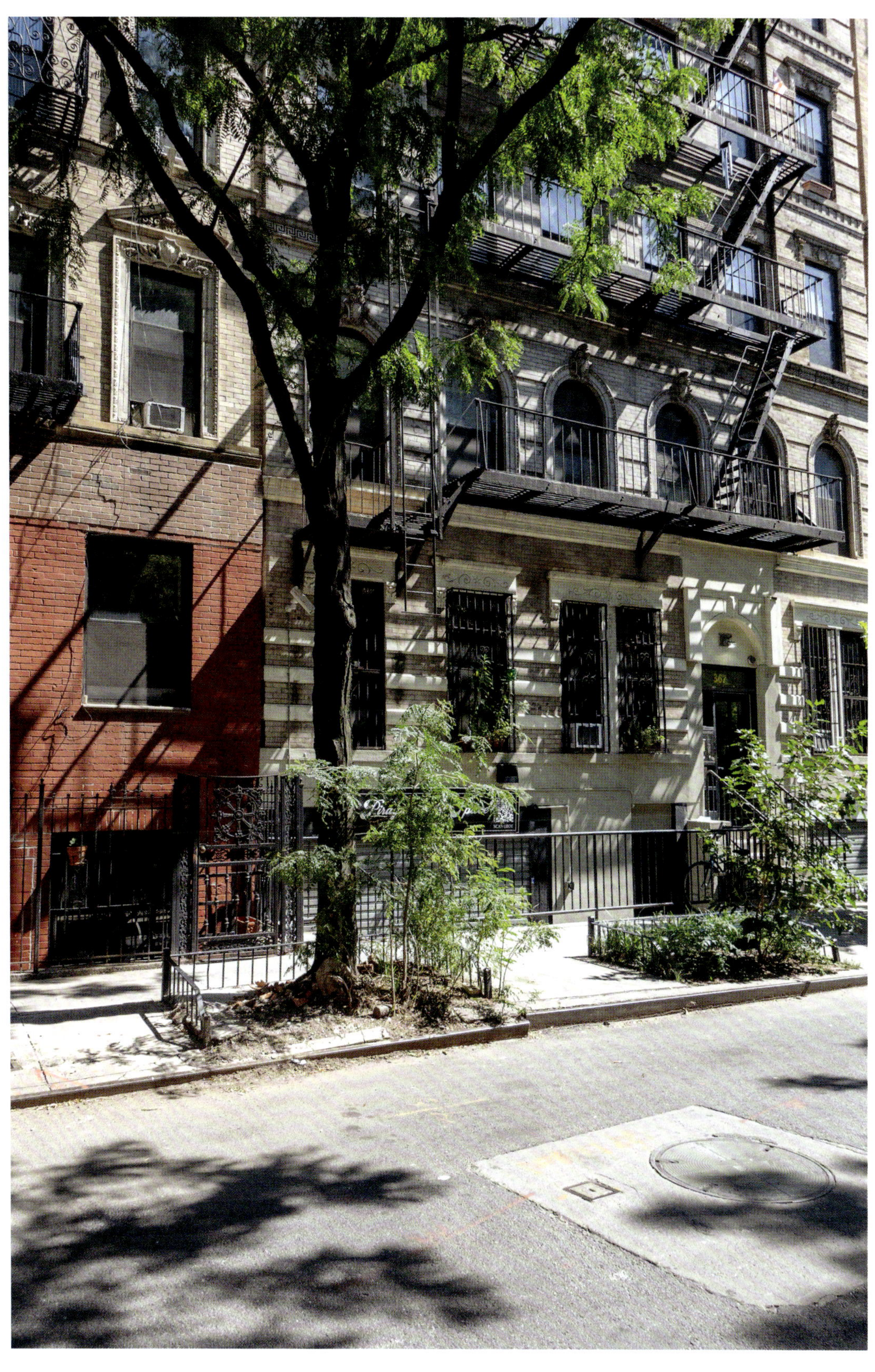

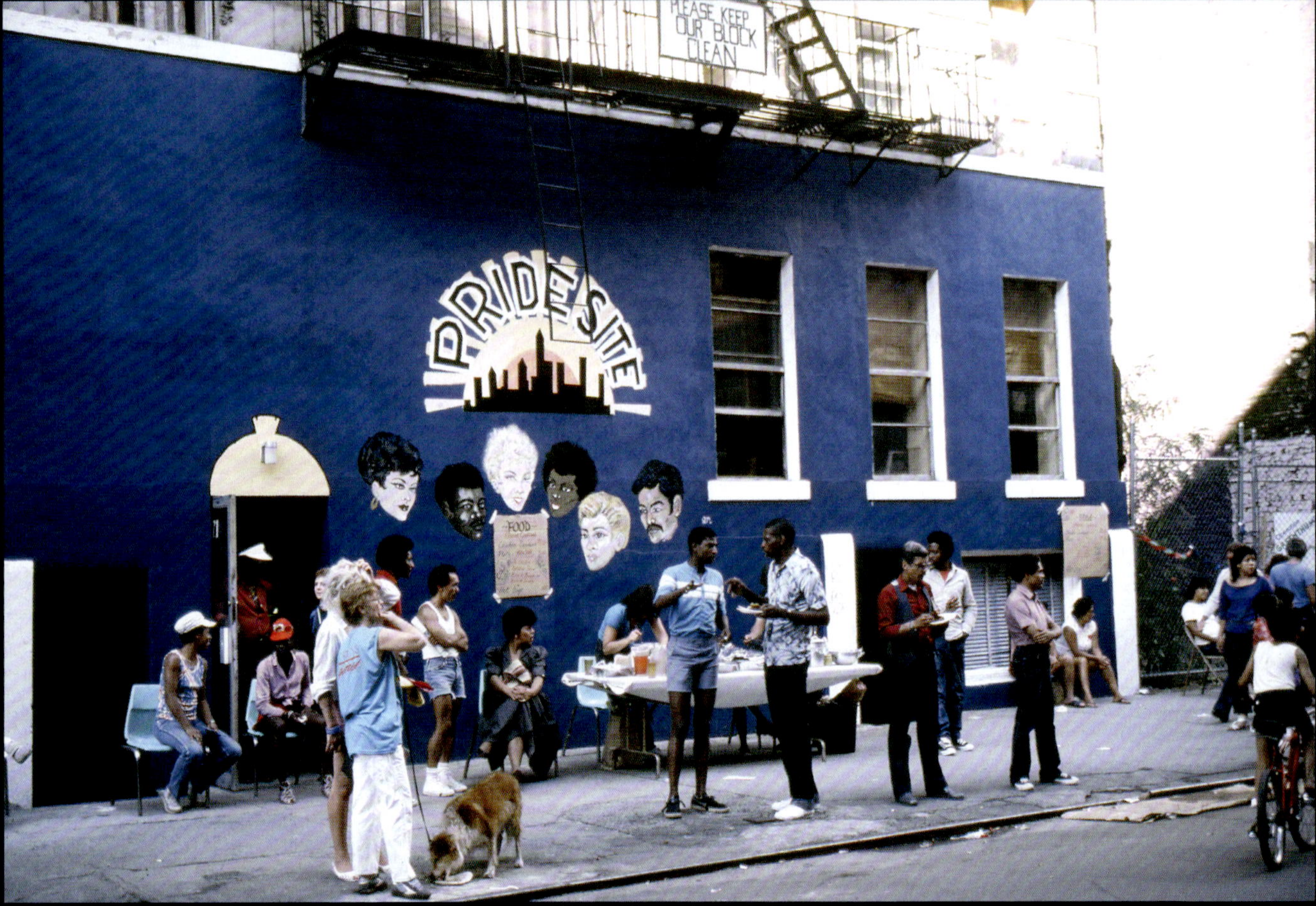

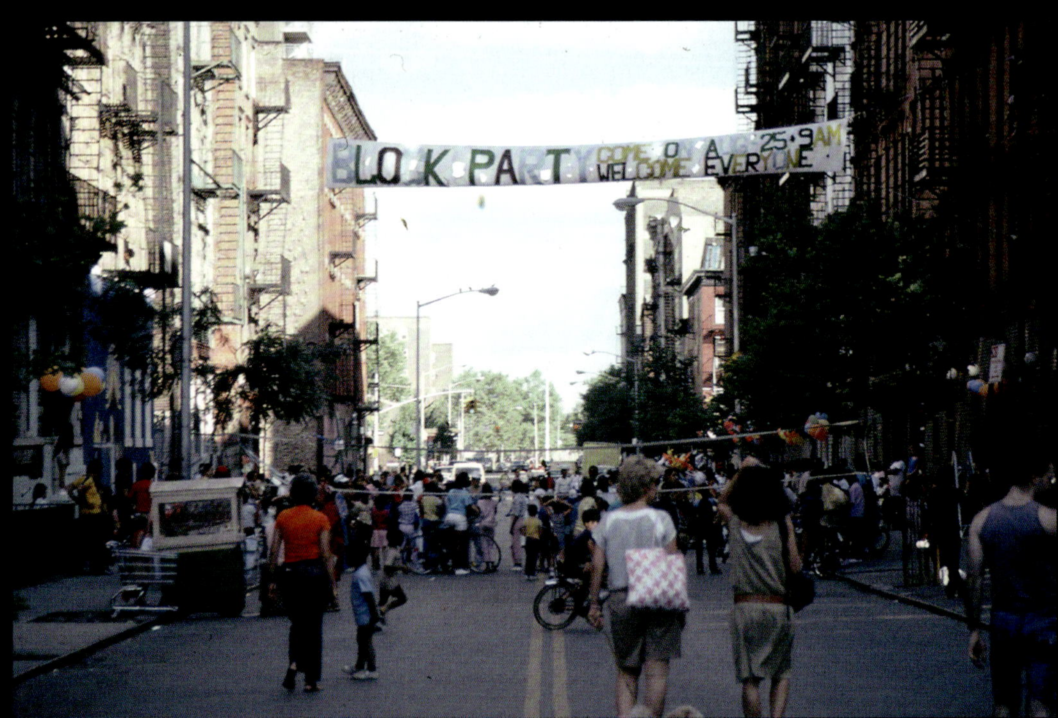

371 EAST 10TH STREET

Community cookout, empty lot.

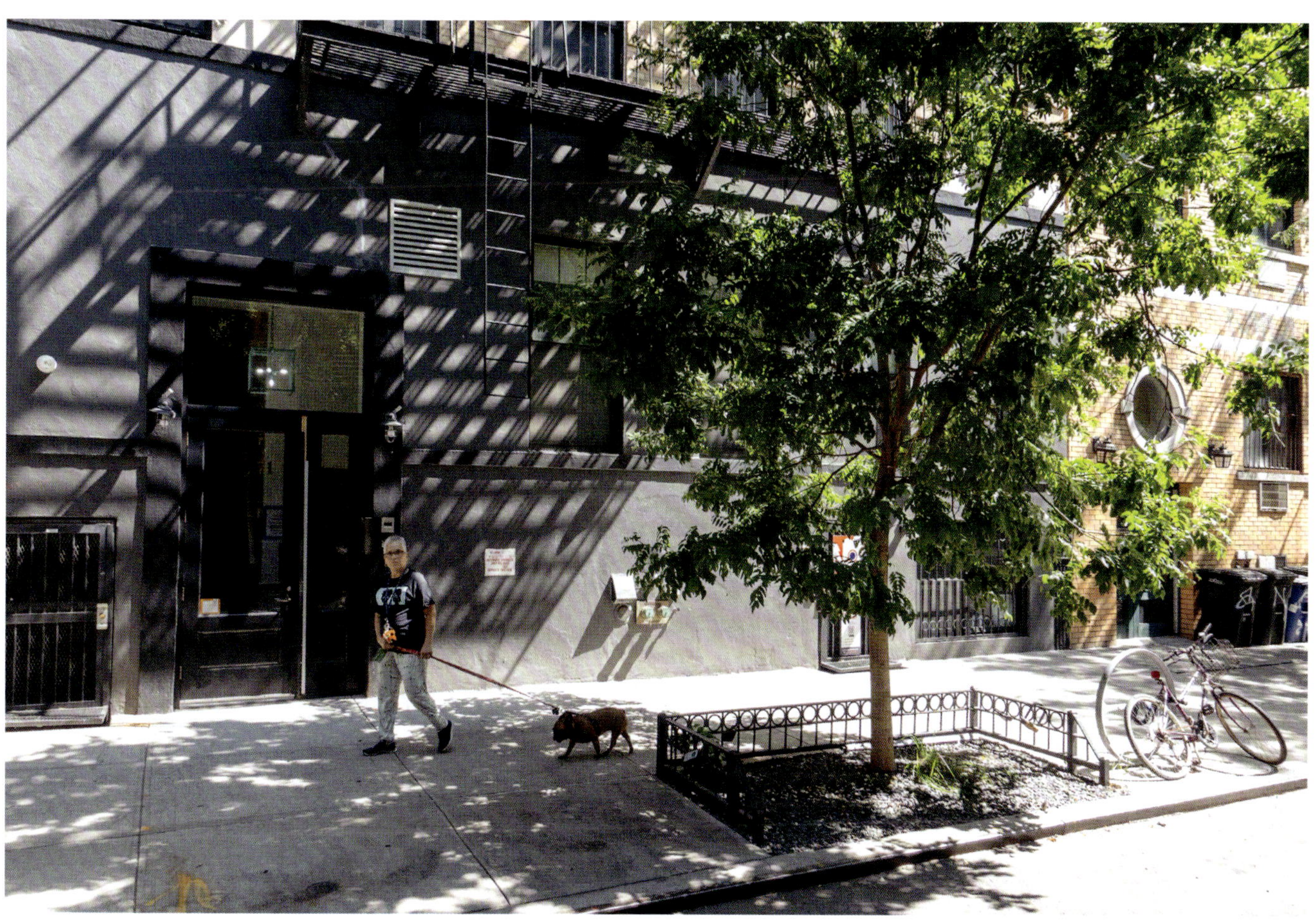

Fixed-up building, new building,
afternoon stroll with the dog.

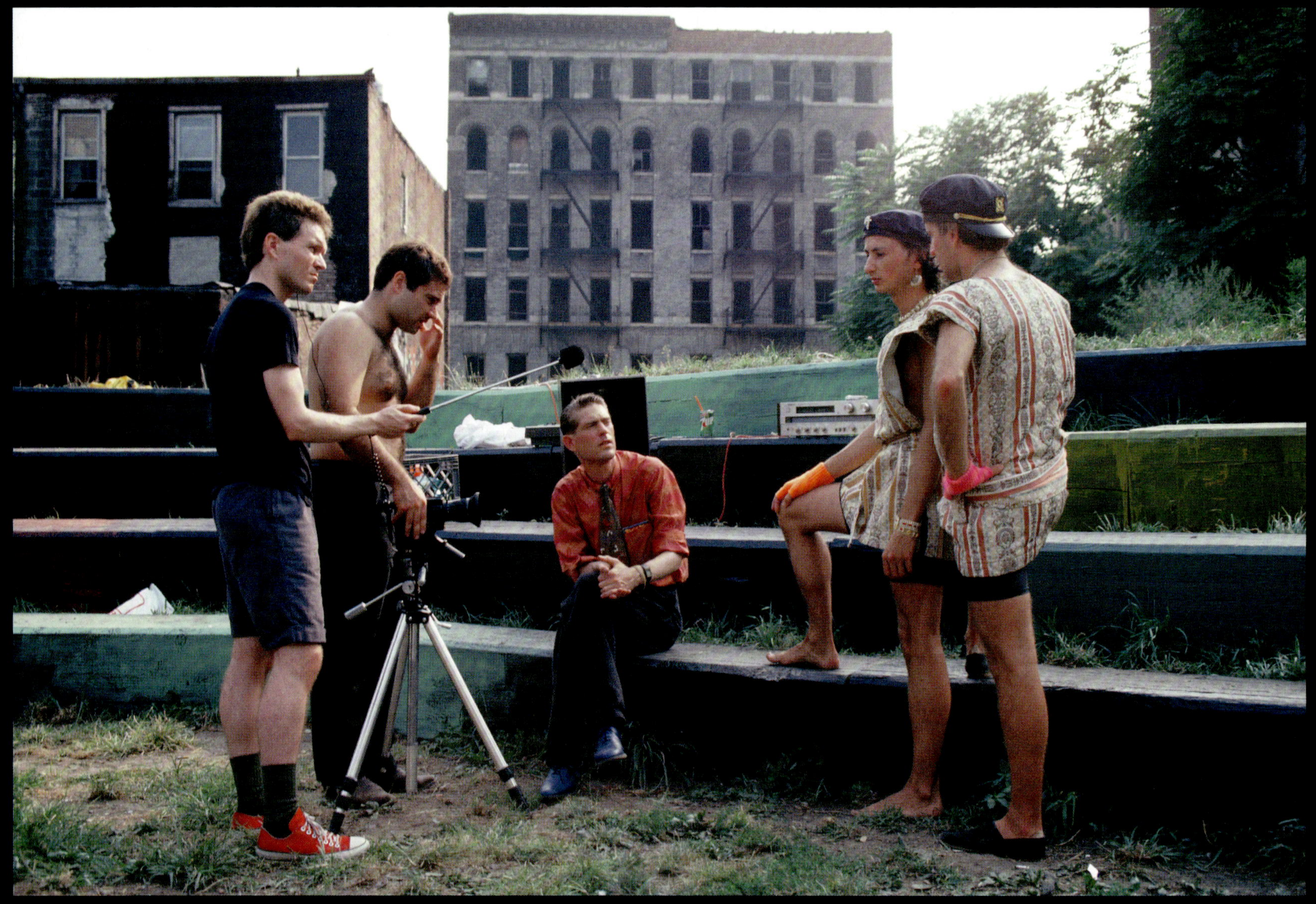

EAST 9TH STREET
AND AVENUE C

Low-budget video in the one of the neighborhood community gardens, with a backdrop of abandoned buildings. My chance meeting with this production crew led to a modest career in shooting pop music. After I photographed them, at their request, I took the photos to the production company, ATI, which was doing Night Flight on the USA Network and some MTV knockoffs.

When ATI asked who else I had photographed, I immediately mentioned Madonna. They hired me, and I started shooting about three to five bands a week for their other USA show, Radio 1990, with Kathryn Kinley and Lisa Robinson. After that I went on to shoot for MTV and then the various record labels.

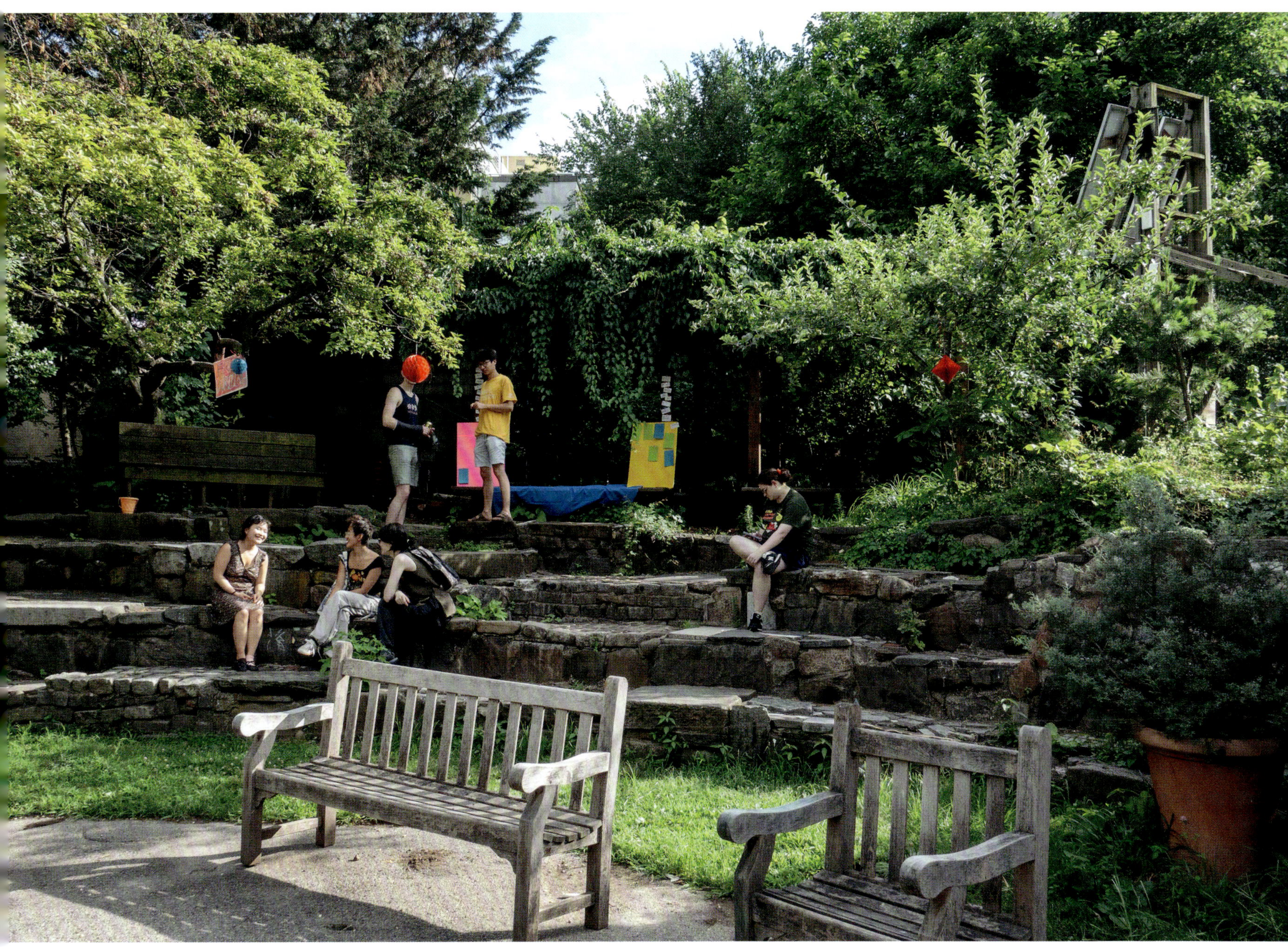

The changes over the years. The willows have come and gone, but all the trees are doing their part. Performance and music continue to be a part of the garden.

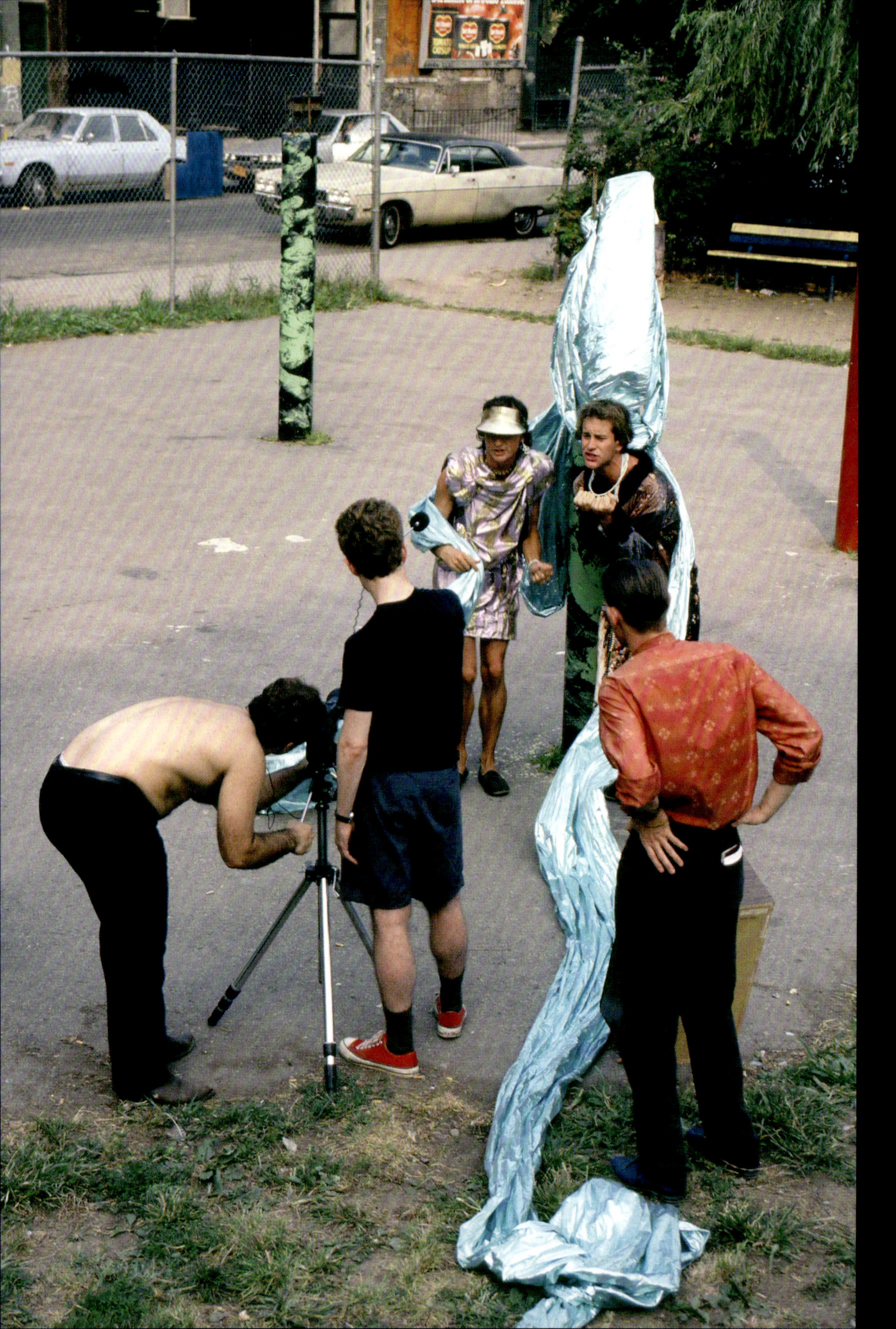

View toward Avenue C.
The video continues.

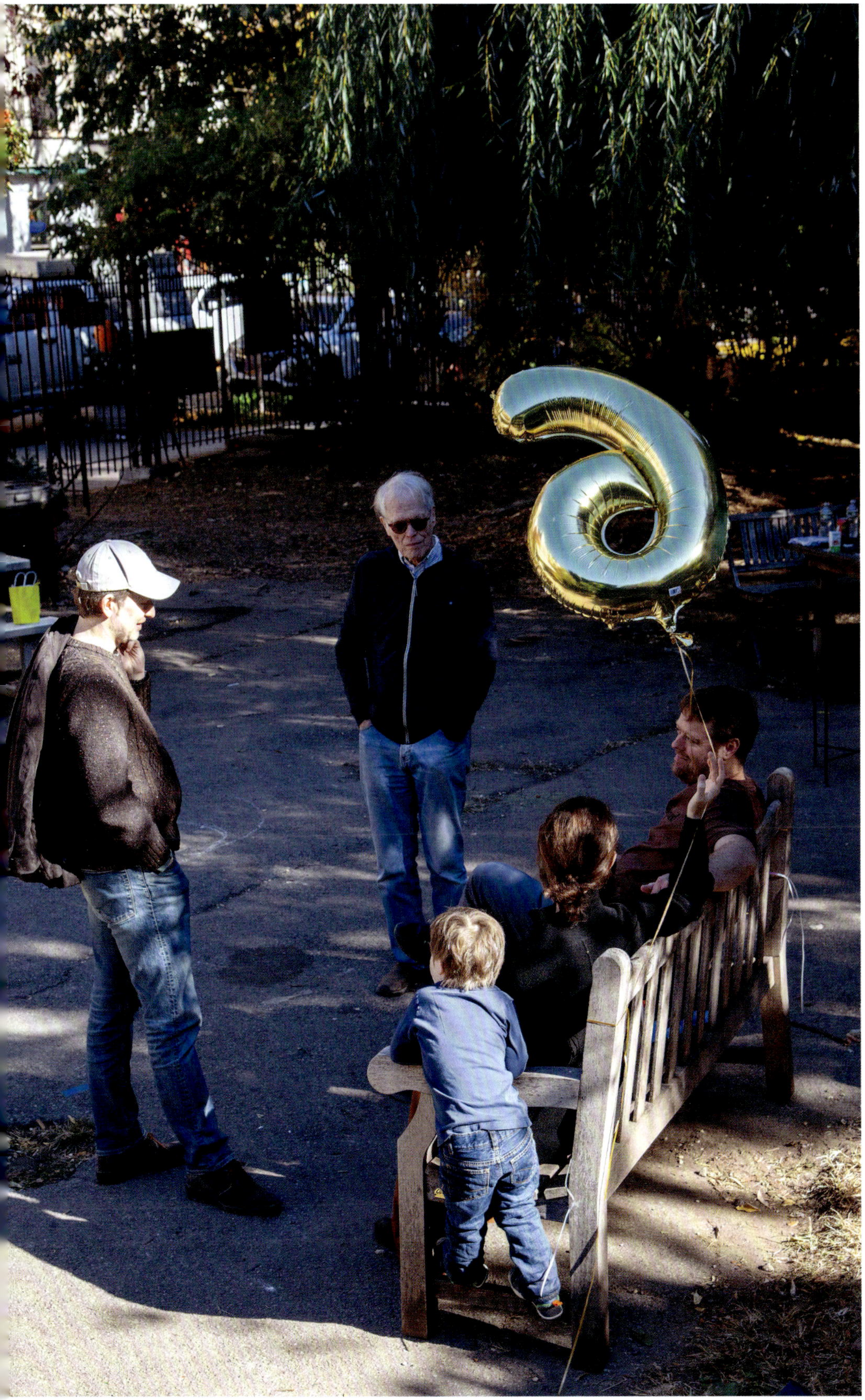

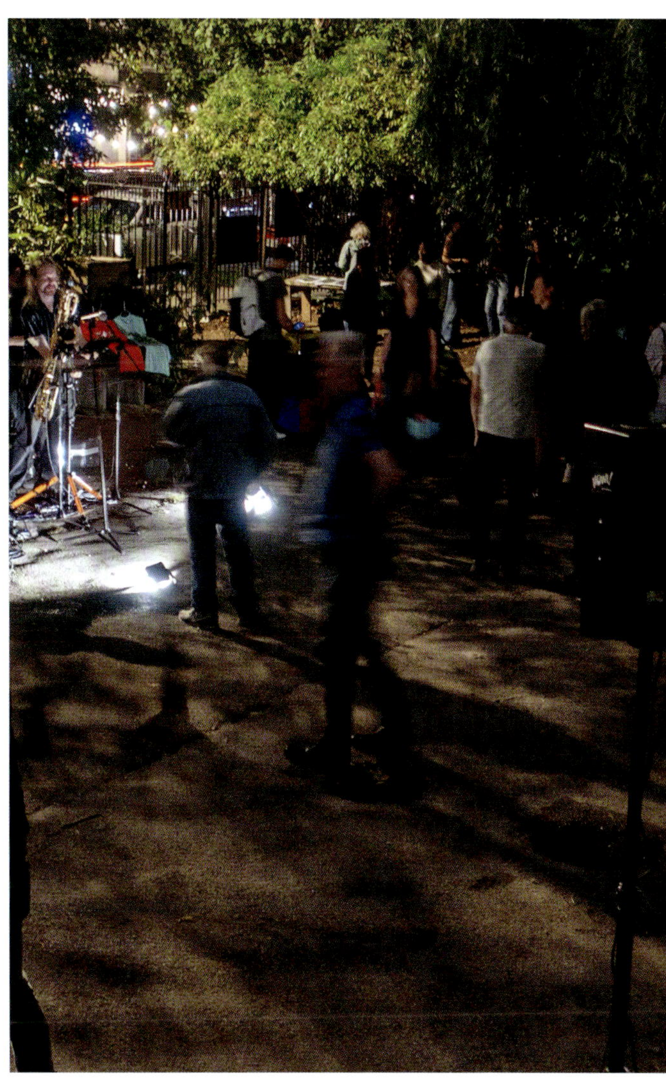

A birthday party for a
neighborhood six-year-old.

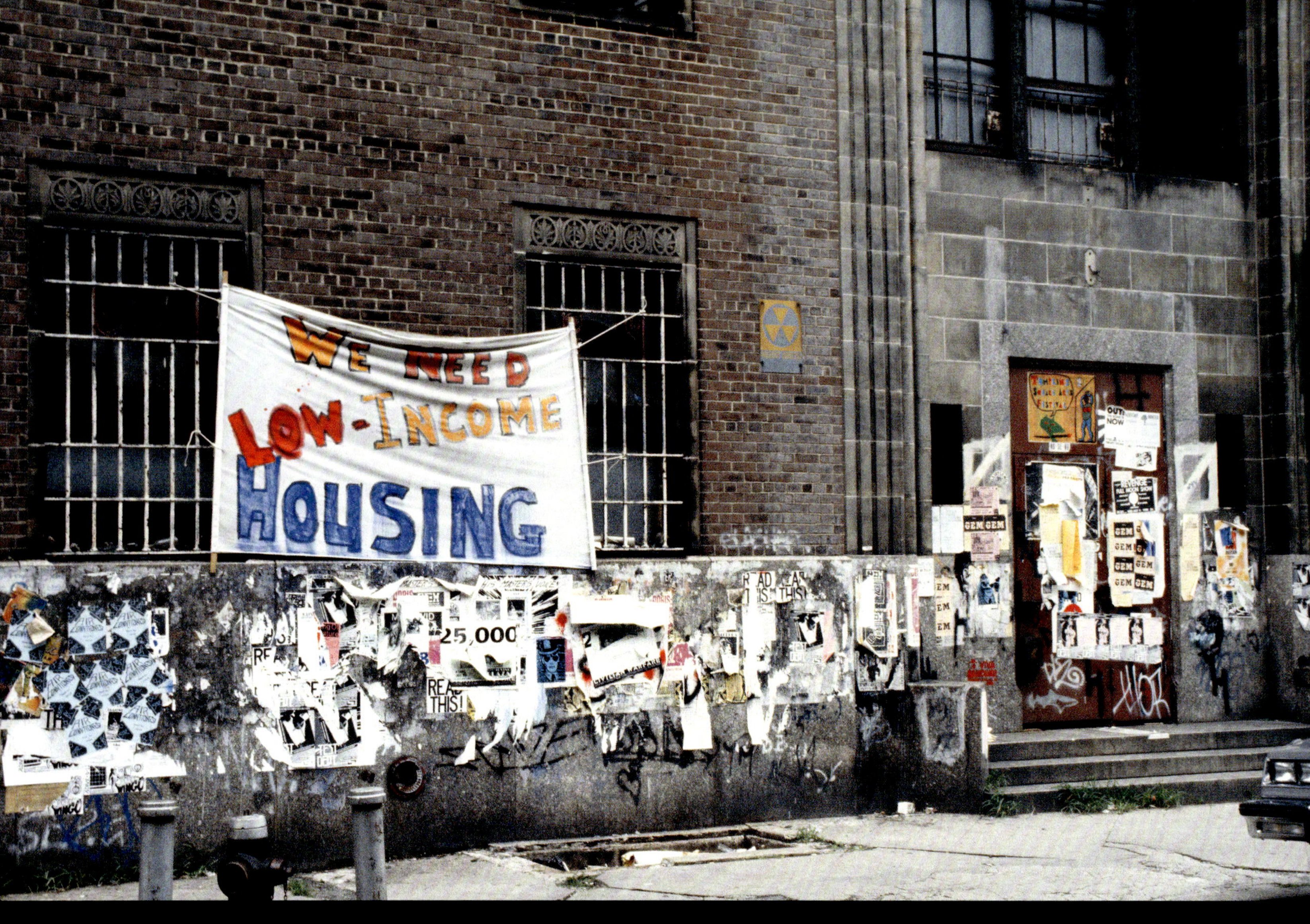
WE NEED
LOW-INCOME
HOUSING
25,000
143 AVENUE B

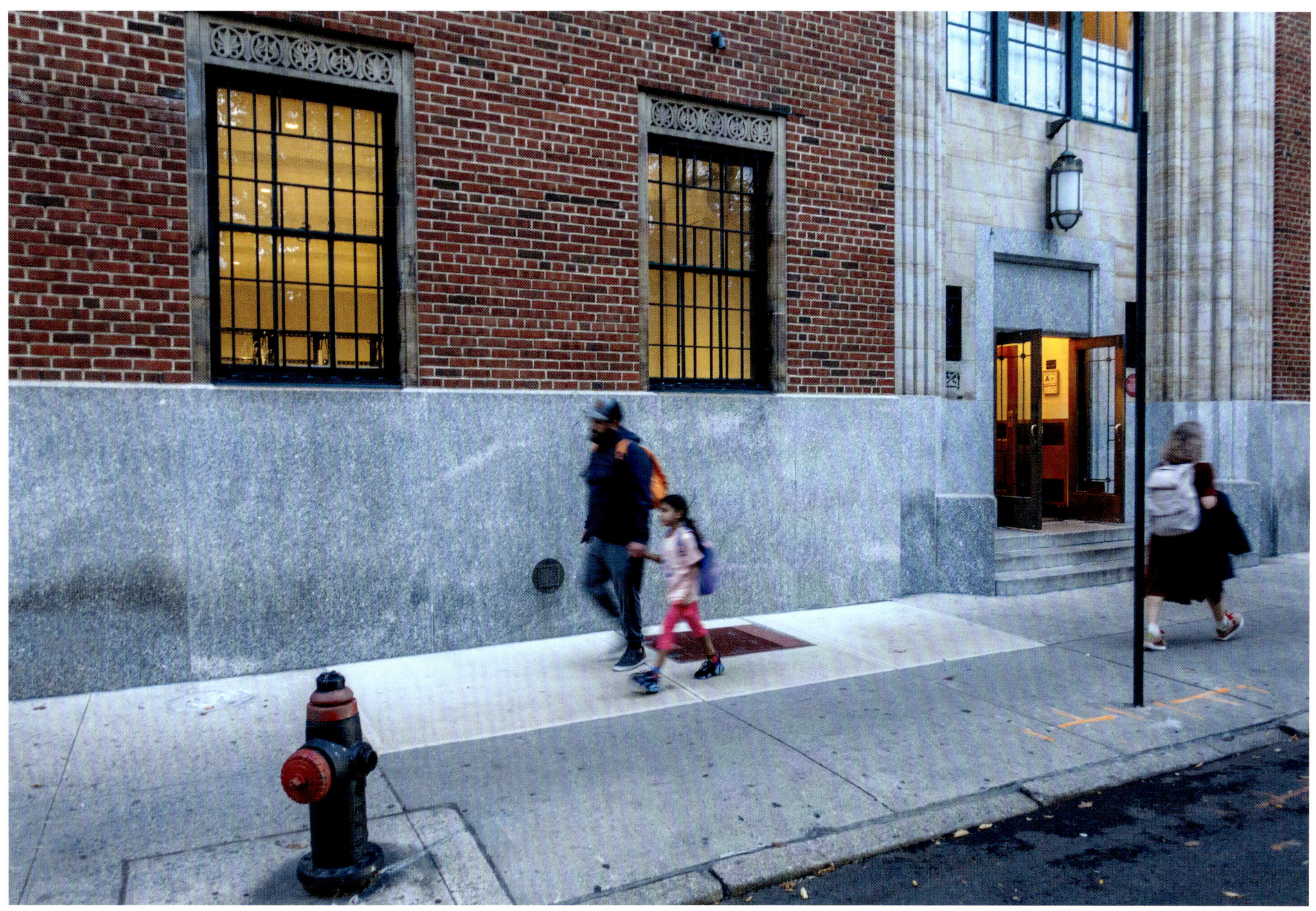

Christodora House,
walking home from school,
walking home from work.

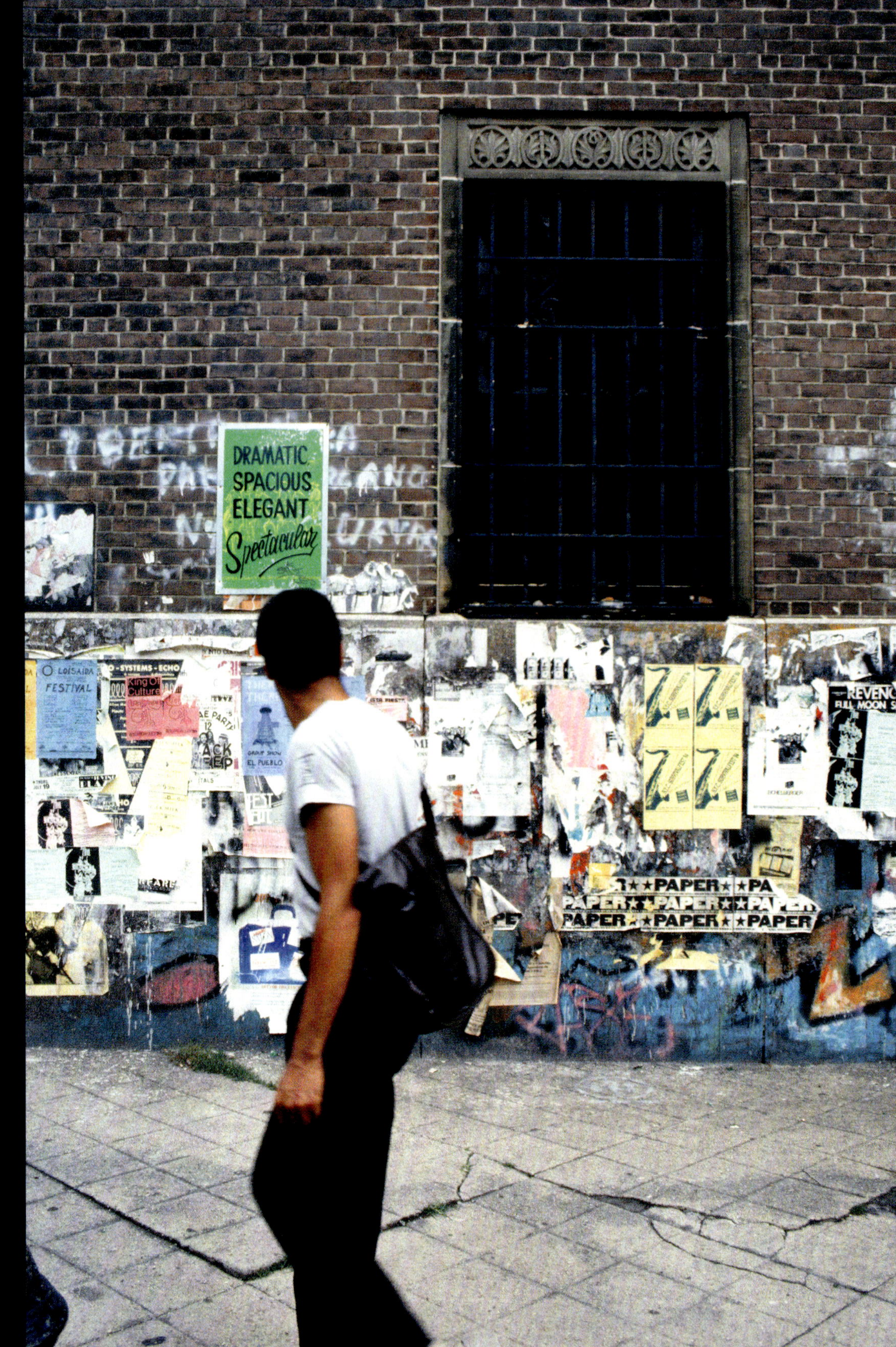

143 AVENUE B

Christodora House: Dramatic,
Spacious, Elegant, Spectacular.

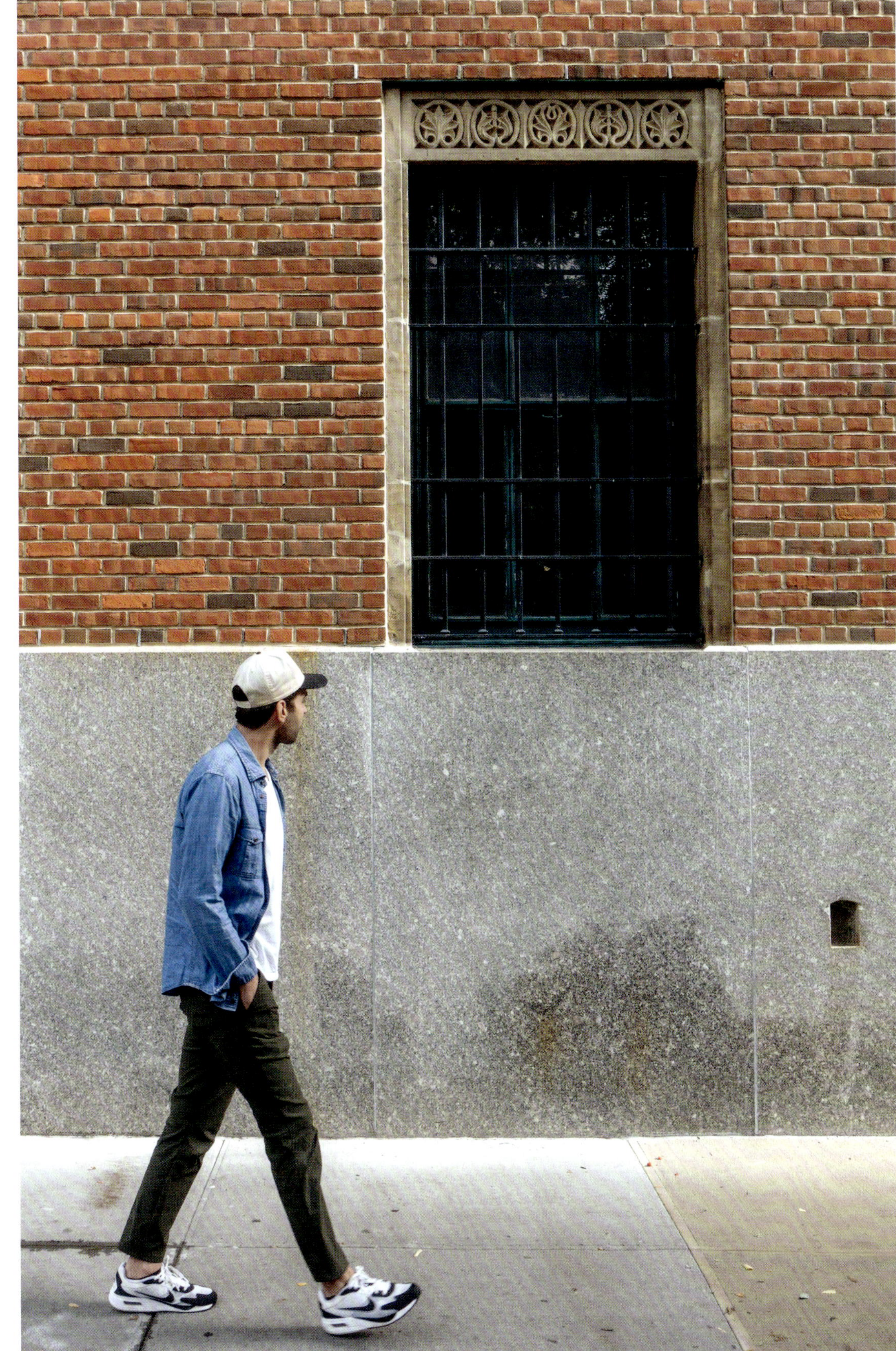

It is!

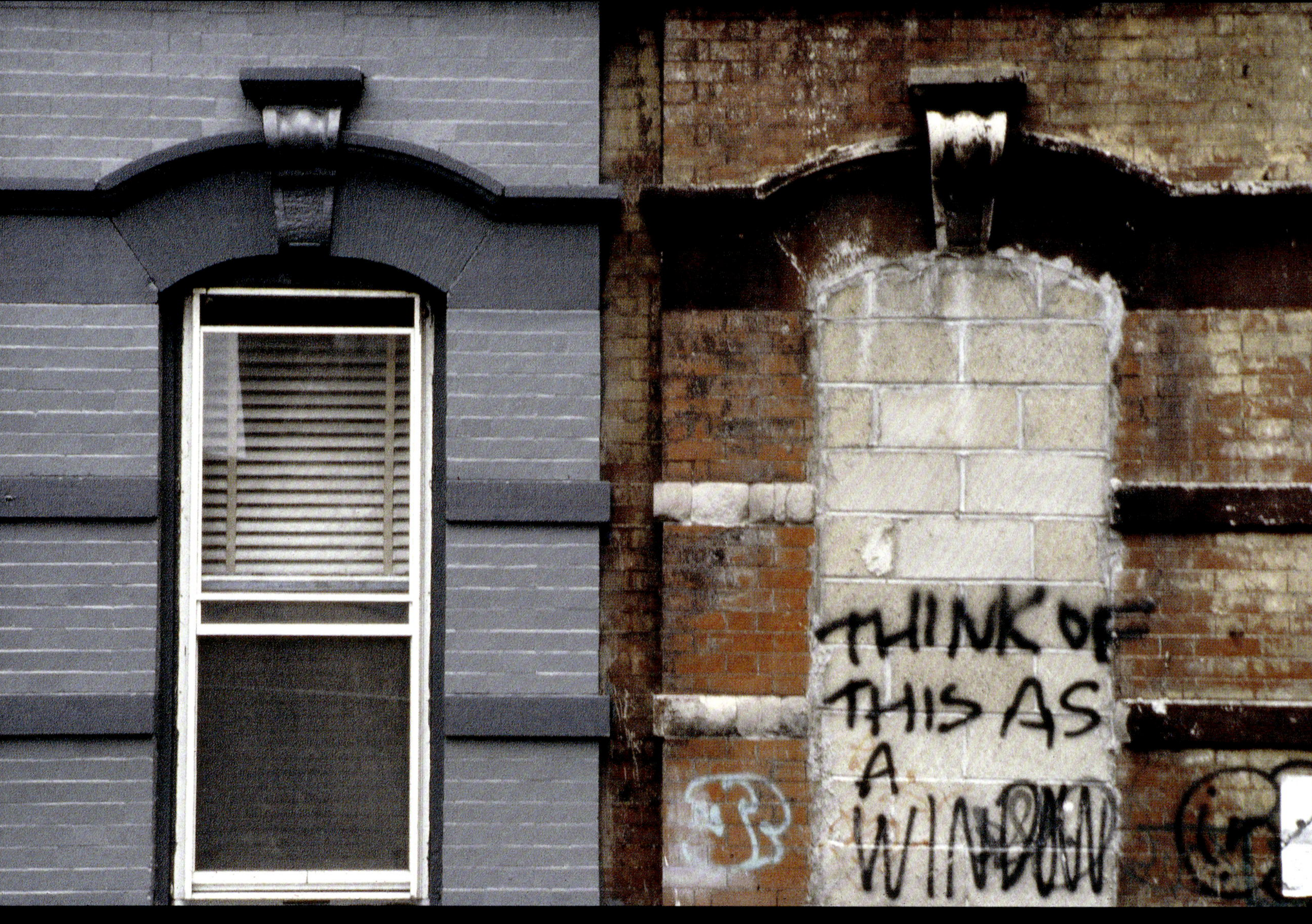

299 AND 301
EAST 8TH
STREET

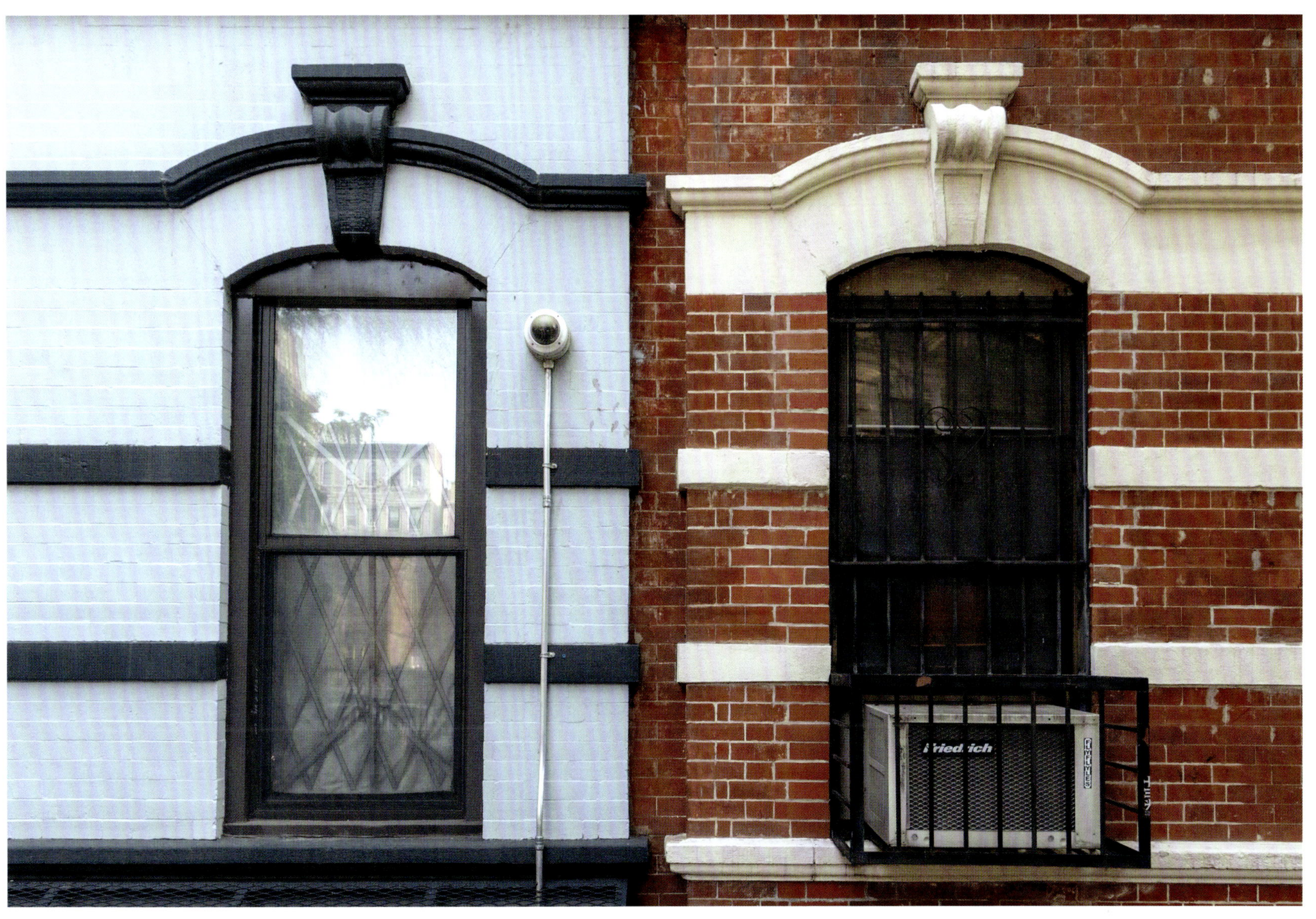

Done.

Abandoned building, cinder-blocked shut,
drug-dealer opened.

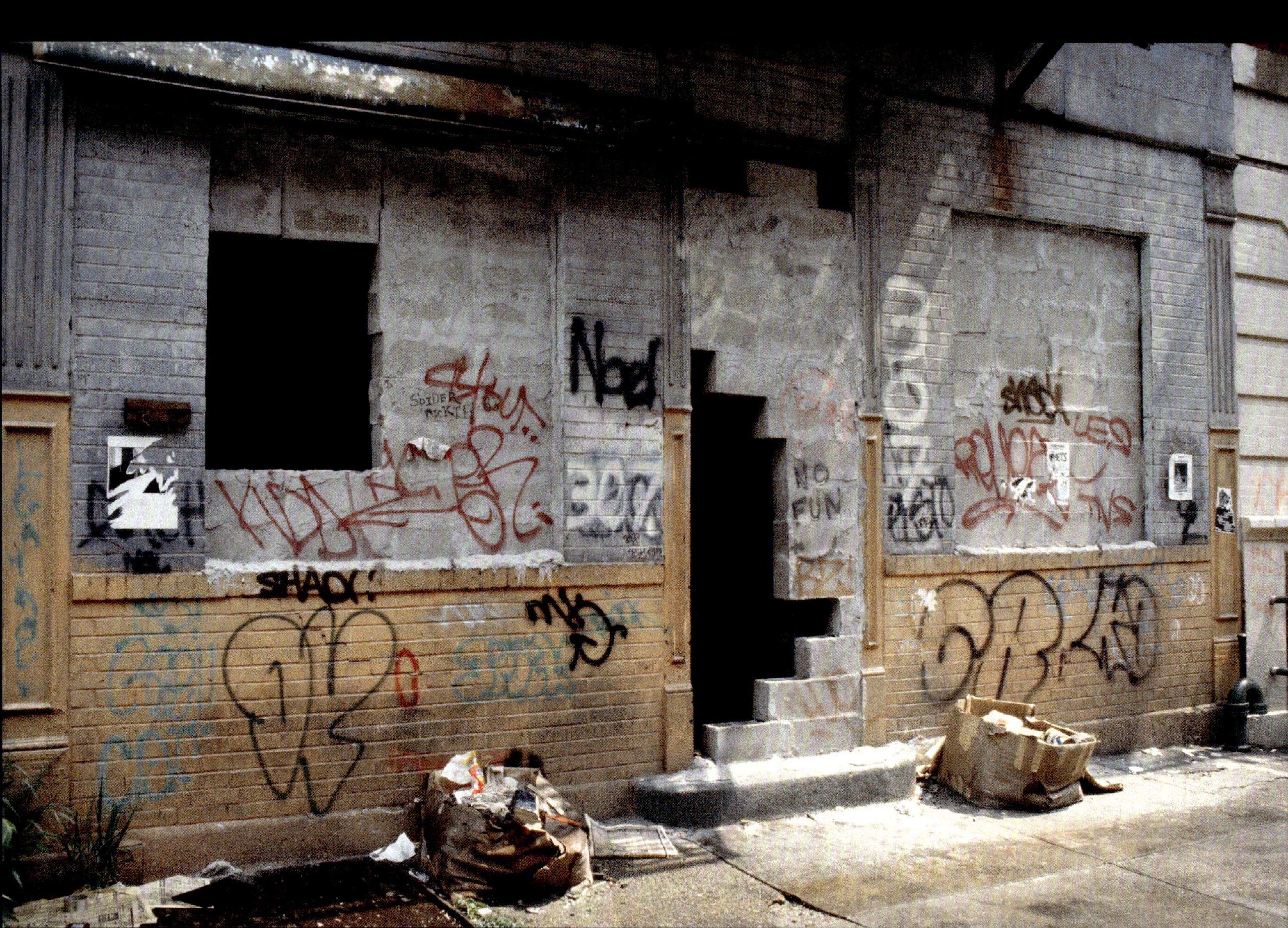

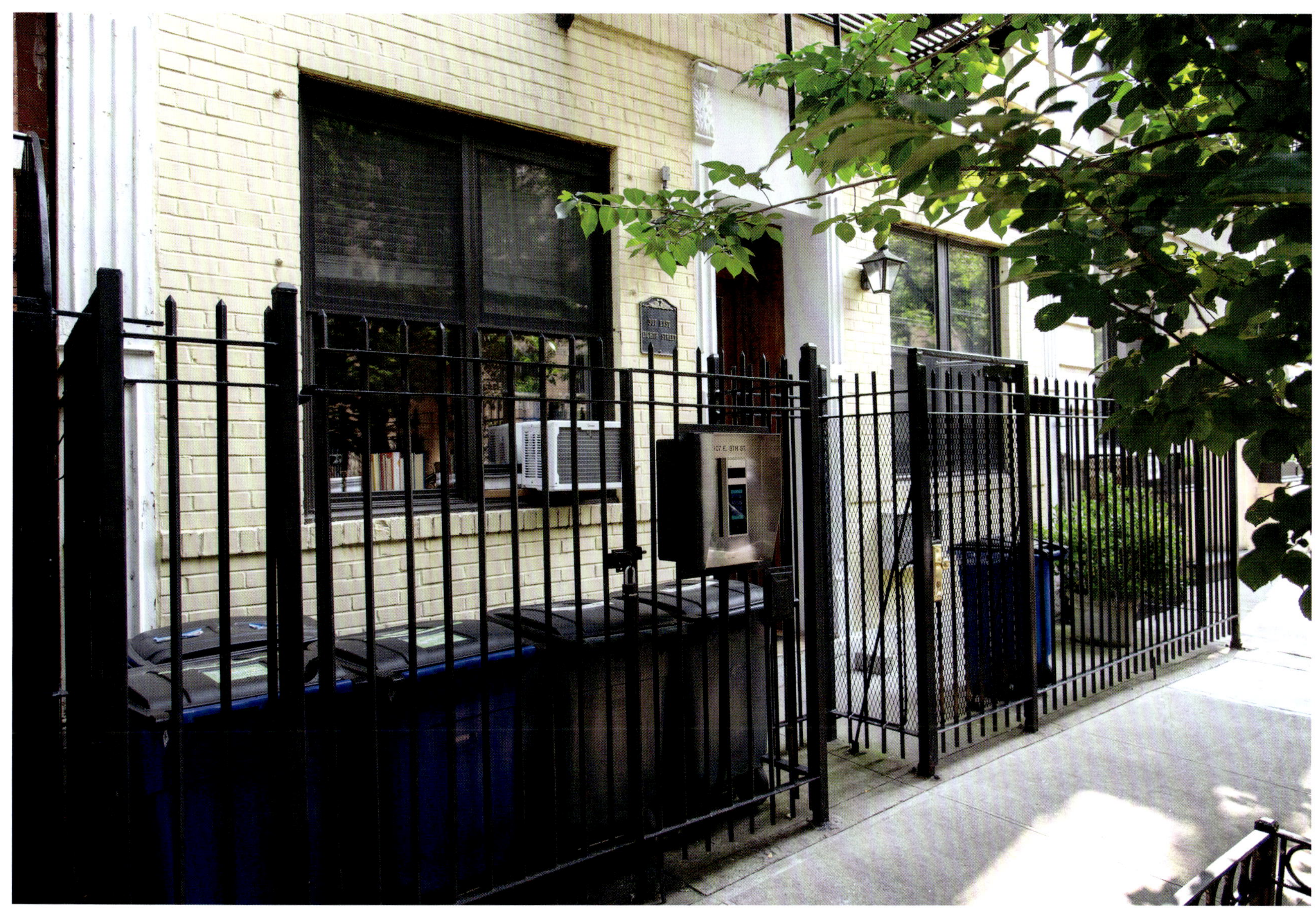

A reclaimed tenement.

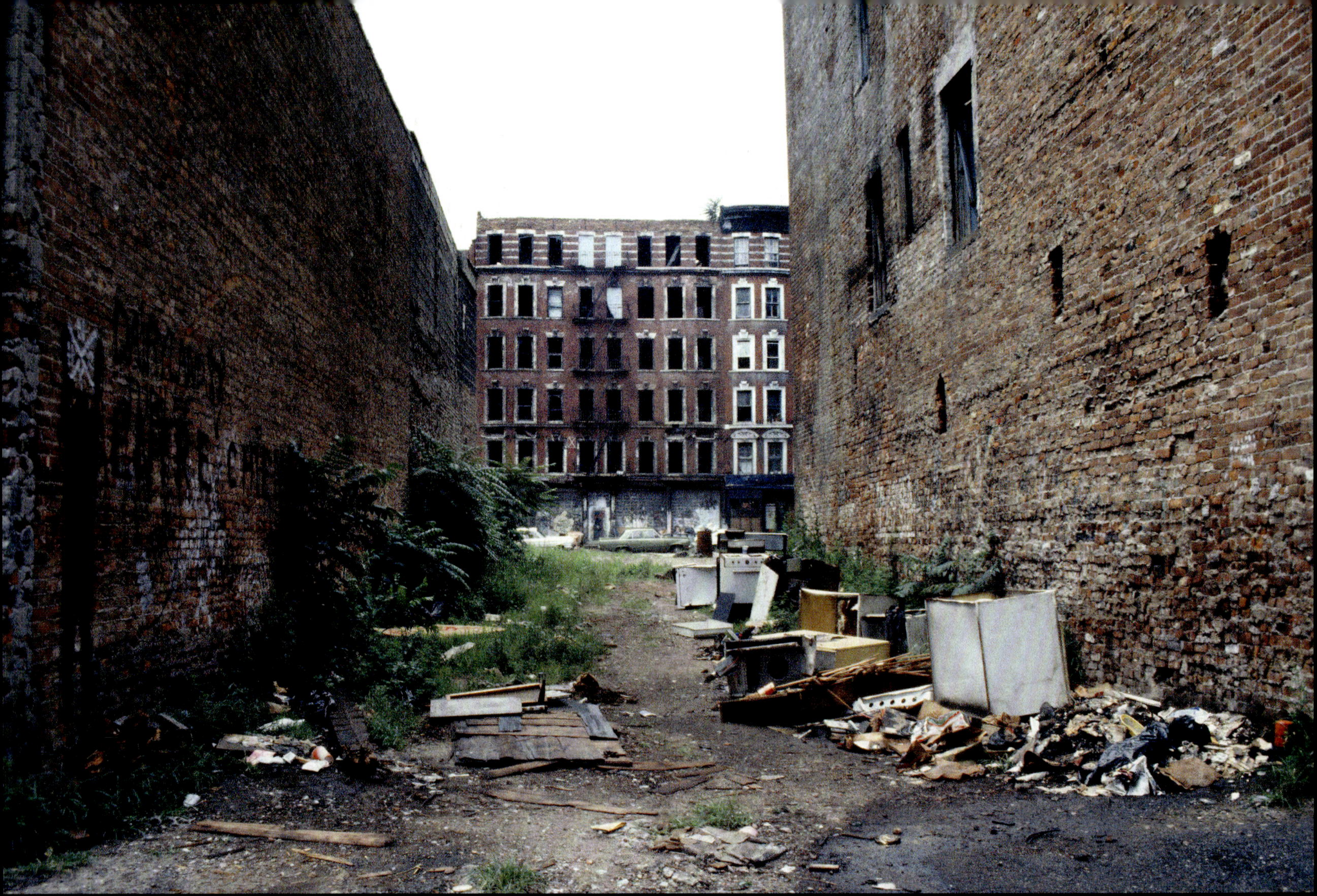

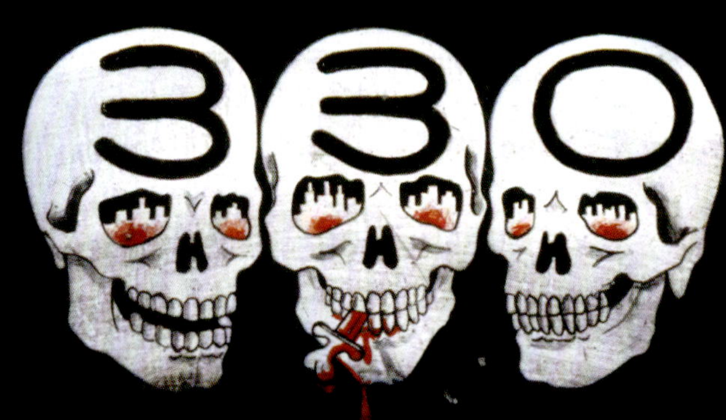
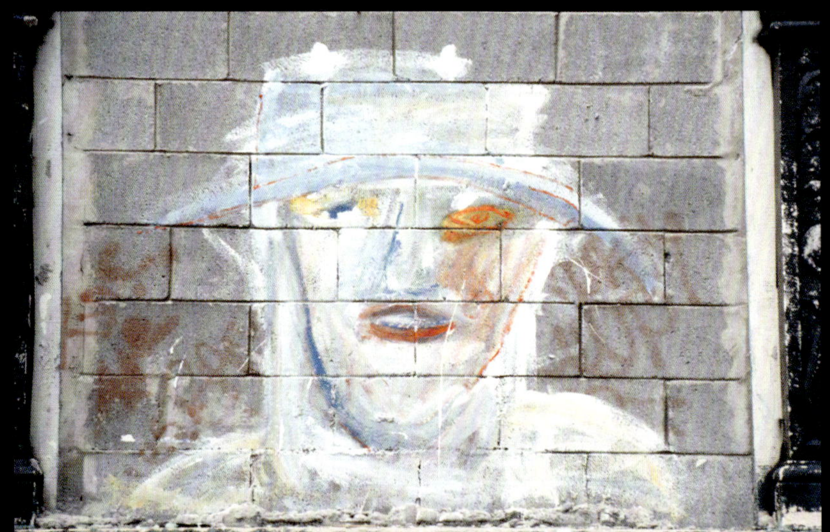

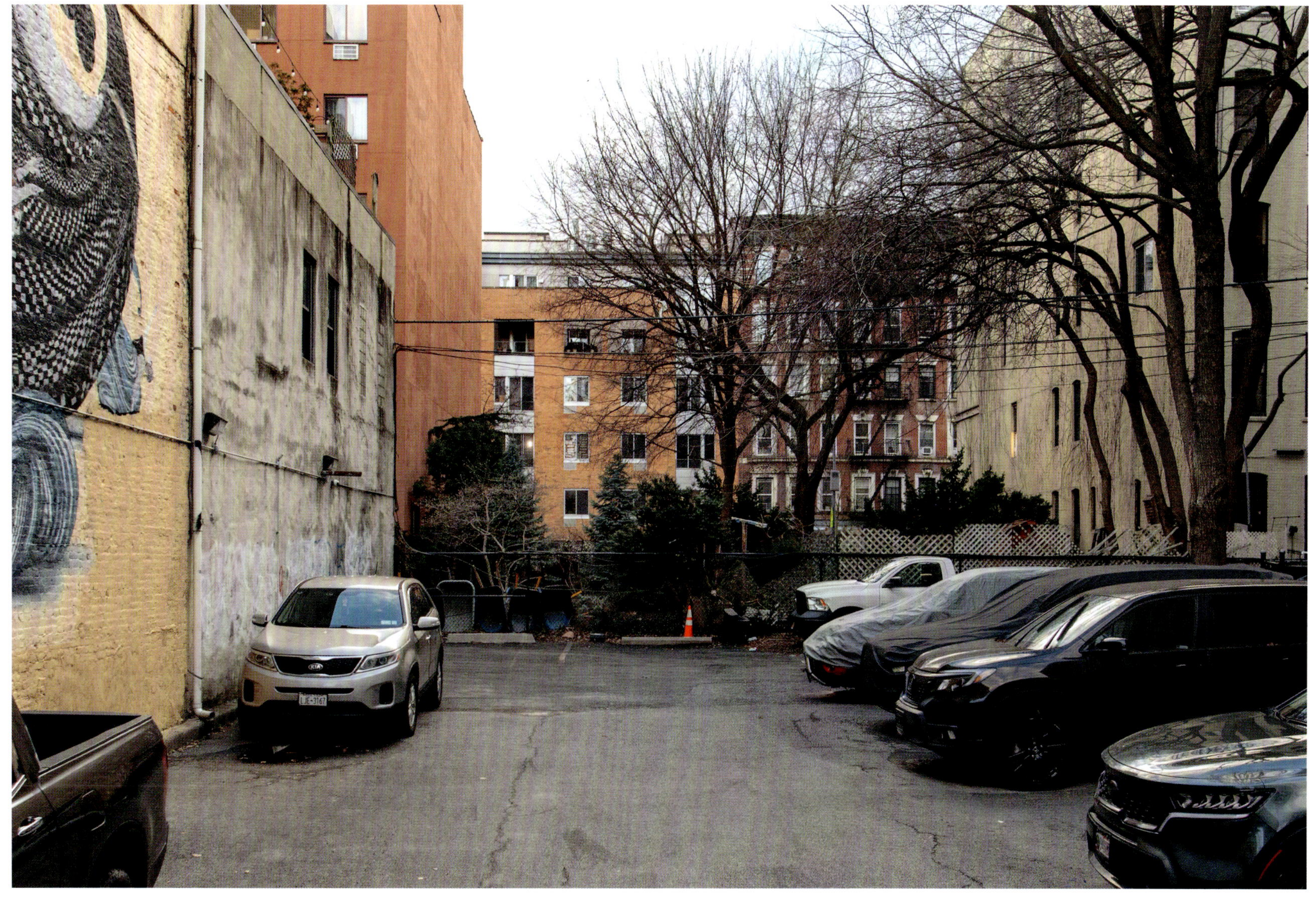

328 EAST 8TH STREET

then Looking through to East 7th Street. The open lot, past the discarded appliances, is now the Lower East Side Ecology Center. The building straight through is gone and replaced; the building on the near right is gone and now part of the parking lot for Casa Victoria Housing for the Elderly. The photo of "330" on skulls is the address painted on the door of the little building on the left. The painting on the cinder-block window is from the tenement next to 330.

now The parking lot for Casa Victoria Housing for the Elderly. The greenery is the Ecology Garden, then through to 7th Street and a new building.

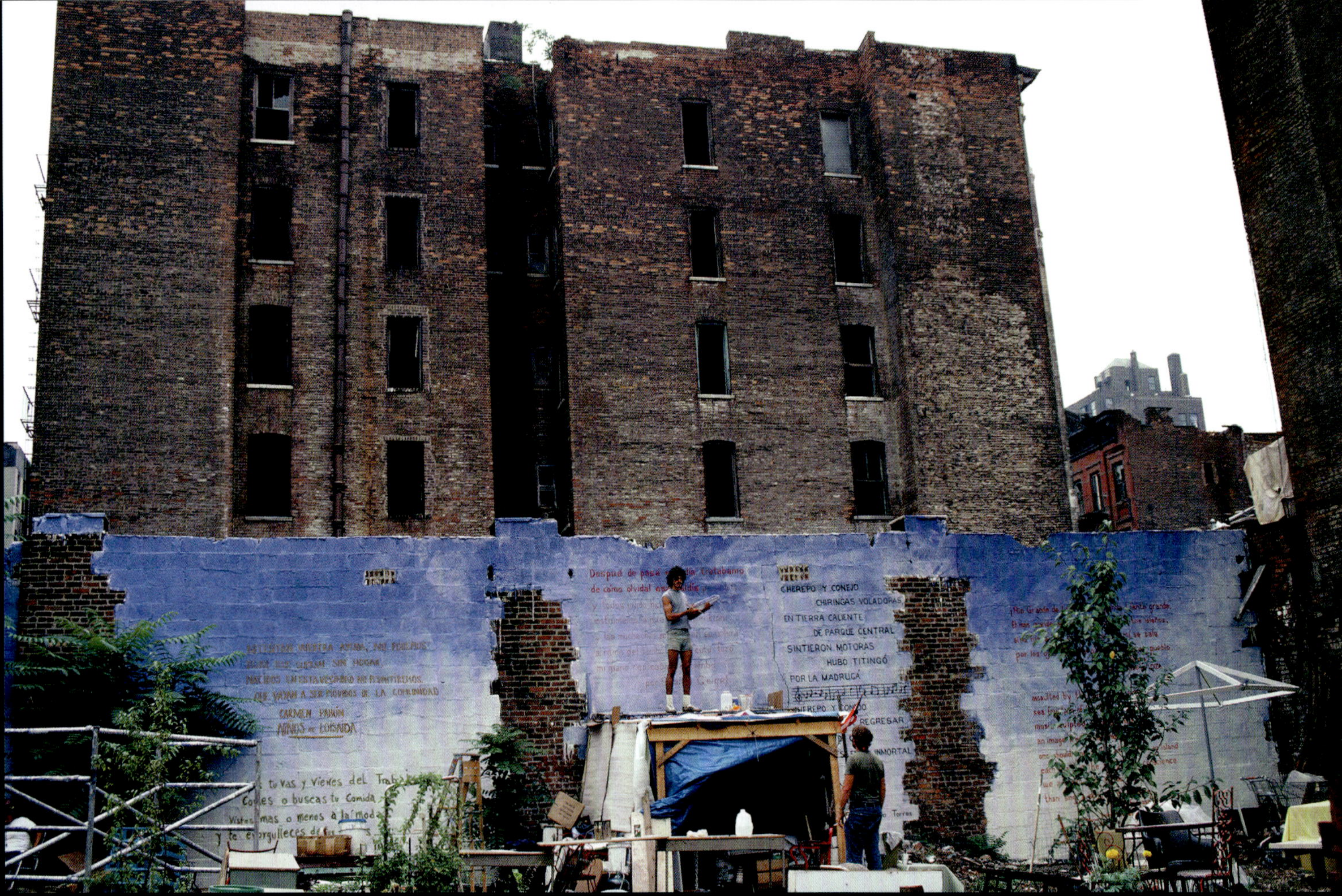

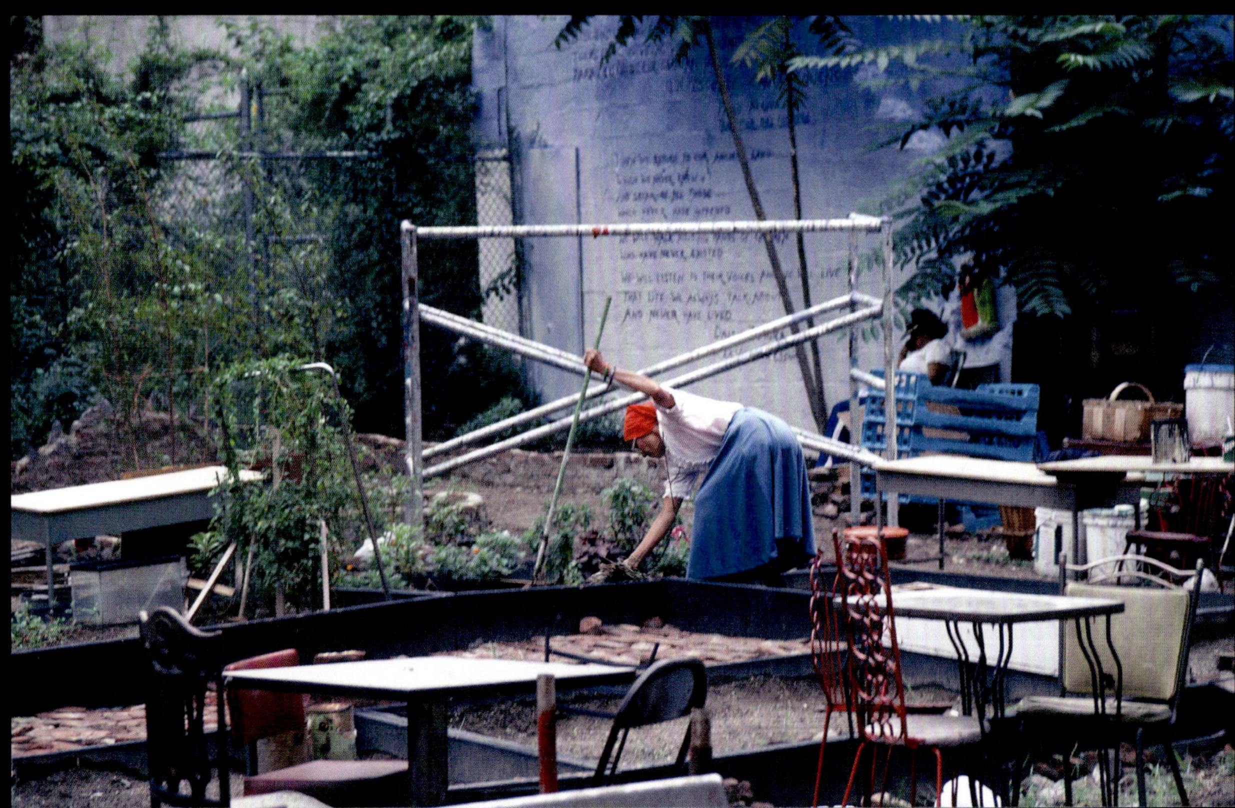

117 AVENUE C

Starting the Carmen Pabón Garden. Clearing rubble, painting walls, planting, and generally cleaning up. Carmen herself working the plant beds.

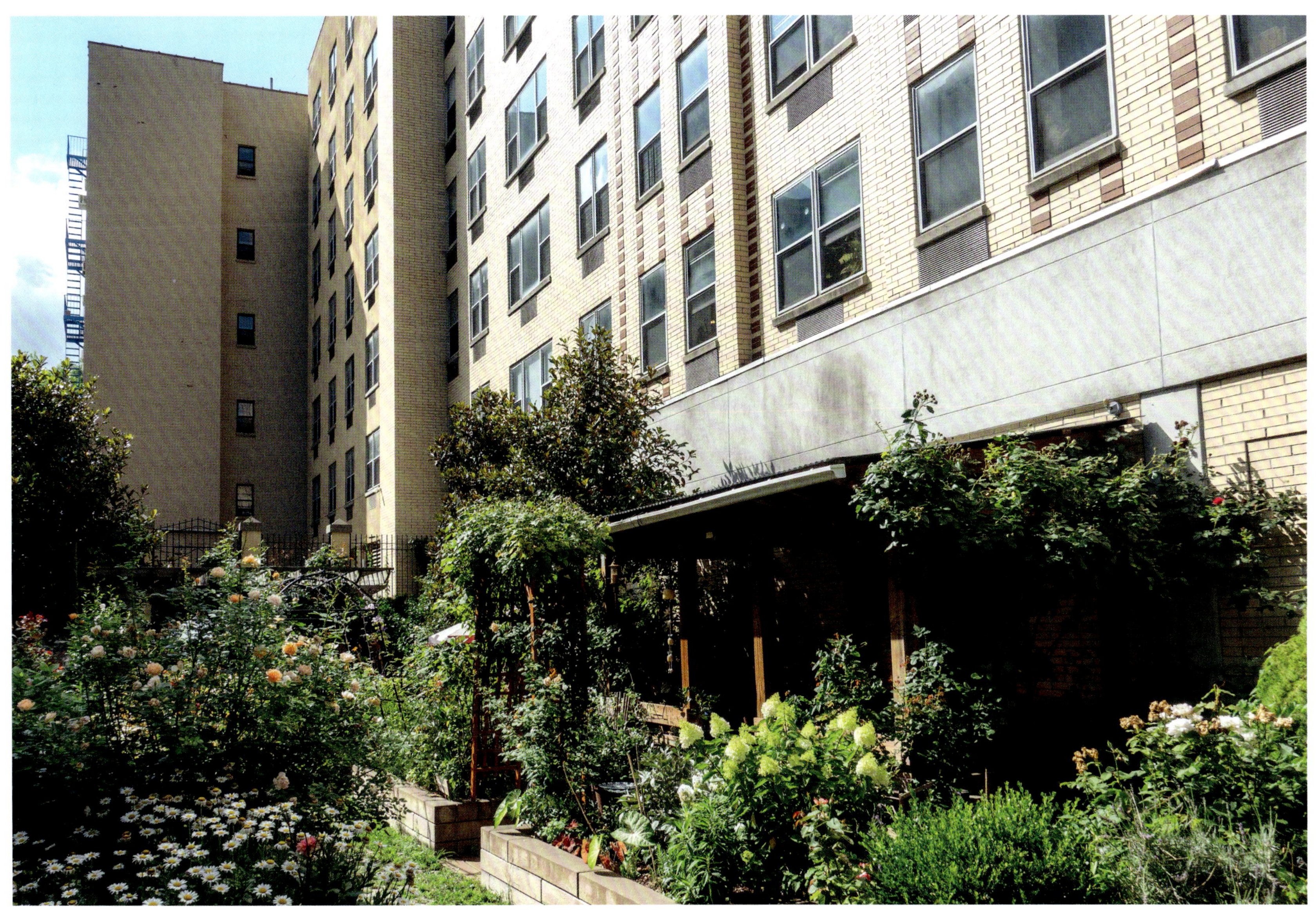

Carmen's garden within the
Eastville Gardens development.

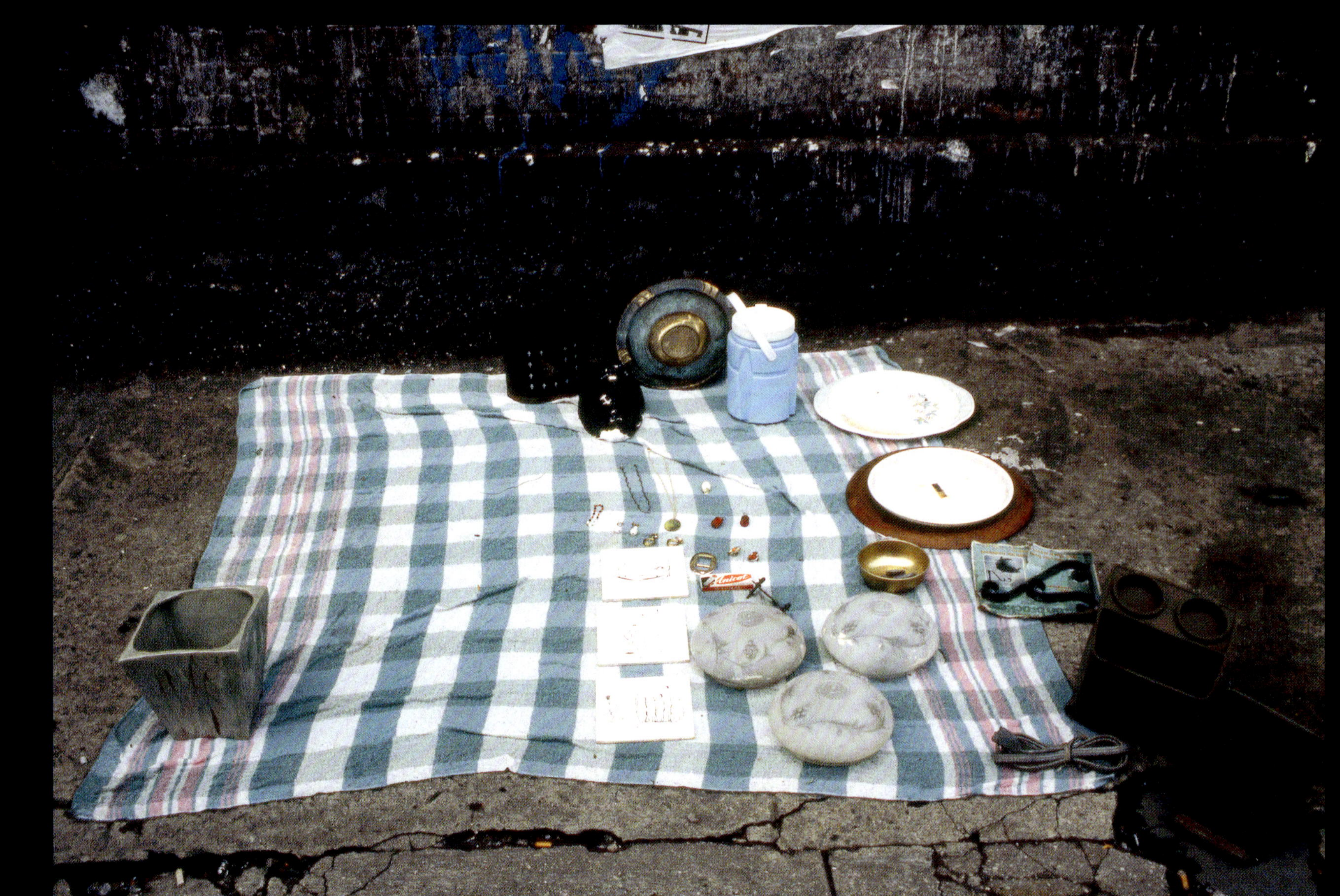

Weekend "den of thieves," one blanket among many lining the blocks. Similar to Second Avenue after 11 p.m. many nights.

Freelance, nothing stolen,
homemade, donated.

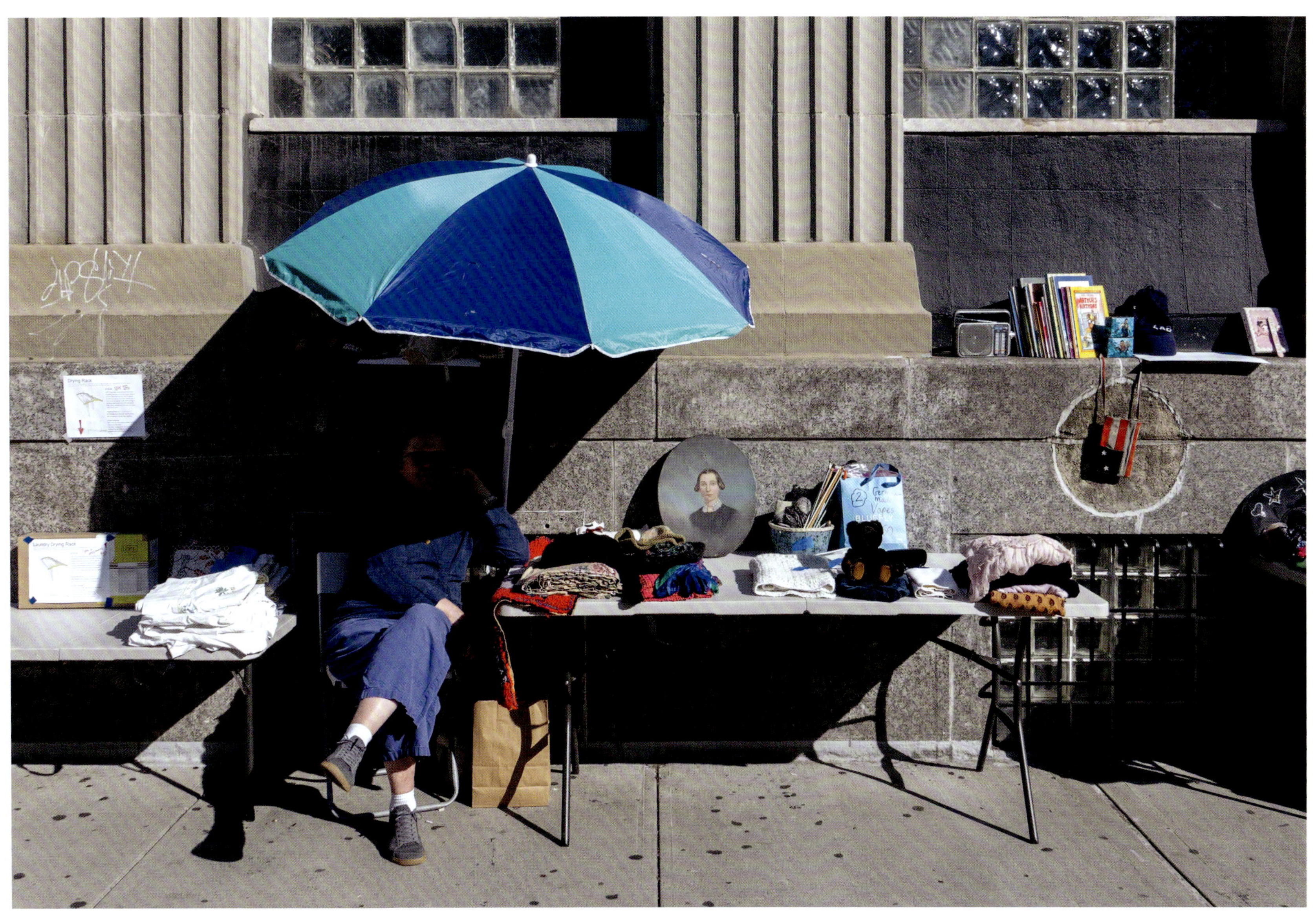

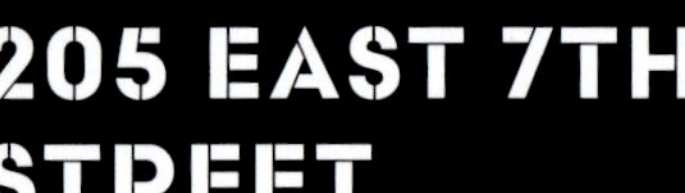

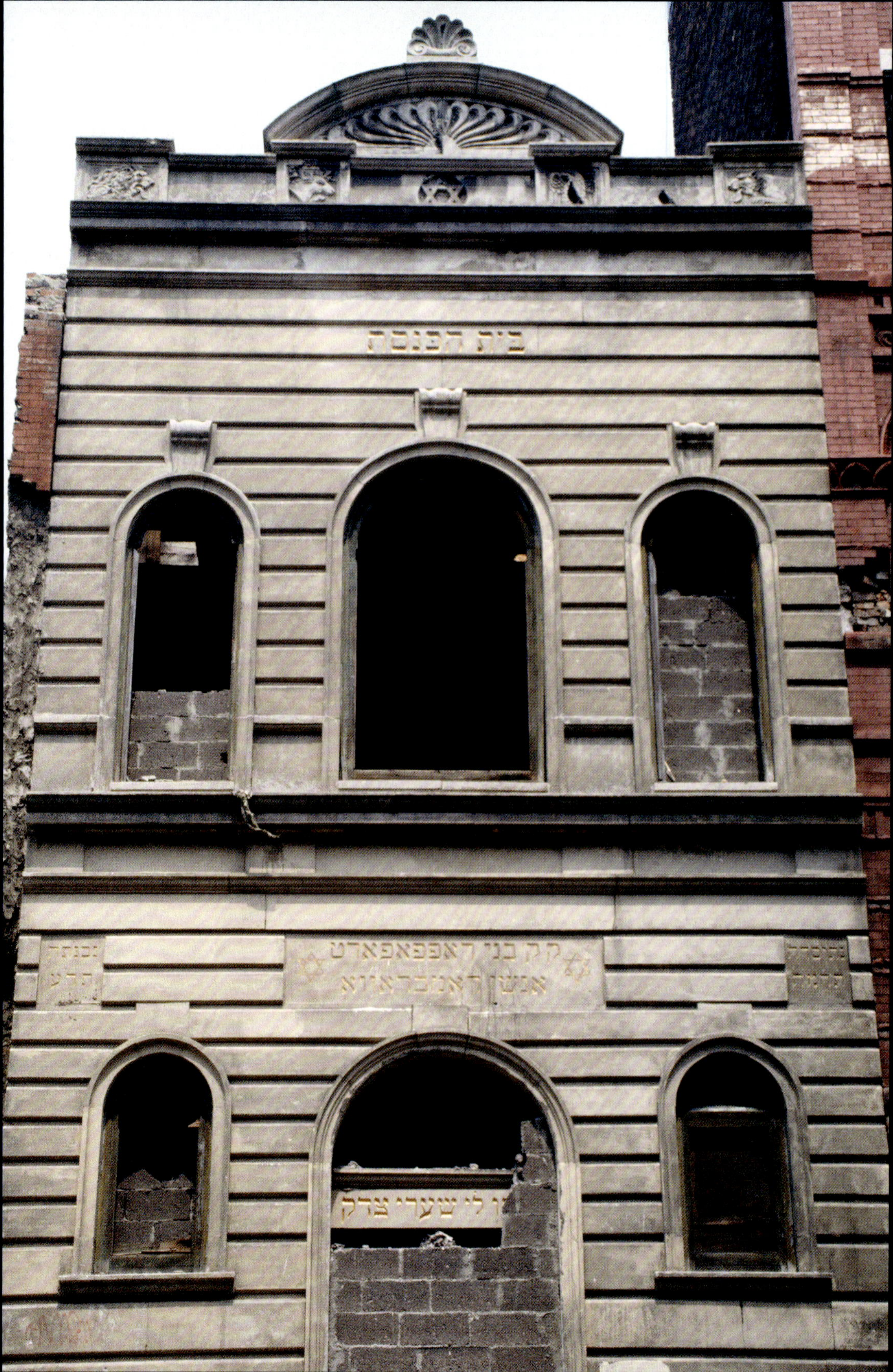

205 EAST 7TH STREET

An old abandoned synagogue. When I asked some neighbors how I could get in to shoot some interiors, I was told I could go in but would get a pipe in the head if I did. Turns out it was where the local heroin trade stored things.

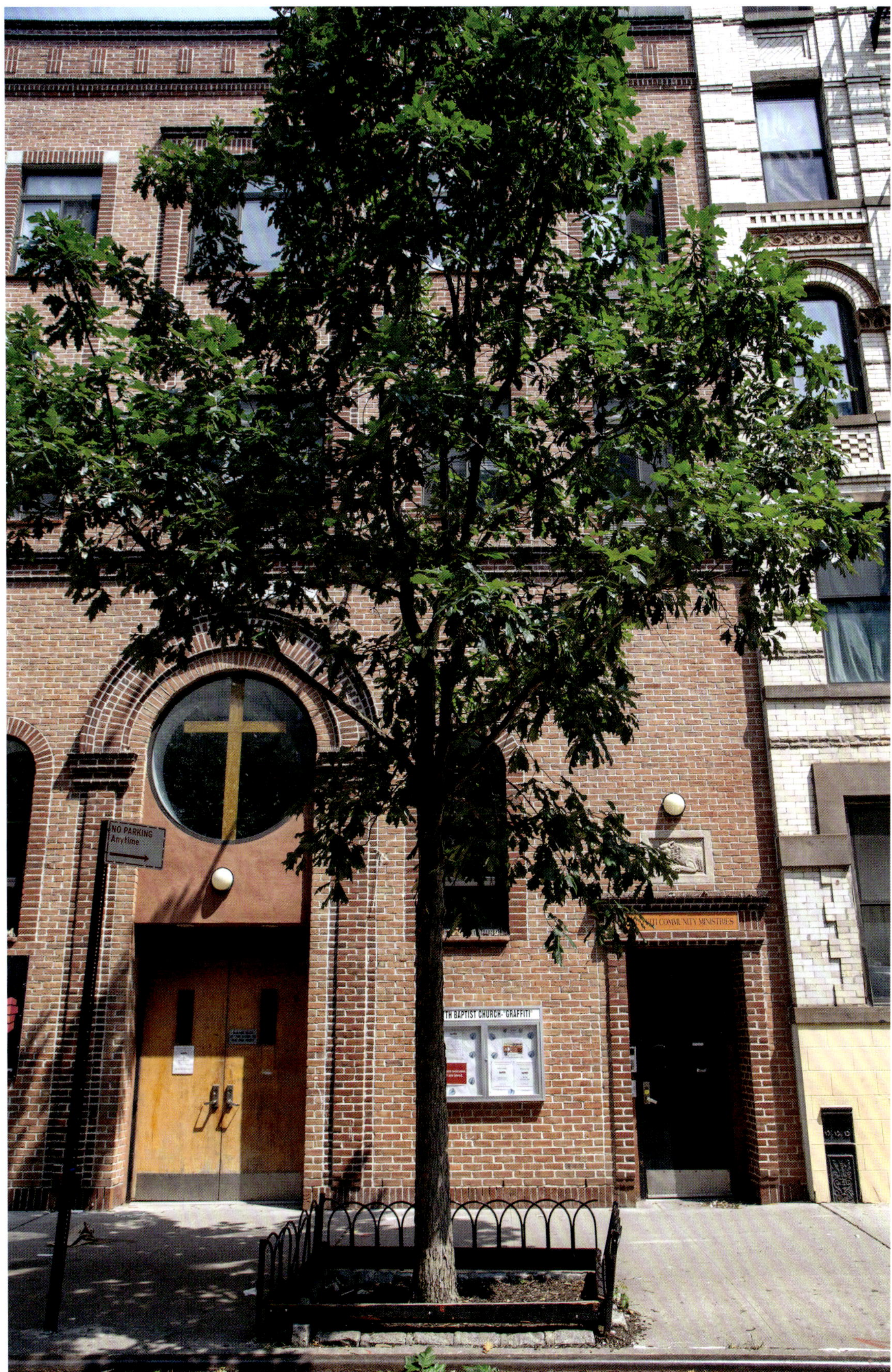

Graffiti Baptist tried to incorporate some of the old synagogue facade, but it was too deteriorated.

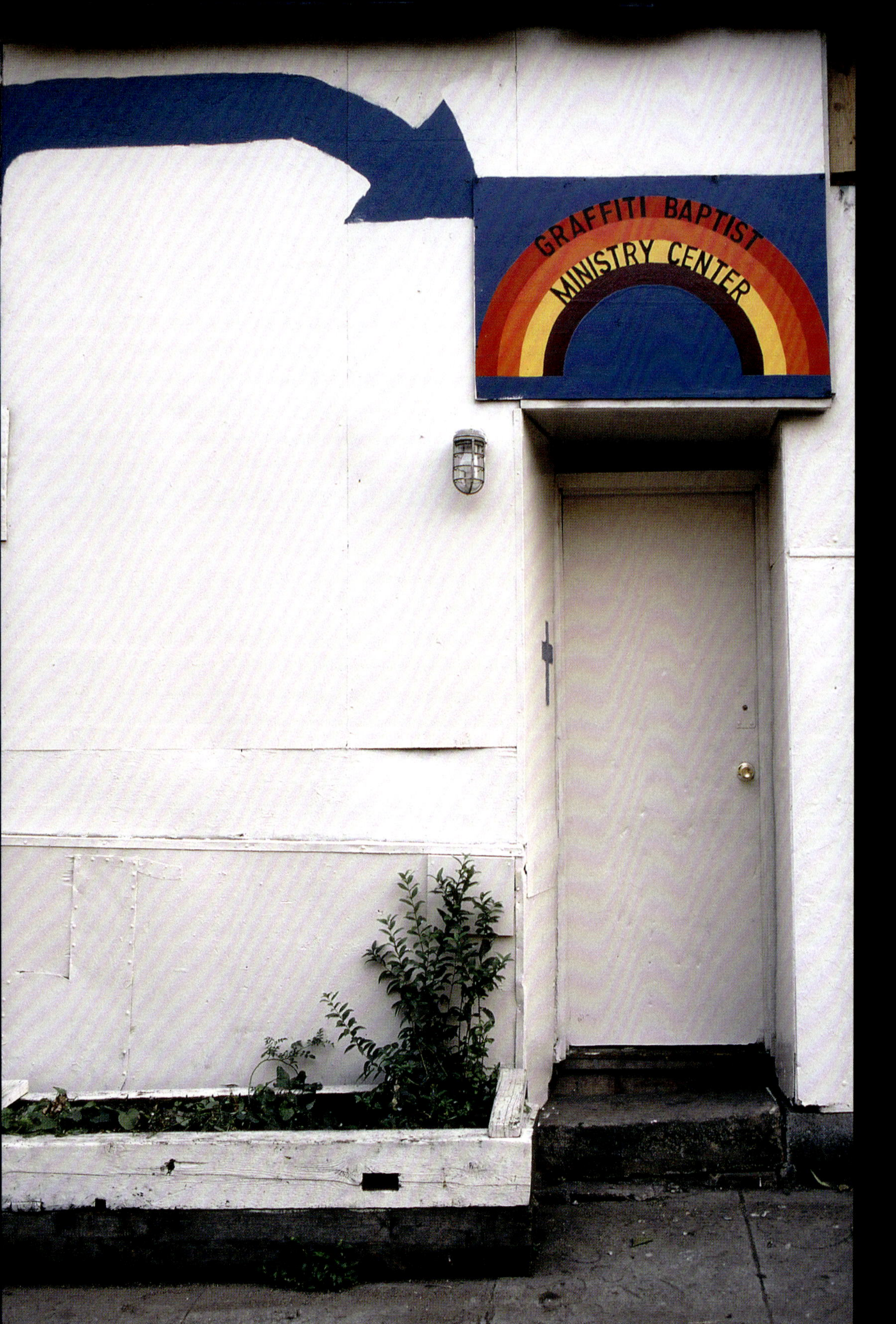

184 EAST 7TH STREET

Original home of Graffiti Baptist

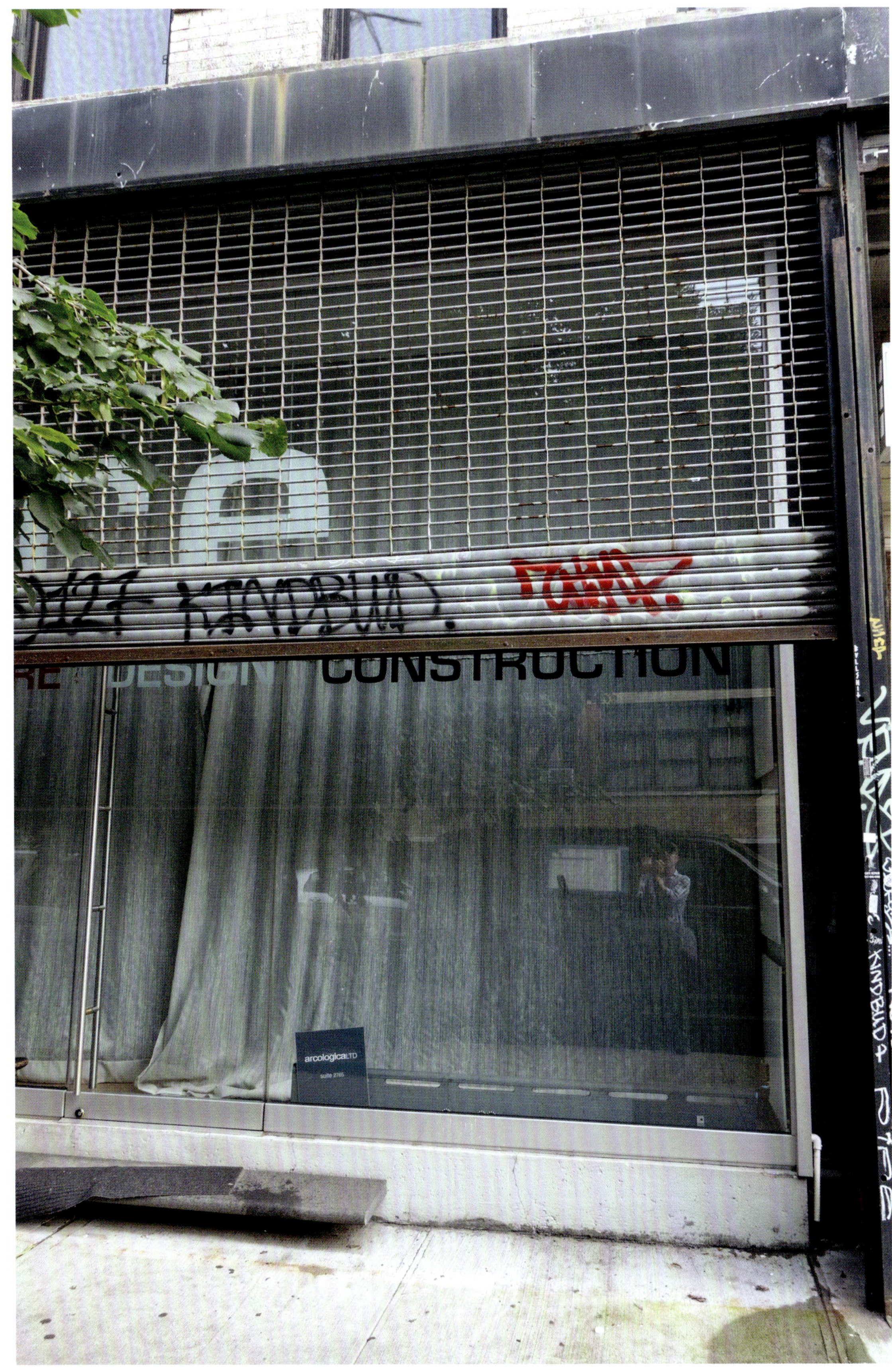

Architectural firm.

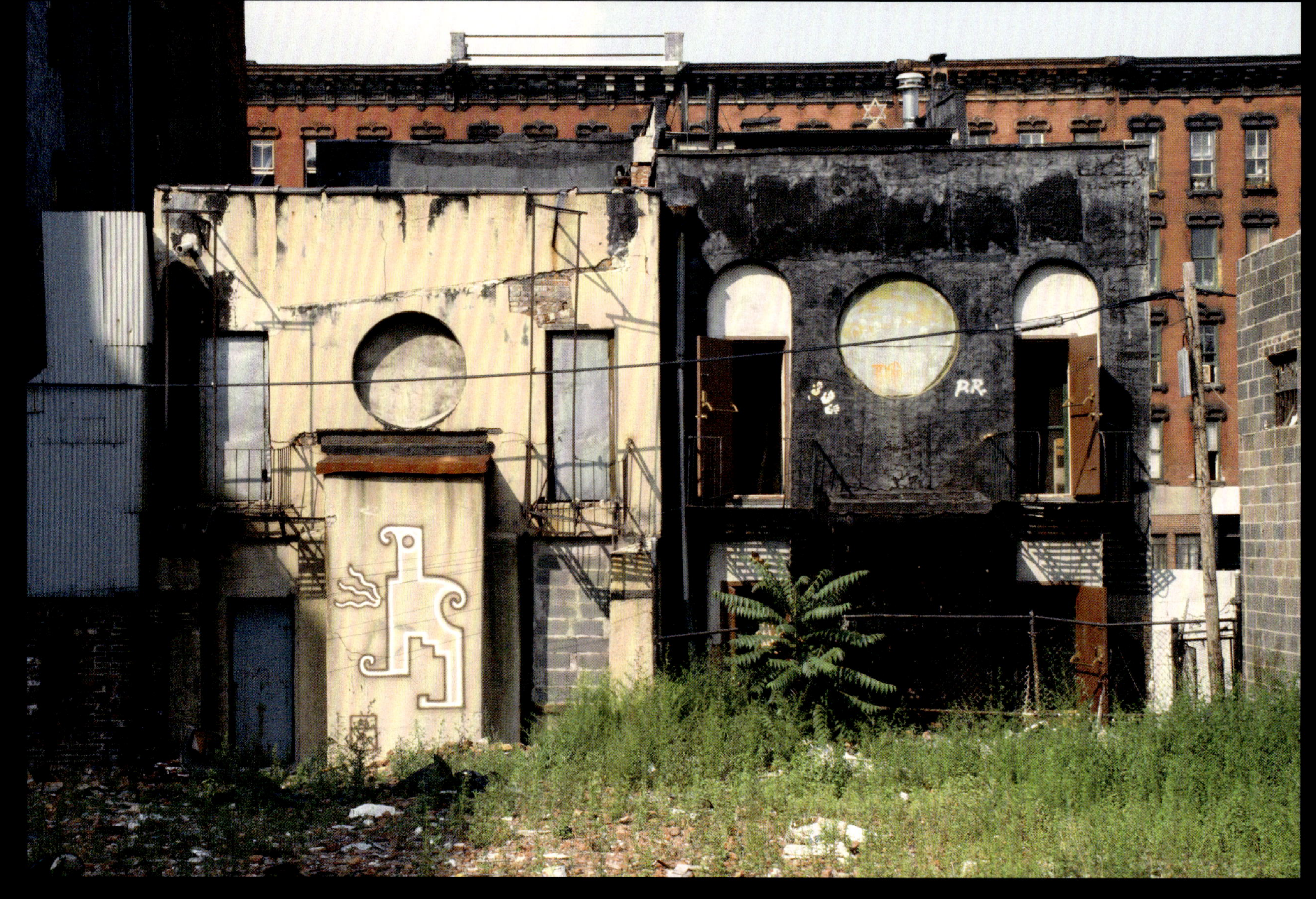

636 AND 638 EAST 6TH STREET

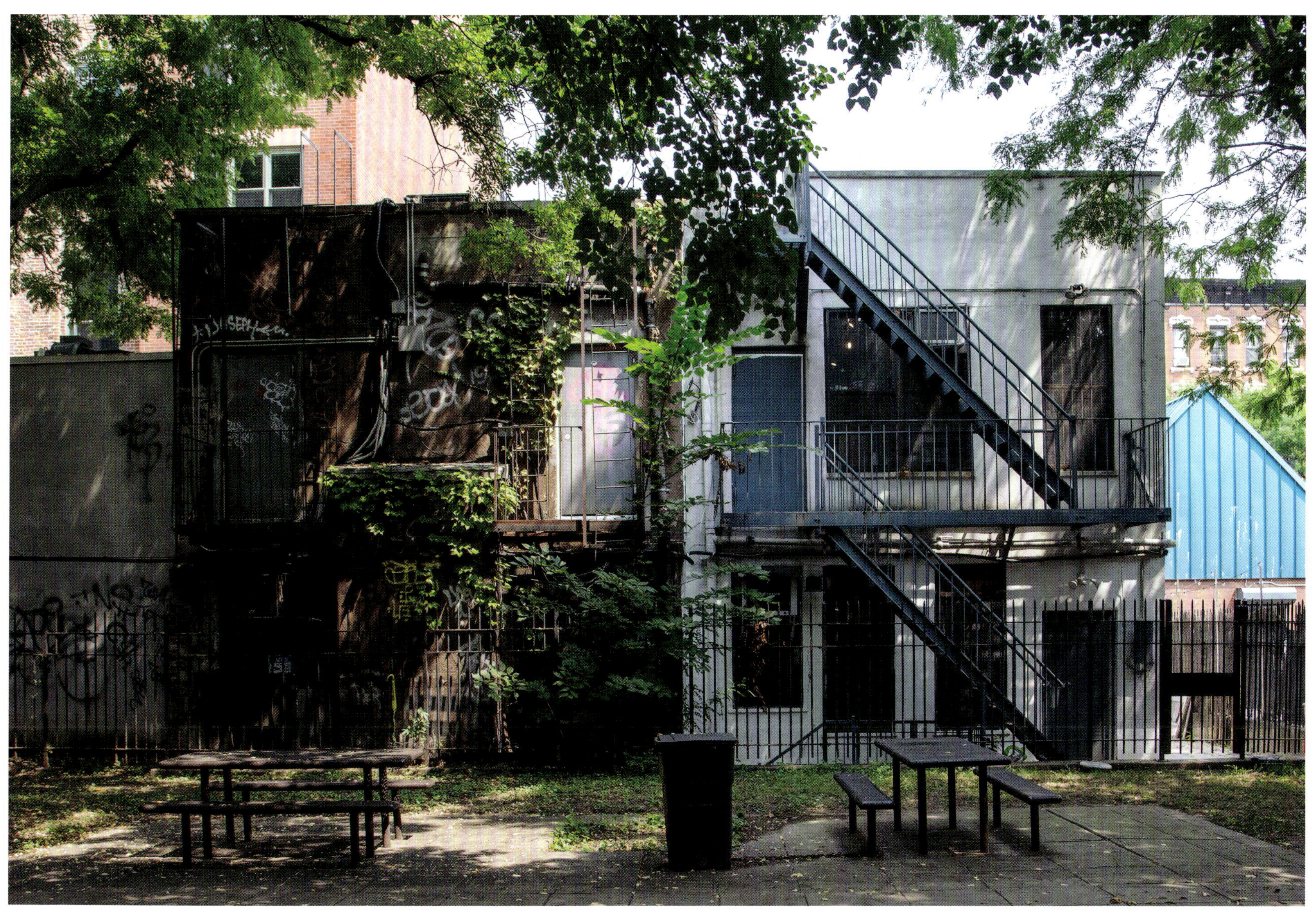

Sixth Street Community Center and the Church of God of 6th Street. Taken from the backyard of the NYCHA housing on East 5th Street. A resident on the sidewalk was nice enough to let me into the backyard.

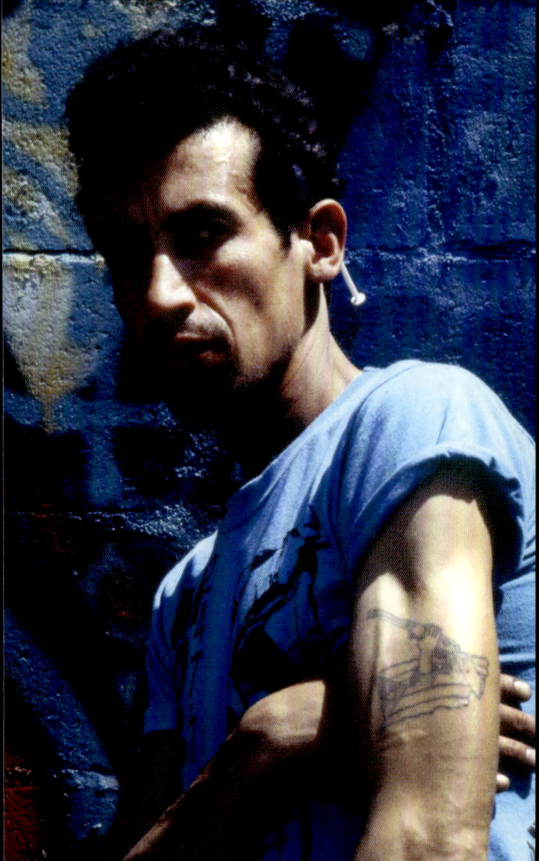

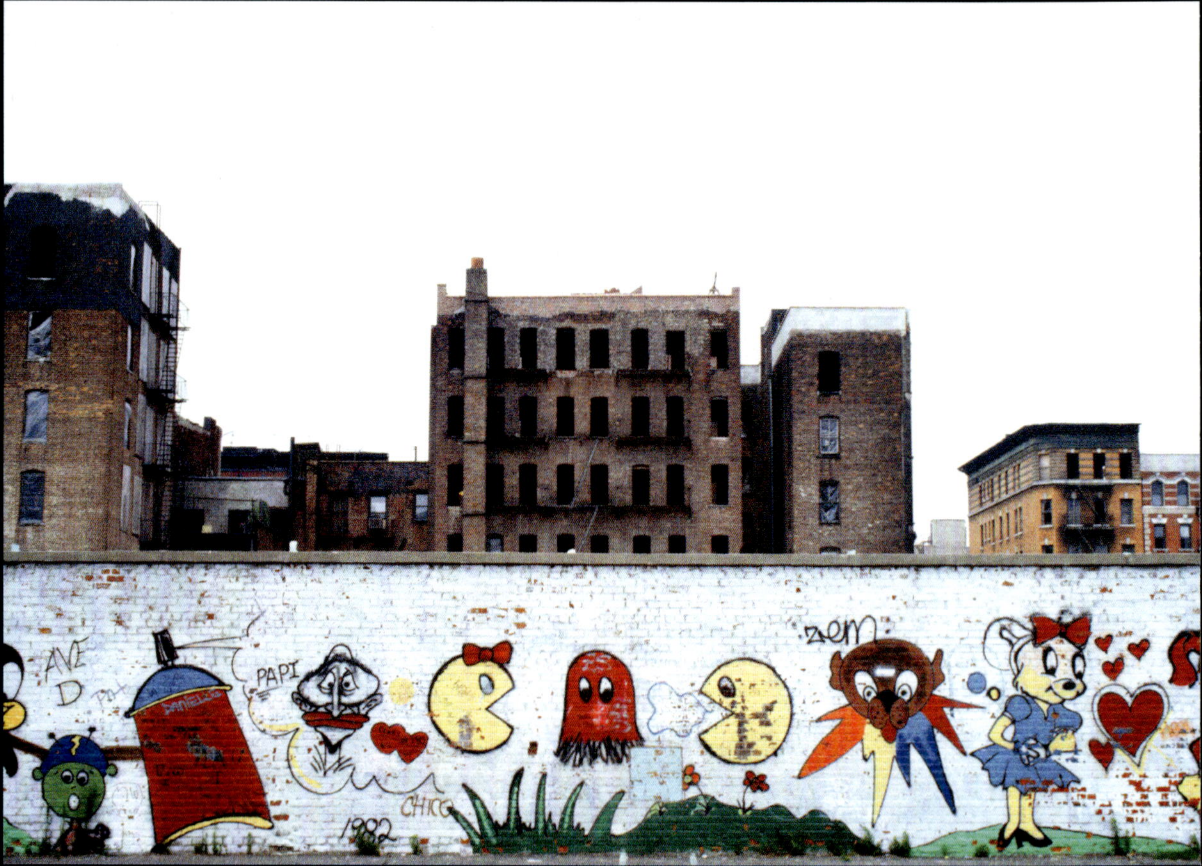

A guy on 5th Street by the playground, a "syringe portrait."

724 EAST 5TH STREET

A playground between Avenues C and D. Pac-Man, "Chico," and burned-out buildings on Avenue C.

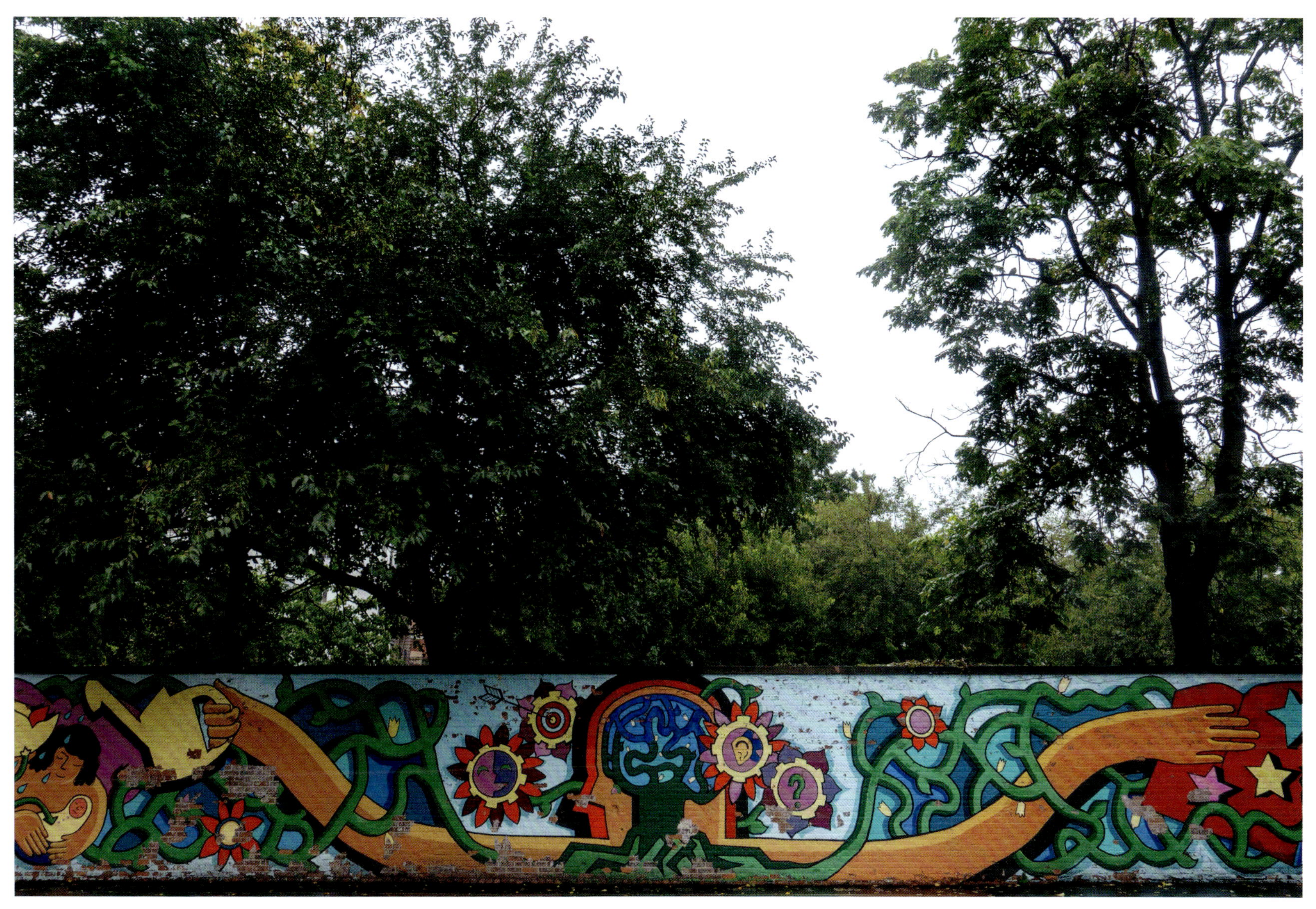

The playground for PS 15, The Roberto
Clemente School. Much more colorful
and many more trees.

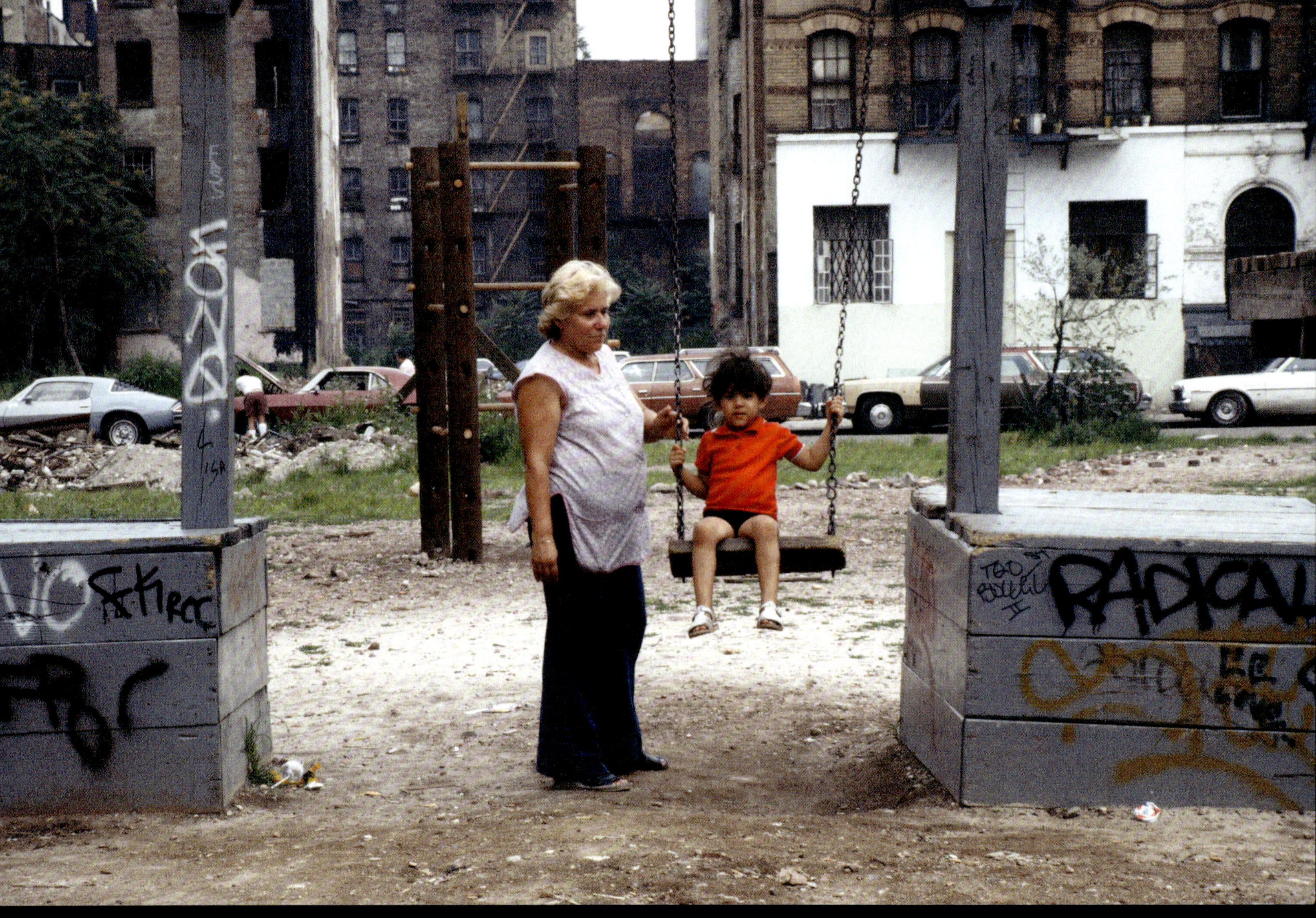

710 EAST 5TH STREET

Making the best of the empty lots. Swing set,
locally made, between Avenues C and D.
Facing south toward 4th Street.

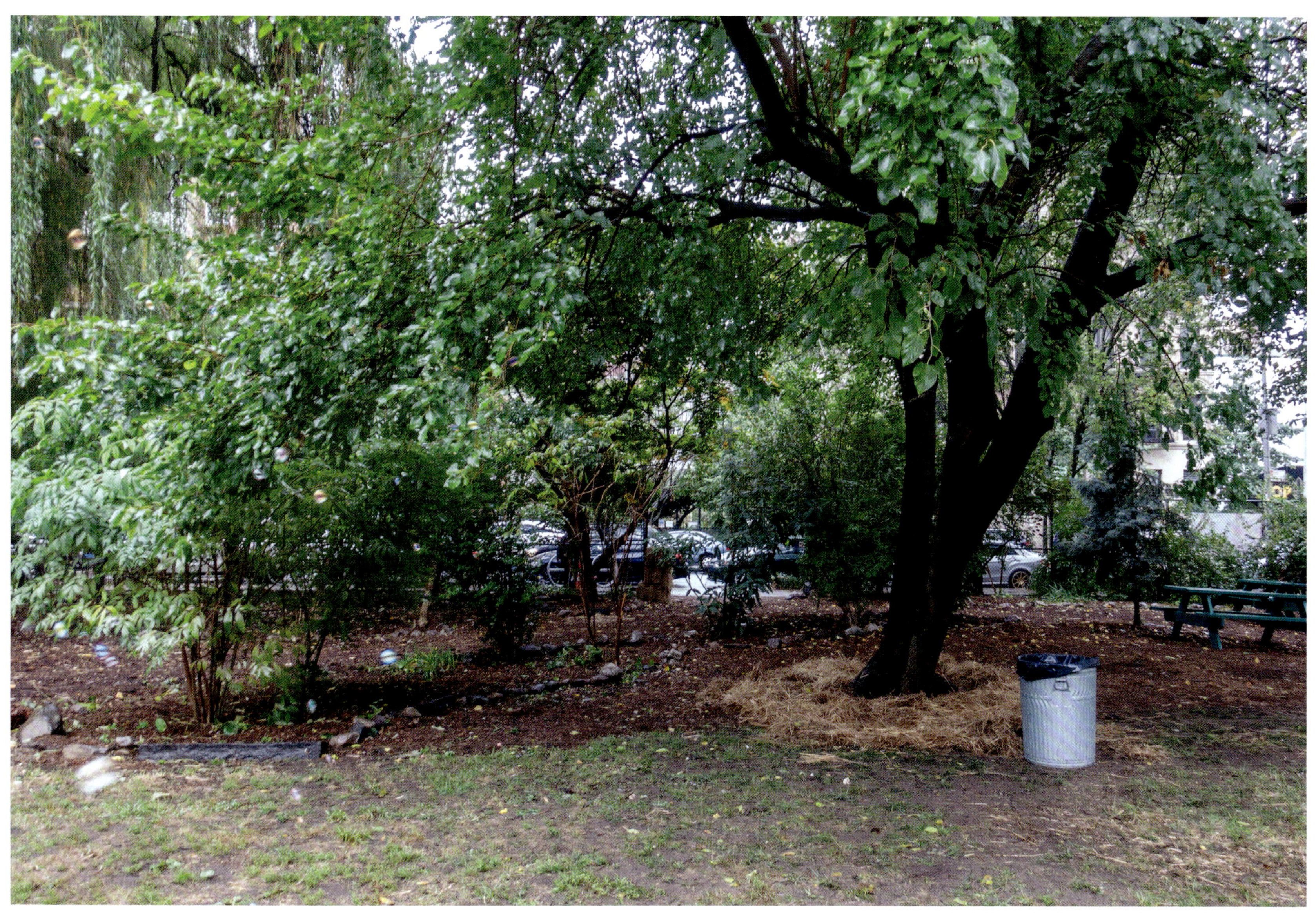

El Jardín del Paraíso:
a community garden in full bloom.

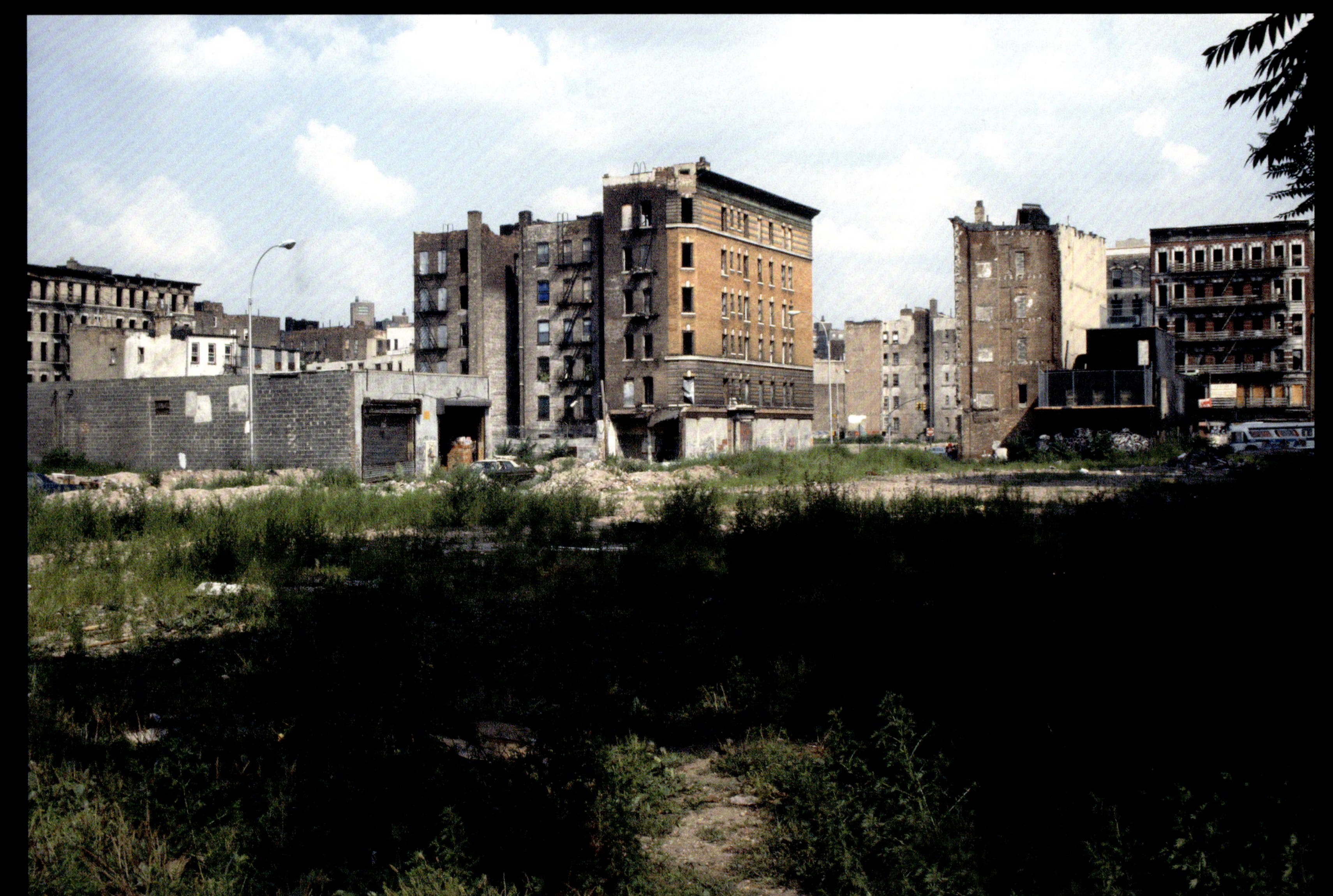

Looking toward Avenue C and East 5th Street. Almost every building is vacant.

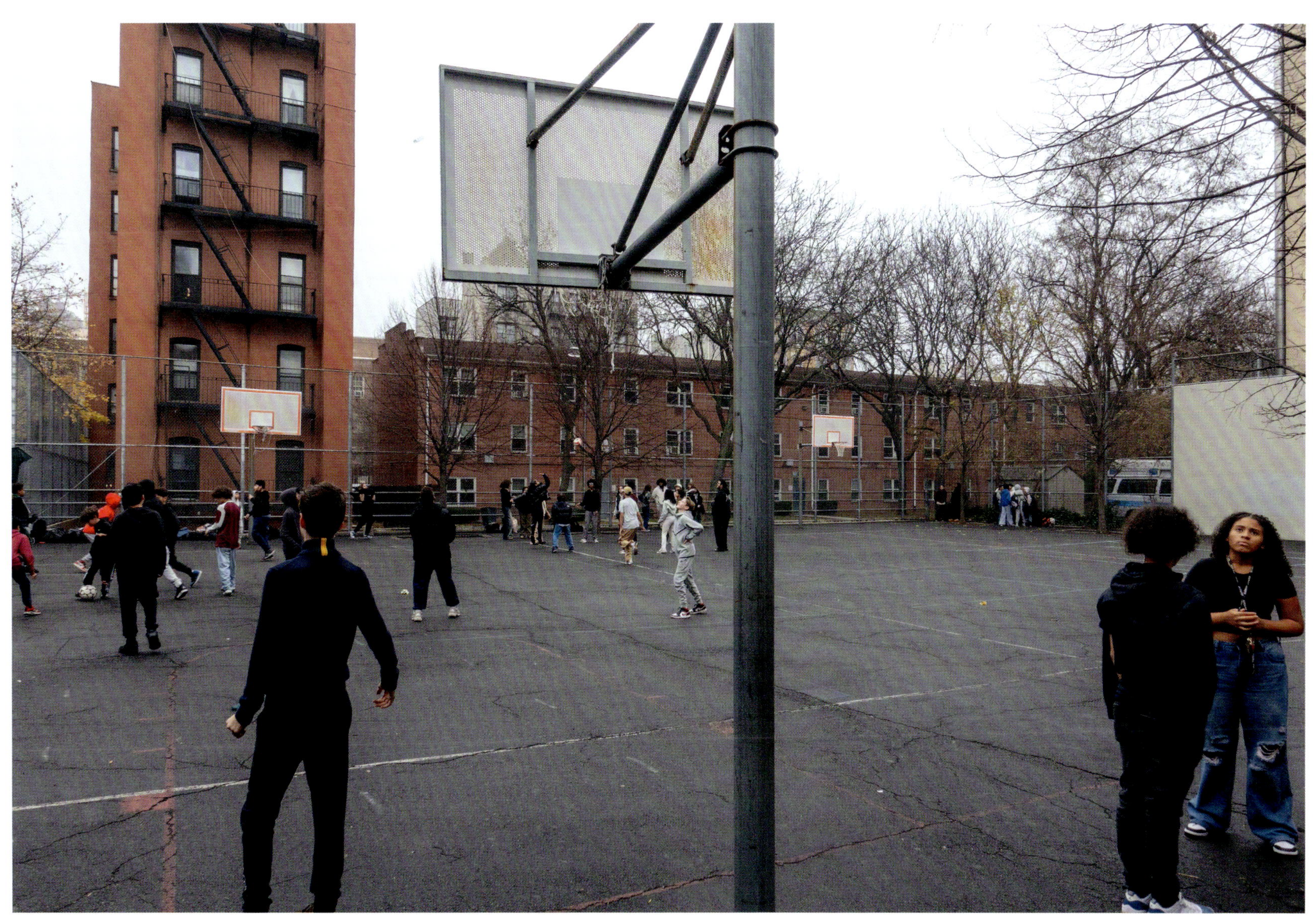

The parking lot and playground for PS 64.

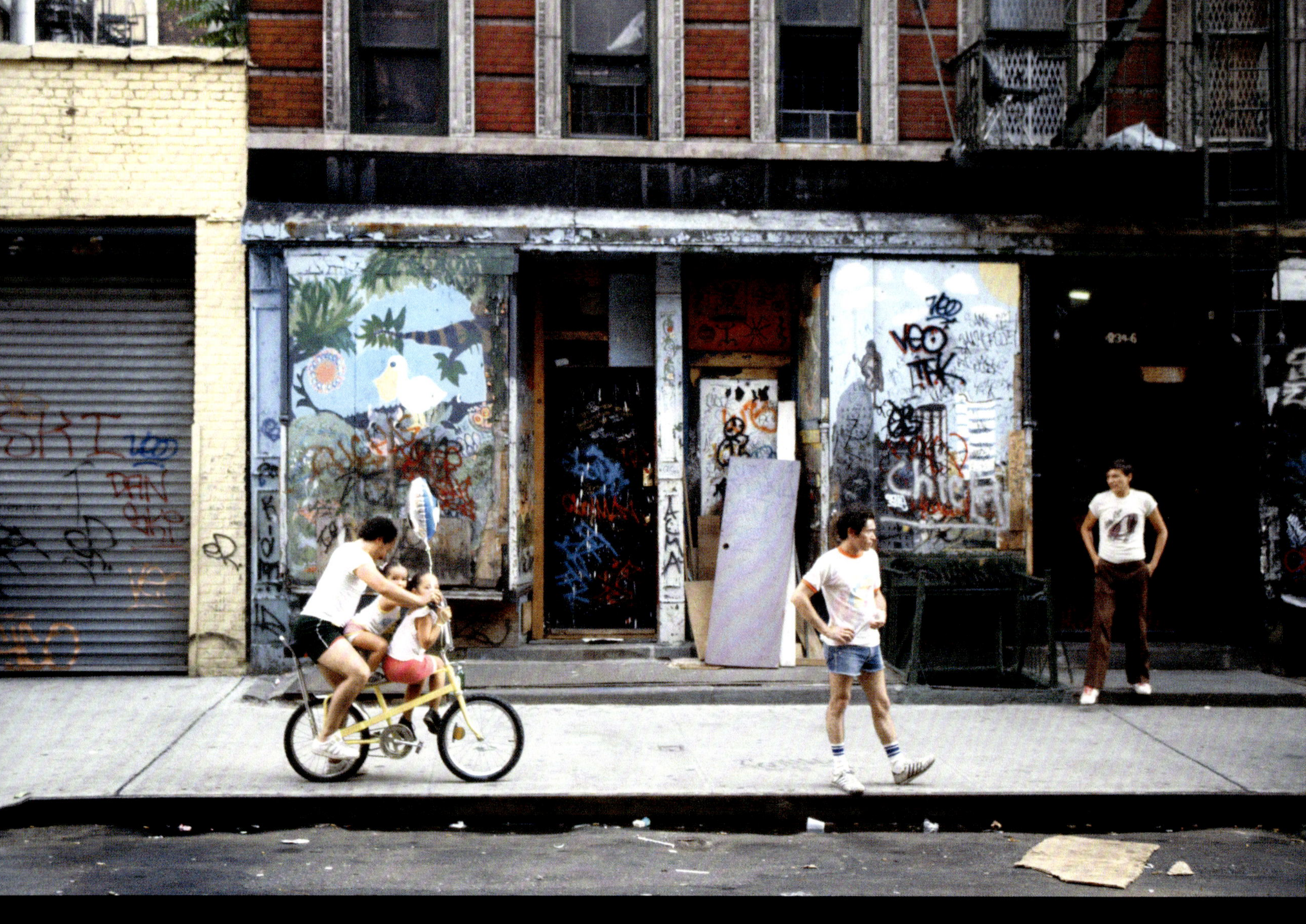

234 EAST 4TH STREET

Gnoccheria East Village. The new building
on the left kept the curb cut.

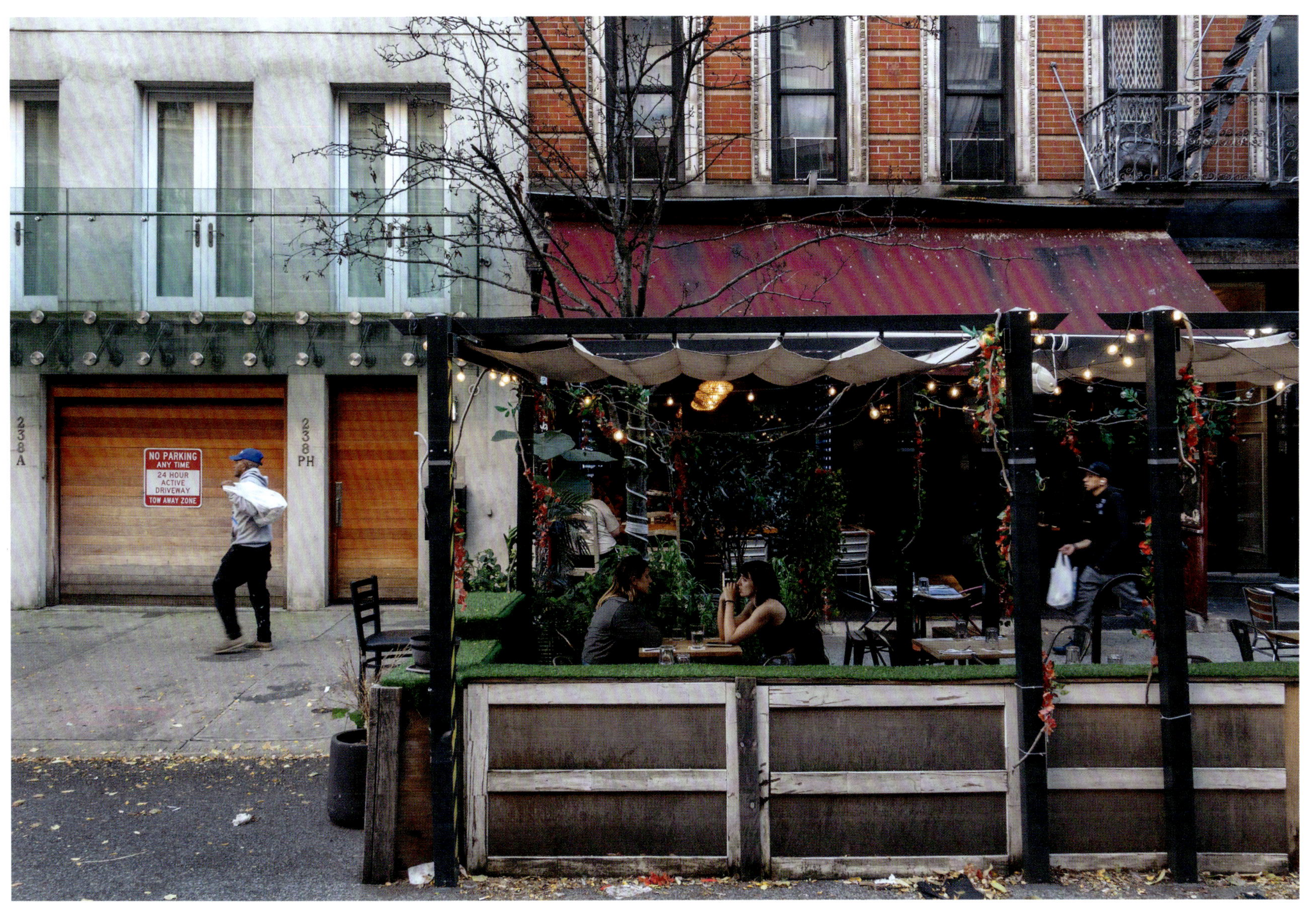

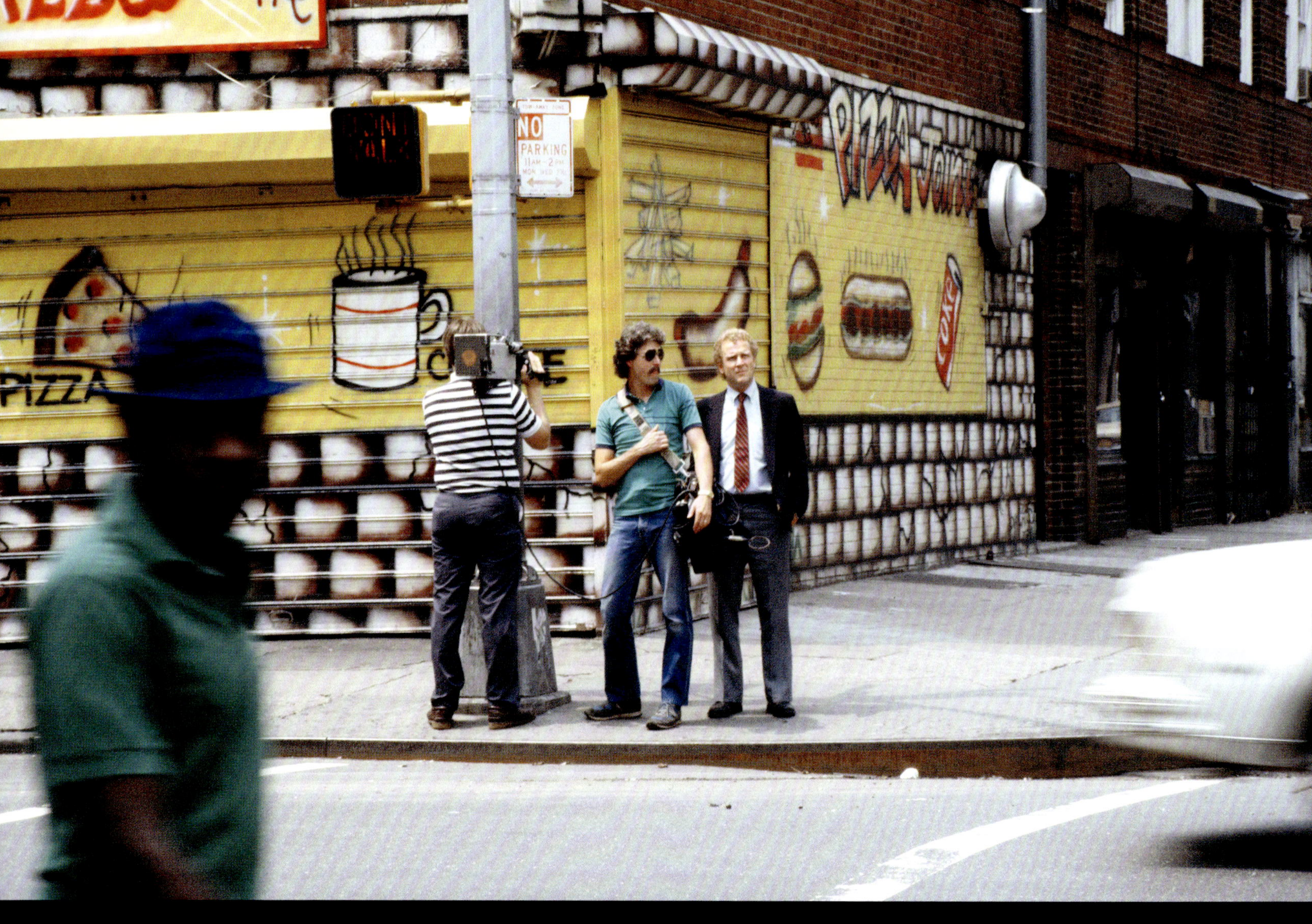

34 AVENUE B

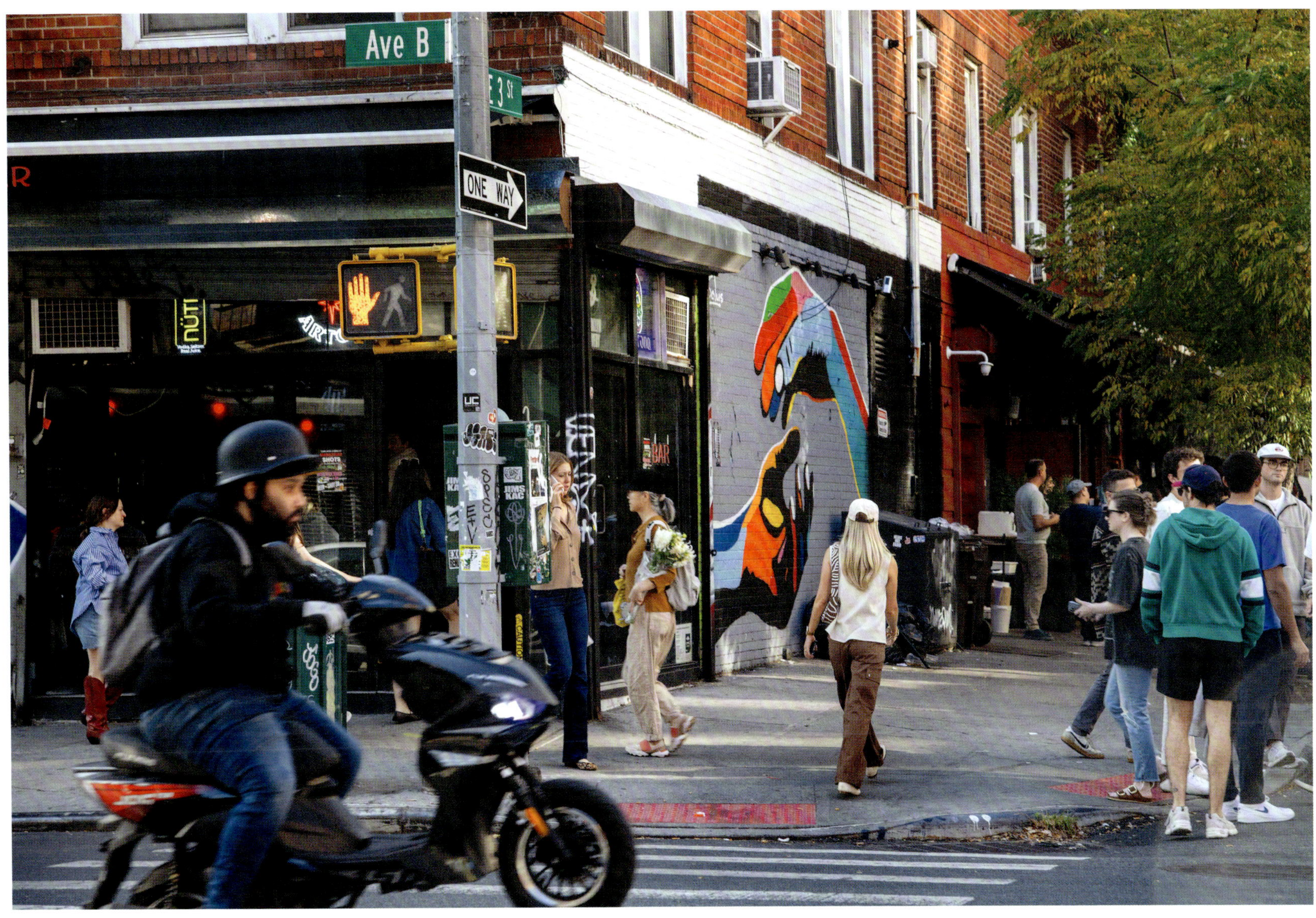

Mama's Bar, Virginia's in the background,
street life in the foreground.

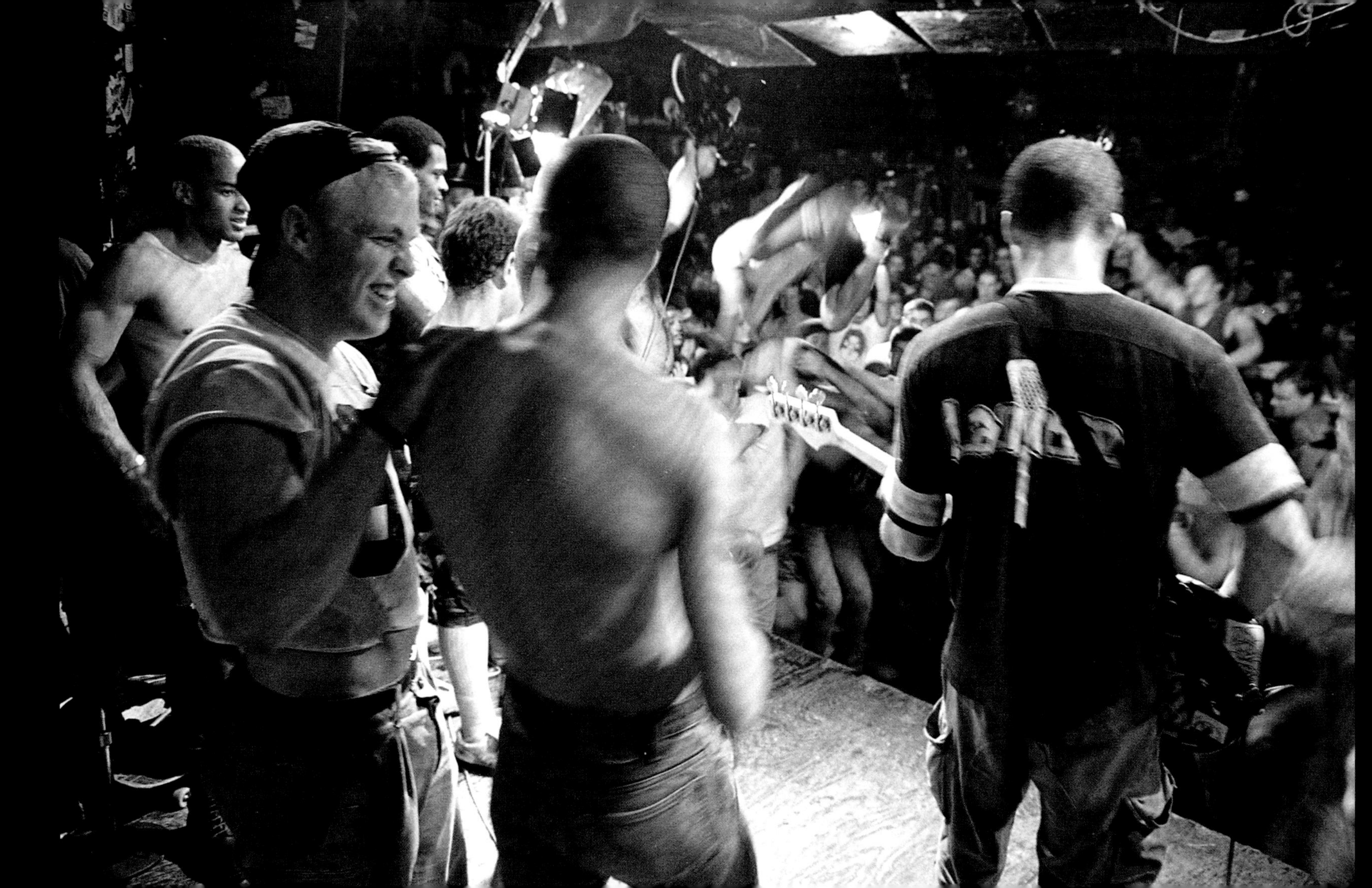

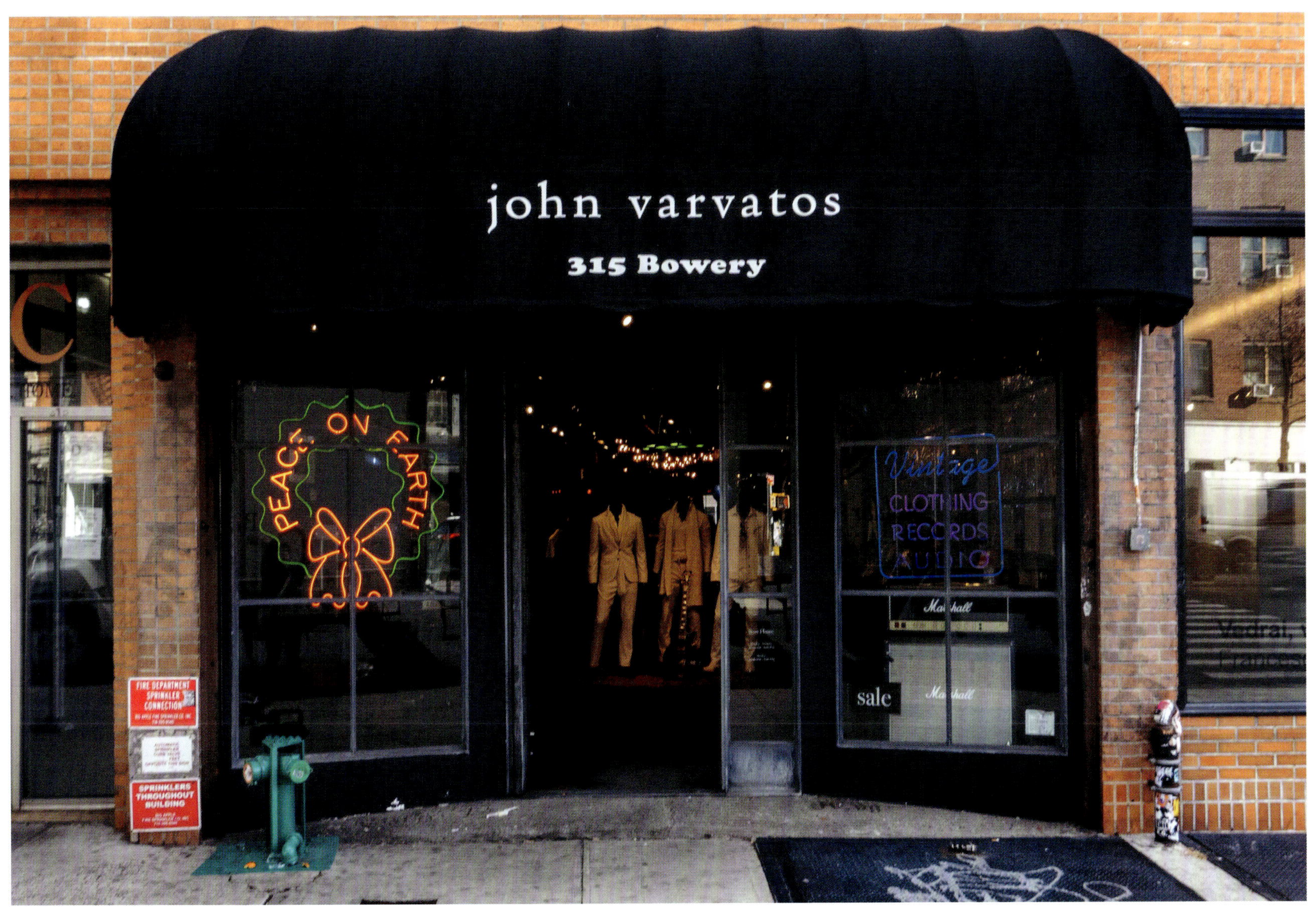

John Varvatos took over the old CBGB spot.

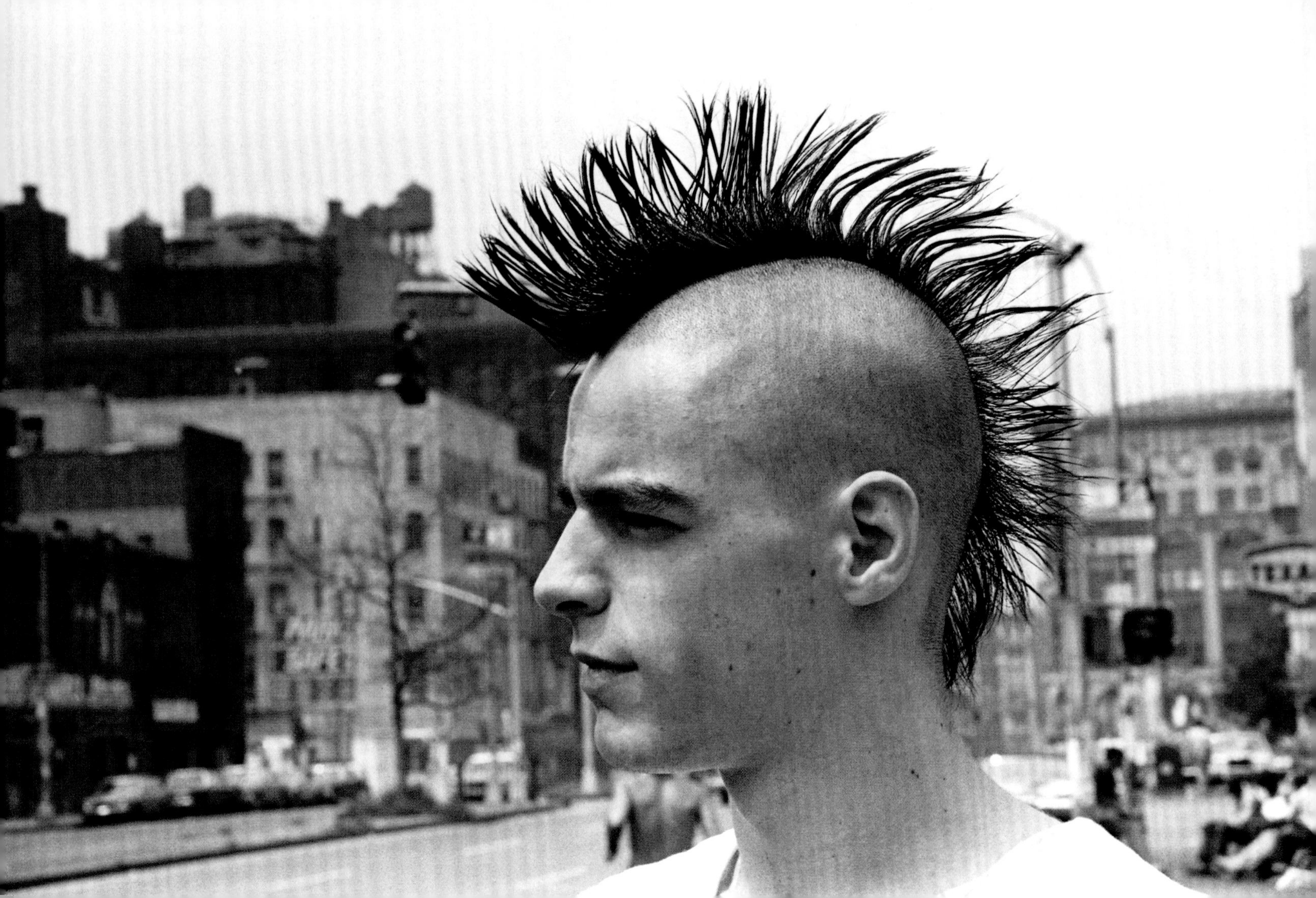

Matt Smith shooting the film
Caught Stealing on East 7th Street.

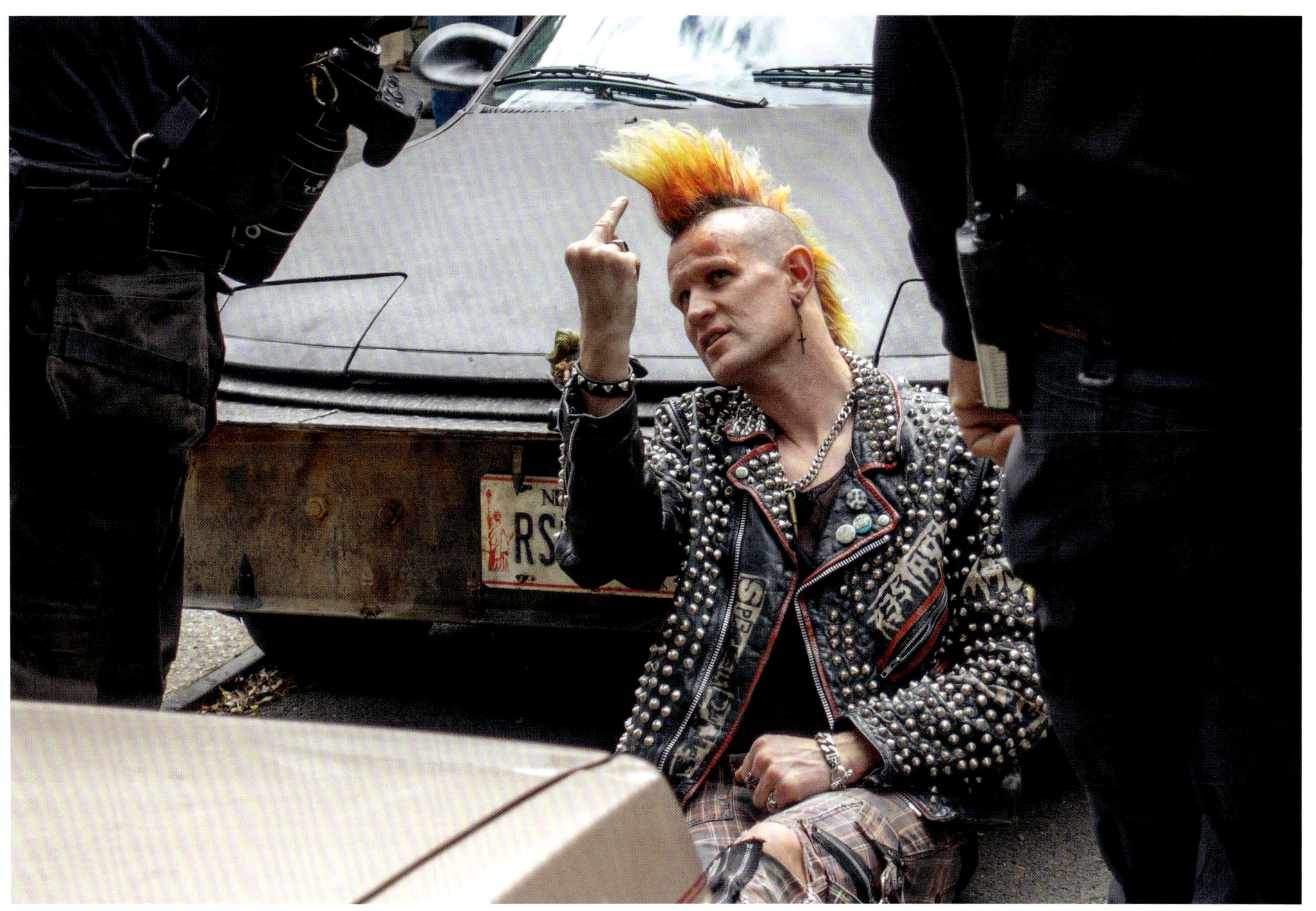

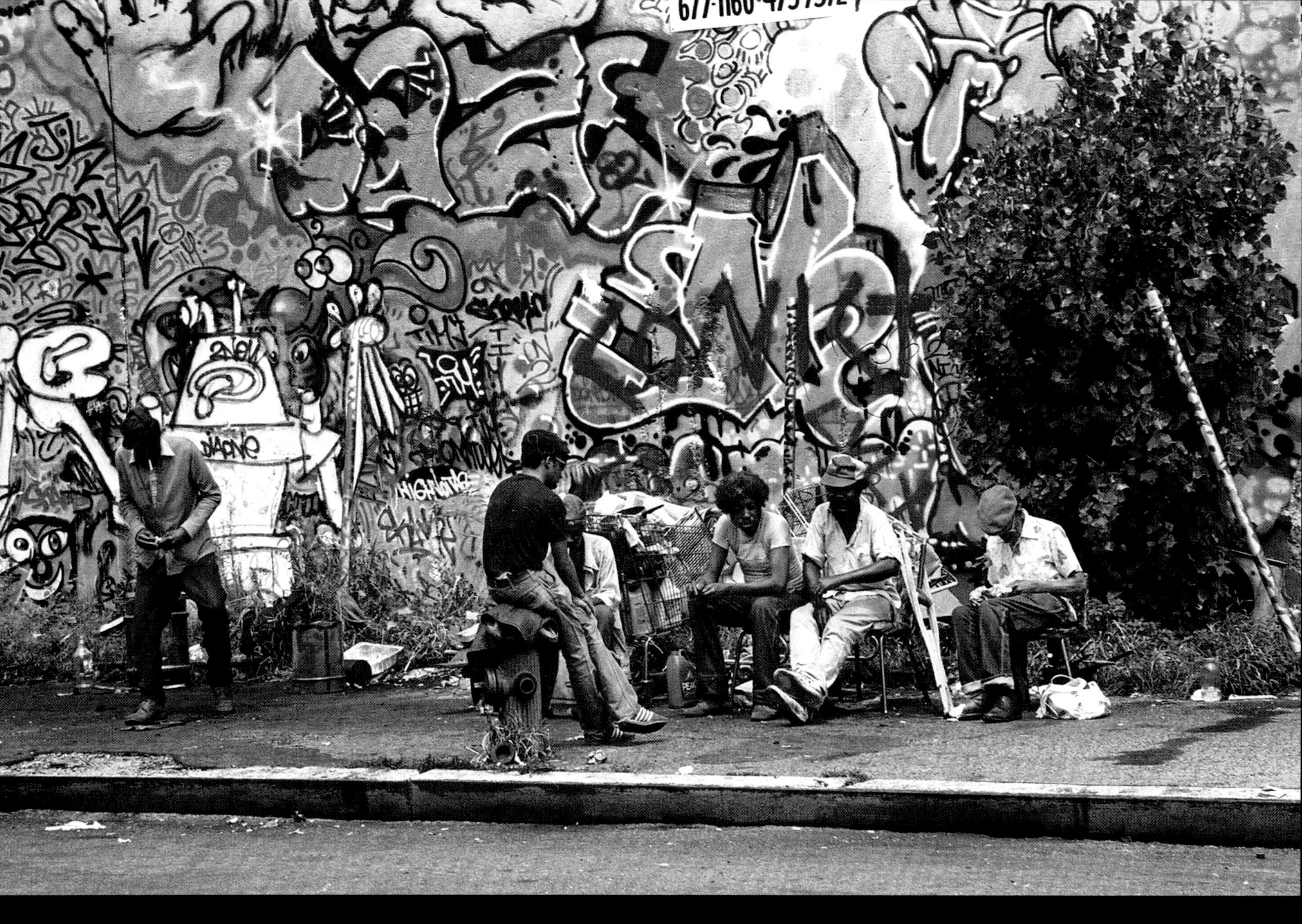

HOUSTON STREET
AND BOWERY

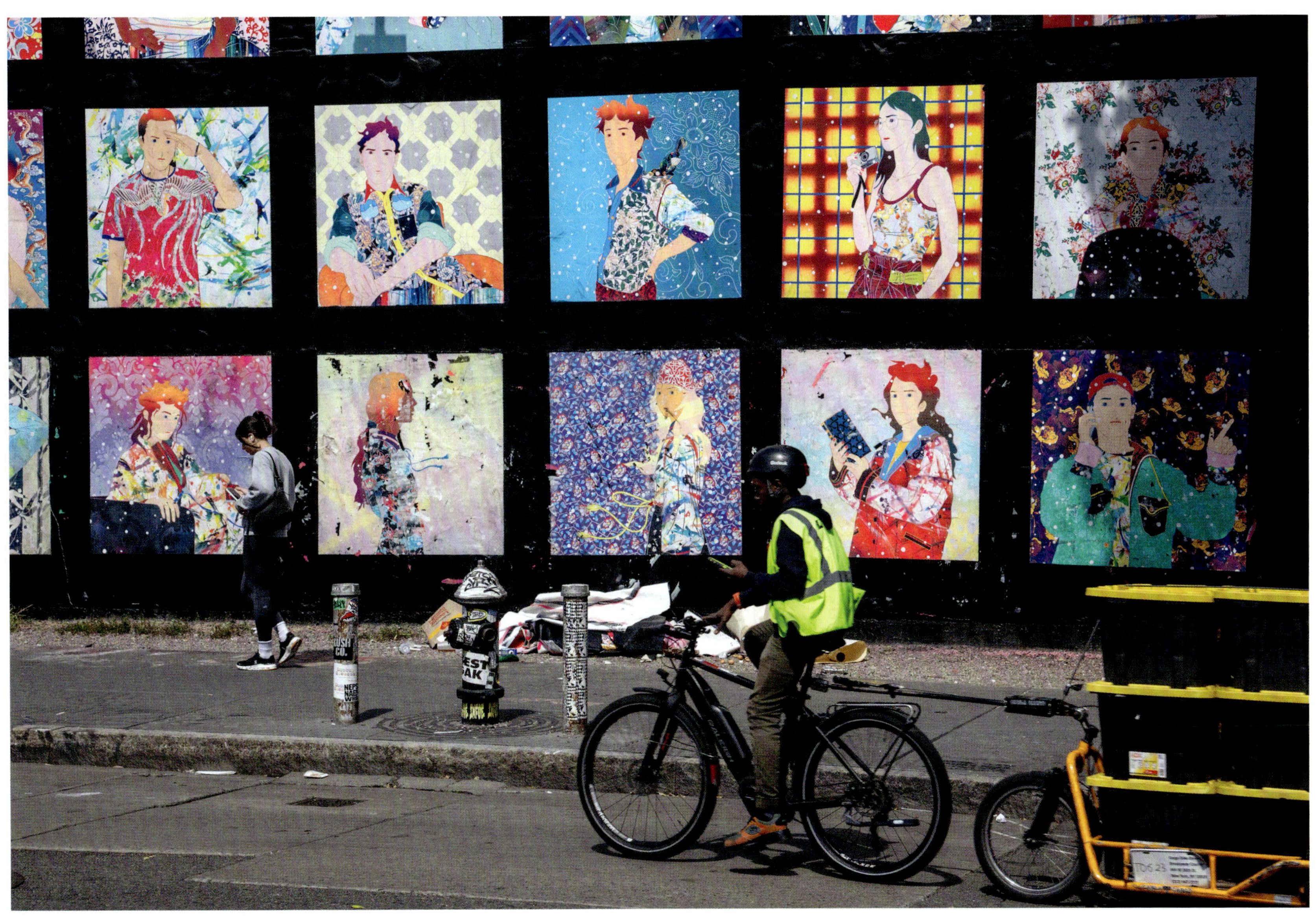

Bowery and Houston shopping.
Amazon delivery guy helping in the cause.
A mural by Tomokazu Matsuyama.

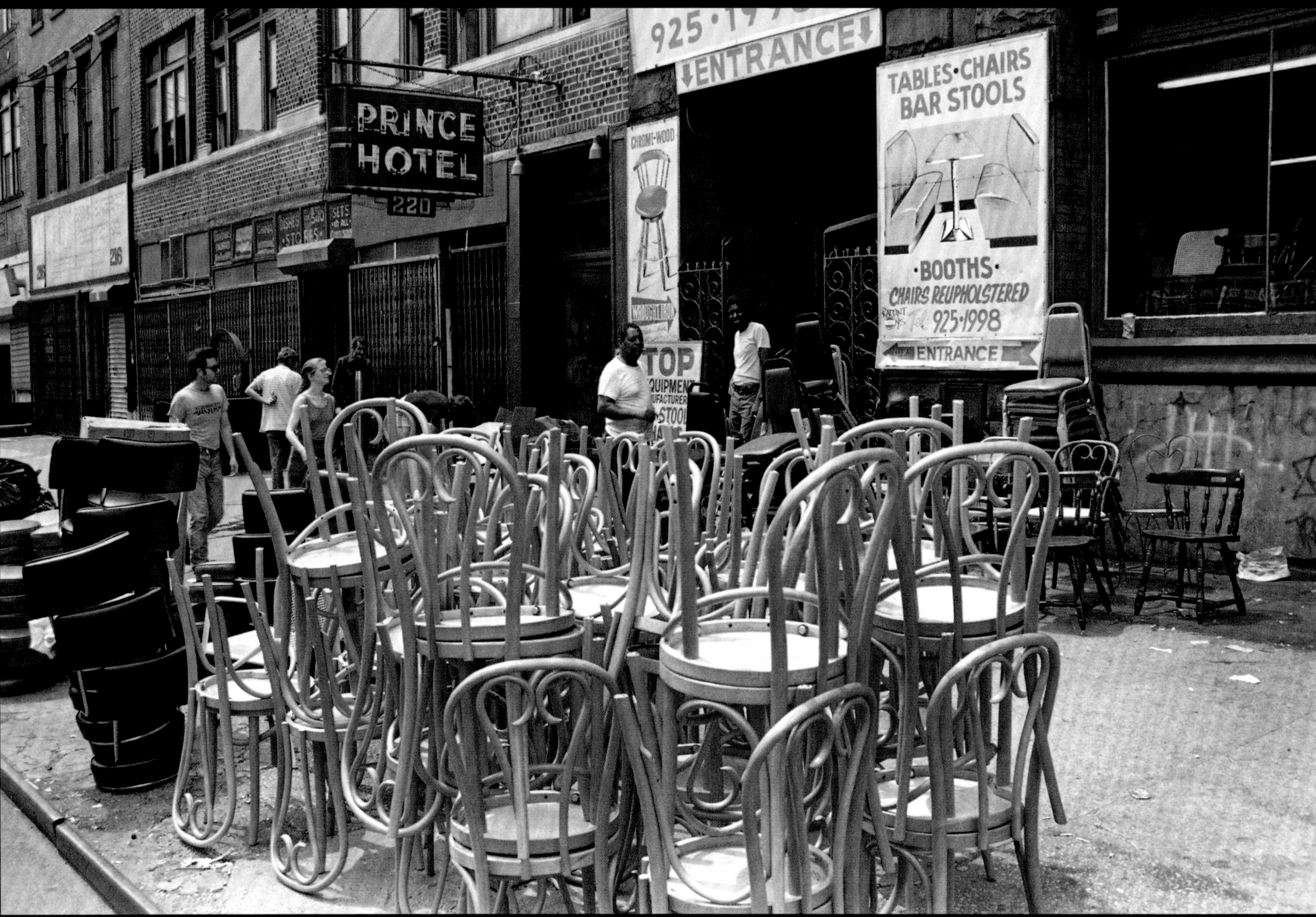

220 AND 222 BOWERY

The Prince Hotel (a flophouse) at 220, and a restaurant supply store and the Bunker at 222. The Bunker was orginally a YMCA, and the writer William Burroughs lived in the former locker room for a number of years. The artist Lynda Benglis lived in the building and also had her studio there. Mark Rothko's studio was in the former basketball gym. The poet John Giornio lived there for almost fifty years and founded Giorno Poetry Systems, a nonprofit "based on the idea of artists supporting other artists," in the building. Today, the nonprofit preserves the Bunker and Burroughs's former bedroom there. A work by Keith Haring is perched above the urinals, a gift to Giorno from a friend.

The Nolita Express Hostel at 220: from flophouse
to hostel. At 222, from YMCA to condos.

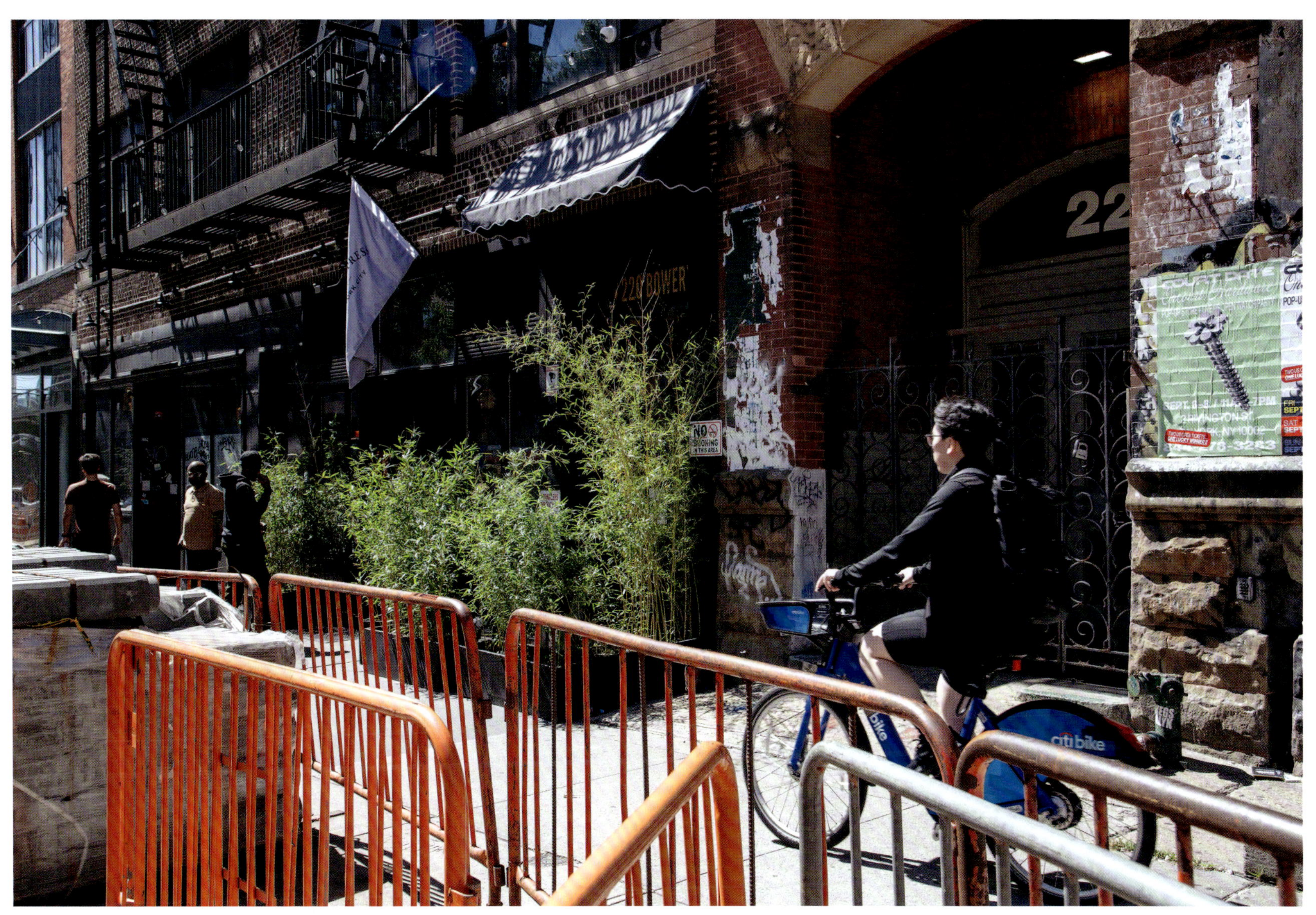

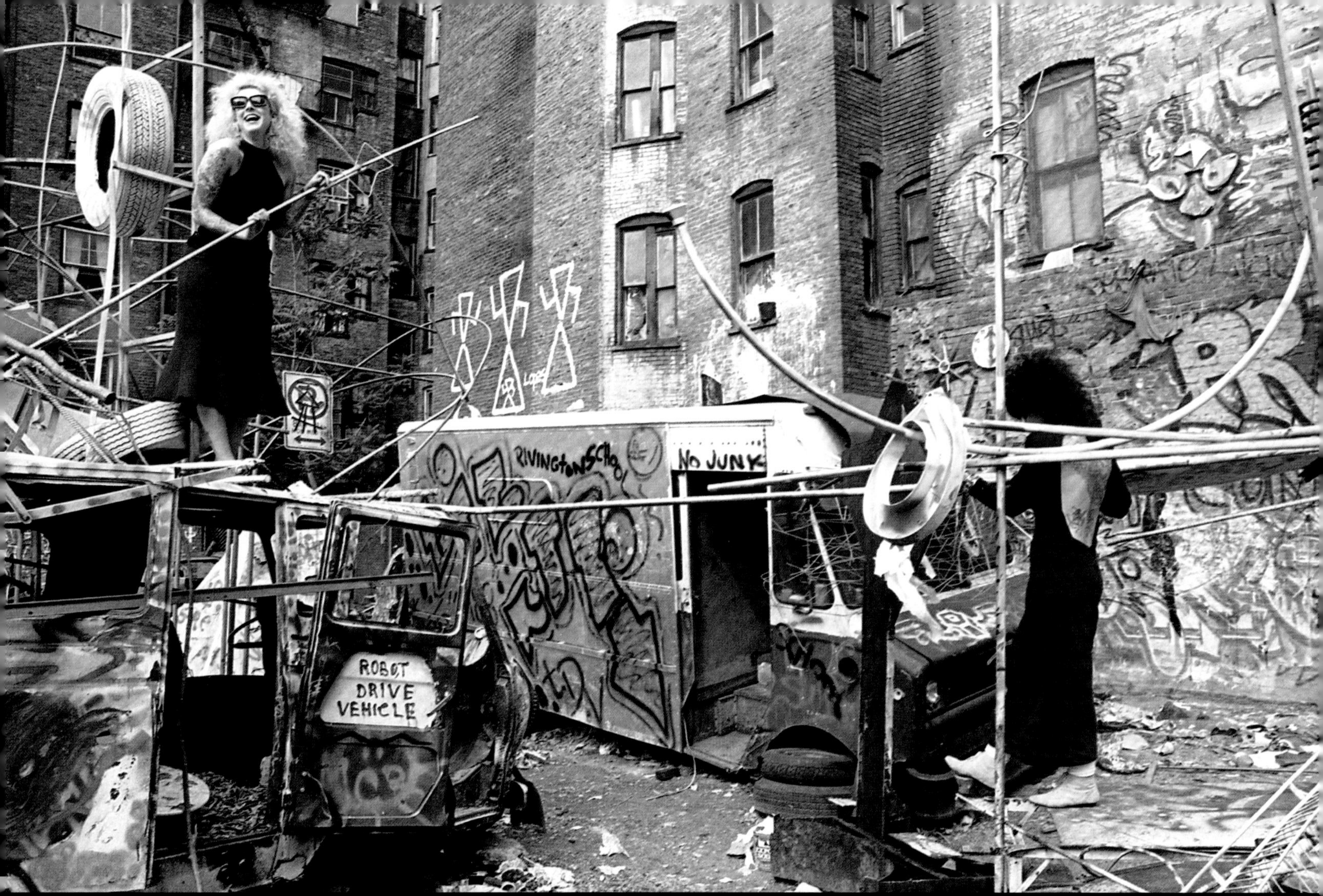

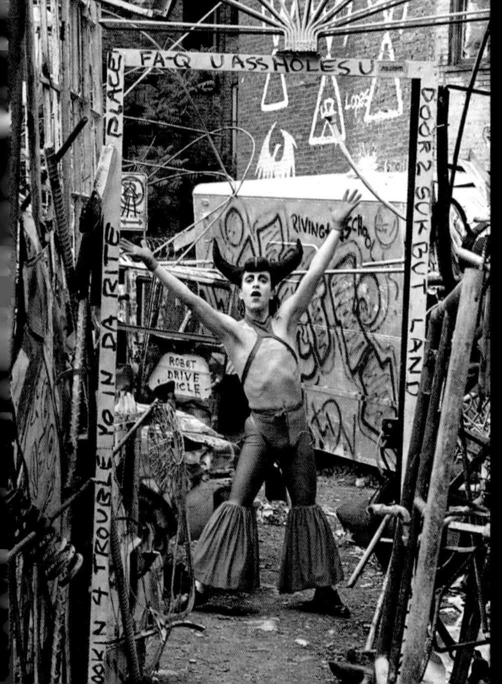
FA-Q U ASSHOLES U
RIVINGTON SCHOOL
DOOR 2 SUK BUT LAND
ROBOT DRIVE VEHICLE
OOK N 4 TROUBLE IO IN DA RITE PLACE

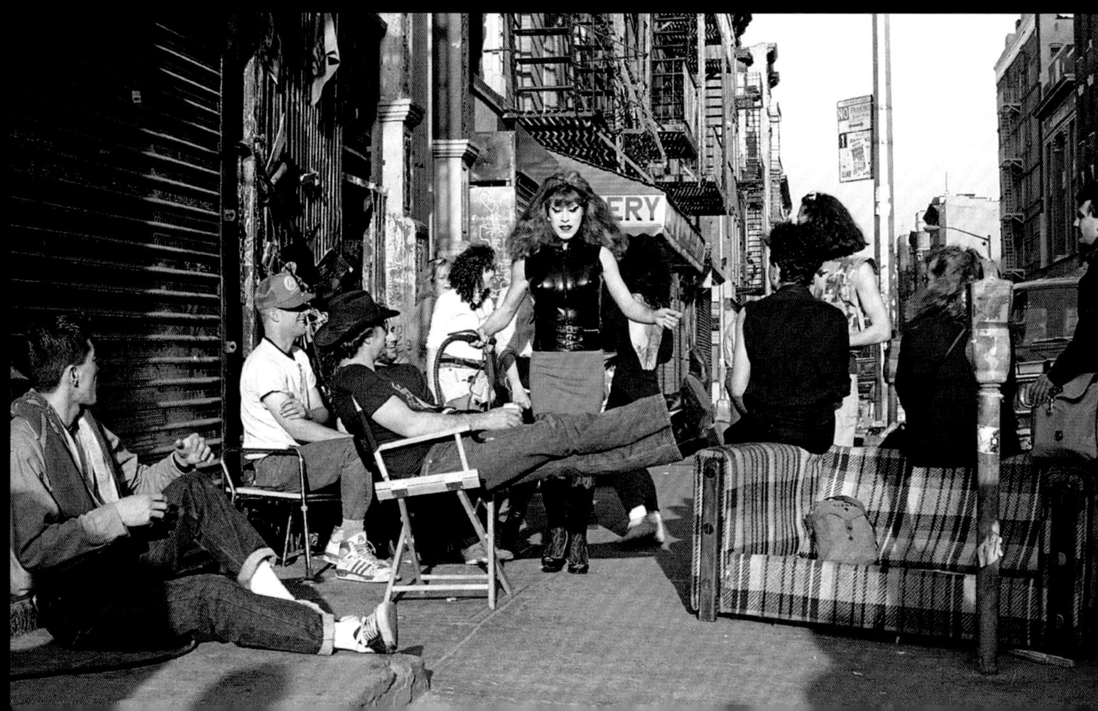
ERY

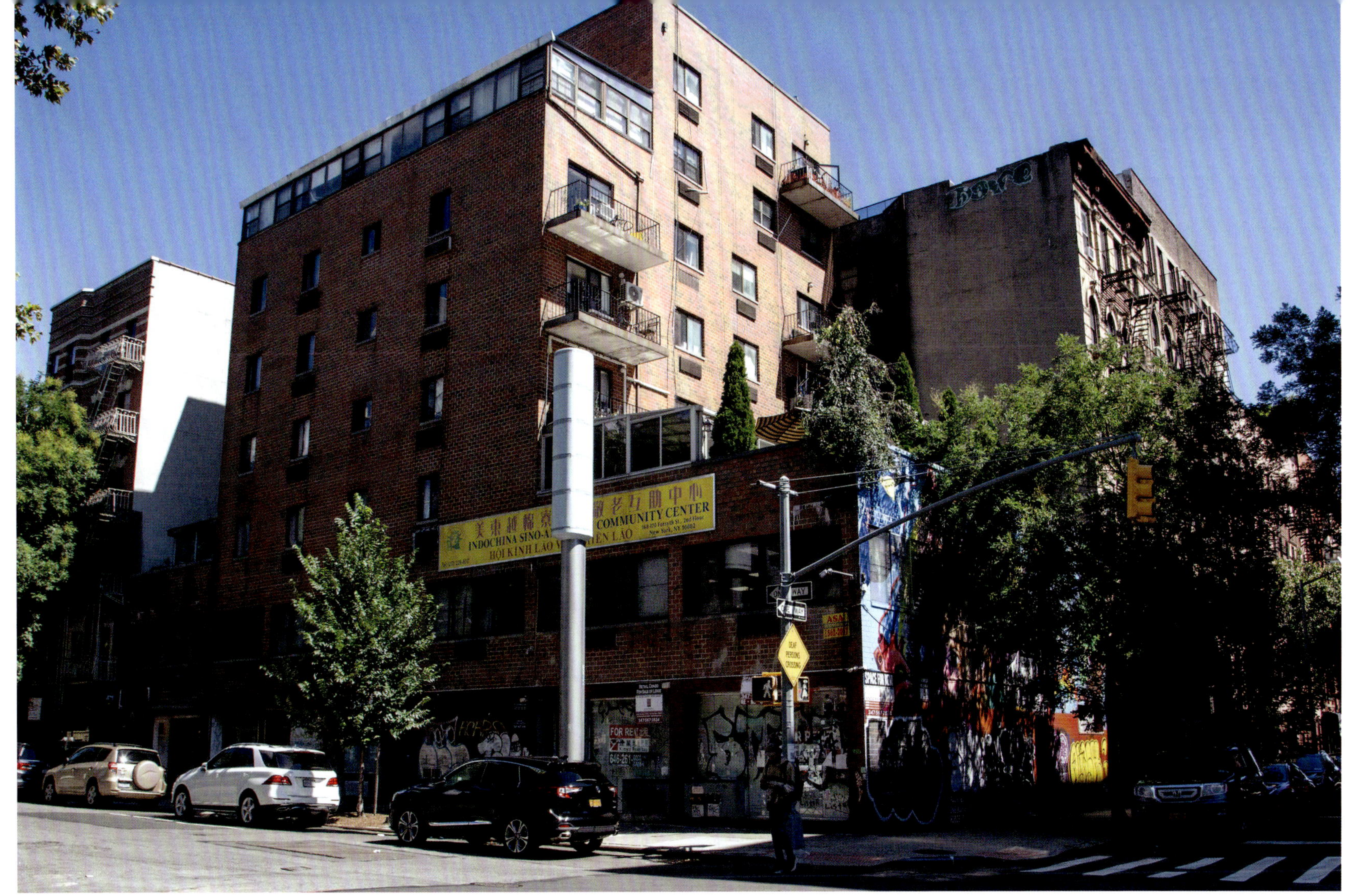

170 FORSYTH STREET

THEN The Rivington Sculpture Garden at Rivington and Forsyth Streets. Part of the Rivington School artists' collective and the No Se No Club. At bottom left, Joey Arias in the sculpture garden, a production still for the movie *Mondo New York*; at bottom right, Arias walking from No Se No on Rivington Street.

NOW The Indochina Sino-American Community Center (ISACC).

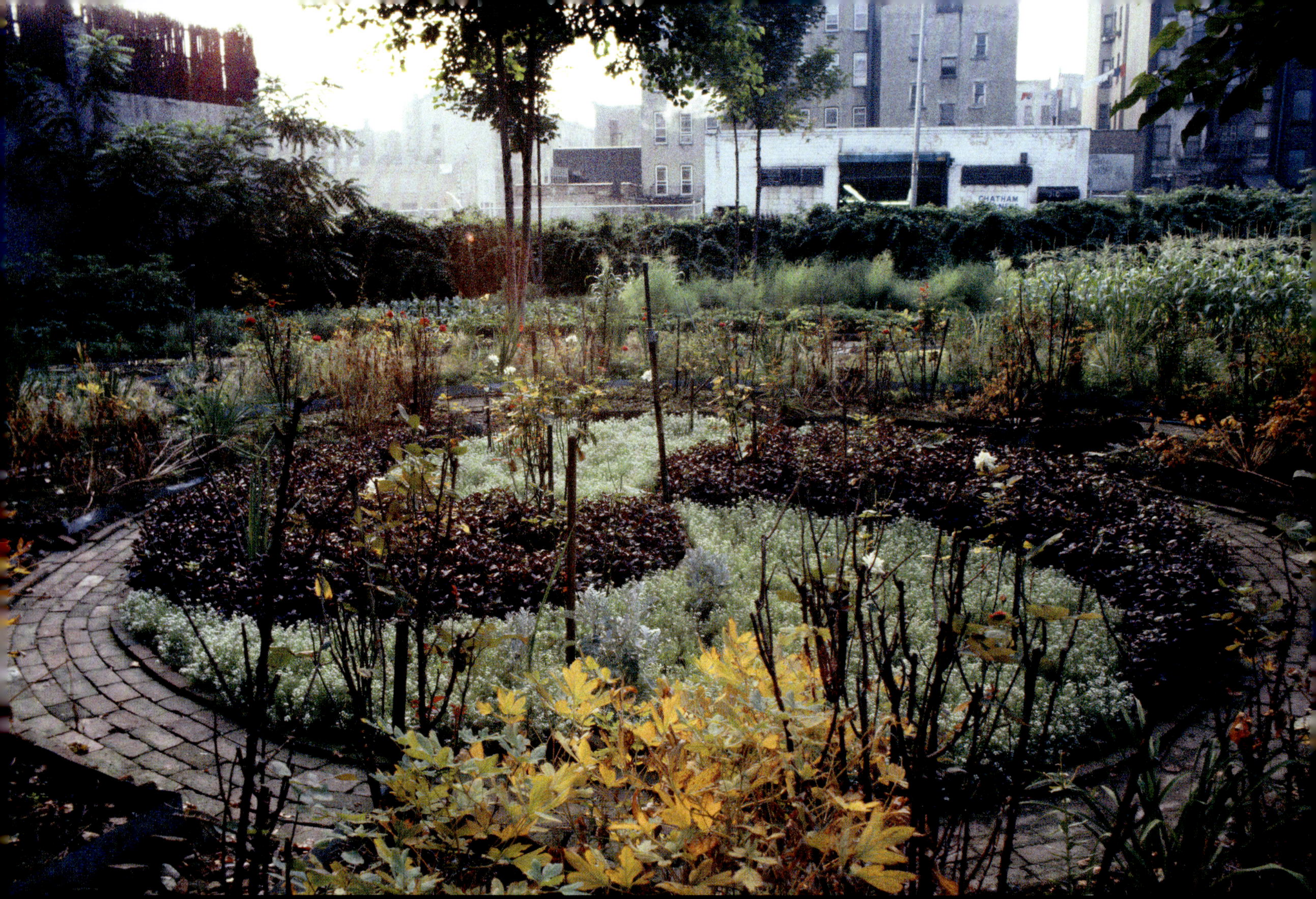

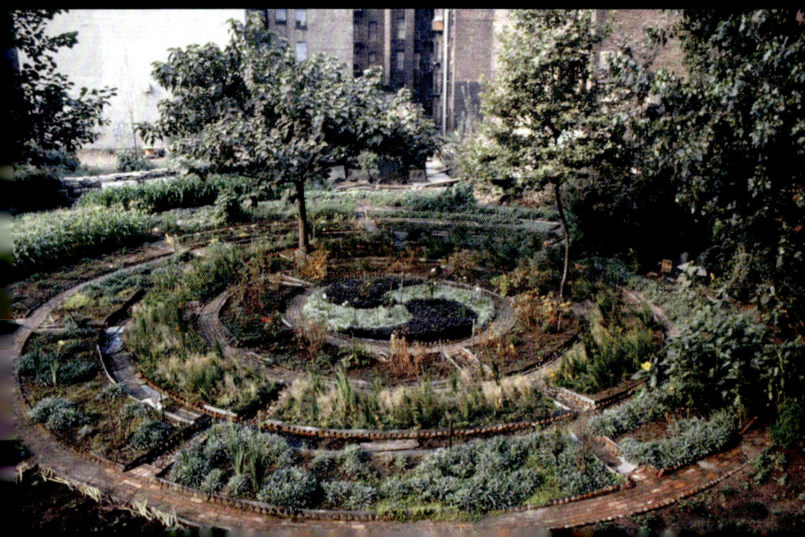

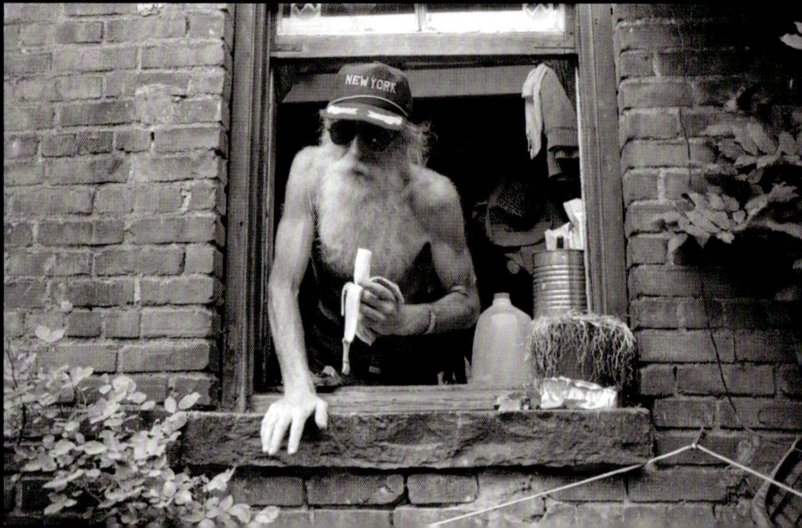

FORSYTH / STANTON / ELDRIDGE STREETS

Adam Purple's Garden of Eden. Adam and "helping hands" created a beautiful garden out of a huge tract of torn-down Lower East Side buildings. They grew food and fed the neighbors. The garden was beautiful, the efforts were enormous, the results were remarkable. One small quibble would be that Adam felt everything should be composted, including his own feces, and that compost is what fertilized all the food fed to the neighbors.

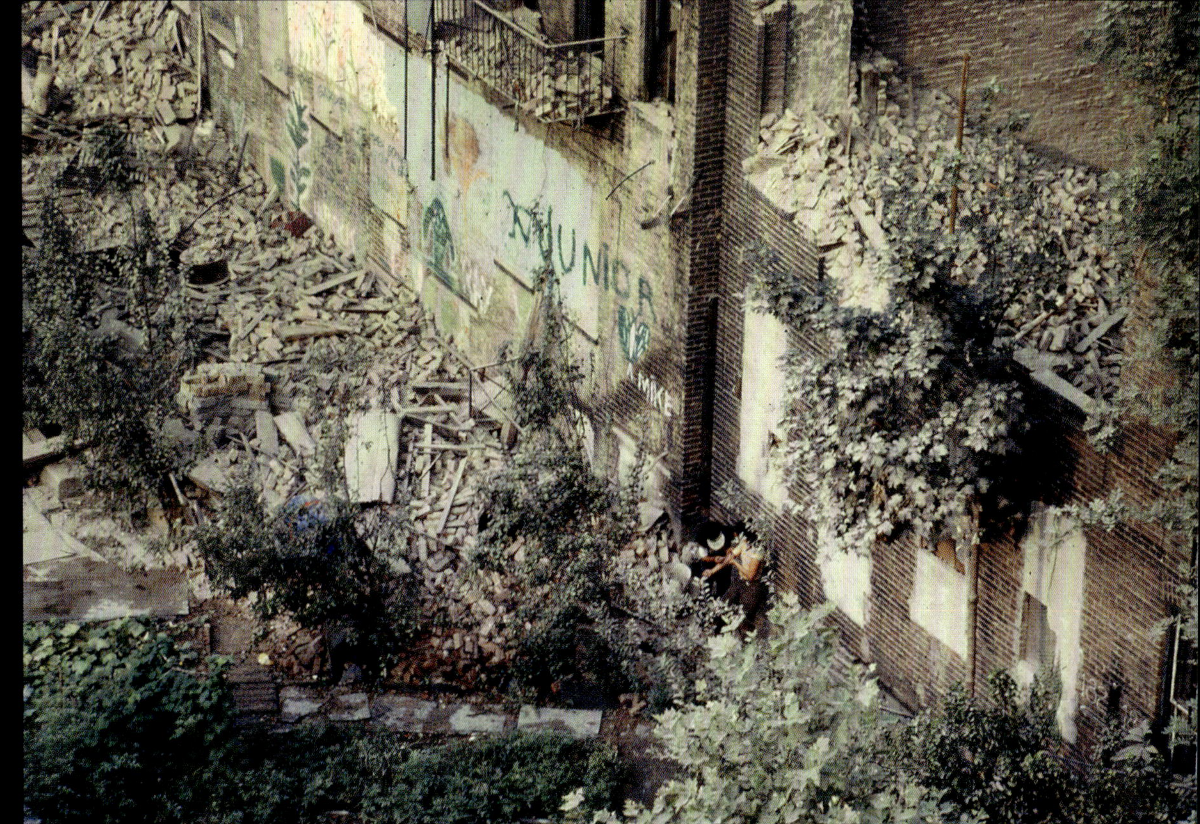

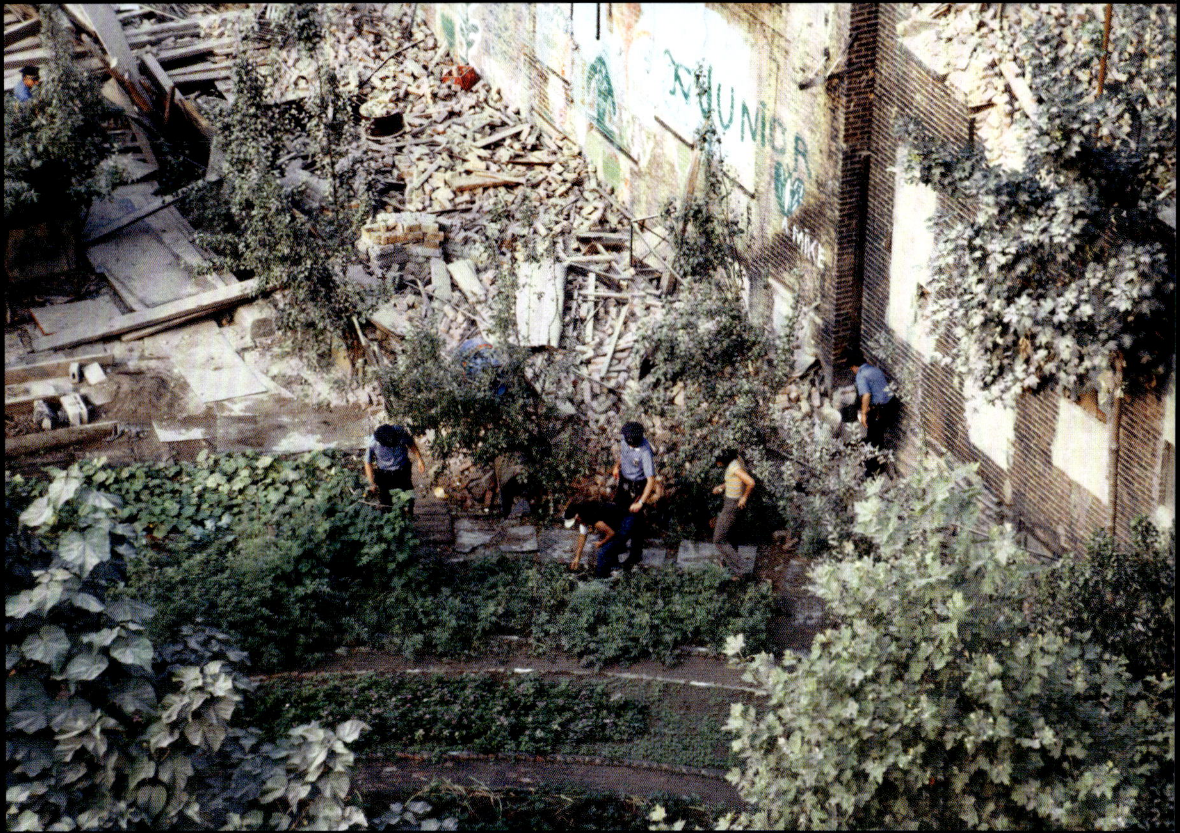

RIGHT From the vantage point of a nearby abandoned building at 6 a.m., I happened to witness some morning drug activity in the Garden of Eden. I could see both the users and the approaching police. Neither could see the other. A big surprise and disruption, for all. I was ignorant of my potential danger, standing on the roof visible to anyone who might look up; it never occurred to me at the time.

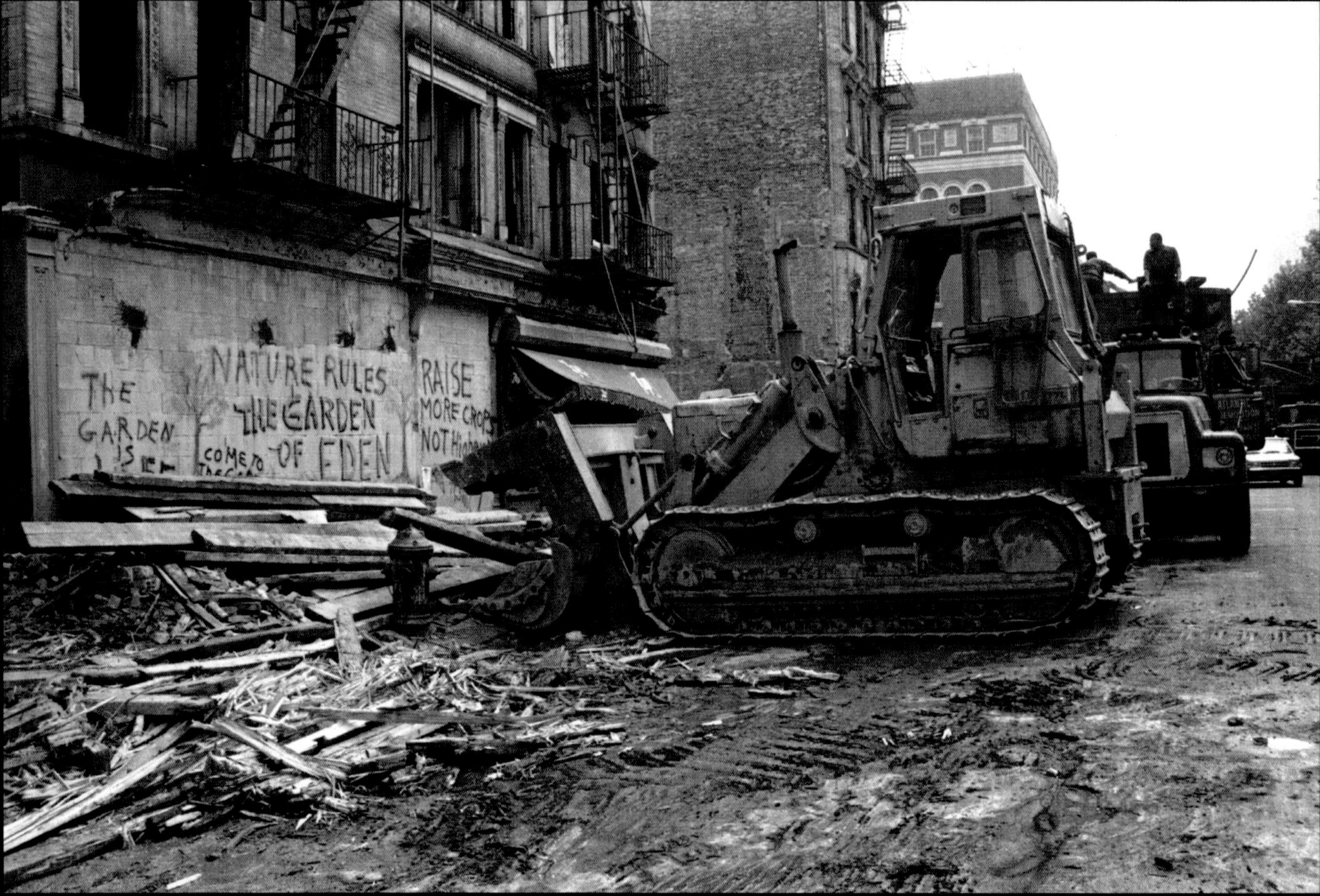

The end of the
Garden of Eden.
Bulldozed for
housing.

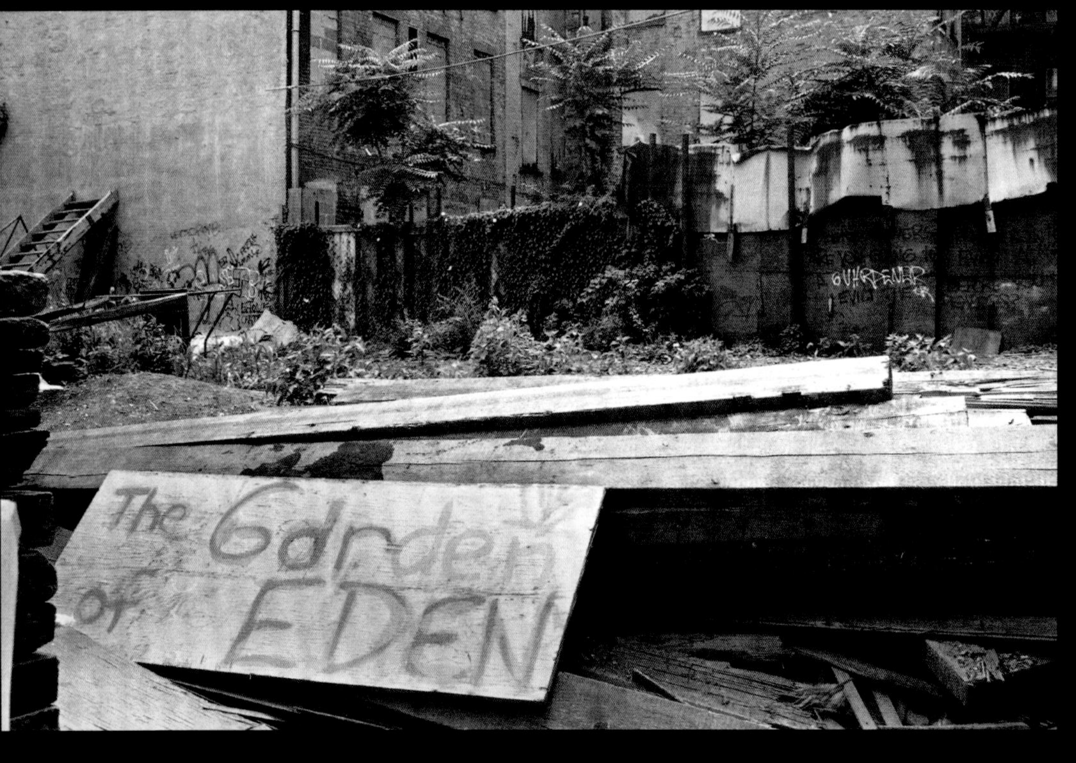

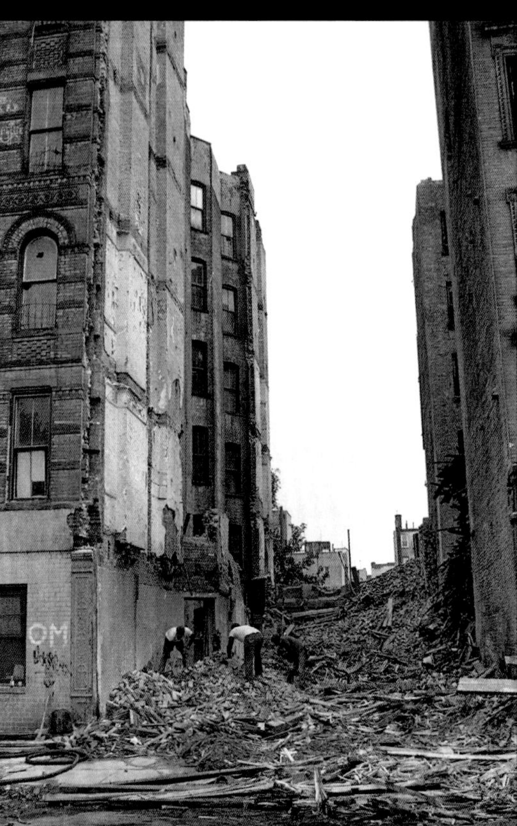

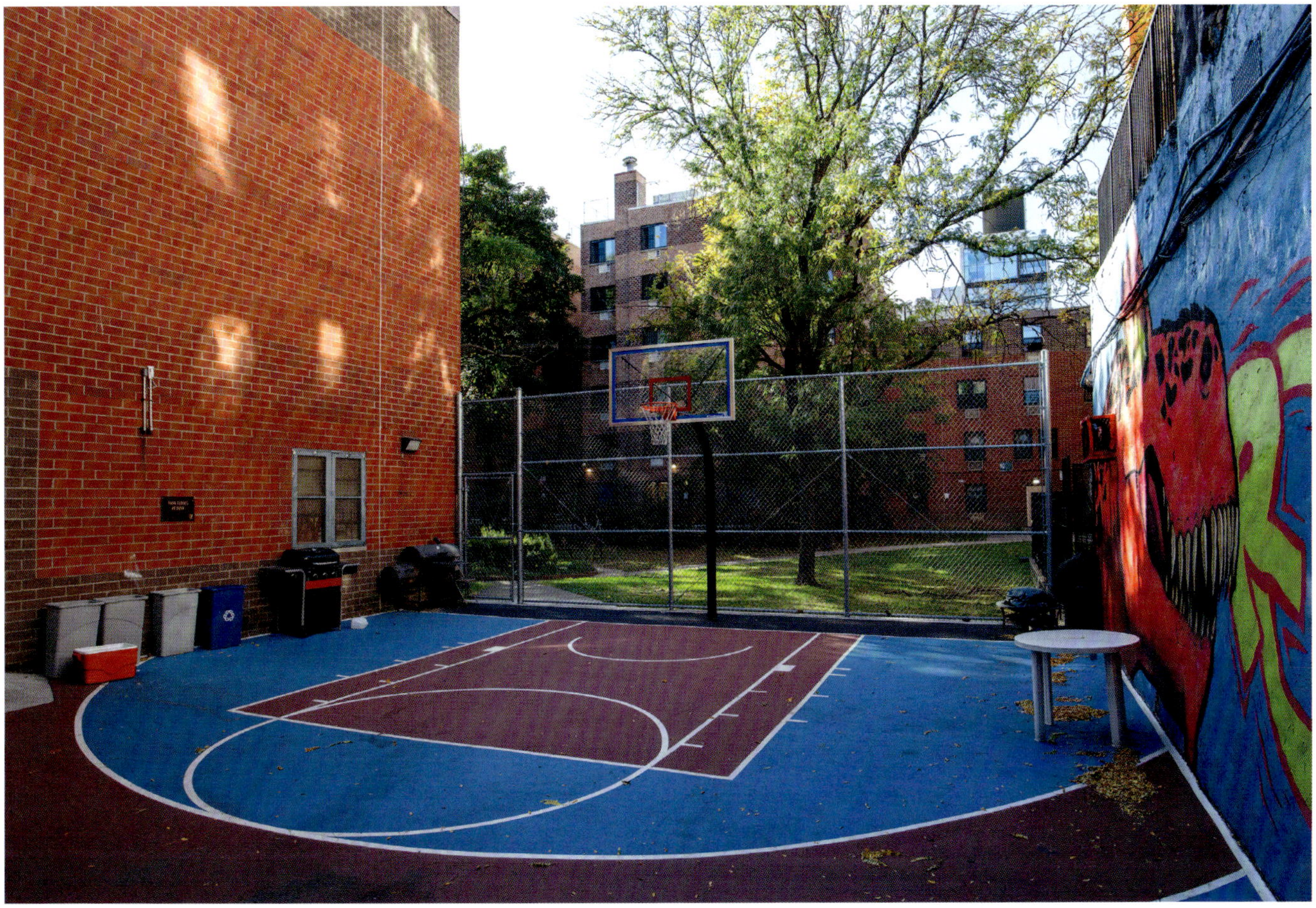

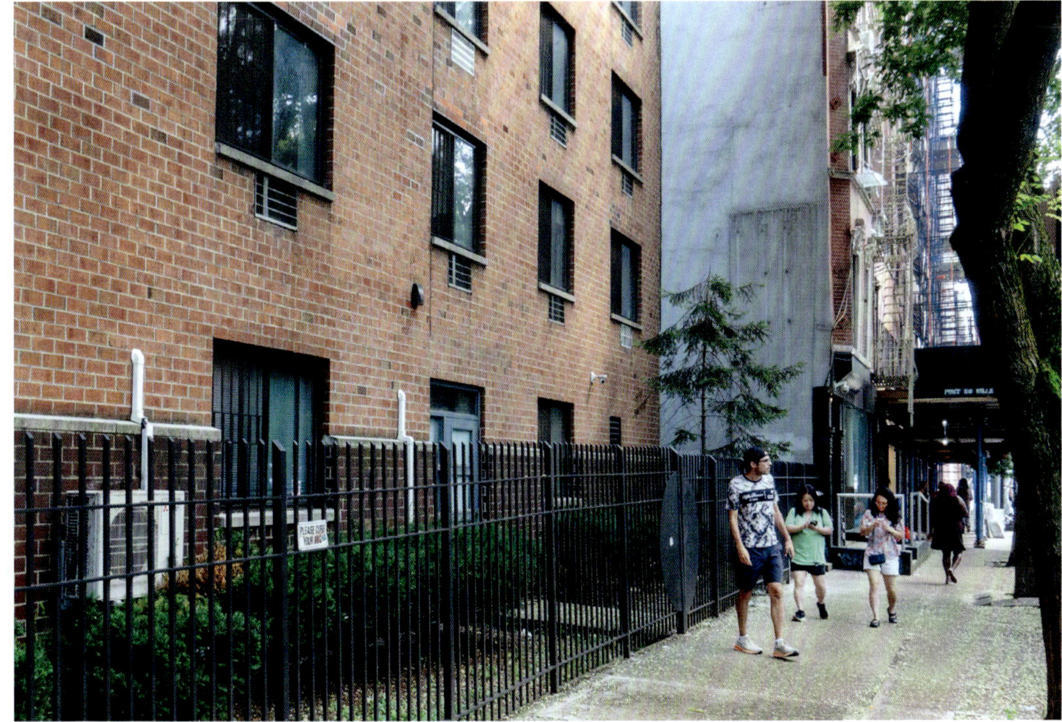

Housing for the deaf
and NYCHA buildings.

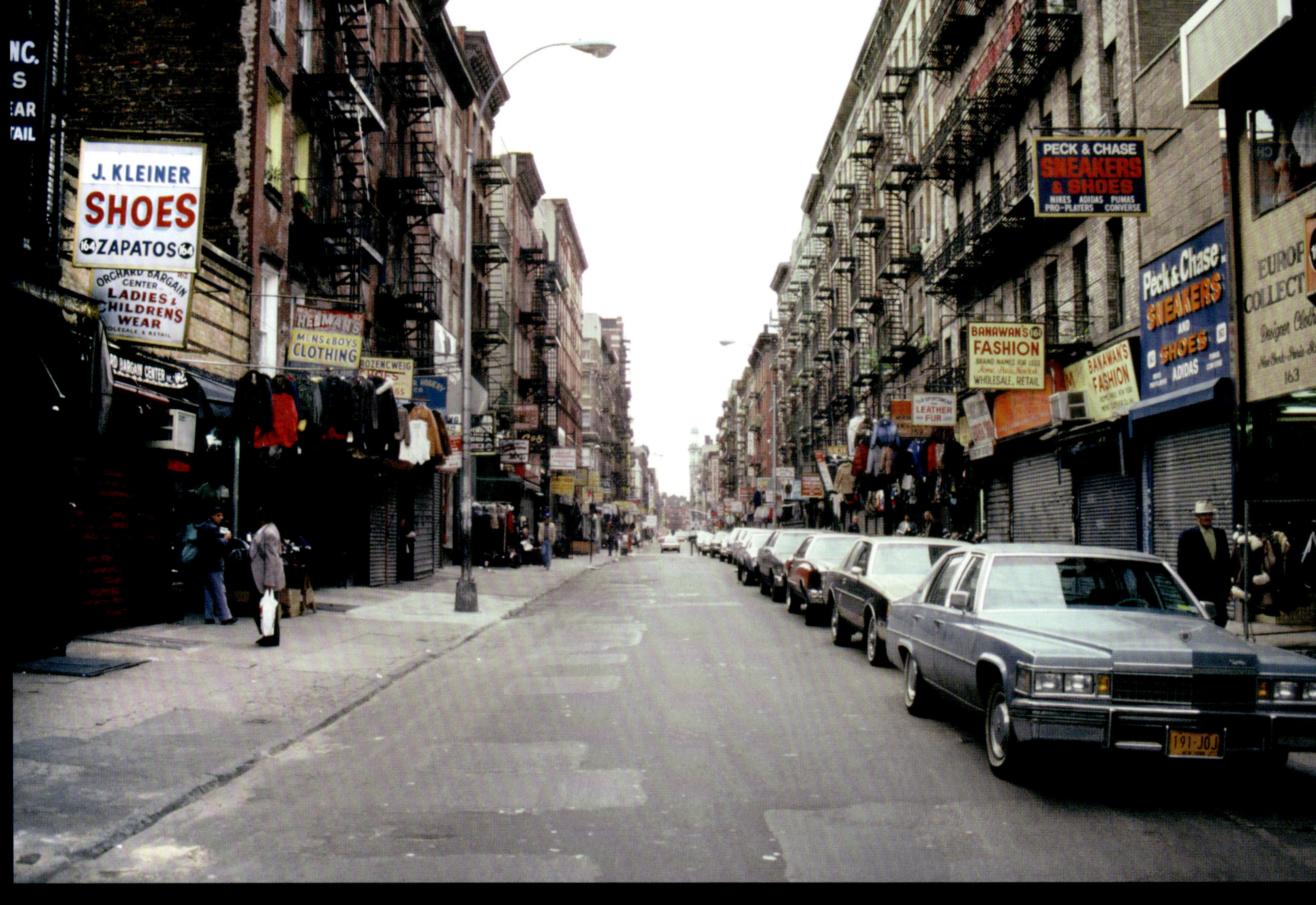
NC.
J. KLEINER
SHOES
ZAPATOS
ORCHARD BARGAIN
CENTER
LADIES &
CHILDRENS
WEAR
WHOLESALE & RETAIL
HELMAN'S
MENS & BOYS
CLOTHING
PECK & CHASE
SNEAKERS
& SHOES
NIKES ADIDAS PUMAS
PRO-PLAYERS CONVERSE
Peck & Chase
SNEAKERS
AND
SHOES
ADIDAS
EUROP
COLLECT
BANAWAN'S
FASHION
BRAND NAMES FOR LESS
WHOLESALE, RETAIL
BANAWAN'S
FASHION
LEATHER
FUR
191-JOJ

164 ORCHARD STREET

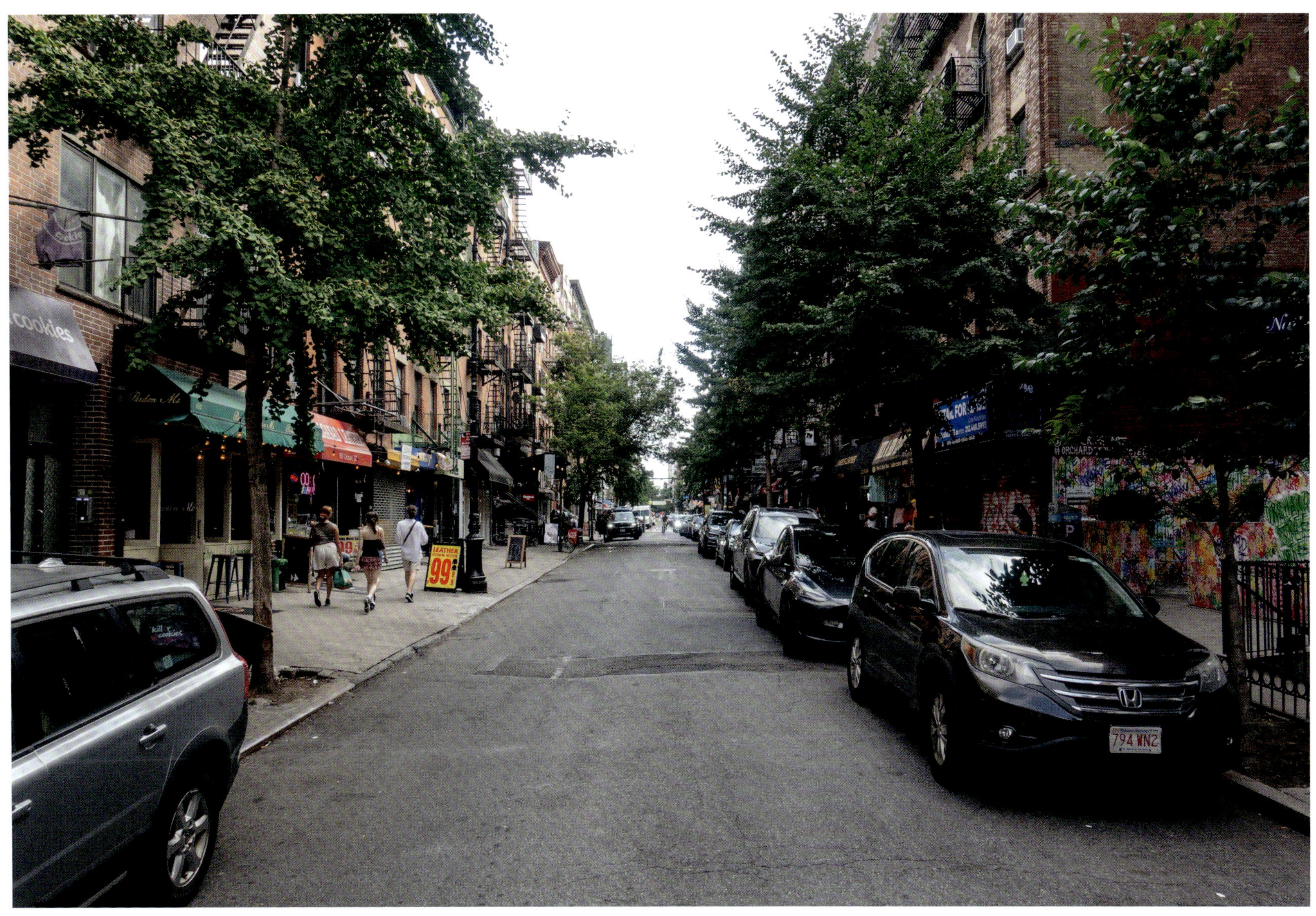

Looking south at Stanton Street—
nails, cookies, bars, fashion. And trees!

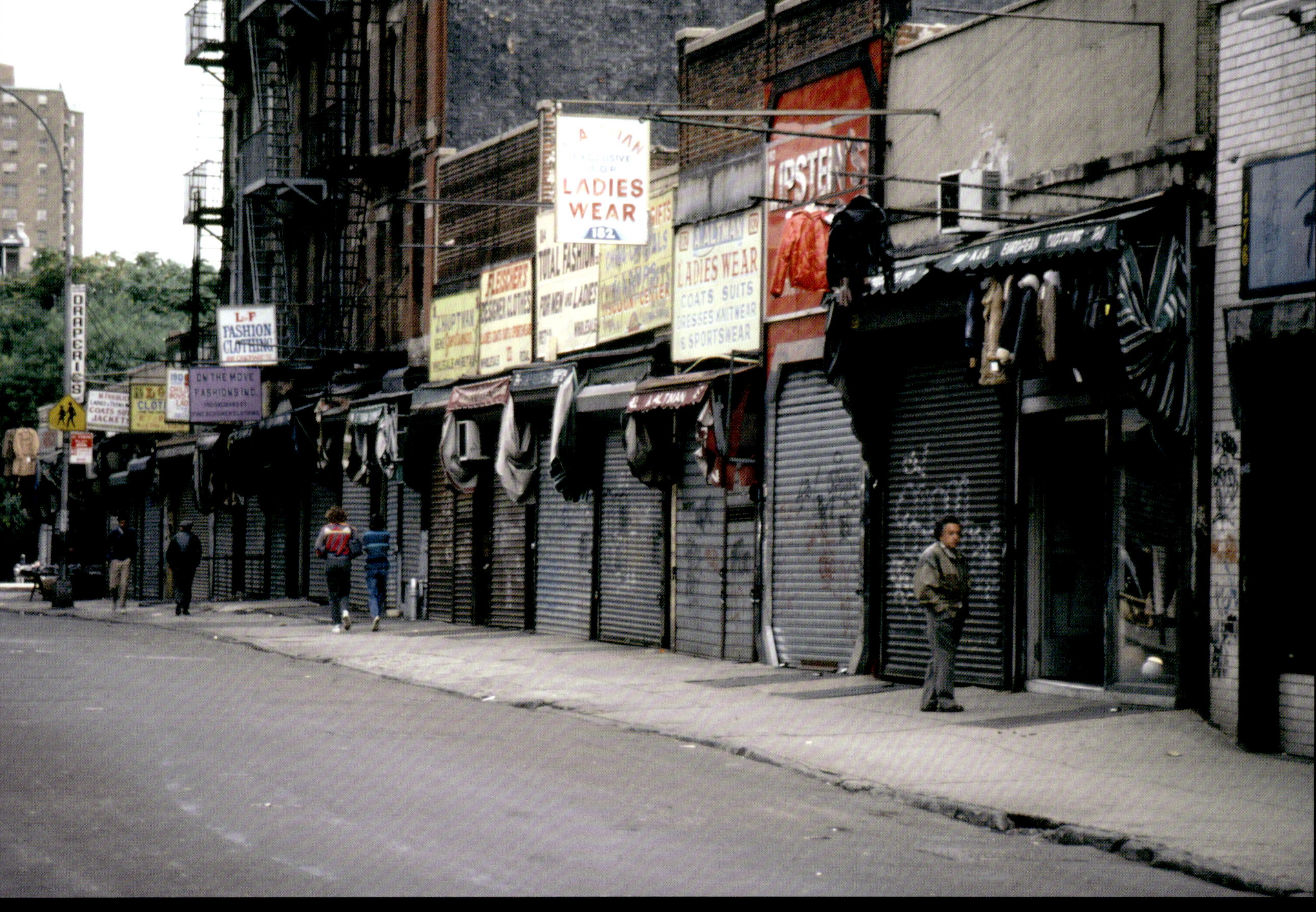

180 ORCHARD STREET

Looking north toward Houston Street.
Fashion at a discount.

P&T Knitwear (an excellent bookstore) and a line for breakfast. Mostly new buildings, all-new look.

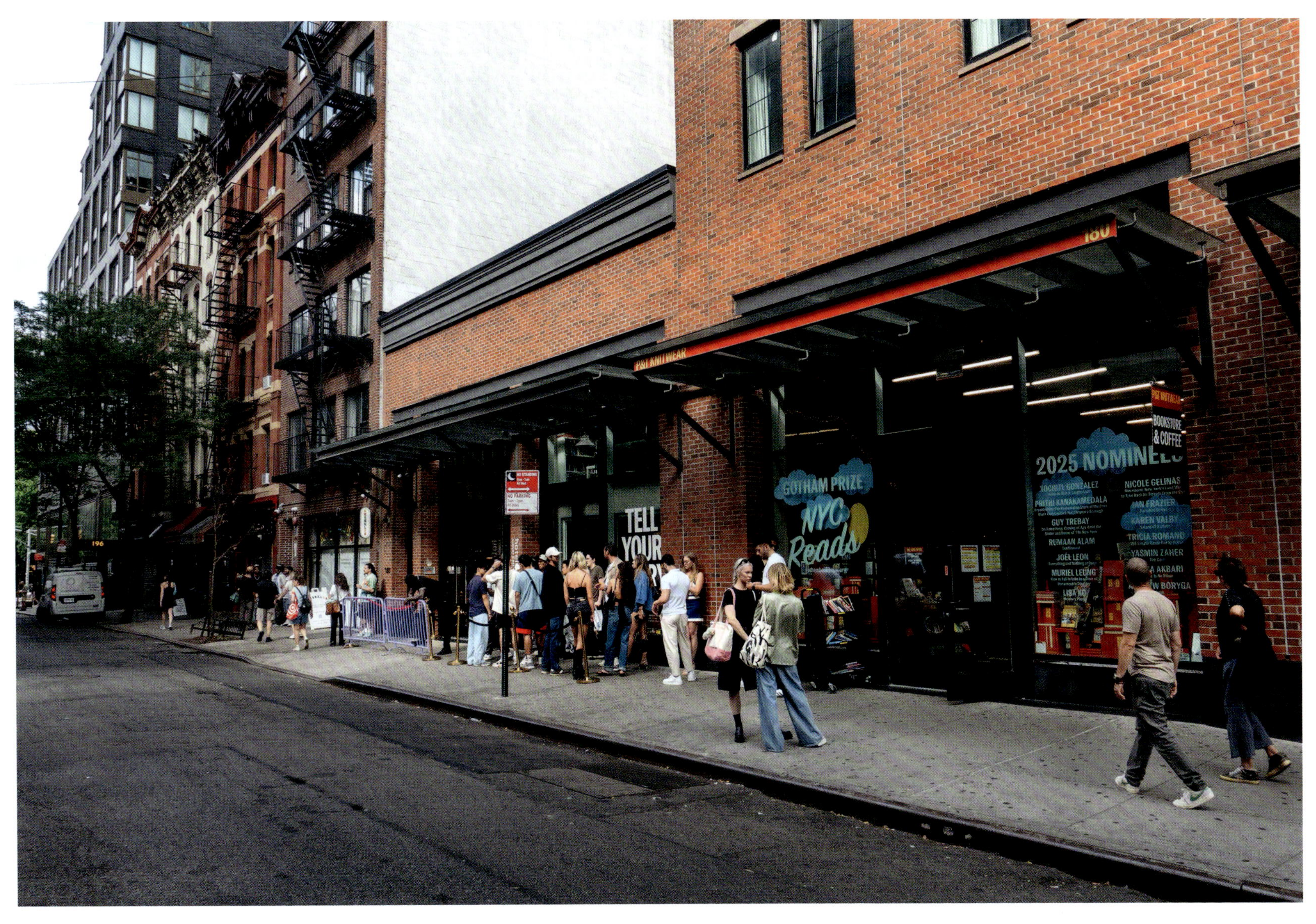

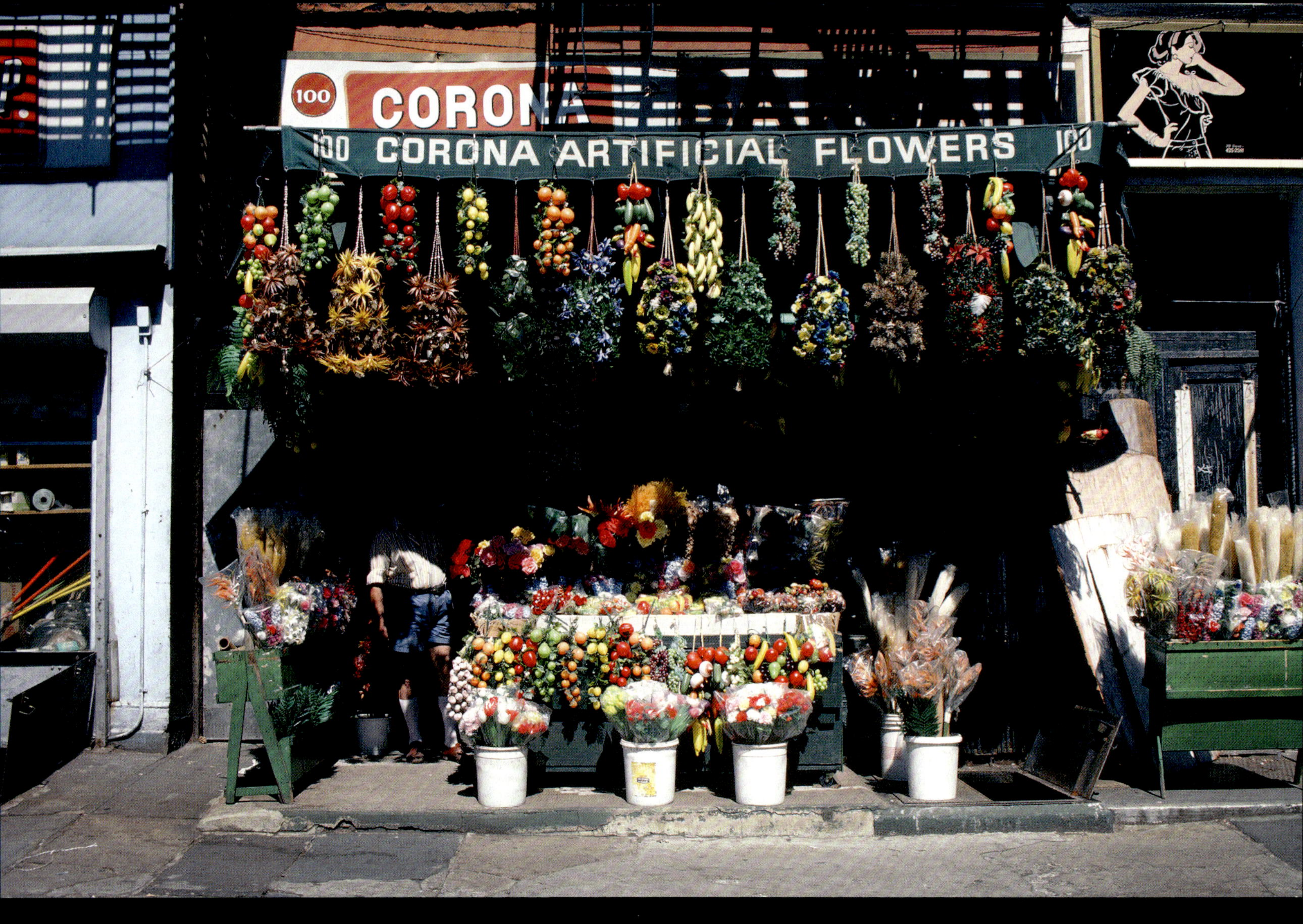

108 STANTON STREET

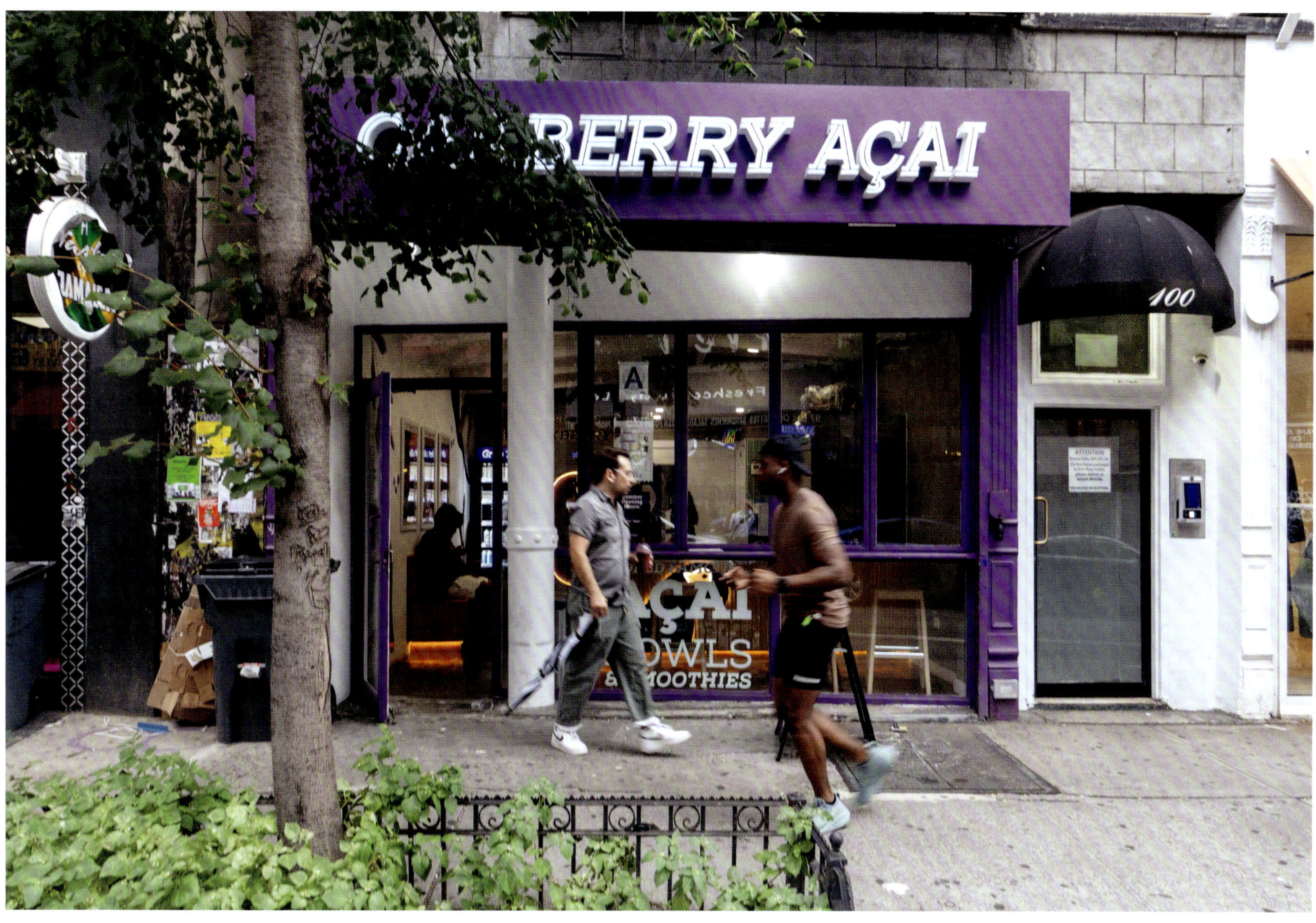

Lower East Side acai bowls at the ready.

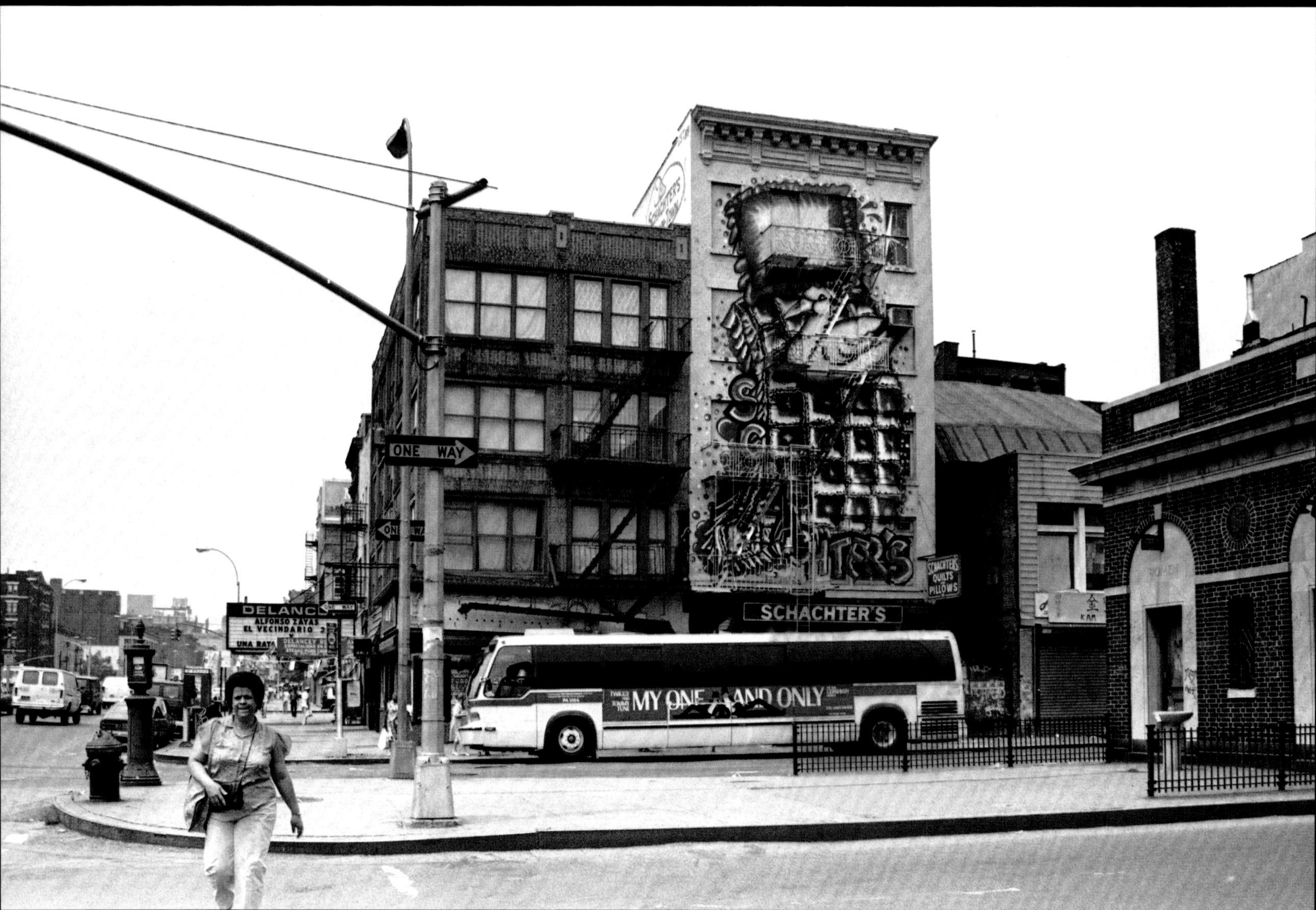

The Allen Street Mall when the bathrooms were actually open. *My One and Only* rolling down Allen, *El Vecindario II* playing at the Delancey.

Buses still rolling, bathrooms now closed,
some buildings torn down, some added to,
movie theater long gone.

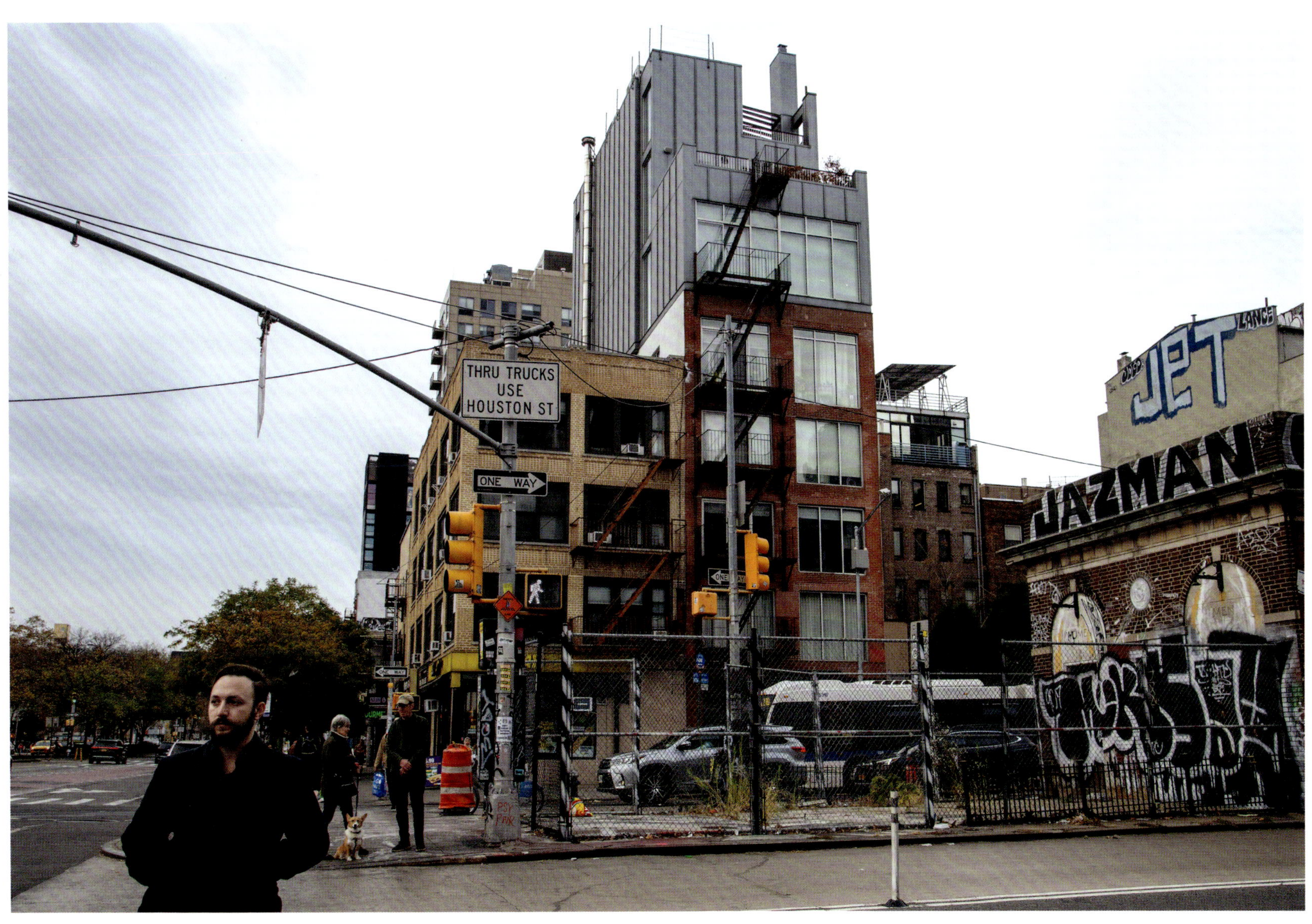

15 PIKE STREET

An abandoned synagogue off East Broadway. In the days when I would climb over fences and through broken windows to see what was inside.

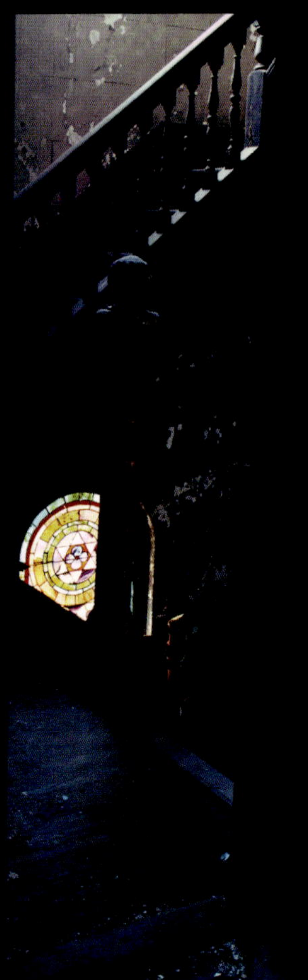

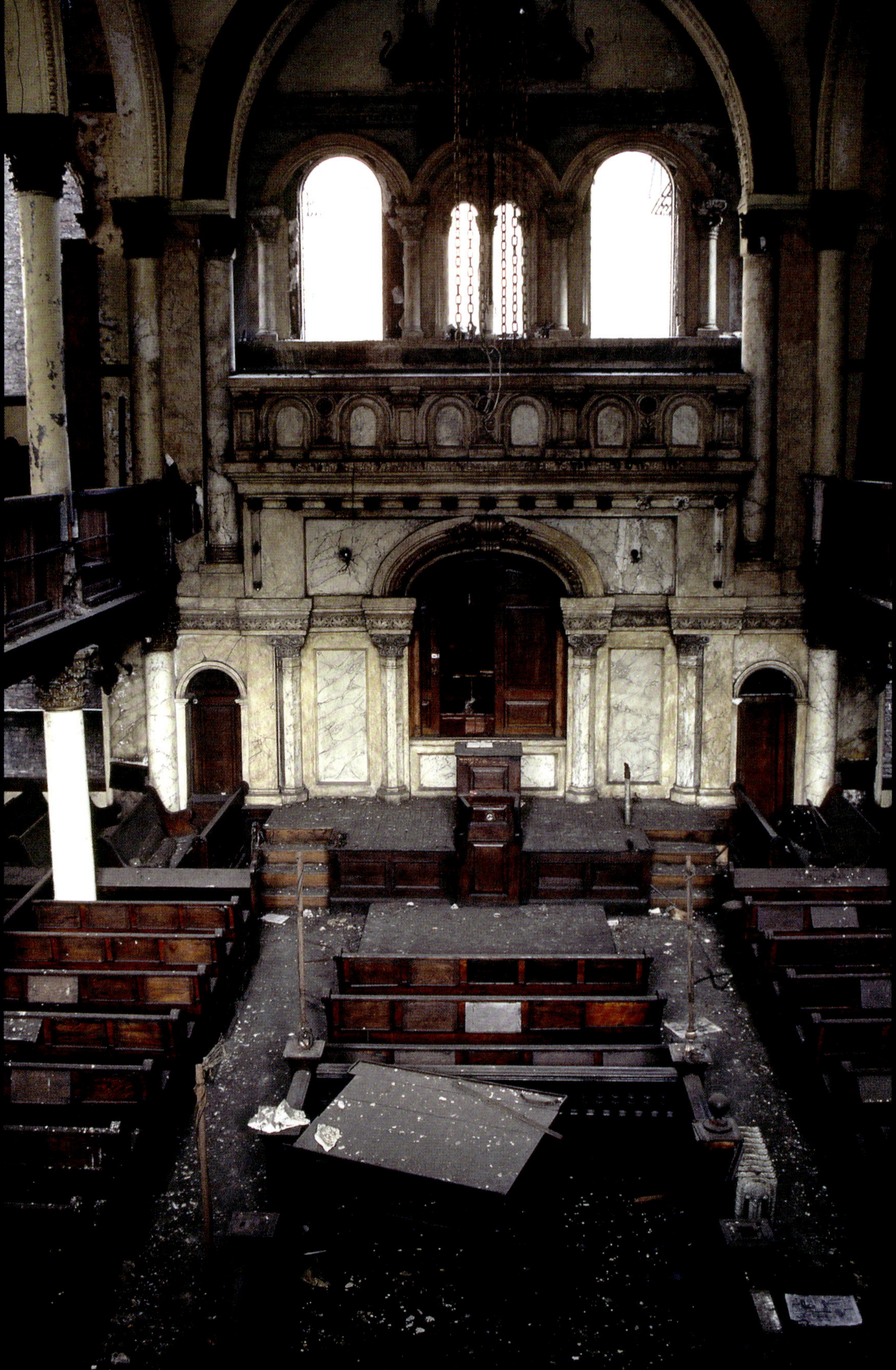

The Sung Tai Buddhist Association
and a very cleaned-up facade.

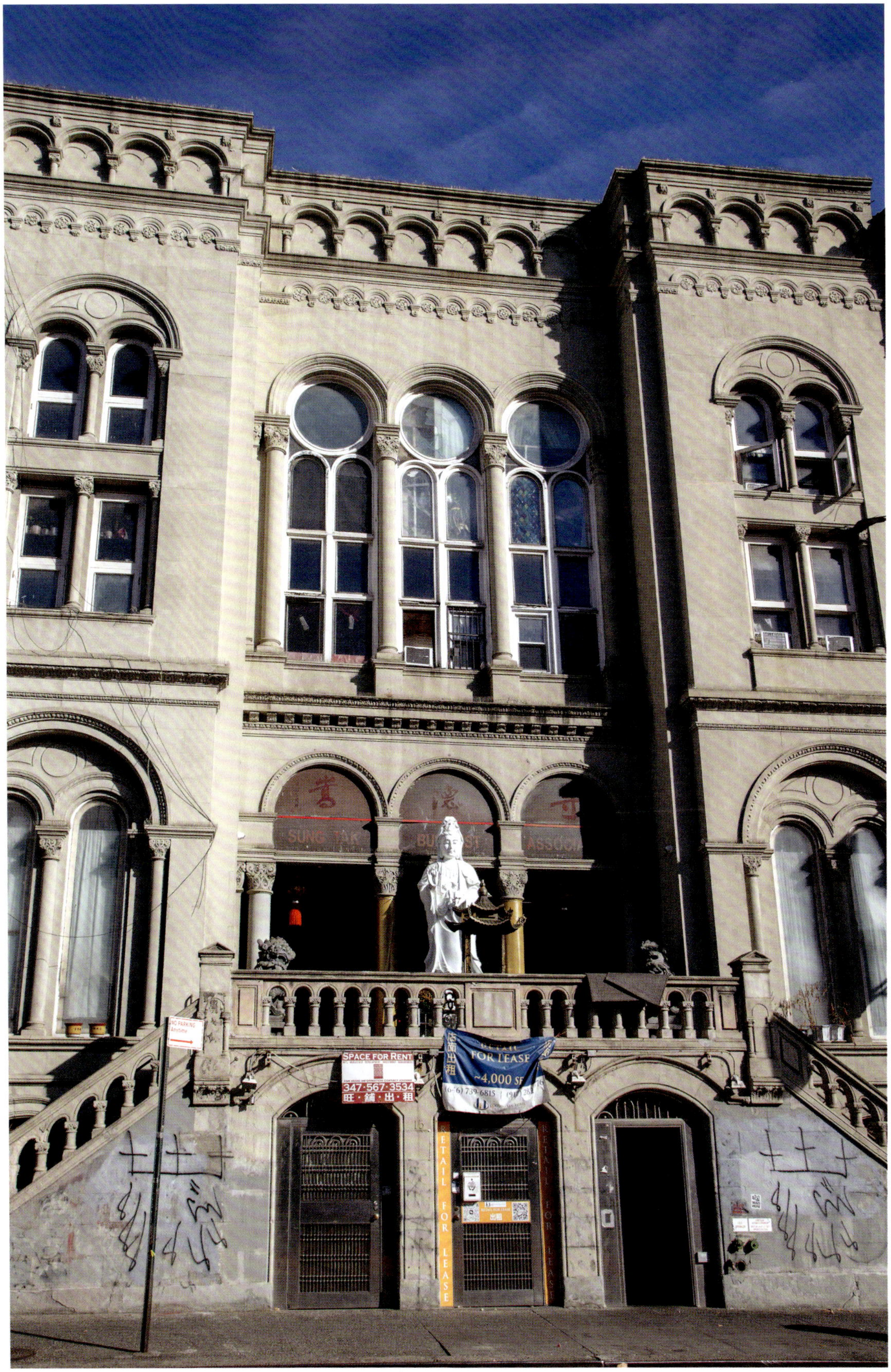

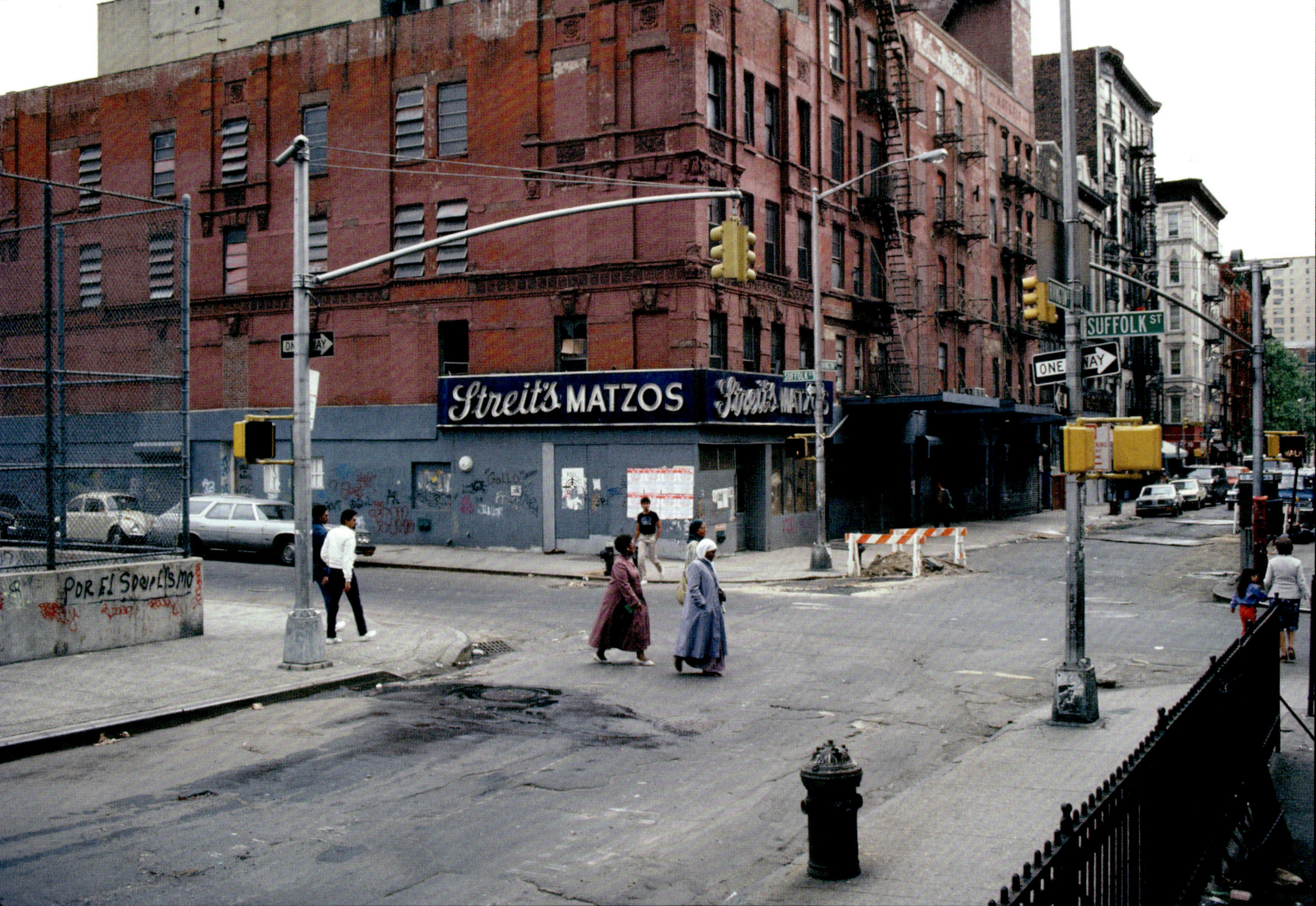

150 RIVINGTON STREET

From the steps of the Clemente Center (the old PS 160), Streit's Matzos. Streit's opened in 1916 and closed these doors in 2015, moving to Rockland County.

School for
Global Leaders
MS 378
is an
IB World School

ONE WAY
ONE WAY
Suffolk St
RETAIL
SPACE
FOR
LEASE

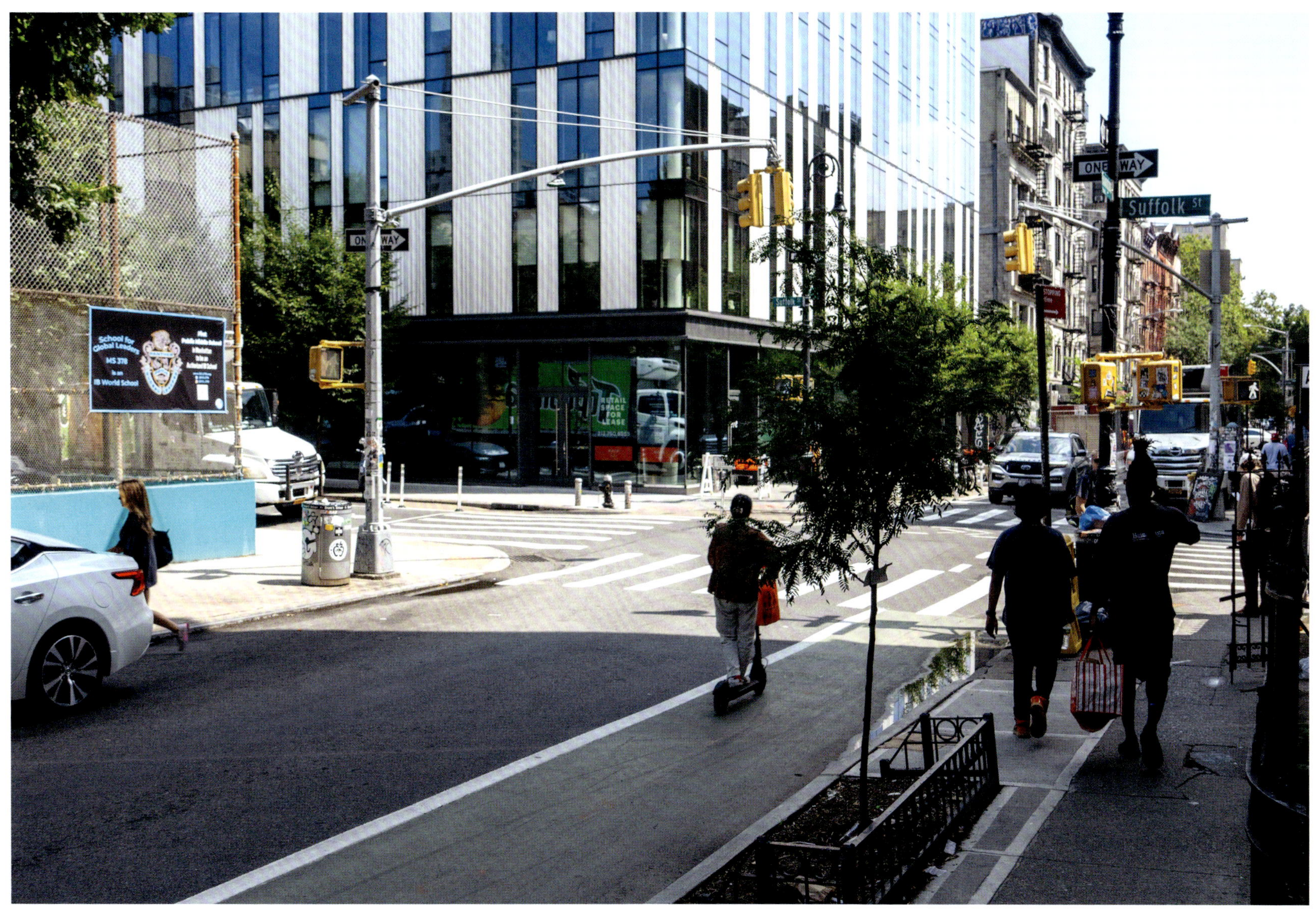

New condos.

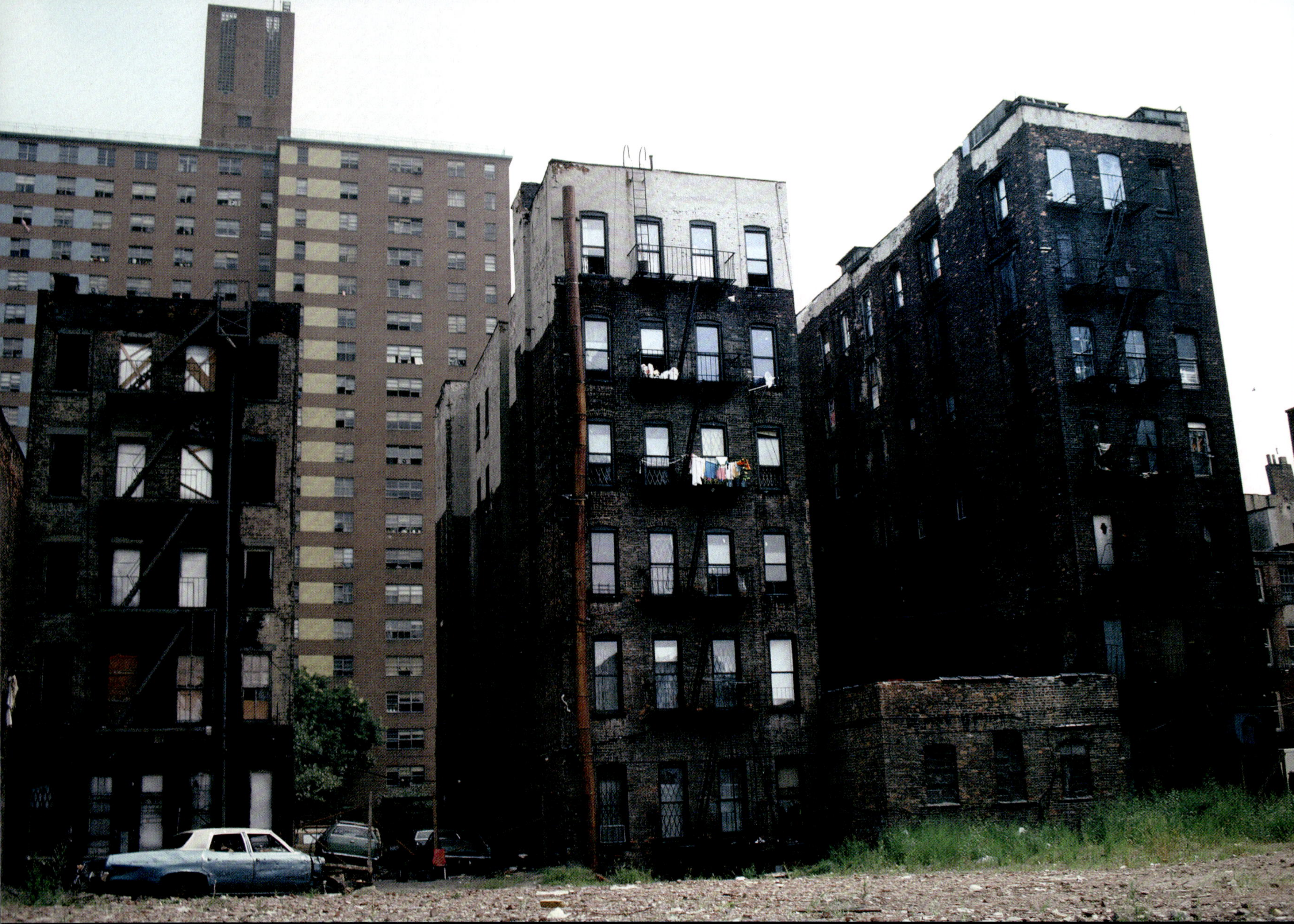

80 RIDGE STREET

Empty lots, empty buildings, empty cars, with the
NYCHA Gompers Houses in the background.

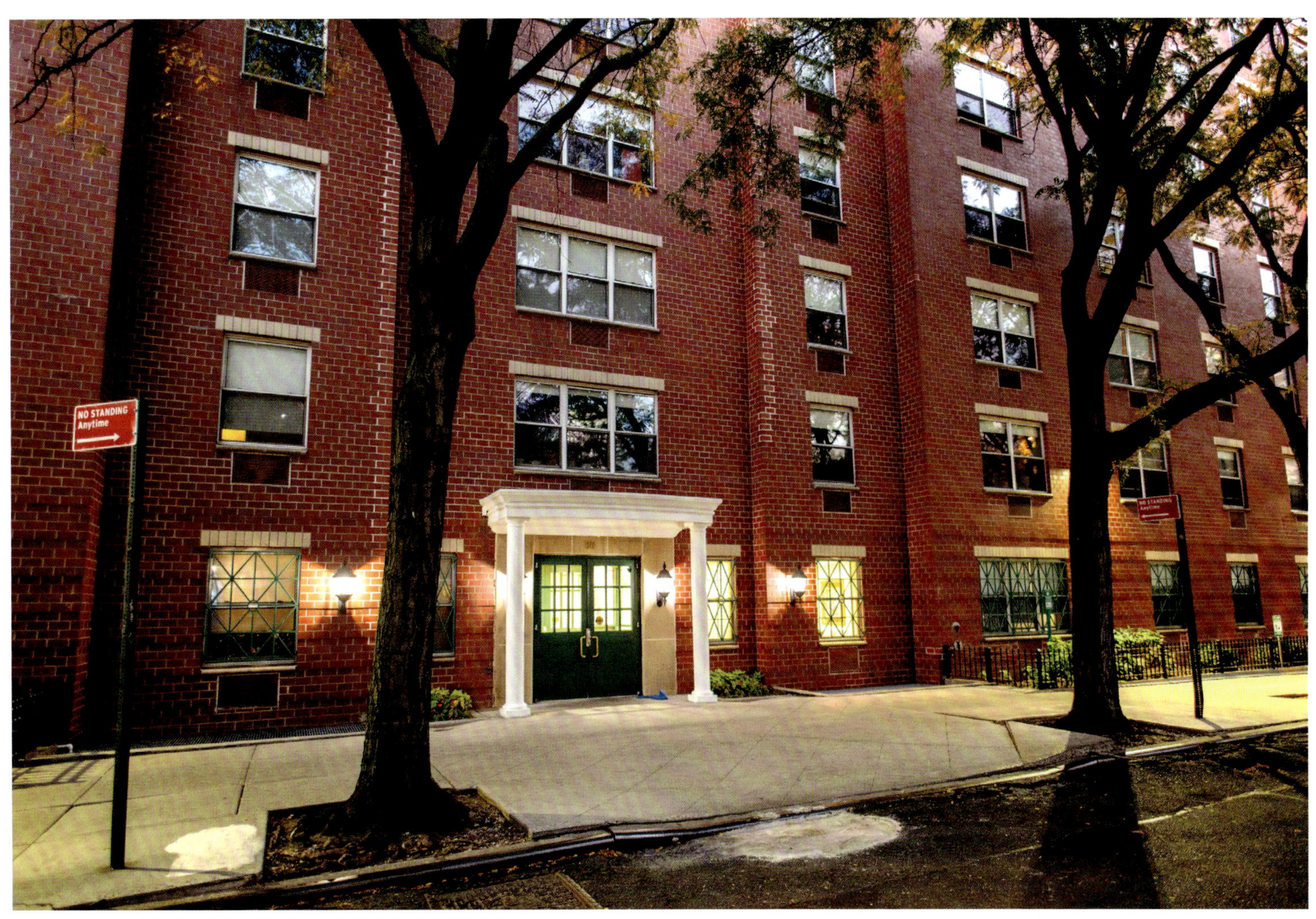

Ridge Street Gardens, the senior housing
complex that was put up on the lot.

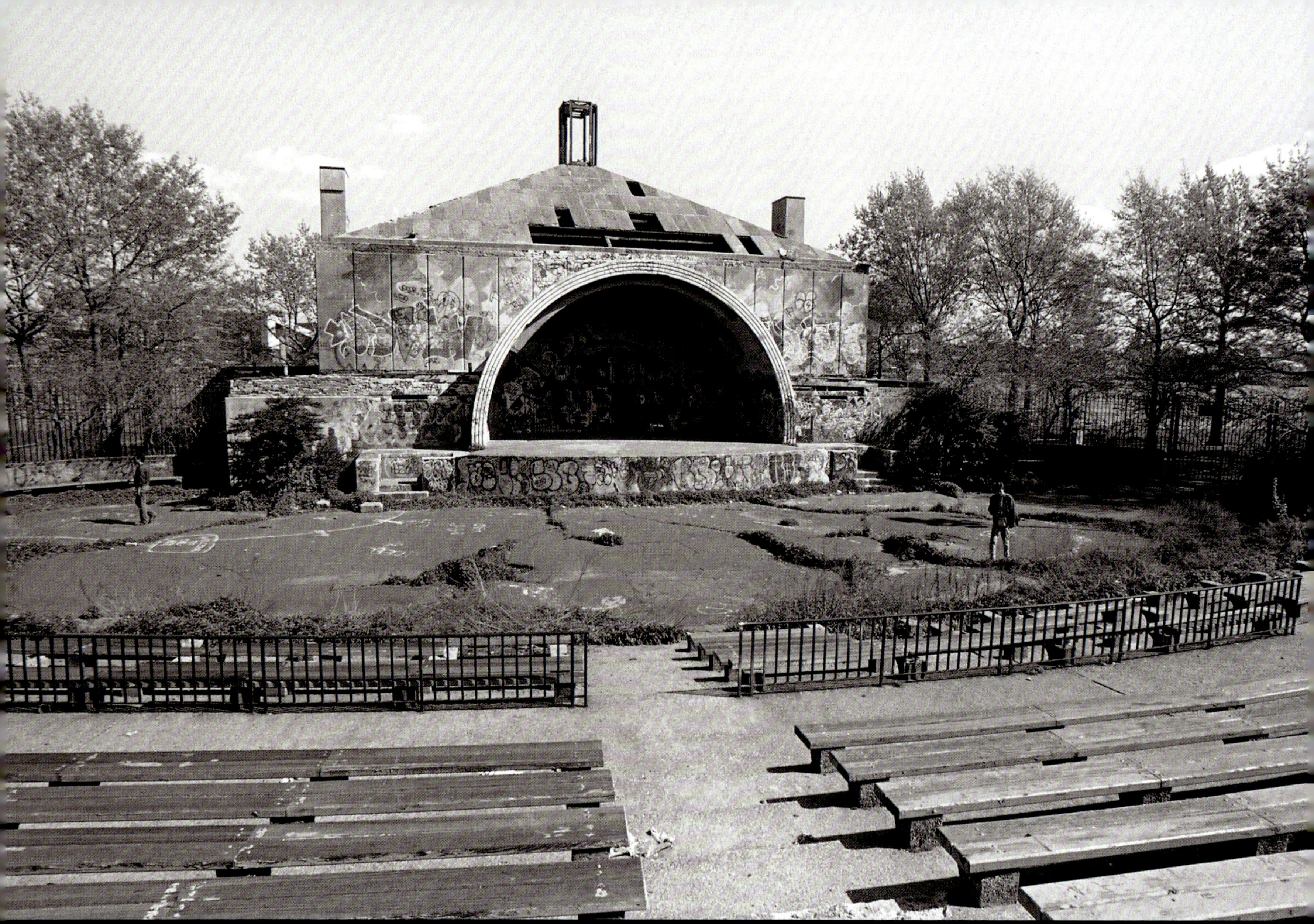

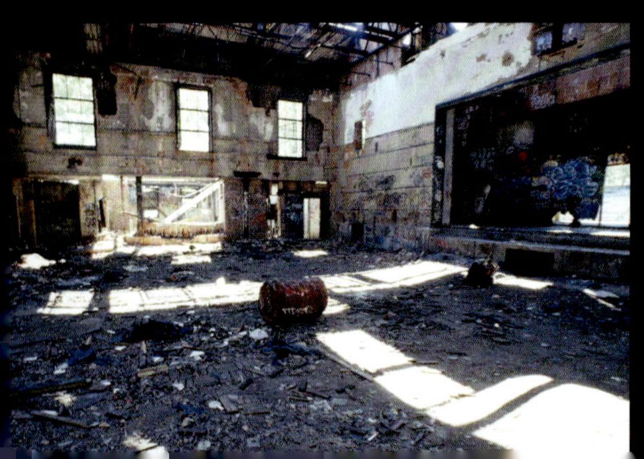
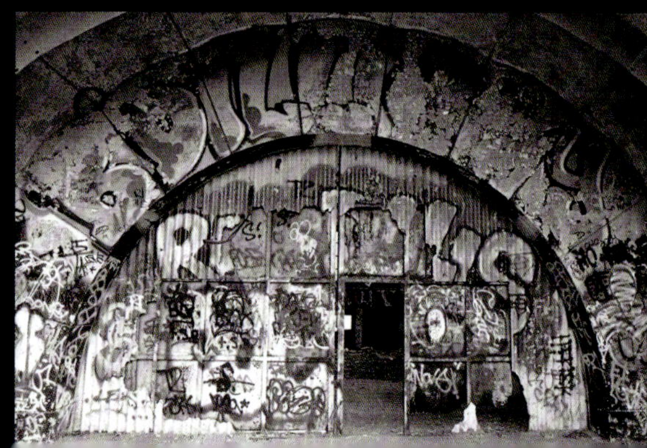
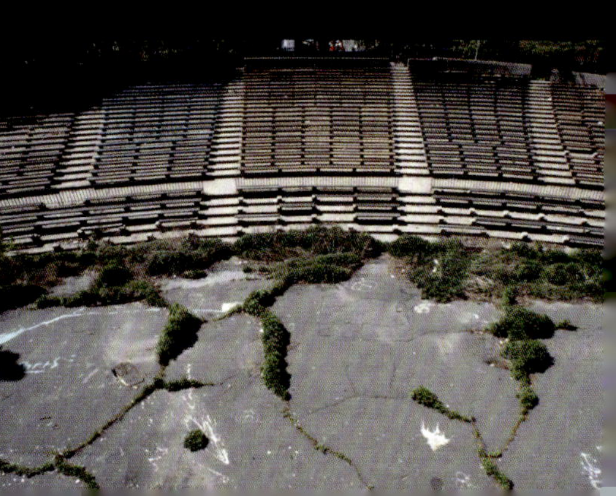

CORLEAR'S HOOK, EAST RIVER PARK

THEN East River Park Amphitheater at Corlear's Hook. The original location for Joseph Papp's Shakespeare in the Park and many other performances. When the bandshell was operational, it had a large backstage area, dressing rooms, and bathrooms. When it started to crumble and deteriorate, it was abandoned and left to the weather.

NOW Same location, post–East Side Coastal Resiliency Project.

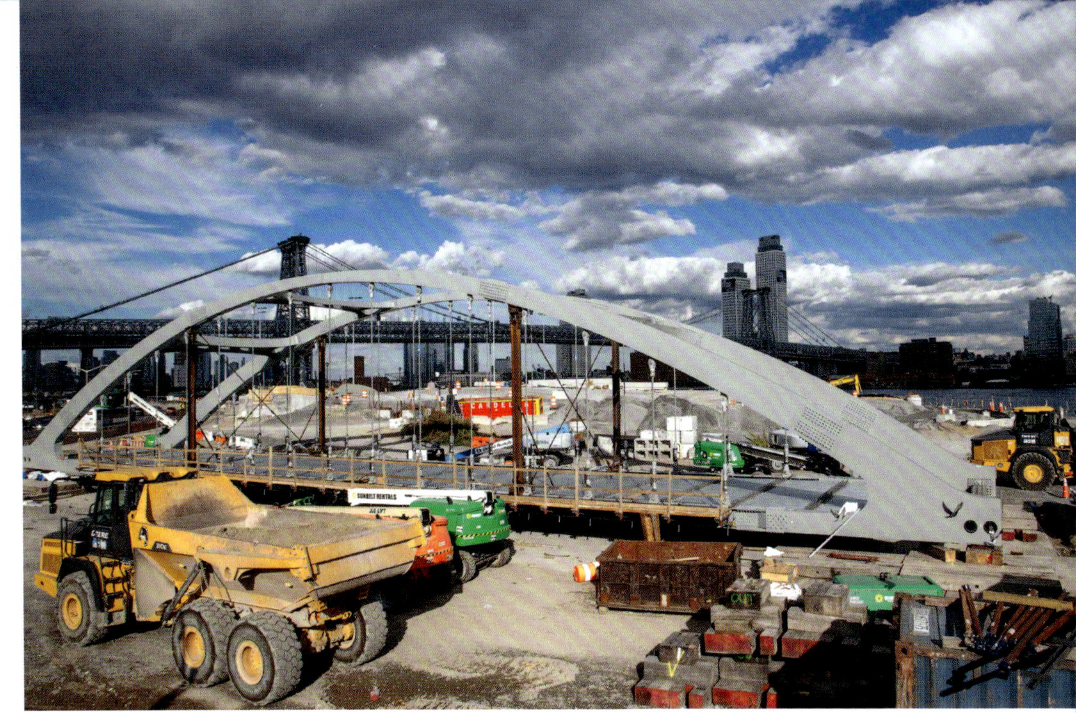

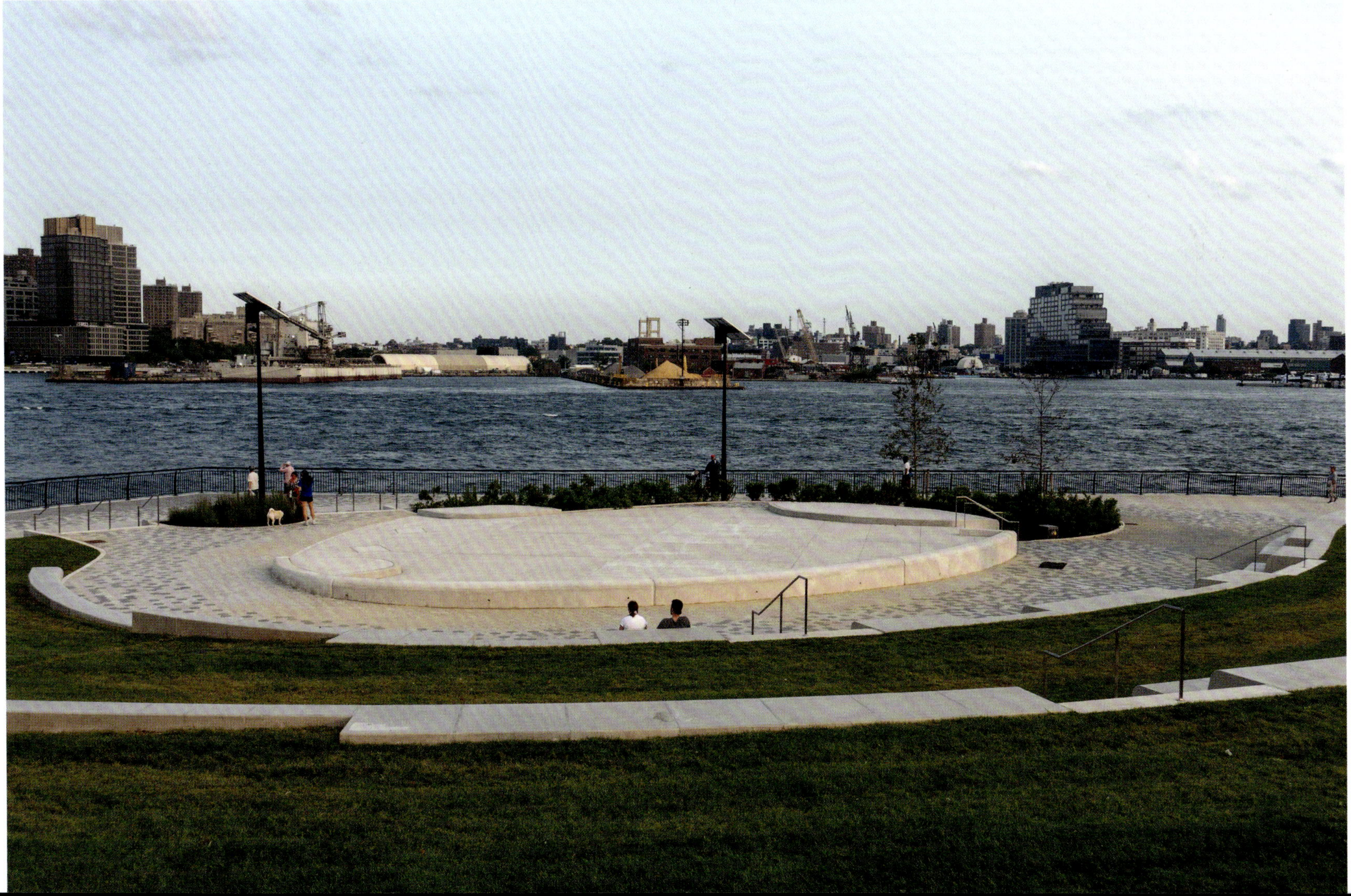

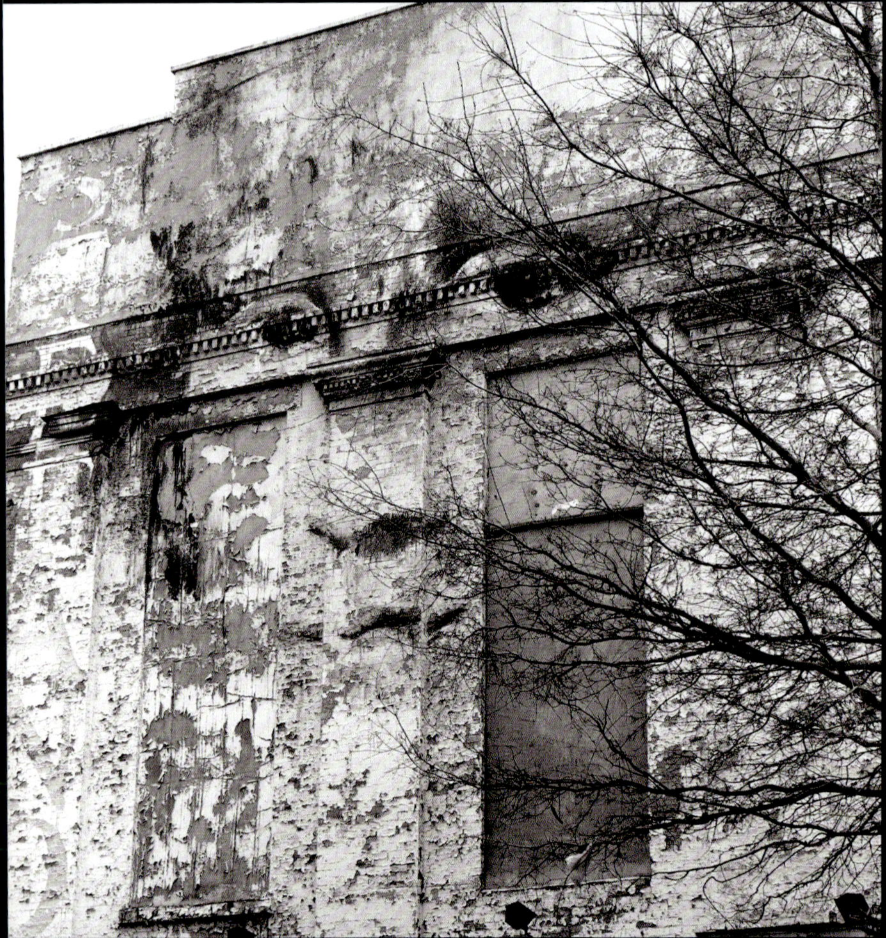

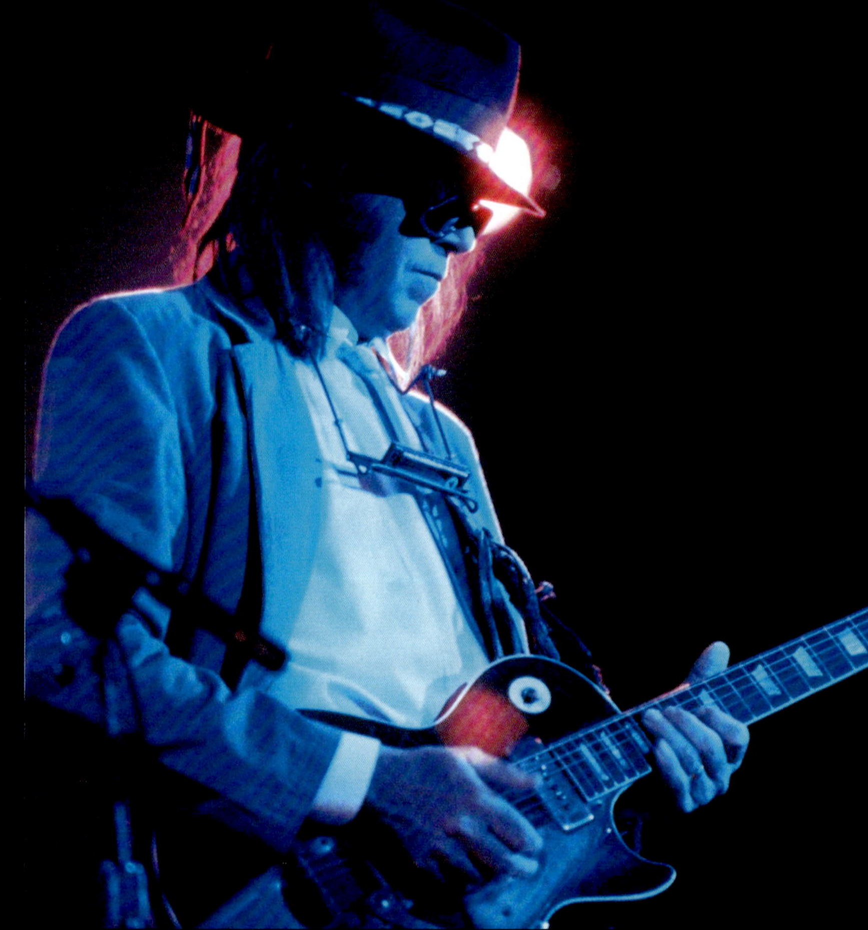

254 EAST 2ND STREET

THEN The World from the street and the painted face on the facade. A nightclub of very questionable structural integrity, a bit off Avenue C, in a very little-trafficked part of the East Village. The balcony looked like it would fall any minute as did the large chandelier, which would be swaying with the music. The World drew very diverse audiences and performers. From performers like Lady Bunny and Dean Johnson (of Dean and the Weenies) to David Bowie and Pink Floyd. Dean also produced the Rock and Roll Fag Bar party every week at the World. The World had a lot of overlap with the Pyramid Club scene. Some people hesitated to go to the World because you'd have to go through the heroin block of 2nd Street between Avenues A and B. Since I lived between Avenues C and Avenue D, I felt like I was kind of going in the back entrance. Plus the dealers on Avenue C knew I lived there, so it was a little less iffy at night. The World closed in 1991 when one of the owners was found shot to death on the balcony.

In 1988 Neil Young performed two nights at the club, which I photographed. The shot seen here became the cover photo for a Neil Young box set (Neil Young Official Release Series Discs 13,14, 20 & 21).

NOW The new apartment building on the site, with the East Side Tabernacle inside.

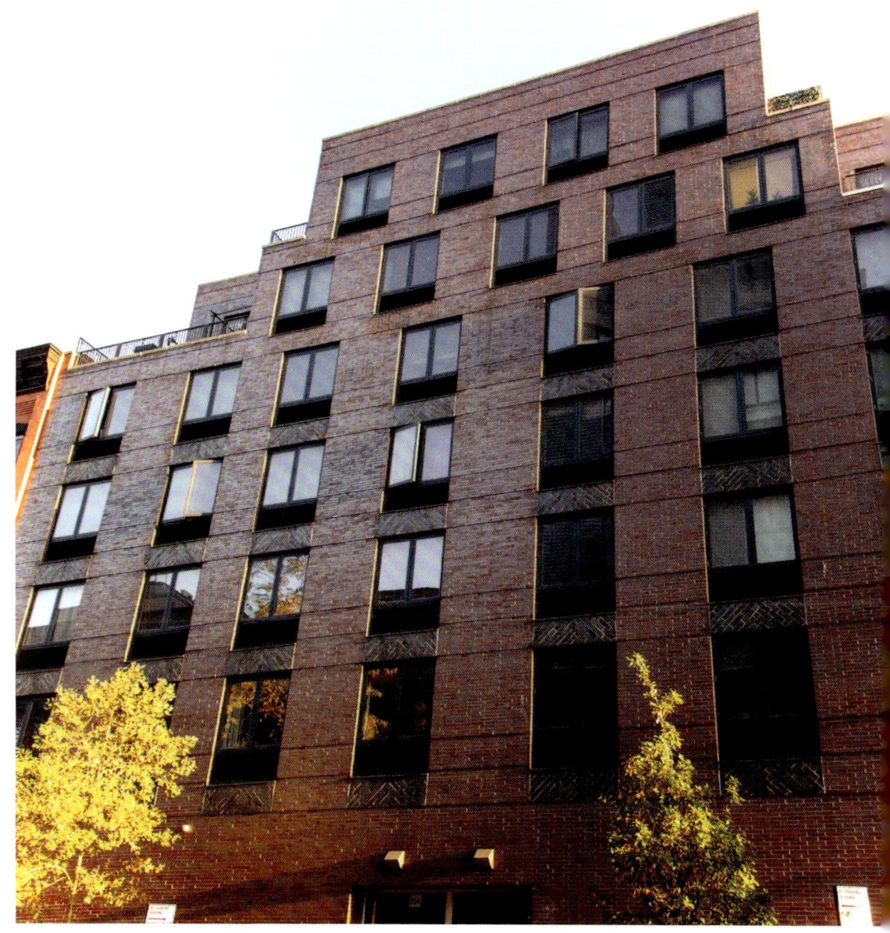

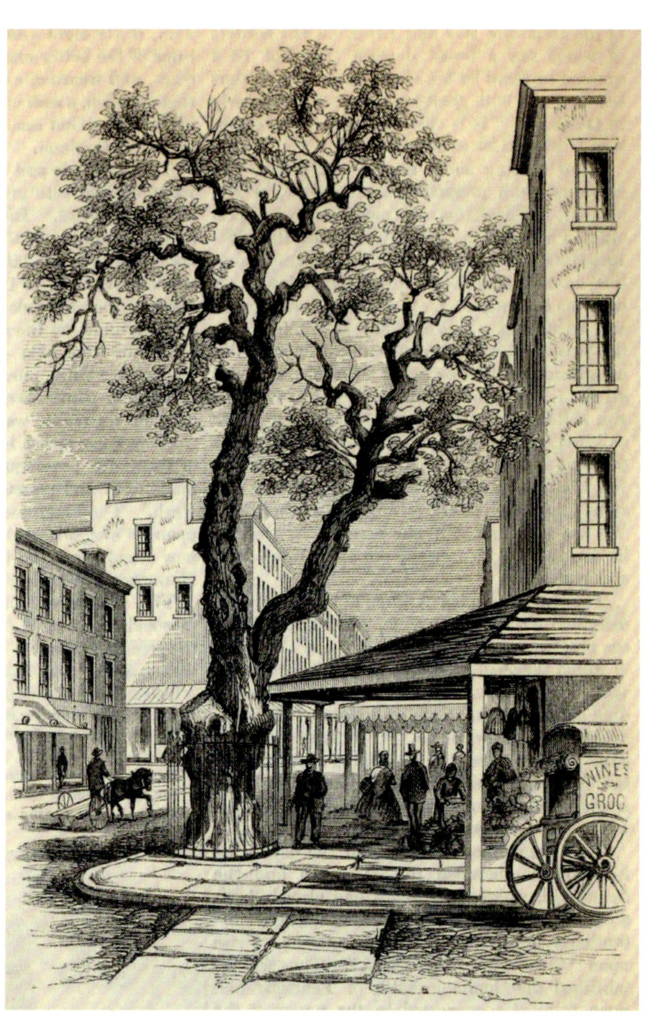

Peter Stuyvesant's pear tree, from Harper's New Monthly Magazine, *May 1862.*

FROM PETER STUYVESANT'S FARM TO CBGB

BILL MORGAN

Three hundred and sixty years ago, the former governor Peter Stuyvesant returned to New York from Holland to live out his retirement in peace on his Great Bouwerie farm of sixty-two acres. On the occasion he planted a commemorative pear tree with the knowledge that it would outlive him. The tree, in his own words, "by which my name may be remembered" survived for exactly two hundred years. It fell in 1867, a victim of a traffic accident when two horse-drawn carts collided and severely damaged the old tree. So beloved was the tree that in 1890 a plaque was erected to commemorate it at the corner of Third Avenue and East 13th Street. Today that plaque still reminds people of the tree planted by the East Village's first landowner.

For obvious reasons, no one is living today who saw the pear tree alive, although a section of it still remains on display at the New-York Historical Society. It is a reminder of things past. A reminder that at one time, this part of Manhattan was lush and beautiful farmland, bounded on the west by Broadway and on the east by the salt marshes of the East River that stretched nearly to today's Avenue A. As the city population grew, the marshes were filled in, houses and apartments were built, and industries popped up along the waterfront. Before long, some of the most important shipyards in the country were clustered between Houston and East 14th Street. In 1865, the William Webb Shipyards launched the most powerful and formidable vessel of the era, a five-thousand-ton ironclad named the *Dunderberg*, from the foot of 7th Street. In their heyday, these boatyards also produced some of America's greatest clipper ships.

Nor does anyone today personally remember that the East Village was once the center of a Bohemian cigar making district, or that Tompkins Square was used as a military parade ground before the majestic elm trees were planted in the late 1800s. Some of those trees are dying now, and the next generation will not enjoy their cool shade in the heat of summer. It is all part of a natural evolution. Change, something that not many of us can embrace fondly, is relentless. Each person who moves into the neighborhood wishes that the streets would remain frozen in amber and never change, but they always do, and new memories will come as certain as the elms will succumb to time.

By the early years of the twentieth century, the fiery revolutionary Emma Goldman was living in the neighborhood, publishing her radical magazine, *Mother Earth*. Two young boys, George and Ira Gershwin, were practicing piano in their apartment on Second Avenue, and John Sloan was painting pictures that would help immortalize McSorley's Old Ale House, the oldest Irish bar in the city.

Whole populations moved through the East Village. Wave after wave of immigrants arrived in America and found affordable housing here, helping to build a community. As time went by, they prospered and moved on to "better" neighborhoods, and their places were taken by other new arrivals. The Germans who arrived in great numbers during the middle of the nineteenth century left their mark on a number of buildings and public institutions like the Ottendorfer Branch of the public library (page 39) and the German Dispensary, a free clinic, both on Second Avenue between St. Mark's Place and East 9th Street. Their community was torn apart in 1904, when a steamboat called the *General Slocum* caught fire and sank in the East River, carrying more than a thousand schoolchildren to their deaths. Until the attacks on the World Trade Center in 2001, it was the worst disaster in the history of New York City. In their grief, many from the area's German population abandoned the neighborhood for Yorkville on the Upper East Side. Since then many other ethnic groups have made the area their home. The Irish, Poles, Ukranians, Puerto Ricans, Russians, Dominicans, Italians, and Jews have all left significant marks on Peter Stuyvesant's old farm as they struggled to become part of America.

However, the remarkable advantage that the East Village has over nearly every other place on earth is that we have been blessed with artists, authors, and photographers who have created works that help preserve the spirit of the neighborhood. Their works have helped to document the passing eras. They show us how we got here and help to point the way forward, to where we might be tomorrow. Daniel Root's masterful images are an excellent example of this. They enable us to view glimpses of the East Village from the early 1980s onward. With luck and good health, he will continue to record the passing scene through the lens of his camera for a long time to come. He has taken on the challenge posed to him of documenting the "now and then" of the neighborhood. He was so thoroughly interested in the neighborhood he moved here in the early 1980s. With that interest, he kept a beautifully detailed photographic record of the things he saw and loved. In 2024 he revisited those sites with his camera, reproducing photos taken earlier and documenting the ongoing change that seems to happen to this spot on Earth with lightning speed.

He isn't the first to do so. Berenice Abbott used her large-format camera to document the architecture in New York fifty years before Root was born, but his pictures capture a different kind of change that hadn't yet begun in the early twentieth century. Abbott focused her lens on notable buildings that were active, vibrant, and viable parts of the community. She celebrated the architecture of her day. Some of Root's earliest photographs document buildings that had experienced decades of neglect, decay, and deterioration, and then he returns to capture their subsequent rebirth. He doesn't just deal with the bricks and mortar of buildings as Abbott did, but traces the changes to the people of the neighborhood, the residents who were part of the countless waves of people who made the East Village what it is today.

I arrived in the East Village around the same time that Root did, moving to a walkup apartment on Avenue A where my wife and I lived for more than a decade. Then, with ever-increasing rents, we were forced to move farther east, to 7th Street between Avenues C and D, where we remained for another twenty years. During those decades, I worked for the poet Allen Ginsberg, one of the neighborhood's widely noted creative residents. As his archivist and editor, I watched with him as the neighborhood changed with the "velocity of money," as he once put it. Allen also wrote a poem by that name—"Velocity of Money"—around the same time the original photographs in this book were taken. The poem is included in this volume (page 13). Often we lamented those economic changes that forced the poor and creative residents out to other parts of the city. But Allen was better than I and could also see the positive aspects of change. He saw the younger residents as more accepting of their neighbors and less inclined to be insular. He realized that what distinguished our neighborhood was its almost unquestioning acceptance of integration, not only of race, but also ethnicity and economic position. The people here seem to embrace change, whereas I could only detest it. I continually looked to the past, longing for the days when a pear tree grew on Third Avenue, but Allen always looked to the future. He was one of the first to join the fight for squatters' rights, neighborhood gardens, and drug rehabilitation centers. He was a champion of younger artists and poets, and always had time to stop on the corner and chat with them. I could only see them as transient harbingers of higher and higher rents.

By coincidence, one of the pictures taken by Daniel Root reminded me of walking through the neighborhood with Ginsberg and his companion Peter Orlovsky. We had stopped in front of a burned-out behemoth of a building on the northeast corner of Avenue B and 10th Street. Peter, who had been looking for his drug connection, paused long enough to examine the vacant building and made the proposal that we should take it over and restore it to the point where we could all live in it, rent-free. Peter was famous as a determined, single-minded, worker when it came to manual labor, but I could see that such an undertaking was much more than we could handle alone. Root captured the derelict building just around the time that Peter, Allen, and I were toying with the idea of homesteading the very same place. Side by side with it is a photo of the building today, restored and occupied by dozens of apartments, a testament to someone else's abilities and vision of urban renovation.

Art documents these changes in a way that nothing else can, and causes people to react to it. All things seem possible in art, especially when creativity is combined with an ideal of social justice. Jacob Riis took photographs of the poverty-stricken immigrants who came to this country looking for opportunity in the last half of the nineteenth century. Many of them found poverty, squalor, and misery instead, but his pictures helped to change the way Americans looked at their "huddled masses yearning to breathe free." Later a Yiddish Rialto sprang up along Second Avenue, which gave hope and entertainment to the huge influx of Jewish refugees escaping the pogroms and wars of Eastern Europe. During mid-century, the Abstract Expressionists found cheap studio space and living quarters in the East Village, and their first galleries exhibited their revolutionary paintings on East 10th Street. Thousands of poets, artists, and musicians have called the area home. They frequented the shops, restaurants, and clubs established by earlier groups. One of Jack Kerouac's favorite bars was on Avenue B at East 7th, Vazac's aka 7B Horseshoe Bar, founded before World War II by a Polish immigrant. Ginsberg spent more than his share of time in the old Ukranian coffee shops near his apartments in the East Village, and William Burroughs found affordable lodgings in an old YMCA on the Bowery (page 196). One day each week Andy Warhol took over the Polish club called the Dom on St. Mark's Place and turned it into the Electric Circus with his Exploding Plastic Inevitable, a nightclub that featured his floating silver balloons. The Velvet Underground and Nico were his house band, and that scene morphed into punk rock. The new music exploded first in the East Village with poet-singers like Patti Smith, Lou Reed, and Laurie Anderson. All that musical energy spilled over into the Bowery with CBGB (page 190), the quintessential punk club, along with other venues.

The value of photography, art, and literature in recording these passing eras is inestimable. The arts have shown us how the East Village came to be what it is today. And the arts can help point the way to where we will be tomorrow. Root's masterful photos give us a slice of the East Village during the 1980s and let us compare these images side by side with photos taken forty years later. For those of us who lament the passage of time, Root reminds us of what once existed. Even though we rebel against the changes that have been wrought, we can now realize that every generation has had its time upon the stage of the East Village. Freedom from repression and social restrictions still thrives here, and we can be encouraged that wonderful things are yet to come for our community.

RIGHT Pottery on the street at the
St. George Ukrainian Festival,
East 6th Street

BELOW Freaky Frige selling his
neighborhood-themed designs,
East 3rd Street and Avenue B

OPPOSITE TOP Elliott Sharp performing
at the LUNGS Harvest Arts Festival,
Green Oasis Community Garden,
370 East 8th Street

OPPOSITE BOTTOM Breakdancing
at the Ukrainian Festival

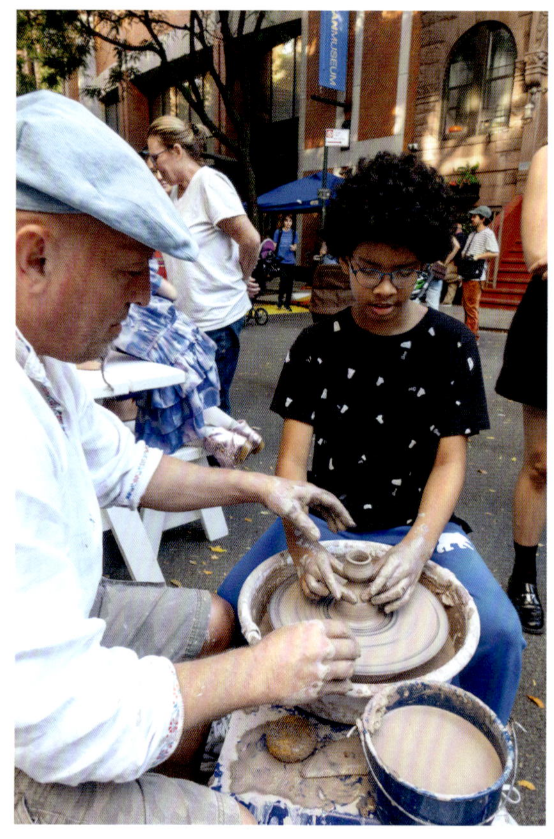

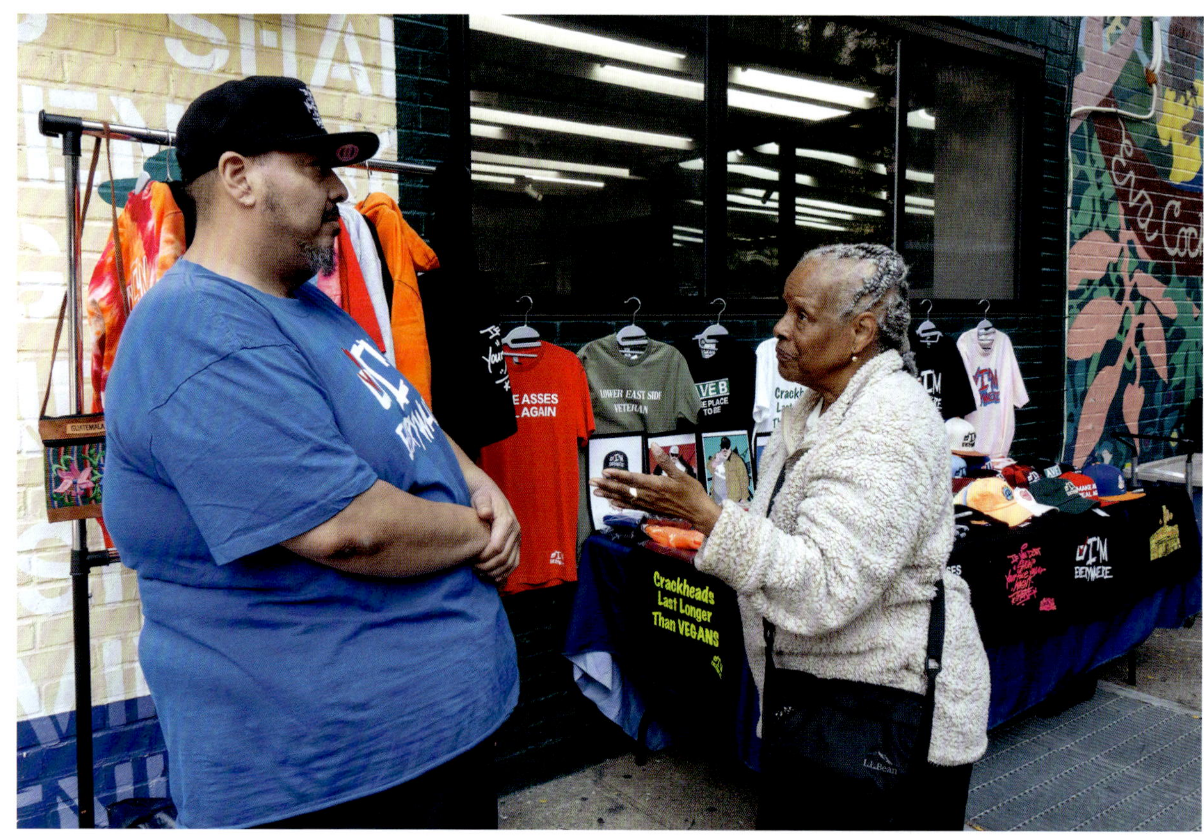

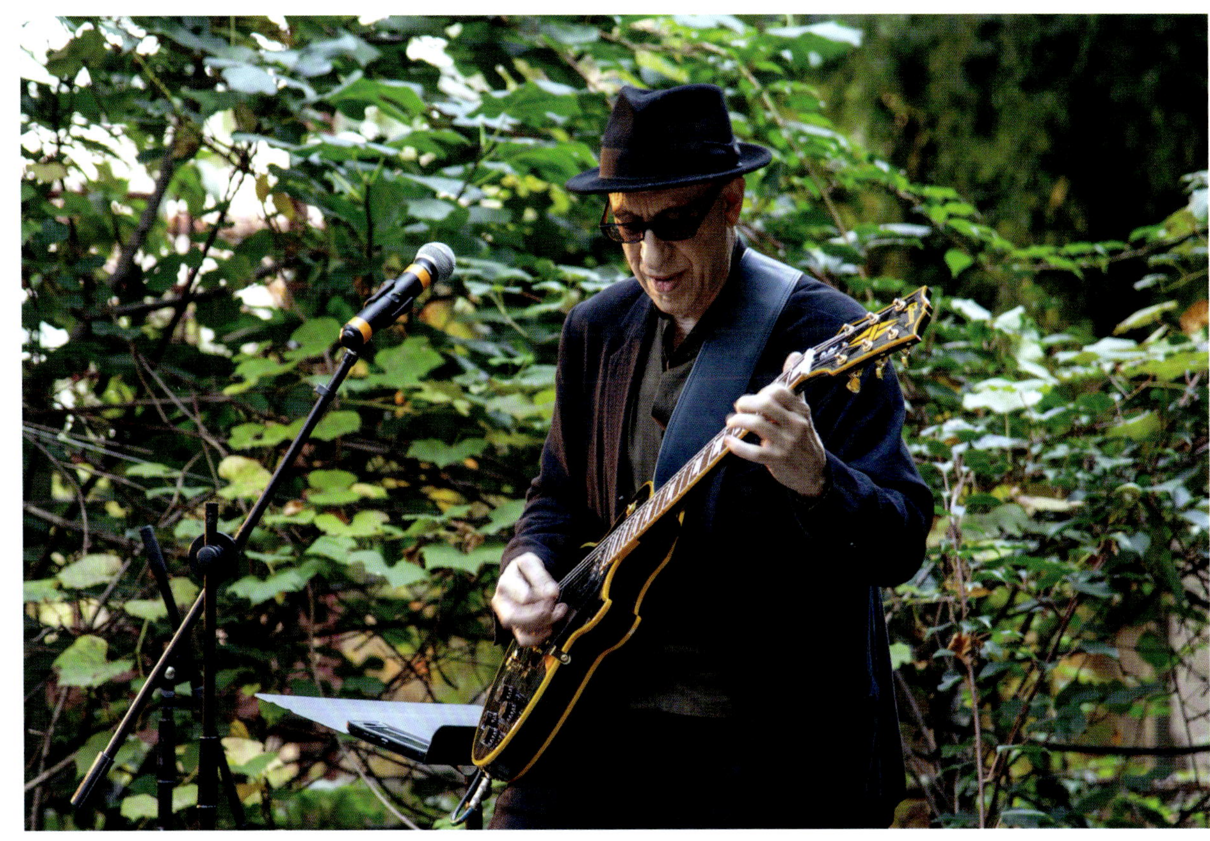

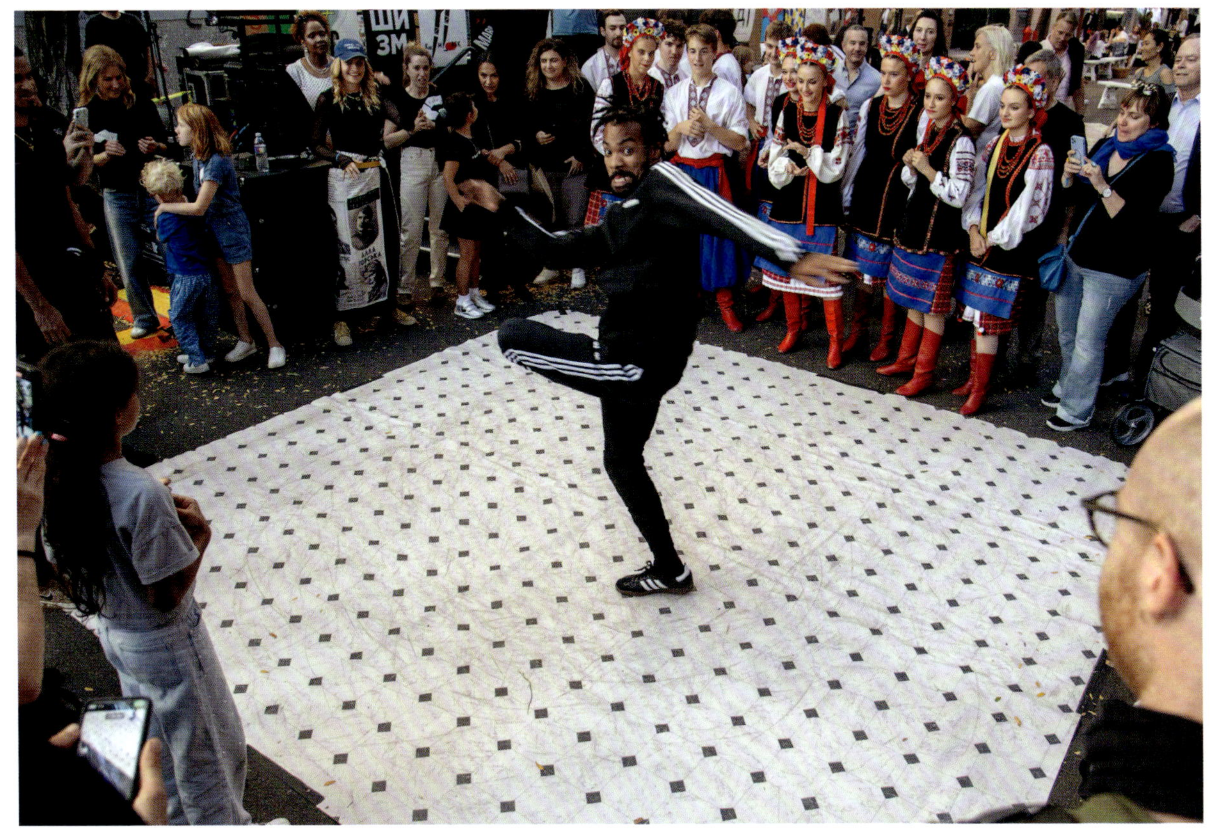

INDEX OF ADDRESSES

Allen Street
and Delancey Street, 210–11

Avenue A, 235
72 Avenue A, 62–63
101 Avenue A, 64–65
109 Avenue A, 68–71
113 Avenue A, 72–73
115 Avenue A, 74–75
141 Avenue A, 80–81
174 Avenue A, 84–85
and East 3rd Street, 44–45
looking south between 7th and
6th Street, 66–67

Avenue B
34 Avenue B, 188–89
143 Avenue B, 160–63
157 Avenue B, 148–49
162 Avenue B, 116–17
165 Avenue B, 144–45
167 Avenue B, 140–41
171 Avenue B, 142–43
175 Avenue B, 120–21
and East 3rd Street, 228
and East 10th Street, 146–47
and East 11th Street, 136–39

Avenue C
108 Avenue C, 172–73
117 Avenue C, 170–71
and East 9th Street, 156–59
burned-out buildings on, 180

Bowery
220 and 222 Bowery, 196–97
315 Bowery, 190–93
and Houston Street, 194–95

Corlear's Hook, 218–19

Delancey Street
and Allen Street, 210–11

East 2nd Street
254 East 2nd Street, 220–21

East 3rd Street
7 East 3rd Street, 72–73
45 East 3rd Street, 74–75
and Avenue A, 44–45
and Avenue B, 228

East 4th Street
234 East 4th Street, 186–87
260 East 4th Street, 184–85

East 5th Street
710 East 5th Street, 182–83
724 East 5th Street, 180–81
photo taken from, 178–79

East 6th Street, 228–29
636 and 638 East 6th Street,
178–79
between First and Second
Avenue, 50–51

East 7th Street
81 East 7th Street, 60–61
184 East 7th Street, 176–77
205 East 7th Street, 174–75

East 8th Street
299 and 301 East 8th Street,
164–65
307 East 8th Street, 166–67
328 East 8th Street, 168–69
370 East 8th Street, 229

East 9th Street
406 East 9th Street, 54–55
440 East 9th Street, 82–83
and Avenue C, 156–59

East 10th Street
254 East 10th Street, 52–53
339 East 10th Street, 108–9
343 East 10th Street, 112–15
367 East 10th Street, 150–53
371 East 10th Street, 154–55
and Avenue B, 146–47

East 11th Street, 1–3
526 East 11th Street, 118–19
633 East 11th Street, from the
roof of, 122–23, 128–31
635 East 11th Street, from the
roof of, 132–33
635 East 11th Street, over the
roof of, 130–31
641 East 11th Street, 124–25
640 East 11th Street, 134–35
and Avenue B, 136–39

East 12th Street, 236–37
15 East 12th Street, 20–21
610 East 12th Street, 122–23
644 East 12th Street, 126–27

East River Park, 218–19

Eldridge Street, 200–3

First Avenue
124 First Avenue, 58–59
132 First Avenue, 48–49
165 and 167 First Avenue,
46–47

Forsyth Street, 200–3
170 Forsyth Street, 198–99

Houston Street
and Bowery, 194–95

Loisaida Avenue
175 Loisaida Ave, 132

Orchard Street
164 Orchard Street, 204–5
180 Orchard Street 206–7

Pike Street
15 Pike Street, 212–13

Ridge Street
80 Ridge Street, 216–17

Rivington Street
150 Rivington Street, 214–15

Second Avenue
126 Second Avenue, 36–37
127 Second Avenue, 34–35
133 Second Avenue, 38–39
136 Second Avenue, 40–41
144 Second Avenue, 42–43
156 Second Avenue, 44–45

St. Mark's Place
2 St. Mark's Place, 16–19, 22–23
3 St. Mark's Place, 14–15
4 St. Mark's Place, 16–17, 20–21
22 St. Mark's Place, 26–27
25 St. Mark's Place, 29
27 St. Mark's Place, 24–25
31 St. Mark's Place, 28
33 St. Mark's Place, 32–33
34 St. Mark's Place, 30–31
97 St. Mark's Place, 56–57
134 St. Mark's Place, 78–79

Stanton Street, 200–3
108 Stanton Street, 208–9

Tompkins Square Park, 86–107

INDEX OF NAMES

2nd Ave Deli, 44
7A, restaurant, 68, 70

Abraço, 61
Alamo Drafthouse Cinema, 64
Allen Street Mall, 211
Alliance Apartments for the
    Elderly, 85
Ama Raw Bar, 139
Arias, Joey, 198
Artforum, 52

BaBaDan Banda de Rua, 107
Barrows, Alan, 118
Basquiat, Jean-Michel, 52
Benglis, Lynda, 196
Best Cleaners on A, 65
Better Health (B & H) Restaurant,
    34–35
Bklyn Macs, 83
Blind Barber, 109
Blue and Gold, 60
Bowie, David, 220
Brasserie Saint Marc (SAINT), 41
Bromley's Hotel, 78
Bunker, 196
Bunny, Lady, 64, 220
Burroughs, William, 196

Cafe Kabul / Khyber Pass (Afghan
    restaurant), 30–31

Campos Community Garden, 127
Carmen Pabón Garden, 170
Casa Victoria Housing for the
    Elderly, 169
Caught Stealing, film shoot, 193
CBGB, 190
Charlie Parker Jazz Festival, 104
Church of God of 6th Street, 179
Christodora House, 128, 160–63
Civilian Warfare Gallery, 118
Clemente Center, 214
Club 101, 65
Commodities, 47
Con Edison, 66, 130
Corlear's Hook, 218–19
Crowbar, 108
Curry Row (Little India; Curry
    Lane), 50

Desperately Seeking Susan, 18, 20
Doc Holliday's, 81
Dom, 26
Dream Baby, 117

East River Park Amphitheater,
    218
East Side Coastal Resiliency
    Project, 219
East Side Tabernacle, 221
East Village Organic, 59
East Village Social (EVS), 77

Empellón Al Pastor, 79
Electric Circus, 26
Elixir Lounge, 141
Estroff Pharmacy, 40

Freaky Frige, 228
Fun Gallery, 52

Garden of Eden, 200–202
Ginsberg, Allen,
    "The Velocity of Money,"
    poem, 13
Giorno, John, 196
Gnoccheria East Village, 187
Golding, Jerome, 52
Good Old Lower East Side
    (GOLES), 143
Graffiti Baptist Church, 175–76
Grateful Dead, 104
Gringo, 14
Green Oasis Community Garden,
    229

Haring, Keith, 52, 196
Harper's New Monthly Magazine,
    222
Harvest Arts Festival, LUNGS, 229
Hekate Café, 141

Indochina Sino-American
    Community Center, 199

El Jardín del Paraíso, 183
John Varvatos, 191
Johnson, Dean, 220
Joseph Papp's Shakespeare in the
    Park, 218

Kerouac, Jack, 84
    The Subterraneans, 84
Khyber Pass / Cafe Kabul (Afghan
    restaurant), 30–31
Kiev, 38
Kim's Produce (later Kim's Dry
    Cleaners, then Kim's Video), 64
Kinley, Kathryn, 156
Kurowycky Meat Products, 58
Kurowycky, Jerry (Jaroslaw), 58

Lakeside Lounge, 116
Lankton, Greer, 118
Led Zeppelin
    Physical Graffiti cover, 48–49
Lee, Alene, 84
Life Café, 110, 112
Life magazine, 110, 112
Little India, 50
Lower East Side Coalition
    Housing Development, 148
Lower East Side Ecology Center
    Garden, 169

M-13 Gallery, 82
Machado, Agosto, 31
Mack, Stan, map of Tomkins
    Square Park, 106
Madonna, 18, 20, 64, 156
Maiden Lane, 111
Mama's Bar, 189
Manic Panic, 32
Mast Books, 63
Matsuyama, Tomokazu, mural by,
    195
Miss Lily's 7A, 69, 71
Mona Lisa, smoking, 52
Mondo Kim's, 64
Mondo New York, 198
Morrissey, Paul, 26
Museum of Modern Art, 31
My One and Only, 210

New York Public Library, 39
NewComers Motorcycle Club, 138
Night Flight, 156
Nirvana, 64
No Se No Club, 198
Nolita Express Hostel, 197
NYCHA Gompers Houses, 216

Odessa Restaurant, 74
Orpheum Theatre, 36
Ottendorfer Library, 39

P&T Knitwear (bookstore), 207
Pabón, Carmen, 170
Paradise Alley, remains of, 84
Paradise Deli, 121
Patchin Place, 84
Penny's General Store (Natural
    Healing Products), 76
Perbacco, 186
Pharmacy, restaurant, 80
Physical Graffiti, 48–49
Pink Floyd, 220
Pioneer, grocery store, 66
Piragua Art Space, 151
Prince Hotel, flophouse, 196
Purple, Adam, 200
Pyramid Club, 64, 220

Radio 1990, 156
Ray's Candy Store, 72–73
Red Hot Chili Peppers, 64
Ridge Street Gardens, 217
Rivington School artists'
    collective, 198
Rivington Sculpture Garden, 198
Roberto Clemente School, PS 15,
    181
Rock and Roll Fag Bar, 220
Rolling Stones, 48–49
    "Waiting on a Friend," music
        video, 48–49

Rothko, Mark, studio of, 196
RuPaul, 64

Samuel Cox, statue, 86–87
Savard, Dean, 118
Scharf, Kenny, 52
Search & Destroy, 29

Sharp, Elliot, 229
Sixth Street Community Center, 179
Smith, Matt, 193
St. Dymphna's bar, 75
St. George Ukranian Festival, 228–29
St. Mark's Bar and Grill, 48
St. Mark's Cinema, 38
St. Mark's Hotel, 21
Stomp, 36
Streit's Matzos, 214
Stromboli Pizza, 48
Stuyvesant, Peter, 222
The Subterraneans, 84

Sung Tai Buddhist Association, 213
Syp's Produce, 64

Tompkins Square Halloween Dog Parade, 89
Tompkins Square Park, 86–107
    bandshell, 96, 98, 104
    map of, 106
Trash and Vaudeville, 16, 20, 22

Ukrainian Restaurant and Caterers (Ukrainian East Village Restaurant), 42
USA Network, 156

Valencia Hotel, 16, 20
El Vecindario II, 211
"The Velocity of Money," poem, 13
Velvet Underground, 26
Verhovyna, 60
Verizon, 39

Veselka, 42
Village East Towers, 134–35
Virginia's restaurant, 189

"Waiting on a Friend," music video, 48–49
Warhol, Andy, 26
Whitman's, 55
Wojnarowicz, David, 118
World nightclub, 220
World Trade Center (WTC)
    One World Trade Center (One WTC), skyline, 129
    skyline, 128

Xing Futang, 39

Yaffa Café, mural, 56
Yiddish Theatre District, 36, 44
Yiddish Walk of Fame, 44–45
YMCA, 196–97
Young, Neil, 220

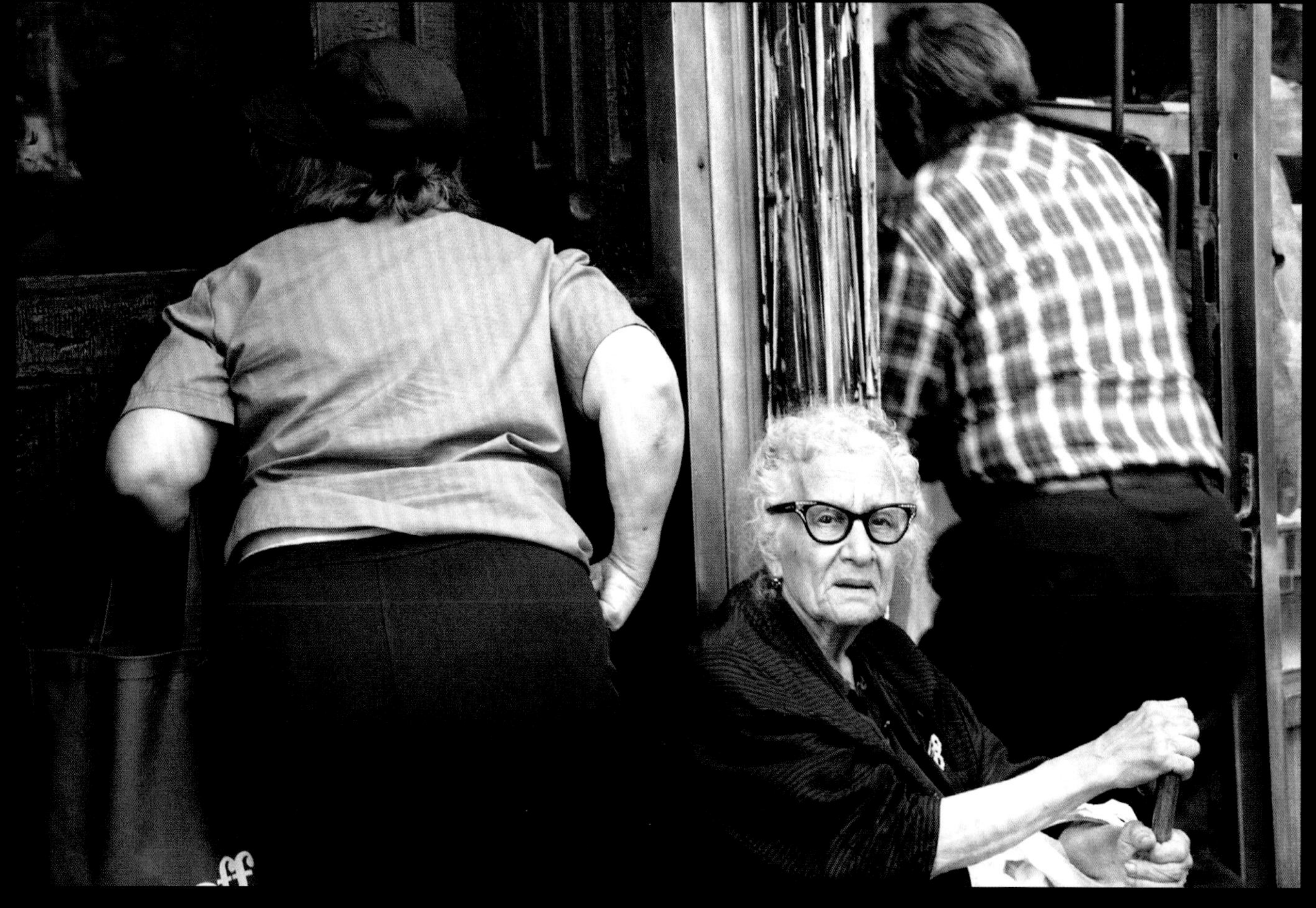

Getting some fresh air with the neighbors on Avenue A (I think).
Some agreeable, some a little less so. Like the one on the left,
putting her butt toward the camera, while keeping an eye on the
reflection to make sure I was "getting it."

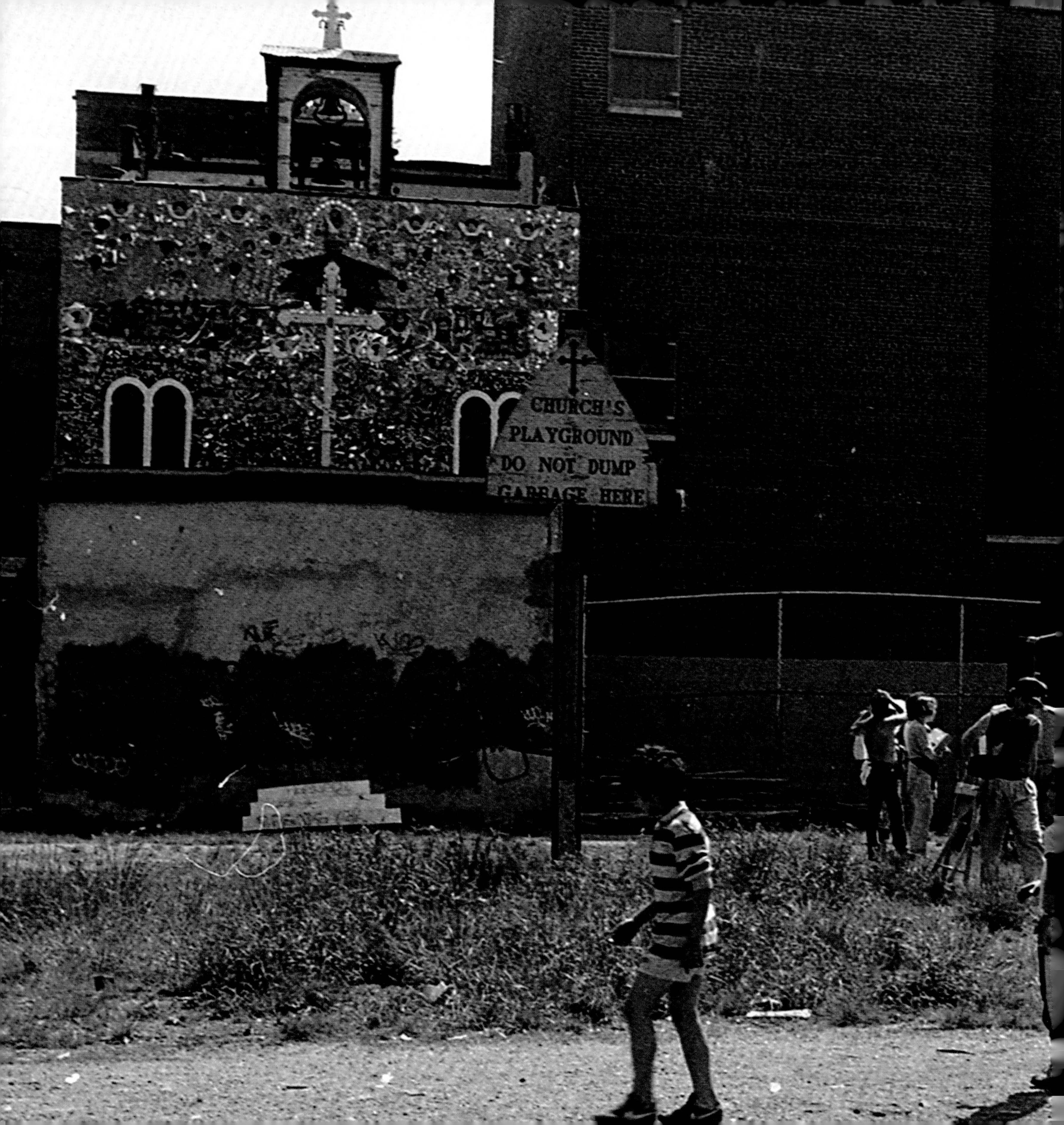

CHURCH'S
PLAYGROUND
DO NOT DUMP
GARBAGE HERE

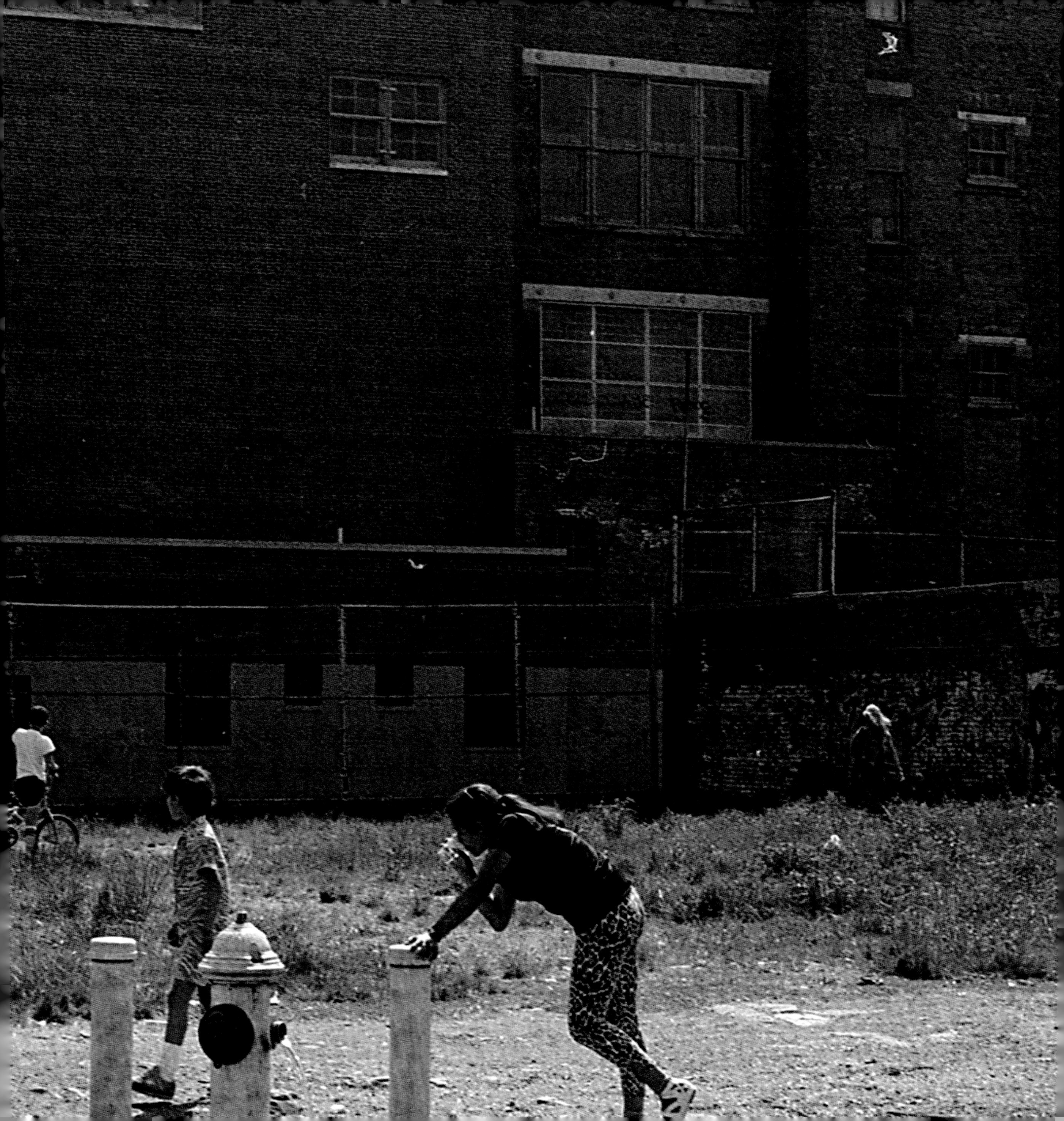

ACKNOWLEDGMENTS

This book is dedicated to **Rina** *for listening and looking and listening and looking some more, and then drawing the beautiful map of the East Village and the Lower East Side.*

SPECIAL THANK YOU TO

David Fabricant . . . for saying yes to this book and keeping a detailed eye on the entire project.

Peter McGough . . . for writing and sharing his ideas and memories.

Bill Morgan . . . for suggesting the Allen Ginsberg poem and writing the afterword. Also for making an introduction to the Allen Ginsberg estate.

Peter Hale, the "mainstay" of the Allen Ginsberg estate . . . for making introductions and directing me through the process of getting rights to use Allen's poem.

Bob Krasner . . . for being a very good photographer . . . and . . . introducing me to Peter McGough, who wrote the foreword; doing an article about my photography, then another article about my previous book, *New York Bars at Dawn*; and being my interview partner for a dialogue about the East Village.

Jeff Katz of the New York Public Library . . . for taking the time to go through this book in its earliest form and then suggesting writers whose words would complement the photographs.

Nadira Husain . . . for prodding me along to believe there was a book in the collection.

Stan Mack . . . for letting me use his wonderful cartoon of Tompkins Square Park.

Jerry Kurowycky . . . for taking the time to confirm some "then" photos.

And . . . Nell, Rosa Sherson, Hannah Root, Agosto Machado, Bill Tucker, Laura Hand, Anton Relin, Miriam Burwasser, Peter Burwasser.

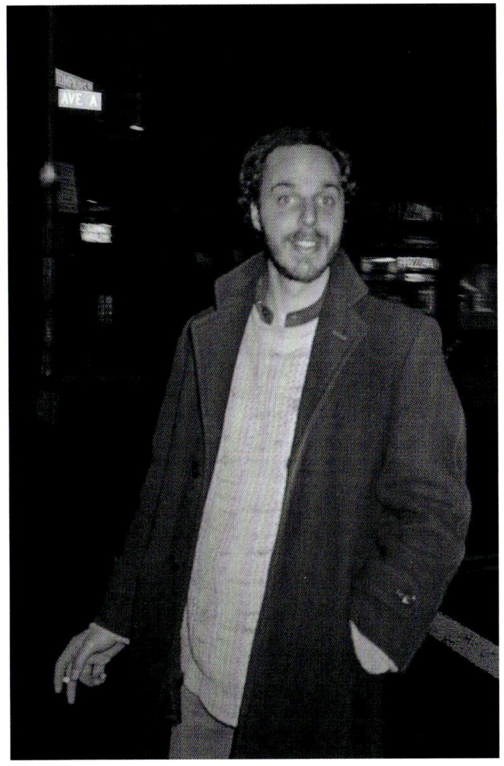

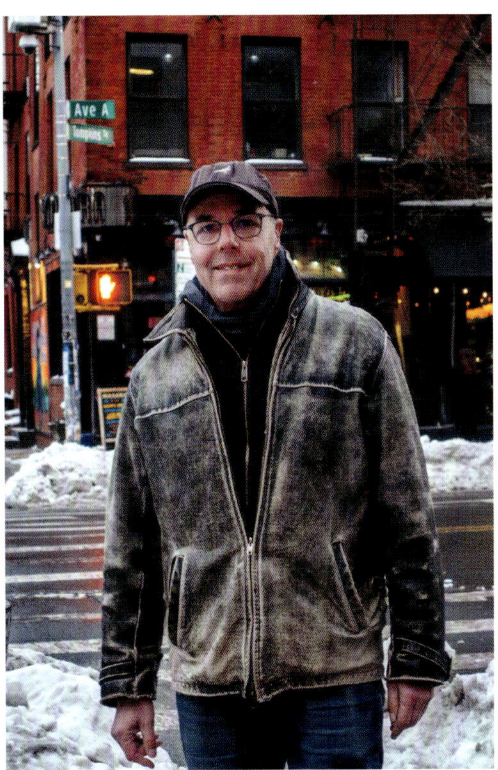

PHOTOS: RINA ROOT

Daniel Root, pictured here in 1984 and 2026, is a fine art photographer and a principal in the visual arts firm The Root Group. His popular pre-dawn photographs of Manhattan watering holes were collected in the book *New York Bars at Dawn* (Abbeville). Root has lived in the East Village since the early 1980s.

Peter McGough is a visual artist and author of the critically acclaimed memoir *I've Seen the Future and I'm Not Going: The Art Scene and Downtown New York in the 1980s.*

Bill Morgan is the author of numerous books about the Beat Generation, as well as *I Celebrate Myself: The Somewhat Private Life of Allen Ginsberg.*

Front cover: 2 Saint Mark's Place then and now, with Madonna on the set of *Desperately Seeking Susan* in 1984. See pp. 18–19.

Back cover: Ray's Candy Store, 113 Avenue A, then and now. See pp. 72–73.

pp. 1–3: Hydrant spray on East 11th Street, 1984.

p. 6: Tenement window, 1984.

pp. 236–37: Outside PS 361, East 12th Street, 1984.

Editing and layout: David Fabricant
Designer: Misha Beletsky
Production editor: Kayla Hassett
Production manager: Louise Kurtz

Permissions
p. 4: Map of the East Village copyright © Rina Root.
p. 13: Allen Ginsberg, "The Velocity of Money," from *Collected Poems 1947–1997*. Copyright © 2006 the Allen Ginsberg Trust. Used with the permission of HarperCollins Publishers.
p. 106: Map of Tompkins Square Park copyright © Stan Mack.

First edition
10 9 8 7 6 5 4 3 2 1

ISBN 978-0-7892-1515-4

Library of Congress Cataloging-in-Publication Data available upon request

For bulk and premium sales and for text adoption procedures, write to Customer Service Manager, Abbeville Press, 655 Third Avenue, New York, NY 10017, or call 1-800-Artbook.

Visit Abbeville Press online at www.abbeville.com.